RESEARCH DESIGN EXPLAINED

Fourth Edition

MARK MITCHELL
Clarion University

JANINA JOLLEY
Clarion University

HARCOURT COLLEGE PUBLISHERS

Fort Worth   Philadelphia   San Diego   New York   Orlando   Austin   San Antonio
Toronto   Montreal   London   Sydney   Tokyo

Publisher	Earl McPeek
Acquisitions Editor	Bradley J. Potthoff
Market Strategist	Katie Matthews
Developmental Editor	Christine Abshire
Project Editor	Elaine Richards
Art Director	Brian Salisbury
Production Manager	James McDonald

Cover: Karl Thibodeaux Photography

ISBN: 0-15-507505-5
Library of Congress Catalog Card Number: 00-102764

Address for Domestic Orders
Harcourt College Publishers, 6277 Sea Harbor Drive, Orlando, FL 32887-6777
800-782-4479

Address for International Orders
International Customer Service
Harcourt, Inc., 6277 Sea Harbor Drive, Orlando, FL 32887-6777
407-345-3800
(fax) 407-345-4060
(e-mail) hbintl@harcourt.com

Address for Editorial Correspondence
Harcourt College Publishers, 301 Commerce Street, Suite 3700, Fort Worth, TX 76102

Web Site Address
http://www.harcourtcollege.com

Harcourt College Publishers will provide complimentary supplements or supplement packages to those adopters qualified under our adoption policy. Please contact your sales representative to learn how you qualify. If as an adopter or potential user you receive supplements you do not need, please return them to your sales representative or send them to: Attn: Returns Department, Troy Warehouse, 465 South Lincoln Drive, Troy, MO 63379.

Printed in the United States of America

1 2 3 4 5 6 7 8 9   039   9 8 7 6 5 4 3 2

Harcourt College Publishers

PREFACE

This textbook began as a search for a textbook. When we first began teaching research design, we looked around for a textbook that conveyed the excitement that accompanies scientific discovery. We also wanted a user-friendly book that could engage our students while offering practical advice about how to read, conduct, and write up research.

Unfortunately, we couldn't find such a book. Existing books conveyed one of two messages: "Research design is easy—just memorize these terms and research studies" or "Research design is hard—it's something so complicated to understand that it should be left to the professionals."

We wanted to replace the sense of mystery and confusion that students bring to scientific psychology with an appreciation of science's excitement and relevance to psychology. To enable students to explore uncharted psychological frontiers, we envisioned a book that explained fundamental concepts so clearly and with so many real-life analogies and examples that students would understand these ideas rather than simply memorize terms.

In short, we discovered we were going to have to write the textbook ourselves. And, once we got started, we discovered that all those frustrations that we—and our students—had experienced in the past were actually helpful. We were able to translate these difficulties into a textbook that explained research concepts in a way that was easy to grasp. Here are some of our methods (methods that you probably use in your teaching):

- We make a concerted effort to stimulate students' interest in the course. For example, we show students how understanding scientific psychology can make them more sophisticated consumers and more marketable job/graduate school applicants.

- We use numerous, clear examples—especially for concepts with which students have trouble, such as statistical significance and interactions.

- We focus on important, fundamental concepts, show students why those concepts are important, relate those concepts to what students already know, and directly attack common misconceptions about those concepts.

- We show the logic behind the process of research design so that students know more than just terminology—they learn how to think like research psychologists.

- We explain statistical concepts (not computations) because statistics need to be considered before doing research, not afterward.

In addition, unlike most texts on the market, each chapter has

- tables that help students see the relationships between concepts
- a glossary that not only defines key terms, but shows the inter-relationships between the terms

DISTINCTIVE CHAPTERS AND APPENDICES

The goal of this book is to encourage students to value, read, and conduct ethical research. Therefore:

- We introduce ethical issues in Chapter 1 and discuss them throughout the book. In addition, we include a separate appendix on ethical issues. Appendix A contains the entire ethical code of APA relating to human and animal research, a sample informed consent form, a sample ethical review form, and practical tips for conducting ethical research.
- We focus on how to read research in Chapter 10, and Appendix B covers ways of searching the literature.
- We discuss how to generate research ideas in Chapter 2.
- We devote Chapter 13 to survey research—the research method that students will most likely use after they leave school.
- We include practical tips about how to conduct a research study in Appendix C.
- We demonstrate in Chapter 14 how to write research proposals and articles in APA style.

FLEXIBLE ORGANIZATION

We know that most professors share our goals of teaching students to be able to read, evaluate, defend, and produce scientific research. We also know that professors differ in how they go about achieving these goals and in the emphasis professors place on each of these goals. For example, about half of all research methods professors think that the best way to help students understand design is to cover nonexperimental methods first, whereas the other half think that students must understand experimental methods first.

To accommodate these differences, we have made the chapters relatively self-contained modules. Because each chapter focuses on ethics, construct validity, external validity, and internal validity, it's easy to skip chapters or cover them in different orders. To give you even more flexibility, we have moved the computationally oriented statistical sections from the chapters to Appendix F. Thus, whether you want to focus exclusively on the basic conceptual issues in analysis or you want students to have a thorough knowledge of basic statistical terms and computations, this text will meet your needs.

ANCILLARIES

To help meet your needs, this book comes with many more ancillaries than you would expect from a research methods text:

- a class-tested **test bank**
- sample lectures in **PowerPoint**®, HTML, and even printed form

- handouts
- lab exercises
- **detailed answers to the end-of-chapter exercises**
- a Web site (**http://www.researchmethods.com**) with an area for professors and a separate area for students

WHAT'S NEW IN THE FOURTH EDITION

By being even clearer and even more focused on helping students critically evaluate research, this edition promises to be more helpful to students and teachers alike. Although we would like to take credit for the improvement in this edition, we can't. Most of the credit belongs to our reviewers. We are especially indebted to an English professor, Dr. Darlynn Fink, and a professional editor, Karen Weyant. Neither individual had any background in psychology and neither was afraid to comment when they had difficulty understanding a section. As a result of their work, this book has more advance organizers, more summary statements, more tightly organized chapters, and fewer hard-to-read paragraphs.

Some of the credit for the improved clarity also belongs to our students. As in previous editions, we had students review the text. However, this time, we each received feedback as a result of teaching the research methods course using our text and the mastery system. Specifically, (1) the wrong answers students gave on quizzes and exercises, and (2) the problems students had in reading articles, writing up lab reports, and writing proposals led us to:

- state some concepts more clearly
- state other concepts more emphatically
- make some examples more closely match what students might see in journal articles
- revise some of the exercises and test items

The product of these revisions is a book that does a slightly better job of reaching "A" students and a much better job of reaching the average student.

Finally, much of the credit for the numerous improvements in this edition belongs to the psychology professors who reviewed the text. Every chapter is better because of their efforts. Below, we list just a few of the changes that have been made in the text.

CHAPTER-BY-CHAPTER CHANGES

We added examples, diagrams, and cartoons to Chapter 1 to emphasize:

- the distinction between the scientific method and other ways of knowing
- the differences between the types of validity
- the fact that most studies will not be perfect in terms of all forms of validity

- the value of testability and replication
- the reasons why people enjoy research

In this edition, Chapter 2 is significantly shorter, there is more emphasis on refining hypotheses, more focus on techniques that students actually use in generating hypotheses, more groundwork laid for writing the introduction, and less discussion of the esoteric aspects of theory.

In this edition, we tried to engage students by relating the information in Chapter 3 to psychological testing. We made the information clearer by adding examples of hypothetical data to help students visualize test-retest reliability and other forms of validity. Our pilot testing suggests that these data sets are much easier for students to understand than verbal descriptions or graphs. We also added examples that were closer to what students were most likely to see in journal articles or in descriptions of psychological tests. In addition, we focused on making the following relationships clearer: reliability and validity, bias and random error, and interobserver agreement and interobserver reliability. Finally, we removed the discussion of factor analysis because many faculty thought that went beyond the abilities of their students.

In Chapter 4, we give a clearer explanation of the assumptions involved in viewing rating scale data as interval, discuss magnitude estimation, and more closely relate the material to helping students critically examine the validity problems with "tests" that appear in popular magazines.

In Chapter 5, we have revised our examples of regression to focus more on real-life implications of regression, and we added some figures to help students understand how the threats to internal validity hinder our ability to determine whether a treatment causes an effect. In addition, we have sharpened the distinctions between maturation and history as well as between testing and instrumentation. Finally, we allude to random assignment as a simple solution for dealing with the threats to internal validity.

In this edition, we shortened Chapter 6 by putting the material on hand-calculating the t-test into Appendix F. Thus, professors who want to teach the t-test in depth can assign that section of the appendix and use the test questions relating to that material. If the professor does not assign Appendix F, the student will still get a solid grounding in statistics. By the end of the chapter, even the student with no previous background in statistics should have a good understanding of such key concepts such as statistical significance, power, Type 1 errors, and Type 2 errors. The student will even understand the essence of the findings of APA's committee on significance testing. In short, rather than focus on the mathematics of the t-test, the chapter has been reorganized to focus on showing: (1) how statistics affects the design of the experiment, and (2) how to interpret statistics.

In Chapter 7, we complied with reviewers and moved the instructions for hand-calculating ANOVA to Appendix F. In addition, we made the connections between analysis and design clearer and incorporated more examples of the value of having multiple control groups.

In Chapter 8, we added a section that teaches students how to make sense of graphs. In addition to making just about every section even clearer, we placed greater emphasis on the fact that if you do include a nonexperimental variable in a factorial design, you cannot make causal statements about that factor.

In this edition, we moved the hand calculations of the dependent groups' t from Chapter 9 to Appendix F, and we added a box on using the Latin Square design with three or more levels of a variable. We also reorganized some material to help students better understand how to interpret the results of a counterbalanced, within-subjects design.

In Chapter 10, we included more practical tips for choosing and evaluating articles. In addition, we expanded our discussion of how to interpret results sections. Finally, we made a few changes so that students could more easily go directly from this chapter to Chapter 14, "Writing Research Proposals and Reports," because we learned that many professors like to assign these two chapters together.

We expanded the discussions of single-n designs and quasi-experiments in Chapter 11 to now include both the controversy about the internal validity of single-n designs and the applied concerns that cause a researcher to use a quasi-experimental design. In addition, we slightly expanded our coverage of psychophysical designs.

To keep in touch with what many see as a change in the field, we have placed more emphasis on content analysis and observational research in Chapter 12.

The improvements in Chapter 13 are due, in large part, to Dave VanAmburg, a professional market researcher who shared his insights into the process and problems of modern, applied survey research with us.

For this edition, it was wonderful to have an English professor, Darlynn Fink, help revise Chapter 14 on how to write papers and proposals. We are also grateful to several reviewers for valuable tips on how to deal with writing a "results" section for a research proposal.

Appendix F is a statistical appendix new to this edition. This appendix can do what many research methods professors end up doing: teach a short course in statistics. It contains five sections, any one of which can be understood without reading the others. The first is a short module about how to select the right statistical test.

The second gives an in-depth explanation of logic of computing the independent groups t-test. By in-depth, we mean that we discuss the logic and computations of the standard deviation, the standard error of the mean, confidence intervals, the standard error of the difference. The second module is, in essence, a short course on parametric statistics. Much of the material in the second module was originally contained in Chapter 6.

The third section takes students step by step through computing a one-way ANOVA; this information previously appeared in Chapter 7. The major change is that we have used a more orthodox formula for calculating the Between Groups Sum of Squares.

The fourth section steps students through the dependent groups t-test. This material was originally in Chapter 9.

The fifth module is a free-standing unit on correlational analyses. It contains four independent, but connected, sections. The first is an in-depth explanation of the logic behind the formula for the Pearson r. The second explains why and how to determine whether a Pearson r is significantly different from zero. The third shows, step by step, how to compute a Chi-Square and a phi coefficient. The fourth describes the basic logic behind factor analysis.

Finally, we should note that two appendices were removed. These two appendices, "Marketing your research skills in the real world" and "The field experiment," are available on our Web site **http://www.researchmethods.com**.

....

ACKNOWLEDGMENTS

Writing *Research Design Explained* was a monumental task that required commitment, love, effort, and a high tolerance for frustration. If it had not been for the support of our friends, family, publisher, and students, we could not have met this challenge.

Robert Tremblay, a Boston journalist, and Lee Howard, a Connecticut journalist, have our undying gratitude for the many hours they spent critiquing the first three editions of this book. We are also grateful to Darlynn Fink, an English professor, and Karen Weyant, a professional editor, for their work on this edition. We also give special thanks to Christine Abshire, Lisa Hensley, Michael Cobb, Christina Oldham, Susan Pierce, Susan Meyers, Kirsten Olson, Elaine Richards, Brian Salisbury, James McDonald, and the rest of the folks at Harcourt College Publishers for sharing and nurturing our vision. In addition to thanking Bob, Lee, Darlynn, Karen, and Harcourt College Publishers, we would like to thank three groups of dedicated reviewers, all of whom were actually co-authors of this text:

First, we would like to thank the competent and conscientious professors who shared their insights with us: Louis Banderet, Quinsigamond Community College; James H. Beaird, Western Oregon State College; John P. Brockway, Davidson College; Tracy L. Brown, University of North Carolina–Asheville; Edward Caropreso, Clarion University; Walter Chromiak, Dickinson College; James R. Council, North Dakota State University; Helen J. Crawford, University of Wyoming; Raymond Ditrichs, Northern Illinois University; Patricia Doerr, Louisiana State University; Linda Enloe, Idaho State University; Mary Ann Foley, Skidmore College; George L. Hampton III, University of Houston–Downtown; Robert Hoff, Mercyhurst College; Lynn Howerton, Arkansas State University; John C. Jahnke, Miami University; Randy Jones, Utah State University; Sue Kraus, Fort Lewis College; Scott A. Kuehn, Clarion University; Kenneth L. Leicht, Illinois State University; Charles A. Levin, Baldwin-Wallace College; Joel Lundack, Peru State College; Steven Meier, University of Idaho; Charles Meliska, University of Southern Indiana; Kenneth B. Melvin, University of Alabama; Stephen P. Mewaldt, Marshall University; John Nicoud, Marion College of Fond du Lac; David Pittenger, Marietta College; Carl Ratner, Humboldt State University; Ray Reutzel, Brigham Young University; Anrea Richards, University of California–Los Angeles; Margaret Ruddy, Trenton State College; James J. Ryan, University of Wisconsin–La Crosse; Rick Scheidt, Kansas State University; Gerald Sparkman, University of Rio Grande; Sylvia Stalker, Clarion University; Sandra L. Stein, Rider College; Ellen P. Susman, Metropolitan State College of Denver; Russ A. Thompson, University of Nebraska; Benjamin Wallace, Cleveland State University; Paul Wellman, Texas A&M University; and Christine Ziegler, Kennesaw State College.

Second, we would like to thank our student reviewers, especially Susanne Bingham, Mike Blum, Chris Fenn, Jess Frederick, Kris Glosser, Melissa Gregory, Barbara Olszanski, Shari Poza, Rosalyn Rapsinski, and Melissa Ustik.

Third, we would like to thank the English professors who critiqued the previous editions of our book: William Blazek, Patrick McLaughlin, and John Young. In addition to improving the writing style of the book, they also provided a valuable perspective—that of the intelligent, but naïve, reader.

Finally, we would like to thank our daughter Moriah for allowing us the time to complete this project.

ABOUT THE AUTHORS

After graduating summa cum laude from Washington and Lee University, Mark L. Mitchell received his M.A. and Ph.D. degrees in psychology at The Ohio State University. He is currently a professor at Clarion University.

Janina M. Jolley graduated with "Great Distinction" from California State University at Dominguez Hills and earned her M.A. and Ph.D. in psychology from The Ohio State University. She is currently a consulting editor of *The Journal of Genetic Psychology* and *Genetic Psychology Monographs.* Her first book was *How to Write Psychology Papers: A Student's Survival Guide for Psychology and Related Fields,* which she wrote with J. D. Murray and Pete Keller. She is currently a professor of psychology at Clarion University.

Dr. Mitchell and Dr. Jolley are married to research, teaching, and each other—not necessarily in that order. You can write to them at the Department of Psychology, Clarion University, Clarion, PA 16214; contact them through their Web site (http://www.researchmethods.com); or send e-mail to them at either Mitchell@clarion.edu or Jolley@clarion.edu.

CONTENTS

CHAPTER 3 MEASURING AND MANIPULATING VARIABLES: RELIABILITY AND VALIDITY 71

CHAPTER 13   SURVEY RESEARCH   468

CHAPTER 14   PUTTING IT ALL TOGETHER: WRITING RESEARCH PROPOSALS AND REPORTS   511

APPENDIX A ETHICS   A-2

APPENDIX B SEARCHING THE LITERATURE (Electronically and the Old-Fashioned Way)   B-1

APPENDIX C CONDUCTING A STUDY   C-1

APPENDIX D SAMPLE RESEARCH PAPER   D-1

APPENDIX E STATISTICS AND RANDOM NUMBERS TABLES   E-1

APPENDIX F INTRODUCTION TO STATISTICS   F-1

To Anna, Glen, and Neal

PSYCHOLOGY AND SCIENCE

The whole of science is nothing more than the refinement of everyday thinking.
—ALBERT EINSTEIN

Since the beginning of the twentieth century, people's innate desire to understand themselves—and the human condition—has found a new avenue toward the answer: the scientific method.
—JACQUELINE SWARTZ

OVERVIEW

In this chapter, you will learn why psychologists embrace scientific research. Then, you will learn about the problems psychologists encounter when they try to apply traditional scientific techniques to the study of human behavior. Finally, you will learn how you will benefit from understanding research design.

WHY PSYCHOLOGY USES THE SCIENTIFIC APPROACH

Since humans were first able to reason, they have asked themselves: "Why are people the way they are?" A little more than 100 years ago, a few individuals tried a novel approach to answering this question—the scientific approach. As a result, psychology was born.

Today, thousands of psychologists believe in the scientific approach. Why do psychologists find the scientific approach so attractive?

THE CHARACTERISTICS OF SCIENCE

Psychologists find the scientific approach attractive because it is a useful tool for getting accurate answers to important questions. Detectives use the scientific approach to solve crimes; biologists use the scientific approach to track down the genes responsible for inherited disorders; and behavioral scientists use the scientific approach to unravel the mysteries of the human mind. In short, "if you want to do good, science puts in your hands the most powerful tools to do so" (Dawkins, 1998).

What is it about the scientific approach that makes it such a useful tool for people who want answers to important questions? As you will soon see, the eight strengths of the scientific approach are that it:

- finds general rules
- collects objective evidence
- makes testable statements
- adopts a skeptical, questioning attitude about all claims
- remains open-minded about new claims

- is creative
- is public
- is productive

General Rules

Just as detectives assume that crimes have motives, scientists assume that events happen for reasons. Furthermore, scientists are optimistic that they can find general rules that will allow us to better understand the world. Their hope is that by finding the underlying reasons for events, they will find simplicity, order, and predictability in what often seems a complex, chaotic, and random universe. Thus, contrary to what happens in some science classes, the goal of science is not to make the world more complex and confusing. Instead, science's goal is to make the world more understandable. One way to make the world more understandable is to find simple rules that explain, describe, and predict behavior.

Objective

Scientists must be careful, however, not to be blinded by the desire to see the world as a simple and predictable place. We all know people who, in their desire to see the world as simple and predictable, "see" rules and patterns that reflect their prejudices and biases, rather than fact. For example, some people think they can "size up" a person based on the person's race, astrological sign, attractiveness, handwriting, body build, or some other superficial characteristic. However, when we objectively test the ability of these people to predict other people's behavior, they fail miserably—as more than 100 studies have shown (Dawes, 1994).

Scientists believe in objective facts because they know from past experience that we can't always accept people's subjective opinions. In the past, physicians believed that destroying parts of patients' brains (lobotomies) made patients "better." Some even issued reports about the number of patients who were "cured" and the number who were better off—but both "cured" and "better off" were based on the surgeon's subjective judgment rather than on an objective report of observable changes in the patients, such as returning to work (Shorter, 1997).

To avoid being swept away by either unfounded speculations or biased perceptions, scientists collect observable evidence. That is, they compile concrete data that can be verified by independent observers, as well as by skeptics. The scientific laws of gravity, magnetism, and operant conditioning were discovered through objective observation of physical evidence (Ruchlis & Oddo, 1990). Consequently, these laws are not opinions but facts.

Testable

Although we have attacked *unsupported* speculation, we are not saying that scientists don't speculate—they do. Like detectives, scientists are encouraged to make bold, specific predictions and then to find evidence that either supports or refutes their speculations.

Similarly, although we would argue that unsupported opinions are of limited value, we are not saying that scientists don't have opinions. Scientists, like everyone else, have opinions. Unlike almost everyone else, however, scientists willingly put those opinions to the test.

Why risk finding out that a cherished opinion is wrong and that you must change your mind? There are at least two reasons. First, a major goal of science is to identify myths, superstitions, and false beliefs. Second, one of science's major strengths is that it allows scientists to learn from mistakes. Thus, to be a scientist, you do not need to start with intuitively accurate insights into how the world works. You just need to learn when your initial insights are wrong. The key to learning from your mistakes is to make statements that are *testable:* statements that may possibly be shown to be wrong. The goal in making a testable statement is not to make a statement that will be wrong, but rather to put yourself in a position so that if you are wrong, you admit it and learn from your mistake.

At first, it may seem strange to risk being wrong. To understand why it is okay to make statements that can potentially be proven false, let's consider people who don't. These people do not allow facts to change their beliefs. For example, one individual predicted that the earth would be destroyed in 1998. Has he admitted his mistake? No, he claims that the earth, in fact, *was* destroyed in 1998, but that we are now living on an alternate earth in another dimension, and we are unaware of the destruction of our "previous" world. We cannot prove him wrong.

We can, however, point out that he has made an untestable statement—a statement that no amount of evidence can disprove. Furthermore, we can point out that untestable statements can never be changed, refined, or corrected by the discovery of new facts. Because scientists know the problems with untestable statements, they avoid making vague statements and blindly accepting after-the-fact explanations.

Vague statements may be untestable   Vague statements are as useless as they are untestable (see Figure 1-1). Thus, a detective who claims that the murderer lives in this galaxy can neither be proven wrong nor given credit for solving the case.

Because these vague statements are untestable, they are often the province of "sucker bets" and of pseudosciences, such as palmistry and astrology. For example, suppose a stranger bets you that Wednesday will be a good day, but doesn't define what a good day is. No matter what happened on Wednesday, the stranger may come back on Thursday, demanding payment because Wednesday, by the stranger's definition, was a great day. Similarly, one of the authors' horoscopes once read: "Take care today not to get involved with someone who is wrong for you and you for him or her. Trouble could result." This horoscope tells us nothing. No matter what happens, the astrologer could claim to have predicted it.

One reason the astrologer can be so slippery is because he used vaguely defined terms. For example, the astrologer does not give us a clue as to what "wrong for you" means. Thus, if trouble had resulted, the astrologer could say, "The person was wrong for you." If trouble had not resulted, the astrologer could say, "The person

UNTESTABLE STATEMENTS

Vague predictions that are never wrong may be useless.

was right for you." Note that because the horoscope does not tell us anything, it can't be proven wrong. But because it does not tell us anything, it is also useless.

One way that scientists avoid making vague statements is by defining their concepts in precise and objective terms. Instead of talking only in terms of vague, invisible, and hard-to-pin-down abstractions such as "love," psychologists talk in terms of the specific, observable procedures they use to measure love.

More technically, scientists use **operational definitions:** the specific, observable, concrete steps that are involved in measuring or manipulating the concept being studied. Thanks to operational definitions, researchers are not limited to talking about psychological variables such as stress, love, and intelligence in vague, abstract, and poetic ways. Instead, researchers can also talk about a psychological concept in terms of the specific recipes they have invented for measuring that variable.

As you will see in Chapter 3, these recipes may range from measuring brain wave activity to scoring a multiple-choice test. Some of these recipes will be clever and do a good job of capturing the psychological variable they are supposed to measure, whereas others will not be quite so good. But no matter what the recipe is, it is a recipe that other scientists can follow. Because the operational definition is an objective recipe that anyone can follow, there is no disagreement about what each participant's score is.

When researchers state their predictions in such clear, concrete, and objective terms, they can objectively determine whether the evidence supports their predictions. For example, no matter what their biases, they can objectively establish whether scores on a given happiness test are correlated with scores on a certain IQ test.

You have seen that vague statements lead to untestable predictions. You have also seen that one way of making a vague statement is to avoid using operational definitions. By not using operational definitions, "quacks" can avoid being pinned down about what they really mean. Scientists, on the other hand, want to make testable predictions so that they can change their views if they are wrong. To better understand why scientists like testable predictions, let's contrast testable predictions with after-the-fact explanations.

After-the-fact explanations may be untestable   After-the-fact explanations, like vague statements, are difficult to prove wrong. For example, if we say that a person committed a murder because of some event in his childhood, how can we be proven wrong? Most people would accept or reject our claim based on whether it sounded reasonable. The problem, however, with accepting "reasonable-sounding" explanations is that after something happens, almost anyone can generate a plausible-sounding explanation for why it happened. Although these explanations may seem reasonable, they may be incorrect.

To dramatize the fact that plausible-sounding explanations may be wrong, psychologists have asked people to explain numerous "facts," such as why "opposites attract," and why changing your original answer to a multiple-choice test question usually results in changing from a right answer to a wrong answer. Participants were able to generate logical, persuasive reasons for why those "facts" were true—even though all of those "facts" are false (Dawes, 1994; Myers, 1999; Slovic & Fischoff, 1977; Stanovich, 1990; Weiten, 1992).

Skeptical

Scientists are not just skeptical about after-the-fact explanations. Scientists, like detectives, are so skeptical that they want evidence before they believe even the most "obvious" of statements. As Carl Sagan (1993) noted, scientists have the courage to question conventional wisdom. For example, Galileo tested the obvious "fact" that heavier objects fall faster than lighter objects—and found it to be false. Like the skeptical detective, scientists respond to claims by saying things like "show me," "let me see," "let's take a look," and "can you verify that?" Neither detectives nor scientists accept notions merely because an authority says it's true or because everyone is sure that it is true. Instead, both detectives and scientists demand objective evidence.

Even after scientists have objective evidence, they continue to be skeptical. They realize that evidence is not the same thing as proof. In other words, like detectives, scientists ask themselves, "What other explanations are there for these facts?" Consequently, scientists are experts at considering alternative explanations for events. For example, *malaria* means "bad air" ("mal" means bad as in "malpractice," "aria" means air) because people thought malaria was caused by breathing the bad-smelling air around swamps. People pointed out that malaria cases were more common around swamps and that swamps contained foul-smelling marsh gas. Scientists countered by pointing out that the presence of marsh gas is not the only difference between dry areas and swampy areas. For instance, there are more insects, such as mosquitoes, in swamps. As we now know, it is mosquitoes—not marsh gas—that cause people to contract malaria.

Being skeptical also means realizing that "convincing proof" may merely be the result of a coincidence. A suspect may be near the victim's house on the night of the murder for perfectly innocent reasons; a patient may suddenly get better even after getting a "quack" treatment; a volcano may erupt exactly 20 years after an atomic bomb went off; and we can have one very warm summer for reasons having nothing to do with the "greenhouse effect." Scientists, as Robert Abelson (1995) says, "give chance a chance" to explain events.

Open-minded

Despite being so skeptical, good scientists are extremely open-minded. Just as they are reluctant to accept an idea because everyone believes it, they are reluctant to rule out an idea simply because nobody believes it. That is, just as a good detective initially considers everyone a suspect, scientists are willing to entertain all possibilities. Scientists have the courage to be open to the truth and to see the world as it is (Sagan, 1993). Consequently, scientists will not automatically dismiss anything as nonsense, not even ideas that seem to run counter to existing knowledge, such as telepathy. The willingness to test odd ideas has led scientists to important discoveries such as the finding that certain jungle plants have medicinal properties.

Creative

To test such ideas, scientists have to be creative. Unraveling the mysteries of the universe is not a boring, unimaginative, or routine task. Scientific giants such as Marie Curie (the discoverer of radium), Charles Darwin, and Friederich Kekule (who, while dreaming, solved the riddle of how carbon molecules are structured) are referred to as creative geniuses.

We should point out, however, that you don't need to be "naturally creative" to think in a creative way. Indeed, Darwin, Einstein, and Edison did not attribute their creative success to natural creative ability, but to persistence.

Shares Findings

Although science owes a great debt to individual geniuses like Einstein, science does not depend on the secret knowledge possessed by one individual. Instead, science produces and relies on publicly shared knowledge. That is, science relies on studies that are **replicable:** repeatable.

By making knowledge public, biases and errors can be spotted—and corrected. Thus, if a researcher publishes a biased or flawed study, rival investigators may repeat that study or challenge the researcher's conclusions.

Furthermore, by being public, researchers can build on each other's work. By building on each other's work, scientists can accomplish much more than if each had worked separately.

Without such open sharing of information, science doesn't work, as the debate on cold fusion illustrates. In 1989, two physical scientists announced at a press conference that they had invented a way of creating nuclear fusion, a potential source of safe electric power, without heating atoms to extreme temperatures. (Before the scientists' announcement, all known ways of producing nuclear fusion used more energy to heat atoms than the fusion reaction produced. Thus, nobody could seriously consider using nuclear fusion to produce electricity commercially.) The two scientists, however, did not submit their research to peer-reviewed journals, and they failed to give details of their procedures. Thus, nobody could replicate their work.

All these actions worked against science's self-corrective and unbiased nature. By not sharing their work, they removed the checks and balances that make science the reliable source of evidence that it is. Instead of letting others verify their findings, the two scientists expected people to accept their findings on the basis of a press conference. Fortunately, scientists refuse to accept statements, even statements from other scientists, without objective evidence.

Thus far, we have skeptically assumed that cold fusion did not really happen. But what if it did? The researchers' lack of openness would still be unfortunate because science flourishes only when scientists openly exchange findings.

Productive

Fortunately, scientists usually do share their findings. As a result, in some fields of science, knowledge doubles every five to ten years. The evidence that science is a productive tool for making discoveries and advancing knowledge is all around us. The technology created by science has vaulted us a long way from the Dark Ages or even the pre-VCR, pre-personal computer, pre-microwave early 1970s.

The progress science has made is remarkable considering that it is a relatively new way of finding out about the world. As recently as the 1400s, people were punished for studying human anatomy and even for trying to get evidence on such basic matters as the number of teeth a horse has. As recently as the early 1800s, the scientific approach was not applied to medicine or psychology. Until that time, people were limited to relying on tradition, common sense, intuition, and logic for medical and psychological knowledge.

Once science gained greater acceptance, people used the scientific approach to test and refine commonsense notions, as well as notions derived from intuition, tradition, and logic. As a result of supplementing and complementing other ways of knowing, science helped knowledge progress at an explosive rate.

THE CHARACTERISTICS OF PSYCHOLOGY

Most people agree that the scientific method works. Almost everyone would agree that science has allowed physics, chemistry, and biology to progress at a rapid rate. Almost nobody would argue that we could make more progress in understanding our physical world by abandoning science and going back to pre-scientific beliefs and methods such as alchemy or philosophy (Dawkins, 1998).

Although almost nobody has doubts about the value of the physical sciences, some doubt the value of psychological science. Some of the same individuals who would strongly object to chemists going back to alchemy have no objections to psychologists going back to astrology.

Why do some individuals think the scientific method is wonderful for studying chemistry and the other physical sciences, but not for studying psychology? Often, the reason is that they question whether psychology is a science. That is, they question whether psychologists:

- find general rules
- collect objective evidence
- make testable statements
- are skeptical
- are open-minded
- are creative
- produce publicly shared knowledge that can be replicated
- are productive

General Rules

Perhaps the most serious question about psychology as a science is, "Can psychologists find general rules that will predict, control, and explain human behavior?" Cynics argue that although it is possible to find rules to explain the behavior of molecules, it is not possible to find rules to explain the behavior of people.

These cynics claim that, unlike molecules, people are not all alike. Psychologists respond by saying that even though people are not all alike, they are genetically similar. Perhaps because of this similarity, most of us share many traits, from using language to trying to repay those who help us.

Cynics also claim that, unlike molecules, humans may spontaneously do something for no reason. Psychologists argue that most behavior does not just spontaneously appear. Instead, people usually do things for a reason.

Although both cynics and psychologists make logical arguments for their positions, psychologists have evidence to back up their arguments. That is, psychologists have not only argued that human behavior is governed by rules, they have also found many such rules (Kimble, 1990). For example, psychologists have discovered laws of operant and classical conditioning, laws of perception, laws of memory (Banaji & Crowder, 1989), and even laws of emotion (Frijda, 1988). (If you doubt that emotions follow rules, then ask yourself why people have fairly predictable reactions to certain movies. For example, most people cry or come close to tears the first time they see *Bambi,* whereas most people feel a nervous excitement the first time they see a horror film.)

Resistance to the idea that human behavior follows general rules has affected not only psychology, but medicine. Until recently, people believed that no general rules applied to illness. One person's flu was caused by circumstances that were completely different from another's. As Burke (1985) noted, "Each patient regarded his own suffering as unique, and demanding unique remedies." Consequently, one patient's treatment was totally different from another's. Partly because what cured one person was supposed to be totally ineffective for curing anyone else, knowledge about cures was not shared. As a result, medicine did not progress, and many people died unnecessarily. It was only after physicians started to look for general causes of disease that successful cures (such as antibiotics) were found.

Nevertheless, general rules do not always work. A treatment that cures one person may not cure another. For example, one person may be cured by penicillin, whereas another may be allergic to it. It would be wrong, however, to say that reactions to drugs do not follow any rules. It's simply that how an individual will respond to a drug is affected by many rules. Predicting a person's reaction to a drug would require knowing at least the following: the individual's weight, family history of reactions to drugs, when they last ate, condition of their vital organs, other drugs they are taking, and level of dehydration.

Like human physiology, human behavior is governed by many factors. Because there are so many rules that may come into play in a given situation, predicting what a given individual will do in that situation would be difficult even if you knew all the rules. Psychologists agree with cynics that predicting and explaining an individual's behavior are difficult. Psychologists disagree, however, with the cynic's assumption that there are no rules underlying behavior. Instead, psychologists know that there are rules that are useful in predicting the behavior of many of the people much of the time. As Sherlock Holmes said, "You can never foretell what any man will do, but you can say with precision what an average number will be up to. Individuals may vary, but percentages remain constant."

Some critics mistakenly argue that if you can't predict an individual instance of behavior, then the behavior does not follow general rules. Although this argument sounds convincing, think about trying to predict the outcome of a coin flip. We can't accurately predict the outcome of a coin flip. Why not? Is it because the outcome of a coin flip does not follow any rules? No, it follows very simple rules: The outcome depends on what side was up when the coin was flipped and how many times the coin turned over. Nevertheless, since we do not know how many times the coin will turn over, we can't predict the outcome of a single coin toss. Similarly, most would agree that the weather is determined by specific events. However, because there are so many events and because we do not have data on all events, we can't predict the weather with perfect accuracy.

In short, just because a given behavior in a given situation can't be predicted, we should not conclude that the behavior does not follow rules. The behavior might be perfectly predictable—if we knew the rules and could precisely measure the relevant variables.[1]

Objective Evidence

A second question people raise about psychology's ability to be a science is, "Can psychologists collect objective evidence about the human mind?"

Even though we can't see the mind, we can collect objective evidence about it. That is, although we can't directly measure abstract concepts such as love, aggression, and memory, we can develop observable operational definitions of these concepts.

In the effort to measure the unobservable objectively, psychology can follow the lead of the physical sciences. The physical sciences have a long history of studying things they could not see. Genetics was well advanced before anyone had seen a gene; physicists and chemists were discussing electrons long before electrons were seen; and nobody has seen gravity, time, temperature, pressure, or magnetism. Unobservable events can be inferred from observable events: Gravity can be inferred from observing objects fall, and psychological variables such as love can be assessed by observable indicators such as how long a couple gazes into each other's eyes, pupil dilation at the sight of the partner, physiological arousal at the sight of the partner, and passing up the opportunity to date attractive others.

According to one historian of science, psychology's reliance on operational definitions has made psychology more objective than physics (Porter, 1997). Another indication that psychologists have succeeded in making unbiased observations is that when psychologists replicate (repeat) another's study, they are very likely to get the same pattern of results that the original investigator obtained—even when the reason for repeating the study was skepticism of the original study's results. In fact, the results of psychological research are just as replicable as those of physics research (Hedges, 1987; Stanovich, 1990). In short, both logic and evidence suggest that psychological research is objective.

Testable

A third question people have about psychology is, "Can it make testable statements?" If it can't, then it would share the weaknesses of astrology. Fortunately, most published research articles in psychology make testable predictions. Indeed, our journals are full of articles in which predictions made by the investigators were disconfirmed. For example, to his surprise, Charles Kiesler (Kiesler, 1982; Kiesler & Sibulkin, 1987) found that many mentally ill individuals are hurt, rather than helped, by being put into mental institutions. In summary, the fact

---

[1]In physics, for example, researchers working on chaos theory (also known as complexity theory) have shown that simple processes can produce a complex and hard-to-predict pattern of behavior.

that research frequently disproves researchers' predictions is proof that psychologists make testable statements.

Skeptical

A fourth question about psychology is, "Can psychologists be as skeptical as other scientists?" Some people worry that psychologists will accept, rather than test, existing beliefs about human behavior. After all, many of these beliefs seem logical and have the weight of either popular or expert opinion behind them. Consequently, some fear that, rather than seeing what the evidence says, psychologists will base their decisions about what is true on logic, popularity, or authority.

Although some therapists have ignored the objective evidence, scientific psychologists have been diligent about testing even the most "obviously true" of ideas. For example, Greenberger and Steinberg (1986) performed a series of studies testing the "obviously true" idea that teenagers who have jobs better understand the value of hard work. They found that—contrary to conventional wisdom—teenagers who work are more cynical about the value of hard work than nonworking teens. Similarly, Shedler and Block (1990) tested the "obviously true" idea that drug use is the cause of psychological problems. Their evidence suggested that conventional wisdom was wrong—heavy drug use was a symptom, rather than a cause, of psychological problems. Likewise, Coles (1993) found that "cocaine babies" were not as troubled as many people originally believed. Thus, "obviously true" ideas are often found to be false when objectively tested.

In addition to questioning conventional wisdom, psychologists question observable evidence. For example, psychologists may question the degree to which mental tests or other measures of behavior truly capture the psychological concepts that those instruments claim to capture. Psychologists are not easily convinced that a set of questions labeled as a "love scale" actually measures love or that an "intelligence test" measures intelligence. Instead, psychologists need evidence documenting that these tests really measure what the tests claim to measure.

Psychologists are skeptical about measures because they realize that we never have a direct pipeline into a person's mind. We can't see the mind; we can see only behavior. From observing behavior, we may be able to make educated guesses about what is going on in the mind. Unfortunately, our inferences about what is going on inside a person's head could be wrong. Consequently, we should never assume that we know what a behavior really means. In other words, there is often a gap between the operational definition of a concept and the concept. Therefore, we should always question how well the operational definition really matches the label that the investigator gives it.

Psychologists are also very skeptical about drawing cause–effect conclusions. They realize that it is hard to isolate the one factor that may be causing a certain behavior. Therefore, if they find that better students have personal computers, they do not leap to the conclusion that computers cause academic success. Psychologists realize that academic success may lead to obtaining a computer. For example, some students may have been given a computer because they were doing well in school. Furthermore, psychologists realize that the computer-owning students may be doing better than other students because the computer-owning students went to better preschools, had better nutrition, or received more parental encouragement. Until these and other explanations are eliminated, psychologists would not assume that computers cause academic success.

Finally, many psychologists are skeptical about the extent to which results from a study can be generalized to the real world. They do not assume that a study done in a particular setting with a particular group of people can be generalized to other kinds of participants in a different setting. For instance, they would not automatically assume that a study originally done with gifted 10-year-olds at a private school would obtain the same results if it were repeated with adult participants studied in the workplace.

To review, psychologists are extremely skeptical. What others see as proof, psychologists see as circumstantial evidence. Thus, psychologists question conclusions about (1) thoughts and feelings, (2) causes of behavior, and (3) generalizing the results of a study.

Open-minded

Paralleling the concern that psychologists do not test "obvious facts" is the concern that psychologists are not open to ideas that run counter to common sense. These concerns are groundless. Psychological scientists are skeptical, but not set in their ways or cynical. Consequently, psychologists have tested all sorts of counterintuitive ideas, such as the idea that subliminal, backward messages (backmasking) on records can lead teens to Satanism (Custer, 1985); the idea that people can learn in their sleep; and the idea that ESP can be reliably used to send messages (Swets & Bjork, 1990). Although psychologists found no evidence for any of those ideas, psychology's willingness to try to test virtually anything has led to tentative acceptance of some novel concepts, such as the idea that acupuncture may be effective in relieving pain and the idea that meditating helps people to live longer (Alexander, Langer, Newman, Chandler, & Davies, 1989).

Creative

Whereas psychologists' open-mindedness has been questioned, few have questioned psychologists' creativity. Most people realize that it takes creativity to come up with ideas for psychological research. In fact, a few people even believe that they lack the creativity required to generate research ideas. However, they are wrong—anyone who follows the tips on idea generation in Chapter 2 can come up with a research idea.

The need for creativity doesn't end with generating the research idea. Creativity is also needed to test the idea. For example, creativity is needed to develop accurate measures of the concepts the researcher plans to study. Imagine the challenge of developing measures of such concepts as love, intelligence, and helpfulness. Fortunately, to measure key variables, the individual researcher does not always have to rely on his or her own creativity. As you will see in Chapter 3, the researcher can often rely on the creativity of others. After all, why reinvent the wheel when creative psychologists have already developed ways of measuring all kinds of concepts—from practical intelligence (Sternberg, 1986), to level of moral reasoning (Kohlberg, 1981), to need for exciting stimulation (Zuckerman, 1993)?

Even after finding ways of measuring key concepts, researchers may need to use their creativity to develop a situation that will permit them to test their research idea. Like the inventors of the wind tunnel, they may need to create a scaled-down model of a real-life situation that is simpler and more controllable than real life, yet still captures the key aspects of the real-life situation. For example, to study real-life competition, social psychologists have developed competitive games for participants to play. Similarly, to model the situation in which nothing you do seems to matter, Martin Seligman (1990) had people try to solve unsolvable puzzles. Thus, psychologists have been very creative in their research.

Shares Findings

Psychologists have also been very good at sharing their ideas and findings with others in the field, as shown by the hundreds of journals in which they publish their work. Indeed, psychologists may enjoy more candor and cooperation than scientists in other fields because psychologists usually gain little by keeping results secret. For example, if you wanted to be the first to patent a new technology, it would pay to keep secrets from competitors. In such a race, if you were first, you might make millions. If you were second, you would make nothing. Although such "races for dollars" are common in chemistry, they are rare in psychology because psychologists produce few patents or inventions.

Productive

Perhaps because of this candor, psychologists have made tremendous progress. As Mynatt and Doherty (1999) point out, "a little over a 100 years ago, we started knowing nothing, but look where we are now! In the last 100 years, a few psychologists have learned more about human behavior than the rest of humanity learned in the previous 1,000 years."

To see the effect of research on the teaching and practice of psychology, compare introductory textbooks published in 1910, 1930, 1950, 1980, and 2000. Even a cursory examination of these texts will dramatize two facts. First, research has radically increased the amount of knowledge in every field of psychology. Second, the rate of research discovery is rapidly accelerating—especially in the fields of counseling, developmental, personality, cognitive, physiological, social, and applied psychology.

Because research has contributed to every area of psychology, even former opponents of research now praise it. For example, Abraham Maslow (1970), the founder of the "Third Force," an approach that initially rebelled against scientific psychology and openly questioned whether scientific psychology was relevant to human concerns, later wrote: "Clearly, the next step for this psychology . . . is research, research, research . . ." (p. 1).

Today, because the questions and challenges facing modern society are ever changing, scientific research is as relevant as ever. To take just a few examples, researchers have identified ways of getting people to behave in ways that will stop the spread of the AIDS virus (O'Keeffe, Nesselhof-Kendall, & Baum, 1990); ways of increasing volunteerism (Snyder & Omoto, 1990); ways of encouraging energy conservation (Aronson, 1990); and ways of understanding and helping married couples get along (Gottman, 1993; Holmes & Boon, 1990). No wonder people outside psychology, professionals in areas such as education, communication, marketing, economics, and medicine, now adopt the same research methods that psychologists use. In short, psychological research has been so productive that it has dramatically changed both psychology and the real world.

THE IMPORTANCE OF SCIENCE TO PSYCHOLOGY

Not only is the scientific method responsible for the tremendous progress in psychology, but it is also largely responsible for psychology's uniqueness. Whereas many other fields—from astrology to philosophy—are concerned with the thoughts and behaviors of individuals, only psychology studies individuals scientifically (Stanovich, 1990). Thus, as Stanovich points out, it is no accident that every definition of psychology starts out, "The science of . . ."

What if psychology was not a science? The alternatives to building a field where facts matter are not appealing. Without the scientific method, psychology might simply be a branch of astrology (Stanovich, 1990). Without science, we might just do what tradition and logic tell us, even when tradition and logic tell us to do things that are actually harmful. For example, until very recently, physicians told us that both logic and tradition dictate that premature infants should not be held or rubbed. However, psychological research showed that premature infants benefit from being held and massaged (Field, 1993). Or, psychology might merely be common sense, even though common sense contradicts itself (see Box 1-1). Or, psychologists might arbitrarily decide that human behavior does not follow any rules. In other words, psychologists might choose to believe that we cannot know what people are like or what treatments are helpful.

Psychology is not the only science that has had to free itself from quackery, tradition, common sense, philosophy, and from the belief that its subject matter followed no rules. Since the beginning of recorded history, there have been people who have argued that finding rules or laws that govern nature is impossible. For centuries, most people believed the stars followed no pattern. Not that long ago, it was believed that diseases followed no patterns. Even today, some people believe that human behavior follows no discernible pattern. Yet, each of these assumptions has been disproven. The stars, the planets, diseases, and humans behave for reasons that we can understand. Admittedly, the rules determining human behavior may be complex and numerous—and it may even

---

• BOX 1-1 •

THE INCONSISTENCY OF COMMON SENSE

1. Absence makes the heart fonder,   BUT   Absence makes the heart wander.
2. Birds of a feather flock together,   BUT   Opposites attract.
3. Look before you leap,   BUT   He who hesitates is lost.
4. Too many cooks spoil the broth,   BUT   Two heads are better than one.
5. To know you is to love you,   BUT   Familiarity breeds contempt.

---

be that some behaviors do not follow rules. However, to this point, searching for rules of behavior has been fruitful (see Table 1-1).

Despite the success of scientific psychology, we should point out that the scientific approach has its limitations. If scientists become corrupt, overly arrogant, or stop being skeptical, science's ability to be objective would suffer. Furthermore, science, even at its best, is only one way of obtaining information.

Although science is only one way of knowing, science can work in concert with a variety of other ways of knowing. It can verify knowledge passed down by tradition or from an authoritative expert. It can test knowledge obtained by intuition or common sense. By anchoring speculation in reality, psychology can create, refine, or verify common sense and eliminate superstitions (Kohn, 1988). For example, consider the following six findings from research:

1. Punishment is not very effective in changing behavior.
2. Having teens work in low-wage jobs does not instill the "work ethic."
3. Drug use is often a symptom rather than a cause of psychological problems.
4. Absence makes the heart fonder only for couples who are already very much in love.
5. If you tell somebody what happened, they will tend to think they could have predicted the event, that "they knew it all along."
6. Pessimistic older people are less likely to get depressed.

All of these findings are refinements of the "common sense" of a few years ago. All of these findings are, or will soon become, part of the common sense of this century.

In short, science is a powerful tool that can be used to solve human problems. If we have such a tool, why shouldn't we use it—especially when it does not rule out the use of other tools?

• TABLE 1-1 •

PSYCHOLOGY AS A SCIENCE

CHARACTERISTIC	EXAMPLE
Finds general rules	Helps us understand human behavior through rules such as: laws of operant and classical conditioning, laws of memory (meaningless information is hard to remember, memorizing similar information, such as Spanish and Italian, leads to memory errors), and a wide range of theories from social learning theory to cognitive dissonance theory.
Collects objective evidence	Tests whether beliefs and theories are consistent with objective evidence. Obtains objective evidence by recording participants' behaviors: number of words written down on memory test, ratings made on an attitude scale, responses on personality test, reaction times, etc. One index of how effective we are at being objective is that our research findings are as replicable as research findings in physics.
Makes verifiable statements	Makes specific testable predictions that are sometimes found to be wrong (rewarding someone for doing a task will always increase their enjoyment of that task). That is, we use evidence to correct wrong beliefs.
Skeptical	Demands evidence for almost any statement. Challenges common sense and traditional notions. Does not take evidence (participants' statements or ratings) at face value. Considers alternative explanations for evidence (group given memory pill may do better than another on memory task because they had naturally better memories, because they were tested later in the day, or because they believed the pill would work).
Open-minded	Entertains virtually any hypothesis, from acupuncture relieving pain to meditation prolonging life.
Creative	Measures psychological concepts, generates hypotheses, and devises studies that rule out alternative explanations for findings.
Public	Allows scientists to check and build on each other's work because research is presented at conferences and published in journals.
Productive	Increases psychological knowledge at a dramatic rate.

QUESTIONS ABOUT APPLYING TECHNIQUES FROM PHYSICAL SCIENCES TO PSYCHOLOGY

Although psychologists are excited about using a tool that has been so successful in the physical sciences, they are not blind to the fact that there are problems with applying the scientific method to humans. To appreciate how sensitive psychologists are to the unique challenges and responsibilities involved in studying the behavior of living things, let's see how a psychologist would react if someone ignored those challenges and responsibilities. For instance, suppose that a novice investigator tried to model his psychological research after the following chemistry experiment:

A chemist fills two test tubes with hydrogen and oxygen molecules. She leaves the first test tube alone. She heats the second over a flame. She observes that water forms only in the second test tube. Because there was only one difference between the two test tubes (the flame), she concludes that the flame caused the group of molecules in the second test tube to behave differently than the molecules in the first tube. She then concludes that heat always causes hydrogen and oxygen to combine.

The novice then conducts the following study:

A novice investigator fills two rooms with people. He leaves the group in the first room alone. He heats up the second room. He "observes" that the second group behaves more aggressively than the first. He then concludes that "feeling warmer" always makes people more "aggressive."

Because of the vast differences between humans and molecules, an experienced research psychologist would have four sets of questions about the novice investigator's study. The first three sets (summarized in Table 1-2) deal with the validity of our novice investigator's conclusions: (1) Did the treatment manipulation really *cause* the second group to behave differently than the first?; (2) Did the investigator really measure and manipulate the *psychological variables* that he claimed he did? (Did the manipulation make participants "feel warm" and did the participants' behavior really reflect aggression?); and (3) Would the results *generalize* to other settings and participants? The fourth set of concerns is the most serious: Was it moral and ethical to perform the study?

INTERNAL VALIDITY QUESTIONS: DID THE TREATMENT CAUSE A CHANGE IN BEHAVIOR?

The first set of questions deals with the study's **internal validity:** the degree to which the study demonstrates that the treatment *caused* a change in behavior. If the study establishes that putting the participants into different rooms caused the one group to behave differently from the other group, the study has internal validity. If something else could be causing the groups to differ, then the study does not have internal validity.

For the chemist, establishing internal validity is fairly simple. If the flame condition yields water and the no-flame condition does not, she knows that the flame manipulation caused the water to form. She knows that there are no other differences between the test tubes that could have caused water to form in one tube, but not the other.

She does not have to worry that the oxygen molecules in one tube were naturally more likely to combine with hydrogen than were the molecules in the

• **TABLE 1-2** •

COMMON THREATS TO THE THREE KINDS OF VALIDITY

TYPE OF VALIDITY	MAJOR SOURCES OF PROBLEMS	MISTAKES TO AVOID	EXAMPLES OF PROBLEM IN REAL LIFE
Construct: The names we give to our measures and manipulations are accurate. That is, we are making accurate inferences about what our participants' behaviors mean and about the psychological states that our manipulations produce.	Faulty measures, resulting in mislabeling or misinterpreting behavior. Poor manipulations can also harm construct validity, as can participants figuring out and playing along with (or against) the hypothesis.	Accepting at face value that a test measures what its title claims it does. Anybody can type up some questions and call it an intelligence test—but that doesn't mean the "test" really measures intelligence.	Mislabeling a behavior. Thinking that a shy person is a snob, believing that what people *say* they think and feel is exactly what they think and feel, having complete confidence in lie detectors, "knowing" that a cat loves you because it sits in your chair after you get up.
Internal: Determining *cause–effect* relationship between manipulation and behavior *in* a given study. Establishing that a certain observable event caused (was responsible for, influenced) a change in behavior.	Allowing factors other than the manipulation to vary. For example, if the treatment and the no-treatment group differ before the study begins, we can't conclusively establish that the treatment caused the difference in the groups' behavior.	Failing to ask the question, "Isn't there something other than the treatment that could cause the difference in behavior?"	Misidentifying the causes of a problem. Giving a new president credit or blame for changes in the economy, blaming a new dentist for your existing dental problems, claiming that a parent's child-rearing methods are responsible for the child's autism.
External: The results of the study can be generalized *outside* the study to other situations and participants.	Artificial situations, testing an unusual group of participants, small number of participants.	Believing that any survey, regardless of how small or biased, has external validity.	Stereotyping—based on a very limited sample, people conclude that, "They are all like that. Seen one, seen them all."

other tube. She does not have to worry that she put the flame to the oxygen molecules at a time of day when they are most likely to combine. She does not have to worry that some other chemical or force in the environment was responsible for the oxygen combining with hydrogen in the test tube that she heated, but not the other. By doing her study in a test tube, she can isolate the oxygen from any unwanted influences. In short, isolating the cause of a difference in molecular behavior is relatively easy.

Isolating the cause of a difference in human behavior, on the other hand, is not so easy. There are so many factors, other than the treatment, that could make one group behave differently than another. Some of those factors make the groups different even before the study starts. Others come into play later. To establish internal validity, the psychologist would have to rule out all those nontreatment differences.

In questioning the internal validity of the novice's study, the research psychologist might start by determining whether the warm group was more aggressive even before they entered the warm room. For example, the research psychologist would have to worry about the possibility that the difference in how the two groups behaved was due to the people in the warm room being naturally more aggressive than the people in the other room.

Even if there were no differences between the two groups in how aggressive their members tended to be, the "warm room" group might still start the study in a more aggressive mood than the other group. To illustrate, suppose the novice tested the "normal room" group in the morning and the "warm room" group at night. In that case, the research psychologist would have to worry about the study's internal validity because many events completely unrelated to the room manipulation might cause the "warm room" participants to behave differently from the "normal room" participants. For instance, during the early evening, the "warm room" group may have had a few drinks or heard some bad news. Although neither the alcohol nor the bad news had anything to do with what happened to participants inside the warm room, the alcohol or bad news might affect the participants' behavior. Therefore, if the novice had tested the two groups at different times of day, the research psychologist would worry about the study's internal validity.

As you have seen, there may be differences in mood or personality between the "warm room" group and the "normal room" group even before the groups enter their respective rooms. Therefore, the research psychologist has to worry that these mood and personality differences, rather than the treatment, may cause participants to behave differently. Let's suppose, however, that the research psychologist has determined that the groups were essentially the same before they entered their respective rooms. Can the research psychologist now stop worrying about the study's internal validity? Not yet.

The research psychologist still can't assume that the only difference between the two groups is the manipulation. Instead, she has to worry that the warm room group may still hear, see, smell, or sense things that (1) are different from what the other group hears, sees, smells, and senses and (2) have nothing to do with turning up the thermostat. For example, suppose that during the "warm room" session—but not during the "normal room" session—some event completely unrelated to the treatment manipulation occurred, such as a jackhammer making noise outside, some people yelling nearby, or a thunderstorm starting. That event—rather than the treatment manipulation—could have caused the "warm group" to behave differently than the other group.

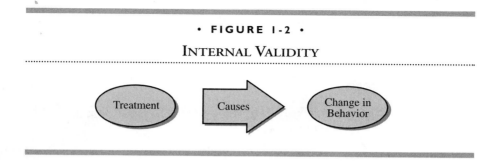

• **FIGURE 1-2** •

INTERNAL VALIDITY

In summary, the novice assumed his study had internal validity—that it showed that the treatment manipulation had an effect (see Figure 1-2). However, it is hard to establish internal validity because it is hard to clearly establish that the treatment manipulation, rather than something else, caused a change in how participants scored on the measure.

CONSTRUCT VALIDITY QUESTIONS: CAN WE MAKE THE LEAP FROM THE PHYSICAL WORLD TO THE MENTAL WORLD?

As we have seen, the novice investigator carelessly assumed that the room manipulation caused the two groups of participants to behave differently. That is, he went from *observing* that the participants in the room where he turned up the thermostat behaved differently than those in the other room to *inferring* that "turning up the thermostat *caused* the two groups to behave differently." However, that was not the only questionable inference he made.

The novice also went from *observing* that the participants in the room where he turned up the thermostat behaved differently than those in the other room to *inferring* that "participants who *felt warm* were more *aggressive*." That is, the novice made the leap from describing the physical world of publicly observable research procedures and participant actions to making inferences about the mental world of private, invisible thoughts and feelings.

In making the leap to talking about the world inside participants' heads, the novice presumed that his manipulation made warm room participants "feel warm" and that he accurately measured "aggression." In other words, the novice assumed that he accurately manipulated and measured psychological **constructs:** mental states that can't be directly observed, such as love, intelligence, hunger, feeling warm, and aggression. That is, the novice assumed that he could (1) control what was going on inside participants' heads by changing their outside environment and (2) know what was going on inside participants' heads by observing their behavior. The experienced researcher would argue that we should be cautious about thinking we know what is going on inside people's heads. We should be careful when leaping from the public, observable, physical

• FIGURE 1-3 •

CONSTRUCT VALIDITY

cathy®   **by Cathy Guisewite**

Knowing what participants do is not the same as knowing what they are thinking.

world of operational definitions to the private, unobservable, mental world of constructs (see Figure 1-3). At the very least, we should know when we are making a leap from observed events to unobserved constructs.

The novice apparently failed to notice that he took two such leaps. First, the novice did not directly go inside participants' minds and make them "feel warm." Rather, the novice investigator only manipulated the outside physical environment by raising the thermostat. Second, the novice investigator did not see participants "feel aggressive." He only observed their outward behavior.

You can see why the experienced researcher sees the novice as recklessly careless. Despite not directly manipulating or directly observing participants' psychological states, the novice investigator is making claims about psychological states. He is *labeling* his room manipulation as a manipulation of "feeling warm" and he is labeling participants' behavior as "aggressive." He is assuming that his concrete operational definitions accurately capture the abstract psychological constructs he wants to measure.

The skeptical scientist would wonder how the novice can be so confident that he has accurately labeled his manipulation and his measure. A skeptic might ask whether the novice should even dare to talk about constructs, which by definition are not observed, but are instead *constructed* (made up). As children learn in the story of "The Emperor's New Clothes," things that you do not see may not exist.

The novice investigator might respond that most scientists go beyond talking about the procedures they use. That is, physical scientists' conclusions do not deal with the actual actions they performed, but with the underlying variables that they manipulated. For example, the chemist's conclusions would not deal with the effects of "a lit Bunsen burner," but rather with the effects of the underlying variable—heat.

The experienced researcher would point out that the leap from observing the flame from the Bunsen burner touch the test tube to saying that the Bunsen burner manipulates the heat of molecules in a test tube is relatively safe and short. It is unlikely that the burner has any other effects. The molecules do not notice the flame's color, are not terrified by its intensity, do not care if it discolors the test tube, and do not smell it. On the other hand, the noise or the smell coming from the heater may annoy people. Thus, manipulating the temperature of molecules is simpler than manipulating how people feel. Furthermore, the chemist makes virtually no inference when it comes to observing the results of the reaction: Water is easy to observe and measure. In contrast, it is difficult to measure "aggression" accurately.

In short, the experienced research psychologist realizes that measuring and manipulating people's thoughts and feelings are more difficult than measuring and manipulating the behavior of molecules. If you are not careful, going from objective, observable, physical events to inferring invisible, subjective, psychological constructs may involve jumping to conclusions. For instance, some people are quick to infer that a person who works slowly is unintelligent; however, the truth may be that the individual is cautious, ill, lazy, or unfamiliar with the task.

Because the possibility of error is so great, psychologists are extremely cautious about inferring private mental states from publicly observable behavior. Therefore, the research psychologist would question the temperature study's **construct validity:** the degree to which the study measures and manipulates the underlying psychological elements that the researcher claims to be measuring and manipulating (see Figure 1-4). In this case, the research psychologist would look for three potential cracks in the study's construct validity:

1. The manipulation was poor, so the construct "feeling warm" was not properly manipulated.
2. The measure was poor, so the construct "aggression" was not accurately measured.
3. Participants figured out what the hypothesis was and played along, so the high scores on the "aggression" measure were due to lying or acting rather than to feeling aggressive.

Construct Validity Problems Caused by the Manipulation: What Does the Treatment Really Manipulate?

To start questioning whether the novice had manipulated and measured the constructs of "feeling warm" and aggression, the researcher might question the manipulation's construct validity. She would ask herself, "Is it right to call this raising-the-thermostat manipulation a 'feeling warm' manipulation?"

• **FIGURE 1-4** •

CONSTRUCT VALIDITY

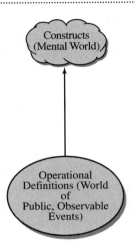

To begin answering that question, she would ask two other questions. First, "Did the manipulation make the 'warm' group really feel warmer than the other group?" Second, "Did the manipulation have any effect besides making the 'warm' group feel warmer?"

The answer to the first question is not as simple as you might think. One reason is because it is impossible to directly get inside participants' minds (1) to change how they feel, and (2) to see that you made that change. Instead, the only possible way for any researcher to manipulate participants' mental states is indirectly—by changing the physical environment. For any indirect manipulation to work, participants must mentally react to the manipulation in the way the researcher expects. Unfortunately, participants may interpret the manipulation differently from the way the researcher intended. Thus, putting one group of participants in a room that is, at the physical level, 10 degrees hotter than another is not the same as making one group, at the psychological level, "feel warmer" than another. For example, participants may take off jackets and sweaters to cool off, they may find the room's temperature "comfortable," or they might not even notice the change in temperature.

If the researcher decides that the manipulation does make participants feel warmer, she still has to answer the question, "Did the manipulation do anything besides make some participants feel warmer than others?" Usually, manipulations are not so pure that their only effect is to change what you intended to change. Instead, manipulations may have "impurities." As we will see, these impurities can be physical or psychological.

The research psychologist might start her search for the manipulation's impurities at the physical level. She would ask, "What did turning up the thermostat do to the participants' environment besides make the room hotter?" Turning up the thermostat in the "warm" room might not only make the room hotter, but also make the room noisier (if the heater was noisy) or decrease the room's air quality (if the heater's filter was dirty). If turning up the thermostat is a temperature manipulation, a noise manipulation, and an air-quality manipulation, how can the novice justify labeling it a "warmth" manipulation? It would be more accurate to call it a "temperature, noise, and air-quality" manipulation.

Even if the manipulation is "pure" at the physical level, it may not be pure at the psychological level. The novice may have made the participants feel frustrated about being unable to open the windows to cool off the room, or he may have made participants feel angry with him for putting them in such an uncomfortable room. Therefore, in addition to being a manipulation of feeling warm, the treatment may have had the additional side effect of making people frustrated and angry. So, how can the novice justify calling the room manipulation a "warmth" manipulation when it may actually be a frustration or anger manipulation?

As you have seen, it is difficult to manipulate variables. Even seemingly straightforward manipulations may not be what they seem. For example, suppose that an "aspirin" manipulation involves giving aspirins to one group, but not to the other. On the surface, the "aspirin" label would seem to describe the manipulation accurately. However, what if the aspirin tablets also contained caffeine? Then, rather than being a pure manipulation of "aspirin," the manipulation is an "aspirin and caffeine" manipulation. What if getting the aspirin makes participants expect to feel better? Then, the manipulation is an "aspirin and positive expectation" manipulation. In conclusion, you should always question the name that a researcher decides to attach to a manipulation. Because of the difficulties of manipulating what one wants to manipulate, the novice should not expect skeptical scientists to take it on faith that he is manipulating the invisible mental state that he claims to be manipulating.

Construct Validity Problems Caused by the Measure: What Does the Measure Really Measure?

Even if the manipulation of "feeling warm" is valid, the measure of aggression may not be. Psychological constructs such as aggression are abstract, invisible, and therefore impossible to measure directly. We can only indirectly assess inner reality from clues we find in outer reality. Because there is no direct pipeline to the mind, participants' behaviors and reactions may be mislabeled. For example, the novice investigator may have misinterpreted "kidding around" and attention-getting behaviors as aggression. Or, the novice investigator may have misinterpreted physiological reactions to being warm (sweating, flushed face) as signs of "nonverbal aggression." Or, the novice may have labeled assertive behavior as "aggressive." Or, the multiple-choice test of aggression may not have any construct validity. In short, it is reckless to assume that an operational definition will perfectly capture the construct that the researcher is trying to measure.

Construct Validity Problems Caused by Participants: Is Their Behavior Genuine or an Act?

Even if the novice had used a good manipulation and a good measure, the results may be misleading because the participants knew they were in a research project. In the novice investigator's study, warm room participants may realize that they have been (1) deliberately placed in an abnormally warm room and then (2) given an opportunity to express aggression. In other words, they may figure out that the researcher wants them to be aggressive. If they like the investigator, they may lie about how aggressive they feel or act aggressively just to help the investigator.

Review: Comparing Internal Validity and Construct Validity

In conclusion, our novice wants both internal and construct validity. He wants to be able to conclude that warmth causes aggression.

If his study had internal validity, but not construct validity, he couldn't legitimately make statements about constructs such as "aggression." Therefore, the only thing he could safely conclude would be that his manipulation caused a change in participants' behavior. For example, he might be limited to concluding, "Turning up the thermostat caused a difference in how participants filled in circles on a multiple-choice answer sheet."

If, on the other hand, his study had construct validity, but not internal validity, he couldn't legitimately make cause–effect statements. He could only conclude that "the group that felt warm was more aggressive." He could not conclude that warmth causes aggression because it might be that individuals in the warm room group had more aggressive personalities than the people in the other group.

EXTERNAL VALIDITY QUESTIONS: CAN THE RESULTS BE GENERALIZED?

Even if the novice researcher actually manipulated "feeling warm" and accurately measured "aggression" (construct validity) and established that differences between the two groups in this particular study were caused by the room manipulation (internal validity), the experienced researcher would still question the study's **external validity**: the degree to which the results could be *generalized* to different participants, settings, or times (see Figure 1-5). There are at least two reasons to question the aggression study's external validity.

Can the Results Be Generalized to Other Participants?

First, since people differ, a result that occurs with one group of people might not occur with a different group of people. The novice investigator might have ob-

• **FIGURE I-5** •

EXTERNAL VALIDITY

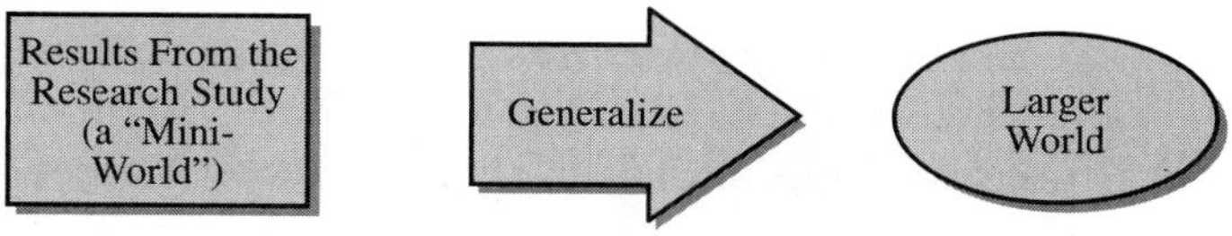

tained different results had he studied Russian sixth-graders instead of Midwestern college students; if he had studied people used to working in very warm conditions; or if he had studied less-aggressive individuals. To maximize external validity, the novice should have tested a large, random sample of participants.

Can the Results Be Generalized to Other Settings?

Second, since people's behavior may change depending on the situation, the results might not hold in another setting. For instance, suppose the novice investigator used a very sterile laboratory setting to eliminate the effects of nontreatment factors. By isolating the treatment factor, the novice investigator may have succeeded in establishing internal validity. However, results obtained under such controlled situations may not generalize to more complex situations, such as the workplace or the home, where other factors, such as frustration and pressure, come into play. Thus, the investigator may have achieved internal validity at the expense of external validity.

In short, even if temperature did increase aggression in this particular lab, with this particular group of participants, at this particular time, the experienced researcher would not automatically assume that temperature would have the same effect in future studies conducted with different participants in different settings. Therefore, to maximize external validity, the experienced researcher might repeat the study using different types of participants and different situations.

ETHICAL QUESTIONS: SHOULD THE STUDY BE CONDUCTED?

As you have seen, the novice failed to fully appreciate the differences between humans and molecules. The novice's failure to take into account the fact that humans are more complex and individualized than molecules would force any research psychologist to question the validity of the novice's temperature study. But in addition to failing to understand that humans are more complex and individualized than molecules, the student also overlooked the two most important differences between molecules and humans:

1. Molecules do not have rights, whereas humans do.
2. Chemists have no responsibility for the welfare of molecules involved in their studies, but psychologists have a responsibility for the welfare of their participants.

Therefore, in the researcher's mind, the most important question about the study is whether it was **ethical:** consistent with the American Psychological Association's principles of right and wrong. Indeed, no professional researcher would do a study without first determining whether the study could be conducted in an ethical manner. If the study can't be conducted ethically, it should not be done.

In deciding whether the study was ethical, the researcher would consult the American Psychological Association's *Ethical Principles of Psychologists and Code of Conduct* (APA, 1992), often referred to as the "*Principles.*" A copy of the ethical guidelines from the *Principles* relating to research is included in Appendix A. In addition to the *Principles,* the researcher might also consult the American Psychological Association's *Ethical Principles in the Conduct of Research With Human Participants* (APA, 1982). By consulting both sources, the researcher should be able to make an informed decision about whether the participants' rights had been protected and whether the novice investigator had lived up to his responsibilities.

Has Potential Harm Been Minimized?

As the *Principles* point out, participants have the right to know what will happen in the study, the right to refuse to be in the study, and the right to anonymity. Thus, according to the *Principles,* the novice should have told participants that the study would involve sitting in a warm room with a group of people. Knowing what the study was about, participants should have freely volunteered to be in the study. Once in the study, they should have been told that they could quit the study at any point. The novice should also have taken extensive precautions to ensure that no one other than the investigator found out how each participant behaved during the study.

The *Principles* not only discuss participant rights, but also discuss investigator responsibilities (see Table 1-3). According to the *Principles,* the investigator's responsibilities begin well before the study begins. As part of the planning phase, the investigator should try to anticipate all possible risks to participants and then protect participants from these risks. In this study, the investigator should consult with physicians to be sure that the temperature was not too hot and to identify people who might have a bad physiological reaction to the heat. In addition, the investigator would have to determine how to make sure that the aggression induced by the heat would not get out of hand, leading to someone getting physically or psychologically hurt.

While the study is being conducted, the investigator is responsible for behaving in an ethical manner. Furthermore, under some circumstances, the investigator may also be responsible for ensuring that others behave ethically. For example, if the novice had others working on the aggression study, the novice would be responsible

---

• **TABLE 1-3** •

SELECTED ETHICAL GUIDELINES FOR STUDIES INVOLVING HUMAN PARTICIPANTS

1. Participants should volunteer to be in the study. They should not be forced to participate.

2. Participants should have a general idea of what will happen to them if they choose to be in the study. In addition, they should be well-informed about anything that they might perceive as unpleasant. That is, they should know about anything that might cause them to decide not to participate.

3. Participants should be told that they can quit the study at any point and they should be encouraged to quit the study if, at any point, they find the study upsetting.

4. Investigators should keep each individual participant's responses confidential.

5. Investigators should make sure all people working for them behave ethically.

6. Investigators should try to anticipate all possible risks to participants and take steps to prevent these potential problems from occurring.

7. At the end of the study, investigators should probe participants for signs of harm and take steps to undo any harm detected.

8. At the end of the study, investigators should explain the purpose of the study and answer any questions participants may have.

9. Researchers should get approval from appropriate committees (such as the school's animal care and use committee, the institution's human participants committee) before conducting research.

---

for their conduct. In other words, if the people working with or for the novice behaved unethically, the novice could not avoid responsibility by saying that he personally did not misbehave or that he did not know what the others were doing.

After each participant has finished taking part in the study, the investigator should **debrief** participants: Explain the purpose of the study, answer any questions, and undo any harm that the participant may have experienced. During debriefing, the investigator should actively look for evidence of harm. The investigator can't merely assume that no one has been harmed. Instead, the investigator must accept the possibility that some participants may have been harmed. The investigator must also realize that some participants may be reluctant to tell the researcher that they have been harmed. Once harm is detected, the researcher should try to undo that harm.

Fortunately, most studies do not harm participants. Thus, the main function of debriefing is usually to explain the study to participants. Educating participants about the study is the least an investigator can do to compensate people for their participation. Telling participants about the study may also help participants by assuring them that their reactions are not unusual. For example, participants might think that they were antisocial or highly aggressive unless they were told that the study was designed to make them act and feel that way.

Unfortunately, you can't determine that the novice's study was ethical merely by observing that the novice followed a few simple guidelines. Instead, as the introduction to *The Ethical Principles in the Conduct of Research With Human Participants* (APA, 1982) states, "the decision to undertake research rests upon a considered judgment by the individual psychologist about *how to best contribute to psychological science and human welfare*" [emphasis added].

This statement has two important implications. First, it means that even if the novice fulfilled all his responsibilities to the participants, the study might still be unethical if the study were unlikely to contribute to psychological science and human welfare. Second, it means that even if the investigator violated certain participant rights (such not telling participants what the study is trying to find out), the study might still be ethical if the expected benefits of the study would compensate for those violations. Consequently, an important step in determining whether a study is ethical is determining the likelihood that the study will benefit humanity.

Have Potential Benefits Been Maximized?

The researcher would begin to determine the likelihood that the study would benefit humanity by determining the importance of the research question. Unfortunately, determining the value of the research question is highly subjective. One person may find the idea very important, another may find it unimportant. In the aggression study, the novice may believe that determining the relationship between temperature and aggression is extremely valuable, arguing that it might lead to ways of preventing riots. Others, however, may disagree.

To further complicate the problem of assessing the potential value of a piece of research, no one knows what the researcher will discover. A study that looks promising may discover nothing. On the other hand, many scientific studies designed to answer one question have ended up answering a very important, but unrelated question (Burke, 1978; Coile & Miller, 1984). For example, Pavlov set out to discover the role of saliva in digestion, yet ended up discovering classical conditioning. Because it is so hard to judge the value of a research question, the researcher would probably acknowledge that the novice's research question has some merit.

As you have seen, judging the importance of a research question is difficult. Therefore, to estimate the potential value of the novice's study, the research psychologist would put less emphasis on her subjective impression of the importance of the research question and put more emphasis on the more objective judgment of how well the study would answer the research question. That is, she would ask, "Is the study likely to provide valid data?"

By "valid data," she would not necessarily mean that the study must have all three types (construct, internal, and external) of validity. Indeed, few studies even attempt to have all three validities. Thus, rather than seeing whether the study has all three forms of validity, her focus would be on determining whether the study has the validity or validities necessary to answer the research question. To illustrate that different research goals require different validities, let's look at three examples.

First, suppose that an investigator wants to describe what most people do in a given situation. In that case, the investigator is not interested in the causes of behavior. Therefore, the investigator would not strive for internal validity. However, because the investigator is interested in generalizing the results to most people, the investigator would strive for external validity.

Second, suppose that a researcher is trying to develop a test of social intelligence. If the researcher's only goal is to show that the test accurately measures the construct of social intelligence, the researcher needs only construct validity.

Third, suppose that an investigator is trying to explain or control behavior. In that case, the investigator needs to discover the causes of a behavior. Therefore, such an investigator would need internal validity.

After carefully considering whether the study had the validity or validities necessary to answer the research question and after considering the importance of the research question, the research psychologist would have some sense of the potential value of the study. Then, the research psychologist would again consider the potential risks to participants. If steps had been taken to avoid harm and if the benefits outweighed the risks, the researcher would believe that conducting the study was ethical.

That does not mean, however, that the researcher would grant the novice permission to conduct the study. Indeed, even if the researcher wanted to conduct the study herself, she would not just go out and do it. Instead, she—like most researchers—would consult with others before doing the research.

Consulting with others is vital for two reasons. First, when weighing the benefits of one's own research against the costs to participants, it is hard to be fair and impartial. Second, consulting with others may lead to insights about how to protect participants from harm.

Because consulting with others is so important, some researchers will not do a research study until their department's ethics committee has approved the study. At many schools, researchers must obtain permission from a campus-wide ethics committee (often called *an internal review board* or *IRB*) before conducting any study that involves human participants. In any event, a novice investigator should always get approval from a higher authority before conducting a study. To reiterate: *Never conduct a study without first obtaining approval from your professor!*

As you have seen, the psychological researcher's most important concerns about the novice's aggression study are ethical concerns. Indeed, since ethical concerns include concerns about validity and human betterment, one could argue that ethical concerns are the researcher's only concerns (see Table 1-4).

But what if the novice's study had used animals instead of human participants? In that case, some might think that the psychologist would not have been concerned about ethics. As you can see from Table 1-5, nothing could be further from the truth. Indeed, in recent years, animal rights have received more attention from the American Psychological Association than human rights. If the aggression study had used animals as participants, the researcher would

• **TABLE I-4** •

Determining Whether a Research Study Is Ethical

Does it maximize the potential benefits to psychological science and human welfare?

1. Is the research question important?

2. Will the research study provide valid answers to the research question? The type of validity needed will depend on the research question.

   • If the research question concerns finding out whether a certain factor causes a change in behavior (e.g. "Does a certain type of school environment increase student attendance?"), the study should have internal validity. That is, the study should take steps to rule out the possibility that other factors may be responsible for the effect.

   • If answering the research question hinges on accurately measuring abstract psychological concepts, construct validity would be very important. That is, the researchers should be able to make a strong case that the psychological variables they are talking about are the variables they actually measured. Construct validity would be the main concern in a research study that was trying to develop a psychological test.

   • If the main purpose of the research is to provide results that can be generalized to the real world, external validity would be very important. In such a case, the researchers would want to show that their participants did not represent a limited sample of people. External validity is very important for polls because polls try to determine how most people would respond to certain questions.

Does it minimize the potential for harm to participants?

1. Does it conform to the ethical principles of the American Psychological Association?

   • Are participants volunteers?

   • Did they know what the study involved before they agreed to participate?

   • Were participants told they could quit the study at any point?

   • Were participants debriefed?

2. If participants will be subjected to stress,

   • Have less-stressful alternatives been considered?

   • Has the amount of stress been minimized?

   • Have procedures for helping distressed participants been established?

have consulted the ethical standards listed in Table 1-5 (APA, 1992) as well as APA's 1996 booklet, *Ethical Principles for the Care and Use of Animals,* a copy of which is included in Appendix A. If the study had been done unethically, the investigator would be severely punished.

CONCLUSIONS ABOUT THE QUESTIONS THAT RESEARCHERS FACE

You have seen that research psychologists are aware of the responsibilities and challenges of studying human and animal behavior. What you have not seen is the wide range of methods psychologists use to meet these challenges and re-

· **TABLE 1-5** ·

CARE AND USE OF ANIMALS IN RESEARCH

The ethical standards below are considered enforceable rules of conduct. Violating these rules may result in being expelled from the American Psychological Association and/or being sued or arrested.

a. Psychologists who conduct research involving animals treat them humanely.

b. Psychologists acquire, care for, use, and dispose of animals in compliance with current federal, state, and local laws and regulations, and with professional standards.

c. Psychologists trained in research methods and experienced in the care of laboratory animals supervise all procedures involving animals and are responsible for ensuring appropriate consideration of their comfort, health, and humane treatment.

d. Psychologists ensure that all individuals using animals under their supervision have received instruction in research methods and in the care, maintenance, and handling of the species being used, to the extent appropriate to their role.

e. Responsibilities and activities of individuals assisting in a research project are consistent with their respective competencies.

f. Psychologists make reasonable efforts to minimize the discomfort, infection, illness, and pain of animal subjects.

g. A procedure subjecting animals to pain, stress, or deprivation is used only when an alternative procedure is unavailable and the goal is justified by its prospective scientific, educational, or applied value.

h. Surgical procedures are performed under appropriate anesthesia; techniques to avoid infection and minimize pain are followed during and after surgery.

i. When it is appropriate that the animal's life be terminated, it is done rapidly, with an effort to minimize pain, and in accordance with accepted procedures.

SOURCE: From Ethical Principles of Psychologists and Code of Conduct (1992), *American Psychologist, 47,* 1597–1611 by the American Psychological Association. Reprinted with the kind permission of the American Psychological Association.

sponsibilities. Depending on ethical considerations, the type of validity the researcher is after, and the research problem, investigators may use a single participant or thousands of participants, human participants or animal participants, laboratory studies or field studies, experiments or surveys.

WHY YOU SHOULD UNDERSTAND RESEARCH DESIGN

Thus far, we have explained why professional psychologists are interested in scientific research. Psychologists see research as a useful tool to obtain answers to their questions. But why should you know how to use this tool?

TO UNDERSTAND PSYCHOLOGY

The classic answer is that you can't really understand psychology—the science of behavior—unless you understand its methods. Without understanding psychology's scientific aspects, you may know some psychological facts and theories, but you will not understand the basis for those facts and theories. Thus, to major in psychology without knowing about research would be like buying a car without looking at its engine or a house without inspecting its foundation.

A more practical answer is that psychology's value in the real world often comes not from its facts but from its methods. As a "young" science, psychology has not yet produced as much knowledge as some other sciences. Consequently, in some complex, applied situations, the most useful thing psychology can offer is not a prepackaged answer to the problem based on established facts, but rather its method of getting answers to problems (Levy-Leboyer, 1988).

TO READ RESEARCH

When research gets answers to problems that interest you, you will want to take advantage of that research. Often, to take advantage of that research, you must be able to read and interpret scientific research reports. For instance, you may want to know something about the latest treatment for depression, the causes of shyness, factors that lead to better relationships, or new tips for improving workplace morale. If you need the most up-to-date information, if you want to draw your own conclusions, or if you want to look at everything that is known about a particular problem, you need to be able to read the research yourself.

You can't rely on reading about research in textbooks, magazines, or newspapers. Textbooks will give you only sketchy summaries of the few, often out-of-date, studies selected by the textbook's authors. Magazine and newspaper articles, on the other hand, often talk about up-to-date research, but these reports may not accurately represent what happened.

Knowing research terminology and logic will allow you to bypass second-hand accounts of research. Consequently, you will be able to read the original source and come to your own conclusions.

With psychology progressing at a rapid rate, you really will need to keep up with the field. As an employee, you will want to make more money every year. How can you justify receiving raises if, with every year, your knowledge is more and more out-of-date? If you see clients, you should be giving them treatments that work, and you should be acting on the best information available. After all, you would not be pleased to go to a physician whose skills were 10 years out-of-date.

TO EVALUATE RESEARCH

If you understand research, you will not only be able to get recent, first-hand information, but you will also be in a position to evaluate that information. You also may be able to evaluate many second-hand reports of research in magazines and newspapers.[2] Thus, you will be able to take full advantage of the knowledge that psychologists are giving away, knowledge that is available to you in libraries, in newspapers, and on television. Your critical abilities will also enable you to judge how much weight you should place on a particular research finding—a very useful skill, especially when you encounter two conflicting research findings.

TO PROTECT YOURSELF FROM "QUACKS"

Perhaps more important than encountering conflicting research findings is the problem of identifying phony experts or "quacks." Free speech protects quacks, just as the free market protected "snake oil" salespeople in the days before the United States government created the Food and Drug Administration. Back then, patent medicine vendors could sell the public almost anything, even pills that contained tapeworm segments.

Today, "experts" are free to go on talk shows and the Internet to push "psychological tapeworms." Common "psychological tapeworms" include unproven and sometimes dangerous tips on how to lose weight, quit smoking, discipline children, and solve relationship problems.

We do not mean that all experts are giving bad advice. Instead, we mean that it's hard to tell what's good advice and what is not. Although the truth is out there, so are a lot of lies. Science, nonscience, and pseudoscience exist side by side on the shelves of the "psychology" section in the bookstore, on talk shows, on the Internet, and on televised "news magazines." We live in the Information Age, but we also live in the *Mis*information Age. As a result, without some training in research, it is hard to distinguish which "expert" information is helpful and which is potentially harmful.

TO BE A BETTER THINKER

Not only can understanding the scientific approach improve your access to psychological knowledge, but it can also improve your thinking. As you will see, science is an elaboration of everyday thinking. The skills you learn in this course—problem-solving skills, decision-making skills, looking for objective information, and being able to judge and interpret information—are transferable to your everyday life. Consequently, the same scientific thinking skills you will learn in this book are taught in books that purport to raise your practical intelligence (e.g., Lewis & Greene, 1982). Furthermore, those same skills are measured by some tests of "practical intelligence" (Frederikson, 1986) and are

---

[2]Assuming, of course, that the articles provide you with enough information about the study's procedures. If they do not, you will have to find the original scientific publication.

necessary for understanding certain real-life situations (Lehman, Lempert, & Nisbett, 1988). In addition, Lehman's research suggests that learning about research methodology in psychology transfers to understanding real-life applications of methodological principles better than does learning about other sciences, such as chemistry.

Put another way, people would like to be able to separate fact from fiction. They like to believe that they "tend to be skeptical and will not accept statements without adequate proof" (Forer, 1949). However, without understanding science, how can they know what "adequate proof" is?

TO BE SCIENTIFICALLY LITERATE

Another reason students take psychological research methods courses is that taking such courses is a relatively easy way to learn about how science works. Intelligent people are supposed to be able to profit from experience, and in today's world, many of our experiences are shaped by scientific and technological changes. Yet many people do not know how science works.

Some argue that this scientific illiteracy threatens our democracy—and they have a point. How can we make intelligent decisions about the so-called "greenhouse effect" if we can't properly interpret the data about global warming? We would like to rely on experts, but experts contradict each other on many important issues. Therefore, if we are going to make an informed decision about global warming, addressing the crime problem, or a host of other problems, we need to know how to interpret scientific research.

Regrettably, it appears that many people are not scientifically literate. Most high school students (and some high-ranking politicians) believe in astrology. Furthermore, many of astrology's skeptics can easily be made into believers (Glick, Gottesman, & Jolton, 1989). In addition to astrology, other scientifically invalid procedures such as handwriting analysis, foot reflexology, and numerology also enjoy surprising popularity (Lardner, 1994).

Given this low level of scientific literacy, perhaps it is not surprising that hype often seems to carry more weight than objective facts. Politicians, for example, often say, "We don't need to do research on the problem; we know what we need to do," or "I don't care what the research says, I feel. . . ." Similarly, many consumers are buying products that include "secret, ancient remedies" rather than products that have been proven to be effective through open, public, scientific testing.

With flagrant disregard for internal validity, people often make careless cause–effect statements. Leaders take credit for random or cyclical changes in the economy. Advertisers try to convince us that certain products cause professional models to be attractive. Even people who are not trying to sell us products use very weak evidence. For example, *Sports Illustrated* presented the following evidence "proving" that teens are being killed for high-priced sneakers: a young man was found dead, and his money, cocaine, and shoes had been stolen. Couldn't it be that he was killed for the money, the drugs, or some other reason? Does it have to be the shoes alone?

With blatant disregard for internal, external, and construct validity, talk show hosts periodically parade a few people who claim "success" as a result of some dieting or parenting technique. With similar contempt for our ability to think about and evaluate the internal, external, and construct validity of claims, advertisers still successfully hawk products using testimonials from a few satisfied users, and political leaders "prove" what our country needs by telling us stories about one or two individuals rather than "boring" us with facts (Kincher, 1992). Unfortunately, research shows that, to the naïve, these nonscientific and often misleading techniques are extremely persuasive (Nisbett & Ross, 1980).

TO INCREASE YOUR MARKETABILITY

Besides making you a more informed citizen and consumer, knowing about research makes you more employable. In today's job market, you probably will not be hired based upon what technical information you possess because such information is quickly obsolete and, in all likelihood, is already available from a computer database at the punch of a keystroke. Instead, you will probably be hired for your ability to evaluate and create information. That is, you will be hired for your analytical abilities rather than your knowledge of facts. For example, even marketing majors are told that, at least for their first few years, their scientific skills, not their marketing intuition, are what will pave the way to future career success (Edwards, 1990). In other words, if you have the analytical skills that enable you to distinguish between good and bad information, and the ability to turn data into useful information, companies want you. These same analytical skills will, of course, also be helpful if you plan to go to graduate school in business, law, medicine, or psychology.

TO DO YOUR OWN RESEARCH

To get into graduate school or to enhance your marketability, you may want to do your own research. Doing your own research shows that you are organized, persistent, and capable of getting things done.

Or, you may need to do research as part of your job. Some of our former students have been surprised that they ended up doing research to get government grants or to get more staff for their social services agencies. Perhaps they should not have been surprised. More and more organizations—from Wal-mart to museums—are doing research to find out if what they are doing works (Ralof, 1998). Others do research to find out whether what they are planning to do will work. For example, movie moguls do research to determine whether a movie's ending is effective—and how to change the ending if it is not.

But beyond the employment angle, you may find that doing research is its own reward. Some students like research because it allows them to "do" psychology rather than read about it. Some enjoy the teamwork aspect of working with professors or other students. Some enjoy the creativity involved in designing a study, seeing it like writing a script for a play. Some like the acting that is involved in conducting certain kinds of studies (some researchers claim that a valuable research skill is the ability to say "oops" convincingly). Some enjoy the challenges of solving the practical problems that go along with completing any project. Others enjoy the excitement of trying to get answers to questions about human behavior. They enjoy the search so much that some even consider psychology research as "me-search" (Field, 1993). Certainly, many have found the passion for discovery much more exciting than learning terms and definitions. Thus, not surprisingly, such poor-to-average students as John Watson (the father of behaviorism) and Charles Darwin enjoyed exploring the mysteries of human behavior. Once you start an investigation into one of the many uncharted areas of the human psyche, we think you will understand what Carl Rogers (1985) meant when he said, "We need to sharpen our vision of what is possible . . . to that most fascinating of all enterprises: the unearthing, the discovery, the pursuit of significant new knowledge" (p. 1).

Concluding Remarks

In conclusion, no matter what you do in the future, understanding scientific research will be useful (see Table 1-6). The skills you learn will allow you to refine your critical thinking skills and become a scientifically literate citizen and consumer—almost necessities in our science-dominated world.

Similarly, no matter what you do in the future, you may find it necessary to read and evaluate the merits of specific psychological research findings. If you become a counseling psychologist, you will want to use the best, most up-to-date treatments with your clients. Partly for this reason, licensing exams for counseling psychologists include questions testing knowledge of research methods. If you become a manager, you will want to know the most effective management techniques. If you become a parent, you will want to evaluate the relative effectiveness of different child-rearing strategies. To get accurate answers in any of these areas, you will need to understand research. Unless you understand the research process, you may be limited by insufficient, out-of-date, or inaccurate information.

Finally, knowing about research will help you get the tools you need to get answers to your own questions. By reading this book, you will learn how to generate research ideas, manipulate and measure variables, collect objective data, ensure validity, choose the right design for your particular research question, treat participants ethically, interpret your results, and communicate your findings. We hope you will use this knowledge to join the most fascinating quest of our time—exploring the human mind.

• **TABLE 1-6** •

EIGHT REASONS TO UNDERSTAND
PSYCHOLOGICAL RESEARCH METHODS

....

1. To understand psychology better
2. To keep up with recent discoveries by reading research
3. To evaluate research claims
4. To protect yourself from quacks and frauds
5. To be a better thinker
6. To be scientifically literate and thus a better-educated citizen and consumer
7. To improve your marketability in our Information Age
8. To do your own research

Summary

1. Psychologists use the scientific approach to unearth observable, objective evidence that either supports or refutes their preconceived notions.

2. Because scientists make their evidence public, they can check each other's work, as well as build on each other's work. Because of the public, group-oriented nature of science, scientific progress can be rapid.

3. Because scientists make their evidence public, informed people can make use of new discoveries.

4. Science is both open-minded and skeptical. It is skeptical of any idea that is not supported by objective evidence; it is open-minded about any idea that is supported by objective evidence.

5. One goal of science is to find simple, general rules that will make the world more understandable.

6. One reason psychological research is objective is that psychologists use concrete, operational definitions of abstract concepts.

7. Psychologists realize that concrete operational definitions may not really capture the invisible mental constructs the operational definitions are designed to capture. Thus, they question the labels that researchers give to their measures and manipulations.

8. When investigators actually are studying the psychological/mental states they claim to be studying, their research has construct validity.

9. Threats to construct validity include poor measures of variables, poor manipulations, and participants figuring out the purpose of the research and basing their actions on the researchers' expectations, rather than acting in a "genuine" manner.

10. Psychologists realize that it is hard to prove that a certain treatment causes an effect. Often, the "proof" is really only circumstantial evidence: Other factors may be responsible for the change in behavior. Therefore, psychologists often question cause–effect statements.

11. If a study establishes that a particular, observable, physical stimulus or manipulation causes a certain, observable response, then it has internal validity.

12. Psychologists realize that what happens with one group of participants in one setting may not generalize to another type of participant or to a different setting. For example, they realize that a study done with one group of students in a lab setting may not apply to a group of people working in a factory. Therefore, they are appropriately cautious about generalizing the results of a study to real-world situations.

13. If a study's findings can be generalized to other people, places, and times, the study has external validity.

14. There is no psychology without science. Without science, psychology would have fewer facts than it does now and would be little better than palmistry, astrology, graphology, or any other "pseudoscience." More specifically, using the scientific approach in psychology has allowed psychologists to (1) improve common sense, (2) disprove certain superstitions, and (3) make enormous progress in understanding how to help people.

15. Scientific research is a logical, proven, and ethical way of obtaining important information about human behavior.

16. Human participants in research studies have many rights, including the right to decide whether they want to be in the study, the right to privacy, and the right to learn the study's purpose.

17. *Do not conduct a study without the approval of your professor.* In addition, obtain approval from the appropriate ethics committees. For example, if you are doing animal research, you may need approval from your school's animal care and use committee. If you are doing research with human participants, you may need approval from your school's internal review board (IRB).

18. If you are involved with a study that harms a participant, you cannot avoid responsibility by arguing that you did not know the rules, that you did not mean to harm the person, that you were just doing what the lead investigator told you to do, or that your assistant, rather than you, was involved in the harmful behavior.

19. According to APA's ethical principles, the potential benefits of a study should outweigh the study's potential for harm. Thus, there are two ways to increase the chances that your study is ethical: Reduce the potential for harm, and maximize the potential gains of your research.

20. To maximize the gains of your research, you should make sure that your study has the kind of validity that your research question requires. Your research question will determine which type—or types—of validity you need.

21. If your research question is about whether something causes a certain effect, your study should have internal validity.

22. If your research question concerns what percentage of people engage in some behavior, you need a study that has external validity. One key to having external validity is to have a large, random, representative sample of participants.

23. If your research question involves measuring or manipulating some state of mind (hunger, stress, learning, fear, motivation, love, etc.), then you need construct validity.

24. Skills learned in research design are transferable to real life.

Key Terms

construct: a mental state that can't be directly observed or manipulated, such as love, intelligence, hunger, feeling warm, and aggression (p. 2).

operational definition: a "recipe" for how you are going to measure or manipulate a construct; the specific, observable, concrete steps involved in measuring or manipulating that particular construct. (p. 5)

construct validity: the degree to which the study actually measures and manipulates the elements that the researcher claims to be measuring and manipulating. If the operational definitions of the constructs are poor, the study will not have good construct validity. For example, a test claiming to measure "aggressiveness" would not have construct validity if it really measured assertiveness. (p. 23)

internal validity: the degree to which the study demonstrates that the treatment caused a change in behavior. If a study lacks internal validity, the researcher may falsely believe that a factor causes an effect when it really doesn't. Most studies involving humans do not have internal validity because they can't rule out the possibility that some other factor may have been responsible for the effect. Unfortunately, steps taken to increase internal validity (such as keeping nontreatment factors constant) could harm the study's external validity. (p. 18)

external validity: the degree to which the results of the study can be generalized to other places, people, or times. (p. 26)

ethical: conforming to a profession's principles of what is morally correct behavior. In the case of psychological research, the American Psychological Association has established guidelines and standards of morally appropriate behavior. To learn more about these guidelines and standards, see Table 1-3 and Appendix A. (p. 28)

debrief, debriefing: Explaining the purpose of the study, answering any questions, and undoing any harm that the participant may have experienced as a result of participating in the study. (p. 29)

replicable: repeatable. A skeptical researcher should be able to repeat another researcher's study and obtain the same pattern of results. (p. 7)

Exercises

1. Why is it important for scientists to make testable statements?
2. How do operational definitions help psychology to
   a. be objective?
   b. make testable statements?
   c. be public?
   d. be productive?
3. How does the ability of psychologists to replicate each other's work help psychology to be
   a. skeptical?
   b. open-minded?
   c. productive?
4. Match the following to the qualities of science.

   ___Testable   **a.** Learn from mistakes.

   ___Skeptical   **b.** "Show me the evidence."

   ___Open-minded   **c.** Avoid bias.

   ___Objective   **d.** Publish studies.

   ___Public   **e.** Question authority.

   ___Productive   **f.** Science works.

5. List at least two similarities between a scientist and a detective.
6. Physicists can't accurately predict certain simple events. For example, physicists have trouble with such questions as, "If you drop a basketball from a table, how many times will it bounce—and what will be the pattern of those bounces?" Which characteristic of science is threatened by physicists' failure to answer this question? What implications, if any, does this failure have for psychology?
7. Some early psychologists studied and reported on their own thoughts. For example, a person would solve a mathematical problem and then report on everything that went on in his mind during the time that he worked on the problem. What quality of science was missing in these studies?
8. From what you know about astrology, grade it on a "pass/fail" basis on how well it does on the following characteristics of science:

Characteristic	Grade
Makes testable statements	
Productive (knowledge refined, new discoveries made)	
Seeks objective, unbiased evidence to determine the accuracy of beliefs	

9. According to some, iridology is the science of determining people's health by looking at their eyes. Practitioners of this "science" learn it through secret, closed-door seminars; don't try to verify their diagnoses through other means; and different practitioners will diagnose the same patient very differently. What characteristics of science does iridology have? Where does it fall short?

10. Some claim that psychoanalysis is not a science. They attack it by claiming that it lacks certain characteristics of science. Below are three such attacks. For each attack, name the characteristic of science that psychoanalysis is being accused of failing to achieve.
    a. "Psychoanalytic explanations for a person's behavior often fit with the facts, but are generally made after the fact."
    b. "The unconscious is impossible to observe."
    c. "The effectiveness of psychoanalysis does not appear to have improved in the last 20 years."

11. Match the concept to the type of validity.

    ____ construct validity   **a.** generalize

    ____ external validity   **b.** cause–effect

    ____ internal validity   **c.** mental states

12. Match the threat to the type of validity.

    ____ construct validity   **a.** poor measure

    ____ external validity   **b.** treatment and no-treatment groups were unequal before the study began

    ____ internal validity   **c.** small, biased sample of participants

13. Abraham Maslow and other humanistic psychologists have argued that psychologists have studied rats and neurotic individuals but have not studied exceptionally well-adjusted people. This is a criticism about the_____ validity of research.

14. The professor of a psychology of women class notes that a study used only male participants. The professor is probably attacking the _____validity of that study.

15. The professor of a psychology of women class notes that a study claiming that women are more conforming than men could be interpreted as showing that women are more cooperative than men. The professor is probably attacking the _____ validity of that research.

16. A survey finds that Diet Coke drinkers are less irritable than Diet Pepsi drinkers. The investigator concludes that consuming Diet Pepsi causes enhanced irritability. This conclusion lacks _____ validity.

17. Don and Julie are engaged to be married this summer. However, upon taking a "couple compatibility" test in a popular magazine, they find they are

not compatible. Before breaking off their engagement, Don and Julie should determine the _____ validity of the test.

18. A medical school asks people to volunteer for a "study that involves taking drugs and undergoing psychological testing." The researchers conclude that the drug calms people down. Given the type of participants used in this study, the _____ validity of the research could be questioned.

19. Near the end of the last lecture before an exam, a professor asks two students whether they have any questions. Both say "no." As a result, the professor concludes that those two students know and understand everything that was covered in class. The professor's measure of "knowing and understanding everything" may lack _____ validity.

20. Match the criticism to the type of validity (internal, external, or construct) being questioned.

Criticism	Validity Being Questioned
Measure is biased.	
Two groups differ, not because of treatment, but by chance.	
Participants studied are not typical of an average cross-section of people.	
Only males were used.	
Measure used is not very good.	
Participants included only gifted 10-year-olds.	
Groups were not the same before treatment was introduced.	
Participants' reports of their feelings may be inaccurate.	
Participants may have guessed hypothesis and played along.	
Measure does not capture construct.	
Participants may have changed even without treatment, so researcher should not conclude that treatment caused the change.	
Results would not hold in a real-life situation.	
Task was boring and meaningless, so participants were not psychologically involved in the study.	
Manipulation may not have produced the intended effect on participants' psychological states.	

21. "A rose by any other name would smell as sweet." Perhaps. But if a scale that measured conservatism were relabeled "close-mindedness scale," there would be _____ validity problems with studies using this "close-mindedness" scale.

22. *Teen* magazine printed a survey form in a recent issue. Of those who reply, 40 percent claim to have used drugs. As a result, the magazine concludes that 40 percent of teens have used drugs. Even assuming the respondents are honest, the study may lack _____ validity.

23. The author of the book, *The Hidden Life of Dogs,* claims that her dogs fell in love and got married, had moral fiber, and that a male dog told a female dog that he knew she was younger than he and inferior to him in every way that mattered to dogs, but he didn't care about that since he felt unrequited love for her. A psychologist might question the _____ validity of these observations. Why?

24. A police officer puts a drunk in a blue room. The prisoner acts in a way that the officer describes as "violent." Then, the officer moves the prisoner to a pink room. This prisoner then acts in a way that the officer describes as "less violent."

    a. A scientist doubts that the pink room changed the prisoner's behavior. Instead, she thinks the change in the prisoner's behavior in the pink room might just be a coincidence. The prisoner may have changed his behavior for reasons that have nothing to do with the pink room at all (for example, the prisoner has calmed down by the time he enters the pink room). Since the scientist is doubting that the pink room caused the effect, she is questioning the study's _____ validity.

    b. A second scientist believes that even if the pink room changed this prisoner's behavior (that is, the study had _____ validity), there would be serious doubts as to whether the pink room would change the behavior of sober prisoners. The second scientist is questioning the degree to which the results would generalize. Thus, this scientist is questioning the study's _____ validity.

    c. A third scientist agrees that the prisoner's behavior changed, but does not agree that the behavior became "less violent." Instead, the scientist thought that the prisoner was simply less active in the pink room. Since the scientist is disputing the way the behavior was labeled, the scientist is attacking the study's _____ validity. Specifically, the scientist is attacking the _____ validity of the study's measure of aggression.

25. What type of validity are chemists most interested in? Why don't chemists do more research in natural settings like bakeries? What implications does this have for psychological research?

26. Is it ethical to treat a patient with a method that has not been scientifically tested? Why or why not? Is it ethical to withhold a treatment that is believed to work in order to find out if it does indeed work? Why or why not?

27. What APA ethical principles (see Table 1-3) are violated by television shows such as *Candid Camera* and *America's Funniest Home Videos?*

28. Would the studies done by the U.S. government in the 1950s to determine the effects of nuclear radiation—studies done without the participants' knowledge—be ethical according to APA's ethical code? Why or why not?

29. Two of the most ethically questionable studies in the history of psychology are Milgram's obedience study (where participants were told to deliver dangerous shocks to an accomplice of the experimenter) and Zimbardo's prison study (where well-adjusted students pretended to be either prisoners or guards). In both of these studies, there would have been no ethical problems at all if participants had behaved the way common sense told us they would; that is, no one would have obeyed the order to shock the accomplice, and none of the "guards" would have mistreated the prisoners.

Points to ponder:

a. Does the inability to know how participants will react to a research project mean that research should not be done?

b. Does people's inability to know how they and others will react in many situations mean that certain kinds of research should be performed so we can find out the answers to these important questions?

30. What ethical principles, if any, were violated in Milgram's shock experiment? (See Table 1-3.)

31. From the brief description of Zimbardo's prison study in question 29, what ethical principles, if any, were violated in Zimbardo's prison study? (See Table 1-3.)

32. Assume that a participant in a study in which you were involved suffered intense distress. According to the APA ethical guidelines, which of the following are legitimate excuses that would relieve you of responsibility? Explain your answers.

a. "I was just following orders."

b. "My assistant conducted the session and behaved inappropriately, not me."

c. "I didn't notice that the participant was upset."

d. "I just didn't think that we had to tell participants that they would get mild electrical shocks."

e. "I didn't think that asking questions about suicide would be upsetting—and for most of my participants it wasn't."

f. "When the participant got upset, it surprised me. I just didn't know what to do and so I didn't do anything."

g. "Our subjects were mice. We can cause mice whatever distress we want."

GENERATING AND REFINING RESEARCH HYPOTHESES

Much of what we take to be true is seriously wrong.
—GORE VIDAL

Science is a way to . . . distinguish truth from fraud.
—RICHARD FEYNMAN

....

OVERVIEW

Research does not begin with variables, equipment, or participants. It begins with questions. Thus, at one level, this is a book about how you can get answers to questions.

In this chapter, you will first learn how to get questions. Then, you will learn how to develop your questions into workable research **hypotheses:** testable predictions about the relationship between two or more variables.

....

GENERATING RESEARCH IDEAS FROM COMMON SENSE

One way to generate research ideas is to adopt the skeptical attitude that characterizes science. Thus, you should see whether the objective evidence supports or refutes ideas that you or others believe.

In trying to find out what is and is not true, you could question "time-tested" treatments as well as new treatments. These treatments may range from palm-reading courses to the value of the Internet for teaching.

Another avenue for your skepticism is to test common sense. As one scientist (Stern, 1993) put it, a major goal of psychology should be to "separate common sense from common nonsense." Many psychologists have tested common-sense assumptions. For example, Stanley Schachter (1959) tested the saying that "misery loves company." Robert Zajonc (1968) found the saying, "familiarity breeds contempt," to be false in many situations. Ellen Berscheid and her colleagues (1971) found that "birds of a feather flock together." Don Byrne (1971) found that opposites don't attract. Latane, Williams, and Harkins (1979) found evidence for the idea that "too many cooks spoil the broth." Wohlford (1970) found that fathers who smoked were more likely to have sons who smoked. Thus, he found some support for the saying, "like father, like son."

If we mentioned a saying that you were planning to test, do not automatically abandon plans to test that saying. Sayings are usually broad enough that all aspects of them can't be completely tested in a single study. For example, researchers still do not have definitive answers on the extent to which many of a son's behaviors (other than smoking) are modeled after his father's. Similarly, even though in 1971, Byrne found evidence that opposites (in terms of attitudes) don't attract, it wasn't until 7 years later that researchers found that opposites—in the form of psychologically "masculine" males and psychologically "feminine" females—don't attract in short-term blind dates (Ickes & Barnes, 1978). And it wasn't until 12 years later that researchers discovered that psychologically "masculine" males and psychologically "feminine" females don't attract in long-term marriage relationships (Antill, 1983). Thus, you can test a saying that has already been partially tested. However, if you want to test completely untested sayings, there are many from which to choose.

Where do you find a commonsense assumption that you could dispute? You might find one in a fortune cookie, in a package of Salada tea (Dillon, 1990), in a book of quotations, in a self-help or advice book such as *Life's Little Instruction Book,* in a song, in an ad, on a bumper sticker, on a T-shirt, or in an editorial column. Another way to find an assumption you want to test is to talk to a person who always seems to disagree with you. If both of you make sensible arguments, but neither one of you can prove that the other is wrong, then it is time to get objective evidence to show that your acquaintance is wrong.

Yet another way to find questionable assumptions is to attack a real-life, practical problem (cheating, prejudice, rudeness, apathy, too many false fire alarms in the dorms, etc.). Usually, you will find that different people have different "solutions" to almost any practical problem. You could collect objective evidence to find out which of these "solutions" work best.

If you decide to attack a practical problem, you may find that you have two research projects. The first is to document that a problem really exists; the second is to compare the effectiveness of different approaches to solving the problem. For example, you might first conduct a study to find out how prevalent the problem of cheating (or prejudice, apathy, superstitious thinking, etc.) is on your campus. Then, your second study might see which approaches to solving the problem are most effective. For instance, you might see if any of the following four methods designed to stop students from cheating on exams are more effective than what teachers normally do:

1. a lecture-based training program emphasizing the ways that cheating harms the cheater
2. group discussion about how cheating is unfair to other students
3. more serious penalties for cheaters
4. more observers walking around during the exam

In summary, questioning common sense is a time-tested way to generate research ideas. In the distant past, famous discoveries—such as that the earth revolves around the sun and that light objects fall just as fast as heavy objects—came from researchers who were willing to question common sense. More recently, a fourth-grader made national news by doing research that questioned whether a "healing technique" adopted by over 100 nursing schools was effective (Rosa, Rosa, Sarner, & Barrett, 1998). As you can see from these examples, just by being skeptical, other people have been able to generate important research ideas. If you are naturally somewhat skeptical and use Box 2-1, you too

---

• **BOX 2-1** •

SIX WAYS TO TAP YOUR INTUITION

1. Base your idea on "old sayings," assumptions or predictions made in songs, assumptions made in classic or popular literature, or statements made by experts, by asking:

   a. Is it true?

   b. Is there anything I know that seems to contradict that?

   c. When isn't it true? When is it more likely to be true?

   d. Is it true only in moderation?

   e. Why is it true (What is the cause-effect relationship? What is the mediating variable?)

   f. Why do people believe it's true?

2. Collect data on your own behavior, try to find rules that govern your behavior, and then see if those rules apply to other people.

3. Transform an argument into a research idea—find facts to settle a battle between two opinions.

4. Ask six key questions about any interesting phenomenon:

   a. Who does the behavior?

   b. How do people who are high performers and low performers of the behavior differ?

   c. What precisely is the behavior?

   d. When (under what circumstances) is the behavior most likely to occur?

   e. Why do people engage in the behavior?

   f. What are the long- and short-term effects of the behavior?

5. Determine why bad/irrational actions occur.

6. Attack a practical problem (ecology, illiteracy, prejudice, apathy, alcoholism, violence).

   a. Document that it exists.

   b. Evaluate the effectiveness of potential cures for the problem.

---

can generate an important research idea. However, testing your own insights is not the only—or even the most preferred—way to generate research ideas.

GENERATING RESEARCH IDEAS FROM PREVIOUS RESEARCH

A more preferred way to generate research ideas is to base an idea on previous research. For a beginning researcher, basing an idea on previous research has at least three major advantages.

First, a hypothesis based on previous research is more than a guess, it is an educated guess. Consequently, you have a reasonable chance of obtaining results that support your hypothesis.

Second, regardless of whether your hypothesis is supported, your study will be relevant to what other scientists have done. Consequently, your research will not produce an isolated, trivial fact.

Third, doing research based on other people's work is easier than starting from scratch, especially when you are a beginning researcher. Just as a beginning cook might find it intimidating to make a pizza from scratch without a recipe, some beginning researchers find it intimidating to design a study from scratch. However, just as the beginning cook would feel comfortable adding a few toppings to a store-bought pizza, a beginning researcher might feel comfortable building on someone else's study. That is, after learning how one study was done, the beginning researcher might feel comfortable designing a similar study.

SPECIFIC STRATEGIES

You have seen that there are advantages to developing research ideas from previous research. But how can you take advantage of other people's work?

Repeat Studies

The simplest way to take advantage of other people's work is to repeat (*replicate*) someone else's study. Since science relies on skepticism, you should repeat studies when you find the study's results difficult to believe—especially if those results conflict with results from other studies, seem inconsistent with established theory, or have not been replicated.

Do a Study Suggested by a Journal Article's Author(s)

Almost as simple as replicating a study is doing a study suggested by an article's authors. At the end of many research articles, the authors suggest additional studies that should be done. Often, they point out that the research should be repeated either using a different sample of participants or using a different setting.

Improve the Study's External Validity

Even if the researchers do not suggest it, you may decide to test the external validity (generality) of their findings. For example, you might ask:

1. Should I redo a study, but include types of participants that were not adequately represented in the original sample? That is, are there reasons to believe that the original study's results would not apply to most people, or to most women, or to most members of some other group?

2. Should I redo a lab study by taking it outside of the lab and into the real world? In other words, is there any important element of real life that was not only left out of the study, but that might moderate the relationship found in the original study?

3. Should I repeat the study using stimulus materials more like stimuli that people are exposed to in real life? Sometimes, stimuli in research are highly artificial. For example, many studies have asked participants to form impressions of a person based on reading a list of traits that supposedly describe that person, and many have asked participants to memorize

lists of nonsense syllables. Therefore, you might replace the list of words, nonsense syllables, or traits that participants saw in the original study with a videotape.

4. Can I think of any other situations where the relationship between the variables observed in the original study may not hold?

Improve the Study's Internal Validity

Instead of improving a study's external validity, you may choose to improve its internal validity. As you learned in Chapter 1, establishing that one factor caused an effect is very difficult, partly because it is hard to control other factors. For example, Gladue & Delaney (1990) argued that a study finding that "girls get prettier at closing time" at bars (Pennebaker et al., 1979) left unanswered the question of whether time or alcohol consumption was responsible for increased perceptions of attractiveness. Therefore, they modified the original study to control for the effects of alcohol consumption.

Similarly, although Frank and Gilovich (1988) found that teams switching to black uniforms were called for more penalties, their finding did not prove that wearing black causes a team to get more penalties. After all, it could be that aggressive coaches like to have their teams wear black. Therefore, as you can see in Appendix D, Frank and Gilovich devised a study that allowed them to make sure that uniform color was the only difference between their teams. Consequently, they were able to isolate black as the cause of the increased aggression.

Improve the Study's Construct Validity

Rather than improving a study's external or internal validity, you may choose to improve a study's construct validity. As you learned in Chapter 1, when trying to guess what is going on inside participants' minds, researchers may guess wrong. Usually, the problem is either that the researchers used poor operational definitions of their constructs (the manipulation or measure was poor) or that participants figured out the hypothesis and that discovery affected their responses.

When thinking about improving a study's construct validity, the first place to start is by seeing whether you can use a better manipulation or measure than the original researchers used. Is there a better "stress" manipulation than the one the original researchers used? Was their "conformity" measure really a measure of cooperativeness? Even if they used a relatively good measure of the construct they wanted to measure, it is unlikely that any single measure of a broad construct such as conformity, intelligence, aggression, or memory will fully capture the entire construct. Therefore, if the original study finds a relationship using one set of operational definitions, you might replicate the study using different operational definitions of the construct(s). Thus, when early research suggested that men have greater "spatial ability" than women, critics questioned whether the tasks used to measure spatial ability fully captured the construct of spatial ability. This questioning led to further research. That research has given us a better picture of how men and women differ on spatial ability. (On the average, men are much faster than women at mentally rotating objects, are slightly better at picking out figures that are hidden in a complex background, and are not as good at remembering where objects are.)

Even when the measures and manipulations are fine, a study's construct validity will be poor if participants figure out what the hypothesis is. Therefore, when reading a study, you should ask, "If I were a participant, would I know what results the researcher expected?" If your answer to this question is "yes," you may decide to repeat the study but improve it by reducing the biasing effects of participants' expectations.

One way to avoid the biasing effects of participants' expectations is to use the **double-blind technique:** the tactic of keeping both the participants and the research assistants who interact with the participants from knowing which treatment the participants are getting. You are probably most familiar with the double-blind technique from studies examining the effects of new drugs. In such studies, the participants all receive a pill, but only some of the pills have the real medicine in them. Since neither the physician nor the participant knows who has received the real drug, differences between the real-pill group and fake-pill (placebo) group will be due to the drug itself rather than to the patient's or physician's belief that the drug will work.

Look for Practical Implications of the Research

Even if you are satisfied with the original study's validity, the study will still leave many questions unanswered. If the study involves basic (nonapplied) research, do the findings apply to a practical situation? For example, can a technique that helps participants remember more words on a list in a laboratory experiment be used to help students on academic probation? Similarly, if a study finds that a treatment affects the way people think, you could do a study to see if the same treatment also affects what people actually do. It is one thing to show that a treatment makes participants remember certain information, feel more sympathy for a crime victim, or produce more of a certain kind of chemical. It is something else to show that the treatment changes the way participants actually act in real-life situations.

Try to Reconcile Studies That Produce Conflicting Results

When you find studies that produce conflicting results, there is obviously a need to reconcile the apparent contradiction. One strategy for resolving the contradiction is to look for subtle differences in how the studies were conducted. What do the studies that find one pattern of results have in common? What do the studies that find a different pattern have in common? Asking these questions may alert you to a possible **moderator variable:** a variable that intensifies, weakens, or reverses the relationship between two other variables.

Trying to uncover the moderator variable is a creative and potentially productive task. For example, consider the research on the effect of having people watch you. Many studies found a "social facilitation" effect—the presence of an audience improved performance. Many other studies, however, found a "social inhibition" effect—the presence of others decreased performance. By studying both the studies that found a "social facilitation effect" and the studies that found a "social inhibition" effect, Robert Zajonc (Zajonc, 1965; Zajonc & Sales, 1966) discovered how the two sets of studies differed: Studies finding social facilitation involved tasks that were easy for participants to do, whereas studies finding social inhibition involved tasks that were hard for participants to do. Zajonc then designed several studies where he varied both the presence of others and task difficulty. His results supported the hypothesis that task difficulty was a moderator variable. That is, the effect that other people's presence had on task performance depended on how difficult the task was.

CONCLUSIONS ABOUT GENERATING RESEARCH IDEAS FROM PREVIOUS RESEARCH

In conclusion, existing research is a rich source of research ideas. At the very least, you can always just repeat the original study. If you wish to modify the existing study, there are numerous ways you can go. You could improve its internal, construct, or external validity. Or, you may decide to pursue the practical applications of the study. Or, you may try to find situations where the findings would not hold. Or, you could try reconciling a study's findings with a study that obtained different findings. Or. . . .

Not only does using existing research help you generate ideas, but it also helps you test those ideas. For instance, if you decide to repeat a study, reading the original study will tell you almost everything you need to do. Even if you develop a follow-up study, reading the original article closely will help you determine how to measure your variables, what to say to your participants, and so forth.

....

CONVERTING AN IDEA INTO A RESEARCH HYPOTHESIS

If you used any of the strategies we have discussed thus far, you should have some research ideas. However, you may not have a research hypothesis. That is, you may not have a testable prediction about the relationship between two or more variables. Although converting an idea into a workable research hypothesis can be difficult, it is absolutely essential. It is essential because the goal of all research is to test hypotheses.

Admittedly, different types of research may test different kinds of hypotheses. For example, laboratory experiments test cause-effect hypotheses. They try to find out whether a treatment causes a certain effect. Survey research, on the other hand, tries to test descriptive hypotheses. Rather than find out why the behavior occurs, survey research tries to focus on who does the behavior, how they do the behavior, or when and where they do the behavior. Thus, a lab experimenter's hypothesis may involve seeing whether a given intervention stops people from cheating, whereas a survey researcher's hypothesis may deal with finding out whether men are more likely to cheat than women. Despite their differences, however, both researchers will have hypotheses.

Not only do all researchers have hypotheses, they have their hypotheses before they conduct their research. If they started their research without having a hypothesis to help them know what to look for, it is unlikely that they would have found anything. Consequently, most professors and many ethics committees require you to state the hypothesis you plan to test before they will even consider allowing you to do research. Because having a hypothesis is so important, the rest of this chapter is devoted to helping you generate a workable research hypothesis.

MAKE IT TESTABLE

When converting an idea into a hypothesis, you must be sure that your hypothesis is testable. In general, a testable hypothesis has the same basic characteristics as a fair bet.

As with any bet, you must be able to define your terms. For example, if you bet that, "Gene will be in a bad mood today," you need some publicly observable way of determining what a bad mood is. Similarly, if you hypothesize a relationship between two variables, you must be able to obtain operational definitions of your key variables. Thus, if you plan to measure the effects of physical attractiveness on how much a person is liked, you must be able to define attractiveness according to publicly observable criteria, and you must be able to measure liking objectively.

Also, as with any bet, your prediction should be specific so that it is clear what patterns of results would indicate that your hypothesis "won" and what results would indicate that your hypothesis "lost." You do not want to do a study and then have to debate whether the results supported or refuted your hypothesis. Usually the easiest way to avoid such disputes is to make your hypothesis as specific as possible. Therefore, when stating your hypothesis, specify not only a relationship between two or more variables, but also the direction of that relationship. That is, rather than saying aggression will vary with temperature, it would be better to say increases in aggression will correspond to increases in temperature. Ideally, you would be even more specific. For example, you might predict that increasing the temperature from 80 to 90 degrees Fahrenheit will increase aggression more than increasing the temperature from 70 to 80 degrees. To check that your prediction is precise enough, ask yourself, "What kind of result would disconfirm my prediction?" and "What kind of result would support my prediction?" Then, graph both of these patterns of results.

By being precise, you can avoid making predictions that are so vague that no pattern of results will disprove them. Unlike some fortune tellers and unscrupulous gamblers, you want to be fair by giving yourself the opportunity to be proven wrong.

MAKE IT SUPPORTABLE

Besides giving your hypothesis a chance to be refuted, you also want to give your hypothesis the opportunity to be supported. That is, you not only have to beware of making bets you can't lose, but also of bets you can't win.

You must be especially wary of one kind of bet you can never win—trying to prove the **null hypothesis:** a prediction that there is no relationship between your variables. Even if your treatment group scores exactly the same as the no-treatment group, you have not proven the null hypothesis.

To understand why you can't prove the null hypothesis, suppose you hypothesize no relationship between attraction and liking. Even if you find no relationship, you can't say that there isn't a relationship. You can only say that you didn't find the relationship. Failing to find something—whether it be your keys, a murder weapon, a planet, or a relationship between variables—is hardly proof that the thing doesn't exist.[1]

The fact that you can't prove the null hypothesis has two important implications. First, you can't do a study to prove that a treatment has no effect. If you find no difference between your treatment group and no-treatment group, you can't say that your treatment has no effect: You can only say that you *failed* to find a treatment effect. Second, you can't do a study to prove that two treatments have the same effect. That is, if you find no difference between your two treatment groups, you can't say that the treatments have the same effect: You can only say that you *failed* to find a difference between them.

BE SURE TO HAVE A RATIONALE: HOW THEORY CAN HELP

In addition to making sure that your hypothesis is testable, make sure that you have a solid rationale for your hypothesis. If you can't think of a good reason why your hypothesis should be correct, your hypothesis is probably a "bad bet." For example, if you hypothesized, without giving any rationale, that people would be more creative after drinking seven glasses of water, it is doubtful that your prediction would pan out. Instead, it would appear that you were simply going on a hopeless fishing expedition. Therefore, always write out the reasons for making your prediction. Your rationale can come from previous research that has found results similar to what you are hypothesizing, common sense, or theory.

Do not overlook the fact that theory can provide a rationale for your hypothesis, even when your hypothesis did not originally come from theory. For example, suppose that, on a hunch, you predicted that having pets would

---

[1]But why might you fail to find an effect? We'll answer that question in Chapter 6. For now, just realize that we can't say "there is no effect." Instead, we can only say "no effect has been found."

cause the elderly to be more mentally alert and healthy. You might then use theory to help you clearly articulate a logical rationale for your prediction. For example, according to learned helplessness theory, a lack of control over outcomes may cause depression. Therefore, having a pet may give one more of a sense of control and thus make one less vulnerable to helplessness (Langer & Rodin, 1976).

DEMONSTRATE ITS RELEVANCE: THEORY VERSUS TRIVIA

In addition to giving yourself a reasonable chance of finding support for your hypothesis, you should explain how your research fits in with existing theory and research or how it solves a practical problem. Scientists frown on doing research just to find isolated bits of trivia. For example, without any other rationale, doing a study to show that alcohol decreases Ping-Pong performance is meaningless, except possibly to people who bet on Ping-Pong. Psychological research should not be a trivial pursuit.

Theory can transform your hypothesis from trivial to relevant. To see how, consider the following two examples.

First, consider the following hypothesis: Around age 7, children stop believing in Santa Claus. In its own right, this is a relatively trivial hypothesis. However, when put in the context of Piaget's theory, which states that around age 7, children are able to think logically about concrete events (and thus realize that Santa Claus can't be everywhere at once and can't carry that many toys), the finding has deeper significance.

Second, suppose you were to make a hypothesis about a gender difference. At first, this hypothesis might seem quite trivial. If you were, however, able to tie your hypothesis to the theory of evolution, your hypothesis would be more interesting.

How could you tie a hypothesis about gender differences to the theory of evolution? The key is to assume that although both genders have the evolutionary goal of having as many offspring that survive into adulthood as possible, the strategies that will achieve this aim for men are different from the strategies that will achieve this aim for women (Buss, 1994). Consequently, it is consistent with the theory of evolution that men would be more:

- promiscuous (They have virtually no limit on how many offspring they can have.)

- jealous (Unlike women, men can't be sure that they are the biological parent.)

- impressed by youth (Younger women are more fertile than older women.)

- influenced by physical attractiveness (Attractiveness is a rough indicator of health, and the woman's health is vital because the potential offspring will live inside the woman's body for 9 months.)

You are not limited to using a single theory to make your hypothesis seem relevant. Indeed, the most interesting hypotheses are the ones in which you can show that one theory predicts one outcome, whereas a second theory predicts the opposite outcome. For example, researchers tested the psychoanalytic prediction that if you express hostility toward a person, you'll release pent-up anger and consequently feel better about the person. They pointed out that cognitive dissonance theory, on the other hand, predicts that if John is mad at Bob and then hurts Bob, John will justify his aggression by viewing Bob in a negative way. That is, according to dissonance theory, after you express aggression toward a person, you will feel more hostility toward that person. Experiments support the dissonance prediction (Aronson, 1990).

REFINE IT: 10 TIME-TESTED TIPS

One reason you may have trouble demonstrating your hypothesis's relevance is that you are not used to using past research and theory to justify testing an idea. However, another reason you may have trouble selling people on the value of testing your idea is that you need a better hypothesis to sell. Below are 10 tips that have helped students improve their hypotheses.

1. Don't Be Afraid to Be Wrong

It is nice to have the results support your hypothesis. It is also nice to have a powerful rationale for why the hypothesis will be supported. However, if you accomplish these goals by proposing a study that has been replicated time and time again, you will probably have difficulty explaining why the study needs to be replicated yet again. Remember, scientists are allowed to make mistakes. Indeed, scientists often learn more from predictions that do not turn out than from those that do.

2. Don't Be Afraid to Deal With Constructs

It is difficult to accurately measure and manipulate constructs. However, if you avoid dealing with constructs, you may propose a study that is easy to test, but hard to find interesting. For example, you might propose the hypothesis that alcohol will decrease reaction time. To avoid proposing hypotheses that lack both constructs and excitement, realize that there are valid ways to manipulate and measure constructs (as you will see in the next chapter).

3. Don't Avoid Theory

Theory can help you make the leap from just having a general topic to having a specific prediction, especially if your topic is an applied problem. As Kurt Lewin said, "There is nothing so practical as a good theory."

Before seeing how theory can help you attack a practical problem, let's first look at cognitive dissonance theory (see Figure 2-1). According to cognitive dissonance theory, if a person holds two thoughts that the person considers contra-

• FIGURE 2-1 •

COGNITIVE DISSONANCE

Dilbert reprinted by permission of United Features Syndicate, Inc.

dictory, the person will experience an unpleasant state called dissonance (see Table 2-1). Since dissonance is unpleasant, the person will try to reduce it, much as the person would try to reduce hunger, thirst, or anxiety (Aronson, 1990).

• TABLE 2-1 •
BASIC PROPOSITIONS OF COGNITIVE DISSONANCE THEORY

1. If an individual has two thoughts that the individual considers inconsistent, then that individual will experience dissonance.
2. Dissonance is an unpleasant state, like anxiety or hunger.
3. An individual will try to reduce dissonance.
4. Changing one of the thoughts to make it consistent with the other is one way of reducing dissonance.

To better understand cognitive dissonance, suppose a man thinks he is generous, but also knows he doesn't give money to charity. If he notices and perceives that these two thoughts are inconsistent, this inconsistency will bother him. In other words, he will feel dissonance. To reduce this dissonance, he may change his thoughts or his actions. To reconcile the perceived inconsistency, he may decide that he is not generous, or that the charities he refused were not worthwhile, or that he will give more money to charity.

Now that you have some understanding of cognitive dissonance theory, let's see how two sets of researchers used dissonance theory to go from a general practical problem to a specific prediction. The first set were concerned with the general problem of how to get people to buy condoms. According to cognitive dissonance theory, people will buy condoms if buying condoms will reduce their feelings of cognitive dissonance. That is, if John is aware that he has two contradictory thoughts ("I believe that people should use condoms when having sex," and "I have had sex without condoms"), John will feel dissonance. To reduce that dissonance, he can perform an action that will be consistent with what he has just preached—buy condoms. Thus, cognitive dissonance theory led to this hypothesis: Participants will be motivated to buy condoms if researchers (a) have participants publicly advocate the importance of safe sex and then (b) remind each participant about times when that participant had failed to use condoms. As predicted, participants who were made to see that their past behavior was inconsistent with their publicly stated position were more likely to buy condoms (Stone, Aronson, Crain, Winslow, & Fried, 1994).

The second set of dissonance researchers were concerned about the general problem of getting introductory psychology students to believe that it was important to learn about research methods. Although many general psychology professors have worried about the problem, Miller, Wozniak, Rust, Miller, & Sleezak (1996) consulted cognitive dissonance theory to find a specific treatment. The hypothesis suggested by cognitive dissonance theory was that having students write essays about why it was important to know about research methods would be more effective than lecturing to students about the value of research. This hypothesis was supported: Students were most likely to believe in the value of research methods when they had "convinced themselves."

You have seen that theory can be useful. A theory, however, can only help you if you know about it and understand it. How can you get to know a theory?

Your first step to getting introduced to a theory might be to read textbook summaries of theories. These summaries will allow you to select a theory that can help you. Once you have selected a theory, you must go beyond textbook summaries because such summaries may oversimplify the theory. The researcher who relies exclusively on textbook summaries may be accused of ignoring key propositions of the theory or of using a **straw theory:** an exaggerated, oversimplified caricature of the theory. Therefore, in addition to reading textbook summaries, you should also see how other researchers have summarized the theory. To find these summaries, consult journal articles that describe studies based on the theory (e.g., "Elation and depression: A test of opponent process theory"). The beginnings of these articles usually include a brief description of the theory that the study tests.

Once you have selected a theory, read the original statement of the theory (the citation will be in the texts or articles that you read). Then, to keep up-to-date about changes in the theory, use *Psychological Abstracts* or *Social Sciences Citation Index* to find books and review articles devoted to the theory. (For more information on how to conduct a literature review, see Appendix B.)

4. Be Manipulative

Rather than trying to describe what happens, try to change what happens. That is, think about how you can manipulate variables. For example, the authors of the sample article in Appendix D, like many other people, had observed that wearing dark uniforms was associated with aggression. They went beyond what others had done, however, by manipulating whether participants wore black or white uniforms and observing its effect on aggressiveness.

5. Look for Other Effects

Almost any variable will have more than one effect. There are short-term effects, long-term effects, good effects, bad effects, and side effects. So, if people are looking at the good effects of pursuing the American dream, you could look for the bad effects. Similarly, if others look for the good effects of attractiveness, you could look at the bad effects.

6. Reverse Cause and Effect

Suppose you have a rather ordinary hypothesis such as "If a person is attractive, participants will be more likely to help him/her than if the person is not attractive. That is, being attractive causes one to be helped." Your idea is to make a friend look either moderately attractive or very attractive and see if the friend is helped more when she looks very attractive. You could make this hypothesis more interesting by changing which variable is the cause and which is the effect.

That is, you could hypothesize that being helped leads to being perceived as attractive. For example, you might give some participants a chance to do your friend a favor and see if the participants who had a chance to help your friend rate her as being more attractive than those who are not given that opportunity.

7. Look for Moderator Variables

If you have a hypothesis about the relationship between two variables that is too obvious and too well-documented, ask yourself, "Under what circumstances doesn't this relationship hold?" Think of exceptions to the rule. For instance, imagine that Leslie Zebrowitz had decided to test the old saying "people from a different race all look alike." This hypothesis would not be that interesting because much research had shown support for it. Instead, she and her colleagues thought about exceptions to that rule. She and her colleagues (Zebrowitz, Montepare, & Lee, 1993) found that, under certain conditions, people could do a good job of distinguishing between members of other racial groups. For example, they found that attractiveness moderated the "all look alike" effect: People could distinguish between attractive and nonattractive members of a different race.

In addition to looking for variables that moderate relationships that both common sense and research have established, you could look for moderator variables that would allow you to reconcile the inconsistencies of common sense. For example, when does "like attract like," and when do "opposites attract"? When does "absence make the heart grow fonder," and when does absence mean "out of sight, out of mind"? Under what circumstances are "two heads better than one," and under what circumstances is it better to do it yourself (after all, "too many cooks spoil the broth" and "nothing is worse than a committee")?

One type of moderator variable you might look for could be your intervention program. For example, you might predict that people who went through your "how to work better in groups" training program might follow the "two heads are better than one" rule, whereas those who had not would follow the "too many cooks spoil the broth" rule. In other words, untrained people might work better alone, whereas trained people might work better in groups.

8. Look for Mediating Variables

Rather than look for factors that moderate a relationship between two variables, you might look for the **mediating variable:** the mental or biological mechanism by which the stimulus affects the response. Understanding the mediating processes inside the participant that come between the observable stimulus and the observable response allows you to understand how a cause has its effects. That is, a stimulus may have an effect by first changing some mediating variable inside the participant (thoughts, feelings, or physiological reactions) which, in turn, triggers a change the participant's behavior.

Even the most mundane hypothesis may become quite interesting by focusing on the "behind the scenes" mediating processes that are responsible for the proposed relationship. For example, the hypothesis that football fans feel bad when their team loses is not that interesting. It is interesting, however, to hypothesize about the bodily or psychological mechanisms that create this effect. What inside the person causes him to feel bad? Is there a decrease in testosterone? A change in their self-concept? Similarly, hypothesizing that attractive people are more persuasive is not that interesting. It is more interesting to find out how that works. What mediates that relationship? Is the mediator perceived honesty? That is, are attractive people more persuasive because they are perceived as more honest? If you suspect that a mediating variable is responsible for the effect of a certain factor, you should do an experiment that manipulates that mediating variable (Sigall & Mills, 1998).

9. Be More Specific

Sometimes, you can improve your hypothesis by being more specific. For instance, the hypothesis that exercise reduces stress is, by itself, not that interesting. However, it would be interesting and valuable to graph the functional relationship between exercise and stress so that we could specify how much exercise leads to how much stress reduction. Can you get away with exercising for 15 minutes, or do you need an hour to get the full effect? Is exercising for 2 hours twice as effective as exercising for 1 hour? In terms of stress reduction, is exercising for 3 hours better, worse, or the same as exercising for 1 hour? For many treatments, people would like to know how much is too little, how much is too much, and how much is just right. The best way to estimate the effects of different amounts (doses) of a treatment is to map the shape of the **functional relationship:** the extent to which changes in one variable are accompanied by changes in another variable.

10. Look at Components

Another way to be more specific is to break down a broad construct into its components (see Figure 2-2). Thus, rather than hypothesizing that love will increase over time, you might hypothesize that certain aspects of love (commitment, intimacy) will increase over time, whereas other parts (passionate love) will not. Similarly, rather than saying that stress will interfere with memory, you might try to find what part of memory is most affected by stress. Is it encoding, rehearsal, organization, or retrieval?

MAKE SURE THAT TESTING THE HYPOTHESIS IS BOTH PRACTICAL AND ETHICAL

Once your hypothesis is testable, reasonable, and relevant, you must still ask two additional questions. The first question is, "*Can* your hypothesis be tested?" Sometimes you may not have the skills or the resources to test it. For example, testing some hypotheses in physiological psychology may require equipment or surgical skills that you do not have. The second question is, "*Should* your hypothesis be tested?" That is, can the hypothesis be tested in an ethical manner?

• **FIGURE 2-2** •

Two Examples of How Component Measures Generate New Relationships to Explore

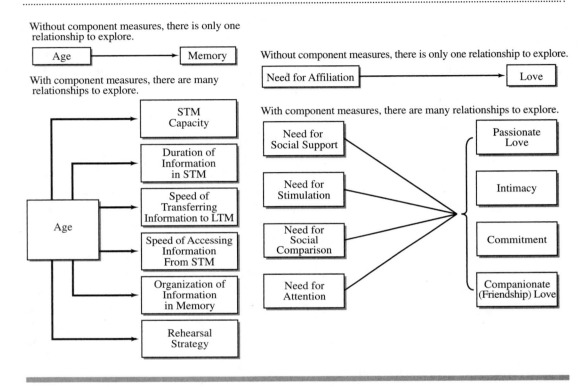

You have a serious obligation to make sure that your study is ethical. Clearly, you do not have the right to physically or psychologically harm another. Reading Appendix A can help you to decide whether your study can be done in an ethical manner. However, because conducting ethical research is so important, do not make the decision to conduct research without consulting others. Before doing a study, you and your professor will probably need to have your project reviewed by an ethics committee. In any event, *never conduct a study without your professor's approval!* (See Table 2-2.)

CHANGING UNETHICAL AND IMPRACTICAL IDEAS INTO RESEARCH HYPOTHESES

In their present form, some of your ideas may be unethical or impractical. However, with a little ingenuity, many of your ideas can be converted into workable

---

• TABLE 2-2 •

QUESTIONS TO ASK ABOUT A POTENTIAL HYPOTHESIS

1. Can it be proven wrong?
   - Can you obtain operational definitions of the variables?
   - Is the prediction specific?

2. Can it be supported?
   - Are you predicting that you will find an effect or a difference? (Remember, your results can never prove the null hypothesis.)

3. Are there logical reasons for expecting the prediction to be correct?
   - Is it predicted by theory?
   - Is it consistent with past research findings?
   - Does it follow from common sense?

4. Would the results of the test of your prediction be relevant to:
   - previous research?
   - existing theory?
   - a practical problem?

5. Is it practical and ethical to test your prediction?
   - Do you have physical and financial resources to test this idea?
   - Would testing the hypothesis cause physical or psychological harm to the participants? (See Appendix A.)
   - Do you have approval from your professor?
   - If your school has an internal research review board (IRB), do you have approval from that board?

---

research hypotheses. As you will see, many practical and ethical obstacles can be overcome by making the key variables more abstract, constructing a smaller scale model of the situation, toning down the strength of the manipulation, not using manipulations, or finding ways to operationalize the crucial variables.

To understand how these principles can turn even the most impractical and unethical idea into a viable research hypothesis, consider the following hypothesis: Receiving severe beatings causes one to be a murderer. How could we convert this idea into a workable research hypothesis?

MAKE VARIABLES MORE GENERAL

One possibility is to make your key variables more abstract. That is, you might view murder as a more specific instance of aggression. Similarly, you might view beating as a specific instance of either aggression, pain, or punishment. Thus, you now have three research hypotheses that have been studied in controlled settings: "aggression leads to more aggression," "pain causes aggression," and "punishment causes aggression."

USE SMALLER SCALE MODELS OF THE SITUATION

Of course, you are not going to have human participants hitting each other to measure aggression. Instead, you may give participants an opportunity to destroy something that supposedly belongs to the target of their anger, an opportunity to write a negative evaluation, an opportunity to press a button that supposedly (but doesn't really) delivers a mild shock to another person, and so on. As you can imagine, working with a small scale model of aggressive situations is more ethical than manipulating real-life aggression.

Smaller scale models of the situation not only have ethical advantages, but also have practical advantages as well. For example, if you are interested in the effects of temperature on aggression, you can't manipulate the temperature outside. However, you can manipulate the temperature in a room. Similarly, you can't manipulate the size of a crowd at a college football game to see the effect of crowd size on performance, but you can manipulate audience size at a dart contest that you sponsor. By using a dart contest, testing your audience-size hypothesis is not only possible, but also practical. For instance, if audience size has an effect, you could probably find it by varying the size of the audience from zero (when you are hiding behind a one-way mirror) to three (yourself and two friends).

Once you have a small scale model of a phenomenon, you can test all kinds of ideas that previously seemed impossible to test. For example, can you imagine using the dart contest situation to test the effects of audience involvement or size of reward on performance?

Because smaller scale models of situations are so valuable, researchers often review research literature to discover if someone else has already made a smaller scale model of the phenomenon they wish to study. That is, just as an airplane designer may use a wind tunnel to test new airplane designs, researchers may use someone else's model of a situation to see if their ideas fly.

CAREFULLY SCREEN POTENTIAL PARTICIPANTS

In some research, you might decrease the ethical problems by choosing participants who are unlikely to be harmed by the manipulation. Therefore, if you were to do a frustration-aggression study, you might only use participants who:

1. were, according to a recently administered personality profile, well-adjusted
2. were physically healthy
3. volunteered after knowing about the degree of discomfort they would experience

USE "MODERATE" MANIPULATIONS

Not only can you limit who will be in the study, but you can also limit how much of the manipulation you use. By reducing the extent to which you use unpleasant stimuli, you reduce the harm to participants. Thus, if you were to induce frustration to observe its effect on aggression, you might decide not to use a very high level of frustration. Even though a high level of frustration would be more likely to produce aggression, you might decide to use lower levels of frustration to lower the risks of harming your participants.

DO NOT MANIPULATE VARIABLES

Finally, you may decide not to manipulate the variables at all. To understand the basic advantages and disadvantages of not manipulating variables, let's return to the original hypothesis: Receiving severe beatings causes one to be a murderer. You might pursue this idea by interviewing murderers and nonmurderers to see whether murderers were more likely to report being beaten as children. Unfortunately, even if you found that murderers were more likely than nonmurderers to have been beaten, your results would not necessarily mean that the beatings caused the murders. Beatings may have no impact on murders. Instead, murderers may have been beaten more than nonmurderers because, even when they were younger, murderers were more aggressive and more disobedient than nonmurderers. Although interviewing wouldn't allow you to discover whether beatings cause children to become murderers, it might allow you to address a related research hypothesis: "Murderers are more likely to claim to be beaten by their parents than nonmurderers."[2]

Concluding Remarks

In this chapter, you have learned how to generate research ideas. Consequently, if you spend a little time reviewing this chapter, you should be able to generate several hypotheses about how two or more variables are related. Once you have those ideas, you may want to test them. However, before you can test those ideas, you must find a way to obtain or generate operational definitions of your variables. Chapter 3 will help you do that.

Summary

1. The purpose of scientific research is to test ideas. Thus, one way to get research ideas is to test commonsense ideas.

2. Hypothetical constructs are abstract variables that can't be directly observed (love, learning, thirst, etc.). Researchers can deal with abstract constructs by

---

[2]Unfortunately, you will not know whether murderers actually were beaten more than other people because murderers may exaggerate the extent to which they were beaten.

devising "recipes" for these variables called operational definitions: concrete ways of manipulating or measuring abstract constructs.

3. Building on other people's research is an easy way to get good research ideas.

4. Strategies for developing research ideas from previous research include: improving the original study's external, internal, or construct validity; repeating the study; seeing if the finding has any practical implications; doing a follow-up study suggested by the study's authors; and trying to determine why two studies produced conflicting findings.

5. You can sometimes improve a study's construct validity by using the double-blind technique.

6. Never do a study without first obtaining your professor's permission.

7. A null hypothesis states that there is no relationship between two variables. While it can be disproven, it can't be proven.

8. When possible, use theory and past research to provide a rationale for your prediction and to show that the results of your study may have implications for evaluating theory and previous research findings.

9. If your hypothesis involves a prediction that one variable influences a second variable, you can refine that hypothesis by: (a) studying the functional relationship between those two variables, (b) trying to find the physiological or mental variable mediating that relationship, or (c) finding a variable that moderates that relationship.

10. A research hypothesis must be testable and must be testable in an ethical manner.

11. Even the most impractical and unethical of ideas may be converted into a practical and ethical hypothesis if you carefully screen your participants, use a small scale model of the phenomenon you wish to study, make key variables more general or abstract, tone down the intensity of your manipulation, or don't use manipulations.

Key Terms

double-blind technique: strategy for improving construct validity that involves making sure that neither the participant nor the researcher who has direct contact with the participant knows what treatment the participant has received. (p. 53)

functional relationship: the extent to which changes in one variable are accompanied by another. For example, the graph of a functional relationship may find that beyond a certain point, increasing the amount of the treatment does not lead to additional improvement (p. 63)

null hypothesis: a prediction that there is no relationship between your variables. (p. 56)

hypothesis: a testable prediction about the relationship between two or more variables. (p. 48)

straw theory: an exaggerated or oversimplified view of the real theory. Some people claim to be attacking a theory when they are actually attacking a straw version of that theory. (p. 61)

mediating variable: when a stimulus causes a response, it does so by changing something inside the organism (such as a person's thoughts, feelings, or physiological reactions). In other words, the stimulus has its effect because it causes changes in mediating variables, which, in turn, cause changes in behavior. Because knowing the mediating variables leads to understanding how a stimulus causes an effect, researchers are often interested in tracking down mediating variables. For example, not only have researchers found that smelling a certain fragrance (stimulus) improves performance on a task (response), but they have also tried to find the underlying mechanisms (the mediating variables) responsible for the fragrance's effect. Some have used brain imaging techniques to look for physiological mediators; others have used questionnaires to try to see if the fragrance has its effect on behavior by changing mood. (p. 62)

moderator variable: a variable that intensifies, weakens, or reverses the relationship between two other variables. For example, the effect of wearing perfume on being liked may be moderated by gender: If you are a woman, wearing perfume may make you more liked; if you are a man, wearing perfume may make you less liked. (p. 53)

Exercises

1. Look up a research study that tests a commonsense notion or proverb. What is the title of the article? What are its main conclusions?
2. Generate a research idea based on testing a commonsense notion.
3. Are moderator variables more associated with internal, external, or construct validity? Why?
4. Writing an essay that expresses opinions that go against your beliefs may cause you to change your beliefs. According to dissonance theory, what factors may moderate the effect of writing such a counterattitudinal essay?
5. What would you guess would be the mediating variable in astrology? Do you think that variable could cause people to have different personalities?
6. Premature infants who are held more tend to gain more weight. What is a possible mediating variable for this effect?
7. According to dissonance theory, what is an important variable that mediates attitude change?
8. People work harder when they are alone than when they are in groups. In addition, the bigger the group, the less work they tend to do. What variables might moderate the relationship between group size and effort?

9. Find a research article that tests a hypothesis derived from theory. Give the citation for the article and describe the main findings.

10. Derive a research hypothesis from a theory. Theories you might use would include: Bandura's social learning theory, Skinner's theory of operant conditioning, Solomon's opponent process theory, learned helplessness theory, Piaget's theory, dual memory theory, cognitive dissonance theory, attribution theory, equity theory, reactance theory, or sociobiology.

11. Describe the relationship between moderator variables and external validity.

12. Design a study to improve the construct validity of the study reported in Appendix D.

13. Design a study to test the generalizability of the findings of the study reported in Appendix D.

14. The study reported in Appendix D finds a relationship between two variables. Design a study to map out the functional relationship between those two variables.

15. Design a study to test the practical implications of the findings from the study reported in Appendix D.

16. In terms of the null hypothesis, discuss what is wrong with the following research conclusions:

    a. There is no difference in outcome among the different psychological therapies.

    b. There is no difference in effectiveness between generic and brand-name drugs.

    c. Viewing television violence is not related to aggression.

    d. Nutrasweet® has no side effects.

    e. There are no gender differences in emotional responsiveness.

MEASURING AND MANIPULATING VARIABLES: RELIABILITY AND VALIDITY

Science begins with measurement.
—LORD KELVIN

OVERVIEW

In the last chapter, you learned how to generate ideas about how two or more variables are related. But before you can test any of your ideas about those variables, you must generate operational definitions of those variables. For example, if you wanted to test the idea that "bliss causes ignorance," you would first have to define the vague, general, abstract, and invisible variables "ignorance" and "bliss" in a clear, specific, concrete, and visible way. That is, you must spell out the exact procedures you would follow to create "bliss" and the exact procedures you would follow to measure "ignorance." There are two main advantages to using operational definitions.

First, because **operational definitions** are concrete recipes for your variables, they allow you to talk about your variables in concrete, specific, objective terms rather than in abstract, vague, poetic, subjective terms. Rather than saying, "My opinion is that they are happy," you can say, "They scored 94 on the happiness scale." By letting you talk about facts rather than opinions, operational definitions make it possible for you to test your hypothesis objectively.

Second, by being specific and public, operational definitions allow others to replicate your study. Thus, operational definitions allow other scientists to check on, as well as build on, your research.

In short, to be a science, a field must produce publicly observable facts. Therefore, if psychology is to be a science, psychologists must be able to develop publicly observable ways to measure and manipulate variables.

Most people correctly believe that the ability of psychology to be a science depends on the ability of psychologists to measure psychological variables objectively and accurately. Unfortunately, most people also believe one of two myths about measuring psychological variables.

On the one extreme, there are cynics who believe the myth that psychological variables cannot be measured. These people think that psychology is not—and cannot—be a science.

On the other extreme, there are extremely trusting individuals who believe the myth that psychological variables are easy to measure. These trusting souls believe that anyone who says they are measuring a psychological variable is really doing so. Consequently, these gullible people are unable to distinguish between pseudoscientific claims and scientific claims.

The truth is that measuring and manipulating psychological variables is not easy. However, measuring abstract constructs such as love, motivation, shyness, religious devotion, or attention span is not impossible. By the end of this chapter, you will not only know how to develop operational definitions of such abstract concepts, but also how to determine whether such operational definitions have a high degree of construct validity. Put another way, by the end of this chapter, you will have completed a short course in psychological testing.

CHOOSING A BEHAVIOR TO MEASURE

How can we develop tests or measures of abstract constructs? Although we might like to see abstract, invisible, psychological variables like love, we cannot. However, we can see behavior. Thus, if we are to measure a psychological variable objectively, we must measure behavior.

But what behavior should we observe? We need to choose a behavior that, according to theory, past research, or intuition, is an indicator of the concept we are trying to measure. Usually, operational definitions will involve measuring one of the following four types of behavior:

1. verbal behavior: what participants say, write, rate, or report
2. overt actions: what participants do
3. nonverbal behavior: participants' body language
4. physiological responses: brain-wave activity, heart rate, blood pressure, sweating, pupil dilation, etc.

ERRORS IN MEASURING BEHAVIOR

Choosing a behavior that you can measure accurately is an important first step on the path to developing a measure. However, the path from choosing a behavior to developing a measure is not as straightforward as you might first think. To understand why choosing a measure involves more than choosing a behavior, imagine that you want to measure how fast participants run a 40-yard dash. To measure this behavior, (1) you must set the stage for the behavior to occur,

(2) the participants must perform the behavior, and (3) you must record the behavior. What happens at each of these three stages will affect what time is recorded as the participants' 40-yard dash time.

First, the conditions of the test will affect how fast a participant runs. The instructions you give, the clothes the participant wears, whether the test is indoors or outdoors, whether the participant is tested on a grass field or on a track, the temperature at the time of the test, and how many people are watching will all affect how fast the participant runs.

Second, the participant will affect how fast he or she runs. For example, the participant's mood, energy level, and desire will affect how fast he or she runs.

Third, the observer will affect the 40-yard dash time that is actually recorded for each participant. For example, if the observer starts the stopwatch after a participant starts running, that participant's recorded time will be faster than the participant's actual time.

All three of these factors—conditions, participants, and observers—can vary. For example, instructions and other conditions of the test may not be the same from day to day, moment to moment, and participant to participant. Energy level and motivation may also vary from day to day, moment to moment, and participant to participant. Finally, the timer's accuracy may vary from day to day, moment to moment, and participant to participant.

✳ OVERVIEW OF TYPES OF ERRORS

When these factors vary, they affect participants' scores. The way these factors affect participants' scores depends on the whether these factors vary (1) systematically or (2) randomly.

Bias

If these factors vary systematically, the result is **bias.** Bias may cause a researcher to "find" whatever he or she expects to find. For example, suppose a research team believes that one group of individuals, the individuals given a special treatment, will run faster than the no-treatment group. There are at least three ways in which the team may unintentionally bias the results. First, the researcher may consistently give the participants who are expected to run faster more time to warm up than the other participants. Second, the researcher may be more enthusiastic and attentive when dealing with the runners who are expected to run fast. Third, the researcher may click off the stopwatch just *before* the runners who received the treatment reach the finish line, while always clicking off the stopwatch just *after* the other runners reach the finish line. If the researcher does any of these things, the researcher will "find" that the group that he expected to run faster has faster recorded times than the other group.

Random Error

You have seen that if the conditions of the test, the participants' expectations, or the scoring of the test consistently favor one group, the result is bias. But what if these factors vary in an unpredictable, inconsistent way? Then, you have **random errors of measurement.** For instance, suppose the wind at the time participants run the race varies in an unsystematic way. It unpredictably blows at the back of some runners, in the face of other runners, but, on the average, it does not significantly aid the runners receiving the treatment more than the other runners.

This random measurement error makes individual scores less trustworthy. Some runners' times will benefit from the gusts of wind, while other runners' times will be hurt by the wind. Thus, if there is a substantial amount of random measurement error, comparing individuals' scores may be very misleading.

Although random measurement error has a strong effect on individual scores, its impact is less on the average of a group of scores because random measurement error tends to balance out. For example, it is unlikely that individuals who received the treatment were much more aided by the wind than individuals who did not receive the treatment.

Admittedly, random measurement error will probably not balance out perfectly. Fortunately, however, you can use statistical techniques to estimate the extent to which random measurement error might fail to balance out. For example, a statistical analysis might tell you that it is unlikely that wind and other random error would have caused the groups to differ by more than 5 seconds.

If your groups' average times differed by 10 seconds, you could conclude that the groups probably do not differ due to random error alone. Instead, they probably really are different. But what if the groups differed by 4 seconds?

The good news is that if this difference is just due to random error, you will not be fooled into saying that the groups really differ. You know, thanks to the statistical analysis, that the groups could reasonably be expected to differ by as much as 5 seconds by chance alone.

The bad news is that if this difference is due to a real difference between the groups you will *fail* to say that the groups really differ. You know, thanks to the statistical analysis, that the groups could reasonably be expected to differ by as much as 5 seconds by chance alone. Therefore, you are not going to claim that the observed difference represents a treatment effect. In such a case, unsystematic random measurement error would hide true differences between groups.

As you have just seen, statistical analyses cannot always compensate for having a great deal of random error. To illustrate, suppose there had been less random measurement error in your study. In that case, the statistical analyses might have told you that it was unlikely that wind and other random error would have caused the groups to differ by more than 2 seconds. Since the observed difference was 4 seconds, you would know that the groups really differed. By reducing the amount of random error, you would have been able to see that your groups really were different.

In short, although random measurement error and bias in measurement are both measurement errors, the two errors are different. Random error is not bias. Thus, random error would not create a systematic difference between your groups. It might, however, make it hard to determine whether a difference between your groups was due to the treatment.

To better understand the difference between bias and random error, imagine that two people are weighing themselves over a period of days. Although neither is losing weight, the first is content with her weight, whereas the second is trying to lose weight. Both will probably not record the same weight each time. For example, they may record the following data:

DAY	PERSON 1	PERSON 2
Day 1	150	151
Day 2	149	150
Day 3	151	149

In the case of Person 1, the errors are random. The errors do not make it look like she is losing weight. Despite the errors, we know that her weight is around 150 pounds. Thus, although the weight of the clothes she is wearing while being weighed, the time of day she weighs herself, and how she reads the needle on the scale are not exactly the same from measurement to measurement, they are not varying in a systematic way. Person 2, however, may now think he is losing weight. His errors are following a pattern. Maybe the pattern is due to moving the scale to a more sympathetic part of the floor, maybe it is due to weighing himself at a time of day when he tends to weigh less (before meals), or maybe it is due to his optimistic reading of the scale's needle. Regardless of how he is biasing his measurements, the point is that he is seeing what he wants to see. He is not being objective.

TWO TYPES OF OBSERVER ERRORS

To review, errors of measurement can come in at three points: (1) from the person administering the measure, (2) from the participant being measured, and (3) from the person observing and scoring the participant's behavior. Furthermore, at each of these three points, two types of errors can occur: (1) systematic biases and (2) random errors. Let's start by seeing how these two errors come into play when people observe, score, and record behavior.

Observer Bias (Scorer Bias)

The first, and by far the most serious, mistake is that people's subjective biases may prevent them from making objective observations. Observers may be more likely to count, remember, or see data that support their original point of view. In other words, a measure of behavior may be victimized by **observer bias**: observers recording what they expect participants will do rather than what participants are actually doing.

To see how serious a problem observer bias can be, suppose that observers record the cigarette-smoking behavior of smokers before and after the smokers go through a "stop smoking" seminar. Suppose also that the observers were biased. For example, before a smoker entered the program, if the smoker took one puff from a cigarette, the observer counted that as smoking an entire cigarette. However, after completing the program, the observer did not score "only one puff" as smoking. In such a case, observer bias would be systematically pushing cigarette smoking scores in a given direction—down. By decreasing the average smoking score, observer bias may lead us to believe that a smoking prevention program worked, even if it did not.

If we can't control observer bias, we can't do scientific research. There is no point in doing a study if, regardless of what actually happens, you are going to "see" the results you want to see. Thus without objective measures, we go from the scientific ideal of believing what we see to seeing whatever we believe.[1]

Random Observer Error

The second type of mistake that observers make in scoring behavior is due to carelessness. By being careless, they will make unsystematic random errors. These random errors will inconsistently increase and decrease scores. For example, a participant who should get a score of "3" could get a score of "2" one moment, a "4" the next.

If your observers are that inconsistent, you should stop thinking of participants as getting a "3," but rather in terms scoring somewhere in the 2–4 range. For example, you might say, "Participant x scored a 3, but random observer error may easily have added or subtracted a point from that score. Since random observer error has made that score inaccurate, we shouldn't think of it as a 3, but as a score somewhere between 2 and 4."

The good news is that because random errors are inconsistent and unsystematic, they will probably not substantially affect a group's overall average score. The points that random observer errors add to some group members' scores will tend to be balanced out by the points that random errors subtract from other group members' scores. Thus, unlike observer bias, random observer error will probably not significantly change a group's average score.

Minimizing Observer Errors

To get accurate information from our measures, we would like to reduce the influence of both observer bias and random observer error. In this section, we will discuss techniques that reduce both kinds of errors, techniques that specifically reduce observer bias, and techniques that reduce random error. We will begin the section, however, by explaining why it is more important to reduce observer bias than to reduce random error.

---

[1] Fortunately, science does have a safeguard against subjective measures: replication. If a skeptic having different beliefs replicates the study, the skeptic will obtain different results—results consistent with the skeptic's beliefs. As a result of the failure to replicate the original study's results, the flaw in the measure will be exposed.

Why It Is More Important to Reduce Observer Bias Than Random Error
To understand why observer bias is more of a problem than random error, let's consider two error-prone basketball referees. The first makes many random errors, the other is biased. Which would you want to referee your team's big game?

Your first reaction might be to say, "Neither!" After all, the referee who makes many random errors is aggravating. Who wants an inattentive, inconsistent, and generally incompetent ref? However, in the course of a game, those random errors will tend to balance out. Consequently, neither team will be given a significant advantage. On the other hand, a referee who is biased against your team will consistently give the opponent a several-point advantage. Thus, if you had to choose between the two error-prone officials, which one would you pick? Most of us would pick the one who made many random errors over the one who was biased against us.

Eliminating Human Observer Errors by Eliminating the Human Observer
Often, we don't have to choose between minimizing random error and minimizing observer bias because the steps that reduce observer bias also tend to reduce random observer error. For example, one way to eliminate observer bias is to replace human observers with scientific instruments. Eliminating the human observer eliminates both bias due to the observer and random error due to human observers.

Limiting Human Observer Errors by Limiting the Human Observer's Role
If you can't eliminate observer bias and random observer error by eliminating the observer, you may still be able to limit observer bias and random observer error by limiting the observer's role. For instance, rather than having observers interpret participants' answers to essay questions, you could limit the observers' role to recording participants' answers to multiple-choice questions.

As you might imagine, almost any time you make the observer's job easier, you reduce both observer bias and random observer error. Thus, if you follow the tips in Table 3-1 for making the observer's job easier, your measure will be less vulnerable to both observer bias and random observer error.

Reducing Observer Bias by Making Observers "Blind"   Although Table 3-1 includes a wide variety of strategies that will help reduce observer bias, those tactics may not eliminate observer bias. To understand why they won't, suppose you were having observers judge essays to determine whether men or women used more "aggressive" words. Even if you conducted a thorough training program for your raters, the raters might still be biased. That is, if they knew that the writer was a man, they might rate the passage as more aggressive than if they thought the same passage was written by a woman. Instead of letting your raters know whether an essay was written by a man or woman, you should consider making your raters **blind**: unaware of the participant's characteristics and situation.

• TABLE 3-1 •
TECHNIQUES THAT REDUCE BOTH RANDOM OBSERVER ERROR AND OBSERVER BIAS

1. Use machines (such as computers and automatic counters) rather than humans to observe and record behavior.

2. Simplify the observer's task by:

   a. using objective measures such as multiple-choice tests rather than essay tests.

   b. replacing tasks that require observers to judge a behavior's intensity with tasks that merely ask observers to count how many times the behavior occurs.

   c. reducing the possibility for memory errors by making it very easy to immediately record their observations. For example, give your observers checklists so they can check off a behavior when it occurs, or counters that observers can click every time a behavior occurs.

3. Tell observers that they are to record and judge observable behavior rather than invisible psychological states.

4. Photograph, tape record, or videotape each participant's behavior so that observers can recheck their original observations.

5. Carefully define your categories so that all observations will be interpreted according to a consistent, uniform set of criteria.

6. Train raters and motivate them to be accurate.

7. Use only those raters who were consistent during training.

8. Keep observation sessions short so observers don't get tired.

The importance of making observers blind has been illustrated in several studies. In one such study, people rated a baby in a videotape as much more troubled if they were told they were watching a baby whose mother had used cocaine during pregnancy than if they were not told such a story (Woods, Eyler, Conlon, Behake, & Wobie, 1998).

Conclusions About Reducing Observer Bias   In essence, the tactics you would use to reduce observer bias are the same tactics a professor would use to avoid favoritism in grading. The professor who is concerned with avoiding favoritism in grading would certainly not determine students' grades solely by sitting down at the end of term and trying to recall the quality of each student's class participation. Instead, a professor who was solely concerned with avoiding favoritism would give multiple-choice tests that were computer scored. If the favoritism-conscious professor were to give an essay exam, the professor would establish clear-cut criteria for scoring the essays, follow those criteria to the letter, and not look at students' names while grading the papers.

Reducing Random Observer Error Making observers blind should eliminate observer bias, but it will not eliminate random observer error. Blind observers can still be careless, inattentive, forgetful, or inconsistent about how they interpret behavior. For example, suppose a history professor grades 100 essay exams over the weekend. Even if the professor grades all those exams "blind," fatigue and other factors may result in the professor's scoring not being perfectly consistent from test to test. For example, the professor may not be consistent in how much partial credit he gives for a certain essay answer, and the professor may make errors on some papers in adding up all the points.

We do not mean to imply that the steps you take to reduce observer bias will never reduce random observer error. On the contrary, the steps you take to reduce any type of observer error will usually reduce both observer bias and random observer error. Indeed, except for the blind technique, every step that you take to reduce observer bias will also tend to reduce random observer error.

ERRORS IN ADMINISTERING THE MEASURE

By using blind procedures and by eliminating or reducing the observer's role, you can reduce the amount of measurement error that is due to observers making mistakes when they score participants' behaviors. However, not all errors in measurement are due to the scorer. Some errors are made in administering the measure. As was the case with scoring, there are two kinds of errors that people can make in administering the measure: bias and random error.

When you administer the measure, you hope to avoid introducing either bias or random error. However, to avoid both these errors completely, you would have to keep all of the factors that influence a participant's response constant. For example, if you were administering an IQ test, you would have to keep everything—the noise level, lighting, instructions to participants, your facial expressions, voice inflections, and gestures—the same.

Keeping all these factors perfectly constant is impossible. However, most researchers—and people who administer psychological tests—strive for a high level of **standardization:** treating each participant in the same (standard) way. Thus, you should try to test all your participants in the same soundproof, temperature-controlled setting. You should also write out a detailed description of how you are going to test your participants, and then you should stick to those procedures. For example, you might write down whatever instructions you were going to give participants and then read those instructions to every single participant. You might even present your instructions on a videotape. To further standardize procedures, you might put the instructions and measures in a booklet, or you might even have a computer administer the measure.

Because perfect standardization is usually impossible, there will be some error in measurement due to imperfect standardization. If we must have error, we would prefer that this error be random error rather than bias. For example, it would be disastrous if the researcher biased the results by being more attentive, enthusiastic, and patient when administering the test to the treatment group than to the no-treatment group.

To avoid bias in the administering of a measure, you should try to keep the person who administers the measure "blind." For example, you might have one researcher who administers the treatment and a second researcher—who is blind to what the first researcher did—administer the measure. Since the researcher administering the measure is blind to whether the participant had received the treatment, this researcher could not administer the measure one way to participants receiving the treatment and another way to participants not receiving the treatment.

ERRORS DUE TO THE PARTICIPANT

To this point, we have focused on two sources of measurement error: errors made by the person administering the measure and errors made by the person scoring the measure. We will now turn to a third source of both random error and bias—the participant. That is, we will now discuss two reasons why participants may produce responses that don't perfectly reflect their true behavior or feelings: (1) random error due to participants and (2) bias due to participants (**subject bias**).

Random Participant Error

First, participants themselves are not perfectly consistent. Their behavior is variable. Some of this variability is random. One moment they may perform very well, and the next moment they may perform very poorly. For example, participants may misread questions, lose their concentration, make lucky guesses, or make unlucky guesses.

One way to overcome this random variability in participants' behavior is to get a large sample of their behavior. Thus, if you wanted to know how good a free-throw shooter someone was, you wouldn't have her shoot only two free throws. Instead, you would probably have her shoot at least 20. Similarly, if you wanted to know how outgoing she was, you wouldn't base your conclusion on a two-item test. Instead, you would probably use a test that had at least 20 questions on it so that random participant error would tend to balance out.

Subject Biases

The second, and more troublesome, reason why participants' actions may not reflect their true behavior is because participants' responses may be biased. That is, participants may change their behavior to impress you or to help you (or, perhaps, to thwart you).

One of the earliest documented examples of the problem of subject bias was the case of Clever Hans, the mathematical horse (Pfungst, 1911). Hans would answer mathematical problems by tapping his hoof the correct number of times. For example, if Hans's owner asked Hans what 3 times 3 was, Hans would tap his hoof 9 times. Hans's secret was that he would watch his owner. His owner would stop looking at Hans's feet when Hans had reached the right answer. Thus, although people interpreted Hans's hoof tapping as evidence that Hans was mentally performing mathematical calculations, the hoof tapping really only meant that Hans was watching and reacting to his owner's gaze. Hans did not know math, but he did know how to give the "right" answer.

If animals can produce the "right" answer when they know what you are measuring, so can humans. In fact, for humans, there are two kinds of "right" (biased) responses: (1) obeying demand characteristics and (2) social desirability.

Obeying Demand Characteristics   The first kind of "right" answer is the one that makes you, the researcher, look good by ensuring that your hypothesis is supported. Orne (1962) believed that participants are very willing to give researchers whatever results the researcher wants. In fact, participants are so eager to please that they look for clues as to how the researcher wants them to behave. That is, participants look for hints about what the hypothesis is. According to Orne, if a participant finds a hint, the participant will follow that hint as surely as if the researcher had demanded that the participant follow the hint. Orne refers to such hints as **demand characteristics**.

To give you some idea of the power of demand characteristics, consider how they operate in everyday life. Imagine you and a friend are at a restaurant. The service is slow, and the food is poor. You and your friend grumble about the food through much of the meal. Then, at the end of the meal, your server asks you, "Was everything all right?" Do you share your complaints, or do you succumb to demand characteristics and say that everything was fine?

To see how demand characteristics might affect the results of a study, imagine that you do the following study. First, you have participants rate how much they love their partner. Next, you give them fake feedback, supposedly from their partner, showing that their partner loves them intensely. Finally, you have participants rate how much they love their partner a second time. In this study, participants may realize that they are supposed to rate their love higher the second time. Therefore, if participants reported that they loved their partner more the second time, you would not know whether learning about their partners' devotion really changed the participants' feelings or whether participants merely obeyed the study's demand characteristics.

How did participants know what you wanted them to do? Your measure made it obvious that you were measuring love. Once participants knew that you were measuring love, they were able to guess why you showed them their partners' ratings. You gave them all the clues (demand characteristics) they needed to figure out what you would consider a "good" response.

Fortunately, you do not have to use measures that make it so easy for participants to follow demand characteristics. You can use measures that either (1) make it difficult for participants to figure out what you are measuring or (2) make it difficult for participants to play along with the hypothesis.

• BOX 3-1 •

WAYS TO AVOID SUBJECT BIASES WHEN MEASURING LOVE

TECHNIQUE	EXAMPLE
Measure participants in nonresearch settings	Observe hand-holding in the college cafeteria.
Unobtrusive observation	Observe hand-holding in the lab through a one-way mirror.
Unobtrusive measures (nonverbal)	Observe how much time partners spend gazing into each other's eyes.
Unobtrusive measures (physical traces)	Measure how close together the couple sat by measuring the distance between their chairs.
"Unexpected Measures"	Ask participant to repair the damage "caused" by his/her partner.
Disguised Measures	Ask participants to rate themselves and their partners on several characteristics. Then, infer love from the extent to which they rate their partner as being similar to themselves.
Physiological Responses	Measure pupil dilation to see if it increases when their partner comes into the room.
Important Behavior	See if the participant passes up the opportunity to date a very attractive person.

As Box 3-1 shows, there are at least two ways you could make it harder for participants to figure out what you are measuring. Unfortunately, both ways raise ethical questions because they may involve compromising the principle of informed consent: Participants should freely decide whether to participate in the study only after being told what is going to happen to them.[2]

The first way involves making it hard for participants to know that you are observing them. In technical terminology, you use **unobtrusive measurement**: recording a particular behavior without the participants knowing you are measuring that behavior. For example, you might spy on them outside of the laboratory or through a one-way mirror.

The second way involves disguising your measure. You might let participants think you were measuring one thing when you were actually measuring

---

[2]In the next chapter, we discuss the ethical issues involved in choosing a measure.

something else. For instance, you might take advantage of the fact that people in love tend to overestimate how similar they are to their partner. Therefore, you could have participants rate themselves and their partners on a variety of characteristics. Participants would probably think you are interested in how accurately or positively they rate their partners. Instead, you'd be seeing the extent to which participants believed that they were similar to their partner—and using perceived similarity as a measure of love.

But what if you can't stop your participants from figuring out the hypothesis? Even if participants figure out the hypothesis, you can still do two things to prevent participants from playing along with it.

First, you could make it almost impossible for participants to play along with the hypothesis. For instance, if you used brain-wave activity as a measure of love, participants couldn't easily play along with the hypothesis.

Second, you could make it costly for participants to play along with the hypothesis. For example, if you made it so participants would have to spend more time doing a dull task (watching people fill out questionnaires) to help out their partner, many would not be willing to play along with the hypothesis.

Social Desirability Bias

Unfortunately, subject bias and deceit do not stop at participants trying to give you the results they think you want. In addition to wanting you to look good, participants also want to look good themselves. Thus, another kind of subject bias is the **social desirability bias**: the participant acting in a way that makes the participant look good.

• FIGURE 3-1 •

SOURCES AND TYPES OF MEASUREMENT ERROR

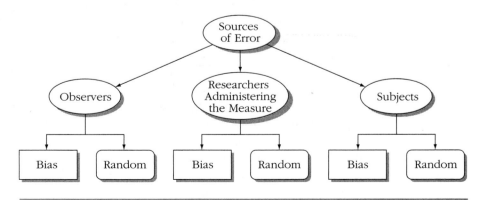

Participants want to look good, and on most questionnaires, it is easy for participants to check the answer that makes them look good. Consequently, many studies have shown that people claim to be much more helpful (Latane & Darley, 1970) and less conforming (Milgram, 1974) than they really are.

The same two tactics that reduce the problem of demand characteristics also reduce the problem of social desirability. Participants won't try to impress the researcher if (1) they don't know they are being watched or (2) showing off is difficult. For example, they probably won't try to be more generous than they are if they don't know you are watching them or if it costs them time and money to show how generous they are.

Despite the effectiveness of those two techniques, the easiest and most commonly used tactic to deal with the social desirability bias is to make participants' responses anonymous. If participants cannot get credit for their answers, they cannot impress the researcher by putting down exaggerated or false information. Therefore, participants should not be motivated to make socially desirable, but false, responses.[3]

Conclusions About Reducing Subject Biases

Note that making responses anonymous—the most commonly used method to reduce social desirability bias—was not mentioned as a method to reduce bias caused by following demand characteristics. It wasn't mentioned because making responses anonymous does not necessarily eliminate the bias caused by obeying demand characteristics. That is, even though anonymous participants can't make themselves look good, they can still try to make you look good. Thus, even though they won't get credit for it, anonymous participants may still figure out the hypothesis and try to help you out.

SUMMARY OF TYPES OF MEASUREMENT ERROR

We have discussed three major sources of measurement error: errors due to the person scoring the measure, errors due to the person administering the measure, and errors due to the participant. We have also stressed that each of these sources can contribute two types of measurement error: random error and systematic bias (see Figure 3-1). Furthermore, we have stressed that bias is a much more serious threat to validity than random error. We showed how observer bias was worse than random observer error, how researcher bias was worse than random errors in administering a measure, and how subject bias was worse than random participant error.

---

[3]Unfortunately, participants may still give false or misleading information. For example, some adolescents may display a sense of humor or a sense of rebelliousness by putting outrageous answers on an anonymous questionnaire.

RELIABILITY: THE (RELATIVE) ABSENCE OF RANDOM ERROR

As you have seen, bias is a much more serious threat to validity than random error. Indeed, at this point, you might be saying to yourself, "Bias is bad. It should be eliminated. But random error doesn't seem that serious. Why should we bother to devise a measure that is free from random error?" In the next section, we will answer that question. That is, we will explain why you want a measure that is **reliable**: producing stable, consistent scores that are not strongly influenced by random error (chance).

THE IMPORTANCE OF BEING RELIABLE: RELIABILITY AS A PREREQUISITE TO VALIDITY

You want your measure to be stable and reliable because you assume that you are measuring a stable characteristic. That is, you assume that a person's traits, such as intelligence, shyness, and height, don't change from minute to minute. If you measure the same person at two different times, you should get basically the same results each time. Thus, if you measure someone's height to be 5′6″ one day and 6′2″ the next, you know something is wrong. Because you are not getting the same results each time, you know that your measurements are being affected by something other than the stable trait (height) that you are trying to tap. Instead, your measurements are probably being affected by random error.

Clearly, you don't want your measurements to be wildly bounced around by the erratic winds of chance. Consequently, when deciding whether to use a measure, you want to know whether it is strongly contaminated by chance (random error).

USING TEST-RETEST RELIABILITY TO ASSESS OVERALL RELIABILITY: TO WHAT DEGREE IS A MEASURE "RANDOM ERROR FREE"?

To find out to what extent your measurements are affected by random error, you should find out the measure's reliability. Perhaps the most straightforward way to find out the degree to which the measure produces consistent results is to obtain its **test-retest reliability**.

As the name suggests, test-retest reliability requires participants to be tested and then retested. Often, developers of psychological tests give participants a psychological test and then test those same participants again about 3 months later. Then a test-retest coefficient is computed by comparing the score each participant received the first time they took the test with the score each received the second time they took the test.

The more participants' scores on the first measurement correspond to their scores on the second measurement, the higher the test-retest coefficient. Usually, test-retest coefficients range between .30 (poor reliability) and .98 (excellent reliability). However, it is conceivable to get any number from 0.00 to 1.00.[4]

At one level, the test-retest coefficient tells you the percentage of variation in scores that is stable and consistent from test to retest. Thus, a test-retest coefficient of 1.00 would mean that there was a perfect (100%) correspondence between the first and second time of measurement—all those who scored high the first time also scored high the second time. The data below reflect a 1.00 test-retest coefficient.

PARTICIPANT	SCORE FIRST TIME	SCORE SECOND TIME
Carol	3	3
Mary	4	4
Tom	5	5

At another level, the test-retest coefficient tells you the *percentage* of variation in scores that is not due to random error. Thus, a test-retest coefficient of 1.00 tells us that 100% of the differences between scores are not due to random error. The measure is "100% random error free."

What we often want to know, however, is the extent to which differences between scores are due to random error. To find out how much of the variation is due to random error, you have to subtract the amount of variation that is not due to random error from the total amount of variation. Specifically, you have to subtract the test-retest correlation from 1.00.

To illustrate, suppose your test-retest correlation was .90 (it's 90% random error free). Then, since 1.00 − .90 = .10, then .10 (10%) of the variation in your scores was due to random error. (You could use this same subtraction method to find out how much fat is in a hot dog that is 93% fat-free, but that might be too depressing.) If a measure's test-retest correlation is 1.00, scores are not at all (0%) affected by random error (because 1.00 − 1.00 = 0 = 0%).

A test-retest coefficient of 0, on the other hand, would mean that there was absolutely no (0%) relationship between scores participants received the first time they took the test and the scores they received when they were retested. The only way a participant would get the same score on both the test and retest was by chance. Put another way, 100% (1.00 − 0 = 1.00 = 100%) of the variation in scores was due to random error. As you can see from the next table, a zero test-retest coefficient means that there is no connection between how a person scored the first time and how he scored the second time.

---

[4] The test-retest reliability coefficient is usually not a correlation coefficient. If it were, it could range from −1 to +1. However, it is usually the square of the test-retest reliability correlation (Anastasi, 1982). This squared term represents the percentage of variation that is **not** due to random error. To find out how much of the variation of scores is due to random error, you subtract the test-retest coefficient from 1. Thus, if your test-retest coefficient is 1, none of the variation in your scores is due to random error (because 1 − 1 = 0). If, on the other hand, your test-retest coefficient is 0, then all of the variation in your scores is due to random error (because 1 − 0 = 1).

Participant	Score First Time	Score Second Time
Carol	3	5
Mary	4	3
Tom	5	5

If you are examining a previously published measure, the test-retest reliability coefficient may have already been calculated for you. The measure's test-retest reliability coefficient may be cited in the original researcher report, in the test's manual, in *Mental Measurements Yearbook* (Kramer & Conoley, 1992), in *Test Critiques* (Keyser & Sweetland, 1984), in *Tests in Print* (Mitchell, 1983), or in *Directory of Unpublished Experimental Mental Measures* (Goldman & Mitchell, 1990).

When interpreting these test-retest reliability coefficients, remember that they are telling you the extent to which the measure is not affected by random error. Thus, although a test-retest correlation of .70 does not sound bad, it means that .30 (1.00 − .70 = .30 = 30%) of the differences between participants' scores on this measure are due to random error.

Normally, you would not choose a measure in which more than 30% of the differences between participants' scores was due to random error. In other words, you would probably not choose a measure that had a test-retest reliability coefficient below .70.

IDENTIFYING (AND THEN DEALING WITH) THE MAIN SOURCE OF A MEASURE'S RELIABILITY PROBLEMS

What if your measure's test-retest reliability is below .70? Then, more than 30% of the variation in scores is due to random error. Where is this random error coming from? As we discussed before, there are three likely sources:

1. random error due to the observer
2. random error due to the way the measure is administered
3. random error due to the participant

It would be nice if we could know how much of measure's unreliability is due to each of these sources. If we knew the source of a measure's unreliability, we might then be able to fix the problem at the source. For example, if we knew that the scores varied from test to retest because the observers varied from test to retest in how they scored the behavior, then we could work on making the observers more consistent. Therefore, if possible, we should try to determine which of the three likely sources is most to blame for the measure's poor reliability.

Are Observers to Blame for Low Test-Retest Reliability?
Assessing Observer Reliability

The first question many researchers ask is whether the observer is to blame for the measure's poor reliability. However, random observer error is not always the source of a measure's reliability problems. Indeed, we can often immediately determine that the observer is *not* a major source of random error because the scoring system is relatively objective. For example, in a multiple-choice test, observers are probably not going to make many errors.

But what about when observers judge or rate behavior? Then, we must realize random observer error may be hurting our measure's reliability. In that case, we should estimate the extent to which random observer error is lowering our test-retest reliability. That is, we should try to find out how much of our random measurement error is due to the observer.

We can estimate how much our measure is affected by random observer error by assuming that if two trained raters score the same behavior differently, these differences are due to random observer error. For example, the observers may produce different scores because one or both observers guessed about which category to put the behavior in, misread the stopwatch, or made any number of other random mistakes. To show that the scores on a measure are not being affected by such random errors, researchers show that two or more observers who independently (without talking to one another) rate the same behavior come up with similar scores. To express the degree to which observers agree, researchers use one of two indexes: interobserver agreement and interobserver reliability.

Sometimes, the researchers will report the **interobserver (judge) agreement:** the percentage of times the raters agree. For example, the researchers might report that the raters agreed 98% of the time. Interobserver agreement is simple to calculate and understand. If observers are agreeing 100% of the time, then there is no random error due to the observer.

Usually, researchers will report another, slightly more complicated index of the degree to which different raters give similar ratings: **interobserver reliability.** To obtain interobserver reliability, researchers calculate a correlation coefficient between the different raters' judgments of the same behaviors and then square that correlation.[5]

Like test-retest reliability coefficients, interobserver reliability coefficients can range from 0 to 1. An interobserver reliability coefficient of 1.00 means there is a 100% correspondence between the raters. Knowing how one observer rated a behavior allows you to know perfectly (with 100% accuracy) how the other observer rated the behavior. The following data reflect an interobserver reliability coefficient of 1.00.

---

[5]To show you the connection between interobserver agreement and interobserver reliability, imagine that we are having observers rate whether a behavior falls into one of two categories. If observers were just flipping a coin to determine what category the behavior belonged, they would agree 50% of the time. Thus, if the observers' judgments are completely affected by chance, interobserver agreement would be 50% and the interobserver reliability coefficient would be zero. If, on the other hand, random error had no effect on judgments, interobserver agreement would be 100% and interobserver reliability coefficient would be 1.00.

PARTICIPANT	OBSERVER 1'S RATING	OBSERVER 2'S RATING
Tom	1	1
Jim	2	2
Sue	3	3
Allen	4	4
Robert	5	5
Mary	6	6

The 1.00 interobserver reliability coefficient tells you the extent to which your measure is not affected by random observer error. Specifically, the 1.00 interobserver reliability coefficient shows that the measure is "100% random observer error free." But you want to know the extent to which the measure is affected by random observer error. To find out, subtract the interobserver reliability from 100%. Since 100% − 100 = 0, you know that 0% of the differences between participants' scores on this measure are due to random observer error. Thus, with an interobserver reliability of 1.00, raters' judgments are not at all (0%) influenced by random observer error.

An interobserver reliability coefficient of zero, on the other hand, indicates that there is no relationship between the observers' ratings. Knowing how one observer rated a behavior gives you no idea about how the other observer rated the same behavior. Put another way, when interobserver reliability is zero, 100% (100% − 0 = 100%) of the variation in scores is due to random error. To see a case in which observers' judgments are completely a function of random error, look at the data below.

PARTICIPANT	OBSERVER 1'S RATINGS	OBSERVER 2'S RATINGS
Tom	1	5
Jim	1	1
Sue	3	3
Allen	4	4
Robert	4	2
Mary	3	3

As you can see, there is no connection between Observer 1's ratings and Observer 2's ratings. Since scores are completely a function of random observer error, the measure has no interobserver reliability.

Nonobserver Sources of Random Error

Because observers usually agree to some extent, and since journal editors will usually only publish articles that have a high degree of interobserver reliability, you will almost never see a published study that includes an interobserver reliability coefficient below .60. In other words, you will rarely see a published article where more than 40% (1.00 − .60 = .40 = 40%) of the differences between scores are due to random observer error. Therefore, when reading a study, your question will not be, "Did the observers agree?" but rather, "To what extent did the observers agree?" Generally, you will expect interobserver reliability coefficients of around .90.

You want a measure with a high interobserver reliability coefficient for two reasons. First, you want your measure to be objective—you want trained raters to report the same scores. Second, *interobserver reliability puts a ceiling on test-retest reliability.* For example, if interobserver reliability is .60, test-retest reliability can't be above .60.

To better understand how interobserver reliability puts a ceiling on test-retest reliability, imagine the following scenario. We perfectly standardize how we administer the measure. Each participant behaves exactly the same way each time he or she is observed. To reiterate, the way they behaved on the retest is exactly the same as how they behaved the first time they were tested. To this point, it looks like you are going to have perfect test-retest reliability. There is no random variation in scores due to either the participant or to how the measure is administered. Unfortunately for you, however, there is a serious problem with random error due to the observer: Your observers decide what score to give the behavior by flipping a coin. In this scenario, you will have no interobserver reliability. Scores will differ from each other for only one reason—random observer error. Because the only reason scores differ from each other is random error, you will have no test-retest reliability.

To understand the mathematical reason why interobserver reliability puts a ceiling on test-retest reliability, let's think about what each coefficient represents. To be more specific, let's think about what you find out when you subtract each coefficient from 1.00.

To understand what happens when you subtract each coefficient from 1.00, you must first understand what 1.00 represents. It represents the total amount of variation in scores. It represents every reason why one score on the measure differs from another. If you think about differences among scores as a pie, 1.00 represents the whole pie.

When you subtract the interobserver reliability coefficient from 1.00, you find out how much of the variability is due to a single source of random error: the observer. When you subtract the test-retest reliability coefficient from 1.00, you find out how much of the variability in scores is due to the *combined effects* of all sources of random error, including the observer. Thus, an interobserver reliability coefficient of .60 means that .40 (1.00 − .60 = .40) of the variation in scores is due to one source of random error: random observer error. Forty percent of the "pie" is consumed by random observer error. A test-retest coefficient of .60, on the other hand, means that .40 (100 − .60 = .40) of the variation in scores is due to all sources of random error combined. That is, the total, combined impact of random error due to the observer, plus the random error due to the person administering the measure, plus the random error due to the participant consume 40% of the "pie."

Now, you are ready to understand why interobserver error puts a ceiling on test-retest reliability. If one source of random error—random observer error—accounts for .40 (40%) of the variation in scores (interobserver reliability is .60), then all sources of random error combined must account for at least .40

(40%) of the variation in scores. That is, even if nothing else creates random variation in scores, random error due to the observer will create .40 (40%) of the variation in scores. If at least .40 of the variation in scores is due to random observer error, then no more than .60 (1.00 − .40 = .60) of the variation in scores could possibly be due to nonrandom factors. Forty percent of the pie has been eaten before all the other sources of random error have had a chance.

If those other sources of random error eat up more of the pie, test-retest reliability could be below the ceiling set by the .60 interobserver reliability. For example, if imperfect standardization and inconsistency in participants added another 30% of random variation in participants' scores, then 70% (40 + 30) of the differences between participants' scores would be due to random error. As a result, the test-retest coefficient would be an incredibly low .30 (1.00 − .70 = .30).

If interobserver reliability is low, then you probably need to reduce random observer error. Sometimes you can reduce random observer error by training, motivating, or replacing your observers. Often, however, you will find that you need to simplify the observers' job or find a way of measuring behavior that does not involve observers. One reason multiple-choice tests and rating scale measures are so popular in psychology is that these measures essentially eliminate observers, thereby eliminating the random observer error that human observers produce.

Estimating Random Error Due to Participants

So far, we have discussed the situation where interobserver reliability is low, thus dooming test-retest reliability to be low. But what if interobserver reliability is high, yet test-retest reliability is still low? For example, suppose you have the following data:

| | TEST | | RETEST | |
PARTICIPANT	OBSERVER 1	OBSERVER 2	OBSERVER 1	OBSERVER 2
Joe	3	3	5	5
Mary	4	4	3	3
Steve	5	5	5	5

Then, you know your low test-retest reliability is not due to the observer. If the low test-retest reliability is not due to the observer, then it must be due to poor standardization and/or to the participant.

Ideally, you would figure out how much of the random error was due to poor standardization and how much was due to random changes in the participant. Unfortunately, it is impossible to directly assess how much random error is due to poor standardization, and it is very difficult to assess how much of the random error is due to the participant. However, there is a way to get a rough index of how much random error is due to the participant—if you are using a test, scale, or survey that can be objectively scored.

Internal Consistency: Test Questions Should Agree With Each Other   How can we determine how much random error on a test is due to the participant? The key is to assume that each question on the test is measuring the same thing.

For example, let's assume that all questions on a shyness test are measuring shyness. If this assumption is correct, people who score "shy" on one question should score "shy" on all the other questions. In other words, the test should agree with itself. But what if it doesn't? What if a participant is "shy" according to some questions, but "outgoing" according to others?

Then, if our assumption that all the questions are measuring the same thing is correct, this inconsistency between how questions are answered is due to random error. As you may recall, random error, ordinarily, could be due to one or more of the following:

1. the observer
2. the testing environment
3. the participant

Random Error Due to Participants May Cause Low Internal Consistency

When we use an objective, multiple-choice test, however, we know that the random measurement error is not due to the observer because objectively scored, multiple-choice measures are not vulnerable to observer error. Thus, when we use an objectively scored measure, random error in measurement could be due to:

1. the observer
2. the testing environment
3. the participant

Furthermore, we are pretty sure that the testing environment and instructions are not changing *during* the test, so we are pretty sure that the random fluctuations in the participants' behavior are not due to changes in the testing environment. That is, we expect that the testing environment is basically the same when the participant answers question 2 as it is when the participant answers question 3. If the random error is not due to the scorer or to the testing environment, it must be due to the participant. Consequently, we would conclude that the inconsistency in answers to different questions was due to the participant. Therefore, in this case, random error in measurement could be due to:

1. the observer
2. the testing environment
3. the participant

Specifically, the measure's inconsistency may reflect (1) temporary random fluctuations in how participants think or feel; or (2) guessing on the part of participants.

Two Solutions to Problems Caused by Random Participant Error

If your measure's reliability problems are due to the participant, what can you do? Your plan of attack will depend on whether the inconsistency is due to participants changing from moment to moment or to participants guessing at the answers to questions.

Add Questions to Let Random Participant Error Balance Out   If participants fluctuate considerably from moment to moment on how they think or feel, the best you can do is ask many questions. By asking many questions, you allow random fluctuations to balance out.

Asking many questions should also help balance out the effects of guessing. For example, suppose you are unprepared for a physics quiz and the only thing you can do is guess at the answers. If the quiz is composed of one multiple-choice question, you might get 100% just by guessing. However, if the quiz is composed of 100 multiple-choice questions, random guessing is not going to get you a high score.

Ask Better Questions to Reduce Random Participant Error   Asking more questions is not the only way to deal with the problem of guessing. Sometimes the solution is to ask better questions. Your participants may be guessing at the answers because the questions are so poorly worded that participants are guessing at what the questions mean. Thus, you may be able to reduce random error due to guessing by rewording or eliminating some of your questions. By rewording and eliminating questions, you should boost your measure's **internal consistency:** the degree to which answers to each question correlate with the overall test score.

Measuring Internal Consistency

But how would you know whether you have boosted your measure's internal consistency? How would you know whether your measure's internal consistency was poor in the first place?

There is a wide range of indexes of internal consistency that you can examine—from average inter-item correlations to split-half reliabilities to Cronbach's alpha. Despite their differences, all of these indexes are designed to measure the degree to which answers to one item (question) of the test correspond to answers given to other items on the test. Thus, the following data would produce a high score on any index of internal consistency:

PARTICIPANT	QUESTION 1	QUESTION 2	QUESTION 3
Joe	1	1	1
Mary	3	3	3
Susan	5	5	5

Average Inter-Item Correlations as Indexes of Internal Consistency   One very direct index of the extent to which answers to one test item (question) correlate with answers to other test items is the *average inter-item correlation*. As the name suggests, this index involves computing a correlation between the answers to each question (item) and then averaging those correlation coefficients.

Depending on how you average those correlation coefficients, you will either end up with the mean inter-item correlation or the median inter-item correlation. If you use the mean as your average (you add up all the correlation coefficients and divide by the number of correlation coefficients), you have the *mean inter-item correlation.* If your average is the median (you arrange the correlation coefficients from lowest to highest and pick the middle one), you have the *median inter-item correlation.*

Usually, there is little difference between the median inter-item correlation and the mean inter-item correlation. For example, if you had a three-item test, you might find the following:

Correlation of item 1 with item 2	.2
Correlation of item 1 with item 3	.3
Correlation of item 2 with item 3	.4
Mean inter-item correlation:	.3
Median inter-item correlation:	.3

Split-Half Reliability Coefficients as Indexes of Internal Consistency   Other indexes of internal consistency are less direct than the average inter-item correlation. Many rely on essentially splitting the test in half and comparing how participants scored on one half versus how they scored on the second half. For example, researchers may (1) calculate each participant's score for the first half of the test, (2) calculate each participant's score for the second half of the test, and then (3) correlate scores on the first half of the test with scores on the last half of the test. This correlation between the score for the first half of the test and the score for the second half is a type of *split-half reliability.* Thus, the following data would yield a perfect (1.00) split-half reliability and suggest that the scale was internally consistent:

SCORE ON FIRST 10 QUESTIONSSCORE ON LAST 10 QUESTIONS

PARTICIPANT	(FIRST HALF OF TEST)	(SECOND HALF OF TEST)
Joe	50	50
Mary	10	10
Susan	30	30

Another type of split-half reliability involves splitting the test in half by comparing answers to the odd-numbered questions (1, 3, 5, etc.) with answers to the even-numbered questions (2, 4, 6, etc.). Specifically, researchers may calculate a score based on only the answers to the odd-numbered questions, a score based only on the answers to even-numbered questions, and then correlate the "odds" with the "evens." This result would be the measure's "odd-even correlation."

Additional Indexes of Internal Consistency   In addition to the measures of internal consistency that we have described, there are more mathematically sophisticated measures of internal consistency, such as Cronbach's alpha and

Kuder-Richardson reliabilities. At this point, we do not want you to know the advantages and disadvantages of each measure of internal consistency. Instead, we want you to realize whenever you see odd-even correlations, average inter-item correlations, Cronbach's alpha, split-half reliabilities, or Kuder-Richardson reliabilities, the researchers are just trying to tell you the extent to which their measure is internally consistent.

In general, you can treat these indexes of internal consistency as all being pretty much alike—except that the score suggesting good internal consistency is very different for the average inter-item correlation than for the other indexes of internal consistency. For the other indexes we have mentioned, you need a score of at least .70 (and preferably above .80) to say that the measure is internally consistent. Thus, you would probably not use a measure with an odd-even correlation of .60 or a Cronbach's alpha of .50. However, the cutoff for acceptable internal consistency of the average (or median) inter-item correlation index is .30. Thus, most experts would say that a measure that had a median inter-item correlation of .35 has an adequate degree of internal consistency.

Conclusions About Internal Consistency's Relationship to Reliability

An adequate degree of internal consistency suggests that your measure's reliability problems are not due to its questions. Nor are your reliability problems due to minute-to-minute fluctuations in your participants. Instead, your reliability problems, if you have any, are probably due to participants changing over time or to improper standardization.

Low internal consistency, on the other hand, suggests that there are problems with the questions on your test. These problems will tend to hurt your test's overall reliability, especially if your test is relatively short. Therefore, you may want to boost your test's internal consistency by eliminating or refining some of the test questions.

CONCLUSIONS ABOUT RELIABILITY

Up to now, this chapter has focused on reliability. We have shown you why reliability is important, how to determine if a measure has sufficient reliability, and how to determine where a measure's reliability is breaking down (for a review, see Table 3-2 and Figure 3-2). Specifically, we have stressed that:

1. Reliability is a prerequisite for validity.
2. Test-retest reliability tells you the total extent to which random error is influencing your measure.
3. If test-retest reliability is low, you may want to calculate other types of reliability coefficients (interobserver reliability, internal consistency) to find out the main source of the measure's unreliability.

However, we have not talked about the main limitation of reliability: *Reliability does not guarantee validity.* For example, consider the following data:

• TABLE 3-2 •

KEY POINTS TO REMEMBER ABOUT RELIABILITY

1. Two major *avoidable* sources of unreliability are:
   a. random fluctuations in the measurement environment.
   b. random fluctuations in how observers interpret and code observations.
2. All reliability coefficients are not the same.
3. Test-retest reliability tells you the total extent to which random error is influencing your measure.
4. Other types of reliability can help you find the source of the measure's unreliability. For example, a low interobserver reliability coefficient tells you that random observer error is seriously reducing your measure's overall reliability.
5. Reliability is necessary for validity: Valid measures are reliable.
6. Reliability does not guarantee validity: Reliable measures are not always valid.
7. Unreliability weakens validity, but does not introduce systematic bias into the measure.
8. Reliability is an important, but not all-important, consideration in choosing a measure.

PARTICIPANT	SCORE ON AGGRESSION TEST	SCORE ON RETEST	NUMBER OF FIGHTS
Joe	50	50	3
John	60	60	4
Tim	70	70	1

As you can see, individuals score the same on the retest as they did when they were first tested. Thus, the test has high test-retest reliability. However, individuals' scores on the test do not correspond with how many fights they get into. Thus, the test is not a valid measure of aggression. Consequently, the measure is reliable, but not valid.

BEYOND RELIABILITY: ESTABLISHING CONSTRUCT VALIDITY

One reason that a reliable measure may not be valid is because it is reliably and consistently measuring the wrong thing. How can we know that a measure has **construct validity:** the degree to which the measure is measuring the construct that it claims to measure?

We can never know for certain that our measure has construct validity. However, we can make a case for a measure's construct validity, especially if it has good content validity, internal consistency, convergent validity, and discriminant validity.

• **FIGURE 3-2** •

DETERMINING WHETHER—AND HOW—TO IMPROVE A MEASURE'S RELIABILITY

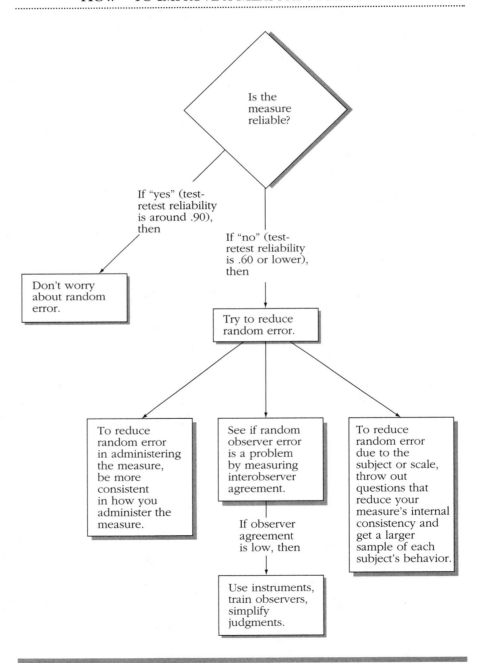

CONTENT VALIDITY: DOES YOUR TEST HAVE THE RIGHT STUFF?

Often, the first step in devising a valid test is to establish its **content validity**: the extent to which it represents a balanced and adequate sampling of relevant dimensions, knowledge, and skills. Before even writing any test questions, you should consult the established theories and definitions of the concept you wanted to measure. Your definition would then guide you in writing your questions. For example, if you defined love as, "feeling sexual attraction toward a person and a willingness to make sacrifices for that person," then you would make sure your measure had questions that measured both sexual attraction and willingness to sacrifice. In fact, to make sure that you had an adequate number of both types of questions, you might break your scale into two subscales: a "sexual attraction" subscale and a "sacrifices" subscale.

As you can see, there are two main points to content validity: (1) *sampling* from every dimension of the construct you are trying to measure and (2) having a big enough *sample* of questions from each of those *content* areas. Thus, it is not surprising that content validity is sometimes called *content sampling*.

When evaluating classroom tests and other tests of knowledge or skills, content validity may be extremely important. For example, a test to assess everything you have learned about psychology should not consist of only one multiple-choice question. Beyond having many questions, such a test should cover all areas of psychology, not just one. For example, if such a test consisted of 500 questions about classical conditioning, it would not have content validity.

INTERNAL CONSISTENCY REVISITED: EVIDENCE THAT YOU ARE MEASURING ONE CHARACTERISTIC

It is valuable to make a logical argument that you are measuring what you say you are measuring. If you cannot show how your measure logically follows from an accepted definition of the concept, then few would accept your measure as valid. However, it is not enough to claim that all your questions are measuring a certain construct. You need objective, statistical evidence of that claim.

A first step toward making the case that all your questions are measuring the right construct is to show that all your questions are measuring the same thing. In other words, one step toward construct validity is to show that your scale—or subscales—are internally consistent.

Earlier, when we discussed measuring internal consistency as a possible way to measure how much random error was due to participants, we were *assuming* that all the questions were measuring the same construct. If that assumption is correct, a participant whose answer to question 1 indicates that she is willing to make personal sacrifices for her partner should answer question 2 in a way that also indicates that she is willing to make personal sacrifices for her partner. If she does not answer question 2 the same way—and our assumption that all the questions measure the same construct is correct— then random error has affected her answer to one or both of those questions.

But what if the assumption that all the questions are measuring the same construct is wrong? Then the differences in how participants answer question 1 versus how they answer question 2 are not due to random error. Instead, the differences are due to question 1 measuring one thing and question 2 measuring something else. For example, question 1 may be measuring how much participants are willing to make personal sacrifices for their partner, whereas question 2 may be measuring how much they trust their partner.

To reiterate, people who score a certain way on one of the "personal sacrifices for partner" subscale questions should score similarly to all the other "personal sacrifices for partner" questions. If the answer to one question suggests a participant is willing to sacrifice for his partner, the answers to the other questions should also echo this suggestion. It may help you to think of each question as a judge of whether participants have a certain characteristic. If one judge's scores are far apart from everyone else's, we would doubt that judge's competence. We might ask, "Was she watching the same thing everybody else was?" Similarly, if answers to a certain question on the test do not correspond to answers to the other questions, we would have questions about that question. Because low internal consistency raises questions about our questions, we want our measure to have high internal consistency.

As we mentioned earlier, there are several ways you can determine whether a measure has high internal consistency. If we found high inter-item correlations, split-half reliabilities, or Cronbach's alpha values, we would be more confident that all the questions on our test were measuring the same construct. For example, the following data would support the view that the questions agree with each other:

PARTICIPANT	QUESTION 1	QUESTION 2	QUESTION 3
Joe	1	1	1
Mary	3	3	3
Susan	5	5	5

However, what if the data were like this?

PARTICIPANT	QUESTION 1	QUESTION 2	QUESTION 3
Joe	1	1	5
Mary	3	3	1
Susan	5	5	3

Then, we would probably want to reword or eliminate question 3. By the time you get through eliminating questions, you should end up with a measure that had high split-half reliability. You may have had a teacher or professor describe the basics of this process when reviewing a classroom test. For example, the teacher may mention that most of the people who did well on the exam got a certain question wrong; whereas, the students who did poorly on the exam got that question right. The teacher, therefore, argues that that there was something wrong with that question and vows not use that question on future exams.

By eliminating and rewording questions, we should be able to achieve a reasonable level of internal consistency. Thus, if we were to take participants' scores on the first half of a 20-question test and correlate them with their scores on the last half of the test, we should find a high degree of agreement, like this:

PARTICIPANT	SCORE ON FIRST 10 QUESTIONS (FIRST HALF OF TEST)	SCORE ON LAST 10 QUESTIONS (SECOND HALF OF TEST)
Joe	50	50
Mary	10	10
Susan	30	30

The data above strongly suggest that the test is measuring one thing. Thus, internal consistency seems like a good idea if you are measuring a simple construct that has only one dimension. But what if you are measuring a complex construct that you think has two separate aspects? Suppose you want to measure love and you think that love has two different dimensions (sexual attraction and willingness to sacrifice for the other). You also believe that these dimensions are relatively independent. That is, you believe that a person could be high on sexual attraction, but low on willingness to sacrifice. In such a case, you don't expect a high level of internal consistency because you are measuring two different things.

One solution would be to make up a love scale that had two different subscales. You would then expect that each of the individual subscales would have a high degree of internal consistency but that the subscales would not correlate highly with each other. That is, all the responses to questions related to sexual attraction should correlate with one another; all the responses to items related to sacrifice should correlate with one another; but the sexual attraction scale should not correlate highly with the sacrifice scale. For example, the following results would support the case that your two subscales were measuring two different constructs:

Split-half reliability for Sacrifice Subscale: .84

Split-half reliability for Sexual Attraction Subscale: .89

Correlation between the Sacrifice and Sexual Attraction Subscales: .10

CONVERGENT VALIDATION STRATEGIES: STATISTICAL EVIDENCE THAT YOU ARE MEASURING THE RIGHT CONSTRUCT

Internal consistency can help you build the case that you are measuring the number of constructs you claim to be measuring. For example, the data just presented strongly suggest that the test is measuring two things. But does it tell us what those two things are? No.

The data just presented give us no objective evidence that we are measuring "sacrifice" and "sexual attraction." Indeed, if one subscale were measuring intelligence and the other were measuring political attitudes, we might obtain those same data.

To make a case that your measure is measuring a certain construct, you should show that your measure correlates with other indicators of that construct. For example, you might establish that:

1. People who score high on accepted measures of the construct also score high on your measure.
2. People who belong to a group composed of individuals known to possess a high level of the construct score high on your measure.
3. Participants given a treatment that should cause them to have a high level of the construct score high on your measure.
4. People who exhibit behaviors known to correlate with the construct tend to score high on your measure.

In technical terminology, you need to obtain evidence for your measure's **convergent validity:** the extent to which your measure correlates with other indicators of the construct. The general idea is that your measure and these other indicators correlate with each other because they are all converging on the same thing—your construct.

Perhaps the most obvious step in convergent validation is to show that your measure correlates with other measures of the same construct. Thus, if you were measuring love, you might correlate your measure with another measure of love, such as Rubin's Love Scale (Rubin, 1970). Since both measures are supposed to be measuring the same thing, the two measures should correlate highly with one another. That is, participants scoring high on your love measure should score high on the other love measure, and participants scoring low on your love measure should score low on the other love measure. Ideally, you would find a convergent validity correlation between your measure and the existing measure of .80 or higher, as in this example:

PARTICIPANT	ESTABLISHED LOVE MEASURE	YOUR MEASURE
Joe	100	100
Mary	20	20
Susan	60	60

Another obvious tactic is to find two groups: one known to possess a high degree of the characteristic you want to measure and one known to possess a low degree of that characteristic. You would hope that participants known to have a high level of the construct would score higher on your measure than participants known to have a low level of the construct. This tactic is called the **known-groups technique.** Thus, in validating your love scale, you might give your scale to two groups—one that is known to be in love (dating couples) and one that is known to not be in love (strangers). For example, scores on the love scale might approximate the following:

STRANGERS	DATING COUPLES
55	90

In addition to looking at whether your measure distinguishes between two existing groups, you could determine if your measure predicts that participants will later belong to different groups. For instance, you might see if your measure could predict which dating couples would get engaged and which would soon split up (Rubin, 1970).

You could also see if your measure distinguishes between two groups exposed to different experimental manipulations. For example, if you had an experimental group that was expecting a shock and a control group that was not, you would expect the experimental group to score higher on your measure of anxiety than the control group.

Finally, you could determine whether your measure correlated with other indicators of the concept. Thus, you might correlate scores on the love scale with a behavior that lovers tend to do, such as look into each other's eyes. For instance, Rubin showed that couples with low scores on his love scale were less likely to gaze at each other than couples with high scores.

DISCRIMINANT VALIDATION STRATEGIES: SHOWING THAT YOU ARE NOT MEASURING THE WRONG CONSTRUCT

Convergent validity uses the "if it looks like a duck and walks like a duck, it must be a duck" approach to building the case for construct validity. Unfortunately, something may look like a duck and walk like a duck, but actually be a related bird. Thus, an "intelligence test," despite correlating with some measures of intelligence, may really measure mathematical knowledge. Similarly, a "love measure" that has some convergent validity with other measures of love may be measuring liking rather than love.

To illustrate the limits of convergent validity, suppose you correlate your love scale with another love scale. Imagine you have the following data:

PERSON	SCORE ON YOUR SCALE	SCORE ON OTHER LOVE SCALE
Person 1	30	38
Person 2	52	49
Person 3	70	60

You have some good evidence for convergent validity because people who score one way on your test score about the same way on an established love test. But are you really measuring love? Before you say "yes," let's look at a table that combines the previous data with data from a "liking" scale:

PERSON	LIKING SCALE	YOUR SCALE	OTHER LOVE SCALE
Person 1	30	30	38
Person 2	52	52	49
Person 3	70	70	60

As you can see from the previous data, you seem to be measuring liking rather than love. Because you cannot show that your so-called "love" measure is different from a "liking" measure, you cannot say that the "love" measure is valid. Thus, convergent validity alone is not enough to establish construct validity. It is not enough to show that a measure correlates with measures of the right construct. We must also show that our measure has **discriminant validity:** showing that it is *not* measuring a different construct. Typically, you establish discriminant validity by showing that your measure does not correlate too well with measures of different constructs.

What does it mean that your measure should not correlate too well with measures of different constructs? In other words, what pattern of results would support the idea that your measure has discriminant validity? This is a tricky question, because it depends on whether you are trying to show discriminant validity relative to a related construct or whether you are trying to show discriminant validity relative to an unrelated construct.

Showing Discriminant Validity Relative to Related Constructs

If you are trying to show discriminant validity relative to a related construct, you do not need a zero correlation between your measure and a measure of that related construct. Instead, you would expect that scores on your measure would be related to scores on a measure of that related construct. Since the constructs are related, you would expect at least a modest correlation between your measure and a measure of that related construct. For example, you might expect that your love scale would correlate moderately (.60) with the liking scale because people who love each other tend to like each other. However, if your love scale correlated very highly with the liking scale, then you would be worried that you were measuring liking instead of love. You would especially be concerned if your scale correlated more highly with a liking scale than it did with other love scales.

Similarly, if you had a measure of practical intelligence, you would not be alarmed if it correlated moderately with a measure of conventional intelligence. However, if the correlation was around .80 (about as high as different IQ tests correlate with each other), then you would have a hard time arguing that you had devised a test of a different type of intelligence. Instead, the evidence would suggest that you had devised yet another measure of conventional intelligence.

In short, to establish discriminant validity relative to a related construct, you do not need to show that there is a near-zero correlation between your measure and a measure of the related construct. Indeed, if the constructs are highly related, even a moderately high correlation of .60 might provide evidence of discriminant validity—as long as that was significantly lower than your measure's convergent validity correlations.

Showing Discriminant Validity Relative to Unrelated Constructs

If, on the other hand, you need to show discriminant validity relative to an unrelated construct, you would need a near-zero (anywhere from −.20 to +.20) correlation between your measure and a measure of the unrelated construct. For example, you, like most test developers, may need to show that your measure is not affected by social desirability bias. How would you do that?

The first step is to have participants complete your measure and a social desirability scale. Social desirability scales, sometimes called "lie scales," measure the degree to which the participant gives answers that—rather than being truthful—would impress most people. Basically, a social desirability scale includes questions that ask you to describe yourself by choosing one of two responses:

• a socially desirable response that would fit how you should ideally be, according to society, but that actually fits very few people

• a truthful, but less flattering response (what you really do)

An example of such a question would be: "True or False: I always help other people out." The socially desirable response is "true," the truthful response is "false." People who lie by picking the socially correct responses will score high on the social desirability scale. On the other hand, people who pick the truthful, but less flattering, answers will score low in social desirability.

After administering both your measure and the social desirability scale, you would correlate the two measures. A correlation of around zero (between -.20 and +.20) would suggest that your measure is not strongly influenced by the social desirability bias. That is, a near-zero correlation between your scale and a social desirability scale suggests that you are measuring people's true feelings rather than people's willingness to make a good impression.

If, on the other hand, scores on the social desirability scale correlate highly with responses on your scale, then your measure may be strongly affected by the social desirability bias. Thus, rather than measuring what people really think, you may just be measuring their willingness to make a good impression. For example, do you think the following data support the idea that the "friendliness test" really measures friendliness?

PERSON	FRIENDLINESS SCORE	SOCIAL DESIRABILITY SCORE
Person 1	30	30
Person 2	52	52
Person 3	70	70

Clearly, they do not. The "friendliness test" is really a measure of social desirability.

As you can imagine, showing that a new measure has a near-zero correlation with social desirability is often one of the first steps that researchers take in establishing discriminant validity. Unfortunately, social desirability is only one of several constructs that you may need to show that you are not measuring; you may also need to show that your measure has discriminant validity relative to a variety of other constructs. For example, if you have a love measure, you may have to show that it does not correlate too highly with measures of related constructs such as liking, lust, loyalty, and trust. Consequently, when trying to decide whether to use a certain measure, you should ask two questions:

1. What else might this measure be measuring?
2. Is there evidence that this measure does not measure those other constructs? That is, does the measure show a low to moderate correlation with measures of those other constructs?

SUMMARY OF CONSTRUCT VALIDITY

As you can see from Box 3-2 and Figure 3-3, building a strong case for your measure's construct validity is several research projects in itself. To assess convergent validity, researchers often have to consult theory and past research to see what manipulations would affect their construct and then see if those manipulations affect scores on their own measure. In addition, they may need to consult theory and past research to see what behaviors correlate with high levels of the construct and then see if people scoring high on their measure exhibit those behaviors. To assess discriminant validity, they have to correlate their measure with measures of other constructs. To assess internal consistency, they

---

• **BOX 3-2** •

VALIDATING A LOVE MEASURE: RUBIN'S LOVE SCALE

Reliability	Showing that measure was not excessively affected by random error: Test-Retest Reliability of .85
Content Validity	All three dimensions of love are represented (predisposition to help, dependency, and possessiveness).
Convergent Validity	Predicts how much two individuals will gaze at each other. Predicts probability that individuals will eventually get married. People who are engaged score higher than people who are casually dating.
Discriminant Validity	Love scores correlate only moderately with scores on a liking scale, suggesting that the scale is not a measure of liking.

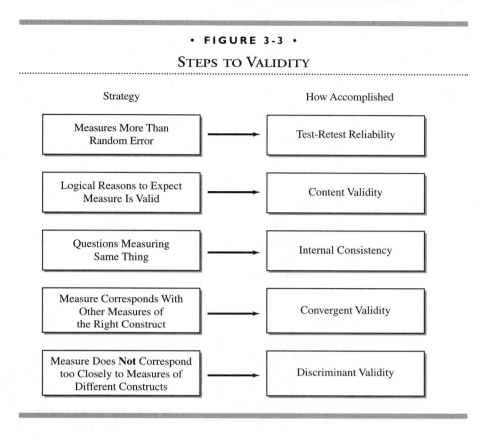

• FIGURE 3-3 •

STEPS TO VALIDITY

Strategy | How Accomplished

Measures More Than Random Error	→	Test-Retest Reliability
Logical Reasons to Expect Measure Is Valid	→	Content Validity
Questions Measuring Same Thing	→	Internal Consistency
Measure Corresponds With Other Measures of the Right Construct	→	Convergent Validity
Measure Does **Not** Correspond too Closely to Measures of Different Constructs	→	Discriminant Validity

need to administer the measure and calculate some measure of internal consistency. Since validating a measure takes so much time and since most researchers are interested in finding out new things about a construct rather than finding new ways to measure it, most researchers do not invent their own measures. Instead, they use measures that others have already validated. (In fact, while reading about what it would take to validate your own love scale, you may have been saying to yourself, "Let's use Rubin's Love Scale instead.")

MANIPULATING VARIABLES

There are two reasons why we have devoted most of this chapter to measuring, rather than manipulating, variables. First, all research involves measuring variables, whereas not all research involves manipulating variables. Second, many of the things you should think about when measuring variables also apply to manipulating variables—as you will soon see.

COMMON THREATS TO A MANIPULATION'S VALIDITY

When evaluating manipulations, for example, you have the same concerns as you have when you measure variables:

1. Can we reduce random error?
2. Can we reduce bias due to the researcher?
3. Can we reduce bias due to the participant?
4. Can we provide evidence that the operational definition we are using is valid?

Random Error

Just as you want to minimize random error when measuring variables, you want to minimize random error when manipulating variables. Therefore, just as you standardized the administration of your measure, you want to standardize the administration of your treatment. That is, you want to administer the treatment the same way every time.

Experimenter Bias

Just as you were worried about researchers being biased in their observations, you will also be worried about **experimenter bias**: experimenters being biased when they administer the treatment. For instance, researchers may be friendlier to the participants who are getting the treatment. As was the case with observer bias, the key is to use scientific equipment to administer the manipulations, to use paper and pencil instructions, to standardize procedures, or to make the researcher *blind* to what condition the participant is in.

Subject Biases

Just as you were concerned that your *measure* might tip participants off to how they should behave, you should also be concerned that your *manipulation* might tip participants off as to how they should behave. One of the most frequently cited examples of how a treatment could lead to demand characteristics was a series of studies begun in the 1920s at the Hawthorne Electric Plant. The investigators, Roethlisberger and Dickson (1939), were looking at the effects of lighting on productivity. At first, everything seemed to go as expected. Increasing illumination increased productivity. However, when they reduced illumination, productivity continued to increase. The researchers concluded that the treatment group was reacting to the special attention rather than to the treatment itself. This effect became known as the **Hawthorne Effect.**

Although many experts now believe that Roethlisberger and Dickson's results were not due to the "Hawthorne Effect," no one disputes that participants may act differently simply because they think they are getting a treatment. Therefore, researchers use a wide variety of techniques to avoid the "Hawthorne Effect." Some of these techniques are similar to the techniques used to make a measure less vulnerable to subject biases. For example, just as researchers may reduce subject biases by measuring participants in nonresearch settings, experimenters may reduce subject biases by manipulating the treatment in a nonresearch setting.

A more common way of reducing subject biases is to give the "no-treatment" group a **placebo:** a treatment that is known to have no effect. For example, in most studies examining the effect of a drug, some participants get the real pill (the treatment), whereas others get a sugar pill (the placebo). If both groups improve equally, then researchers would be concerned that the treatment group's improvement might be due to participants expecting to get better. If, however, the treatment group improves more than the placebo group, we know that the treatment group's improvement was not due to participants' expectations.

EVIDENCE USED TO ARGUE FOR A MANIPULATION'S CONSTRUCT VALIDITY

As with measures, you would like to provide evidence that your treatment is doing what you claim it is. The difference is that making a case for the validity of a treatment is usually less involved than making a case for the validity of a measure.

The two most common ways of establishing validity are (1) to argue that your treatment is consistent with a theory's definition of the construct and (2) to use a **manipulation check:** a question or set of questions designed to determine whether participants perceived the manipulation in the way that the researcher intended.

Consistency With Theory

To illustrate the value of these two ways of establishing construct validity, suppose that you wanted to manipulate cognitive dissonance: a state of arousal caused when participants are aware of having two inconsistent beliefs. You would want to argue that your manipulation meets three general criteria that dissonance theory says must be met for dissonance to be induced:

1. Participants must believe they are voluntarily performing an action that is inconsistent with their attitudes (a smoker writing an essay about why people shouldn't smoke).

2. Participants should believe that the action is public and will have consequences (before writing the essay, participants must know that others will read their essay and know that the participant wrote it).

3. Participants must not feel that they engaged in the behavior for a reward (you didn't pay them for doing the behavior).

To make the case that the manipulation is consistent with dissonance theory, you might argue that:

1. You told participants their cooperation was voluntary and they could refuse.

2. You told them that their essay would be signed and that children who were thinking about smoking would read it.

3. You did not pay participants for writing an anti-smoking essay.

Manipulation Checks

Your procedures would seem to induce the mental state of dissonance—assuming that participants perceived the manipulation as you intended. To check on that assumption, you might use a manipulation check. For example, you might ask participants if they felt aroused and uncomfortable, if they felt that their attitudes and behavior were inconsistent, if they felt they were coerced, if they felt that their behavior was public, whether they foresaw the consequences of their behavior, and so on. Many researchers believe that you should always use a manipulation check when doing research on human participants (Sigall & Mills, 1998).

But what if giving people the manipulation check tips participants off to the study? In that case, manipulation check advocates would say to use the manipulation check, but only after the participant has responded to your measure. Or, you might conduct a mini-study in which the only thing that happens is that participants are given the manipulation and then they respond to the manipulation check.

But what if it's obvious that you are manipulating whatever you think you are manipulating (physical attractiveness, concrete versus abstract words, etc.)? Even then, manipulation check advocates would urge you to go ahead with a manipulation check for two important reasons. First, a manipulation check could establish the discriminant validity of your treatment. For example, wouldn't it be nice if you could show that your attractiveness manipulation increased perceptions of attractiveness, but did not change perceptions of age or wealth? Second, since you are doing research to test assumptions rather than to make assumptions, you should be willing to test the assumption that you are manipulating what you think you are manipulating (see Table 3-3).

TRADEOFFS AMONG THREE COMMON TYPES OF MANIPULATIONS

Choosing a manipulation usually involves making tradeoffs because there is no such thing as the perfect manipulation. Different manipulations have different strengths and weaknesses. In the next sections, we will briefly highlight the strengths and weaknesses of three common kinds of manipulations: instructional manipulations, environmental manipulations, and stooge manipulations.

Instructional Manipulations

Perhaps the most common treatment manipulation is the **instructional manipulation**: manipulating the variable by giving written or oral instructions. The advantage of an instructional manipulation is that you can standardize your manipulation easily. Often, all you have to do is give each participant the same

• **TABLE 3-3** •

SIMILARITIES BETWEEN
MEASURING AND MANIPULATING VARIABLES

MEASURE	MANIPULATION
Reduce random error by standardizing administration of the measure.	Reduce random error by standardizing administration of the manipulation.
Reduce observer bias by training, standardization, instruments, and making researcher "blind" about the participant's condition.	Reduce researcher bias by training, standardization, instruments, and making the researcher "blind" about the participant's condition.
Participants may figure out what the measure is measuring and then act in such a way as to make a good impression or give the researcher the "right" results. Sometimes, the problem of subject biases is dealt with by not letting participants know what the measure is or what the hypothesis is.	Participants may figure out what the manipulation is designed to do and then act in such a way as to make a good impression or to give the researcher the "right" results. Sometimes, the problem of subject biases is dealt with by not letting participants know what the manipulation is or what the hypothesis is.
Show that your operational definition is consistent with the theory's definition of the construct.	Show that your operational definition is consistent with the theory's definition of the construct.
Convergent validity is shown by correlating the measure with other measures of construct.	Convergent validity is sometimes demonstrated by showing that the manipulation has same effect that other manipulations of the construct have and that it has an effect on a simple, direct measure of the construct (the manipulation check).

photocopied sheet of instructions. This standardization reduces both random error and experimenter bias.

However, just because you can consistently present instructions to participants, don't assume that your instructions will be perceived the same way every time. Participants may ignore, forget, or misinterpret instructions.

To reduce random error due to participants interpreting your instructions differently, be sure to repeat and paraphrase your most important instructions. Many researchers advise you to "hit participants over the head" with your manipulation. Thus, if you were manipulating anonymity, you would tell "anonymous" participants that their responses would be anonymous, confidential, and private, and that no one will know how they responded. Furthermore, you would also tell them not to write their name on the paper. In the public condition, you would do just the opposite. You would tell "public" participants that everyone would see their paper, that you were going to make copies of their paper, and you would make a big deal of their signing their names to the paper.

If participants do not understand or do not pay attention to the manipulation, the instructional manipulation will have little effect on your participants. However, by making the instructions clear, this problem can be overcome. Unfortunately, participants may understand your manipulation too well. That is, participants may figure out what you are trying to manipulate and then play along. Fortunately, you can reduce this threat to your study's construct validity by using placebo treatments, counterintuitive hypotheses, and clever ways of measuring your construct. (For examples of clever measures, see Box 3-1 p. 83).

Environmental Manipulations

If you are concerned that participants will "play along" with an instructional manipulation, you may use an **environmental manipulation:** changing the participants' surroundings. Some environmental manipulations take the form of "accidents." For instance, smoke may fill a room, the participant may be induced to break something, or the participant may overhear some remark.

When considering an environmental manipulation, ask two questions. First, will participants notice the manipulation? Even when manipulations have involved rather dramatic changes in participants' environments (smoke filling a room), a sizable proportion of participants report not noticing the manipulation (Latane & Darley, 1970).

Second, can you present the manipulation the same way every time? Fortunately, many environmental manipulations can be presented in a consistent, standardized way. Most animal research, for example, involves environmental manipulations that can be consistently presented (food deprivation). Likewise, research in perception, sensory processing, cognition, and verbal learning usually involves environmental manipulations (presenting illusions or other stimuli). These manipulations vary from the routine—presentation of visual stimuli by computer, tachistoscope, memory drum, or automated slide projector—to the exotic. For example, Neisser (1984) has done studies in which the manipulation consists of silently moving the walls of the participant's cubicle.

Manipulations Involving Stooges

A special kind of environmental manipulation employs **stooges:** confederates who pretend to be participants, but are actually the researcher's assistants. By using stooges, social psychologists and others get participants to respond openly, thus avoiding the demand characteristics that accompany instructional manipulations. Unfortunately, there are two problems with using stooges.

First, using stooges raises ethical questions because, by deceiving your participants, you are violating the principle of informed consent. Your attempt to reduce demand characteristics is coming at the cost of participants' rights. The decision to try to deceive participants should only be made after careful consideration of the alternatives. Thus, for ethical reasons, you or your professor may decide against using stooges.

• TABLE 3-4 •

COMPARING THE ADVANTAGES AND DISADVANTAGES

OF THREE DIFFERENT KINDS OF MANIPULATIONS

INSTRUCTIONAL	ENVIRONMENTAL	STOOGES
Easy to do.	Not as easy to do.	Not easy to do.
Easily standardized.	Not easily standardized.	Not easily standardized.
Reduces:	May lead to concerns about:	May lead to concerns about:
1. Random error	1. Random error	1. Random error
2. Potential for experimenter biases.	2. Potential for experimenter biases.	2. Potential for experimenter biases.
Vulnerable to subject biases.	Less vulnerable to subject biases.	Not very vulnerable to subject biases.

Second, it's very hard to standardize the performance of a stooge. At best, inconsistent performances by stooges create unnecessary random error. At worst, stooges may bias the results. Some researchers solve the standardization problem by having participants listen to tapes of actors rather than relying on stooges to give the exact same performance time after time. For example, both Aronson and Carlsmith (1968) and Latane and Darley (1970) made participants believe they were listening to people talking over an intercom when participants were actually listening to a tape recording.

As you can see, choosing manipulations usually means making tradeoffs (see Table 3-4). To choose the right manipulation for your study, you must determine what your study needs most. Is experimenter bias your biggest concern? Then, you might use an instructional manipulation. Are you most concerned with demand characteristics? Then, you might use an environmental manipulation.

MANIPULATING VARIABLES: CONCLUSIONS

As you have seen, when manipulating variables, you have many of the same concerns you have when measuring variables. However, when manipulating variables, you have one set of concerns that you don't have when measuring variables: How much of the treatment should you administer—and who gets what amount? To be more specific, how many different amounts or types of the treatment should you have, how different should these amounts be, and who gets which amount? We will deal with these important issues in Chapters 6 and 7.

Concluding Remarks

In Chapter 2, you developed a research idea: a prediction about how two or more variables were related. In this chapter, you learned how to determine whether you had valid operational definitions of those variables. Now that you have the raw materials to build a research design, you can take advantage of the rest of this book.

Summary

1. *Reliability* refers to whether you are getting consistent, stable measurements. Reliable measures are relatively free of random error.

2. A way to measure the extent to which a test is free of random error is to compute its test-retest reliability.

3. Three major sources of unreliability are random errors in scoring the behavior, random variations in how the measure is administered, and random fluctuations in the participant's performance.

4. You can assess the degree to which random errors due to the observer/scorer are affecting scores by computing an interobserver reliability coefficient. Interobserver reliability puts a ceiling on test-retest reliability.

5. For objective tests, you may get some idea about the degree to which scores are affected by random, moment-to-moment fluctuations in the participant's behavior by using a measure of internal consistency. Average inter-item correlations, split-half reliabilities, and Cronbach's alpha are all indexes of internal consistency.

6. Random error is different from bias. Bias is a more serious threat to validity. In a sense, random error dilutes validity, whereas bias poisons validity.

7. *Validity of a measure* refers to whether you are measuring what you claim you are measuring.

8. Reliability puts a ceiling on validity. Therefore, an unreliable measure cannot be valid. However, reliability does not guarantee validity. Therefore, a reliable measure may be invalid.

9. A valid measure must have some degree of reliability and be relatively free of observer bias and subject biases.

10. Two common subject biases are social desirability (trying to make a good impression) and obeying the study's demand characteristics (trying to make the researcher look good by producing results that support the hypothesis).

11. By not letting participants know what you are measuring (unobtrusive measurement), you may be able to reduce subject biases (see Box 3-1).

12. Establishing internal consistency, discriminant validity, convergent validity, and content validity are all ways of building the case for a measure's construct validity.

13. Choosing a manipulation involves many of the same steps as choosing a measure.

14. Placebo treatments and unobtrusive measurement can reduce subject bias.

15. "Blind" procedures and standardization can reduce experimenter bias.

16. You can use manipulation checks to make a case for your manipulation's validity.

Key Terms

bias: systematic errors that can push the scores in a given direction. Bias may lead to "finding" the results that the researcher wanted. (p. 74)

observer bias: bias created by the observer seeing what the observer expects to see, or selectively remembering/counting/looking for data that support the observer's point of view (also known as *scorer bias*). (p. 76)

blind, blind observer: an observer who is unaware of the participant's characteristics and situation. Using blind observers reduces observer bias. (p. 78)

operational definition: a publicly observable way to measure or manipulate a variable; a "recipe" for how you are going to measure or manipulate your factors. (p. 72)

random error of measurement: inconsistent, unsystematic errors of measurement. Carelessness on the part of the person administering the measure, the person taking the test, and the person scoring the test can cause random error. (p. 75)

reliable, reliability: the extent to which a measure produces stable, consistent scores. Measures are able to produce such stable scores if they are not strongly influenced by random error. A measure can be reliable, but not valid. However, if a measure is not reliable, it cannot be valid. (p. 86)

test-retest reliability: a way of assessing the total amount of random error in a measure by administering the measure to participants at two different times and then correlating their results. Low test-retest reliability could be due to inconsistent observers, inconsistent standardization, or poor items. Low test-retest reliability leads to low validity. (p. 86)

interobserver agreement: the percentage of times the raters agree. (p. 89)

interobserver reliability: like interobserver agreement, interobserver reliability is an index of the degree to which different raters rate the same behavior similarly. Low interobserver reliability probably means that random observer error is making the measure unreliable. (p. 89)

internal consistency: the degree to which all the items on a measure correlate with each other. If you have high internal consistency, all the questions seem to be measuring the same thing. If, on the other hand, answers to some questions are inconsistent with answers to other questions, this inconsistency may be due to some answers being (1) strongly influenced by random error or being (2) influenced by different constructs. Internal consistency can be estimated through average correlations, split-half reliability coefficients, and Cronbach's alpha. (p. 94)

subject biases: ways the participant can bias the results. The two main subject biases are (1) trying to help the researcher out by giving answers that will support the hypothesis, and (2) giving the socially desirable response. (p. 81)

social desirability bias: participants acting in a way that makes the participant look good. (p. 84)

demand characteristics: aspects of the study that allow the participant to figure out how the researcher wants that participant to behave. (p. 82)

unobtrusive measurement: recording a particular behavior without the participant knowing you are measuring that behavior. Unobtrusive measurement reduces subject biases such as social desirability bias and obeying demand characteristics. (p. 83)

Hawthorne Effect: when the treatment group changes its behavior not because of the treatment itself, but because group members know they are getting special treatment. (p. 108)

instructional manipulation: manipulating the variable by giving written or oral instructions. (p. 110)

environmental manipulation: a manipulation that involves changing the participant's environment rather than giving the participant different instructions. (p. 112)

stooges: confederates who pretend to be participants, but are actually the researcher's assistants. (p. 112)

construct validity: the degree to which an operational definition reflects the concept that it claims to reflect. Establishing content, convergent, and discriminant validity are all ways of arguing that your measure has construct validity. (p. 97)

content validity: the extent to which a measure represents a balanced and adequate sampling of relevant dimensions, knowledge, and skills. (p. 99)

convergent validity: validity demonstrated by showing that the measure correlates with other measures, manipulations, or correlates of the construct. (p. 102)

known-groups technique: a convergent validity tactic that involves seeing whether groups known to differ on a characteristic differ on a measure of that characteristic (e.g., ministers should differ from atheists on a measure of religious beliefs). (p. 102)

discriminant validity: the extent to which the measure does not correlate strongly with measures of constructs other than the one you claim to be measuring. (p. 104)

experimenter bias: experimenters being more attentive to participants in the treatment group or giving different nonverbal cues to treatment group participants than to other participants. (p. 108)

standardization: treating each participant in the same (standard) way. Standardization should reduce experimenter bias. (p. 80)

manipulation check: a question or set of questions designed to determine whether participants perceived the manipulation in the way that the researcher intended. (p. 109)

placebo treatment: a treatment that is known to have no effect. To reduce the impact of subject bias, the group getting the real treatment is compared to a group getting a placebo treatment—rather than to a group that knows it is getting no treatment. (p. 109)

Exercises

1. What is an operational definition? Give an example of an operational definition. How does an operational definition differ from a dictionary definition?
2. What two general types of errors may cause an observation of behavior to be inaccurate? If you were doing a study, which of these two factors would have the greater impact on the average score of your treatment group?
3. What is reliability?
4. Why do we want reliability?
5. Can you have a test-retest reliability coefficient of below zero? Why or why not?
6. Is observer bias a major cause of unreliability?
7. In which situation will interobserver reliability be higher?
    a. scoring an essay exam
    b. scoring a multiple-choice test
8. True or False: If the interobserver agreement were 100%, interobserver reliability would be 1.
9. If your measure's test-retest reliability was .90, should you try to discover what your interobserver reliability was? Why or why not? (Hint: See Figure 3-2)
10. If your measure's test-retest reliability was .50, would you go about trying to discover what your interobserver reliability was? Why or why not? (Hint: See Figure 3-2)
11. If your measure's interobserver reliability is .70, can your test-retest reliability be .80? Why or why not?
12. Assume that test-retest reliability is .50 and interobserver reliability is 1.00. What is the source of your measure's reliability problems? What would you do to increase reliability? (Hint: See Figure 3-2)
13. Assume that test-retest reliability is .50 and interobserver reliability is .60. What is the main source of your measure's reliability problems? What would you do about it? (Hint: See Figure 3-2)
14. True or False: Reliability guarantees validity.
15. True or False: A measure's reliability puts a ceiling on validity.
16. True or False: Unreliability dilutes a measure's validity.
17. True or False: Unreliability poisons a measure's validity.

18. True or False: Validity guarantees reliability.
19. How would assessing interobserver reliability differ from assessing test-retest reliability?
20. What are the two primary types of subject bias? What are the differences between these two sources?
21. List four basic tactics for reducing the possibility of subject bias.
22. Suppose you are interested in measuring procrastination. You have students write an essay on a computer. Unknown to them, the computer measures how long it takes them to begin, how many breaks they take, and how long each of those breaks is. What would be the advantages of having the computer secretly record the information?
23. What is convergent validity? What are four basic ways of establishing convergent validity?
24. What is discriminant validity? Why is it necessary?
25. What is the value of internal consistency?
26. What is content validity? For what measures is it most important?
27. True or False: Shortening a test would probably harm its content validity.
28. True or False: Shortening a test would probably harm its internal consistency.
29. True or False: Internal consistency may be assessed by split-half reliability coefficients.
30. If lovers score higher on a "love" test than strangers, the love test has _____ validity, established by the _____ _____ technique.
31. If friends do not score higher on a "love" test than strangers, the test has _____ validity.
32. A test of empathy that did not correlate with intelligence would have _____ validity.
33. If therapists with high scores on an empathy test have better success rates than therapists with lower scores, then the empathy test has _____ validity.
34. If a test over Chapters 1–3 has 30 questions on Chapter 1, 15 questions on Chapter 2, and only 5 questions on Chapter 3, we might suspect that the test lacked _____ validity.
35. Why might it always be a good idea to correlate scores of a new personality test with a social desirability scale?
36. If you were going to develop a "Social Skills Scale," what subscales would you include? Why?
37. If researchers use an aggression scale to see if they have increased the participants' level of aggression, what two threats to validity should they particularly be concerned about?
38. What information about an aggression test would suggest that the test is a good instrument?
39. Measuring the degree to which someone is thinking is difficult. However, imagine that you are to try to measure thinking by using a measure of facial tension. How would you validate that measure?

40. A researcher wants to measure "aggressive tendencies." The researcher is trying to decide between a paper-and-pencil test of aggression and observing actual aggression.
    a. What problems might there be with observing aggressive behavior?
    b. In evaluating the test, what should the researcher beware of?
    c. What information about the test would suggest that the test is a good instrument?

41. Think of a construct you would like to measure.
    a. Name that construct.
    b. Define that construct.
    c. Locate a published measure of that concept (see Appendix B) and write down the reference for that source.
    d. Develop a measure of that construct.
    e. What could you do to improve or evaluate your measure's reliability?
    f. If you had a year to try to validate your measure, how would you go about it? (Hint: Refer to the different kinds of validities discussed in this chapter.)
    g. How vulnerable is your measure to subject and observer bias? Why? Can you change your measure to make it more resistant to these threats?

42. What problems do you see with measuring "athletic ability" as 40-yard dash speed? What steps would you take to improve this measure? (Hint: Think about solving the problems of bias and reliability).

43. Think of a factor that you would like to manipulate.
    a. Define this factor as specifically as you can.
    b. Find one example of this factor being manipulated in a published study (see Appendix B). Write down the reference citation for that source.
    c. How would you manipulate that factor? Why?
    d. How could you perform a manipulation check on the factor you want to manipulate? Would it be useful to perform a manipulation check? Why or why not?

44. Compare the relative advantages and disadvantages of using an instructional manipulation versus an environmental manipulation.

CHAPTER 4

BEYOND RELIABILITY AND VALIDITY: CHOOSING THE BEST MEASURE FOR YOUR STUDY

When possible, make the decisions now, even if action is in the future. A reviewed decision usually is better than one reached at the last moment.
—WILLIAM B. GIVEN, JR.

There is very little difference between one man and another; but what little there is, is very important.
—WILLIAM JAMES

....

OVERVIEW

Some people buy the most powerful software available, only to find out that it doesn't work well for them. The program may be incompatible with other software they have, or it may not have a certain feature they want. As a result, they have a decent program, but one that doesn't work well for what they want to do. Similarly, when selecting a measure, some people choose the most valid measuring instrument available, yet find out that it doesn't work well for what they want to do.

At first, choosing the most valid measure seems perfectly sensible. After all, who wouldn't want to make sure that their instrument measures what it is supposed to measure?

After giving it some thought, however, you probably realize that most important decisions involve weighing more than one factor. Every measure, like every computer program, has weaknesses. The key is to find the measure whose weaknesses are least likely to get in the way of what you want to do.

The extent to which a measure's weaknesses will get in the way of what you want to do depends on what you want to do. For example, imagine that you find three measures that, although they have similar overall levels of validity, have different specific weaknesses in terms of validity. The first measure is vulnerable only to biased observers. The second measure is a rating scale measure vulnerable only to subject biases. The third measure's only weakness is unreliability. Which measure should you choose? The answer depends on your particular study.

If you were able to keep observers "blind," you would not be concerned with observer bias. For example, observers could not bias the results in favor of the treatment group if they didn't know whether the person they were rating was in the treatment group or the no-treatment group. Thus, if you could make observers "blind," you might choose the measure that is vulnerable only to observer bias.

If you had a hypothesis that is easy to figure out, you would avoid the measure that is vulnerable to subject bias. For example, suppose you hypothesized that participants would like a product more after seeing an ad for the product. Unfortunately, even if the ad was ineffective, participants may still rate the product higher after seeing the ad because they thought you wanted the ad to be effective. In this case, the combination of a hypothesis that is easy to guess and a rating scale measure that is easy to fake would be deadly to your study's construct validity. Therefore, you would not use the rating scale measure. Suppose, however, you had a hypothesis that participants probably wouldn't figure out. For example, suppose your hypothesis was that the ad would actually decrease liking for the product. In that case, you might choose the rating scale measure because its vulnerability to subject biases should not hurt you.

Finally, if you were very concerned about avoiding both subject and observer bias, you would choose the measure that was unbiased, but unreliable. Admittedly, such a measure would have limited validity, and its random error would make it difficult for you to obtain a statistically reliable difference between your treatment and no-treatment groups. However, if you found a significant difference between the treatment and no-treatment groups, you could be confident that the difference wasn't due to bias.

As you can see, even if validity were your only concern, you would not always choose the measure that, in general, was most valid. Instead, you would choose the measure that would be most valid for your particular study. However, validity is never your only concern. For starters, ethical and practical concerns will always affect your choice of measure. Furthermore, you should also choose a measure based on whether it will allow you to answer your research question.

SENSITIVITY: WILL THE MEASURE BE ABLE TO DETECT THE DIFFERENCES YOU NEED TO DETECT?

To understand how a measure could prevent you from answering your research question, imagine a cell biologist's reaction to being told that she could only use a magnifying glass. Obviously, she would be surprised. Without a microscope, the cell biologist could not detect small differences between cells.

Like cell biologists, psychologists often look for subtle differences. Consequently, like cell biologists, psychologists usually want their measure to be **sensitive:** to have the ability to detect differences among participants on a given variable. For example, we might try to increase participants' empathy for others. Realistically, we realize that one short treatment is probably not going to have enormous effects on a trait that has been shaped by heredity and a lifetime of experiences. If we have been able to make even a small improvement in this characteristic, we would like to know about it.

ACHIEVING THE NECESSARY LEVEL OF SENSITIVITY

How can you find or develop a sensitive measure? Often, you can evaluate or improve a measure's sensitivity by simply using common sense. For example, if participants must receive either a score of "1" or "2," the measure will not be sensitive to subtle differences among participants (just as "weighing" people as either "light" or "heavy" would skip over differences). But beyond such commonsense considerations, look at the measure's validity and reliability: A sensitive measure will tend to be more valid and more reliable than an insensitive measure.

Look for High Validity

The desire for sensitivity is a major reason that researchers often insist on having the most valid measure available. That is, even though they have several valid measures to choose from, they want the most valid one because it will tend to be the most sensitive.

Why does the most valid measure tend to be the most sensitive? To answer this question, keep two related facts in mind. First, the most valid measure is the one in which scores are least affected by factors that are irrelevant to what you are trying to measure. Second, the less a measure's scores are affected by irrelevant factors, the more it will be sensitive to changes in the relevant factor. For example, if you were weighing people to determine whether a diet had an effect, you would be more likely to find the diet's effect if participants were weighed unclothed rather than clothed. Both the clothed and unclothed measures would be valid. However, because the unclothed measure is not assessing the weight of the clothes, it is more valid and more sensitive to actual weight changes.

For similar reasons, measures that involve fewer inferences tend to be both more valid and more sensitive. Consequently, scientists would prefer to measure a person's weight on a scale rather than by the depth of the impression the person's footprint left in the sand. Likewise, they would prefer to measure body fat using calipers rather than by estimating it from overall body weight.

There are two concrete steps you can take to increase the chances that your measure is both valid and sensitive. First, spend the time to figure out precisely what it is you want to measure. When you first come up with a research idea, you may have a general sense of what you want to measure. For example, you may start out thinking that you want to measure attraction. Upon reflection, however, you may decide that you really want to measure lust. One way of helping you focus on what you want to measure is to look up the term you think you want to measure in the *Psychological Thesaurus*. The *Thesaurus* will help you clarify what you want to measure by alerting you to more specific terms, as well as related terms.

Second, ask if there is a more direct way of measuring your construct. For example, if you are interested in measuring aggression in football, do not simply measure how many penalties a team gets. Instead, measure how many penalties they get for unsportsmanlike conduct. Similarly, rather than assuming that fear will lead children to sit closer to each other and then measuring fear by how closely children sit to each other, take the more direct approach of asking children how afraid they are. By thinking about the simplest, most direct way to measure what you want to measure, you can often reduce the extent to which your measure is affected by things you don't want to measure, thereby increasing sensitivity.

Look for High Reliability

As you have seen, the desire for sensitive measures is one reason why psychologists value validity. As you will soon see, the desire for sensitive measures is also a reason psychologists value reliability. To the extent that a measure is varying due to random error, it is not varying due to differences in participants. That is, the less reliable the measure is, the less sensitive it is to differences.[1] For example, suppose you weighed yourself every day on a highly unreliable scale. Furthermore,

---

[1]The less reliable the measure, the more it is affected by random error—provided that whatever you are measuring is stable. If you are measuring intelligence—and if intelligence is stable—any unreliability in your measure reflects random error. If, however, you are measuring something that changes (knowledge about research methods), then unreliability might not reflect random error.

suppose you had gained 2 pounds. Some days your scale would make it seem like you had gained 6 pounds, while on other days your scale would make it seem like you had lost 2 pounds. Instead of realizing that you'd gained weight, you might think that the different readings on the scale were entirely due to random error.

As the example above suggests, unreliability is to data what static is to radio reception. With a little static, you can still listen to the radio news. As the static increases, it becomes increasingly difficult to understand the news. Similarly, with a lot of random error in your measurements, it becomes hard to pick up the news your data are sending you. If your measures are very unreliable, even a large difference between your groups may be due to random measurement error. Consequently, if you use an unreliable measure and see that your groups score differently on that unreliable measure, you don't know if these differences are due to random measurement error or whether they represent actual differences.

To visualize how random error makes it hard to see the message in your data, imagine you were measuring the time it took two different rats to run a maze. Suppose that Rat *A* and Rat *B* ran the maze four times each. Their actual times were:

	TRIAL 1	TRIAL 2	TRIAL 3	TRIAL 4
Rat *A*	6 seconds	6 seconds	6 seconds	6 seconds
Rat *B*	5 seconds	5 seconds	5 seconds	5 seconds

If you had obtained these data, you could clearly see that Rat *B* was the faster rat. However, suppose your measuring system was unreliable. For example, suppose you were having some problems with the stopwatch or you weren't always paying close attention. Then, you might record the rats' times as follows:

	TRIAL 1	TRIAL 2	TRIAL 3	TRIAL 4
Rat *A*	7 seconds	6 seconds	5 seconds	6 seconds
Rat *B*	8 seconds	4 seconds	6 seconds	2 seconds

Despite the random error in your measurements, you correctly calculated that Rat *A* averages 6 seconds to run the maze and Rat *B* averages 5 seconds to run the maze. Thus, random error does not bias your observations. However, because of the unreliable, erratic nature of your measuring system, it is hard to determine whether Rat *B* really is the faster rat. The unreliability of the measuring system causes static that makes it harder to get a clear picture of the message your data should be sending you.

You have seen that too much random error in your measuring system can prevent you from detecting true differences between participants. In other words, all other things being equal, the more reliable the measure is, the more sensitive it is. Therefore, if you want to have a sensitive measure, you should probably choose a measure that has a high (above .70) test-retest reliability coefficient.

Find Measures That Provide a Variety of Scores

Thus far, we have discussed cases in which you could increase sensitivity by increasing both reliability and validity. The more scores on the measure are affected by the characteristic you want to measure (rather than by bias, a different trait, or random error), the more the measure is likely to be sensitive to differences between individuals on that characteristic. However, a reliable and valid measure might still be insensitive because—like a scale that will only measure you to the nearest 100 pounds—it fails to allow participants who differ slightly on a trait to receive different scores.

If a measure is to be sensitive to subtle differences between participants, participants who differ on the characteristic must get different scores. Thus, if you measured participants who varied widely on the characteristic, you should get a wide range of scores. Some participants should get extremely low scores, and others should get extremely high scores. Very few participants should get the exact same score.

What could prevent a valid measure from producing the wide variety of scores necessary to reflect the full extent of the variation among your participants? To answer this question, let's imagine that you are trying to detect small changes in how much a man loves a woman. What could stop you from detecting changes in the man's love?

Avoid Behaviors That Are Resistant to Change One reason you might be unable to detect small changes in love is that you choose to measure a behavior that is very resistant to change. Measures based on such behaviors are insensitive. Therefore, if sensitivity is a big concern, you should not choose to measure a behavior that is resistant to change. But what behaviors are resistant to change?

Important behaviors, such as getting married or buying a car, and well-ingrained habits, such as smoking or cursing, are resistant to change. Consequently, unlike ratings on a rating scale, these behaviors may not change as readily as the underlying construct they are supposed to measure. For instance, suppose your measure of love was whether a man asked a woman to marry him. Since a man would only ask a woman to marry him once his love had reached a high level, this measure would be insensitive to many subtle changes. It would not be able to detect a man's love changing from a near-zero level of love to a moderate level.

So, if you are interested in sensitivity, stay away from measures that cannot detect low levels of a construct. Don't use death as a measure of stress, tile erosion in front of a painting as a measure of the painting's popularity, or quitting smoking as a measure of willpower. Instead, use more sensitive measures, such as rating scales.

Avoid Measures That Produce a Limited Range of Scores A second thing that could prevent you from distinguishing between the subtly different levels of the man's love is if your measure did not represent all these different levels. Consequently, a second reason that a marriage proposal is an insensitive measure is that there are only two scores the man could receive (asked or didn't ask). You are trying to distinguish between numerous subtly differing degrees of love, but you are only letting your participant respond in two different ways. If a measure is going to discriminate between many different degrees of love, participants must be able to give many different responses.

Ask "How Much" Instead of "Whether"   One obvious way to allow participants to get a variety of scores on a measure is to add scale points to your measure. Adding scale points to your measure may increase its sensitivity just as adding $1/2$-inch marks to a yardstick makes the yardstick more useful for detecting subtle differences in the length of boards. If you are measuring generosity, don't just record whether someone gave to charity. Instead, record how often she donated, or how much she gave, or how long you had to talk to her before she was willing to give. Similarly, if you are using maze running to measure motivation, don't simply record whether or not the rat ran the maze. Instead, time the rat to determine how fast the rat ran the maze.

Using scientific equipment can help you add scale points to your measure. For instance, with the proper instruments, you can measure reaction time to the nearest thousandth of a second. Or, by using a sound meter to measure how loudly a person is speaking, you can go beyond saying that the person was speaking softly or loudly: You can specify exactly how many decibels the person produced.

Add Scale Points to a Rating Scale   You can also add scale points to self-report measures. For example, don't measure love by asking the question: "Are you in love? (1—no, 2—yes)." Instead, ask: "How much in love are you? (1—not at all, 2—slightly, 3—moderately, 4—extremely)." Similarly, rather than having an observer rate whether a child was aggressive, you could have the observer rate the extent to which the child was aggressive.

There comes a point, however, where adding scale points to a measure will not enhance sensitivity. Asking people to report their weight to the nearest 1/1,000th of a pound or asking them to report their love on a 1,000-point scale will probably not boost sensitivity. That is, after a certain point, any apparent gains in precision are wiped out by the fact that responses are unreliable guesses. Besides, such questions may cause participants to be frustrated or to doubt your competence. Therefore, to boost sensitivity without frustrating your participants, you should not add scale points beyond a certain point. But what is that point?

According to conventional wisdom, that point could be after you reach 3 points or after you reach 11 points, depending on the kind of question you are asking. If you are asking about something that your participants think about a lot, you might be able to use an 11-point scale. If, however, you are asking about an issue that your participants are relatively ignorant of (or apathetic toward), there may be no point in going beyond a 3-point scale. When in doubt, use either a 5- or 7-point scale.

Pilot Test Your Measure   If you have followed our advice, you now have a measure that *potentially* provides a range of scores. However, just because there are many possible scores a participant could get on your measure, it does not mean there are many different scores that your participants will get.

To determine whether scores will actually vary, *pilot test* your measure: Try out your study and your measure on a few participants before conducting a full-blown study. If you do a pilot test, you will often find that participants' scores on the measure do not vary as much as you expected. If you do not conduct a pilot test, you will only discover the problem with your measure after you have completed the study. For example, one investigator performed an experiment to see if reading along with a videotape would help children remember more than if they just saw the videotape. To measure memory, she asked the children 24 questions about the story. She thought participants' scores might range from almost 0 (none correct) to 24 (all correct). Unfortunately, the questions were so hard that none of the children got any of the questions right. Even though the children's memories for the material probably differed, they all got the same score—zero. Thus, the results of her study were hard to interpret.

SENSITIVITY: CONCLUSIONS

You have seen that if a measure is to be sensitive to differences between participants, participants must differ on the measure. However, it is not enough that different participants get different scores. Instead, different participants must get different scores because they differ on what you are trying to measure. If participants are getting different scores due to random error, the measure will not be sensitive. For example, if you have people respond, on a 100-point scale, to a question they don't understand, you will get a wide range of scores, but your measure will be insensitive. In general, to the extent that participants' scores vary because of factors unrelated to your construct, the measure is not sensitive.

To boost sensitivity, then, you should minimize the extent to which participants' scores vary because of factors unrelated to your construct. Thus, if you use simple, anonymous behaviors as measures (such as self-rating scales), you may be more likely to detect differences between participants than if you observe complex, public behaviors that are influenced by many factors other than your construct.

As you can imagine, the goal of sensitivity sometimes conflicts with the goal of validity. For example, to avoid subject biases, you might want to use a complex, public behavior (sacrificing for one's partner) as your measure of love. However, to have a sensitive measure, you might want to use a simple rating scale. Do you choose the complex behavior that might be insensitive? Or, do you use the rating scale, even though it would be invalid if participants simply give you the ratings they think you want?

In certain situations, some researchers would choose the more sensitive rating scale. To understand why, realize that a sensitive measure can help you find small differences so that you can make discoveries. An insensitive measure, on the other hand, may stop you from making discoveries. Consequently, some scientists would use a sensitive measure that would first allow them to find differences; they would later debate what those differences mean (the construct validity question). They would prefer debating what their difference meant to not finding any differences at all.

In short, even though validity is important, it is not the only factor to consider when selecting a measure. Depending on the circumstances, having the ability to detect subtle differences may be equally important. After all, an insensitive measure may—by making sure that you fail to find anything—prevent you from being able to answer your research question.

SCALES OF MEASUREMENT: WILL THE MEASURE ALLOW YOU TO MAKE THE KINDS OF COMPARISONS YOU NEED TO MAKE?

An insensitive measure is not the only kind of measure that can prevent you from answering your research question. Indeed, perhaps a more important aspect of the measure is whether it allows you to make the kind of comparison you need to make.

The kind of comparison you need to make is determined by your research question. For example, consider these four questions:

1. Do the two groups *differ* on the quality?
2. Does one group have *more* of the quality than the other?
3. *How much more* of the quality does one group have than the other group?
4. Does one group have more than three *times as much* of the quality than the other group?

All four of these questions could be answered by using numbers. All measures can provide numbers. However, very few measures could help you answer the fourth question. Why?

The answer lies in the fact that not all measures produce the same kinds of numbers. To repeat, *not all numbers are alike.* Just as some descriptive phrases are more informative and specific than others ("Joe doesn't look the same as Tom" versus "Joe is twice as attractive as Tom"), some numbers are more informative than others.

THE DIFFERENT SCALES OF MEASUREMENT

Rather than saying that some numbers provide more specific information than other numbers, psychologists say that some numbers represent a *higher scale of measurement* than others. In the next few sections, we will show you:

- how numbers representing different scales of measurement differ
- why some measures provide more informative numbers than others
- how to determine what kind of numbers you need

Nominal Numbers: Different Numbers Representing Different States

The least informative numbers are **nominal scale numbers:** numbers that substitute for names. Like names, nominal numbers can be used to identify, label, and categorize things. Things having the same number are alike (they belong in the same category); things having different numbers are different (they belong to different categories).

Like names, nominal numbers cannot meaningfully be ordered. In other words, just as we do not say that Jane is a bigger name than Jim, we do not say that someone having the uniform number 36 is better than someone wearing number 35.

In everyday life, we run into these name-like, orderless, nominal numbers constantly. For example, social security numbers, players' uniform numbers, charge card numbers, license plate numbers, and serial code numbers are all nominal numbers.

In psychological research, the best use of nominal numbers is when the participants can be clearly classified as either having a certain quality or not. In those cases, we can use numbers to substitute for category names. For example, we may put people into categories such as male/female or student/faculty. In other words, this most basic way of using numbers is perfect when you aren't interested in measuring different amounts, but different kinds or types. For example, someone scoring a "1" might think of love as an addiction, a person scoring a "2" might think of love as a business partnership, a person scoring a "3" might think of love as a game, and a person scoring a "4" might think of love as "lust" (Sternberg, 1994).

Unfortunately, sometimes you are interested in measuring different amounts of a construct, but you are stuck with nominal numbers because the measuring system is so crude. That is, in the early stages of developing a measure, we may have such a poor idea of what scores on the measure mean that we can't even say that a high score means we have more of a construct than a low score. For instance, suppose that when participants see their partner, some participants produce one pattern of brain-waves, whereas others produce a different pattern. Labeling the first brain-wave pattern "1" and the other pattern "2" is arbitrary. We could have just as easily labeled the first pattern "2" and the other pattern "1." Consequently, we have nominal scale measurement because we do not know whether "2" indicates a greater reaction than "1." We only know that "2" is a different pattern than "1."

Once we find out that one pattern indicates more love than another, it would be meaningful to give that pattern the higher number. At that point, we would have moved beyond nominal scale measurement.

Ordinal Numbers: When Bigger Means More

As you shall see, we often want to move beyond nominal scale measurement. Rather than always being limited to saying only that participants getting different numbers differ, we often want to say that participants receiving higher scores have more of a given quality. That is, beyond saying that people scoring "3" are similar to each other and different from people scoring "1," we want to also state that people scoring "3" have *more* of a certain quality than those scoring "1." In other words, we may want to be able to meaningfully *order* scores from lowest to highest. We want higher scores to mean more of the quality. For example, people scoring a "5" feel more love than people scoring "4," who feel more love than people scoring "3," and so on.

If you can assume that higher numbers indicate more love than lower numbers, your measure is producing at least **ordinal scale numbers**: numbers that can be meaningfully *ordered* from lowest to highest. When you assume that you have ordinal data, you are making a very simple assumption: The numbers are ordered. Note, however, that you are not assuming that the difference between "2" and "1" is the same as the difference between "3" and "2." To reiterate, you are assuming that "2" means more of the construct than "1," and "3" means more of the construct than "2," but you have no idea how much more of the construct a person scoring "3" has than a person scoring "2."

To illustrate what ordinal scaling does and does not assume, suppose you successfully ranked 10 couples in terms of how much they loved each other. Because the numbers can be meaningfully ordered from highest to lowest, these are definitely ordinal data. Yet, because they are ordinal data, the psychological difference between "1" and "2" may be very different from the psychological difference between "9" and "10." For example, there might be very little difference between the couple getting rank 1 and the couple getting rank 2, but there might be an enormous difference between the couple getting rank 9 and the couple getting rank 10. In short, ranked data, like all ordinal data, can tell you whether one participant has more of a quality than another, but are limited in that they can't tell you how much more of a quality one participant has than another.

Interval Scale Numbers: Knowing How Much More

Because of the limitations of ordinal numbers, you may decide you want a higher scale of measurement. For example, in addition to assuming that numbers can be ordered, you might also want to be able to assume that the psychological distance (the difference in participants' minds) between a score of "1" and "2" is exactly the same as the psychological difference between "2" and "3," which is the same as the psychological distance between any two consecutive whole numbers. In technical terminology, you are assuming that your numbers are on an **interval scale**: a scale for which equal numerical intervals represent equal psychological intervals.

Unfortunately, the assumption of equal intervals is not easy to defend—no matter what measure you use. As we have seen, ranked data are typically assumed to be only ordinal—not interval. If you use a measure of nonverbal behavior, you could still fail to meet the assumption of equal intervals. For example, suppose that while you had couples wait alone in a small room for 10 minutes, you recorded the total amount of time the couple stared into each other's eyes. It would be risky to assume that the difference in love between a couple who looks for 360 seconds and a couple who looks for 300 seconds is the same as the difference between a couple who looks for a total of 60 seconds and a couple who does not look at all.

Likewise, if you use a physiological measure, it is hard to justify the assumption that equal changes in bodily responses correspond to equal changes in psychological states. It seems unlikely that changes in the body correspond perfectly and directly to changes in the mind. For example, if, on seeing their partner, one participant's blood pressure increases from 200 to 210 and another's goes from 90 to 100, would you say that both were equally in love?

How could you possibly get interval scale data? One possibility is to ask participants to do the scaling for you. That is, ask participants to rate their feelings on a scale, trusting that participants will view the distances between each scale point as equal psychological distances.

Although many psychologists assume that rating scales produce interval scale data—and there is some evidence to support this assumption—this assumption of equal intervals is controversial. To see why this assumption is hard to justify, suppose you had people rate how they felt about their spouse on a −30 (hate intensely) to a +30 (love intensely) scale. Would you be sure that someone who changed from −1 to +1 had changed to the same degree as someone who had changed from +12 to +14?

Ratio Scales: Zeroing in on Perfection

If you are extremely demanding, it may not be enough for you to assume that your measure's numbers can be meaningfully ordered from lowest to highest and that equal intervals between numbers represent equal psychological distances. You may want to make one last, additional assumption—that your measure has an absolute zero. In other words, you might assume that someone scoring a zero on your measure feels absolutely no love. If a score of zero on your love measure represented absolutely no love, and you had equal intervals, then you could make ratio statements such as: "The couple who scored a '1' on the love measure was 1/2 (a ratio of 1 to 2) as much in love as the couple scoring a '2.'" Because measures that have both an absolute zero and equal intervals allow you to make ratio statements, these measures produce **ratio scale numbers**.

The assumption of having an absolute zero is not automatic, even when measuring physical reality. For example, 0 degrees Fahrenheit doesn't mean no (zero) temperature. If it did, we could make ratio statements such as saying that 50 degrees is half as hot as 100 degrees.

As you have seen, meeting the assumptions of ratio scale measurement is not automatic even when measuring physical reality. It is even harder to meet the requirements of ratio scale measurement when measuring a psychological characteristic. Indeed, it is difficult to meet either of the assumptions of the ratio scale. First, it is hard to say that a zero score means a complete absence of a psychological characteristic. Second, it is hard to say that the numbers generated by a measure correspond *perfectly* to psychological reality. It's tough enough to have some degree of correspondence between scores on a measure and psychological reality, much less to achieve perfection.

Because of the difficulty of achieving ratio scale measurements, most researchers do not ask participants to try to make ratio scale judgments. They usually do not ask participants to think of "zero" as the absence of the quality. Indeed, they often do not even let participants have a zero point. Instead, participants are more likely to be asked to make their ratings on a 1-to-5 scale than on a 0-to-4 scale. Furthermore, even when participants rate on a 0-to-4 scale, participants are rarely asked to think of "2" as having twice as much of the quality as "1," "3" as three times "1," and "4" as four times as much as "1."

Occasionally, however, participants are asked to make ratio scale judgments, a process called *magnitude estimation.* For example, participants might be told that the average amount of liking that people feel for a roommate is a "50." If they feel one-fifth as much liking toward their roommate as that, they should estimate the magnitude of their liking toward their roommate as 10. If they like their best friend twice as much as they think most people like their roommates, they should estimate the magnitude of their liking for their best friend as 100. Participants would then be asked to rate the magnitude of their liking of a variety of people.

Magnitude estimation doesn't always involve using numbers. Instead, participants might draw lines. For example, they may be shown a line and told to imagine that the length of that line represents the average extent to which people like their roommates. Then, they may be asked to draw lines of different lengths to express how much they like various people. If a participant likes Person *A* three times as much as Person *B,* the participant's line representing his or her liking for Person *A* should be three times longer than their Person *B* line.

Advocates of magnitude estimation believe that the numbers or line lengths that participants produce provide ratio scale data. However, as you might imagine, critics have doubts. Even when participants are asked to make ratio scale judgments in magnitude estimation, there is no guarantee that participants will be able to do so.

WHY OUR NUMBERS DO NOT ALWAYS MEASURE UP

You can see why ratings and even subjective estimates of magnitude might not provide ratio scale numbers. But why don't you get ratio scale numbers from your behavioral measures? For example, why isn't time staring into each other's eyes a ratio scale measure?

Isn't zero the complete absence of gazing? Isn't 3 seconds of gazing three times as much as 1 second? Yes and no. Yes, seconds of gazing is a ratio scale measure if you are interested in knowing about gazing. But you aren't measuring gazes for gazing's sake. You are using gazes to measure love. You are not trying to measure physical reality (gazes); you are trying to use physical reality to measure psychological reality (love). As an indirect, imperfect reflection of love, time of gaze is not a ratio scale measure (see Box 4-1). Similarly, although we can all agree that a heart rate of 60 beats per minute is twice as fast as a heart rate of 30 beats per minute, we can't all agree that a person with a heart rate of 60 beats per minute is twice as excited as a person with a heart rate of 30 beats per minute.

To reiterate, you cannot measure excitement, love, or any other construct, directly. You can only measure constructs indirectly. It is unlikely that your indirect measure of a construct will measure that construct with the perfect accuracy that ratio scale measurement requires.

WHICH LEVEL OF MEASUREMENT DO YOU NEED?

You have seen that there are four different levels of measurement: nominal scale, ordinal scale, interval scale, and ratio scale. As you go up the scale from nominal to ordinal to interval to ratio scale measurement, the numbers become increasingly informative (for a review, see Table 4-1).

You have also seen that as you go up the scale, it becomes harder to find a measure that provides the required level of measurement. For example, if you need ordinal data, you could use almost any measuring system—from ranked data to magnitude estimation. However, if you needed ratio scale data, magnitude estimation might be your only option. You could not use a measure that involved ranking participants from lowest to highest—no matter how valid that ranking system was. The scale of measurement you needed, rather than validity, would determine what measure you would use.

The scale of measurement you need should always influence what measure you use. Therefore, when choosing a measure for a study, you should ask two questions:

1. What scale of measurement do I need to answer the research question?
2. Which of the measures that I am considering will give me this level of measurement?

The next sections and Tables 4-2 and 4-3 will help you answer these questions.

When You Need Ratio Scale Data

Suppose you want to find out whether engaged couples are twice as much in love as dating couples who are not engaged. Since you are hypothesizing a 2-to-1 ratio, you need a measure that gives you ratio scale numbers. As Table 4-3 indicates, there are very few measures that you can use if you need ratio scale numbers.

Fortunately, you only need ratio scale level of measurement if you are trying to make ratio statements like married women are twice as happy as widows.

• BOX 4-1 •

NUMBERS AND THE TOLL TICKET

Toll by Vehicle Class (in dollars)

Exit No.	# Miles	1	2	3	4
1	3	.25	.35	.60	.35
2	10	.40	.45	1.00	.60
3	40	.50	.60	1.35	.80
4	45	.80	.90	2.15	1.30
5	49	.90	1.10	2.65	1.55
6	51	1.45	1.65	3.65	2.15
7	117	3.60	4.15	9.95	5.85

The toll ticket shows us many kinds of numbers in action. For example, the numbers representing vehicle class (1–4) at the top of the ticket (under toll by vehicle class) are nominal numbers. The only reason the toll people used numbers instead of names is that numbers take less room. So, instead of writing "car," "16-wheeled truck," "small truck," etc., they wrote 1, 2, 3, and 4. There's no particular order to these numbers as shown by the fact that a "3" is charged more than any other number.

The exits, when used as an index of distance, represent ordinal data. You know that if you have to get off at exit 4, you will have to go farther than if you get off at exit 5, but—without looking at the miles column—you don't know how much farther. Thus, missing exit 4 isn't too bad, the next exit is only 4 miles away. Missing exit 6, on the other hand, is terrible—the next exit is 66 miles farther down the road!

Money, as a measure of miles, is also an ordinal measure. That is, although you know that the more money you spend on tolls, the farther you have gone, you can't figure out how much farther you have gone merely by looking at how much money the toll was. For example, if you are vehicle class number 1, it costs you 25 cents to go 3 miles, 15 cents more to go 7 additional miles, and only 10 more cents gets you 30 additional miles.

As you have seen, both the amount of money spent and the number of exits passed are just ordinal measures when they are used to try to estimate the amount of another variable (distance). Similarly, some behavioral and physiological measures (eye-gazing or blood pressure increases) may only be ordinal measures when used to estimate the amount of another variable, such as the invisible psychological state of love.

When You Need at Least Interval Scale Data

Since you will probably not be comparing groups to find out whether one group is twice as much in love as another group, you will rarely need to assume that your measure has ratio properties. You may, however, have to assume that your measure does have interval properties. For example, suppose you are trying to estimate the effects of therapy on relationships. Before relationship counseling is offered on your campus, you measure the degree to which couples are in love. Next, you observe who goes to counseling and who doesn't. Finally, at the end of the term, you measure the couples' love again. Let's say that you got the following pattern of results:

• TABLE 4-1 •

THE MEANING AND LIMITATIONS OF DIFFERENT SCALES OF MEASUREMENT

SCALE	MEANING	MAIN LIMITATION
Nominal	Different scores represent *different* types of behavior or different amounts of the construct. ("3" is a different kind of love than "1" or a different amount of love.)	Since there is no order to nominal numbers, we can't say that "3" indicates more love than "1."
Ordinal	Different scores indicate different amounts *and* higher scores represent greater amounts of what is being measured. ("3" is more love than "1.")	Since the distances between numbers do not correspond to psychological reality, we can't say *how much* more of a quality one participant has than another.
Interval	Different scores indicate different amounts *and* higher scores represent more of the construct *and* equal distances between numbers represent equal psychological differences. Therefore, we can say *how much* more love one participant feels than another. ("3" is more love than "1" to the same extent that "5" is more love than "3.")	Since we do not have an absolute zero, we cannot say *how many more times* love one participant has than another.
Ratio	Higher scores represent more of the construct *and* equal distances between numbers represent equal psychological differences *and* zero means a complete absence of the construct. The mathematical ratio between two scores perfectly corresponds to reality. ("3" is 3 *times as much* love as "1.")	None

	BEGINNING OF TERM	END OF TERM
Didn't go to counseling	3.0	4.0
Went to counseling	5.0	7.0

(The higher the score, the more in love. Scores could range from 1 to 9.)

Did the couples who went for counseling change more than those who didn't? At first glance, this seems like an easy question. The no-counseling group changed one unit and the counseling group changed two units, so isn't two units more than one unit? Not necessarily.

If we have interval or ratio scale data, we can assume that each unit of change represents the same psychological distance. Therefore, we can say that, psychologically, two units of change is more than one unit of change. Thus, if we have interval or ratio scale data, we can say that the counseling group changed more than the no-counseling group.

But what if we had nominal or ordinal data? With nominal or ordinal data, we can't safely assume that each unit of change represents the same psychological distance. If our data were nominal or ordinal, the psychological distance between 3 and 4 could be much more than the psychological distance between 5 and 7. Thus, if we had nominal or ordinal data, we could not have answered the question, "Did couples who went for counseling change more than those who didn't?" As you can see from this example, if your research question involves asking whether one group changed more than another group, then you must use a measure that has at least interval properties.

When Ordinal Data Are Sufficient

Suppose you don't care how much more in love one group is than the other. All you want to know is which group is most in love. For example, suppose you want to be able to order these three groups in terms of amount of love:

Didn't go to counseling at all	3.0
Went to counseling for 1 week	5.0
Went to counseling for 8 weeks	7.0

(The higher the score, the more in love. Scores could range from 1 to 9.)

If you had ordinal data, you could conclude that participants who went to counseling for 8 weeks were most in love, those who went for 1 week were less in love, and those who didn't go to counseling were least in love. So, if you simply want to know which group is higher on a variable and which group is lower, then all you need is ordinal data. If all you need is ordinal data, you are in luck. As you can see from Table 4-3, most measures produce data that meet or exceed the requirements of ordinal level measurement.

When You Only Need Nominal Data

It's conceivable that you aren't interested in discovering which group is more in love. Instead, you might have the less ambitious goal of just trying to find out whether the different groups differ in terms of their love for each other. If that's the case, nominal data are all you need. Since you only need to make the least demanding and safest assumption about your numbers (that different numbers represent different things), any valid measure you choose will measure up.

• **TABLE 4-2** •

DIFFERENT RESEARCH QUESTIONS REQUIRE
DIFFERENT LEVELS OF MEASUREMENT

RESEARCH QUESTION	SCALE OF MEASUREMENT REQUIRED
Can more members of Group *A* be categorized as _____ (in love, neurotic, etc.) than members of Group *B*?	At least nominal
Is Group *A* more _____ than Group *B*?	At least ordinal
Is the difference between Group 1 and Group 2 more than the difference between Group 3 and Group 4?	At least interval
Did Group *A* change more than Group *B*?	At least interval
Is Group *A* three times more _____ than Group *B*?	Only ratio scale

CONCLUSIONS ABOUT SCALES OF MEASUREMENT

As you have seen, different research questions require different scales of measurement. If you are only asking whether two groups *differ,* any scale of measurement, even *nominal,* will do. If, however, you are asking whether one group

• **TABLE 4-3** •

MEASURING INSTRUMENTS AND
THE KIND OF DATA THEY PRODUCE

SCALE OF MEASUREMENT	MEASURING TACTICS ASSUMED TO PRODUCE THOSE KINDS OF NUMBERS
Ratio	Magnitude estimation
Interval	Rating scales (Magnitude estimation)
Ordinal	Nonverbal measures Physiological measures Rankings (Rating Scales) (Magnitude estimation)
Nominal	Any valid measure (All of the above)

Note: Any measurement technique that provides data that meet a certain level of measurement also provides data that meet the less stringent requirements of lower levels of measurement. Thus, a measure that provides data that meet the requirements of interval scale measurement also provides data that meet the requirements of ordinal and nominal scale measurement.

has *more* of a quality than another, you need at least *ordinal* level data. If your research question involves asking *how much* more of a quality one group has than another, then you need to use a measure that provides at least *interval* data. If you need to find out *how many times more* of a quality one group has than another, then you need *ratio* level data.

If your research question requires a given level of measurement, you must use a measure that provides that level of measurement. Consequently, you may find that the type of data you need will dictate the measure you choose. You may find that the only measure that will give you the type of data you want is not as sensitive or as free from biases as another measure.

Let's look at one example that illustrates this point. Suppose you want to know if a treatment is more effective for couples having relationship problems than it is for couples who are very much in love. You are reluctant to use a rating scale measure because rating scale measures are extremely vulnerable to subject biases. However, rating scale measures are commonly assumed to produce interval data—and your research question requires at least interval scale data.

To illustrate why you require interval data, imagine that a problem couple's score on the measure goes from a "1" to a "3," whereas a happy couple's increases from an "8" to a "9." To say that the problem couple actually experienced more improvement, you must assume that the difference between "1" and "3" is greater than the difference between "8" and "9." This is not an assumption you can make with either nominal or ordinal data. It is, however, an assumption you can make if you have interval data (because with interval data, the psychological distance between "1" and "2" is the same as the distance between "8" and "9").

Because your research question requires interval data, you must use a measure that provides at least interval data. Consequently, if the rating scale is the only measure that gives you interval scale data, you will have to use it—despite its vulnerability to subject bias—because it is the only measure that will allow you to answer your research question.

ETHICAL AND PRACTICAL CONSIDERATIONS

Clearly, you want to use a measure that will allow you to answer your research question. However, there may be times when you decide not to use a certain measure even though that measure allows you to answer your research question. For example, suppose you have a measure that gives you the right scale of measurement and is more valid than other measures because it is not vulnerable to subject biases. However, it avoids subject bias by surprising or tricking participants. In that case, you may decide against using a measure because you believe participants should be fully informed about the study before they agree to participate. Similarly, you may reject field observation because you feel those tactics threaten participants' privacy.

Although you should always be concerned about ethical issues, you often have to be concerned about practical issues. You may have to reject a measure because it is simply too time-consuming or expensive to use. Practical concerns may even force you to either reject or use a measure based on its **face validity**: the extent to which the measure seems to the nonexpert to be valid. Usually, because face validity has nothing to do with real, scientific validity, you would not choose a measure for its face validity any more than you would judge a book by its cover. Normally, you would choose a measure based on a careful evaluation of scientific evidence, rather than on participants' opinions.

Indeed, under many circumstances, you might avoid a measure that had high face validity because high face validity could harm real validity. That is, if people think that questions from a "test" in a popular magazine are measuring a certain construct, then people can "fake" the test to get the results they want. Conversely, a measure with no face validity may be valid precisely because participants don't see what it is measuring.

As we have pointed out, when evaluating the validity of a measure, you will usually have little use for face validity. However, face validity may be important to the consumer (or the sponsor) of your research. For example, how loud a person yells and how many widgets a person produces may be equally valid measures of motivation. But if you were going to get a manager to take your research seriously, which measure would you use?

Concluding Remarks

In this chapter, you have seen that choosing a measure is a complex decision. It is not enough to just pick the most valid measure. Instead, you need to pick the measure that will be most likely to answer your research question. To pick the best measure for your particular study, you must decide what threats to validity are most serious, decide how much sensitivity you need, decide what level of measurement your research question requires, and carefully weigh ethical, as well as practical, considerations.

Clearly, in designing a research project, choosing a measure is an important decision. However, it is only one of several decisions a researcher may make. For example, the researcher has to decide whether to do a survey, an experiment, or some other type of research. Then, if the researcher decides to do an experiment, the researcher must decide on what type of experiment to do. In the next few chapters, you will learn how to make these key design decisions.

Summary

1. Since no measure is perfect, choosing a measure involves making tradeoffs.
2. Sensitivity, reliability, and validity are highly valued in a measure.

3. Sensitivity is a measure's ability to detect small differences.

4. An unreliable measure cannot be sensitive, but a reliable measure may be insensitive.

5. By asking "how much" rather than "whether," by knowing what you want to measure, by avoiding unnecessary inferences, and by using common sense, you may be able to increase a measure's sensitivity.

6. Different kinds of measures produce different kinds of numbers. These numbers range from the least informative (nominal) to the most informative (ratio).

7. Nominal numbers only let you say that participants differ. However, they do not let you say that one participant has more of a characteristic than another. With nominal measurement, the number you give each group is arbitrary. For example, if you coded men as "1" and women as "2," that is entirely arbitrary. You could even go back and recode women as "1" and men as "2."

8. Ordinal numbers let you say that one participant has more of a quality than another. However, ordinal numbers do not allow you to talk about specific amounts of a quality. They only let you talk about having more of it or less of it, but not about how much more.

9. Interval and ratio numbers let you say how much more of a quality one participant has than another.

10. Ratio scale numbers let you say how many times more of a quality one participant has relative to another.

11. Depending on the research question, a measure's sensitivity and its level of measurement may be almost as important as validity.

12. You must always consider ethical and practical issues when choosing a measure.

Key Terms

face validity: the extent to which a measure looks valid to the ordinary person. Face validity has nothing to do with scientific validity. However, for practical or political reasons, you may decide to consider face validity when comparing measures. (p. 139)

nominal scale numbers: numbers that substitute for names. Different numbers represent *different* types, kinds, categories, or qualities, but larger numbers do not represent more of a quality than smaller numbers. (p. 129)

ordinal scale numbers: numbers that can be meaningfully ordered from lowest to highest. With ordinal numbers, we know that the higher scoring participant has *more* of a quality than the lower scoring participant, but we don't know how much more of the quality the higher scoring participant has. (p. 130)

interval scale data: data for which equal numerical intervals represent equal psychological intervals. That is, the difference between scoring a "2" and a

"1" and the difference between scoring a "7" and a "6" is the same not only in terms of scores (both are a difference of 1), but also in terms of the actual amount of the psychological characteristic being measured. Interval scale measures allow us to compare participants in terms of *how much* of a quality they have. (p. 130)

ratio scale numbers: numbers having all the qualities of interval scale numbers, but that also result from a measure that has an absolute zero (zero on the measure means the complete absence of the quality). As the name implies, ratio scale numbers allow you to make ratio statements about the quality that you are measuring (Steve is two *times as* friendly as Tom). (p. 131)

sensitivity: a measure's ability to detect differences among participants on a given variable. (p. 122)

Exercises

1. Researchers have used a measure to find small differences between groups. Based on this information, would you infer that the measure's reliability was low or high? Why?
2. List the scales of measurement in order from least to most accurate and informative.
3. Becky wants to know how much students drink.
   a. What level of measurement could Becky get? Why?
   b. Becky asks participants: How much do you drink?
      a) 0–1 drinks
      b) 1–3 drinks
      c) 3–4 drinks
      d) more than 4 drinks
      What scale of measurement does she have?
   c. Becky ranks participants according to how much they drink. What scale of measurement does she have?
   d. Becky assigns participants a "1" if they are a wine drinker, and a "2" if they are a beer drinker. What scale of measurement is this?
   e. Becky asks participants: How much do you drink?
      a) 0–1 drinks
      b) 1–3 drinks
      c) 3–4 drinks
      d) more than 4
      e) don't know
      If she codes the data as follows: a=1, b=2, c=3, d=4, e=5, what scale of measurement does she have? Why?
4. Assume that facial tension is a measure of thinking.
   a. How would you measure facial tension?
   b. What scale of measurement is it on? Why?
   c. How sensitive do you think this measure would be? Why?

5. Suppose a researcher is investigating the effectiveness of drug awareness programs.
   a. What scale of measurement would the investigator need if she were trying to discover whether one drug awareness program was more effective than another?
   b. What scale of measurement would the investigator need if she were trying to discover whether one program is better for informing the relatively ignorant than it is for informing the fairly well-informed?
6. In an ideal world, car gas gauges would be on what scale of measurement? Why? In practice, what is the scale of measurement for most gas gauges? Why do you say that?
7. Find or invent a measure.
   a. Describe the measure.
   b. Discuss how you could improve its sensitivity.
   c. What kind of data (nominal, ordinal, interval, or ratio) do you think that measure would produce? Why?

INTERNAL VALIDITY

All things are possible until they are proved impossible.
—PEARL S. BUCK

We seek causal explanations in order to intervene, to govern the cause so as to govern the effect.
—EDWARD TUFTE

OVERVIEW

This chapter is about **internal validity.** As you may recall from Chapter 1, you need internal validity if you are going to show that your treatment had an effect. If you need to determine whether a treatment, intervention, training program, lecture, or therapy works, you need to conduct a study that has internal validity.

For a study to have internal validity, it must clearly demonstrate that a specific factor causes an effect. Thus, if you establish that turning on blue lights in a room causes higher scores on a happiness questionnaire, your study has internal validity.

The logic of establishing internal validity is simple. First, you determine that changes in a treatment (blue lighting) are followed by changes on an outcome variable (increased happiness). Then, you determine that the treatment (blue lighting) is the only factor responsible for the effect (increased happiness). That is, you show that the results could not be due to anything other than the lighting. Or, as a psychologist would say, you rule out **extraneous factors:** factors other than the treatment.

The most direct way to rule out the possibility that your results are due to the effects of extraneous factors is to eliminate all extraneous factors from your study. If there are no extraneous factors in your study, extraneous factors obviously can't be responsible for your results. In the abstract, there are two ways you can get rid of extraneous factors:

1. Get two identical groups, treat them identically, except that you only give one of the groups the treatment, then compare the treatment group to the no-treatment group.

2. Get some participants, measure them, make sure that nothing in their life changes except that they get the treatment, then measure them again.

In actual practice, however, neither of these methods succeeds in eliminating extraneous variables. As a result, these approaches—contrary to what a naïve person might believe—can't prove that a treatment caused an effect.

In this chapter, you will learn why these two approaches fail to establish internal validity. Specifically, you will learn about Campbell and Stanley's (1963) eight general threats to internal validity:

1. selection
2. selection by maturation interactions
3. regression
4. mortality
5. maturation
6. history

7. testing
8. instrumentation

In addition, you will know enough about these eight threats to:

1. Detect their presence in research that erroneously claims to prove that a certain factor has an effect.
2. Avoid using a design that is vulnerable to these threats.
3. Take steps to prevent these threats from corrupting the internal validity of your research.

....

TWO-GROUP DESIGNS

To begin our exploration of Campbell and Stanley's eight threats to validity, let's examine the first approach for ruling out extraneous variables: getting two identical groups. Specifically, suppose you get two groups of participants and treat them identically, except that only one of the groups gets the treatment (blue lighting). Then, you give both groups the happiness scale and note that they have different levels of happiness.

WHY WE NEVER HAVE IDENTICAL GROUPS

What do you conclude? If the groups were identical before you introduced the treatment, you would correctly conclude that the treatment caused the groups to differ. However, if the groups were not identical before you introduced the treatment, the effect could be due to **selection**: choosing groups that were different from one another before the study began.

Self-Assignment to Group Produces Selection Bias

How can you avoid the selection error? A first step toward avoiding selection error is to prevent participants from choosing what condition they want to be in (self-selection). If your participants choose their own conditions, you know that the groups will differ on at least one dimension: One group chose the treatment whereas the other chose to avoid the treatment. Furthermore, the groups probably differ in ways that you do not know about. As a result, if you let participants choose what condition they will be in, you will probably end up comparing apples and oranges.

Sometimes the effects of self-selection are obvious. For example, suppose you compare two groups—one group volunteers to stay after work to attend a seminar on "Helping Your Company"; the other does not. If you find that the seminar group is more loyal to the company than the no-seminar group, you can't conclude that the effect is due to the seminar. The groups obviously differed in loyalty before the study began.

Sometimes the effects of self-selection are not as obvious. For instance, what if you let participants choose whether they get blue lighting or no lighting? If you find that the blue lighting group is happier than the no-lighting group, you can't conclude that the effect was due to the blue lighting. People who prefer blue lighting may be happier than people who prefer no lighting. You really do not know how participants who choose one condition differ from those who choose another condition. But you do know that they differ—and those differences may cause the groups to differ at the end of the study.

Researcher Assignment to Group Produces Selection Bias

We've seen that letting participants assign themselves to a group creates unequal groups. However, if you assign participants to groups, you might unintentionally bias your study. For example, you might put all the smiling participants in the blue light condition and all the frowning participants in the no-treatment condition.

Arbitrary Assignment to Group Produces Selection Bias: Choosing Groups Based on Their Differences Results in Having Groups That Are Different

To avoid the bias of "picking your own team," you might assign participants to groups on the basis of some arbitrary rule. For example, why not assign students on the right-hand side of the room to the no-treatment group and assign students on the left side of the room to the treatment group? The answer is simple: "Because the groups are not equal." At the very least, the groups differ in that one group prefers the right side, while the other group prefers the left side. They probably differ in many other ways. For example, if the left side of the room is near the windows and the right side is near the door, we can list at least four reasons why "left-siders" might be happier and/or more energetic than "right-siders":

1. People sitting on the left side of the room may be more energetic because they walked the width of the room to find a seat.

2. People sitting on the left side of the room may be early-arrivers (students who came in late would tend to sit on the right side so they would not disrupt class by crossing the width of the room).

3. People sitting on the left side may be more interested in the outdoors since they chose to have access to the window.

4. People sitting on the left side may have chosen those seats to get a better view of the professor's performance (if the professor shows the typical right-hander's tendency of turning to the right, which would be the students' left).

You can probably come up with many other differences between left-siders and right-siders in a particular class. But the point is that the groups definitely

• **FIGURE 5-1a** •

Every other person . . .

The rule of choosing "every other person" to get the treatment is not random. The problem with this rule is most obvious when applied to situations where people are encouraged to line up "boy/girl."

differ in at least one respect (choice of side of room), and they almost certainly differ in numerous other respects (see Figure 5-1).

What's true for the arbitrary rule of assigning participants to groups on the basis of where they sit is true for any other arbitrary rule. Thus, any researchers who assign participants on the basis of an arbitrary rule (the first-arriving participants assigned to the treatment group, people whose last names begin with a letter between A and L in the treatment group, etc.) make their research vulnerable to selection bias.

The reason that arbitrarily assigning participants to groups does not work is because you are assigning participants to groups based on their differences. Your groups can't be equal when you are deliberately ensuring that they are different on some variable (preference for side of the room, etc.).

• FIGURE 5-1b •

The arbitrary rule of assigning the front of the class to one treatment and the back of the class to no treatment does not work. Ask any teacher! The two groups are definitely different.

Matching: A Valiant, but Unsuccessful Strategy for Getting Identical Groups

If you can assign participants in a way that guarantees they are different, why can't you assign participants in a way that guarantees they are identical? In other words, why not use **matching:** choosing your groups so that they have identical characteristics?

The Impossibility of Perfectly Matching Individual Participants: Identical Participants Do Not Exist In the abstract, matching seems like an easy, foolproof way of making sure that your two groups are equal. In practice, however, matching is neither easy nor foolproof. Imagine the difficulty of finding two people who match on every characteristic and then assigning one to the no-treatment condition and the other to the treatment condition. It would be impossible. Even identical twins would not be exactly alike—they have different first names, different injuries, and different experiences.

• FIGURE 5-1c •

Assigning by left side versus right side ruins an attention study's internal validity. Students on the window-side of the room are sitting there because they want to look out the window or at the clock. The students on the other side of the room may be sitting there to avoid distractions.

The Difficulty of Matching Groups on Every Variable: There Are Too Many Variables   Obviously, you can't create the situation in which each member of the treatment group has an identical clone in the no-treatment group. Try as you might, there would always be some variable on which you had not matched—and that variable might be important. Even if you created two groups that had the same average age, same average intelligence, same average income, same average height, and same average weight, there would still be thousands of variables on which the groups might differ. The groups might differ in how they felt on the day of the study, how they were getting along with their parents, how many books they had read, their overall health, and so forth.

Two Difficulties With Matching Groups on Every Relevant Variable   You know you can't match your no-treatment and treatment groups on every single characteristic, but do you need to make the groups identical in every respect? No, you only need them to be identical in respect to the variable you want to measure. For example, suppose you were studying happiness. Then, all you would need to do is match your groups on every characteristic that will influence their score on your happiness measure.

Unfortunately, there are two problems with this "solution." First, matching only on those factors that influence the key variable may be impossible because there may be thousands of factors that influence happiness. Second, you probably do not know every single characteristic that influences happiness. After all, if you knew everything about happiness, you would not be doing a study to find out about happiness.

Problems With Matching on Pretest Scores

Instead of matching participants on every characteristic that affects the variable you want to measure, why not match participants on the variable you want to measure? In your case, why not match participants on the happiness scores? That is, before you assign participants to groups, test people on the happiness scale (what psychologists call a pretest). Next, match your groups so that the treatment group and no-treatment group have the same average pretest score. Finally, at the end of the study, test the participants again, giving participants what psychologists call a posttest. If you find a difference between your groups on the posttest, then you should be positive that the treatment worked, right? Wrong!

Even if the treatment had no effect whatsoever, there are two reasons why two groups that scored the same on the pretest could differ on the posttest. That is, as you will see in the next two sections, there are two reasons why matching on pretest scores doesn't make your groups equivalent. First, even if the groups are similar on the pretest variable, they may differ in other ways. If even one of these differences causes the two groups to differ on the posttest, then the groups will score differently on the posttest—even when the treatment has no effect. Second, because of measurement error, groups that score similarly on the pretest measure may not really be similar on the pretest variable.

Selection by Maturation Interactions: Participants Growing in Different Ways

The first reason matching on pretest scores doesn't work is the **selection by maturation interaction**: The groups started out the same on the pretest, but afterward developed at different rates or in different directions. That is, participants who start out the same on a dimension may grow apart because they differ in other respects.

To visualize the strong impact that selection by maturation interaction can have, imagine you found a group of fourth-grade boys and girls. You put all the boys in one group. Then, you had them lift weights. You saw that the average weight they could lift was 40 lbs. You then picked a group of fourth-grade girls who could also lift 40 lbs. Thus, your groups are equivalent on the pretest. Then, you introduced the treatment: strength pills. You gave the boys strength pills for 8 years. When both groups were in the 12th grade, you measured their strength. You found that boys were much stronger than the girls. This difference might be due to the strength pills. This difference, however, might instead be due to the boys naturally developing strength at a faster rate than the girls. That is, the difference may be due to failing to match on a variable (gender) that influences muscular maturation.

You have seen that groups may grow apart because of different rates of physical maturation. Groups may also grow apart because of different rates of social, emotional, or intellectual maturation. To illustrate this point, let's examine a situation where the two groups are probably changing in different ways on virtually every aspect of development.

Suppose a researcher matched—on the basis of job performance—a group of 19-year-old employees with a group of 63-year-old employees. The researcher then enrolled the 19-year-olds into a training program. When the researcher compared the groups 2 years later, the researcher found that the 19-year-olds were performing better than the 63-year-olds. Why?

The difference may have been due to training. The difference, however, may have nothing to do with the training. Instead, the difference may have been due to (1) the 19-year-olds' productivity increasing because they are just learning their jobs and (2) the 63-year-olds' productivity, on the other hand, naturally declining as this group anticipates retirement. Therefore, the apparent treatment effect may really be a selection by maturation interaction.

You may be saying to yourself that you would never make the mistake of matching 19-year-olds and 63-year-olds on pretest scores. If so, we are glad. You intuitively know that you can't make groups equivalent by merely matching on pretest scores. We would caution you, however, to realize that age is not the only—or even the most important—variable that might affect maturation.[1] Many factors, such as intelligence, motivation, and health, might affect maturation. Thus, if you are going to match on pretest scores, you must also match on all of the variables that might affect maturation. Otherwise, you run the risk of a selection by maturation interaction.

To repeat, matching on pretest scores is incomplete. Pretest scores are good predictors of posttest scores, but not perfect predictors. Many factors affect how a participant does on the posttest. If the groups are not matched on these other relevant variables, two groups that started out the same on the pretest may naturally grow apart. Thus, what looks like a treatment effect may really be a selection by maturation interaction.

If you were somehow able to match on pretest scores and all other relevant variables, you would be able to rule out selection by maturation. However, you

---

[1]Note that, contrary to ageist stereotypes, we might find that the older workers improved more than the younger workers. That is, older workers are much more productive and involved than they are often given credit for. Indeed, this ageism is probably why our poor researcher was forced to do such a flawed study. The researcher was able to get management to invest in training for younger workers but not for the older workers. That is, the researcher used the older workers as a comparison group because management gave her no choice—not because she wanted to.

would not be able to rule out the second reason that matching on pretest scores doesn't work: regression. You wouldn't be able to rule out regression because your matched groups might not be equal on the pretest variable.

The Regression Effect   How could your groups not be equal if you measured them and made sure that they were equal? The problem is that you can't measure them to make sure they are equal. That is, because measurement is not perfect, measuring groups as equal does not mean they are equal.

Even though you tend to assume that measurement is perfect, it is not. For example, if a police officer stops you for speeding, the officer might say, "You were going 75." Or the officer might say, "I clocked you at 75." The officer's two statements are very different. You may have been going 40 and the radar mistimed you (radars have clocked trees at over 100 miles per hour), or you may have been going 95. In any event, you probably were not going at exactly the speed that the officer recorded. Even in this age of advanced technology, something as simple as measuring someone's height is not immune to measurement error. In fact, one of the authors fluctuates between 5'5" and 5'8", depending on which physician's office she is measured at. If measurements of variables as easy to measure as height are contaminated with random error, measurements of psychological variables—variables that are not as easy to measure as height—may also be victimized by random measurement error.

Because of random measurement error, a measure of an individual's height, weight, mood, free-throw shooting ability, or almost anything else might be inaccurate. Thus, two individuals having the same score on a measure might actually differ on the variable being measured.

But would random error cause two groups that have the same average score to differ? At first, you might say "not by very much because random error is, by definition, unsystematic and unbiased." That is, because random error tends to balance out, it should affect each group to about the same extent. For example, it would seem unlikely that random measurement error would inflate the free-throw shooting percentage of individuals in the treatment group, but deflate the free-throw percentage of the individuals in no-treatment group. Despite the merits of these arguments, your first reaction would be wrong: Random error may have one effect on the treatment group and another on the no-treatment group.

Given that random error tends to balance out, how could random error have one effect on the treatment group and another effect on the no-treatment group? To answer this question, imagine a group of extremely high scorers and a group of extremely low scorers. For the purpose of this example, let's imagine having hundreds of people each shoot five free throws. From those hundreds, we will select two groups of foul shooters: (1) a group in which all members hit five of five free throws, and (2) a group in which all members hit none of five free throws.

Why is the extremely high-scoring group doing so well? It's unlikely that these scores reflect each individual's true score. Indeed, probably none of the people in the group that hit all five foul shots really are 100% foul shooters. It's more likely that most of these foul shooters are good, but they are also benefiting from some good fortune. A few may be average or even poor foul shooters whose scores are being pushed up by random error. One thing we know for sure—nobody in this group had random error push their free-throw percentage down. Thus, it's likely that you have chosen scores that have been pushed up by random error. In short, although random error probably pushed some people's scores down, this group is made up of only those people whose scores were boosted by random error.

Now, let's look at the group of extremely low scorers. Why are they scoring so low? Perhaps all of them really are 0% foul shooters. It is more likely, however, that many are poor to average foul shooters experiencing a run of bad luck. One thing we know for sure—nobody in this group had random error inflate their free-throw percentage. Thus, it's likely that, for this group, you have chosen scores that have been pushed down by random error.

What will happen if we retest both groups? The first group will tend to do a bit worse than before: Their average will not be 100%. On the pretest, random error was pushing almost all their scores up. That won't happen on the retest. As a result, their scores will revert to more normal levels on the retest. Similarly, the second group will also tend to score at more normal levels on the retest: Their average will not be 0%. Random error was pushing all of their scores down on the pretest. That won't happen two times in a row.

As we have seen, the 0% group will do better on the retest, but the 100% group will do worse. Put another way, both groups' average scores become less extreme on the retest.

Why does each group's average score become less extreme on the retest? Why do their scores revert back to more normal levels? The short answer is that, on the retest, each group's average score is less influenced by random error. The long answer is that: (1) the groups were initially selected because of their extreme pretest scores; (2) their extreme pretest scores were due, in part, to random measurement error pushing their scores toward an extreme; and (3) random error, which by its very nature is inconsistent, probably won't push all the groups' scores in that same direction on the retest.

Thus far, we have considered the case where two groups that score much differently on the pretest (0% versus 100% on a foul-shot test) might appear to grow more similar on a retest. But how could two groups seem to be (1) similar on a pretest and then (2) seem to grow apart on the retest? For example, how could two groups that appeared to be 60% shooters on the pretest end up scoring very differently on the retest? The key to seeing how this illusion would work is to realize that extreme scores are only extreme relative to the group average.

To illustrate, suppose we have a large group of 90% career free-throw shooters and a large group of 30% career free-throw shooters. We then have people from each group shoot 10 free throws. We find that several from each group shoot 60% (6 out of 10) on our pretest. For the career 30% free-throw shooters, 60% is extremely good. For the career 90% free-throw shooters, 60% is extremely bad.

We now have two groups that each shot 60% on our pretest. The first group was taken from extreme scorers from the 90% group, the second group was taken from extreme scorers from the 30% group. The two groups match on the pretest, but this matching is just a mirage due to random measurement error. On the posttest, this mirage will disappear. On the posttest, participants' scores will be affected by chance to a more usual (and lesser) degree. The first group will score closer to its average score of 90% and the second group will score closer to its average score of 30%. In technical terminology, both groups will exhibit **regression (toward the mean)**: the tendency for scores that are extremely unusual to revert back to more normal levels on the retest.

As you might imagine, regression toward the mean could mimic a treatment effect. If, in our free-throw shooting example, you administered a treatment between the pretest and the posttest, people might mistakenly believe that the treatment was responsible for the groups scoring differently on the pretest. For example, if you yelled at the first group after their poor (for them) pretest performance, people might think that your yelling is what caused them to do better on the posttest.

A deceiving swindler might intentionally use regression toward the mean to make it look like a worthless treatment had a positive effect. The key would be to intentionally take advantage of random measurement error to make it look like two dissimilar groups were really similar on the pretest.

Unfortunately, a researcher might unintentionally rely on measurement error to match two groups on a factor in which they differ. For instance, suppose a researcher working at an institution for the mentally retarded wants to see whether a specially developed training program can increase intelligence. The researcher wants to have two groups that are identical in intelligence, give one group the training program, and see whether the training program group does better on a second intelligence test than the no-training group. The researcher, however, also wants both groups to have near-normal intelligence. Unfortunately, after testing all the patients, the researcher only finds eight patients who score between 85 and 95 on the IQ test.

The researcher decides that eight participants are only enough for the treatment group. Therefore, he still needs to find a no-treatment group, preferably one that has the same IQ as his treatment group. As he drives by your school, he has an idea: Use some of your school's students as participants. After clearing it with your school and taking precautions so that no one will be harmed by his procedures, he begins work. He sets up an office at your school and offers $25 to anyone who will take the IQ test.

After testing many people, he finds eight college students who score around 90 on the IQ test. He makes this group his no-treatment group. At the end of the study, he gives both groups IQ tests. When he looks at his results, he's horrified. He finds that the eight college students score much higher on the second IQ test (the posttest) than the institutionalized people. On closer examination, he finds that the college students' IQ scores increased dramatically from the pretest to posttest while the institutionalized patients' IQ scores dropped from pretest to posttest.

What happened? Did the true intelligence of the college students increase even though the researcher did nothing? No. Did the training program shrink the true intelligence of institutionalized patients? No.

What happened was that the investigator selected scores that were likely to be heavily contaminated with measurement error. To understand how this occurred, think about what would cause your classmates to score 90 on an IQ test. They are scoring well below the mean for your school, probably because of some factors having nothing to do with intelligence. Perhaps pulling an all-nighter, being hung-over, or suffering from the flu would cause such poor performance. If they did score a 90 on an IQ test because they were very ill, would it be likely that they would score a 90 the second time? No, chances are that they would not be as ill the second time they took the test. As a result, their second score should be higher because it would probably be a closer reflection of their true intelligence.

Likewise, the investigator chose those retarded patients' scores that were most likely to be loaded with measurement error. Consider how a retarded person could score 90 on the IQ test. What could account for a person scoring so far above his true score? Probably some form of luck would be involved. Just as a few students occasionally, by sheer luck, get a decent score on a multiple-choice test for which they were unprepared, a few retarded individuals might get lucky the first time the IQ test was administered. That is, if you test 8,000 retarded people, eight might score fairly high due to chance. But would these same eight be as lucky the next time? It's a good bet that they would not. Instead, their second score should be a more accurate reflection of their true score. Consequently, they would get lower scores than they did the first time.

Conclusions About Matching on Pretest Scores   In conclusion, there are two reasons why matching on pretest scores does not make your groups equal. First, matching on pretest scores is incomplete. It is incomplete because the pretest performance is not a perfect indicator of posttest performance. Many factors determine how participants will change from pretest to posttest. Therefore, to predict a participant's posttest score, you need to match not only on the pretest score, but on every other variable that might affect how participants will change. If you do not, you may have two groups that started out the same, but naturally grew apart—no thanks to the treatment. In other words, you may have what appears to be a treatment effect, but is really a selection by maturation effect.

Second, you match on scores, which are flawed indicators of actual characteristics, rather than on the actual characteristics themselves. Because of measurement error, it's possible to get two groups that match on pretest scores but that are actually very different. That is, random error may create the illusion that two dissimilar groups are similar.

As convincing as the illusion of similarity may be, it is only a temporary mirage. The mirage is temporary because it is based on choosing those participants whose scores had been blown in a certain direction by random error, which by its nature is inconsistent and directionless. Thus, on retesting, the winds of chance will probably not blow those scores in the same direction.

Put another way, the illusion of similarity was built by choosing those participants whose scores were extremely influenced by random error. On retesting, random error will probably exert a less extreme influence on scores (just as lightning is unlikely to strike the same person twice). Consequently, the extremely deviant scores will revert back to more typical levels (regression toward the mean). As a result, the mirage that made the groups look similar on the pretest probably won't last until the posttest.

If the pretest mirage of similarity evaporates by the posttest, then the groups will look different on the posttest. That is, the two groups that appeared to be similar on the pretest will reveal their true differences during the posttest. To the naïve observer, the groups "became different" because of the treatment. However, you realize that:

1. The groups did not become different. They were really different all along—they only seemed similar at the beginning because of an illusion created by random measurement error.

2. Since the groups did not become different, there is no reason to say that the treatment made them become different. That is, there is no reason to say that the treatment had an effect.

CONCLUSIONS ABOUT TWO-GROUP DESIGNS

You have seen that we can't create identical groups. If we don't match, our groups are different. If we do match, our groups are still different (see Figure 5-2). So, differences between our groups at the end of the study may be due to our groups being different to start with, rather than to the treatment.

Even if our groups were identical to start with, they might not stay that way because of participant mortality: participants dropping out of the study. To understand the threat posed by mortality, suppose we have designed a program for high-risk youth. To test the program's effectiveness, we put 40 at-risk youth into our intense training program and compare them to a no-treatment group consisting of 40 other at-risk youth. We find that youth who complete our training program are much more likely to gain and keep employment than the youth in the no-training group. However, 75% of the treatment group youth drop out of our rigorous program. Thus, we are comparing the 10 elite survivors of the treatment group against everyone in the no-treatment group. Consequently, our training program's apparent "success" may simply be due to comparing the best of one group against everyone in the other group.

In the example above, mortality seriously threatened the validity of our study. Even if the groups had been the same to start with, they were not the same at the end of the study. However, with two-group designs, we usually have

• **FIGURE 5-2** •

MAKING TWO GROUPS IDENTICAL: A GAME YOU CAN'T WIN

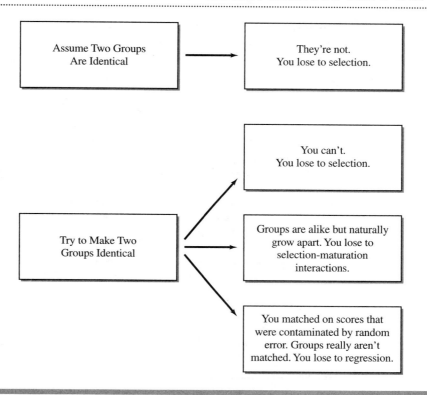

a big problem even before mortality has a chance to be a problem: Our two groups were not identical at the start of the study (see Table 5-1).

PROBLEMS WITH THE PRETEST–POSTTEST DESIGN ✳

The only way we could get two identical groups of participants would be to have the same participants in both groups. That is, each participant could be in both the no-treatment group and in the treatment group.

For instance, we might use a pretest–posttest design: a design in which we give each participant the pretest, administer the treatment, then give each participant the posttest. If we make sure that the participants in the treatment group are the same participants who were in the no-treatment group, we have eliminated the threat of selection.

• TABLE 5-1 •

WHY THE SELECTION PROBLEM IS DIFFICULT TO ELIMINATE

1. Self-assignment causes selection bias.

2. Researcher assignment can cause selection bias.

3. Arbitrary assignment to a group causes selection error by making the groups differ in at least one respect.

4. We can't match participants on every single variable.

5. We can't even match participants on all relevant variables. Therefore, "matched" groups may differ from each other in terms of "unmatched" variables. These "unmatched" variables may cause the groups to behave differently on the posttest.

6. We have to worry about the effects of "unmatched" variables even when we match on pretest scores. As cases of selection by maturation interactions demonstrate, just because participants scored the same at pretest, it does not mean they will score the same at posttest.

7. Even if there were no selection by maturation interactions, matching on pretest scores is imperfect because scores may be heavily influenced by random error. The groups may only appear to be similar because one or both groups' pretest scores are heavily influenced by random error.

At first glance, the pretest–posttest design seems to be a perfect way to establish internal validity. However, the pretest–posttest design can only have internal validity if the treatment is the only reason that posttest scores differ from pretest scores.

Unfortunately, the treatment is not the only reason that participants' scores may change from pretest to posttest. Instead, there are two sets of reasons why participants' scores may change from pretest to posttest. First, participants may change over time, even without the treatment. Second, even if participants do not change from pretest to posttest, their posttest scores may differ from their pretest scores because of changes in scoring accuracy or scoring method. In the next few sections, you will get a clearer idea of how (1) participants may change their behavior for reasons having nothing to do with the treatment, and (2) participants' scores may change, even when their behavior does not.

THREE REASONS PARTICIPANTS MAY CHANGE BETWEEN PRETEST AND POSTTEST

Even without the treatment, participants may change over time. For instance, a participant's mood may change by the minute. To be more specific, besides the treatment, there are at least three reasons that participants may change from pretest to posttest. These three threats to the pretest–posttest study's internal validity are maturation, history, and testing.

• **FIGURE 5-3** •

A HAPPY CASE OF MATURATION

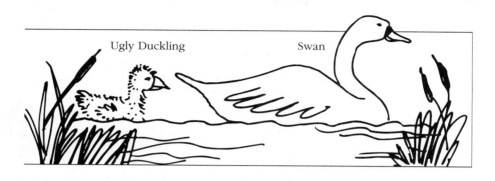

Ugly Duckling   Swan

✳ Maturation ✳

A participant may change between the time of the pretest and the time of the posttest as a result of natural biological changes that occur inside the participant (see Figure 5-3). People are constantly changing. From one moment to the next, they may become hungrier or more fatigued. From one month to the next, they will grow older, and they may grow more mature.

To see how maturation might masquerade as a treatment effect, suppose you instituted a weightlifting program for high school sophomores. You find that—as seniors—they can lift 40 lbs. more than they could as sophomores. Your problem is that you do not know whether the weight training or natural development is responsible for the change. Similarly, if you give a baby 10 years of memory training, you will find that her memory improves. However, this difference is probably not due to the training, but to **maturation**: changes due to natural physiological changes such as growth and development.

✳ History ✳

In addition to changing because of events that occur inside the participant, the participant may change because of events—other than the treatment—that occur in the outside world. Thus, even if the treatment has no effect, a participant may change between pretest and posttest because the participant's *environment* has changed between pretest and posttest (see Figure 5-4). All these environmental changes that have nothing to do with the treatment are called **history**.

To understand the effects of history, suppose two social psychologists have a treatment they think will change how Americans feel about space exploration. However, between pretest and posttest, a spacecraft explodes. Or, suppose an

• **FIGURE 5-4** •

A MYTHICAL CASE OF HISTORY

investigator was examining the effect of diet on maze-running speed. However, between pretest and posttest, the heat went off in the rat room, and the rats nearly froze to death. As you might imagine, events that happen in a participant's life (history) between the pretest and the posttest can have a powerful effect on a participant's posttest score.

Testing: Measuring Participants Changes Participants

One event that always occurs between the start of the pretest and the start of the posttest is the pretest itself. If the pretest changes participants, you have a testing effect. For example, if your instructor gave you the same test twice, you would score better the second time around. Your improvement would be due to finding out and remembering the answers to questions you missed. Because of the testing effect, people who have taken many intelligence tests (for example, children of clinical psychologists) may score very high on IQ tests regardless of their true intelligence.

The testing effect is not limited to knowledge tests. Rather, the testing effect can occur with virtually any measure. To illustrate, let's look at a pretest that has nothing to do with knowledge. For instance, suppose we were to ask people their opinions about Greenland entering the World Bank. Would we get another answer the second time we asked this question? Yes, because the very action of asking for their opinion may cause them to think about the issue more and to develop or change their opinion. In short, by measuring something, you may change it.

HOW MEASUREMENT CHANGES MAY CAUSE SCORES TO CHANGE BETWEEN PRETEST AND POSTTEST

Obviously, participants' scores may change over time because participants have changed. What is less obvious is that participants' scores may change over time even when the participants themselves have not changed. That is, participants' scores may change because of changes in how participants are measured. Specifically, scores may change because of the following three threats to internal validity: instrumentation, regression, and mortality.

Instrumentation: Changes in How Participants Are Measured

An obvious reason for a participant's score changing from pretest to posttest is that the measuring *instrument* used for the posttest is different from the one used during the pretest. If the difference between pretest and posttest scores is due to changes in the measuring instrument, you have an instrumentation effect.

Sometimes, changes in the measuring instrument are unintentional. For example, suppose you are measuring aggression using the most changeable measuring instrument possible: the human rater. As the study progresses, raters may broaden their definition of aggression. Consequently, raters may give participants higher posttest scores on aggression, even though participants' behavior has not changed. Unfortunately, there are many ways that raters could change between pretesting and posttesting. Raters could become more conscientious, less conscientious, more lenient, less lenient, and so forth. Any of these changes could cause an instrumentation effect.

Sometimes, changes in the instrument occur because the researcher is trying to make the posttest better than the pretest. For example, the researcher may retype the original questionnaire to make the scales look nicer, to fix typographical errors, or to eliminate bad questions. Unfortunately these changes, no matter how minor they may seem and no matter how logical they may be, are changes. And these changes may cause instrumentation effects.

We are not saying that you should not administer the best measure possible. You should. But you should refine the measure before beginning the study.

Regression Revisited

Even if the measuring instrument is the same for both the pretest and posttest, the degree to which random measurement error affects scores may differ from pretest to posttest. In other words, with a pretest–posttest design, you still have to deal with regression toward the mean.

To show that you do not get away from regression toward the mean by using the pretest–posttest design, think back to the researcher who was investigating the effects of a training program on intelligence. Suppose that he had decided not to compare the eight highest-scoring patients with a group of college students. Instead, after having the eight patients who scored highest on the pretest complete the training program, he re-administered the IQ test as his posttest. What would he observe?

As before, he would have observed that the patients' IQ scores dropped from pretest to posttest. This drop is not due to the training program robbing patients of intelligence. Rather, the posttest scores more accurately reflect the patients' true intelligence. The posttest scores are lower than the pretest scores only because the pretest scores were inflated with random measurement error.

The pretest scores were destined to be inflated with measurement error because the investigators selected only those participants whose scores were extreme. Extreme scores tend to have extreme amounts of measurement error.

To understand why extreme scores tend to have extreme amounts of measurement error, realize that a participant's score is a function of two things: the participant's true characteristics and measurement error. Thus, an extreme score may be extreme because measurement error is making the score extreme. To take a concrete example, let's consider how a student might get a perfect score on a quiz. There are three basic possibilities for the perfect score:

1. The student is a perfect student.
2. The student is a very good student and had some good luck.
3. The student is an average or below-average student but got incredibly lucky.

As you can see, if you study a group of people who got perfect scores on the last exam, you are probably studying a group of people whose scores were inflated by measurement error. If participants were measured again, random error would probably be less generous. (After all, random error could not be more generous. There's only one place for scores to go—down.) Therefore, if you were to give them a treatment (memory training) and then look at their scores on the next exam, you would be disappointed. The group that averaged 100% on the first test might average "only" 96% on the second test.

In the case we just described, regression's presence is relatively obvious because it's taking advantage of a rather obvious source of measurement error—error in test scores. But regression may take advantage of less obvious sources of random measurement error.

The sneakiest form of measurement error seems more like an error in sampling than an error of measurement. For example, suppose you are trying to make inferences about a participant's typical behavior from a sample of that participant's behavior. If the behavior you observe is not typical of the participant's behavior, you have measurement error. Even if you measured the behavior you observed perfectly, you have measurement error because you have not measured the participant's typical behavior perfectly. This measurement error can lead to regression toward the mean.

To see how a sample of behavior may not be typical of normal behavior, let's look at a coin's behavior. Suppose you find a coin that comes up heads six times in a row. Although you have accurately recorded that the coin came up heads six times in a row, you might be making a measurement error if you concluded that the coin was biased toward heads. In fact, if you were to flip the coin 10 more times, you probably would not get 10 more heads. Instead, you would probably get something close to five heads and five tails.

Coins are not the only things to exhibit erratic behavior. Virtually every behavior is inconsistent and therefore prone to atypical streaks. For example, suppose you watch someone shoot baskets. You accurately observe that she made five out of five shots. Based on these observations, you may conclude that she is a great shooter. However, you may be wrong. Perhaps if you had observed her shooting on a different day, you would have seen her make only one of five shots.

To illustrate how this subtle form of measurement error can lead to regression toward the mean, suppose a person who has been happy virtually all of her life feels depressed. This depression is so unlike her that she seeks therapy. Before starting the therapy, the psychologist gives her a personality test. The test verifies that she is depressed. After a couple of sessions, she is feeling better. In fact, according to the personality test, she is no longer depressed. Who could blame the psychologist for feeling proud?

But has the psychologist changed the client's personality? No, the patient is just behaving in a way consistent with her normal personality. The previous measurements were contaminated by events that had nothing to do with her personality. Perhaps her depressed manner reflected a string of bad fortune: getting food poisoning, her cat running away, and being audited by the IRS. As this string of bad luck ended and her luck returned to normal, her mood returned to normal.

Regression toward the mean is such a clever impersonator of a treatment effect that regression fools most of the people most of the time. Many people swear that something really helped them when they had "hit bottom." The baseball player who recovers from a terrible slump believes that hypnosis was the cure; the owner whose business was at an all-time low believes that a new manager turned the business around; and a man who was at an all-time emotional low feels that his new girlfriend turned him around. What these people fail to take into account is that things are simply reverting back to the norm (regressing toward the mean). When listening to stories about how people bounced back due to some miracle treatment, remember comedian Woody Allen's line: "I always get well, even without the leeches."

Mortality: Changes in How Many Participants Are Measured

The last, and perhaps most obvious, reason that you could find differences between pretest and posttest scores would be that you were measuring fewer participants at posttest than you were at pretest. In other words, your study may fall victim to mortality.

To illustrate how much of an impact mortality can have, imagine that you are studying the effect of diet on memory in older adults. You pretest your participants, give them your new diet, and test them again. You find that the average posttest score is higher than the average pretest score. However, if the pretest average is based on 100 participants and the posttest average is based on 70 participants, your results may well be due to mortality. Specifically, the reason posttest scores are higher than pretest scores may be that the people who scored very poorly on the pretest are no longer around for the posttest.

Although death is the most dramatic way to lose participants, death is not the most common way to lose participants. Usually, mortality results from participants deciding to quit the study, participants moving away, or from participants failing to follow directions.

CONCLUSIONS ABOUT TRYING TO KEEP EVERYTHING EXCEPT THE TREATMENT CONSTANT

We tried to create a situation where we manipulated the treatment, while keeping everything else constant. However, nothing we tried worked.

When we tried to compare a treatment group versus a no-treatment group, we had to worry that our groups were not identical before the study started. Even when we matched our groups, we realized that the groups might not be identical because:

1. We could not match on every single characteristic.
2. We could not match on participants' true characteristics, so we had to match based on imperfect measures of these characteristics.

Because we could not get equivalent groups at the start of the study, we did not dwell on the additional problems of keeping them equivalent. That is, we did not stress the mortality problem that would result if, for example, more participants dropped out of the treatment group than out of the no-treatment group.

Because of the problems with comparing a treatment group against a no-treatment group (see Table 5-2), we tried to measure the same group before and after giving them the treatment. Although this before–after tactic got rid of some threats to validity, it introduced others (see Figure 5-5). As Table 5-3 shows, participants may change from pretest to posttest for a variety of reasons having nothing to do with the treatment. Participants may change as a result of:

1. natural development (maturation)
2. other things in their lives changing (history)
3. learning from the pretest (testing)

Furthermore, participants may *appear* to change from pretest to posttest as a result of:

1. the posttest measure being a different instrument than the pretest measure (instrumentation)
2. their pretest scores being unduly influenced by chance (setting up regression toward the mean)
3. participants dropping out of the study so that the posttest group is not the same group of individuals as the pretest group (mortality)

RULING OUT EXTRANEOUS VARIABLES

Why couldn't we eliminate extraneous variables? Was it because we used improper designs? No; as you will see in later chapters, matching participants and testing participants before and after treatment are useful research techniques.

• TABLE 5-2 •

QUESTIONS TO ASK WHEN EXAMINING A TWO-GROUP (TREATMENT VERSUS NO-TREATMENT) STUDY

Selection:	Were groups really equal before the study began?
Selection by maturation interaction:	Would the groups have naturally grown apart, even without the treatment?
Regression effects:	Even if the groups appeared equivalent before the study began, was this apparent equivalence merely a temporary illusion created by random measurement error?
Mortality:	Did more participants drop out of one group than the other?

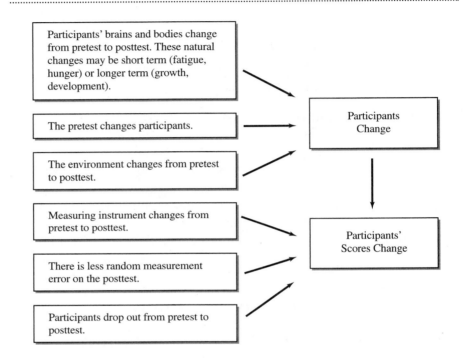

• FIGURE 5-5 •

THE IMPOSSIBLE DREAM: MAKING SURE THE ONLY THING THAT COULD MAKE PARTICIPANTS' SCORES CHANGE IN A PRETEST–POSTTEST DESIGN IS THE TREATMENT

Participants' brains and bodies change from pretest to posttest. These natural changes may be short term (fatigue, hunger) or longer term (growth, development).

The pretest changes participants.

The environment changes from pretest to posttest.

Measuring instrument changes from pretest to posttest.

There is less random measurement error on the posttest.

Participants drop out from pretest to posttest.

Participants Change

Participants' Scores Change

You would like to say that the treatment was the only factor that could cause the change in scores from pretest to posttest, but that's not easy to do.

We couldn't eliminate extraneous variables because it can't be done. Keeping everything the same is impossible. Imagine, in our ever-changing world, trying to make sure that only one thing (amount of blue lighting) in a participant's life changed!

ACCOUNTING FOR EXTRANEOUS VARIABLES

Fortunately, you do not have to eliminate extraneous variables to rule out their effects. As you will learn in Chapter 6, you can combine random assignment and statistics to rule out the effects of extraneous variables.

• **TABLE 5-3** •

QUESTIONS TO ASK WHEN EXAMINING A
PRETEST–POSTTEST (BEFORE–AFTER) STUDY

Maturation:	Could the before–after (pretest–posttest) differences have been due to natural changes resulting from participants becoming older?
History:	Could other events in the participants' lives have caused the pretest–posttest differences?
Testing:	Could participants score differently on the posttest as a result of the practice and experience they got on the pretest?
Instrumentation:	Were participants measured with the same instrument, in the same way, the second time?
Regression:	Were participants selected for their extreme pretest scores? Participants who get extreme scores have a tendency to get less extreme scores the second time around.
Mortality:	Did everyone who took the pretest stick around for the posttest? Or, were the pretest group and the posttest group really two different groups?

Even without using random assignment, you can still try to rule out the effects of extraneous variables. In a sense, your tracking down a treatment's effect without using random assignment is much like a detective tracking down a murderer. Just as the detective is confronted with more than one suspect for a murder, you are confronted with more than one suspect for an effect. Just as the detective can't make the suspects disappear, you can't eliminate extraneous factors. However, like the detective, you can use logic to rule out some suspects and implicate others.

Before you can begin to account for the actions of every suspicious extraneous variable, you have to know "who" each of these variables is. At first glance, identifying all the thousands of variables that might account for the relationship between the treatment and the effect seems as impossible as eliminating all those variables.

IDENTIFYING EXTRANEOUS VARIABLES

Fortunately, identifying the extraneous variables is not as difficult as it first appears because every one of these thousands of factors falls into eight categories: Campbell and Stanley's (1963) eight threats to validity. Thus, you really only have eight suspects (see Table 5-4). If you can show that selection, history, maturation, testing, regression, mortality, instrumentation, and selection by maturation were not responsible for the effect, then you can conclude that the treatment was responsible.

• **TABLE 5-4** •

CAMPBELL AND STANLEY'S EIGHT
THREATS TO INTERNAL VALIDITY

History:	Things other than the treatment that have changed in the participants' environments.
Testing:	Changes resulting from the practice and experience participants got on the pretest.
Instrumentation:	The way participants were measured changed from pretest to posttest.
Regression effects:	If participants are chosen because their scores were extreme, these extreme scores may be loaded with extreme amounts of random measurement error. On retesting, participants are bound to get more normal scores as random measurement error decreases to more normal levels.
Mortality:	Differences between conditions are due to participants dropping out of the study.
Maturation:	Apparent treatment effects are really due to natural, physiological changes, such as growth and development.
Selection:	Treatment and no-treatment groups were different before the treatment was administered.
Selection by maturation interaction:	Treatment and no-treatment groups were predisposed to grow apart.

THE RELATIONSHIP BETWEEN INTERNAL AND EXTERNAL VALIDITY

If you rule out these threats, you have established internal validity. That is, you have demonstrated that a factor causes an effect in a particular study. But you have not demonstrated that you can generalize your results outside your particular study. Internal validity alone does not guarantee that an investigator doing the same study, but with different participants (depressed patients instead of college students), or using a different setting (a library instead of a lab) would obtain the same results. If you want to generalize your results, you need external validity.

If internal validity does not guarantee external validity, why bother with establishing internal validity? One answer is that you may not care about external validity. Some researchers do not care about generalizing their results; they may only want to show that a certain treatment causes a certain effect in a certain setting. For example, therapists may want to show that with their patients, in their hospital, giving the patients an exercise program reduces patients' alcohol consumption. The therapists may not care whether the treatment would work with other kinds of patients at other hospitals (external validity). They only care that they have a method that works for them. However, few people are so single-minded that they are totally unconcerned with external validity.

Although most researchers are concerned about external validity, many research studies do not seem to be designed with external validity in mind. There are at least three reasons why researchers may place little emphasis on external validity in the design of their study.

First, results from internally valid experiments tend to generalize. For example, suppose that an experiment shows that a factor has a certain effect. Suppose further that the experiment, which was done with one type of participant, is replicated (repeated) with a different group of participants. The replication will usually also find that the factor has an effect.

Second, if other researchers using other types of participants and other settings all replicate the findings of the original study, this produces a strong case for the finding's external validity. Indeed, replications by other researchers usually produce stronger evidence that a finding has external validity than anything the original researcher can do.

Third, the things that the original researcher would do to improve a study's external validity may reduce its internal validity (see Table 5-5). Or, to look at it another way, the steps a researcher might take to improve internal validity may end up reducing the study's external validity. For example, to reduce the problem of selection bias, you might use twins as your participants. Although

• TABLE 5-5 •
CLASSIC CONFLICTS BETWEEN THE GOALS OF INTERNAL AND EXTERNAL VALIDITY

TACTIC USED TO HELP ESTABLISH INTERNAL VALIDITY	TACTIC'S IMPACT ON EXTERNAL VALIDITY
Use participants who are very similar to each other to reduce the effects of selection. For example, only study twins or only study rats.	Studying such a narrowly defined group raises questions about the degree to which the results can be generalized to different participant populations. Do the results hold for people who are not twins? Animals that are not rats?
Study participants in a highly controlled laboratory setting to reduce the effects of extraneous factors such as history.	Studying participants in an isolated, controlled environment, such as a lab, raises questions about the extent to which the results might generalize to more complex, real-life settings.

using twins as participants could increase internal validity by reducing differences between your treatment and no-treatment groups, it might hurt the generalizability of your study. Your results might only apply to twins. Similarly, you might reduce the threat of history by testing your participants in a situation (a lab) where they are isolated from nontreatment factors. This highly controlled situation may increase internal validity because the treatment was one of the only things to change during the study. However, you would have to wonder whether the treatment would have the same effect outside this artificial, laboratory situation. Would the results generalize to real life, where the factors from which you isolated your participants come into play?

Concluding Remarks

As you have seen, internal validity and external validity are sometimes in conflict. The same procedures that increase internal validity may decrease external validity. Fortunately, however, internal validity and external validity are not necessarily incompatible. As you will see in future chapters, you can have studies that have both internal and external validity.

If you want to establish both internal and external validity, many would argue that you should first establish internal validity. After all, before you can establish that a factor causes an effect in most situations, you must show that the factor causes an effect in at least one situation.

But how can you establish internal validity? In this chapter, we tried two basic approaches (the no-treatment/treatment group design and the pretest–posttest design), and both failed. In the next chapter, you will learn the easiest and most automatic way to establish internal validity: the simple experiment.

Summary

1. If you observe an effect in a study that has internal validity, you know what caused that effect.

2. Campbell and Stanley (1963) described eight major threats to internal validity: selection, selection by maturation interaction, regression, maturation, history, testing, mortality, and instrumentation.

3. When you compare a treatment group to a no-treatment group, beware of the selection bias: the groups being different even before you administer the treatment.

4. To reduce selection bias, participants should never get to choose what amount of treatment they get. In addition, participants' characteristics, attitudes, or behaviors should have nothing to do with what group (treatment or no-treatment) they are put in.

5. It is impossible to match two groups of participants so that they are identical in every respect: Participants simply differ in too many ways.

6. Even matching participants on pretest scores is not perfect because of the problems of selection by maturation interactions and regression.

7. Selection by maturation occurs when your two groups mature (naturally change) at different rates or in different directions.

8. The fact that extreme scores tend to be a little less extreme the second time around is called regression toward the mean. Regression toward the mean can cause two groups that appear to be matched on a pretest to score differently on the posttest.

9. In the pretest–posttest design, you measure a group, administer the treatment, and measure the group again.

10. Using the pretest–posttest method is not as perfect as it first appears. It is vulnerable to testing, history, regression, maturation, mortality, and instrumentation effects.

11. Regression can occur in the pretest–posttest design because the person may have gotten the treatment when he or she had "hit bottom." There was no place to go but up.

12. Maturation refers to inner, biological changes that occur in people merely as a result of time. In some cases, becoming more mature—not the treatment—accounts for people changing from pretest to posttest.

13. History refers to outside events—other than the treatment—that may influence participants' scores. These events that occur in the participants' world between pretest and posttest can cause participants to change from pretest to posttest.

14. Testing refers to the fact that taking a pretest may affect performance on a posttest.

15. Instrumentation occurs when the posttest measuring instrument is different from the pretest measure.

16. External validity is the degree to which the results from a study can be generalized to other types of participants and settings.

17. Internal and external validity are not necessarily incompatible.

Key Terms

internal validity: the degree to which the study demonstrates that the treatment caused a change in behavior. If a study lacks internal validity, the researcher may falsely believe that a factor causes an effect when it really doesn't.

Most studies do not have internal validity because they can't rule out the possibility that some other factor may have been responsible for the effect. Unfortunately, steps taken to increase internal validity (such as keeping non-treatment factors constant) could harm the study's external validity. (p. 144)

extraneous factors: factors other than the treatment. If we can't control or account for extraneous variables, we can't conclude that the treatment had an effect. That is, we will not have internal validity. History, instrumentation, maturation, mortality, regression, testing, selection, and selection by maturation interactions are all potential sources of extraneous variables. (p. 144)

maturation: internal, biological changes such as growth, aging, and development. Apparent treatment effects may really be due to maturation. (p. 159)

history: external, environmental changes—other than the treatment—that might affect participants' behavior. These outside events can be almost anything—from wars to unusually cold weather. (p. 159)

instrumentation: the way participants were measured changed from pretest to posttest. In instrumentation, the actual measuring instrument changes, the way it is administered changes, or the way it is scored changes. (p. 161)

testing: participants score differently on the posttest as a result of what they learned from taking the pretest. Thus, even if the treatment had no effect, scores might be better on the posttest because of the practice participants got on the pretest. (p. 161)

mortality: differences between conditions are due to participants dropping out of the study. (p. 156)

selection: treatment and no-treatment groups were different before the treatment was administered. (p. 145)

selection by maturation interaction: treatment and no-treatment groups, although similar at one point, would have naturally grown apart (developed differently) even if no treatment had been administered. (p. 150)

regression (toward the mean): if participants are chosen because their scores were extreme, these extreme scores may be loaded with extreme amounts of random measurement error. On retesting, participants are bound to get more normal (average) scores as random measurement error's effects decrease to more normal levels. (p. 154)

matching: choosing your groups so that they are similar (they match) on certain characteristics. Matching reduces, but does not eliminate, selection bias. Because of regression and selection by maturation effects, two groups that were matched on the pretest may score differently on the posttest. (p. 148)

pretest–posttest design: a before–after design in which each participant is given the pretest, administered the treatment, then given the posttest.

The pretest–posttest design is not vulnerable to selection and selection by maturation interactions. It is, however, extremely vulnerable to history, maturation, and testing effects. (p. 157)

Exercises

1. What questions would you ask a researcher who said that the no-treatment and treatment groups were identical before the start of the study?

2. What is the most serious problem for the two-group design? Why?

3. In all of the following cases, the researcher wants to make cause–effect statements. What threats to internal validity is the researcher apparently overlooking?

   a. Employees are interviewed on job satisfaction. Bosses undergo a 3-week training program. When employees are re-interviewed, dissatisfaction seems to be even higher. Therefore, the researcher concludes that the training program caused further employee dissatisfaction.

   b. After completing a voluntary workshop on improving the company's image, workers are surveyed. Workers who attended the workshop are now more committed than those in the "no-treatment" group who did not make the workshop. Researcher's conclusion: The workshop made workers more committed.

   c. After a 6-month training program, employee productivity improves. Conclusion: The training program caused increased productivity.

   d. Morale is at an all-time low. As a result, the company hires a "humor consultant." A month later, workers are surveyed and morale has improved. Conclusion: The consultant improved morale.

   e. Two groups of workers are matched on commitment to the company. One group is asked to attend a 2-week workshop on improving the company's image, the other is the no-treatment group. Workers who complete the workshop are more committed than those in the "no-treatment" group. Researcher's conclusion: The workshop made workers more committed.

4. A hypnotist claims that hypnosis can cause increases in strength. To "prove" this claim, the hypnotist has participants see how many times they can squeeze a hand-grip in 2 minutes. Then, he hypnotizes them and has them practice for 2 weeks. At the end of 2 weeks, they can squeeze the hand-grips together many more times than they could at the beginning. Other than hypnosis, what could have caused this effect?

5. How could a quack psychologist or "healthcare expert" take advantage of regression toward the mean to make it appear that certain phony treatments actually worked?

6. How could a participant's score on an ability test change even though the person's actual ability had not?

7. A memory researcher administers a memory test to a group of residents at a nursing home. He finds grade-school students who score the same as the older patients on the memory pretest. He then administers an experimental memory drug to the older patients. A year later, he gives both groups a posttest.

   a. If the researcher finds that the older patients now have a worse memory than the grade-school students, what can the researcher conclude? Why?

   b. If the researcher finds that the older patients now have a better memory than the grade-school students, what can the researcher conclude? Why?

8. What is the difference between history and maturation?
9. What is the difference between testing and instrumentation?
10. A psychologist's daughter scores much higher on an IQ test than you expect. The score seems extremely inconsistent with the child's grades and your general impressions of the child. What is one possible explanation for the unusually high score?
11. A researcher reports that a certain argument strategy has an effect, but only on those participants who hold extreme attitudes. Why might the researcher be mistaken about the effects of the persuasive strategy?
12. What is the difference between internal and external validity?
13. Provide an example of a study that would have good internal validity, but poor external validity.
14. Provide an example of a study that would have good external validity, but poor internal validity.

THE SIMPLE EXPERIMENT

What you have is an experience, not an experiment.
—R. A. FISCHER

The absence of proof is not the proof of absence.
—MICHAEL CRICHTON

OVERVIEW

Why do people behave the way they do? How can we help people change? To answer these questions, we must be able to isolate the underlying causes of behavior. To be able to isolate the underlying causes of behavior, we must design a study that has **internal validity**: the ability to determine whether a factor causes an effect.

This chapter introduces you to one of the easiest ways to establish that a factor causes an effect: the simple experiment. You will start by learning the basic logic behind the simple experiment. Then, you will learn how to intelligently weigh statistical, ethical, and validity issues in order to design a useful simple experiment. Finally, you will learn how to interpret the results of such an experiment.

BASIC LOGIC AND TERMINOLOGY

The **simple experiment** involves two groups of participants. At the start of the experiment, the two groups should not differ from each other in any systematic way. During the experiment, the experimenter will treat one group differently than the other. For example, the experimenter might give the two groups two different treatments, such as different amounts of a drug, different instructions, different colors of exams, different ads, or different rewards. Often, half the participants (the treatment group) receive a treatment whereas the other half (the no-treatment group) receive no treatment. If, at the end of the experiment, the two groups differ significantly, we can conclude that the treatment—the only systematic difference between the groups—caused that significant difference.

But how do we set up a situation in which the only systematic difference between the no-treatment and the treatment groups is the treatment? The answer is **independent random assignment.** In random assignment, every participant—regardless of that participant's characteristics—has an equal chance of being assigned to either the treatment or no-treatment group.

To review, random assignment, the key to the simple experiment, involves two processes. First, we *randomly* divide our participants into two similar halves. Second, we *assign* one of those halves to get a different treatment than the other.

We have given you a general idea of what random assignment is, but how would you actually randomly assign participants to either a no-treatment or a treatment group? You could flip a coin for each participant. If the coin comes up heads, the participant gets the treatment; if the coin comes up tails, the participant does not get the treatment.[1] Or, you might use a random numbers table to assign participants to condition (see Box 6-1).

EXPERIMENTAL HYPOTHESIS: THE TREATMENT HAS AN EFFECT

Although randomly assigning your participants to two groups is an important aspect of conducting a simple experiment, the most important aspect of designing a simple experiment is generating an **experimental hypothesis:** a prediction that the treatment will *cause* an effect. To generate an experimental hypothesis, you must predict that the treatment and no-treatment groups will differ because of the treatment's effect. For example, you might hypothesize that people getting 3 hours of full-spectrum light will be happier than those getting no full-spectrum light *because* full-spectrum light causes increases in happiness.

---

[1]As you will see in Box 6-1, psychologists usually do not use pure independent random assignment. They typically use independent random assignment with the restriction that an equal number of participants must be in each group.

• BOX 6-1 •

RANDOMLY ASSIGNING PARTICIPANTS TO TWO GROUPS

There are many ways to randomly assign participants to groups. Your professor may prefer another method. However, following these steps guarantees random assignment and an equal number of participants in each group.

STEP 1 On the top of a sheet of paper, make two columns. Title the first "Control Group." Title the second "Experimental Group." Under the group names, draw a line for each participant you will need. Thus, if you were planning to use eight participants (four in each group), you would draw four lines under each group name.

CONTROL GROUP	EXPERIMENTAL GROUP
_____	_____
_____	_____
_____	_____
_____	_____

STEP 2 Turn to a random numbers table, like the one tabled below (or the one in Appendix E). Roll a die to determine which column in the table you will use.

STEP 3 Assign the first number in the column to the first space under Control Group, the second number to the second space, and so on. When you have filled all the spaces for the control group, place the next number under the first space under Experimental Group and continue until you have filled all the spaces. Thus, if you rolled a "5," you would start in the fifth column and your sheet of paper would look like this:

CONTROL GROUP	EXPERIMENTAL GROUP
81647	06121
30995	27756
76393	98872
07856	18876

RANDOM NUMBERS TABLE

COLUMN

ROW	1	2	3	4	5	6
1	10480	15011	01536	02011	81647	69179
2	22368	46573	25595	85393	30995	89198
3	24130	48360	22527	97265	76393	64809
4	42167	93093	06243	61680	07856	16376
5	37570	39975	81837	76656	06121	91782
6	77921	06907	11008	42751	27756	53498
7	99562	72905	56420	69994	98872	31016
8	96301	91977	05463	07972	18876	20922

· BOX 6-1 ·

(CONTINUED)

STEP 4 At the end of each control group score, write down a "C." At the end of each experimental group score, write down an "E." In this example, our sheet would now look like this:

CONTROL GROUP	EXPERIMENTAL GROUP
81647C	06121E
30995C	27756E
76393C	98872E
07856C	18876E

STEP 5 Rank these numbers from lowest to highest. Then, on a second piece of paper, put the lowest number on the top line, the second lowest number on the next line, and so on. In this example, your page would look like this:

06121E

07856C

18876E

27756E

30995C

76393C

81647C

98872E

STEP 6 Label the top line, "Participant 1," the second line "Participant 2," and so forth. The first participant who shows up will be in the condition specified on the top line, the second participant who shows up will be in the condition specified by the second line, and

so forth. In this example, the first participant will be in the experimental group, the second in the control group, the third and fourth in the experimental group, the fifth, sixth, and seventh in the control group, and the eighth in the experimental group. Thus, our sheet of paper would look like this:

Participant Number 1 = 06121E

Participant Number 2 = 07856C

Participant Number 3 = 18876E

Participant Number 4 = 27756E

Participant Number 5 = 30995C

Participant Number 6 = 76393C

Participant Number 7 = 81647C

Participant Number 8 = 98872E

STEP 7 To avoid confusion, recopy your list, but make two changes. First, delete the random numbers. Second, write out "Experimental" and "Control." In this example, your recopied list would look like this:

Participant Number 1 = Experimental

Participant Number 2 = Control

Participant Number 3 = Experimental

Participant Number 4 = Experimental

Participant Number 5 = Control

Participant Number 6 = Control

Participant Number 7 = Control

Participant Number 8 = Experimental

Be aware that not all hypotheses are cause–effect hypotheses. Sometimes, hypotheses involve describing what happens rather than finding out what makes things happen. If you generate a hypothesis that is not a cause–effect statement, then it is not an experimental hypothesis. Thus, if you hypothesize that men are more romantic than women, you do not have an experimental hypothesis. Similarly, if you predict that athletes will be more assertive than nonathletes, you do not have an experimental hypothesis. In short, to have an experimental hypothesis, you must predict that some treatment that you manipulate will cause an effect.

NULL HYPOTHESIS: THE TREATMENT DOES NOT HAVE AN EFFECT

Once you have an experimental (cause–effect) hypothesis, pit it against the **null hypothesis:** the hypothesis that the treatment has no effect. The null hypothesis essentially states that any difference you observe between the treatment and no-treatment group scores could be due to chance. Thus, if our experimental hypothesis was that getting 3 hours of full-spectrum lighting will cause people to be happier, the null hypothesis would be: "Getting 3 hours of full-spectrum lighting will have *no* demonstrated effect on happiness."

If your results show that the difference between groups is probably not due to chance, you can reject the null hypothesis. By rejecting the null hypothesis, you tentatively accept the experimental hypothesis: You conclude that the treatment has an effect.

But what happens if you fail to demonstrate conclusively that the treatment has an effect? Can you say that there is no effect for full-spectrum lighting? No, you can only say that you failed to prove beyond a reasonable doubt that full-spectrum lighting causes a change in happiness. In other words, you're back to where you were before you began the study: You do not know whether full-spectrum lighting causes a change in happiness.[2]

To reiterate a key point: The *failure to find a treatment effect doesn't mean that the treatment has no effect.* If you had looked more carefully, you might have found the effect.

To help yourself remember that you can't prove the null hypothesis, think of the null hypothesis as saying "The difference between conditions *may be* due to chance." Note that saying, "The difference *may be* due to chance" is not the same as saying, "The difference is due to chance."

---

[2]Those of you who are intimately familiar with confidence intervals may realize that null results do not necessarily send the researcher completely back to square one. Admittedly, we do not know whether the effect is greater than zero, but we could use confidence intervals to estimate a range in which the effect size probably lies. That is, before the study, we may have no idea of the potential size of the effect. We might think the effect would be anywhere between −100 units and +100 units. However, based on the data collected in the study, we could estimate, with 95% confidence, that the effect is between a certain range. For example, we might find, at the 95% level of confidence, that the effect is somewhere in the range between +1 units and −3 units.

CONCLUSIONS ABOUT EXPERIMENTAL AND NULL HYPOTHESES

In summary, you have learned four important points about experimental and null hypotheses:

1. The experimental hypothesis is that the treatment has an effect.
2. The null hypothesis is that the treatment has no effect.
3. If you reject the null hypothesis, then you can tentatively accept the hypothesis that the treatment has an effect.
4. If you fail to reject the null hypothesis, you can't draw any conclusions.

To remember these four key points, think about these hypotheses in the context of a criminal trial. In a trial, the null hypothesis is that the defendant did not commit (cause) the crime. The experimental hypothesis is that the defendant did cause the crime. The prosecutor tries to disprove the null hypothesis so that the jury will accept the experimental hypothesis. That is, the prosecutor tries to disprove, beyond a reasonable doubt, the hypothesis that the defendant is "not guilty." If the jury decides that the null hypothesis is highly unlikely, they reject it and find the defendant guilty. If, on the other hand, they still have reasonable doubt, they fail to reject the null hypothesis and vote "not guilty." Note that their "not guilty" verdict is not an "innocent" verdict. Instead, it is a verdict reflecting that they are not sure, beyond a reasonable doubt, that the null hypothesis is false.

MANIPULATING THE INDEPENDENT VARIABLE

Once you have your hypotheses, your next step is to manipulate the treatment. You must administer (assign) the treatment to some participants and withhold it from others. If you are examining the effect of full-spectrum lighting on mood, you must vary the amount of full-spectrum light people get. Furthermore, the amount of full-spectrum light that you give a participant should be independent of (should not depend on or be affected by) the individual's personal characteristics as well as independent of both the participant's and experimenter's preferences. Instead, the amount of full-spectrum light participants receive should be determined by independent random assignment. Since the amount of full-spectrum light *varies* between the treatment group and the no-treatment group, since the amount of full-spectrum light varies *independently* of each participant's characteristics, and since the amount of full-spectrum lighting a participant gets is determined by *independent random assignment,* full-spectrum lighting is the **independent variable.**

In simple experiments, the independent variable will always vary between two amounts or **levels.** In our lighting experiment, participants are randomly assigned to one of the following two levels of the independent variable: (1) 3 hours of full-spectrum lighting, and (2) no full-spectrum lighting.

EXPERIMENTAL AND CONTROL GROUPS: SIMILAR, BUT TREATED DIFFERENTLY

The participants who are randomly assigned to get the higher level of the treatment (3 hours of full-spectrum light) are called the **experimental group**. The participants who are randomly assigned to get a lower level of the treatment (in this case, no treatment) are called the **control group**. In this case, the experimental group is the *treatment group* and the control group is the no-treatment group.

The control group is a comparison group. We compare the experimental (treatment) group to the control (no-treatment) group to see whether the treatment had an effect.

Comparing the experimental group to the control group only makes sense if the groups are roughly equivalent at the start of the experiment. Thus, there should not be any systematic difference between them until the experimenter gives them different levels of the independent variable.

As the terms *experimental group* and *control group* imply, you should have several participants (preferably more than 30) in each of your conditions. The more participants, the more opportunities random assignment has to spread nontreatment factors equally between your groups. Thus, the more participants, the more likely it is that your two groups will be similar at the start of the experiment. Conversely, the fewer participants you have, the less likely it is that your groups will be similar. For example, if you are doing an experiment to evaluate the effect of a strength pill and only have two participants (a 6′4″, 280-lb offensive tackle and a 5′1″, 88-lb person recovering from a long illness), random assignment will not have the opportunity to make your "groups" equivalent. Consequently, your control group would not be a fair comparison group.

THE VALUE OF INDEPENDENCE: WHY CONTROL AND EXPERIMENTAL GROUPS SHOULDN'T REALLY BE "GROUPS"

Although we have noted that the experimental and control groups are groups in the sense that there should be several participants in each "group," that is the only sense in which these "groups" are groups. To conduct an experiment, you do *not* find two groups of participants and then randomly assign one group to be the experimental group and the other to be the control group.

Why You Should Not Choose Two Pre-Existing Groups

To see why not, suppose you were doing a study involving 10,000 janitors at a Los Angeles company and 10,000 managers at a New York company. You have 20,000 people in your experiment—one of the largest experiments in history. Then, you flip a coin and—on the basis of that single coin flip—assign the LA janitors to no treatment and the New York managers to treatment. Even though you have 10,000 participants in each group, your treatment and no-treatment groups differ in a systematic way before the study begins. Your random assignment is no more successful in making your groups similar than it was when you had only two participants. Consequently, to get random assignment to equalize your groups, you need to assign each participant **independently**: individually, without regard to how previous participants were assigned.

Why You Shouldn't Let Your Groups Become "Groups"

Your concern with independence does not stop at assignment. After you have assigned participants to condition, you want each of your participants to remain independent. To maintain independence, do not test the control participants in one group session and the experimental participants in a separate group session. There are at least two reasons why having one testing session for the control group and a second session for the experimental group hurts independence.

First, when participants are tested in groups, they may become group members rather than independent individuals. That is, they may influence each other's responses. For example, instead of giving their own individual, independent responses, participants might respond as a conforming mob.

As a concrete example of the perils of letting participants interact, imagine that you are doing an extrasensory perception (ESP) experiment. In the experimental group, all 60 participants correctly guessed that the coin would turn up heads. In the control group, all 60 participants incorrectly guessed that the coin would turn up tails. If each participant had made his or her decision independently, the results would certainly defy chance. However, if all the experimental group members talked to one another and made a group decision, they were not acting as 60 individual participants, but as one group. In that case, the results would not be so impressive: Since all 60 experimental participants acted as one, the odds of them correctly guessing the coin flip were the same as the odds of one person correctly guessing a coin flip: 50–50.

Although the above example shows what can happen if participants are tested in groups and allowed to interact freely, interaction can disturb independence even when group discussion is prohibited. Participants may influence one another through inadvertent outcries (laughs, exclamations like, "Oh no!") or through subtle nonverbal cues. In our lighting-happiness experiment, one participant who is crying uncontrollably might cause the entire experimental group to be unhappy. In such a case, testing all the experimental participants as a single group would cause us to falsely conclude that the treatment (the lighting) caused unhappiness. If, on the other hand, we tested participants individually, the unhappy participant's behavior would not affect anyone else's responses.

The second reason for not testing all the experimental participants in one session and all the control participants in another is that such group testing turns the inevitable, random differences between testing sessions into systematic effects. For example, suppose that when the experimental group was tested, there was a distraction in the hall, but there was no such distraction while the control group was tested. Like the treatment, this distraction was presented to all the experimental group participants, but to none of the control group participants. Thus, if the distraction did have an effect, its effect might be mistaken for a treatment effect. If, on the other hand, participants were tested individually, it's very unlikely that only the experimental participants would be exposed to distractions. Instead, distractions would have a chance to even out so that participants in both groups would be almost equally affected by distractions.

But what if you are sure you won't have distractions? Even then, the sessions will differ in ways unrelated to the treatment. If you manage to test the participants at the same time, you'll have to use different experimenters and different testing rooms. If you manage to use the same experimenter and testing room, you'll have to test the groups at different times. Consequently, if you find a significant difference between your two groups, you have a problem in interpreting your results. Specifically, you have to ask, "Is the significant difference due to the groups getting different levels of the treatment or to the groups being tested under different conditions (having different experimenters, being tested at different times of day, etc.)?"

To avoid these problems in interpreting your results, make sure that the treatment is the only factor that systematically varies. In other words, use independent random assignment and then test your participants individually (or in small groups) so that random differences between testing sessions have a chance to even out. If you must run participants in large groups, do not run groups made up exclusively of experimental participants or exclusively of control participants. Instead, run groups made up of both control and experimental participants.

THE VALUE OF ASSIGNMENT (MANIPULATING THE TREATMENT)

We have focused on the importance of independence to independent random assignment. Independence helps us start the experiment with two "groups" of participants that do not differ in any systematic way. But assignment is also a very important aspect of independent random assignment.

Random Assignment Makes the Treatment the Only Systematic Difference Between Groups

Assignment is critical because we want the groups to differ in only one systematic way: the treatment. In random assignment, one random sample of participants (the experimental group) is assigned to receive a higher level of the independent variable and the other random sample of participants (the control group) is assigned to receive a lower level of the independent variable. If, at the end of the study, the groups differed by more than would be expected by chance, we could say that the difference was due to the only non-chance difference between them: the treatment.

Without Random Assignment You Do Not Have an Experiment

If you cannot randomly assign participants to your different treatments, then you cannot do a simple experiment. Because you cannot randomly assign participants to have certain personal characteristics, simple experiments cannot be used to study the effects of participant characteristics such as sex, race, personality, and intelligence.[3] For example, it makes no sense to assign a male to be a "female," a 7′2″ person to be "short," or a shy person to be "outgoing."

To see why we need to be able to assign participants, let's imagine that you try to look at the effects of lighting on mood without using random assignment. Suppose you get a group of people who use light therapy and compare them to a group of people who do not use light therapy. What would be wrong with that?

The problem is that you are selecting two groups of people who you know are different in at least one way, and then you are assuming that they don't differ in any other respect. That assumption is probably wrong. We know that people who use light therapy probably differ from those who don't in many ways. To list just a few of these differences: Light users feel more depressed, they live in different climates, are more receptive to new ideas, are richer, and so forth. Because the groups differ in many ways other than in terms of the "treatment," it would be foolish to say that the "treatment"—rather than one of these many other differences between the groups—is what caused the groups to score differently on the happiness measure. Therefore, if the group of light users is more depressed than our sample of nonusers, we could not conclude that the lighting caused their depression. The lighting might be a partial cure—rather than a cause—of their depression. But what if the group of lighting users is less depressed? Even then, we could not conclude that the lighting is causing the light users to be less depressed. They may be less depressed because they are richer, have more spare time, or differ in some other way from those who don't use lights. In short, if you do not randomly *assign* participants to group, you cannot conclude anything about the effects of a treatment.

If, on the other hand, you start with one group of participants and then randomly assign half to full-spectrum lighting and half to no lighting, interpreting differences between the groups would be much simpler. That is, since the groups probably were fairly similar before the treatment was introduced, large group differences in happiness are probably due to the only systematic difference between them—the lighting.[4]

---

[3]You can, however, experimentally investigate how participants react to people who vary in terms of these characteristics. For example, you can have an experiment where participants read the same story except that one group is told that the story was written by a man, whereas the other group is told that the story was written by a woman. Similarly, you can randomly determine, for each participant, whether the participant interacts with a male or female experimenter.

[4]With this experiment, you would know that the lighting manipulation caused the difference between the groups, but you would not know what it was about the lighting manipulation that had the effect. The attention or routine involved in the lighting manipulation may be responsible for the effect. You would be in a better position to say the full-spectrum lighting was responsible if the control group had received normal lighting.

COLLECTING THE DEPENDENT VARIABLE

Before you can determine whether the lighting caused the experimental group to be happier than the control group, you must measure each participant's happiness. You know that each person's happiness will *vary depending* on the individual's personality and you predict that their happiness score will also *depend* on the lighting. Therefore, scores on the happiness measure are your **dependent variable**. Since the dependent variable is what the participant does that you measure, the dependent variable is also called the **dependent measure**.

THE STATISTICAL SIGNIFICANCE DECISION: DECIDING WHETHER TO DECLARE THAT A DIFFERENCE IS NOT A COINCIDENCE

After measuring the dependent variable, you will want to compare the experimental group's happiness scores to the control group's. One way to make this comparison is to subtract the average of the happiness scores for the control (comparison) group from the average of the experimental group's happiness scores.

Unfortunately, knowing how much the groups differ doesn't tell you how much of an effect the treatment had. After all, even if the treatment had no effect, nontreatment factors would probably still make the groups differ. That is, even if the treatment had no effect, the groups may differ due to random error.

How can you determine that the difference between groups is due to something more than random error? To determine the probability that the difference is not exclusively due to chance, you need to use **inferential statistics**: the science of chance.

STATISTICALLY SIGNIFICANT RESULTS: DECLARING THAT THE TREATMENT HAS A RELIABLE EFFECT

If, by using statistics, you find that the difference between your groups is greater than could be expected if only chance were at work, then your results are statistically significant. The term **"statistically significant"** means that you are sure, beyond a reasonable doubt, that the difference you observed is not a fluke.

What is a reasonable doubt? Usually, researchers want to be at least 95% sure that the treatment is responsible for the difference. In other words, they want reasonable doubt to be less than 5% ($100 - 95 = 5$). That is, before they say that a treatment has an effect, they want less than a 5% probability ($p < .05$) that the results could be solely due to random error. Consequently, in journal articles, you will often see statements like, "the results were statistically significant ($p < .05$)."

To review, if you do a simple experiment, you will probably find that the treatment group mean is different than the control group mean. Such a difference is not, by itself, evidence of the treatment's effect. Indeed, because random assignment does not create identical groups, you would expect the two group means to differ to some extent. Therefore, the question is not "Is there a difference between the group means?" but rather "Is the difference between the group means bigger than would be expected if only random factors were at work?" To answer that question, you need to use statistics. Using statistics, you might find that if only chance factors were at work (that is, if the independent variable had no effect), you would get that large a difference less than 5% of the time. Since such a difference occurs less than 5% of the time by chance alone ($p < .05$) when the null hypothesis is true, then you would probably conclude that the independent variable caused a change in the scores on the dependent variable. That is, since it's unlikely that the difference between your groups is due to chance alone, you would probably conclude that some of the difference was due to the treatment. Thus, with statistically significant results, you would be relatively confident that if you repeated the study, you would get the same pattern of results. In short, statistical significance suggests that the results are reliable and replicable.

Statistically Significant Effects Are Not Necessarily Large

Statistical significance does not, however, mean that the results are significant in the sense of being large. Even a very small difference may be statistically reliable. For example, if you flipped a coin 5,000 times and it came up heads 51% of the time, this 1% difference from what would be expected by chance (50% heads) would be statistically significant.

Statistically Significant Results May Have No Practical Significance

Nor does statistical significance mean that the results are significant in the sense of being important. If you have a meaningless hypothesis, you may have results that are statistically significant, but meaningless.

Statistically Significant Results May Not Be in the Direction You Expect

Finally, statistically significant results do not necessarily support your hypothesis. For example, suppose your hypothesis is that the treatment improves behavior. A statistically significant effect for the treatment would mean that the treatment had an effect. But did the treatment improve behavior or make it worse? To find out, you have to look at the means to see whether the treatment group or no-treatment group is behaving better.

Summary of the Limitations of Statistically Significant Results

In short, statistically significant results tell you nothing about the direction, size, or importance of the treatment effect (see Table 6-1). Because of the limitations of statistical significance, the American Psychological Association appointed a task force to examine significance testing. The task force "does not support any action that could be interpreted as banning the use of null significance testing or p values in psychological research and publication" (APA, 1996). However, the task force did recommend that, in addition to reporting

---

• TABLE 6-1 •

LIMITS OF STATISTICAL SIGNIFICANCE

Statistically significant differences are:

1. probably not due to chance
2. not necessarily large
3. not necessarily in the direction you predicted
4. not necessarily important

---

whether the results were statistically significant, authors should provide information about the direction and size of effects.

NULL RESULTS: WHY WE CAN'T DRAW CONCLUSIONS FROM NONSIGNIFICANT RESULTS

You now know how to interpret statistically significant results. But what if your results are not statistically significant? That is, what if you can't reject the hypothesis that the difference between your groups could be due to chance? Then, you have *failed* to reject the null hypothesis. Therefore, your results would be described as "not significant."

As the phrase "not significant" suggests, you can't draw any conclusions from such findings. With **nonsignificant** results (also called **null results**), you do not know whether the treatment has an effect that you failed to find or whether the treatment really has no effect (see Figure 6-1).

Nonsignificant results are analogous to a "not guilty" verdict: Is the defendant innocent, or did the prosecutor present a poor case? Often, defendants get off, not because of overwhelming proof of their innocence, but because of lack of conclusive proof of their guilt.

You have seen that nonsignificant results neither confirm nor deny that the treatment had an effect. Unfortunately, you will find some incompetents treating null results as proof that the treatment has an effect—while other bad researchers will treat null results as proof that the treatment has no effect (see Table 6-2).

Nonsignificant Results Are Not Significant

All too often, people act like nonsignificant results are really significant. For example, they may say, "The difference between my groups shows that the treatment had an effect, even though the difference is not significant." Reread the previous quote because you're sure to see it again: It's the most commonly stated contradiction in psychology. People making this statement are really saying, "The difference is due to the treatment, even though I've found no evidence that the difference isn't simply due to chance."

• FIGURE 6-1 •

THE MEANING OF STATISTICAL SIGNIFICANCE

If the results are statistically significant, we can conclude that the difference between the groups is not due to chance. Since it's not due to chance, it must be due to treatment. However, if the results are not statistically significant, then the results could be due to chance or they could be due to treatment. Put another way, we don't know any more than we did before we subjected the results to statistical analysis.

Before doing a statistical analysis, we know that the difference between groups could be due to *either:*	Treatment OR Chance
After doing a statistical analysis that reveals a significant difference, we know that the difference between the groups is *probably* due to:	Treatment OR ~~Chance~~
If the statistical test fails to reach significance, then the difference could be due to *either:*	Treatment OR Chance

Null Results Do Not Prove the Null Hypothesis: "I Didn't Find It" Doesn't Mean It Doesn't Exist

As we have just discussed, some people act like null results prove the experimental hypothesis. On the other hand, some people make the opposite mistake: They incorrectly assume that null results prove the null hypothesis. That is, they falsely conclude that null results prove that the treatment had no effect. Some individuals make this mistake because they think the term "null results" implies that the results prove the null hypothesis. Those people would be better off thinking of null results as "no results" than to think that null results support the null hypothesis.

• TABLE 6-2 •

COMMON ERRORS IN DISCUSSING NULL RESULTS

STATEMENT	FLAW
"The results were not significant. Therefore, the independent variable had no effect."	"Not that I know of" is not the same as proving "there isn't any."
"The treatment had an effect, even though the results are not significant."	"Not significant" means that you failed to find an effect. Therefore, the statement could be translated as: "I didn't find an effect for the treatment, but I really did." Clearly, that's illogical!

Thinking that nonsignificant results support the null hypothesis is a mistake because it overlooks the difficulty of conclusively proving that a treatment has an effect. People should realize that not finding something is not the same as proving that the thing does not exist. After all, people often fail to find things that clearly exist, such as books that are in the library, items that are in the grocery store, and keys that are on the table in front of them.

Even in highly systematic investigations, failing to find something doesn't mean the thing does not exist. For example, in 70% of all murder investigations, investigators do not find a single identifiable print at the murder scene—not even the victim's. Thus, the failure to find the suspect's fingerprints at the scene is hardly proof that the suspect is innocent. For essentially the same reasons, the failure to find an effect is not proof that there is no effect.

SUMMARY OF THE "IDEAL" SIMPLE EXPERIMENT

Thus far, we have said that the simple experiment gives you an easy way to determine whether a factor causes an effect. If you can randomly assign participants to either a treatment or no-treatment group, all you have to do is find out whether your results are statistically significant. If your results are statistically significant, then your treatment probably had an effect. No method allows you to account for the effects of nontreatment variables with as little effort as random assignment.

ERRORS IN DETERMINING WHETHER RESULTS ARE STATISTICALLY SIGNIFICANT

Unfortunately, however, there is one drawback to random assignment: Differences between groups may be due to chance rather than to the treatment. Admittedly, statistical tests—by allowing you to predict the extent to which chance may cause the groups to differ—minimize this drawback. Statistical tests, however, do not allow you to perfectly predict chance all of the time. Therefore, you may err by either underestimating or overestimating the extent to which chance is causing your groups to differ (see Table 6-3).

TYPE 1 ERRORS: "CRYING WOLF"

If you underestimate the role of chance, you may make a Type 1 error; mistaking a chance difference for a real difference. In the simple experiment, you would make a Type 1 error if you mistook a chance difference between your experimental and control groups for a treatment effect. More specifically, you would make a Type 1 error if you declared that a difference between your groups was statistically significant, when the treatment really didn't have an effect. In nonpsychology settings, examples of Type 1 errors include:

• TABLE 6-3 •

POSSIBLE OUTCOMES OF STATISTICAL SIGNIFICANCE DECISION

STATISTICAL SIGNIFICANCE DECISION	REAL STATE OF AFFAIRS	
	Treatment has an effect	Treatment does not have an effect
Significant: Reject the null hypothesis	Correct decision	Type 1 error
Not significant: Do not reject null hypothesis	Type 2 error	Correct decision

- a jury convicting an innocent person because they mistake a series of coincidences as evidence of guilt
- a person responding to a false alarm, such as thinking that the phone is ringing when it's not or thinking that an alarm is going off when it's not
- a physician making a "false positive" medical diagnosis, such as telling someone she is pregnant when she isn't

Reducing the Risk of a Type 1 Error

What can you do about Type 1 errors? *There is only one thing you can do: You can decide what risk of a Type 1 error you are willing to take.* Usually, experimenters decide that they are going to take a 5% risk of making a Type 1 error. In other words, they say their results must be significant at the .05 level ($p <$ .05) before they decide that their results are significant. That is, they are comfortable with the odds of their making a Type 1 error being less than 5 in 100. But why take even that risk? Why not take less than a 1% risk?

Accepting the Risk of a Type 1 Error

To understand why not, imagine you are betting with someone who is flipping a coin. For all 10 flips, she calls "heads." She wins most of the 10 flips.

Let's suppose that you will refuse to pay up if you have statistical proof that she is cheating. However, you do not want to make the Type 1 error of attributing her results to cheating when the results are really due only to luck. How many of the 10 flips does she have to win before you "prove" that she is cheating?

To help you answer this question, we looked up the odds of getting 8, 9, or 10 heads in 10 flips of a fair coin.[5] Those odds are as follows:

---

[5]You do not need to know how to calculate these percentages.

chances of 8 or more heads	5.47%
chances of 9 or more heads	1.08%
chances of 10 heads	0.1%

From these odds, you can see that you can't have complete, absolute proof that she is cheating. Thus, if you insist on taking 0% risk of falsely accusing her (you want to be absolutely 100% sure), you would not call her a cheat—even if she got 10 heads in a row. As you can see from the odds we listed above, it is very unlikely (.1% chance), but still possible, that she could get 10 heads in a row, purely by chance alone. Consequently, if you are going to accuse her of cheating, you are going to have to take some risk of making a false accusation.

If you were willing to take a 1% risk of falsely accusing her (you wanted to be 99% sure), you would call her a cheat if all 10 flips turned up heads, but not if 9 of the flips were heads. If you were willing to take a 2% risk of falsely accusing her (you wanted to be 98% sure), you would call her a cheat if 9 or 10 of the flips turned up heads. Finally, if you were willing to take a 6% risk of falsely accusing her (you would settle for being 94% sure), you could refuse to pay up if she got eight or more heads.

This betting example gives you a clue about what happens when you set your risk of making a Type 1 error. When you determine your risk of making a Type 1 error, you are indirectly determining how much the groups must differ before you will declare that difference "statistically significant." If you are willing to take a relatively large risk of mistaking a difference that is due only to chance for a treatment effect, then you may declare a relatively small difference "statistically significant." If, on the other hand, you are only willing to take a very tiny risk of mistakenly declaring a chance difference "statistically significant," you must require that the difference between groups be relatively large before you are willing to call it "statistically significant." In other words, all other things being equal, the larger the difference must be before you declare it significant, the less likely it is that you will make a Type 1 error. To take an extreme example of this principle, if you would not even declare the biggest possible difference between your groups "statistically significant," then you would not be taking any risk of making a Type 1 error.

TYPE 2 ERRORS: "FAILING TO ANNOUNCE THE WOLF"

The problem with not taking any risk of making a Type 1 error is that, if the treatment did have an effect, you would be unable to detect it. That is, in trying to be very sure that a difference is due to treatment and not to chance, you may make a **Type 2 error**: overlooking a genuine treatment effect because you think the differences between conditions might be due to chance. Examples of Type 2 errors in nonpsychological situations include:

- a jury letting a criminal go free because they wanted to be sure beyond any doubt and they realized that it was possible that the evidence against the defendant was due to numerous, unlikely coincidences
- a person failing to hear the phone ring or an alarm go off
- a radar detector failing to detect a speed trap
- a physician making a "false negative" medical diagnosis, such as failing to detect that a woman was pregnant

In short, whereas Type 1 errors are errors of commission (yelling "fire" when there is no fire), Type 2 errors are errors of omission (failing to yell "fire" when there is a fire). In trying to avoid Type 1 errors, you may increase your risk of making Type 2 errors. You do not want to be so cautious that you fail to detect real treatment differences. That is, you want your study to have **power**: the ability to find statistically significant differences; or, put another way, the ability to avoid making Type 2 errors.[6]

THE NEED TO PREVENT TYPE 2 ERRORS: WHY YOU WANT THE POWER TO FIND SIGNIFICANT DIFFERENCES

Fortunately, you can have power without increasing your risk of making a Type 1 error. Unfortunately, many people don't do what it takes to have power.

If you don't do what it takes to have power, your study may be doomed to fail to find anything. Even if your treatment has an effect, you will fail to find that effect statistically significant. In a way, looking for a significant difference between your groups with an underpowered experiment is like looking for differences between cells with an underpowered microscope.

As you might imagine, conducting a low-powered experiment often leads to frustration over not finding anything. Unfortunately, beginning researchers frequently frustrate themselves by conducting such low-powered experiments. (We know we did.) Why do beginning researchers often fail to design sufficiently powerful experiments?

STATISTICS AND THE DESIGN OF THE SIMPLE EXPERIMENT

One reason inexperienced researchers fail to design powerful experiments is they simply do not think about power—a "sin" that many professional researchers also commit (Cohen, 1990). But even when novice researchers do think

---

[6]In a sense, power and Type 2 errors are opposites. *Power* refers to the chances (given that the treatment really does have a certain effect) of *finding* a significant treatment effect, whereas a *Type 2 error* refers to the chances (given that the treatment really does have a certain effect) of *failing* to find a significant treatment effect. Mathematically, power = 1.00 – probability of making a Type 2 error. Thus, if power is 1.00 (1.00 – *0* = 1.00), you have a *0%* chance of making a Type 2 error. Conversely, if the treatment has an effect and power is 0 (1.00 – *1.00* = 0), you have a *100%* chance of making a Type 2 error. Often, power is around .40 (1.00 – .60 = .40), meaning that the researcher has a *60%* chance of making a Type 2 error.

about power, they often think that power is a statistical concept and therefore has nothing to do with design of experiments.

Admittedly, power *is* a statistical concept. *Statistical concepts, however, should influence the design of research.* For example, if you take power into account when designing your study, your study will have enough power to find the differences that you are looking for—if those differences really exist.

POWER AND THE DESIGN OF THE SIMPLE EXPERIMENT

To have enough power, you must reduce the likelihood that chance differences will hide the treatment effect (see Figure 6-2). Two ways of stopping random error from overwhelming your treatment effect are: (1) reduce the effects of random error, and (2) increase the size of the treatment effect.

Reduce the Effect of Random Error

One of the most obvious ways to reduce the effects of random error is to reduce the potential sources of random error. The major sources of random variability are random differences between testing situations, random measurement error, random differences between participants, and sloppy coding of data.

Standardize Procedures and Use Reliable Measures   Since a major source of random variability is variation in the testing situation, you can reduce random error by standardizing your experiment. Standardization consists of keeping the testing environment and the experimental procedures as constant as possible. Therefore, to improve power, you might want the noise level, illumination level, temperature, room, and time of testing to be the same for each participant. Furthermore, you would want to treat all your experimental group participants identically and all your control group participants identically. In addition to reducing random error by standardizing procedures, you should also reduce random error by using a reliable dependent measure.

The desire for both reliable measures and strict standardization makes some psychologists love both instruments and the laboratory. Under the lab's carefully regulated conditions, experimenters can create powerful and sensitive experiments.

Other experimenters, however, reject the laboratory setting in favor of real-world settings. By using real-world settings, they can more easily make a case for their study's external validity. The price they pay for leaving the laboratory is that they are no longer able to keep many nontreatment variables (temperature, distractions, noise level, etc.) constant. These variables, free to vary wildly, create a jungle of random error that may hide the treatment's effect.

Because of the large variability in real-world settings and the difficulties of using sensitive measures in the field, even die-hard field experimenters may first look for a treatment's effect in the lab. Only after they have found that the treatment has an effect in the lab will they try to detect the treatment's effect in the field.

• FIGURE 6-2 •

TWO WAYS TO AVOID LOSING YOUR TREATMENT
EFFECT IN A "JUNGLE" OF RANDOM ERROR

• FIGURE 6-2 •

TWO WAYS TO AVOID LOSING YOUR TREATMENT
EFFECT IN A "JUNGLE" OF RANDOM ERROR

Jungle of
Random Error

Lost Treatment Effect

Cut Down on Random Error

Build Up Treatment Effect

Use a Homogeneous Group of Participants   Like differences between testing sessions, differences between participants can hide treatment effects. Even if the treatment effect causes a large difference between your groups, you may overlook that effect, mistakenly believing that the difference between your groups is due to the fact that your participants are years apart in age and worlds apart in terms of their experiences.

To decrease the chances that between-subject differences will mask the treatment's effect, choose participants who are similar to one another. For instance, select participants who are the same sex, same age, and have the same IQ. Or study rats instead of humans. With rats, you can select participants that have grown up in the same environment, have similar genes, and even have the same birthday. By studying homogeneous participants under standardized situations, rat researchers can detect very subtle treatment effects.

Code Data Carefully   Obviously, sloppy coding of the data can sabotage the most sensitively designed study. So, why do we mention this obvious fact?

We mention it because careful coding is a cheap way to increase power. If you increase power by using nonhuman animals as participants, you may lose the ability to generalize to humans. If you increase power by using a lab—rather than a field—experiment, you may lose some of your ability to generalize to real-world settings. But careful coding costs you nothing—except for a little time spent rechecking the coding of your data.

Let Random Error Balance Out   Thus far, we have talked about the most obvious way to reduce the effects of random error—reduce the sources of random error. But there is another way.

You can reduce the effects of random error by giving random error more chances to balance out. To remind yourself that chance does balance out in the long run, imagine flipping a fair coin. If you flipped it six times, you might get five tails—five times as many tails as heads. However, if you flipped it 1,000 times, you would end up with almost as many heads as tails.

Similarly, if you use five participants in each group, your groups probably won't be very equivalent before the experiment begins. Therefore, even if you found large differences between the groups at the end of the study, you might have to say that the differences could very well be due to chance. However, if you use 60 participants in each group, your groups should be fairly equivalent before the study begins. Consequently, a treatment effect that would be undetected if you used 5 participants per group might be statistically significant if you used 60 participants per group. Thus, to take advantage of the fact that random error balances out in the long run, use more participants.

Create Larger Effects: Bigger Effects Are Easier to See

Until now, we have talked about increasing power by making our experiment more sensitive to small differences. Specifically, we have talked about two ways of preventing the "noise" due to random error from making us unable to "hear" treatment effect: (1) reducing the amount of random error, and (2) giving random error a chance to balance out. However, we have left out the most obvious way to increase our experiment's ability to detect the effect: increasing the size of the effect.

As you might imagine, bigger effects are easier to find. But how do we create bigger effects? Your best bet for increasing the size of the effect is to give the control group participants a very low level of the independent variable while giving the experimental group a very high level of the independent variable. The assumption behind this advice is that if the treatment has an effect, then the more treatment, the more effect. That is, the more the groups differ in terms of the treatment, the more the groups should differ in terms of behavior. Hence, to have adequate power in the lighting experiment, rather than giving the control group 1 hour of full-spectrum light and the experimental group 2 hours, you might give the control group no full-spectrum light and the experimental group 14 hours of full-spectrum light.

To see how researchers can maximize the chances of finding an effect by giving the experimental and control groups widely different levels of treatment, let's consider an experiment by Wilson and Schooler (1991). Wilson and Schooler wanted to determine whether thinking about the advantages and disadvantages of a choice could hurt one's ability to make the right choice. In one experiment, they had participants rate their preference for the taste of several fruit-flavored jams. Half the participants rated their preferences after completing a "filler" questionnaire asking them to list reasons why they chose their major. The other half rated their preferences after completing a questionnaire asking them to "analyze why you feel the way you do about each jam in order to prepare yourself for your evaluations." As Wilson and Schooler predicted, the participants who thought about why they liked the jam made lower quality ratings than those who did not reflect on their ratings.

Although the finding that one can think too much about a choice is intriguing, we want to emphasize another aspect of Wilson and Schooler's study: the difference between the amount of time experimental participants reflected on jams versus the amount of time that control participants reflected on jams. Note that the researchers did not ask the control group to do any reflection whatsoever about the jams. To reiterate, Wilson and Schooler did not have the control group do a moderate amount of reflection and the experimental group do slightly more reflection. If they had, Wilson and Schooler might have failed to find a statistically significant effect.

CONCLUSIONS ABOUT HOW STATISTICAL CONSIDERATIONS IMPACT DESIGN DECISIONS

In conclusion, statistical considerations either dictate or influence virtually every aspect of the design process (see Table 6-4). For example, statistical considerations dictate what kind of hypothesis you can test. Because you cannot accept the null hypothesis, the only hypotheses that you can hope to support are hypotheses that the groups will differ. Therefore, you cannot do a simple experiment to prove that two treatments have the same effect or that a certain treatment will be just as ineffective as no treatment.

Not only do statistical considerations dictate what types of hypotheses you can have, but they also mandate how you should assign your participants. Specifically, if you do not assign your participants to groups using independent random assignment, you do not have a valid experiment.

Statistical considerations also dictate how you should treat your participants. That is, you will not have a valid experiment if you let participants influence one another's responses or if you do anything else that would violate the statistical requirement that individual participants' responses must be independent.

Even when statistics are not dictating what you must do, they are suggesting what you should do. To avoid making Type 2 errors, you should:

1. Standardize your procedures.
2. Use sensitive and reliable dependent measures.
3. Carefully code your data.

• **TABLE 6-4** •

IMPLICATIONS OF STATISTICS FOR THE SIMPLE EXPERIMENT

STATISTICAL CONCERN/REQUIREMENT	IMPLICATIONS FOR DESIGNING THE SIMPLE EXPERIMENT
Observations must be independent.	You must use independent random assignment and you cannot allow one participant to influence another participant's response.
Groups must differ for only two reasons—random differences and the independent variable.	You must randomly assign participants to groups.
It is impossible to accept the null hypothesis.	You cannot use the experiment to prove that independent variable has no effect or to prove that two treatments have the same effect.
You need enough power to find a significant effect.	You should: 1. Standardize procedures. 2. Use sensitive, reliable dependent variables. 3. Carefully code data. 4. Use homogeneous participants. 5. Use many participants. 6. Use extreme levels of the independent variable.

4. Use homogeneous participants.

5. Use many participants.

6. Use extreme levels of the independent variable.

NONSTATISTICAL CONSIDERATIONS AND THE DESIGN OF THE SIMPLE EXPERIMENT

Statistical issues, however, are not the only issues that you should consider when designing a simple experiment. If you only considered statistical power, you could harm your participants, as well as your experiment's external and construct validity. Therefore, in addition to statistical issues such as power, you must also consider external validity, construct validity, and ethical issues.

EXTERNAL VALIDITY VERSUS POWER

Many of the things you can do to improve your study's power may hurt your study's external validity. For example, lab experiments, homogeneous participants, and extreme levels of the independent variable all improve power, but may reduce external validity.

By using a lab experiment to stop unwanted variables from varying, you may have more power to find an effect. However, by preventing unwanted variables from varying, you may hurt your ability to generalize your results to real life—where these unwanted variables *do* vary.

By using a homogeneous set of participants (18-year-old, Caucasian males with IQs between 120 and 125), you reduce between-subject differences, thereby enhancing your ability to find treatment effects. However, because you used such a restricted sample, you would not be as able to generalize your results to the average American as a researcher whose participants were a random sample of Americans.

Finally, by using extreme levels of the independent variable, you may be able to find a significant effect for your independent variable. Using those extreme levels, however, may prevent you from determining the effect of realistic, naturally occurring levels of the treatment variable.

CONSTRUCT VALIDITY VERSUS POWER

Not only may your efforts to improve power hurt external validity, but they may also hurt your experiment's construct validity. For example, suppose you had two choices for your measure. The first is a 100-point rating scale that is sensitive and reliable. However, the measure is vulnerable to subject bias: If participants guess your hypothesis, they can easily circle the rating they think you want them to. The second is a measure that is not very reliable or sensitive, but it is a measure that participants couldn't easily fake. If power was your only concern, you would pick the first measure despite its vulnerability to subject bias. With it, you are more likely to find a statistically significant effect. However, many researchers would suggest that you pay attention to construct validity and pick the second measure.

If you sought only statistical power, you might also compromise the construct validity of your independent variable manipulation. For instance, to maximize your chances of getting a significant effect for full-spectrum lighting, you would give the experimental group full-spectrum lighting and make the control group an **empty control group**: a group that doesn't get any kind of treatment. Compared to the empty control group, the treatment group:

1. receives a gift (the lights) from the experimenter
2. gets more interaction with, and attention from, the experimenter (as the experimenter checks participants to make sure they are using the lights)
3. adopts more of a routine than the controls (using the lights every morning from 6:00 a.m. to 8:00 a.m.)
4. has higher expectations of getting better (because they have more of a sense of being helped) than the controls

As a result of all these differences, there is a reasonable chance of finding a significant difference between the two groups. Unfortunately, if you find a significant effect, it's hard to say that the effect is due to the full-spectrum lighting and not due to any of these other side effects of your manipulation.

To minimize these side effects of the treatment manipulation, you might give your control group a **placebo treatment:** a substance or treatment that has no effect. Thus, rather than using a no-light condition, you might expose the control group to light from an ordinary 75-watt incandescent light bulb. You would further reduce the chances of bias if you made both the experimenters and participants *"blind"*: unaware of which kind of treatment the participant was getting. By making experimenters blind, you make it less likely that they will bias the results in favor of the experimental hypothesis. Similarly, by making participants blind, you make it less likely that participants will bias the results in favor of the hypothesis.

In short, the use of placebos, the use of **single blinds** (where either the participant or the experimenter is blind) and the use of **double blinds** (where both the participant and the experimenter are blind) all may reduce the chances that you will obtain a significant effect. If you use these procedures, however, and you still find a significant effect, you can be relatively confident that the treatment itself—rather than some side effect of the treatment manipulation—is causing the effect.

You have seen that what is good for power may harm construct validity—and vice versa. But what tradeoffs should you make? To make that decision, you might find it helpful to see what tradeoffs professional experimenters make between power and construct validity. Do experienced experimenters use empty control groups to get significant effects? Or, do they avoid empty control groups to improve their construct validity? Do they avoid blind procedures to improve power? Or, do they use blind procedures to improve construct validity?

Often, experimenters decide to sacrifice power for construct validity. For example, in their jam experiment, Wilson and Schooler did not have an empty control group. That is, their control group did not simply sit around doing nothing while the experimental group filled out the questionnaire analyzing reasons for liking a jam. Instead, the control group also completed a questionnaire. The questionnaire was a "filler questionnaire" about their reasons for choosing a major. If Wilson and Schooler had used an empty control group, critics could have argued that it was the act of filling out a questionnaire—not the act of reflection—that caused the treatment group to make less accurate ratings than the controls. For example, critics could have argued that the controls' memory for the jams was fresher because they were not distracted by the task of filling out a questionnaire.

To prevent critics from arguing that the experimenters influenced participants' ratings, Wilson and Schooler made the experimenters blind. They employed two experimenters to implement the blind technique. The first experimenter supervised the tasting of the jams and the filling out of the "reasons" and the "filler" questionnaires. After introducing the participants to Experimenter 2, Experimenter 1 left the room. Then, Experimenter 2—who was unaware of (blind to) whether the participants had filled out the reasons or filler questionnaire—had participants rate the quality of the jams.

ETHICS VERSUS POWER

As you have seen, increasing a study's power may conflict with both external and construct validity. In addition, increasing power may also conflict with ethical considerations. For example, suppose you want to use extreme levels of the independent variable (food deprivation) to ensure large differences in the motivation of your animals. In that case, you need to weigh the benefits of having a powerful manipulation against ethical concerns, such as the comfort and health of the participants (for more about ethical concerns, see Chapter 1 and Appendix A).

Ethical concerns determine not only how you treat the experimental group, but also how you treat the control group. Just as it might be unethical to administer a potentially harmful stimulus to your experimental participants, it also might be unethical to completely withhold a potentially helpful treatment from your control participants. For instance, it might be ethically questionable to completely withhold a possible cure for depression from your controls. Therefore, rather than maximizing power by completely depriving the control group of a treatment, ethical concerns may dictate that you give the control group a moderate dose of the treatment. (For a summary of the conflicts between power and other goals, see Table 6-5.)

ANALYZING DATA FROM THE SIMPLE EXPERIMENT: BASIC LOGIC

After carefully weighing both statistical and nonstatistical considerations, you should be able to design a simple experiment that would test your experimental hypothesis in an ethical and internally valid manner. If, after consulting with your professor, you conduct that experiment, you will have data to analyze.

To understand how you are going to analyze your data, remember why you did the simple experiment. You did it to find out whether the treatment would have an effect on a unique population—all the participants who took part in your experiment. More specifically, you wanted to know the answer to the hypothetical question: "If I had put all my participants in the experimental condition, would they have scored differently than if I had put all of them in the control condition?" To answer this question, you need to know the averages of two **populations:**

Average of Population #1: what the average score on the dependent measure would have been if all your participants had been in the control group

• **TABLE 6-5** •

CONFLICTS BETWEEN POWER AND OTHER RESEARCH GOALS

ACTION TO HELP POWER	HOW ACTION MIGHT HURT OTHER GOALS
Use a homogeneous group of participants to reduce random error due to participants.	May hurt your ability to generalize to other groups of participants.
Test participants under controlled laboratory conditions to reduce the effects of extraneous variables.	1. May hurt your ability to generalize to real-life situations where extraneous variables are present.
	2. Artificiality *may* hurt construct validity. If the setting is so artificial that participants are constantly aware that what they are doing is not real and just an experiment, they may **act** to please the experimenter rather than expressing their "true" reactions to the treatment.
Use artificially high or low levels of the independent variables to get big differences between groups.	1. You may be unable to generalize to realistic levels of the independent variable.
	2. May be unethical.
Use an empty control group to maximize the chance of getting a significant difference between the groups.	Construct validity is threatened because the significant difference may be due to the participants' expectations rather than to the independent variable.
Test many participants to balance out the effects of random error.	Expensive and time-consuming.

Average of Population #2: what the average score on the dependent measure would have been if all your participants had been in the experimental group

Unfortunately, you cannot measure both of these populations. If you put all your participants in the control condition, then you won't know how they would have scored in the experimental condition. If, on the other hand, you put all your participants in the experimental condition, you won't know how they would have scored in the control condition.

ESTIMATING WHAT YOU WANT TO KNOW: YOUR MEANS ARE SAMPLE MEANS

Since you can't directly get the population averages you want, you do the next best thing—you estimate them. You can estimate them because, thanks to independent random assignment, you split all your participants (your population of participants) into two random samples. That is, you started the experiment

• **FIGURE 6-3** •

THE CONTROL GROUP AND THE EXPERIMENTAL GROUP ARE TWO SAMPLES DRAWN FROM THE SAME POPULATION

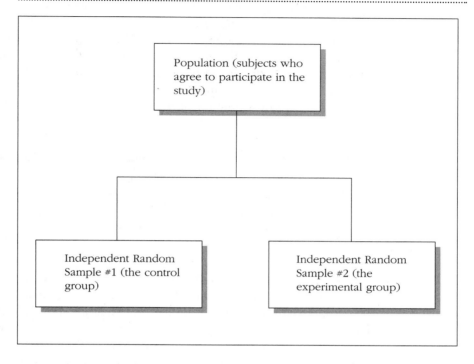

Problem: If the average score for experimental group is different than the average score for the control group, is this difference due to

a. the two groups receiving different treatments?

or

b. random error related to sampling? (Two random samples from the same population may differ.)

with two random samples from your original population of participants. These two "chips off the same block" were the control group and the experimental group (see Figure 6-3).

The average score of the random sample of your participants who received the treatment (the experimental group) is an estimate of what the average score would have been if all your participants received the treatment. The average score of the random sample of participants who received no treatment (the control group) is an estimate of what the average score would have been if all of your participants had been in the control condition.

Calculating Sample Means: Getting Your Estimates

Even though only half your participants were in the experimental group, you will assume that the experimental group is a fair sample of your entire population of participants. Thus, the experimental group's average score should be a reasonably good estimate of what the average score would have been if all your participants had been in the experimental group. Similarly, you will assume that the control group's average score is a fairly good estimate of what the average score would have been if all your participants had been in the control group. Therefore, the first step in analyzing your data will be to calculate the average score for each group. Usually, the average you will calculate is the **mean**: the result of adding up all the scores and then dividing by the number of scores.

Comparing Sample Means: How to Compare Two Imperfect Estimates

Once you have your two sample means, you can compare them. Before talking about how to compare them, let's understand why we are comparing the means. We are comparing the sample means because we know that, before the treatment was administered, both groups represented a random sample of the population consisting of every participant who took part in the study. Thus, at the end of the experiment, if the treatment had no effect, the control and experimental groups would both still be random samples from that population.

As you know, two random samples from the same population will probably be similar to each other. For example, two random samples of the entire population of New York City should be similar to each other, two random samples from the entire population of students at your school should be similar to each other, and two random samples from the entire group of participants who took part in your study should be similar to each other. Thus, if the treatment has no effect, at the end of the experiment, the experimental and control groups should be similar to each other.

WHY WE MUST DO MORE THAN SUBTRACT THE MEANS FROM EACH OTHER

Because two random samples from the same population should be similar to each other, you might think all we need to do is subtract the control group mean from the experimental group mean to find the effect. But such is not the case: Even if the treatment has no effect, the means for the control group and experimental group will rarely be identical. To illustrate, suppose that Dr. N. Ept made a serious mistake while trying to do a double-blind study. Specifically, Dr. N. Ept succeeded in not letting his assistants know whether the participants were getting the real treatment or a placebo, but failed in that all the participants got the placebo. In other words, both groups ended up being random samples of the same population—participants who did not get the treatment. Even in such a case, the two groups may have very different means.

HOW RANDOM ERROR AFFECTS DATA FROM THE SIMPLE EXPERIMENT

Dr. N. Ept's study illustrates an important point: Even if groups are random samples of the same population, they may still differ because of random error. You are probably aware of random error from reading about public opinion polls that admit to a certain degree of sampling error.

To help you see how random error could affect the results of a simple experiment, let's simulate conducting a small-scale experiment. Be warned that this simulation won't show us what would typically happen in an experiment. Instead, this simulation is rigged to demonstrate the worst random error can do. Nevertheless, the simulation does demonstrate a fundamental truth: Random error alone can make your groups fairly unequal.

To conduct this simulation, pretend that you have the following four participants, who would tend to score as follows:

Abby	10
John	20
Mary	70
Paul	40

Now, use Box 6-1 to randomly assign each participant to either the experimental or control group. Then, get an average for each group. Repeat this process several times. If you do this, you will simulate what happens when you do an experiment and the treatment has no effect.

As doing this simulation will reveal, which participants end up in which group varies greatly depending on where on the random numbers table you happen to start—and there are many different places you could start. Not all of these possible ways of splitting participants into control and experimental groups are going to produce identical groups. Indeed, you may even find that random assignment sometimes results in having all men in the experimental group and all women in the control group.

In summary, the control and experimental groups start off as random samples of your participants. At the start of the study, these groups are not identical. Instead, they will probably start off being fairly similar. Occasionally, however, they may start off being fairly different. If they start off as different, then they may score differently on the dependent measure task at the end of the experiment—even when the treatment has no effect. Thus, even if the treatment had no effect, random error might make the experimental group score higher than the control group.

Because random error can affect the results of a study, you need to understand random error to understand the results of a study. More specifically, to interpret the results of a simple experiment, you need to understand two important statistical principles:

1. Random error affects individual scores.
2. Random error may also cause group means to differ.

Fortunately, as you will soon see, you already intuitively understand both of these principles.

Random Error Makes Scores Within a Group Differ

To see that you intuitively grasp the first principle (random error affects individual scores), consider the following scores:

CONTROL	EXPERIMENTAL
70	80
70	80
70	80

Is there something strange about these data? Most students we show these data to correctly realize that these data are faked. Students are suspicious of these data because scores within each group do not vary: There is no within-groups variability in this experiment. The data make it look like the only thing that affects scores is the treatment. With real data, however, scores would be affected by nontreatment factors: There would be within-groups variability.

When asked to be more specific about why they think the data are faked, students point out that there are at least two reasons why scores within each group should differ. First, participants within each group differ from each other, so their scores would reflect those differences. For example, participants in the control group aren't all clones of each other, so their scores won't all be the same. Likewise, participants in the experimental group aren't all identical, so their scores shouldn't all be identical. Second, even if a group's participants were all identical, random measurement errors alone would prevent participants from getting identical scores. For example, even if the control group participants were clones, participants' scores would probably vary due to the measure's less-than-perfect reliability. Similarly, even if all the experimental group participants were identical, their scores would not be: Many random factors—from random variations in how the experimenter treated each participant to random errors in coding of the data—would inevitably cause scores within the experimental group to differ.

In summary, most students have an intuitive understanding that there will be differences within each group (within-groups variability), and these differences are due to factors completely unrelated to the treatment. To be more specific, these differences are due to random error caused by such factors as individual differences, random measurement error, and imperfect standardization.

Random Error Can Make Group Means Differ

To see whether you intuitively grasp the second principle (random error may cause group means to differ from each other), consider the following data:

CONTROL	EXPERIMENTAL
70	70
80	80
70	100

Do you think the experimental group is scoring significantly higher than the control group? Most students wisely say "no." They realize that if the participant who scored "100" had been randomly assigned to the control group rather than the experimental group, the results may have been completely different. Thus, even though the group means differ, the difference may not be due to the treatment. Instead, the difference between these two group means could be entirely due to random error.

As you have just seen, even if the treatment has no effect, random error may cause the experimental group mean to differ from the control group mean. Therefore, we cannot say that there is a treatment effect just because there is a difference between the experimental group's average score and the control group's. Instead, if we are going to find evidence for a treatment effect, we need a difference between our groups that is "too big" to be due to random error alone.

WHEN IS A DIFFERENCE TOO BIG TO BE DUE TO RANDOM ERROR?

What will help us determine whether the difference between group means is "too big" to be due to random error alone? In other words, what will help us determine that the treatment had a statistically significant effect?

To answer that question, we'll look at three sets of experiments. Let's begin with the two experiments tabled below. Which of the following two experiments do you think is more likely to reveal a significant treatment effect?

EXPERIMENT *A*		EXPERIMENT *B*	
CONTROL	EXPERIMENTAL	CONTROL	EXPERIMENTAL
70	70	70	80
71	73	71	81
72	72	72	82

Bigger Differences Are Less Likely to Be Due to Chance Alone

If you picked Experiment *B*, you're correct! All other things being equal, bigger differences are more likely to be "too big to be due to chance alone" than smaller differences. Therefore, bigger differences are more likely to reflect a treatment effect. Smaller differences, on the other hand, provide less evidence of a treatment effect.

To appreciate the fact that small differences provide less evidence of a treatment effect, let's consider an extreme case. Specifically, let's think about the case where the difference between groups is as small as possible: zero. In that case, the control and experimental groups would have identical means. In that case, there would be no evidence of a treatment effect.

"Too Big to Be Due to Chance" Partly Depends on How Big "Chance" Is

You have seen that the size of the difference is one factor that affects whether a result is statistically significant. All other things being equal, bigger differences are more likely to be significant.

However, the size of the difference isn't the only factor that determines whether a result is "too big to be due to chance." To illustrate this fact, compare the two experiments below. Then, ask yourself, is Experiment A or Experiment B more likely to reveal a significant treatment effect? That is, in which experiment is the difference more likely to be too big to be due to chance?

EXPERIMENT A		EXPERIMENT B	
CONTROL	EXPERIMENTAL	CONTROL	EXPERIMENTAL
68	78	70	70
70	80	80	80
72	82	60	90

Differences Within Groups Tell You How Big "Chance" Is

In both experiments, the difference between the control group mean (70) and the experimental group mean (80) is the same. Specifically, in both experiments, the experimental group mean is 10 points higher than the control group mean. Therefore, you can't tell which one is more likely to be "too big to be due to chance" just by seeing which experiment has a bigger difference between group means. Instead, to make the right choice, you have to figure out the answer to this question: "In which experiment is chance alone a less likely explanation for the 10-point difference?"

To help you answer this question, we'll give you a hint. The key to correctly answering this question is to look at the extent to which scores vary within each group. The more variability within a group, the more random error is influencing scores. By looking at how much Experiment A's control group scores differ from one another and by looking at how much Experiment A's experimental group scores differ from each other, you will get an idea of Experiment A's within-groups variability. Similarly, by looking at how much scores differ within Experiment B's control group and how much scores differ within Experiment B's experimental group, you will get an index of Experiment B's within-groups variability. In the experiment with more within-groups variability, random error is having more of an effect on individual scores. All other things being equal, the more random error makes individual scores within a group differ from one another, the more random error will tend to make group means differ from each other.

Now that you've had a hint, which experiment did you pick as being more likely to be significant? If you picked Experiment A, you're correct!

If you were asked why you picked A, you might say something like the following: "In Experiment B, the experimental group may be scoring higher than the control group merely because the participant who scored a 90 randomly ended up in the experimental group rather than in the control group. Consequently, in Experiment B, the difference between the groups could easily be due to random error."

Such an explanation is accurate, but it doesn't fully elaborate the complexity of your reasoning. Let's detail the four steps you went through:

1. You realized that there was more variability within each group in Experiment B than in Experiment A. That is, (1) whereas the control group scores were all pretty close to each other in Experiment A, the control group scores differed considerably from one another in Experiment B; and (2) whereas the experimental group scores were all pretty close to each other in Experiment A, the experimental group scores varied considerably from one another in Experiment B. More technically, the control group scores were farther away from the control group mean, and the experimental group scores were farther from the experimental group mean in Experiment B than in Experiment A.

2. You recognized that within-groups variability could not be due to the treatment. You realized that the differences among participants scores within the control group could not be due to the treatment because none of those participants received the treatment. You also realized that the differences among scores within the experimental group could not be due to the treatment because every participant in the experimental group received the same treatment. Therefore, when scores within a group vary, these differences must be due to factors other than the treatment. For example, scores within a group may differ from each other because of nontreatment factors such as individual differences.

3. You realized that random assignment turned the variability due to nontreatment factors (such as individual differences) into random error. Thus, you realized that the greater within-groups variability in Experiment B meant there was more random error in Experiment B than in Experiment A.

4. You realized that the bigger the differences that random error makes among scores within the control group and among scores within the experimental group, the bigger the difference that random error could make between the control group and the experimental group. That is, the more random error is spreading apart scores within each group, the more random error could be spreading the groups apart.

To review, we have discussed two factors that determine whether a result will be statistically significant. To remember these two factors, it may help you to think of significant results as meaning that the difference between groups is too big to be due to random error.

One factor that affects whether the difference between groups is too big to be due to random error is how big the difference is. However, knowing the absolute size of difference isn't enough. A large difference might not be significant. To be statistically significant, the difference between groups must be large relative to the difference that random error is likely to make.

One factor that affects how much of a difference random error is likely to make is how much random error there is in your data. If there is little random error in your data (as revealed by little variability within the control and experimental groups), then even a modest difference between groups might be too big to be due to random error. If, on the other hand, there is a great deal of variability within each group, then even a large difference between groups may not be statistically significant.

The amount of random error in the data is not the only factor that influences the extent to which random error is likely to influence the results. There is one other factor that affects how big an impact random error is likely to have.

To find out what this factor is, compare Experiments *A* and *B* below. Which is more likely to produce a significant result?

EXPERIMENT *A*		EXPERIMENT *B*	
CONTROL	EXPERIMENTAL	CONTROL	EXPERIMENTAL
68	70	68	70
70	72	70	72
72	74	72	74
		68	70
		70	72
		72	74
		68	70
		70	72
		72	74

In both experiments, the group means are equally far apart, so you can't look at group differences to figure out which experiment is more likely to be significant. In both experiments, the random variability within each group is the same. So looking at within-groups variability will not help you figure out which experiment is more likely to be significant. So, which one do you choose?

With Larger Samples, Random Error Tends to Balance Out

If you chose Experiment *B*, you're correct! Experiment *B* is the right choice because it had more participants.

To understand the benefit of having more participants, you need to keep two facts in mind. First, if the treatment has no effect, the experimental and control groups are random samples of the same population. If we have no treatment effect and both groups are good samples, both groups will be similar to each other. Second, bigger random samples are better samples. If we have no treatment effect and big samples, the control group mean and experimental group mean will be very similar. If, however, we have no treatment effect and small samples, chance might cause the groups to differ a great deal. Thus, the difference in Experiment *A* could easily be due to chance alone, but the difference in Experiment *B* is less likely to be due to chance alone.

Another way to think about the benefits of larger samples is to realize that *with large enough samples, random error tends to balance out.* If you flip a coin four times, you are quite likely to get either 75% heads or 75% tails. That is, random error alone will probably cause a deviation of 25% or more from the true value of 50% heads. If, on the other hand, you flip a coin 4,000 times, you will not get more than 51% heads or fewer than 49% heads. Because 4,000 flips gives random error an opportunity to balance out, random error will not cause a deviation of even 1% from the true value.

Just as having more coin flips allows more opportunities for the effects of random error to balance out, having more participants allows more opportunities for random error to balance out. Thus, Experiment *B*, by having more participants, does a better job than Experiment *A* at allowing the effects of random error to balance out. Consequently, it's less likely that random error alone would cause the groups to differ by a large amount in Experiment *B*. Therefore, a difference between the control group mean and the treatment group mean that would be significant in Experiment *B* might *not* be significant in Experiment *A*.

ANALYZING THE RESULTS OF THE SIMPLE EXPERIMENT: THE *t*-TEST

To actually determine whether a difference between groups is significant, researchers usually use the ***t*-test** (to see how to do a *t*-test, see Appendix E). Although we have not yet talked about the *t*-test, you already understand the basic logic behind it. The basic idea behind the *t*-test is to see *whether the difference between two groups is larger than would be expected by random error alone.* Thus, you should not be surprised to find that the *t*-ratio is the difference between the sample means divided by an index of the extent to which random error might cause the groups to differ. More technically, *t* equals the difference between means divided by the standard error of the difference between means.

USING THE *t*-TABLE

Once you have your *t*-ratio, you need to refer to a *t*-table (see Appendix E) to determine whether your *t*-ratio is significant. To use the *t*-table, you need to know how many degrees of freedom (df) you have.

To calculate your degrees of freedom, simply subtract 2 from the number of participants. Thus, if you used 32 participants, you would look at the *t*-table in Appendix E under the row labeled "30 df."

When comparing the *t*-ratio you calculated to the value in the table, consider your *t*-ratio to be positive. That is, when using the *t*-table, treat your *t* value as if it were a positive *t*-ratio even if your *t* value is actually negative. In other words, take the absolute value of your *t*-ratio.

If the absolute value of your *t*-ratio is not bigger than the number in the table, then your results are not statistically significant at the $p < .05$ level. If, on the other hand, the absolute value of your *t*-ratio is bigger than the number in the table, then your results are statistically significant at the $p < .05$ level.

If your results are statistically significant at the **p < .05 level**, there's less than a 5% chance that the difference between your groups is solely due to chance. Consequently, you can be reasonably sure that your treatment had an effect. You might report your results as follows: "As predicted, the experimental group's mean recall (8.12) was significantly higher than the control group's (4.66), $t(30) = 3.10$, $p < .05$."

ASSUMPTIONS OF THE *t*-TEST

As with any statistical test, the *t*-test requires that you make certain assumptions. For the *t*-ratio, two of these assumptions are especially important.

Two Critical Assumptions

First, because the *t*-test compares the two sample means, the *t*-test requires you to have data that allow you to compute meaningful means. Consequently, you cannot do a *t*-test on ranked data because you cannot meaningfully compute means based on ranked data. For example, although averaging the ranks of second- and third-place finishers in a race would result in the same average rank (2.5) as averaging the ranks of the first- and fourth-place finishers, the average times of the two groups might vary greatly. The average times of the first- and fourth-place finishers could be much faster or much slower than the average of the times of the second- and third-place finishers. Like ranked data, qualitative data do not allow you to compute meaningful means. (Try averaging scores when 1 = nodded head, 2 = gazed intently, and 3 = blinked eyes—what does an average of 1.8 indicate?) Therefore, you cannot do a *t*-test on qualitative data. In short, to perform the *t*-test, you must be able to assume that you have either interval scale or ratio scale data.

Second, the *t*-test requires that observations are independent. If this requirement is violated, the results of the *t*-test are worthless. In the simple experiment, you can meet this requirement by independently and randomly assigning each participant to either the experimental or the control group—and then making sure that the participants do not interact.

To reiterate, to do a meaningful *t*-test in a simple experiment, your data must meet two key assumptions. You must have at least interval scale data, and you must have used independently assigned participants to groups. In addition to these two pivotal assumptions, the *t*-test makes two less-vital assumptions (see Table 6-6).

Two Less-Critical Assumptions

First, the *t*-test assumes that the population from which your sample means was drawn is normally distributed. The reason for this assumption is that if the populations are normally distributed, then the distribution of sample means will tend to be normally distributed. This assumption is usually nothing to worry about because most distributions are normally distributed. But what if the

· **TABLE 6-6** ·

EFFECTS OF VIOLATING THE *T*-TEST'S ASSUMPTIONS

ASSUMPTION	CONSEQUENCES OF VIOLATING ASSUMPTION
Observations are independent (participants are independently assigned and participants do not influence one another's responses).	Serious violation, nothing can be done to salvage your study.
Data are interval or ratio scale (for example, numbers must not represent qualitative categories, nor may they represent ranks [first, second, third, etc.]).	Do not use a *t*-test. However, there are other statistical tests you can use.
The population from which your sample means was drawn is normally distributed.	If the study used more than 30 participants per group, this is not a serious problem. If, however, fewer participants were used, you may decide to use a different statistical test.
Scores in both conditions have the same variances.	Usually not a serious problem.

population isn't normally distributed? Even then, your sample means will probably be normally distributed if you have more than 30 participants per group. That is, as the **central limit theorem** states, with large enough samples, the distribution of sample means will be normally distributed. To understand why the central limit theorem works, realize that if you take numerous large samples from the same population, your sample means will differ from one another for only one reason—random error. Since random error is normally distributed, the distributions of sample means will be normally distributed—regardless of the shape of the underlying population.

The second assumption is that the variability of scores within your experimental group will be about the same as the variability of scores within your control group. To be more precise, the assumption is that scores in both conditions will have the same variance. This is not a very strict assumption. If you have unequal variances, it won't seriously affect the results of your *t*-test, as long as one variance isn't more than 2½ times larger than the other.

QUESTIONS RAISED BY RESULTS

Obviously, if you violate key assumptions of the *t*-test, people should question your results. But even if you don't violate any of the *t*-test's assumptions, your results will raise questions—and this is true whether or not your results are statistically significant.

QUESTIONS RAISED BY NONSIGNIFICANT RESULTS

Nonsignificant results raise questions because the null hypothesis cannot be proven. Therefore, null results inspire questions about the experiment's power, questions such as:

1. Did you have enough participants?
2. Were the participants homogeneous enough?
3. Was the experiment sufficiently standardized?
4. Were the data coded carefully?
5. Was the dependent variable sensitive and reliable enough?
6. Would you have found an effect, if you had chosen two different levels of the independent variable?

QUESTIONS RAISED BY SIGNIFICANT RESULTS

If your results are statistically significant, it means you found an effect for your treatment. Since you found an effect for your independent variable, you don't have to ask any questions about your study's power. But that doesn't mean your results don't raise any questions. On the contrary, a significant effect often raises many questions.

Sometimes, questions are raised because the experimenter sacrificed construct or external validity to obtain adequate power. For example, if you used an empty control group, you have questionable construct validity. Consequently, one question would be: "Does your significant treatment effect represent an effect for the construct you tried to manipulate or is it merely a placebo effect?" Or, if you used an extremely homogeneous group of participants, the external validity of your study might be questioned. For example, skeptics might ask: "Do your results apply to other kinds of participants?" Thus, skeptics might want you to increase the external validity of your study by repeating it with a more representative sample. For example, they might want you to first use random sampling to obtain a representative group of participants and then randomly assign those participants to either the control or experimental group.

At other times, questions are raised because of a serious limitation of the simple experiment: It can only study two levels of a single variable. Therefore, there are two important questions you can ask of any simple experiment:

1. To what extent do the results apply to levels of the independent variable that were not tested?
2. To what extent could the presence of other variables modify (strengthen, weaken, or reverse) the treatment's effect?

Concluding Remarks

As you have seen, the results of a simple experiment always raise questions. Although results from any research study raise questions, some questions raised by the results of the simple experiment are due to the fact that the simple experiment is limited to studying only two levels of a single variable. If the logic of the simple experiment could be expanded to designs that would study several levels of several independent variables at the same time, such designs could answer several questions at once. Fortunately, as you will see in the next two chapters, the logic of the simple experiment can be extended to produce experimental designs that will allow you to answer several research questions with a single experiment.

Summary

1. Psychologists want to know the causes of behavior so that they can understand people and help people change. Only experimental methods allow us to isolate the causes of an effect.

2. Studies that don't manipulate a treatment are not experiments.

3. Many variables, such as age, gender, and personality, can't be manipulated. Therefore, many variables can't be studied using an experiment.

4. The simple experiment is the easiest way to establish that a treatment causes an effect.

5. The prediction that the treatment will cause an effect is called the experimental hypothesis.

6. The null hypothesis, on the other hand, states that the treatment will not cause an observable effect.

7. With the null hypothesis, you only have two options: You can reject it, or you can fail to reject it. You can never accept the null hypothesis.

8. Typically, in the simple experiment, you administer a low level of the independent (treatment) variable to some of your participants (the comparison or control group) and a higher level of the independent variable to the rest of your participants (the experimental group). Near the end of the experimental session, you observe how each participant scores on the dependent variable: a measure of the participant's behavior.

9. To establish causality with a simple experiment, participants' responses must be independent. Because of the need for independence, your experimental and control groups are not really groups. Instead, these "groups" are sets of individuals.

10. Independent random assignment is the cornerstone of the simple experiment. Without independent random assignment, you do not have a simple experiment.

11. Independent random assignment is necessary because it is the only way to make sure that the only differences between your groups are either due to chance or to the treatment.

12. Independent random assignment makes it likely that your control group is a fair comparison group. That is, the control and experimental groups should be fairly equivalent before the treatment is introduced.

13. Random assignment involves manipulating a treatment—assigning a level of a treatment to participants. Random assignment can help internal validity.

14. Your goal in using independent random assignment is to create two samples that accurately represent your entire population of participants. You use the mean of the control group as an estimate of what would have happened if all your participants had been in the control group. You use the experimental group mean as an estimate of what the mean would have been if all your participants had been in the experimental group.

15. Does the treatment have an effect? In other words, would participants have scored differently had they all been in the experimental group than if they had all been in the control group? This is the question that a t-test tries to answer.

16. If the results of the t-test are statistically significant, the difference between your groups is greater than would be expected by chance (random error) alone. Therefore, you reject the null hypothesis and conclude that your treatment has an effect. Note, however, that statistical significance does not tell you that your results are big, important, or of any practical significance.

17. There are two kinds of errors you might make when attempting to decide whether a result is statistically significant.

18. Type 1 errors occur when you mistake a chance difference for a treatment effect. Before the study starts, you choose your "false alarm" risk (risk of making a Type 1 error). Most researchers decide to take a 5% risk.

19. Type 2 errors occur when you fail to realize that the difference between your groups is not solely due to chance. In a sense, you overlook a genuine treatment effect.

20. By reducing your risk of making a Type 1 error, you increase your risk of making a Type 2 error. That is, by reducing your chances of falsely "crying wolf" when there is no treatment effect, you increase your chances of failing to correctly yell "wolf" when there really is a treatment effect.

21. Because Type 2 errors can easily occur, nonsignificant results are inconclusive results.

22. To prevent Type 2 errors: (a) reduce random error; (b) use many participants to balance out the effects of random error; and (c) try to increase the size of your treatment effect.

23. You can easily determine your risks of a Type 1 error, but there's no way you can design your experiment to reduce them. In contrast, it is hard to determine your risk of making a Type 2 error, but there are many ways you can design your study to reduce your risk of making such errors.

24. If your experiment minimizes the risk of making Type 2 errors, your experiment has power. In the simple experiment, *power* refers to the ability to obtain statistically significant results when your independent variable really does have an effect.

25. Sometimes, efforts to improve power may hurt the study's external validity. For example, to get power, researchers may use a highly controlled lab setting rather than a real-life setting. Similarly, power-hungry researchers may study participants who are very similar to each other rather than a wide range of participants.

26. Occasionally, efforts to improve power may hurt the study's construct validity.

27. Using placebo treatments, single blinds, and double blinds can improve your study's construct validity.

28. Ethical concerns may temper your search for power, or even cause you to decide not to conduct your experiment.

29. Because of random error, you cannot determine whether your treatment had an effect simply by subtracting your experimental group mean from your control group mean. Instead, you must determine whether the difference between your group means could be due to random error.

30. The *t*-test involves dividing the difference between means by an estimate of the degree to which the groups would differ when the treatment had no effect. More specifically, the formula for the *t*-test is:

(Mean 1 − Mean 2)/standard error of the difference.

31. The degrees of freedom for a two-group between-subjects *t*-test are two less than the total number of participants.

32. The *t*-test is the most common way to analyze data from a simple experiment.

33. If your data do not meet the assumptions of the *t*-test, your statistical analysis may give you misleading results.

Key Terms

placebo treatment: a fake treatment that we know has no effect, except through the power of suggestion. For example, in medical experiments, a participant may be given a pill that does not have a drug in it. By using placebo treatments, you may be able to make people "blind" to whether a participant is getting the real treatment. (p. 200)

single blind: when either the participant or the experimenter is unaware of whether the participant is getting the real treatment or a placebo treatment. Making the participant "blind" prevents the participant from biasing the results of the study; making the experimenter blind prevents the experimenter from biasing the results of the study. (p. 200)

double blind: where neither the participant nor the experimenter knows what type of treatment (placebo treatment or real treatment) the participant is getting. By making both the participant and the experimenter "blind," you reduce both subject (participant) and experimenter bias. (p. 200)

experimental group: the participants who are randomly assigned to get the treatment. (p. 182)

control group: the participants who are randomly assigned to *not* receive the treatment. The scores of these participants are compared to the scores of the experimental group to see if the treatment had an effect. (p. 182)

empty control group: a control group that does not receive any kind of treatment, not even a placebo treatment. One problem with an empty control group is that if the treatment group does better, we don't know whether the difference is due to the treatment itself or to a placebo effect. To maximize construct validity, most researchers avoid using an empty control group. (p. 199)

independent variable: the treatment variable; the variable manipulated by the experimenter. The experimental group gets more of the independent variable than the control group. Note: Don't confuse independent variable with dependent variable. (p. 181)

levels of an independent variable: the treatment variable is often given in different amounts. These different amounts are called *levels.* (p. 181)

dependent variable (dependent measure): participants' scores—the response that the researcher is measuring. In the simple experiment, the experimenter hypothesizes that the dependent variable will be affected by the independent variable. (p. 186)

independently, independence: a key assumption of almost any statistical test. In the simple experiment, observations must be independent. That is, what one participant does should have no influence on what another participant does, and what happens to one participant should not influence what happens to another participant. Individually assigning participants to treatment or no-treatment condition and individually testing each participant are ways to achieve independence. (p. 183)

independent random assignment: randomly determining, for each individual participant, and without regard to what group the previous participant was assigned to, whether that participant gets the treatment. For example, you might flip a coin for each participant to determine whether that participant receives the treatment. Independent random assignment to experimental condition is the cornerstone of the simple experiment. (p. 177)

experimental hypothesis: a prediction that the treatment will cause an effect. In other words, a prediction that the independent variable will have an effect on the dependent variable. (p. 177)

null hypothesis: the hypothesis that there is no treatment effect. Basically, this hypothesis states that any difference between the treatment and no-treatment groups is due to chance. This hypothesis can be disproven, but it cannot be proven. Often, disproving the null hypothesis lends support to the experimental hypothesis. (p. 180)

simple experiment: participants are independently and randomly assigned to one of two groups, usually to either a treatment group or to a no-treatment group. The simple experiment is the easiest way to establish that a treatment causes an effect. (p. 177)

internal validity: a study has internal validity if it can accurately determine whether an independent variable causes an effect. Only experimental designs have internal validity. (p. 176)

inferential statistics: the science of chance. More specifically, the science of inferring the characteristics of a population from a sample of that population. (p. 186)

population: the entire group that you are interested in. You can estimate the characteristics of a population by taking large random samples from that population. (p. 201)

mean: an average calculated by adding up all the scores and then dividing by the number of scores. (p. 204)

central limit theorem: the fact that, with large enough samples, the distribution of sample means will be normally distributed. Note that an assumption of the *t*-test is that the distribution of sample means will be normally distributed. Therefore, to make sure they are meeting that assumption, many researchers try to have "large enough samples," which they often interpret as at least 15 participants per group. (p. 213)

t-test: the most common way of analyzing data from a simple experiment. It involves computing a ratio between two things: (1) the difference between your group means; and (2) the standard error of the difference (an index of the degree to which group means could differ by chance alone).

As a general rule, if the difference you observe is more than three times bigger than the standard error of the difference, then your results will probably be statistically significant. However, exact ratio that you need for statistical significance depends on your level of significance and on how many participants you have. You can find the exact ratio by looking at the *t*-table in Appendix E and looking for where the column relating to your significance level meets the row relating to your degrees of freedom. (In the simple experiment, the degrees of freedom will be two less than the number of participants.) If the absolute value of the *t* you obtained from your experiment is bigger than the tabled value, then your results are significant. (p. 211)

statistical significance: when a statistical test says that the relationship we have observed is probably not due to chance alone, we say that the results are statistically significant. See also *p* < .05. (p. 186)

p < .05: in the simple experiment, *p* < .05 indicates that if the treatment had no effect, a difference between the groups as big as what was discovered would happen fewer than 5 times in 100. Since the chances of such a difference occurring by chance alone are so small, experimenters usually conclude that such a difference must be due, at least in part, to the treatment. (p. 212)

Type 1 error: rejecting the null hypothesis when it is really true. In other words, declaring a difference statistically significant when the difference is really due to chance. Thus, Type 1 errors lead to "false discoveries." If you set $p <$ .05, there is less than a 5% (.05) chance that you will make a Type 1 error. (p. 190)

Type 2 error: failure to reject the null hypothesis when it is really false. In other words, failing to declare that a difference is statistically significant, even though the treatment had an effect. Thus, Type 2 errors lead to failing to make discoveries. (p. 192)

power: the ability to find differences; or, put another way, the ability to avoid making Type 2 errors. (p. 193)

nonsignificant results: see **null results**.

null results (nonsignificant results): results that *fail* to disprove the null hypothesis. Null results do not prove the null hypothesis because null results may be due to lack of power. Indeed, many null results are Type 2 errors. (p. 188)

Exercises

1. What two conditions must be met to establish that a factor causes an effect? How is the simple experiment able to establish these conditions?
2. Why isn't it necessary to do an experiment in a lab? What advantages are there to doing an experiment in a lab? What advantages are there to doing an experiment in a real-world setting? What are the disadvantages?
3. A professor has a class of 40 students. Half of the students chose to take a test after every chapter (chapter test condition). The chapter tests were taken outside of class. The other half of the students chose to take in-class "unit tests." Unit tests covered four chapters. The professor finds no statistically significant differences between the groups on their scores on a comprehensive final exam. The professor then concludes that type of testing does not affect performance.
   a. Is this an experiment?
   b. Is the professor's conclusion reasonable? Why or why not?
4. Participants are randomly assigned to meditation or no-meditation condition. The meditation group meditates three times a week. The meditation group reports being significantly more relaxed than the no-meditation group.
   a. Why might the results of this experiment be less clearcut than they appear?
   b. How would you improve this experiment?
5. Can gender differences be studied in a simple experiment? Why or why not?

6. Theresa fails to find a significant difference between her control group and her experimental group $t(10) = 2.11$, not significant.

   a. Given that her results are not significant, what—if anything—would you advise her to conclude?

   b. What would you advise her to do? (Hint: You know that her t-test, based on 10 degrees of freedom, was not significant. What does the fact that she has 10 degrees of freedom tell you about the power of her study?)

7. A training program significantly improves worker performance. What should you know before advising a company to invest in such a training program?

8. Jerry's control group is the football team; the experimental group is the baseball team. He assigned the groups to condition using random assignment. Is there a problem with Jerry's experiment? If so, what is it? Why is it a problem?

9. Leslie is examining the effects of caffeine on alertness. Leslie tests the control group at 7:00 a.m. and the experimental group at 7:00 p.m. Is this appropriate? Why or why not?

10. Students were randomly assigned to two different strategies of studying for an exam. One group used visual imagery, the other group was told to study the normal way.

    a. The visual imagery group scores 88% on the test as compared to 76% for the control group. This difference was not significant. What, if anything, can the experimenter conclude?

    b. If the difference had been significant, what would you have concluded? What changes in the study would have made it easier to be sure of your conclusions?

    c. "To be sure that they are studying the way they should, why don't you have the imagery people form one study group and have the control group form another study group?" Is this good advice? Why or why not?

    d. "Just get a sample of students who typically use imagery and compare them to a sample of students who don't use imagery. That will do the same thing as random assignment." Is this good advice? Why or why not?

11. Bob and Judy are doing basically the same study. However, Bob has decided to put his risk of a Type 1 error at .05, whereas Judy has put her risk of a Type 1 error at .01. That is, Bob is willing to take a 5 in 100 risk that the results declared statistically significant are really due to chance, whereas Judy is only willing to take a 1 in 100 risk of "significant results" being due to chance.

    a. If Judy has 22 participants in her study, what t-value would she need to get significant results?

    b. If Bob has 22 participants in his study, what t-value would he need to get significant results?

    c. Who is more likely to make a Type 1 error? Why?

    d. Who is more likely to make a Type 2 error? Why?

12. Why don't participants in the control group all get the same score?

13. Your dependent measure is when people arrive to class. The distribution is not normally distributed. Instead, it tends to be "J" shaped. That is, whereas the average arrival time might be a minute before class, some people show up much earlier, but very few show up much later. Can you do a t-test on these data? Why or why not? (Hint: What does the central limit theorem say?)

14. Gerald's dependent measure is the order in which people turned in their exam (first, second, third, etc.). Can Gerald use a t-test on his data? Why or why not? What would you advise Gerald to do in future studies?

15. Are the results of Experiment A or Experiment B more likely to be significant? Why?

EXPERIMENT A		EXPERIMENT B	
CONTROL GROUP	EXPERIMENTAL GROUP	CONTROL GROUP	EXPERIMENTAL GROUP
3	4	0	0
4	5	4	5
5	6	8	10

16. Are the results of Experiment A or Experiment B more likely to be significant? Why?

EXPERIMENT A		EXPERIMENT B	
CONTROL GROUP	EXPERIMENTAL GROUP	CONTROL GROUP	EXPERIMENTAL GROUP
3	4	3	4
4	5	4	5
5	6	5	6
		3	4
		4	5
		5	6
		3	4
		4	5
		5	6

17. What would be the t-value for the following data? (Hint: After you compute the difference between the group means, you should be able to answer this question.)

EXPERIMENT C	
CONTROL GROUP	EXPERIMENTAL GROUP
3	3
4	4
5	5

18. Why do nonsignificant results raise more questions than they answer?

19. Under what circumstances should you avoid using a t-test?

CHAPTER 7

EXPANDING THE SIMPLE EXPERIMENT: THE MULTIPLE-GROUP EXPERIMENT

"Perhaps too much of everything is as bad as too little."
—EDNA FERBER

OVERVIEW

In Chapter 6, you learned how to perform a simple experiment. You now know that the simple experiment is internally valid and easy to do. However, you are also aware that the simple experiment is limited: With it, you can only study two values of a single independent variable.

In this chapter, you will see why you might want to go beyond studying two values of a single variable. Then, you will see how the logic of the simple experiment (random assignment of participants to two groups) can be extended to experiments that study the effects of three or more values of a single independent variable. Finally, you will learn how to analyze data from such experiments.

THE ADVANTAGES OF USING MORE THAN TWO VALUES OF AN INDEPENDENT VARIABLE

The simple experiment is ideal if an investigator wants to compare a single treatment group to a single no-treatment control group. However, as you will see, investigators often want to do more than compare two groups. They may want to:

1. compare more than two kinds of treatment
2. see whether either of two treatments is better than no treatment
3. compare the effectiveness of three or more different amounts of a treatment
4. compare a treatment group to two different control groups

COMPARING MORE THAN TWO KINDS OF TREATMENTS

Investigators often want to compare three or more different kinds of treatments. For instance, Roediger (1980) wanted to compare five kinds of memory strategies (rote rehearsal, imagery, method of loci, the link method, and the peg system). Clearly, he could not compare all five treatments in one simple experiment.

Instead of randomly assigning participants to two different groups, Roediger randomly assigned his participants to five different groups. To learn how to randomly assign participants to more than two groups, see Box 7-1.

Admittedly, Roediger could have compared the five treatments by using a series of simple experiments. However, using a single multivalued experiment has several advantages over using a series of simple experiments. We will only mention the two most obvious.

First, by doing a single five-value experiment, Roediger greatly reduced the number of experiments he had to perform. To compare all five treatments with one another, Roediger would have had to do 10 simple experiments. Specifically, he would have had to do:

• BOX 7-1 •

RANDOMLY ASSIGNING PARTICIPANTS TO MORE THAN TWO GROUPS

STEP 1   Across the top of a piece of paper write down your conditions. Under each condition draw a line for each participant you will need.

Group 1	Group 2	Group 3
_____	_____	_____
_____	_____	_____
_____	_____	_____
_____	_____	_____

STEP 2 Turn to a random numbers table (there's one in Table E-6, Appendix E). Roll a die to determine which column in the table you will use.

STEP 3 Assign the first number in the column to the first space under Group 1, the second number to the second space, and so forth.

When you have filled the spaces for Group 1, put the next number under the first space under Group 2. Similarly, when you fill all the spaces under Group 2, place the next number in the first space under Group 3.

Group 1	Group 2	Group 3
12	20	63
39	2	64
53	37	95
29	1	18

STEP 4 Assign the first person who participates in your study to the condition with the lowest random number. The second participant will be in the condition with the second lowest random number, and so on. Thus, in this example, your first two participants would be in Group 2, and your third participant would be in Group 1.

1. one experiment to compare rote rehearsal with imagery

2. another experiment to compare rote rehearsal with the method of loci

3. another to compare rote rehearsal with the link method

4. another to compare rote rehearsal with a peg system

5. another to compare imagery with the method of loci

6. another to compare imagery with the link method

7. another to compare imagery with a peg system

8. another to compare method of loci with the link method

9. another to compare method of loci with a peg system

10. another to compare the link method with a peg system

Second, he reduced the number of participants he had to test. If he had done 10 simple experiments, he would have needed 20 groups of participants. To have any degree of power (the ability to find significant differences), he would need at least 15 participants per group or a total of 300 (20 groups × 15 participants per group) participants.[1] With the five-group experiment, he could have the same power with 75 (15 × 5) participants.

✳ COMPARING TWO KINDS OF TREATMENTS WITH NO TREATMENT✳

Even when you are only interested in comparing two types of treatments, you may be better off avoiding the simple experiment. To understand why, let's consider the following fact: For certain kinds of back problems, people going to a chiropractor end up better off than those going for back surgery. Although an interesting fact, it leaves many questions unanswered. For example, is either treatment better than nothing? It could be that chiropractic treatment is the lesser of two evils. On the other hand, both treatments could be substantially better than no treatment. We don't know, because the researchers didn't compare either treatment to a no-treatment control condition.

In psychological research, we often compare two untested treatments. The simple experiment could tell us which is better than the other. However, we would not know whether the better one was the less harmful of two "bad" treatments or the more effective of two "good" treatments. Similarly, we would not know whether the lesser of the two treatments was (1) moderately harmful, (2) merely ineffective, or (3) mildly helpful. However, by using a three-group experiment that has a no-treatment control group, we would be able to judge not only how effective the two treatments were relative to each other, but also their overall, general effectiveness. For example, Allen, Schnyer, & Hitt (1998) compared acupuncture designed to reduce depression to acupuncture not specifically designed to reduce depression. They found that the group receiving acupuncture treatments specifically designed to reduce depression were less depressed than the group getting acupuncture not designed to reduce depression. However, if they had only used these two groups, they would not have known whether both treatments were better than no treatment or whether both treatments were worse than no treatment. Fortunately, they had a third group who received no treatment.[2] As it turned out, Allen, Schnyer, & Hitt's study did not find a clear superiority for acupuncture treatment over no treatment (although this failure to find a significant difference may have been due to not having enough participants).

✳ COMPARING MORE THAN TWO LEVELS (AMOUNTS) OF AN ✳ INDEPENDENT VARIABLE TO INCREASE EXTERNAL VALIDITY ✳

In the simple experiment, you want to pick two **levels (amounts) of the independent variable** that will allow you to find an effect. Intuitively, you realize

[1]Some researchers would say that, under most circumstances, 15 participants per group is too few. Indeed, in many cases, researchers should use 60—not 15—as the absolute minimum number of participants per group (Cohen, 1990). To have 60 participants per group, Roediger would have needed 1,200 participants had he done several simple experiments versus only 300 with a multiple-group experiment.

[2]Although this group of participants received no treatment during the study, they were added to a waiting list for treatment.

that the greater the difference between how the two groups are treated, the greater the chances of finding a significant effect. Therefore, when choosing levels of the independent variable, you may decide to choose levels that differ from each other as much as possible. Thus, if you were investigating the effects of exercise on depression, half of your participants would exercise very little, whereas the other half of your participants would exercise a great deal. Your results might be as follows:

Group 1: Low amounts of aerobic exercise: High levels of depression
Group 2: High amounts of aerobic exercise: High levels of depression

Uncovering Relationships

Based on these results, you would be tempted to conclude that there is no relationship between aerobic exercise and depression. Such a conclusion, however, would be a generalization based on very little evidence. That is, out of the many possible amounts of exercise you could have tested, you have sampled only two. To see how your conclusion about the effects of exercise could be wrong, imagine that aerobic exercise had the following effects on depression (see Figure 7-1):

Low amounts of aerobic exercise: No effect on depression
Medium amounts of aerobic exercise: Reduce depression
High amounts of aerobic exercise: No effect on depression

The u-shaped relationship we have postulated between exercise and depression is fairly common. Psychologists often find u-shaped and upside-down u-shaped relationships. Perhaps the most famous case is the Yerkes-Dodson Law, which states, in part, that:

1. With little motivation, performance is poor.
2. With moderate levels of motivation, performance is good.
3. With too much motivation, performance is poor.

You can probably think of many examples where (to paraphrase the littlest of the three bears) too little of some factor can be bad, too much can be bad, but a medium amount is just right.

If the relationship between aerobic exercise and depression is u-shaped and you pick extreme levels of your independent variable, you will falsely conclude that the treatment has no effect. Therefore, you might be tempted to choose moderate levels of the treatment. However, if the relationship is not u-shaped and you use moderate levels, your levels may not be far enough apart to allow you to detect a treatment effect. As you can see from Figure 7-1, picking the right levels of your independent variable for a simple experiment is a risky business.

To avoid making hard choices about which two levels to use, avoid simple experiments. Instead of choosing two levels, do experiments that use several levels of the independent variable so that you can choose three or more levels.

• **FIGURE 7-1** •

HOW A MULTIPLE-GROUP EXPERIMENT CAN GIVE YOU A MORE ACCURATE PICTURE OF A RELATIONSHIP THAN A SIMPLE EXPERIMENT

(a) A Multiple-Group Experiment

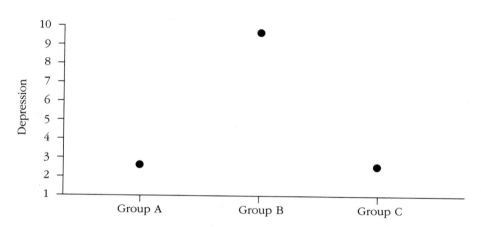

(b) Simple Experiment 1 Finds That Exercise Increases Depression

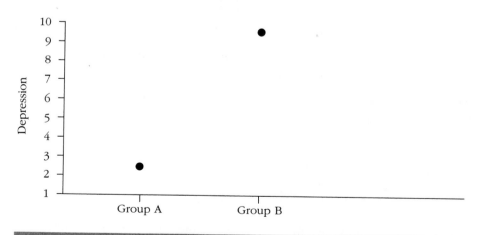

To illustrate the wisdom of using more than two levels, imagine that you used three levels of aerobic exercise in an experiment and obtained the following pattern of results:

• FIGURE 7-1 •

HOW A MULTIPLE-GROUP EXPERIMENT CAN GIVE YOU A MORE ACCURATE PICTURE OF A RELATIONSHIP THAN A SIMPLE EXPERIMENT

(c) Simple Experiment 2 Finds That Exercise Decreases Depression

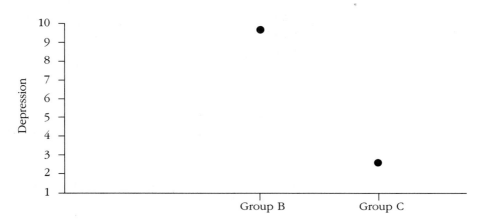

(d) Simple Experiment 3 Fails to Find an Effect of Exercise on Depression

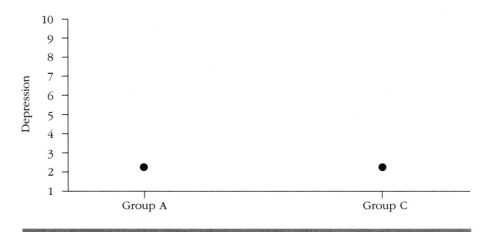

Group 1: Low aerobic exercise: High levels of depression

Group 2: Medium aerobic exercise: Low levels of depression

Group 3: High aerobic exercise: High levels of depression

Based on these results, you would correctly conclude that aerobic exercise affects depression. But what if you had only used two groups? If you had compared Groups 1 and 2, you would have concluded that exercise decreases depression. If you had compared Groups 2 and 3, you would have concluded that exercise increases depression. If you had compared Groups 1 and 3, you would have falsely concluded that exercise has no effect on depression (see Figure 7-1d).

Discovering the Nature of Relationships

You have seen that the researcher using the simple experiment may falsely conclude that a factor has no effect. Even if the researcher using a simple experiment finds a significant effect, that effect may apply only to the two levels used in the experiment. Thus, researchers who rely on simple experiments have difficulty generalizing their results to unexplored levels of the independent variable.

To accurately generalize results to unexplored levels of an independent variable, the researcher must be able to accurately graph the relationship between the independent and dependent variable. That is, the researcher must know the independent and dependent variables' **functional relationship:** the shape of the relationship. Simple experiments do not enable you to uncover the nature of a functional relationship.

To illustrate the weakness of the simple experiment in mapping the shape of a functional relationship, let's consider a simple experiment investigating the effects of aerobic exercise on happiness. Suppose that we obtained the following results:

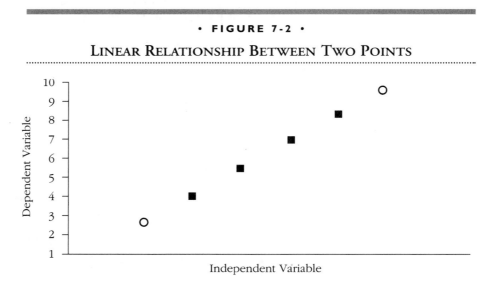

• FIGURE 7-2 •

LINEAR RELATIONSHIP BETWEEN TWO POINTS

Note: The circles represent known data points. The boxes in between the circles are what would happen at a given level of the independent variable if the relationship between the variables is linear. As you can see from the next figure (Figure 7-3), the functional relationship does not have to be linear.

Control group: 0 minutes of exercise per day   1.0 self-rating of happiness

Experimental group: 100 minutes of exercise per day   10.0 self-rating of happiness

From these data, can you determine the functional relationship between aerobic exercise and happiness? Perhaps the functional relationship is **linear** (like a straight line), as in Figure 7-2.

The true relationship, however, between exercise and happiness might not resemble a straight line. Instead, it might be a **nonlinear (curvilinear)** function, such as one of the curved lines in Figure 7-3.

Because many different-shaped lines can be drawn between two points (your two group means), the simple experiment does not help you discover the functional relationship between the variables. Because you would not know the functional relationship, you could do little more than guess if we asked you about the effects of 70 minutes of aerobic exercise. You might assume that the relationship is linear and therefore say that exercising 70 minutes a day would be better than no exercise and would be less effective than exercising for 100 minutes a day. But if your assumption of a linear relationship is wrong (and it well could be), then your guess would be inaccurate.

To get a line on the functional relationship between variables, you need to know more than two points. Therefore, suppose you expanded the simple experiment into a multilevel experiment by adding a group that gets 50 minutes of exercise a day. Then, you would have a much clearer idea of the functional relationship between exercise and happiness. As you can see in Figure 7-4, using three levels can give you a pretty good idea of the functional relationship among variables. If the relationship is linear, you should be able to draw a straight line through all three points. If the relationship is u-shaped, you will detect that too.

Because you can get a good picture of the functional relationship when you use three levels of the independent variable, you can make accurate predictions about unexplored levels of the independent variable. For example, if the functional relationship between aerobic exercise and happiness were linear, you would obtain the following pattern of results:

Group 1: 0 minutes of exercise per day   1.0 self-rating of happiness

Group 2: 50 minutes of exercise per day   5.5 self-rating of happiness

Group 3: 100 minutes of exercise per day   10.0 self-rating of happiness

In that case, you could confidently predict that 70 minutes of exercise would be less beneficial for increasing happiness than 100 minutes of exercise. If, on the other hand, the relationship was **s**-shaped (as in Figure 7-3), you might get the following pattern of results:

Group 1: 0 minutes of exercise per day   1.0 self-rating of happiness

Group 2: 50 minutes of exercise per day   10.0 self-rating of happiness

Group 3: 100 minutes of exercise per day   10.0 self-rating of happiness

• **FIGURE 7-3** •

SOME POSSIBLE NONLINEAR RELATIONSHIPS

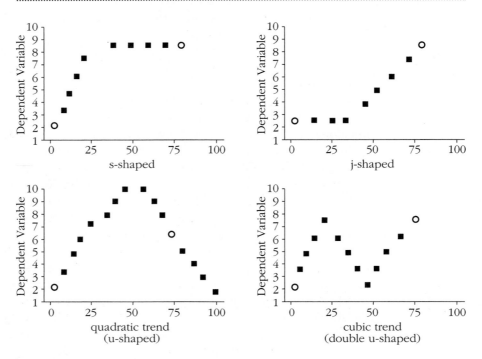

Note: The circles represent the known data points. The boxes in between the circles are what might happen at a given level of the independent variable depending on whether the relationship between the variables is characterized by (a) an s-shaped (negatively accelerated) trend, (b) a j-shaped (positively accelerated) trend, (c) a u-shaped (quadratic) trend, or (d) a double u-shaped (cubic) trend.

In that case, you would predict that a person who exercised 70 minutes would do as well as someone exercising 100 minutes a day.

The more groups you use, the more accurately you can pin down the shape of the functional relationship. Yet, despite this fact, you do not have to use numerous levels of the independent variable. Why? Because nature prefers simple patterns. That is, most functional relationships are linear, and few are more complex than u-shaped functions. Consequently, you will rarely need more than four levels of the independent variable to pin down a functional relationship. In fact, you will usually need no more than three carefully chosen levels to identify the functional relationship among variables.

• FIGURE 7-4 •

HAVING THREE LEVELS OF THE INDEPENDENT VARIABLE (THREE DATA POINTS) AIDS GREATLY IN DETERMINING THE SHAPE OF THE FUNCTIONAL RELATIONSHIP

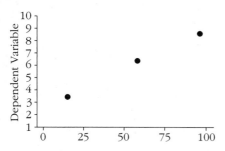

With these three points, we can be relatively confident that the relationship is linear. Most nonlinear relationships (see Figure 7-3) would not produce data that would fit these three data points.

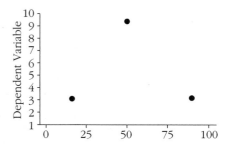

If we got these three data points, we could be relatively confident that the relationship is curvilinear. Specifically, we would suspect we had a quadratic trend.

Summary: Multilevel Experiments and External Validity

In summary, knowing the functional relationship between two variables is almost as important as knowing that a relationship exists. You want to be able to say more than: "If you exercise 100 minutes a day, you will be happier than someone who exercises 0 minutes a day." Who exercises exactly 100 minutes a day? You want to be able to generalize your results so that you can tell people the effects of exercising 50 minutes, 56 minutes, 75 minutes, and so forth. Yet, you have no intention of testing the effects of every single possible amount of exercise a person might do. Instead, you want to test only a handful of exercise levels. If you chose these levels carefully, you would be able to accurately map the functional relationship between the variables. Mapping the functional relationship, in turn, will allow you to make educated predictions about the effects of exercise levels that you have not directly tested.

USING MULTIPLE LEVELS TO IMPROVE CONSTRUCT VALIDITY

You have seen that multilevel experiments—because their results can generalize to a wider range of treatment levels—can have more external validity than simple experiments. In this section, you will learn that multilevel experiments can also have more construct validity than simple experiments.

Confounding Variables in the Simple Experiment

In Chapter 6, you saw that simple experiments—thanks to random assignment—are able to rule out the effects of variables unrelated to the treatment manipulation. For example, because of random assignment, the effects of participant variables such as gender, race, and personality usually will not be confused for a treatment effect. In other words, a statistically significant difference between the control group and the experimental group will probably not be due to the groups being different before the treatment was introduced.

So, simple experiments effectively control for the effects of variables that have nothing to do with the treatment manipulation, such as individual differences among participants. But what if the treatment manipulation is manipulating more than one variable? For example, what if the "exercise" manipulation is also manipulating social support? Simple experiments are not always effective in ruling out the effects of variables that are manipulated along with the treatment.

In an ideal world, this limitation of the simple experiment would not be a problem. Ideally, your treatment would be a pure manipulation that creates one—and only one—difference between the experimental group and the control group. Unfortunately, it is rare to have a perfect manipulation. Instead, the treatment manipulation usually produces not one, but several, differences between how the experimental and control groups are treated. For example, suppose that a simple experiment apparently found that the "attractive" defendant was more likely to get a light sentence than the "unattractive" defendant. We would know that the "attractiveness" manipulation had an effect. However, it could be that, in addition to manipulating attractiveness, the researchers also manipulated perceived wealth. Thus, wealth, rather than attractiveness, might account for the manipulation's effect. For example, people may be less likely to give wealthy defendants long sentences.

Because of impurities in manipulations, the results of simple experiments are often difficult to interpret. That is, you often end up knowing that the treatment manipulation had an effect, but you may have trouble saying what it was about the treatment manipulation that produced the effect. In other words, you may worry that the treatment manipulated more than one variable. In short, simple experiments may lack construct validity because the independent variable manipulation is contaminated by **confounding variables:** variables that are unintentionally manipulated along with the treatment.

The following example[3] illustrates the general problem of confounding. Imagine being in a classroom that has five light switches. You want to know what the middle light switch does. Assume that in the "control" condition, all the light switches are off. In the "experimental" condition, you want to flick the middle switch. However, because it is dark, you accidentally flick on the middle three switches. As the lights come on, the janitor bursts into the room, and

---

[3]We are indebted to an anonymous reviewer for this example and other advice about confounding variables.

your "experiment" is finished. What can you conclude? You can conclude that your manipulation of the light switches had an effect. That is, your study has internal validity. However, because you manipulated more than just the middle light switch, you can't say that you know what the middle light switch did. Put another way, if you were to call your manipulation a "manipulation of the middle switch," your manipulation would have little construct validity.

Because of confounding variables, it is often hard to know what it is about the treatment that caused the effect. In real life, variables are often confounded. For example, someone may know they got a hangover from drinking too much wine, but not know whether it was the alcohol in the wine, the preservatives in the wine, or something else about the wine that produced the awful sensations. A few years ago, a couple of our students joked that they could easily test the hypothesis that alcohol was responsible. All they needed us to do was donate enough money to buy mass quantities of a pure manipulation of alcohol—180 proof, totally devoid of impurities. These students understood how confounding variables can contaminate real-life manipulations, thus making it hard to know what it was about the manipulation that caused the effect.

To understand how confounding variables can contaminate a simple experiment, let's go back to the simple experiment on the effects of exercise that we proposed earlier in this chapter. You will recall that the experimental group got 100 minutes of exercise class per day, the control group got nothing. Clearly, the experimental group participants are being treated very differently than the control group participants. The groups didn't merely differ in terms of the independent variable (exercise). They also differed in terms of several other (confounding) variables: The exercise group received more attention and had more structured social activities than the control group.

Hypothesis-Guessing in Simple Experiments   Furthermore, participants in the experimental group knew they were getting a treatment whereas participants in the control group knew they were not receiving any special treatment. If experimental group participants suspected that the exercise program should have an effect, the exercise program may appear to have an effect—even if exercise does not really improve mood. In other words, the construct validity of the study might be ruined because the experimental group participants guessed the hypothesis (**hypothesis-guessing**).

Because of the impurities (confounding variables) of this manipulation, you cannot say that the difference between groups is due to exercise by itself. Although all manipulations have impurities, this study's most obvious—and avoidable—impurities stem from having an **empty control group:** a group that gets no treatment, not even a placebo. Thus, if you could get rid of—or replace—the empty control group, you could reduce the impact of confounding variables.

How Multilevel Experiments Can Detect Problems With Empty Control Groups   If you insist on using an empty control group, the multilevel experiment may alert you if there are problems with such a group. To illustrate, imagine that you have a three-level experiment where:

1. The first group gets no treatment.
2. The second group gets 20 minutes of aerobic exercise.
3. The third group gets 40 minutes of aerobic exercise.

In this multilevel experiment, the two experimental groups are being treated almost identically. They only differ in terms of how much exercise they get. Consequently, any difference between the experimental groups is probably due to the amount of exercise, rather than to incidental, confounding variables (such as socializing with class members or setting goals).

The participants in the two experimental groups would also have a hard time figuring out the hypothesis and playing along with it. There is no way that they are going to figure out: (1) that there is an empty control group and two exercise groups; (2) that they are in the medium exercise group; and (3) that by acting a certain way, they will get scores that will be higher than the control group's and lower than the high exercise group's.

Probably the best they could do is to figure out that if they are in the no-exercise group they should behave normally, but they should behave differently if they are in an exercise group. That is, participants may be able to guess that they should act one way if they received a treatment and another way if they did not. However, participants would not be able to guess that they should behave one way when they are in one treatment group and a different way when they are in another treatment group. They would probably not even guess that there was more than one treatment group. However, even if they did, they would not know whether their group was getting less of the treatment or more of the treatment than the other treatment group. Therefore, if the treatment didn't have an effect and participants were just trying to play along with the hypothesis, there would be no difference between the two experimental groups. That is, even though the two experimental groups got different levels of treatment, participants would not know that there were two experimental groups and thus would not be able to play along with that part of the hypothesis.

Because participants can only guess and play along with part of the hypothesis, you should be able to determine whether the results of a multilevel experiment are solely due to hypothesis-guessing. To see if you can, go to Table 7-1. There you will find the results of Experiment *A* and Experiment *B*. In one of these experiments, the differences between the groups are due to hypothesis-guessing. Do you think Experiment *A* or Experiment *B* is the flawed experiment? How do you know?

If you think Experiment *B* is the tainted experiment, you are correct! Why did you suspect Experiment *B*? You probably realized that if participants were

• TABLE 7-1 •

A COMPARISON BETWEEN TWO EXPERIMENTS

EXPERIMENT A		EXPERIMENT B	
CONDITION	MOOD	CONDITION	MOOD
No exercise	8.0	No exercise	8.0
Medium exercise	9.5	Medium exercise	11.5
High exercise	11.5	High exercise	11.5

Note: Numbers indicate ratings on a 0–15 self-report scale of mood. Higher numbers indicate better mood.

trying to guess the hypothesis, the experimental groups would differ from the control group, but not from each other. Thus, hypothesis-guessing would produce Experiment *B*'s pattern of results.

To look at the problem a different way, why didn't you suspect Experiment *A*? You probably assumed that if exercise has an effect, a high level of exercise would have a greater effect than a medium level of exercise. Thus, if exercise had an effect, you would expect Experiment *A*'s pattern of results.

It's important to recognize that your assumption that more treatment should lead to more effect is an assumption—an assumption that could be wrong. However, it is remarkable how often nature conforms to this assumption.

Increasing Validity Through Several Control Groups

You have seen that using a multiple-group experiment allows you to do something you cannot do with a simple experiment—have a control group and have more than one treatment group. You have seen that using several treatment groups can sometimes allow you to detect a problem with your control group. In addition to allowing you to use multiple treatment groups, multiple-group experiments allow you to do something else you cannot do with a simple experiment—use multiple control groups.

Because you cannot use multiple control groups in a simple experiment, the person using a simple experiment is often forced to choose between control groups. For example, the researcher may have to choose between using a placebo treatment group that gets a pseudotreatment or an empty control group that gets no treatment whatsoever. With a multiple-group experiment, on the other hand, you do not have to choose. You can have as many control groups as you need.

The Value of a Placebo Group To see how hard it can be to choose between an empty control group and a placebo group, let's go back to the problem of examining the effects of aerobic exercise on mood. If you use an empty control group that has nothing done to them, interpreting your results may be difficult. For example, if the aerobic exercise group does better than this "left alone" group, the results could be due to hypothesis-guessing or to any number of confounding variables (such as socializing with other students in the class, being put into a structured routine, etc.).

If, on the other hand, you use a placebo-treatment group (for example, meditation classes), you would be able to control for many of these confounding variables. Still, your problems are not over.

The Value of an Empty Control Group: "Placebos" May Not Be Placebos

Your problems are not over because you may not know what the effect of your placebo treatment will be. Ideally, you would like to believe that your placebo treatment has no effect. In that case, if the treatment group does worse than the placebo group, the treatment is harmful; if the treatment group does better, the treatment is helpful.

If, however, what you hope is a placebo treatment turns out to be a treatment that really does have an effect, then you are going to have trouble evaluating the effect of your treatment. For example, suppose you find that the exercise group is more depressed than the meditation group. Could you conclude that exercise increases depression? No, because it might be that although exercise reduces depression, meditation reduces it more. Conversely, if you found that the exercise group is less depressed than the meditation group, you could not automatically conclude that exercise decreases depression. It may be that meditation increases depression greatly, and exercise increases depression only moderately. That is, exercise may simply be the lesser of two evils. To find out whether exercise increases or decreases depression, you need to compare the exercise group to a no-treatment group. Thus, if you were interested in the effects of exercise on depression, you have two options: (1) Use a simple experiment and make the hard choice between an empty control group and a placebo group, or (2) Use a multiple-group experiment so that you can include both an empty and a placebo control group.

Using Multiple Imperfect Control Groups to Make up for Not Having the Perfect Control Group

Even if you are sure you do not want to use an empty control group, you may still need more than one control group because you will probably not have the perfect control group. Instead, you may have several groups, each of which controls for some confounding variables but not for others. If you were to do a simple experiment, you may have to decide which of several placebo groups to use. Choosing one control group—when you realize you need more than one—is frustrating. It would be better to be able to use as many as you need.

But how often do you really need more than one control group? More often than you might think. In fact, it is so easy to underestimate the need for control groups that even professional psychologists sometimes underestimate the need for control groups. Indeed, many professional researchers get their research articles rejected because a reviewer concluded that they failed to include enough good control groups (Fiske & Fogg, 1990).

You often need more than one control group so that your study will have adequate construct validity. That is, with even a poor control group, your study has internal validity: You know that the treatment group scored differently than the control group. But what is it about the treatment that is causing the effect? Without good control group(s), you may think that one aspect of your treatment (the exercise) is causing the effect, when the difference is really due to some other aspect of your treatment (the socializing that occurs during exercise).

To illustrate how even a good control group may still differ from the experimental group in several ways having nothing to do with the independent variable, consider the meditation control group. The meditation control group has several advantages over the empty control group. For example, if the exercise group was less depressed than a meditation control group, we could be confident that this difference was not due to hypothesis-guessing, engaging in structured activities, or being distracted from worrisome thoughts for awhile. Both groups received a "treatment," both engaged in structured activities, and both were distracted for the same length of time.

The groups, however, may differ in that the exercise group did a more social type of activity, listened to louder and more upbeat music, and interacted with a more energetic and enthusiastic instructor. Therefore, the exercise group may be less depressed for several reasons having nothing to do with exercise: (1) liking their exercise partners; (2) feeling arousal and positive mood as a result of the music; and (3) being exposed to a very upbeat leader.

To rule out all these possibilities, you might use several control groups. For example, to control for the "social activity" and the "energetic model" explanations, you might add a group that went to a no-credit acting class taught by a very enthusiastic professor. To control for the music explanation, you might add a control group that listened to music or perhaps even watched aerobic dance videos. By using all of these control groups, you may be able to rule out the effects of confounding variables.

ANALYSIS OF MULTIPLE-GROUP EXPERIMENTS

You have just learned that multiple control groups may give you more construct validity than one control group. Earlier, you learned that multiple treatment groups will allow you to more accurately map the functional relationship between the independent variable and the dependent variable than a two-group experiment. Before that, you learned that the multiple-group experiment allows you to compare more treatments at one time than a two-group experiment. In short, you have learned that there are at least three good reasons to conduct a multiple-group experiment:

1. to improve construct validity
2. to map functional relationships
3. to compare several treatments at once

To conduct a good multiple-group experiment, you must understand the logic behind analyzing the results of a multiple-group experiment. To reiterate, you should understand that logic before conducting your study. As you will see, the way that you must analyze your results has implications for what treatment groups you will use, how many participants you will have, and even what your hypothesis will be.

Even if you never conduct a multiple-group experiment, you will read articles that report results of such experiments. To understand those articles, you must understand the logic and vocabulary used in analyzing them. Therefore, in the next few sections, you will learn the logic behind analyzing the results of a multiple-group experiment.

ANALYZING THE MULTIPLE-GROUP EXPERIMENT: AN INTUITIVE OVERVIEW

As a first step to understanding how multiple-group experiments are analyzed, let's look at data from three experiments that compared the effects of no-treatment, meditation, and aerobic exercise on happiness. All of these experiments had 12 participants rate their feelings of happiness on a 0 (not at all happy) to 100 (very happy) scale. Here are the results of Experiment A:

	NO-TREATMENT	MEDITATION	EXERCISE
	50	51	53
	51	53	53
	52	52	54
	<u>51</u>	<u>52</u>	<u>52</u>
Group Means	51	52	53

Compare these results to the results of Experiment B:

	NO-TREATMENT	MEDITATION	EXERCISE
	40	60	78
	42	60	82
	38	58	80
	<u>40</u>	<u>62</u>	<u>80</u>
Group Means	40	60	80

Are you more confident that Experiment A or Experiment B found a significant effect for the treatment variable? If you say B, why do you give B as your answer? You answer B because there is a bigger difference between the groups in Experiment B than in Experiment A. That is, the group means for Experiment B are farther apart than the group means for Experiment A.

Why does having the means farther apart—what statisticians call greater **variability between group means**—make you decide that Experiment B is more likely to be the study that obtained significant results? There are probably at least two reasons why you think bigger between-groups variability gives you a better shot at finding a treatment effect.

First, you intuitively realize that you need between-group variability if you are going to find a treatment effect. That is, if between-group variability were zero, then all the group means would be the same. If all the groups, regardless of how much of the treatment they got, have the same mean, you can't argue that the treatment made the groups different.

Second, you intuitively realize a small difference between group means might easily be due to chance (rather than to the treatment), but a larger difference is less likely to be due to chance.[4] Thus, you realize that the more variability there is between group means, the more likely it is that at least some of that variability is due to treatment.

Now, compare Experiment B with Experiment C. The results of Experiment C are listed below.

	EXERCISE	NO-TREATMENT	MEDITATION
	10	10	100
	80	90	80
	60	60	60
	<u>10</u>	<u>80</u>	<u>80</u>
Group Means	40	60	80

Do you think the results from Experiment B or Experiment C are more likely to indicate a real treatment effect? Both experiments have the same amount of variability between group means. Therefore, unlike in our first example, you cannot use the rule of choosing the experiment with the means that differ the most to choose Experiment B. Yet, once again, you will pick Experiment B. Why?

You will pick Experiment B because you are concerned about one aspect of Experiment C: the extreme amount of variability within each group. You realize that the only reason that the scores within a group vary is because of random error. (The scores cannot differ from each other due to the treatment because all those participants got the same treatment.) Thus, you see that Experiment C is more affected by random error than Experiment B.

The large amount of random error in Experiment C (as revealed by the *within-groups* variability) bothers you because you realize that this random

---

[4]Similarly, if your favorite team lost by one point, you might blame luck. However, if your team lost by 30 points, you would be less likely to say that bad luck alone was responsible for the defeat.

variability—rather than the treatment—might also be the reason the groups differ from one another. That is, the same random variability that makes individual scores within a group differ from each other might also make the group means differ from each other.[5] In Experiment B, on the other hand, the small amount of within-group variability indicates that there is virtually no random variability in the data. Therefore, in Experiment B, you feel fairly confident that random error is not causing the group means to differ from one another. Instead, you believe that the means differ from one another because of the treatment.

Intuitively then, you understand the three most important principles behind analyzing the results of a multiple-group experiment. Specifically, you realize that:

1. Within-group variability is not due to the treatment, but instead is due to random error. That is, differences within a treatment group can't be due to the treatment because everyone in the group is getting the same treatment. Instead, differences among group members must be due to factors such as individual differences and random measurement error.

2. Between-group variability is not a pure measure of treatment effects. Admittedly, treatment effects should cause the groups to differ from one another. However, random variability will also cause the groups to differ from one another. Consequently, even if no treatment were administered, the group means would probably differ. In other words, between-group variability is not a pure index of variability due to treatment (treatment effects) because it also is affected by random error.

3. If you compare between-group variability (the effects of random error plus any treatment effects) to within-group variability (the effects of only random error), you may be able to determine whether the treatment had an effect.

A CLOSER LOOK AT THE ANALYSIS OF A MULTIPLE-GROUP EXPERIMENT

You now have a general idea of how to analyze data from a multiple-group study. To better understand the logic and vocabulary used in these analyses—a must if you are to understand an author's or a computer's report of such an analysis—read the next few sections.

Within-Groups Variability: A Pure Measure of Error

As you already know, within-groups variability does not reflect the effects of treatment. Instead, it reflects the effects of random error. For example, since all

---

[5]To get a sense of how random sampling error might cause the group means to differ, randomly sample two scores from the no-treatment group. Compute the mean of this group. If you do this several times, you will get different means. These different means can't be due to a treatment effect because you are sampling from a group of participants who are all getting no treatment. The reason you are getting different means even though you are sampling the same group is random sampling error. Fortunately, statistics can help us determine how likely it is that the differences among group means are entirely due to random error.

the participants in the meditation group are getting the same treatment (meditation), any differences among those participants' scores can't be due to the treatment. Instead of being due to treatment effects, the differences among scores of meditation group participants are due to such random factors as individual differences, unreliability of the measure, and lack of standardization. Similarly, differences among the scores of participants in the no-treatment group are not due to treatment, but to irrelevant random factors. The same is true for differences within the exercise group. Thus, calculating within-groups variability will tell us the extent to which chance causes individual scores to differ from each other. If we know how much random error causes individual scores to differ from each other, we can estimate the extent to which random error causes group means to differ from each other.

To measure this within-groups variability, we first look at the variability of the scores within each group. To be more specific, we calculate an index of variability called the variance. If we have three groups, we could calculate a variance for each group, giving us three separate indexes of within-groups variability. We would then have three separate estimates of the extent to which the groups could differ due to random error alone. Since we only want one estimate of variability due to random error, we average all these within-group variances to come up with the best estimate of random variability—the within-groups variance. Because the **within-groups variance** gives us an index of the degree to which *random error* alone may cause your group means to differ, within-groups variance is also referred to as **error variance**.

Between-Groups Variability: Error Plus (Possibly) Treatment

Once you have a measure of within-groups variability, the next step is to get an index of the degree to which your groups vary from one another. It is at this step where it becomes obvious that you cannot use a *t*-test to analyze data from a multiple-group experiment. When using a *t*-test, you determine the degree to which the groups differ from one another in a very straightforward manner: You subtract the average score of Group 1 from the average score of Group 2. Subtraction works well when you want to compare two groups, but does not work well when you have more than two groups. You can only subtract two scores at a time. So, if you have three groups, which two groups do you compare? Group 1 with Group 2? Or, Group 2 with Group 3? Or, Group 1 with Group 3?

You might answer this question by saying "all of the above." Thus, with three groups, you would do three *t*-tests: One compares Group 1 against Group 2, a second compares Group 1 against Group 3, and a third compares Group 2 against Group 3. However, that's not allowed!

An analogy will help you understand why you cannot use multiple *t*-tests. Suppose a stranger comes up to you with a proposition: "Let's bet on coin flips. If I get a 'head,' you give me a dollar. If I don't, I give you a dollar." You accept the proposition. He then proceeds to flip three coins at once and then makes you pay up if even one of the coins comes up heads. Why is this unfair? This is unfair because he misled you: You thought he was only going to flip one coin at a time, so you thought he had only a 50% chance of winning. But since he's flipping three coins at a time, his chances of getting at least one head are much better than 50%.

When you do multiple t-tests, you are doing basically the same thing as the coin hustler. You start by telling people the odds that a single t-test will be significant due to chance alone. For example, if you use conventional significance levels, you would tell people that—if the treatment has no effect—the odds of getting a statistically significant result for a particular t-test are less than 5 in 100. In other words, you are claiming that your chance of making a Type 1 error is no more than 5%.

Then, just as the hustler gave himself more than a 50% chance of winning by flipping more than one coin, you give yourself a more than 5% chance of getting a statistically significant result by doing more than one t-test. The 5% odds you quoted would only hold if you had done a single t-test. If you are using t-tests to compare three groups, you will do three t-tests. If you do three t-tests, the odds of at least one turning out significant by chance alone are much more than 5%.

So far, we've talked about the problems of using a t-test when you have a three-group experiment. What happens if your experiment has more than three groups? Then, the t-test becomes even more deceptive (just as you would be in even worse shape if the person you were betting against flipped more than three coins at a time). The more groups you use in your experiment, the greater the difference between the significance level you report and the actual odds of at least one t-test being significant by chance (Hays, 1981). Just to give you an idea of how great the difference between your stated significance level and the actual odds can be, suppose you had six levels of the independent variable. To compare all six groups with one another, you would need to do 15 t-tests. If you did 15 t-tests and used a .05 significance level, the probability of getting at least one significant effect by chance alone would be more than 50%! That is, your risk of making a Type 1 error is 10 times greater than you are claiming it is.

As you have seen, the t-test is not useful for analyzing data from the multiple-group experiment because the t-test measures the degree to which groups differ by using subtraction—and you can only subtract two group averages at a time. To calculate the degree to which more than two group means differ, you need to calculate a variance between those means.

The between-groups variance indicates the extent to which the group means differ. Thus, if all your groups have the same mean, between-groups variance would be zero (because there are no differences between your group means). If, on the other hand, there are large differences between the group means, between-group variance will be large.

So, the size of the between-groups variance depends on the extent to which the group means differ. What affects the extent to which the group means differ? As you saw earlier, two factors affect the extent to which group means differ.

One factor is random error. Even if the treatment has no effect, random error alone may cause differences between the group means. If the experiment is not designed to minimize the effects of random error, random error alone may cause the group means to be quite different from each other. For example, if the experiment is poorly standardized and uses an unreliable measure, heterogeneous participants, and few participants per group, then the average of one treatment group may be quite different from the average of a different treatment group—even though the treatment has no effect. If the effects of random error were kept to a minimum, random error alone would create smaller differences between the group means. Even then, however, random error alone would probably create some between-groups variance. Thus, even when there is no treatment effect, between-groups variance would probably not be zero. Instead, when there is no treatment effect, between-groups variance should be roughly equivalent to a more direct measure of random error—within-groups variance.

The other factor that *may* affect the extent to which the groups differ from each other is the treatment effect. If the treatment has an effect, the differences between the group means should be greater than when the treatment doesn't have an effect. Because of the treatment effect's strong influence on the size of the between-groups variance, the between-groups variance is often called **treatment variance.**

To recap, when there is a treatment effect, the between-group variance is the sum of two quantities: an estimate of random error plus an estimate of treatment effects. Therefore, if the treatment has an effect, between-groups variance (which is affected by the treatment plus random error) will be larger than the within-groups variance (which is only affected by random error).

Comparing Between-Groups Variance to Within-Groups Variance: Are the Differences Between Groups Due to More Than Random Error?

Once you have the between-groups variance (an estimate of random error plus any treatment effects) and the within-groups variance (an estimate of random error), the next step is to compare the two variances. If the between-groups variance is larger than the within-groups variance, then some of the between-groups variance may be due to a treatment effect. Because you will determine whether the treatment had an effect by comparing (analyzing) the between-groups variance to the within-groups variance, this statistical technique is called analysis of variance (ANOVA).

But when doing an ANOVA, how do you compare your two variances? You might think that you would compare your two variances by subtracting them from one another like this:

Between-groups variance (random error + possible treatment effects) − Within-groups variance (random error) = Treatment effect

However, in analysis of variance (ANOVA), you compare your two variances by dividing rather than by subtracting. Specifically, you set up the following ratio:

$$\frac{\text{Between-Groups Variance}}{\text{Within-Groups Variance}}$$

Instead of using the term *variance,* you are more likely to see the term *Mean Square.* Thus, you are more likely to read about authors setting up the following ratio:

$$\frac{\text{Mean Square Between Groups}}{\text{Mean Square Within Groups}}$$

Note that authors tend to leave off the word *groups.* As a result, you are likely to see the ratio described as

$$\frac{\text{Mean Square Between}}{\text{Mean Square Within}}$$

To shorten the expression even further, authors tend to abbreviate Mean Square Between as MSB and Mean Square Within as MSW. Thus, you are likely to see the ratio of the variances described as

$$\frac{\text{MSB}}{\text{MSW}}$$

To complicate things further, recall that authors may not use the terms *between or within.* Rather than use a name that refers to how these variances were calculated, authors may instead use a name that refers to what these variances estimate. Thus, because between-groups variance is, in part, an estimate of treatment effects, authors may refer to MS Between as Mean Square *Treatment* (abbreviated MST). Similarly, because within-groups variance is an estimate of the degree to which random error is affecting estimates of the treatment group means, authors may refer to Mean Square *Within* as Mean Square *Error* (abbreviated MSE).

Regardless of what names or abbreviations they give the two variances, the ratio of the between-groups variance to the within-groups variance is called the **F-ratio.** The following are all *F*-ratios:

$$\frac{\text{MSB}}{\text{MSW}} = \frac{\text{MS Treatment}}{\text{MS Error}} = \frac{\text{MST}}{\text{MSE}}$$

Thus, when reading articles, you may see tables resembling the one below:

SOURCE	MEAN SQUARE	*F*
Treatment	10	2
Error	5	

Conceptually, the *F*-ratio can be portrayed as follows:

$$F = \frac{\text{Random Error + Possible Treatment Effect}}{\text{Random Error}}$$

Why an *F* of 1 Does Not Show That the Treatment Had an Effect   By examining this conceptual formula, you can see that the *F*-ratio will rarely be much less than 1. To illustrate, imagine that there is no (zero) treatment effect. In that case, the formula is (random error + 0)/random error, which reduces to random error/random error. As you know, if you divide a number by itself (e.g., 5/5, 8/8), you get 1.[6] Put another way, if the null hypothesis were true, the between-groups variance and the within-groups variance should be roughly equivalent because both are measuring the same thing—random error.

You now know that if the null hypothesis were true, the *F*-ratio would be approximately 1.00.[7] That is,

$$F = \frac{\text{Random Error + 0}}{\text{Random Error}} = 1.00$$

But what would happen to the *F*-ratio if the treatment had an effect? To answer this question, let's look at what a treatment effect would do to the top and the bottom half of the *F*-ratio.

If the treatment has an effect, the top of the *F*-ratio, the between-groups variance, should get bigger. It now represents random error plus the treatment effect. That is, the three group means are not differing from each other merely because of chance. They now also differ from each other because they received different levels of the treatment.

To repeat, when the treatment does not have an effect, the variance among group means (Mean Square Between) is due only to random error. However, when the treatment does have an effect, the variance among group means is due not only to random error, but also to the treatment causing real differences between the groups. Thus, when the treatment has an effect, the top of the *F*-ratio (MS Between) will get larger.

We have been talking about what a treatment effect does to the *top* of the *F*-ratio, but what does a treatment effect do to the *bottom* of the *F*-ratio? Nothing. Whether or not there is a treatment effect, the bottom of the *F*-ratio, the within-groups variance, always represents only random error. In a three-group experiment, Group 1's scores would differ from one another only because of

---

[6]The only exception is that 0/0=0.

[7]If you get an *F* below 1.00, it indicates that you have found no evidence of a treatment effect. Indeed, in the literature, you will often find statements such as, "There were no other significant results, all *F*s < 1." If you get an *F* substantially below 1.00, you may want to check to be sure you did not make a computation error.

random error. The same is true of Group 2's scores differing from one another, and Group 3's scores differing from one another.

We have discussed the top and the bottom of the F-ratio. You know that both random error and treatment effects affect the top of the F-ratio, whereas only random error affects the bottom of the F-ratio. Thus, treatment effects increase the top of the F-ratio but have no effect on the bottom of the F-ratio.

Let's now use our knowledge of how treatment effects influence the parts of the F-ratio to understand how treatment effects influence the F-ratio. When there is a treatment effect, the differences among group means are due not only to random error (the only thing that affects within-groups variance), but also to the treatment's effect. Consequently, when there is a treatment effect, the between-groups variance should be larger than the within-groups variance. Put more mathematically, when there is a treatment effect, you would expect the ratio of between-groups variance to within-groups variance to be greater than 1. That is:

$$F = \frac{\text{between-groups variance (treatment + random error)}}{\text{within-groups variance (random error)}} > 1,$$

when the treatment has an effect

Using an F-Table However, not all Fs above 1.00 are statistically significant. To determine whether an F-ratio is enough above 1.00 to indicate that there is a significant difference between your groups, you need to consult an F-table, like the one in Appendix E.

Calculating Degrees of Freedom To use the F-table, you need to know two degrees of freedom: one for the top of the F-ratio (between-groups variance, MS treatment) and one for the bottom of the F-ratio (within-groups variance, MS error).

Calculating the degrees of freedom for the top of the F-ratio (between-groups variance) is simple. It's just one less than the number of values of the independent variable. So, if you have three values of the independent variable (no-treatment, meditation, and exercise), you have 2 (3 − 1) degrees of freedom. If you had four values of the independent variable (no-treatment, meditation, archery, aerobic exercise), then you would have 3 (4 − 1) degrees of freedom. Thus, for the experiments we have discussed in this chapter, *the degrees of freedom for the between-groups variance equals the Number of Groups − 1.*

Computing the degrees of freedom for the bottom of the F-ratio (within-groups variance) is also fairly easy. The formula is N (number of participants) − G (groups). Thus, if there are 20 participants and 2 groups, the degrees of freedom = 18 (20 − 2 = 18).[8]

---

[8]As you may recall, you could have used this $N − G$ formula to get the degrees of freedom for the t-test described in Chapter 6. However, because the t-test always compares two groups, people often memorize the formula $N − 2$ for the t-test instead of the more general formula $N − G$.

Let's now apply this formula to some multiple-group experiments. If we have 33 participants and 3 groups, the df for the error term = 30 (because 33 − 3 = 30). If we had 30 participants and 5 groups, the df error would = 25 (because 30 − 5 = 25). To repeat, *the simplest way of computing the error* df *for the experiments we discussed in this chapter is to use the formula* N–G, *where* N = *total number of participants and* G = *total number of groups* (see Table 7-2).

Once you know the degrees of freedom, you can simply find the column in the F-table that corresponds to those degrees of freedom. If your F-ratio is larger than the value listed, then the results are statistically significant at the $p < .05$ level.

The Meaning of Statistical Significance in ANOVA

If your results are statistically significant, what does that mean? As you may recall from Chapter 6, *statistical significance means that you can reject the null hypothesis.* In the multiple-group experiment, the null hypothesis is that the differences among all your group means are due to chance. That is, all your groups are essentially the same. Rejecting this hypothesis means that, because of treatment effects, all your groups are not the same. In other words, you can conclude that at least two of your groups differ. But which ones? Even in a three-group experiment, there are several possibilities: Group 1 might differ from Group 2 and/or Group 2 might differ from Group 3 and/or Group 1 might differ from Group 3. As we just said, a significant F does not tell you which groups differ. Therefore, once you have performed an F-test to determine that at least some of your groups differ, you need to do additional tests to determine which of your groups differ from one another.

Beyond ANOVA: Pinpointing a Significant Effect

You might think that all you would have to do to determine which groups differ is compare group means. Some group means, however, may differ from others solely as a result of chance. To determine which group differences are due to treatment effects, you need to do additional tests. These additional, more specific tests are called post hoc t-tests.

Post Hoc t-Tests Among Group Means: Which Groups Differ?   At this point, you may be saying that you wanted to do t-tests all along. Before you complain to us, please hear our two-pronged defense.

• TABLE 7-2 •

CALCULATING DEGREES OF FREEDOM

SOURCE OF VARIANCE (*SV*)	CALCULATION OF *DF*
Treatment (between groups)	Number of Groups − 1 ($G − 1$)
Within subjects (error variance)	Number of participants minus number of groups ($N − G$)

First, you can only go in and do **post hoc tests** *after* you get a significant *F*-test. That is, you can't legitimately use follow-up tests to ask "which of the groups differ" until you first establish that at least some of the groups do indeed differ. To do post hoc tests without finding a significant *F* is considered statistical malpractice. Such behavior would be like a physician doing a specific test to find out which strain of hepatitis you had after doing a general test that was negative for hepatitis. At best, the test will not turn up anything, and your only problem will be the expense and pain of an unnecessary test. At worst, the test results will be misleading because the test is being used under the wrong circumstances. Consequently, you may end up being treated for a hepatitis you do not have. Analogously, a good researcher does not ask which groups differ from one another unless the more general, overall analysis of variance test has first established that at least some of the groups do indeed differ.[9]

Second, post hoc tests are not the same as conventional *t*-tests. Unlike conventional *t*-tests, post hoc *t*-tests are designed to correct for the fact that you are doing more than two comparisons. That is, as we mentioned earlier, doing more than one *t*-test at the $p = .05$ level and claiming that you only have a 5% risk of making a Type 1 error is like flipping more than one coin at a time and claiming that the odds of getting a "heads" are only 50%. In both cases, the odds of getting the result you hope for are much greater than the odds you are stating. Thus, we cannot simply do an ordinary *t*-test. Instead, we must correct for the number of comparisons we are making. Post hoc *t*-tests take into consideration how many tests are being done and make the necessary corrections.

At this point, we will not require you to know how to do post hoc tests. (If you want to know how to actually conduct a post hoc test, see Appendix E.) You should, however, be aware that if you choose to do a multiple-group experiment, you should be prepared to do post hoc analyses. You should also be prepared to encounter post hoc tests if you read a journal article that reports a significant *F* for a multiple-group experiment. If you read about a Bonferroni *t*-test, Tukey test, Scheffe test, Dunnett test, Newman-Keuls test, Duncan, or LSD test, do not panic. The author is merely reporting the results of a post hoc test to determine which means differ from one another.

Post Hoc Trend Analysis: What Is the Shape of the Relationship?

If you are interested in generalizing your results to unexplored levels of the independent variable, you may not be extremely interested in determining which particular groups differ from one another. Instead, you may be more interested in determining the shape of the functional relationship between the independent and

---

[9]There is not universal consensus on this point. For example, Robert Rosenthal (1992) argued that researchers should almost never do the general, overall *F*-test. Instead, he argues that if you have specific predictions about which groups differ, you should do normal *t*-tests to compare those group means. Those *t*-tests are called "planned comparisons" because you planned to make those comparisons before collecting your data rather than making those comparisons after seeing which means were furthest apart.

dependent variables. For example, as we mentioned earlier in the chapter, you might want to know the shape of the functional relationship to help you generalize to levels of the variable that were not tested. Or, you might be testing a theory that predicts a certain functional relationship. If you are interested in the functional relationship, instead of following up a significant main effect with post hoc tests between group means, follow up the significant effect with a post hoc trend analysis.

But why should you do a trend analysis to determine the shape of the functional relationship between your independent and dependent variables? Can't you see this relationship by simply graphing the group means? Yes and no. Yes, graphing your sample's means allows you to see the pattern in the data produced by your experiment. No, graphing does not tell you that the pattern you observe represents the true relationship between the variables because that pattern could be due to random error. Just as you needed statistics to tell you if the difference between two groups was significant (even though you could easily see whether one mean was higher than the other), you need statistics to know if the pattern you observe in your data (a straight line, a curved line, a combination of a curve and a straight line, etc.) would occur if you repeated the experiment. For example, if random error throws off even one of your sample means, the graph of your data could misrepresent the true functional relationship between your variables. Consequently, to determine if the pattern in your data reflects the real functional relationship, you must do a post hoc trend analysis.

Actually computing a post hoc trend analysis is easy. You can either follow the directions in Appendix E or use a computer program that does the analysis for you. Therefore, you might be tempted to forget about post hoc trend analysis until it comes time to analyze your data. Don't make that mistake!

Before conducting any study, you should always consider how you will analyze the results. The requirements of your statistical tests should always play a role in the decisions you make about how to conduct your study. This is especially true if you hope to use a post hoc trend analysis to find out the functional relationship between your variables. If you do not think about post hoc trend analysis when designing your experiment, you will probably be unable to do a valid post hoc trend analysis on your data. Therefore, if you think that you might want to know about the functional relationship between the variables in your experiment, you should keep three facts in mind *before* conducting that experiment (see Box 7-2).

First, to do a post hoc trend analysis, you must have selected levels of your independent variable that increase proportionally. For example, if you were using three levels of a drug, you would not use 5 mg., 6 mg., and 200 mg. Instead, you might use 10 mg., 20 mg., and 30 mg., or 10 mg., 100 mg., and 1000 mg.

Second, to do a trend analysis, you must have at least an interval-scale measure of your dependent variable. That is, your map of the functional relationship can't be accurate unless your measure of the dependent variable is to scale. For

---

• BOX 7-2 •

REQUIREMENTS FOR CONDUCTING A
VALID POST HOC TREND ANALYSIS

1. Your independent variable must have a statistically significant effect.

2. Your independent variable must be quantitative, and the levels used in the experiment should vary from one another by some constant proportion.

3. Your dependent variable must yield interval or ratio-scale data so that your map of the functional relationship will be to scale.

4. The number of trends you can look for is one less than the number of levels of your independent variable.

---

example, if you tried to find the relationship between the loudness of the music playing on participants' personal stereos and distance walked, you would have to measure distance by feet walked rather than by blocks walked (unless all your blocks are the same length). In short, you can't do a trend analysis if you have ordinal or nominal data.

Third, the more levels of the independent variable you have, the more trends you can look for. As you saw earlier in the chapter, the more points you have, the better you can pin down the shape of the functional relationship between the independent and dependent variables. Specifically, the number of trends you can examine is one less than the number of levels you have. If you had only two levels, you can only test for straight lines (linear component). If you have three groups, you can test for straight lines (linear component), and for a u-shaped curve (quadratic component). With four levels, you can test for straight lines, u-shaped curves, and double u-shaped lines (cubic component). Thus, if you are expecting a double u-shaped curve, you must use at least four levels of the independent variable.

Concluding Remarks

You have seen that you can expand a simple experiment by using more than two values of the independent variable. You have seen that expanding the simple experiment to include three or more values of the independent variable can pay off in two ways. First, using more control groups allows you more opportunities to rule out the effects of confounding variables. Second, using more treatment groups allows you to generalize your results more accurately to more values of the independent variable.

Yet, as valuable as expanding the simple experiment by adding more levels of the treatment can be, there is an even more powerful way to expand the simple experiment—by adding independent variables. As you will see in the next chapter, adding independent variables not only increases construct and external validity, but opens up a whole new arena of research questions.

Summary

1. The multiple-group experiment is more sensitive to nonlinear relationships than the simple experiment. Consequently, the multiple-group experiment is more likely to obtain significant treatment effects and to accurately map the functional relationship between your independent and dependent variables.

2. Knowing the functional relationship allows more accurate predictions about the effects of unexplored levels of the independent variable.

3. To use the multiple-group experiment to discover the functional relationship, you must carefully select your levels of the independent variable, and your dependent measure must provide at least interval scale data.

4. Multiple-group experiments may have more construct validity than a simple experiment because they can have multiple control groups and multiple treatment groups.

5. To analyze a multiple-group experiment, you first have to conduct an analysis of variance (ANOVA). An ANOVA will produce an *F*-ratio.

6. An *F*-ratio is a ratio of between-groups variance to within-groups variance.

7. Random error will make different treatment groups differ from each other. If the treatment has an effect, the treatment will also cause the groups to differ from each other. In other words, between-groups variance is due to random error and may also be due to treatment effects. Because it may be affected by treatment effects, between-groups variance is often called treatment variance.

8. Scores within a treatment group differ from each other for only one reason: random error. That is, the treatment cannot be responsible for variability within each treatment group. Therefore, within-groups variance is an estimate of the degree to which random error affects the data. Consequently, another term for within-groups variance is error variance.

9. The *F*-test is designed to see if the difference between the group means is greater than would be expected by chance. It involves dividing the between-groups variance (an estimate of random error plus possible treatment effects) by the within-groups variance (an estimate of random error). If the *F* is 1 or less, there is no evidence that the treatment has had an effect. If the *F* is larger than 1, you need to look in an *F* table (under the right degrees of freedom) to see whether the *F* is significant.

10. The first degrees of freedom (between groups/treatment) equals the number of groups minus one, abbreviated $G - 1$. The second degrees of freedom (within groups/error) equals the number of participants minus the number of groups, abbreviated $N - G$. Thus, if you had 5 groups and 40 participants, you would look at the F table under 4 $(5 - 1)$ and 35 $(40 - 5)$ degrees of freedom.

11. You are most likely to get a significant F if between-group variability is large (your groups differ from each other), and within-groups variability is small.

12. If you get a significant F, you know that the groups are not all the same. If you have more than two groups, you have to find out which groups differ. To find out which groups are different, do not just look at the means to see which differences are biggest. Instead, do post hoc tests to find out which groups are reliably different.

13. The following table summarizes the mathematics of an ANOVA table.

Source of Variance *(SV)*	Sum of Squares *(SS)*	degrees of freedom *(df)*	Mean Square *(MS)*	F
Treatment (T)	SST	Levels of $T - 1$	$SST / df\,T$	MST/MSE
Error (E)	SSE	Participants – Groups	$SSE/df\,E$	
Total	$SST + SSE$	Participants – 1		

Key Terms

analysis of variance (ANOVA): a statistical test that is especially useful when data are interval, and there are more than two groups. For the experiments discussed in this chapter, ANOVA involves dividing between-groups variance by within-groups variance. (p. 245)

between-groups variance (treatment variance, variability between group means, Mean Square Treatment, Mean Square Between): at one level, between-groups variance is just a measure of how much the group means differ from each other. Thus, if all the groups had the same mean, between-groups variance would be zero. At another level, between-groups variance is an estimate of the combined effects of the two factors that would make group means differ—treatment effects and random error. (pp. 241, 245)

within groups variance (error variance, variability within groups, Mean Square Error, Mean Square Within): at one level, within-groups variance is just a measure of the degree to which scores within each group differ from each other. A small within-groups variance means that participants within each group are all scoring similarly. At another level, within-groups variance is an estimate of the effects of random error (because participants in the same treatment group score differently due to random error, not due to treatment). Thus, within-groups variance is also called **error variance.** (p. 243)

F-ratio: at the numerical level, the F-ratio is the Mean Square Between divided by the Mean Square Within. At the conceptual level, F is the between-groups variance (treatment plus random error) divided by within-groups variance (random error).

If the treatment has no effect, the *F*-ratio will tend to be close to 1.0, indicating that the difference between the groups could be due to random error. If the treatment had an effect, the *F*-ratio will tend to be above 1.0, indicating that the difference between the groups is bigger than would be expected if only random error were at work. (p. 246)

confounding variables: variables, other than the independent variable, that may be responsible for the differences between your conditions. There are two types of confounding variables: ones that are manipulation-irrelevant and ones that are the result of the manipulation. Confounding variables that are irrelevant to the treatment manipulation threaten internal validity. For example, the difference between groups may be due to one group being older than the other, rather than to the treatment. Random assignment can control for the effects of those confounding variables. Confounding variables that are produced by the treatment manipulation hurt the construct validity of the study. They hurt the construct validity because even though we may know that the treatment manipulation had an effect, we don't know what it was about the treatment manipulation that had the effect. For example, we may know that an "exercise" manipulation increases happiness (internal validity), but not know whether the "exercise" manipulation worked because people exercised more, got more encouragement, had a more structured routine, practiced setting and achieving goals, or met new friends. In such a case, construct validity is harmed because we don't know what variable(s) are being manipulated by the "exercise" manipulation. (p. 234)

empty control group: a group that gets no treatment, not even a placebo. Usually, you should try to avoid empty control groups: They hurt construct validity because they don't allow you to discount the effects of treatment-related, confounding variables. For example, empty control groups may make your study very vulnerable to hypothesis-guessing. (p. 235)

hypothesis-guessing: participants trying to figure out what the study is designed to prove. Hypothesis-guessing can hurt a study's construct validity. (p. 235)

levels of the independent variable: values of the independent variable. In the simple experiment, you only have two levels of the independent variable. In the group experiment, you have more than two levels. Having more than two levels of the independent variable can help you determine the functional relationship between the independent and dependent variables. (p. 226)

functional relationship: the shape of the relationship between variables. For example, the functional relationship between the independent and dependent variables might be linear or curvilinear. (p. 230)

linear relationship: a functional relationship between an independent and dependent variable that is graphically represented by a straight line. (p. 231)

nonlinear relationship (curvilinear relationship): a functional relationship be-tween an independent and dependent variable that is graphically repre-sented by a curved line. (p. 231)

post hoc trend analysis: a type of post hoc test designed to determine whether a linear or curvilinear relationship is statistically significant (reliable). (p. 251)

post hoc test: a statistical test done after (1) doing a general test such as an ANOVA and (2) finding a *significant* effect. Post hoc tests are used to fol-low up on significant results obtained from a more general test. Because a significant ANOVA says only that at least two of the groups are signifi-cantly different from one another, post hoc tests may be performed to find out which groups are significantly different from one another. (p. 250)

Exercises

1. A researcher randomly assigns each member of a statistics class to one of two groups. In one group, each student is assigned a tutor. The tutor is available to meet with the student 20 minutes before each class. The other group is a control group not assigned a tutor. Suppose the researcher finds that the tutored group scores significantly better on exams.
   a. Can the researcher conclude that the experimental group students learned statistical information from tutoring sessions that enabled them to perform better on the exam? Why or why not?
   b. What changes would you recommend in the study?
2. Suppose people living in homes for the elderly were randomly assigned to two groups: a no-treatment group and a transcendental meditation (TM) group. Transcendental meditation involves more than sitting with eyes closed. The technique involves both "a meaningless sound selected for its value in facilitating the transcending, or settling-down, process and a specific procedure for using it mentally without effort again to facilitate transcending" (Alexander, Langer, Newman, Chandler, & Davies, 1989). Thus, the TM group was given instruction in how to perform the tech-nique, then "they met with their instructors half an hour each week to ver-ify that they were meditating correctly and regularly. They were to practice their program 20 minutes twice daily (morning and afternoon) sitting comfortably in their own room with eyes closed and using a timepiece to ensure correct length of practice" (Alexander, et al.).
   Suppose that the TM group performed significantly better than other groups on a mental health measure.[10]
   a. Could the researcher conclude that it was the transcendental medita-tion that caused the effect?

---

[10]A modification of this study was actually done. The study included appropriate control groups.

b. What besides the specific aspects of TM could cause the difference between the two groups?

c. What control groups would you add?

d. Suppose you added these control groups and then got a significant F for the treatment variable? What could you conclude? Why?

3. Assume you want to test the effectiveness of a new kind of therapy. This therapy involves screaming and hugging people in group sessions followed by individual meetings with a therapist. What control group(s) would you use? Why?

4. Assume a researcher is looking at the relationship between caffeine consumption and sense of humor.

a. How many levels of caffeine should the researcher use? Why?

b. What levels would you choose? Why?

c. If a graph of the data suggests a curvilinear relationship, can the researcher assume that the functional relationship between the independent and dependent variables is curvilinear? Why or why not?

d. Suppose the researcher used the following four levels of caffeine: 0 mg., 20 mg., 25 mg., 26 mg. Can the researcher do a trend analysis? Why or why not?

e. Suppose the researcher ranked participants based on their sense of humor. That is, the person who laughed least got a score of 1, the person who laughed second-least scored a 2, and so on. Can the researcher use these data to do a trend analysis? Why or why not?

f. If a researcher used four levels of caffeine, how many trends can the researcher look for? What are the treatment's degrees of freedom?

g. If the researcher used three levels of caffeine and 30 participants, what are the degrees of freedom for the treatment? The degrees of freedom for the error term?

h. Suppose the F is 3.34. Referring to the degrees of freedom you obtained in your answer to "g" (above) and to Table E-3 (Appendix E), are the results statistically significant? Can the researcher look for linear and quadratic trends?

5. A computer analysis reports that $F(6, 23) = 2.54$. The analysis is telling you that the F-ratio was 2.54, and the degrees of freedom for the top part of the F-ratio = 6 and the degrees of freedom for the bottom part = 23.

a. How many groups did the researcher use?

b. How many participants were in the experiment?

c. Is this result statistically significant at the .05 level? (Refer to Table E-3.)

6. How is the top part of the F-ratio like the top part of the t-ratio? How is the bottom part of the F-ratio like the bottom part of the t-ratio?

7. A friend gives you the following Fs and significance levels. On what basis would you want these Fs (or significance levels) rechecked?

a. $F(2, 63) = .10$, not significant

b. $F(3, 85) = -1.70$, not significant

    c. $F(1, 120) = 52.8$, not significant

    d. $F(5, 70) = 1.00$, significant

8. Complete the following table.

Source of Variance (SV)	Sum of Squares (SS)	degrees of freedom (df)	Mean Square (MS)	F
Treatment (T) 3 levels of treatment	180	_____	_____	_____
Error (E), also known as within-groups variance	80	8	_____	

9. Complete the following table.

Source of Variance (SV)	Sum of Squares (SS)	degrees of freedom (df)	Mean Square (MS)	F
Treatment (T) (between-groups variance)	50	5	_____	_____
Error (E) (within-groups variance)	100	_____	_____	
Total	_____	30		

10. A study compares the effect of having a snack, taking a 10-minute walk, or getting no treatment on energy levels. Sixty participants are randomly assigned to condition and then asked to rate their energy level on a 0 (not at all energetic) to 10 (very energetic) scale. The mean for the "do nothing" group is 6.0, for having a snack 7.0, and for walking 7.8. The *F*-ratio is 6.27.

    a. Graph the means.

    b. Are the results statistically significant?

    c. If so, what conclusions can you draw? Why?

    d. What additional analyses would you do? Why?

    e. How would you extend this study?

EXPANDING THE SIMPLE EXPERIMENT: FACTORIAL DESIGNS

OVERVIEW

In Chapter 6, you learned how the logic of the simple experiment enables it to be internally valid. However, you also learned that it was limited: With it, you could only study two levels of a single independent variable.

In Chapter 7, you learned that the basic logic behind the simple experiment could be extended to experiments that study three or more levels of a single independent variable. You saw that such multiple-group experiments could possess impressive internal, external, and construct validity.

In this chapter, you will learn how to extend the basic logic of the simple experiment to study the effects of two independent variables in a single experiment. Specifically, you will learn about one of the most commonly used experimental designs: the 2 × 2 factorial. But beyond learning how to design and interpret the results of 2 × 2 factorial experiments, you will learn why you should want to study the effects of two independent variables in a single experiment.

THE 2 × 2 FACTORIAL DESIGN

To illustrate how you can study two independent variables in a single experiment, suppose you wanted to know the effect of two factors—caffeine and exercise—on appetite. You want to use two levels of caffeine (0 mg and 20 mg) and two levels of exercise (no exercise and 50 minutes of exercise). To study the effects of both these factors (caffeine and exercise) in a single experiment, you would randomly assign participants to four groups:

1. a no-exercise, no-caffeine group
2. a no-exercise, 20 mg caffeine group
3. a 50 minutes of exercise, no-caffeine group
4. a 50 minutes of exercise, 20 mg caffeine group

In technical terminology, you would be using a **factorial experiment**: an experiment that examines the effects of two or more independent variables (factors). Specifically, because the exercise factor has two levels and the caffeine factor has two levels, you have a 2 (no exercise/50 minutes exercise) × 2 (no caffeine/20 mg caffeine) factorial experiment.[1]

HOW ONE EXPERIMENT CAN DO AS MUCH AS TWO

If you wanted to study the effects of caffeine and exercise on appetite, you would not absolutely have to do a factorial experiment. Instead, you could do two simple experiments. One simple experiment would look at caffeine's effects on appetite. The other would look at exercise's effects on appetite. To visualize the difference between doing a single 2 × 2 factorial experiment versus doing two simple experiments, refer to Table 8-1.

As you can see, the first three cells of the 2 × 2 experiment have every group that the two simple experiments have. In a sense, those three cells of the 2 × 2 contain two simple two-group experiments.

If the two simple experiments have four groups, how can the 2 × 2 do the same work with only three groups? A close look at Table 8-1 shows that, although the two simple experiments have four groups, they only have three

---

• **TABLE 8-1** •

HOW THREE CELLS OF A 2 × 2 EXPERIMENT CONTAIN THE INFORMATION OF TWO SIMPLE EXPERIMENTS

TWO SIMPLE EXPERIMENTS

Simple experiment #1

Control group	Caffeine group

Simple experiment #2

Control group
Exercise group

THREE OF THE FOUR CELLS OF A 2 × 2 EXPERIMENT

Control group	Caffeine group
Exercise group	

---

[1]If you had three levels of exercise, you would have a 3 (no exercise/50 minutes exercise/100 minutes exercise) × 2 (no caffeine/20 mg caffeine) factorial experiment. With a 3 × 2 factorial, you would have 6 (3 × 2) groups of participants. If, instead of adding a level of exercise, you had decided to add the factor of temperature, you might have a 2 (no exercise/50 minutes) × 2 (no caffeine/20 mg caffeine) × 2 (low temperature/high temperature) factorial design. In a 2 × 2 × 2 factorial, you would have 8 groups of participants.

different kinds of groups. That is, two of those groups do the same thing—serve as a control group. By not duplicating the control group, three cells of the 2 × 2 can contain the three different groups that the two simple experiments have.

To reiterate, by getting double duty out of the control group, three cells of the 2 × 2 incorporate the two simple experiments. As you will soon see, the first row of Table 8-1 contains the first simple experiment and the first column contains the second simple experiment.

By comparing the two groups in the first row of the 2 × 2 (the control group and the caffeine group), you would get a **simple main effect** for caffeine—just as you would have gotten if you had done Simple Experiment #1. Thus, in one sense, the first row is a simple experiment that looks at the effect of caffeine.

Similarly, in one sense, the first column is a simple experiment that looks at the effect of exercise. That is, by comparing the two groups in the first column of the 2 × 2 (the control group and the exercise group), you would get a simple main effect for exercise—just as you would if you had done Simple Experiment #2.

HOW ONE EXPERIMENT CAN DO MORE THAN TWO

As you have seen, the first row and the first column of the 2 × 2 experiment can do everything that the two simple experiments do. If the 2 × 2 can do everything two simple experiments can do with only three groups, why do we have the fourth group? We have the fourth group so we can discover things we could not have discovered had we used two simple experiments.

The 2 × 2 Yields Four Simple Main Effects

As you can see from Table 8-2, because of the fourth group, the 2 × 2 contains four simple experiments. Thus, if we used certain statistical techniques, we could use the 2 × 2 to find four simple main effects:

1. the simple main effect for *exercise* in the no-caffeine conditions (by comparing the *exercise,* no-caffeine group with the *no-exercise,* no-caffeine group)
2. the simple main effect for *exercise* in the caffeine conditions (by comparing the *exercise,* caffeine group with the *no-exercise,* caffeine group)
3. the simple main effect for *caffeine* in the no-exercise conditions (by comparing the no-exercise, *caffeine* group with the no-exercise, *no-caffeine* group)
4. the simple main effect for *caffeine* in the exercise conditions (by comparing the exercise, *caffeine* group with the exercise, *no-caffeine* group)

The simplest way to estimate these simple main effects is to subtract the relevant group means from each other. To illustrate, suppose we had the following means:

• **TABLE 8-2** •

How the 2 × 2 Experiment Contains the Information of Four Simple Experiments

	Simple experiment #1 (Effect of exercise when no caffeine is present)	Simple experiment #2 (Effect of exercise when caffeine is present)
	Control group	Caffeine group
	Exercise group	Caffeine + Exercise group

Simple experiment #3 (Effect of caffeine for subjects who don't exercise)

Control group	Caffeine group

Simple experiment #4 (Effect of caffeine for subjects who do exercise)

Exercise group	Caffeine + Exercise group

A 2 × 2 EXPERIMENT

(This row contains Simple Experiment #3)
(This row contains Simple Experiment #4)

Control group	Caffeine group
Exercise group	Caffeine + Exercise group

(This column contains Simple Experiment #1)   (This column contains Simple Experiment #2)

Mean for exercise, no-caffeine group	2,500
Mean for no-exercise, no-caffeine group	2,000
Mean for exercise, caffeine group	2,900
Mean for no-exercise, caffeine group	2,200

With these means, we could estimate four simple main effects. Let's start by comparing the groups that are the same in terms of caffeine use but differ in how much they have exercised:

1. The simple main effect for *exercise* in the no-caffeine conditions = 500 (2,500 − 2,000).

2. The simple main effect for *exercise* in the caffeine conditions = 700 (2,900 − 2,200).

Now, let's compare the groups that are the same in terms of exercise but differ in terms of caffeine use:

3. The simple main effect for *caffeine* in the no-exercise conditions = 200 (2,200 − 2,000).

4. The simple main effect for *caffeine* in the exercise conditions = 400 (2,900 − 2,500).

The 2 × 2 Yields Two Pairs of Simple Main Effects

We have shown you that the 2 × 2 can yield four simple main effects. Perhaps a better way of looking at the 2 × 2 is that it produces two pairs of simple main effects: (1) a pair of simple main effects relating to the first independent variable (e.g., two exercise simple main effects) and (2) a pair of simple main effects relating to the second independent variable (e.g., two caffeine simple main effects).

Why do we want you to think about two pairs of simple main effects rather than four individual simple main effects? We want you to think about pairs of simple main effects because researchers do not do 2 × 2 factorial experiments with the primary aim of detecting the four simple main effects.

If researchers were only interested in the four simple main effects, researchers could just conduct four separate simple experiments. If researchers were only interested in the four simple main effects, the focus of their statistical analyses would be on teasing out these four effects. In actual practice, analyzing the 2 × 2 does not focus on teasing out these four effects. Indeed, researchers often do not conduct any analyses that would help them isolate these four individual simple main effects. Instead, as you will see in the next two sections, the main focus is on each treatment's pair of simple main effects.

To be more specific, the two areas that researchers' analyses focus on are (1) combining each treatment's two simple main effects and (2) contrasting each treatment's two simple main effects. By *combining* a treatment's simple main effects, researchers can estimate that treatment's overall, average effect in their study. By *contrasting* a treatment's simple main effects, researchers can determine whether the treatment has one effect on one group of participants, but a different effect on a different group of participants.

Averaging a Treatment's Main Effects Lets You Find the Overall Main Effect: The Average Effect of Varying a Factor

To combine a treatment's simple main effects, you average them. The *average* of a treatment's two simple main effects allows you to estimate the average effect of that treatment in your study. This average effect is called the treatment's **overall main effect.**

In the caffeine–exercise study, the researcher would average the two caffeine simple main effects to get an overall main effect for caffeine. To illustrate, suppose the simple main effect of caffeine was 200 in the no-exercise condition (the caffeine, no-exercise group consumed 200 more calories than the no-caffeine, no-exercise group). Furthermore, suppose that the simple main effect of caffeine was 400 in the exercise condition (the caffeine, exercise group consumed 400 more calories than the no-caffeine, exercise group). In that case, the estimate for the overall main effect of caffeine would be 300 (because the average of 200 and 400 is 300).

To estimate the overall main effect for exercise, the researcher would average the two exercise simple main effects. If the overall exercise main effect was significant, it would mean that, on the average, participants getting exercise consumed a different number of calories than the participants getting no exercise.

One reason researchers emphasize overall main effects is convenience. It is easier to talk about one overall main effect than about two simple main effects.

However, a much more important advantage of averaging the two simple main effects into an overall main effect is that it allows us to make more general statements about that variable's effects. For example, consider the advantage of averaging the two simple main effects of caffeine. Because we have combined two simple main effects, we are not confined to saying that caffeine has an effect if you exercise 50 minutes a day. Instead, we can say that, on the average, in a study that varied exercise levels, caffeine has an effect. The implication is that we can be more confident that the effect of caffeine generalizes across a variety of exercise levels.

Comparing a Factor's Simple Main Effects Lets You Find the Interaction

But what if the simple main effect of caffeine is very different in the exercise condition than in the no-exercise condition? In that case, you should not make a general statement about the effects of caffeine without mentioning that the caffeine effect changes depending on how much exercise one does. In that case, you should be happy that we can compare one of a treatment's simple main effects with that treatment's other simple main effect. In this case, by comparing the two simple main effects of caffeine, you could tell that the effect of caffeine depends on whether the participant has exercised.

If the simple main effects of caffeine differ depending on the level of exercise, there is an **interaction** between caffeine and exercise (see Table 8-3). If, on the other hand, they do not differ (caffeine has the same effect in the no-exercise condition as it has in the exercise condition), then you do not have an interaction. If you do not have an interaction, you can predict that the effect of combining those variables is what you would get from adding up their separate, individual effects.

Interactions Are Important: Moderating Variables in Real Life   Interactions are a fact of life (see Table 8-4). Treatments will tend to have one effect on one group of individuals, but another effect on other individuals. For example, eating grapefruit is good for most people, but not for people who are taking certain kinds of medications. For those people, eating grapefruit may kill them! In other words, there is a positive main effect for eating grapefruit, but there is a dangerous grapefruit-drug interaction.[2]

---

[2]A popular and effective allergy medicine was taken off the market because of this deadly interaction.

• **TABLE 8-3** •

SIMPLE MAIN EFFECTS, OVERALL MAIN EFFECTS, AND INTERACTIONS

Simple Main Effects

Definition:	The effects of one independent variable at a specific level of a second independent variable. The simple main effect could have been obtained merely by doing a simple experiment.
How Estimated:	By comparing the mean for one group with the mean for a second group (for instance, comparing the no-caffeine, no-exercise group mean to the caffeine, no-exercise group mean).
Question Addressed:	What is the effect of the caffeine in the no-exercise condition?

Overall Main Effect

Definition:	The average effect of a treatment.
How Estimated:	By averaging a treatment's simple main effects. If the average of the two simple main effects is significantly different from zero, there is an overall main effect.
Question Addressed:	What is the average effect of caffeine in this study?

Interaction

Definition:	The effect of a treatment is different, depending on the level of a second independent variable. That is, the effect of a variable is not consistent across conditions.
How Estimated:	By looking at the *differences* between a treatment's simple main effects. If the treatment's simple main effects are the same, there is no interaction. If, however, the treatment's two simple main effects differ significantly, there is an interaction.
Question Addressed:	Does caffeine have the same effect on appetite for those who exercise as it has on those who don't exercise?

We do not mean that all interactions, or even all drug interactions, have to be dangerous. The only requirement for an interaction is that the effect of combining treatments is different from the sum of their individual effects. For example, there is a very interesting interaction involving caffeine and nicotine, both of which are stimulants. Consuming caffeine increases physiological arousal—unless people have nicotine in their system. For people who have a lot of nicotine in their system, caffeine actually reduces physiological arousal: The person who has smoked a bunch of cigarettes may actually wind down by having a cola.

In dealing with others, most people believe that interactions play a key role. That is, people think that the effect of an action depends on (interacts with) other factors.

Sometimes, those interacting factors involve context. For example, telling someone "congratulations" will have a good effect if she has just been promoted, but a bad effect if she has just been fired.

• TABLE 8-4 •

WAYS OF THINKING ABOUT INTERACTIONS

VIEWPOINT	HOW VIEWPOINT RELATES TO INTERACTIONS
Chemical Reactions	Lighting a match, in itself, is not dangerous. Having gasoline around is not, in itself, dangerous. However, the *combination* of lighting a match in the presence of gasoline is explosive. Because the explosive effects of combining gas and lighting a match are different from simply adding their separate, individual effects, gasoline and matches interact.
Personal Relationships	John likes most people. Mary is liked by most people. *But* John dislikes Mary. Based only on their individual tendencies, we would expect John to like Mary. Apparently, however, like gasoline and matches, the combination of their personalities produces a negative outcome.
Sports	The whole is not the same as the sum of the parts. That is, a team is not the sum of its parts. The addition of a player may do more for the team than the player's abilities would suggest—or the addition may help the team much less than would be expected because the team "chemistry" is upset. In other words, the player's skills and personality may interact with those of the other players on the team or with the team's strategy. Sometimes, the result is that adding the player will help the team more that what would be expected by knowing only the team's characteristics and the player's characteristics. Sometimes, adding the player will help the team less than what would be expected if one only knew the team's characteristics and the player's characteristics. Knowing the interaction between the team and the player—how the two will mesh together—may be almost as important as knowing the player's abilities. Good pitchers get batters out. Poor hitters are easier to get out than good hitters. *However,* sometimes a poor hitter may have a good pitcher's "number" because the pitcher's strengths match the hitter's strengths. Similarly, some "poor" pitchers are very effective against some of the league's best batters. Managers who can take advantage of these interactions can win more games than would be expected by knowing only the talents of the individual team members.
Prescription Drugs	Drug *A* may be a good, useful drug. Drug *B* may also be a good, useful drug. But, taking Drug *A* and *B* together may result in harm or death. Increasingly, doctors and pharmacists have to be aware of not only the effects of drugs in isolation, but their combined effects. Ignorance of these interactions can result in deaths and in malpractice suits.
Making General Statements	Interactions indicate that you cannot make a general, simple statement that one variable always has a specific effect. You cannot talk about the effects of one variable without mentioning that the effect of that variable depends on a second variable. Therefore, if you have an interaction, when discussing a factor's effect, you need to say "but," "except when," "depending on," "only under certain conditions." Indeed, you will often see results sections say that the main effect was "qualified by a _____ interaction" or "the effect of the _____ variable was different depending on the level of (the other) variable."
Visually	If you graph an interaction, the lines will not be parallel. That is, the lines either already cross or if they were extended, they would eventually cross.
Mathematically	If you have an interaction, the effect of combining the variables is *not* the same as adding their two effects together. Rather, the effect is better captured as the result of multiplying the two effects. That is, when you add 2 to a number, you know the number will increase by 2, regardless of what the number is. However, when you multiply a number by 2, the effect will depend on the other number. When doubling a number, the effect is quite different when the number to be doubled is 2 than when it is 1,000 or than when it is −40. To take another example of the effect of multiplication, consider the multiplicative effects of interest rates on your financial condition. If interest rates go up, that will have a big, positive effect on your financial situation if you have lots of money in the bank; a small, positive effect if you have little money in the bank; and a negative effect on your finances if you owe money to the bank (you will have to pay more interest on your debt).

At other times, those interacting (moderating) factors are personal characteristics. That is, an approach that works with one type of person may not work with another type of person. For instance, some people assume that lecturing may be the best strategy for teaching shy students, but that group activities are the best way to teach outgoing students (Shute, 1994).

As the above examples illustrate, people often suspect that variables interact. Research supports the popular notion that some treatments will have one effect on one group of participants, but a different effect on another group. For instance, if you have a group of participants who believe they have no control over the noise level in the room, increasing the noise level seriously harms performance. For participants who believe they can control the noise level, however, increasing the noise level does not harm performance. Thus, noise level interacts with perceived control (Glass & Singer, 1972).

Because of this interaction, you cannot simply say noise hurts performance. You have to say the effect of noise level on performance depends on perceived control. In other words, rather than stating a simple rule about the effects of noise, you have to state a more complex rule. This complex rule puts qualifications on the statement that noise hurts performance. Specifically, the statement that noise hurts performance will be qualified by some word or phrase such as "depending on," "but only if," or "however, that holds only under certain conditions."

Because the concept of interaction is so important, let's consider one more example. As a general rule, we can say that getting within 1 inch of another person will make that person uncomfortable. Thus, the main effect of getting physically closer to someone is to produce a negative mood. However, what if you are the other person's romantic partner? Then, getting closer may elicit positive feelings. Because the effect of interpersonal distance is moderated by initial liking of the target person, we can say that there is an interaction between distance and the participant's initial feelings toward the target person.

In short, you now know two facts about interactions. First, if there is an interaction involving your treatment, it means that the treatment has one effect under one set of conditions, but another effect under another set of conditions. Second, interactions play an important role in real life.

Interesting Questions in Modern Psychology Are Often Questions About Interactions   As psychology has progressed, psychologists have focused increasingly more attention on interactions. Part of the reason psychologists focus on interactions is because psychologists have already discovered the main effects of many variables. We know how many individual variables act in isolation. Now, it is time to go to the next step—addressing the question: "What is the effect of combining these variables?" Put another way, once we learn what the general effect of a variable is, we want to find out what specific conditions may modify (moderate) this general, overall effect. Consequently, in Chapter 2, we encouraged you to generate research ideas that involved moderating variables. In other words, we encouraged you to do what many psychologists do—focus on interactions involving moderating variables rather than on main effects.

Another reason psychologists focus on interactions is because we realize that (1) individuals rarely are exposed to one and only one variable, and (2) interactions are common. Consequently, psychologists now frame general problems and issues in terms of interactions. That is, rather than saying, "What is the (main) effect of personality and what is the (main) effect of the situation?" psychologists are now asking, "How do personality and the situation interact?" Asking this question has led to research indicating that some people are more influenced by situational influences than others (Snyder, 1984).

Similarly, rather than looking exclusively at the main effects of heredity and the main effects of environment, many scientists are looking at the interaction between heredity and environment. In other words, rather than asking, "What is the effect of a certain environment?" they are asking, "Are the effects of a certain environment different for some people than for others?"

Looking for these interactions sometimes produces remarkable findings. For example, psychologists have found that certain children may benefit from an environment that would be detrimental to children who had inherited a different genetic predisposition (Plomin, 1993). Eventually, such research may lead to new ways of educating parents. For instance, rather than telling parents the one right way to discipline children, parent education may involve teaching parents to identify their child's genetic predispositions and then alter their parenting strategies to fit that predisposition. In short, much of the recent research in psychology has involved asking questions that relate to interactions, such as "Under what conditions do rewards hurt motivation?"

External Validity Questions Are Questions Involving Interactions   We do not mean to imply that the interest in interactions is an entirely new phenomenon. Anyone interested in external validity is interested in interactions. If you are concerned that a treatment won't work on a certain type of person (women, minorities, the elderly), you are concerned about a treatment × type of person interaction. If you are concerned that a treatment that worked in one setting (a hospital) won't have the same effect in a different setting (a school), you are concerned about a treatment × setting interaction. If you are concerned that a treatment won't have the same effect in another culture, you are concerned about a treatment × culture interaction. If you are concerned that the superiority of one treatment over another will diminish over time, you are concerned about a treatment × time interaction. In summary, determining the external validity of your findings is often a matter of determining whether your treatment interacts with setting, culture, or type of participant.

Questions in Applied Psychology Are Often Questions Involving Interactions
Understandably, applied psychologists have always been interested in interactions. One of the founders of applied psychology, Walter Dill Scott, was

fascinated by the fact that some people will like an advertisement that others will hate. In other words, he wanted to investigate personality × type of ad interactions. Most applied psychologists after Scott have shared his interest in determining which treatments work on which type of people. For example, therapists know that a therapeutic approach (behavior therapy, drug therapy) that works well for some people (phobics) may not work as well for others. That is, they know that there are treatment × type of patient interactions.

In conclusion, the applied psychologist is keenly interested in interactions. When people pay for advice, they do not want the expert to only know about main effects. That is, they do not want the expert to stop at saying, "My recommended course of action works in the average case, so it may work for you." Instead, they may quiz the expert about interactions involving their treatment: "Under what circumstances might that action make things worse—and do my situations fit those circumstances?" To know when a treatment will be helpful and when it will be harmful boils down to knowing the interactions involving that treatment.

EXAMPLE OF QUESTIONS ANSWERED BY THE 2 × 2 FACTORIAL EXPERIMENT

Now that you have a general understanding of main effects and interactions, let's apply this knowledge to a specific experiment. If you were to do the caffeine and exercise experiment we described earlier, you would look for three different kinds of effects:

1. the main (average) effect of caffeine
2. the main (average) effect of exercise
3. the interaction between caffeine and exercise

The main effect of caffeine is caffeine's *average* effect. Therefore, it would be calculated by *averaging* the caffeine simple main effects. Likewise, the main effect of exercise is the average effect of varying exercise. Therefore, it would be calculated by averaging the two exercise simple main effects.

The interaction, on the other hand, reflects the extent to which caffeine's effect *differs* depending on exercise level. Therefore, the interaction is estimated by finding the extent to which caffeine's effect in the no-exercise condition *differs* from its effect in the exercise condition. You can find the interaction by subtracting the two caffeine simple main effects from each other.

If there is a significant difference between caffeine's effect in the no-exercise condition and its effect in the exercise condition, then you have an interaction. The effect of caffeine depends on how much participants exercise.

If, on the other hand, there is no difference between the two caffeine simple main effects, there is no interaction. That is, if caffeine main effects are the same (the difference between them is 0), the effect of caffeine does not depend on level of exercise.

To review, a significant main effect for caffeine would mean that, on the average, varying caffeine had an effect on calories consumed. A significant main effect for exercise would mean that, on the average, varying exercise had an effect on calories consumed. Finally, a significant interaction would mean that the combination of exercise and caffeine produces an effect that is not simply the sum of their two separate effects (see Table 8-5). That is, an interaction means that combining the variables makes them either more effective or less effective than you would expect from knowing only their individual effects. For example, suppose that the average effect of exercise was to boost calorie consumption by 100 calories, and the average effect of caffeine was also to boost calorie consumption by 100 calories. If we asked you to guess how many more calories the group that got both exercise and caffeine consumed than the control group, you might say "200." Your guess of 200 seems reasonable, based on adding up the individual effects of exercise and caffeine. After all, 100 + 100 = 200. If we have an interaction, however, your guess would be off. The exercise plus caffeine group might consume only 100 more calories than the controls—or might consume 300 more. In short, if you had a caffeine-exercise interaction, you couldn't predict how much the exercise plus caffeine group would consume merely by knowing the individual effects of exercise and caffeine.

As you can imagine, significant interactions force scientists to answer such questions as, "Does caffeine increase calorie consumption?" by saying, "Yes, but it depends on . . ." or "It's a little more complicated than that." Psychologists do not give these kinds of responses to make the world seem more complicated than it is.

On the contrary, psychologists would love to give simple answers. Like all scientists, they love parsimony (they prefer simple explanations to more complex explanations). Therefore, they would love to report main effects that are

---

• **TABLE 8-5** •

QUESTIONS ADDRESSED BY A 2 × 2 EXPERIMENT

EFFECT	QUESTION ADDRESSED
Overall main effect for exercise	On the average, does varying exercise levels have an effect?
Overall main effect for caffeine	On the average, does varying caffeine levels have an effect?
Interaction between caffeine and exercise	Does the effect of caffeine *differ depending on* how much exercise participants get?
	Put another way:
	Does the effect of exercise *differ depending on* how much caffeine participants get?

not qualified by interactions. They would like to say that exercise is always good, and drinking caffeine is always bad. However, if interactions occur, scientists have the obligation to report them—and in the real world, interactions abound. Only the person who says, "Give me a match, I want to see if my gas tank is empty," is unaware of the pervasiveness of interactions. Time and time again, you learn that when variables combine, the effects are different than you would expect from knowing only their individual, independent effects.

Because we live in a world where we are exposed to a variety of variables and because these variables interact, you may be compelled to do experiments that capture some of this complexity. But how would you describe the results from such a factorial experiment?

POTENTIAL RESULTS OF A 2 × 2 FACTORIAL EXPERIMENT

You would describe the results of a 2 × 2 factorial experiment in terms of (1) whether you got a main effect for your first independent variable, (2) whether you got a main effect for your second independent variable, and (3) whether you got an interaction. As you can see from Table 8-6, getting a main effect for your first independent variable does not mean that you will be more likely to get a main effect for your second independent variable or that you will be more likely to get an interaction. Instead, like flipping a coin three times or playing a slot machine, the three different results are independent. Consequently, as you can see from the table, there are eight basic patterns of results you could obtain.

If you did a study, how would you know which of these patterns of results you obtained? At some point, you would need to do a statistical analysis, such as analysis of variance. Without such a statistical analysis, the patterns you observed in your data might be due to random error rather than to statistically reliable treatment effects. Before or after doing such an analysis, however, you would probably like to see what patterns exist in your data. Therefore, you might calculate the mean response for each group and then make a table of those means. To show how a table of means can help you, let's examine tables depicting six different patterns of results:

1. main effect and no interaction
2. two main effects and no interaction
3. two main effects and an interaction
4. no main effects and an interaction
5. one main effect and an interaction
6. no main effects and no interaction

• **TABLE 8-6** •

EIGHT POTENTIAL OUTCOMES
OF A 2 × 2 FACTORIAL EXPERIMENT

1. A Main Effect for Variable 1	No Main Effect for Variable 2	No Interaction
2. No Main Effect for Variable 1	A Main Effect for Variable 2	No Interaction
3. A Main Effect for Variable 1	A Main Effect for Variable 2	No Interaction
4. A Main Effect for Variable 1	A Main Effect for Variable 2	An Interaction
5. No Main Effect for Variable 1	No Main Effect for Variable 2	An Interaction
6. A Main Effect for Variable 1	No Main Effect for Variable 2	An Interaction
7. No Main Effect for Variable 1	A Main Effect for Variable 2	An Interaction
8. No Main Effect for Variable 1	No Main Effect for Variable 2	No Interaction

Note that having (or not having) a main effect has no implications whatsoever for whether you will have an interaction.

A MAIN EFFECT AND NO INTERACTION

Let's start by supposing you obtained the results displayed in Table 8-7. To understand your results, you might start looking at the experiment as though it were four separate simple experiments. Thus, if you look only at the first row, it is just like you are looking at a simple experiment that manipulated exercise (while not giving any of the participants caffeine). Put another way, looking at the first row shows you what happened in the no-caffeine groups.

As you can see, the no-exercise group consumed just as many calories (2,000) as the exercise group. That is, for the no-caffeine groups, varying exercise had no noticeable effect.

To find out what happened in the caffeine groups, look at the second row. Note that looking at the second row is just like looking at a simple experiment that varied exercise (while giving all the participants 20 mg of caffeine). As you can see by the fact that both the no-exercise and the exercise groups consumed 2,200 calories, varying exercise had no noticeable effect in the caffeine conditions. Averaging the effect of exercise over both the no-caffeine and the caffeine conditions, you find that exercise's average (overall) effect was zero. The exercise group's scores, on the average, were the same as the no-exercise group's. Thus, there was no overall main effect for exercise.

Looking at the columns tells you about the effect of caffeine. That is, each column is like a simple experiment that looks at the effect of caffeine. For example, looking at the first column is like looking at a simple experiment that varied caffeine (while not having any participants exercise). Thus, looking at

• **TABLE 8-7** •

MAIN EFFECT FOR CAFFEINE, NO INTERACTION

	No Exercise	Exercise	Exercise simple main effects
No Caffeine	2,000	2,000	+0 (2,000 – 2,000 = 0)
Caffeine	2,200	2,200	+0 (2,200 – 2,200 = 0)

Caffeine simple main effects	+200 (2,200 – 2,000 = +200)	+200 (2,200 – 2,000 = +200)

Averaging a treatment's simple main effects gives us its overall main effect:

Simple main effect of **Caffeine** in the no-exercise condition	+200
Simple main effect of **Caffeine** in the exercise condition	+200
Average effect (overall main effect) of **Caffeine**	+400/2 = +200

Simple main effect of **Exercise** in the no-caffeine condition	+0
Simple main effect of **Exercise** in the caffeine condition	+0
Average effect (overall main effect) of **Exercise**	0/2 = +0

Comparing a treatment's simple main effects tells us whether there is an interaction:

Since there are no differences between the two simple main effects for caffeine (both are +200), then there is no interaction. In other words, since the effect of caffeine is not affected by how much participants exercised, there is no interaction.

the first column (the no-exercise conditions) shows you the effect of varying caffeine in the no-exercise groups. As you can see, for these no-exercise groups, caffeine appears to boost calorie consumption by about 200 calories.[3]

Looking at the second column shows you the effect of caffeine for the exercise groups. That is, looking at the second column is like looking at a simple experiment that manipulated caffeine (while having all participants exercise). As you can see, the caffeine group consumes 200 more calories than the no-caffeine group. Thus, there appears to be a simple main effect for caffeine in the exercise condition.

Since caffeine increases calorie consumption in both the no-exercise and the exercise conditions, it appears that there is an overall main effect for caffeine. In other words, the average effect of caffeine is to increase calorie consumption.

---

[3]Because of random error, we don't know what the effect actually is. Furthermore, without using statistical tests, you can't claim that you have a significant main effect or interaction. However, since (1) our purpose in this section is to teach you how to interpret tables and graphs and since (2) you will rarely see tables and graphs in journal articles without an associated statistical analysis, we will pretend, in this section, that any differences you observe are (1) due entirely to treatment effects and (2) statistically significant.

Because the effect of caffeine does not differ depending on the level of exercise, there is no interaction. That is, the effect of caffeine is the same in the no-exercise condition as it is in the exercise condition: In both cases, it boosts calorie consumption by about 200.

Instead of having no interaction and a main effect for caffeine, you could have no interaction and a main effect for exercise. This pattern of results is shown in Table 8-8. From the top row, you can see that, when there was no caffeine, exercise increased calorie consumption by 500. Looking at the bottom row, you see that exercise also increased calorie consumption by 500 in the caffeine conditions. Averaging the effect of exercise over both the no-caffeine and the caffeine conditions, you estimate that exercise's average (overall) effect, the overall main effect of exercise, was 500.

Looking at the columns tells you about the effect of caffeine. Looking at the first column tells you about the effect of caffeine in the no-exercise conditions. By looking at the first column (the no-exercise column), you can see that, in the no-exercise conditions, the participants getting caffeine consumed the same number of calories (2,000) as participants in the no-caffeine condition.

• **TABLE 8-8** •

MAIN EFFECT FOR EXERCISE, NO INTERACTION

	No Exercise	Exercise	Exercise simple main effects
No Caffeine	2,000	2,500	+500 (2,500 − 2,000 = +500)
Caffeine	2,000	2,500	+500 (2,500 − 2,000 = +500)
Caffeine simple main effects	+0 (2,000 − 2,000 = +0)	+0 (2,500 − 2,500 = +0)	

Averaging a treatment's simple main effects gives us its overall main effect:

Simple main effect of **Caffeine** in the no-exercise condition	+0
Simple main effect of **Caffeine** in the exercise condition	+0
Average effect (overall main effect) of **Caffeine**	+0/2 = 0

Simple main effect of **Exercise** in the no-caffeine condition	+500
Simple main effect of **Exercise** in the caffeine condition	+500
Average effect (overall main effect) of **Exercise**	1,000/2 = +500

Comparing a treatment's simple main effects tells us whether there is an interaction:

Since there are no differences between the two simple main effects for exercise (both are +500), then there is no interaction. In other words, since the effect of exercise is not affected by how much caffeine participants consumed, there is no interaction.

Looking at the second column tells you about the effect of caffeine in the exercise conditions. By looking at the second column (the exercise column), you can see that, in the exercise conditions, the participants getting caffeine consumed the same number of calories (2,500) as participants in the no-caffeine group. Since there was no effect for varying caffeine in either the no-exercise conditions (the first column) or the exercise conditions (the second column), it appears that there is no main effect for varying caffeine.

Combining the exercise simple main effects told you that there is an exercise main effect. Comparing the exercise simple main effects tells you that you don't have an exercise by caffeine interaction. Comparing the exercise main effects tells you that there is no interaction because the effect of exercise is unaffected by the level of caffeine. As Table 8-8 demonstrates, exercise increases food consumption by 500 calories, regardless of the amount of caffeine that participants consumed.

Although making tables of means is a useful way to summarize data, perhaps the easiest way to interpret the results of a factorial experiment is to graph the means. To see how useful graphing can be, graph the data in Table 8-8. Your graph should look something like Figure 8-1. If it doesn't, please consult Box 8-1.

• **FIGURE 8-1** •

MAIN EFFECTS FOR EXERCISE, NO INTERACTION

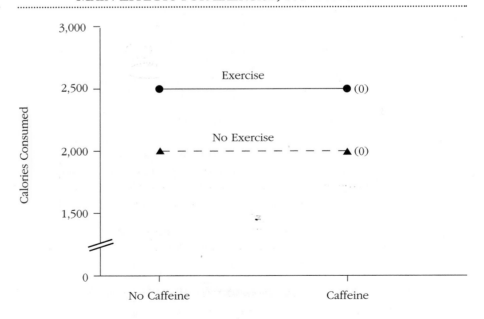

Note: Numbers in parentheses represent the simple main effects of caffeine. Thus, the simple main effect of caffeine is zero in both the no-exercise and the exercise conditions.

• **BOX 8-1** •

TURNING A 2 × 2 TABLE INTO A GRAPH

If you have never graphed a 2 × 2 before, you may need some help. How can you graph three variables (the two factors and the dependent variable) on a two-dimensional piece of paper? The short answer is that you need to use two lines instead of one.

To see how to actually make such a graph, get a sheet of notebook paper and a ruler. Starting near the left edge of the sheet, draw a 4-inch line straight down the page. This vertical line is called the *y*-axis. The *y*-axis corresponds to scores on the dependent measure. In this case, your dependent measure is calories consumed. So, label the *y*-axis "Calories Consumed."

Now that you have a yardstick (the *y*-axis) for recording calories consumed, your next step is to put marks on that yardstick. Having these marks will make it easier for you to plot the means accurately. Start marking the *y*-axis by putting a little hash mark on the very bottom of the *y*-axis. Label this mark "0." A half an inch above this mark, put another mark. Label the mark "500." Keep making marks until you get to "3,000."

Your next step is to draw a horizontal line that goes from the bottom of the *y*-axis to the right side of the page. (If you are using lined paper, you may be able to trace over one of the lines that goes across the page.) The horizontal line is called the *x*-axis. On the *x*-axis, you should put one of your independent variables. It doesn't really matter which independent variable you put on the *x*-axis. However, for the sake of this example, put "Caffeine (mg)" about an inch below the middle of the *x*-axis. Then, put a mark on the left-hand side of the *x*-axis and label this mark "No Caffeine." Next, put a mark on the right side of the *x*-axis and label it "20 mg Caffeine."

You are now ready to plot the means in the left column of Table 8-8. Once you have plotted those two means, draw a straight line between those two means. Label that line "No Exercise." Next, plot the two means in the right column of Table 8-8. Then, draw a line between those two points. Label this second line (which should be above your first line) "Exercise." Your graph should look something like Figure 8-1.

Figure 8-1 confirms what you saw in Table 8-8. Exercise increased calorie consumption, as shown by the exercise line being above the no-exercise line. Caffeine did not increase calorie consumption, as shown by the fact that both lines stay perfectly level as they go from no caffeine to 20 mg caffeine.

Finally, there is no interaction between exercise and caffeine on calorie consumption, as shown by the fact that the lines are parallel. The lines are parallel because exercise is having the same effect on the no-caffeine group as it is on the caffeine group. In this case, exercise is having no (0) effect on both the no-caffeine and caffeine groups.

Thus, if you graph your data, you only need to see whether the lines are parallel to know if you have an interaction. *If your lines are parallel, you do not have an interaction.* If, on the other hand, your lines have very different slopes, you may have an interaction.

TWO MAIN EFFECTS AND NO INTERACTION

Table 8-9 reflects another pattern of effects you might obtain. From the first row, you can see that, in the no-caffeine groups, exercise increased calorie consumption by 500 calories. Looking at the second row, you see that, in the caffeine groups, exercise also increased calorie consumption by 500. Averaging the effect of caffeine over all caffeine conditions, you find that the average effect of exercise (the overall main of exercise) was to increase calorie consumption by 500.

Looking at the columns tells you about the effect of varying caffeine levels. The first column tells you about what happens in the no-exercise conditions. As you can see, in the no-exercise conditions, the participants who get caffeine consume 200 more calories than those who don't get caffeine. Looking at the second column, you learn that, in the exercise condition, the caffeine group also consumes 200 more calories than the no-caffeine group. Because caffeine increases calorie consumption in both the no-exercise and the exercise groups, it appears that there is a caffeine main effect.

• **TABLE 8-9** •

MAIN EFFECTS FOR CAFFEINE AND EXERCISE, NO INTERACTION

	No Exercise	Exercise	Exercise simple main effects
No Caffeine	2,000	2,500	+500 (2,500 – 2,000 = +500)
Caffeine	2,200	2,700	+500 (2,700 – 2,200 = +500)
Caffeine simple main effects	+200 (2,200 – 2,000 = +200)	+200 (2,700 – 2,500 = +200)	

Averaging a treatment's simple main effects gives us its overall main effect:

Simple main effect of **Caffeine** in the no-exercise condition	+200
Simple main effect of **Caffeine** in the exercise condition	+200
Average effect (overall main effect) of **Caffeine**	+400/2 = +200

Simple main effect of **Exercise** in the no-caffeine condition	+500
Simple main effect of **Exercise** in the caffeine condition	+500
Average effect (overall main effect) of **Exercise**	1,000/2 = +500

Comparing a treatment's simple main effects tells us whether there is an interaction:

Since there are no differences between the two simple main effects for exercise (both are +500), then there is no interaction. In other words, since the effect of exercise is not affected by how much caffeine participants consumed, there is no interaction. Put another way, since the simple main effect for caffeine is the same in both the no-exercise and the exercise conditions (+200), there is no interaction.

• **FIGURE 8-2** •

MAIN EFFECTS FOR CAFFEINE AND EXERCISE, NO INTERACTION

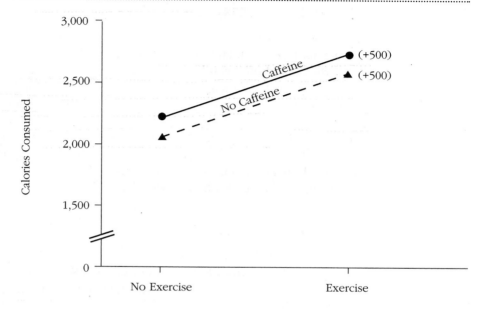

Note: Numbers in parentheses represent the simple main effects of exercise. Thus, the simple main effect of exercise was +500 in the no-caffeine condition and also in the caffeine condition.

Finally, you also know that there is no interaction because the effect of caffeine is unaffected by the level of exercise. As Table 8-9 demonstrates, the effect of caffeine is independent of (does not depend on) the amount of exercise. That is, caffeine increases food consumption by 200 calories in both the exercise and the no-exercise conditions.

To look at this lack of caffeine × exercise interaction from a different perspective, the effect of exercise is unaffected by the level of caffeine. Specifically, exercise increases food consumption by 500 calories for both the caffeine and no-caffeine groups.

If you graph the means, as we did in Figure 8-2, you can see that the graph confirms what you saw in Table 8-9. Caffeine increased calorie consumption, as shown by the caffeine line being above the no-caffeine line. Similarly, exercise increased calorie consumption, as shown by the fact that both lines slope upward as they go from no exercise to exercise. That is, the left (no exercise) side of the graph is lower than the right (exercise) side of the graph. Finally, the graph tells you that there is no interaction between exercise and caffeine on calorie consumption because the lines are parallel. The lines are parallel because exercise affects the no-caffeine groups the same (parallel) way that it affects the caffeine groups.

TWO MAIN EFFECTS AND AN INTERACTION

Now imagine that you got a very different set of results from your study. For example, suppose you found the results in Table 8-10.

As the table shows, you have main effects for both exercise and caffeine. The average effect of caffeine is to increase calorie consumption by 500, and the average effect of exercise is to increase calorie consumption by 500 calories.

However, the effect of caffeine varies depending on how much exercise participants get. In the no-exercise condition, caffeine increases calorie consumption by 200, In the exercise condition, on the other hand, caffeine increases consumption by 800 calories. Since the effect of caffeine differs depending on the amount of exercise, you have an interaction.

• TABLE 8-10 •

MAIN EFFECTS FOR CAFFEINE AND
EXERCISE WITH AN INTERACTION

	No Exercise	Exercise	Exercise simple main effects
No Caffeine	2,000	2,200	+200 (2,200 – 2,000 = +200)
Caffeine	2,200	3,000	+800 (3,000 – 2,200 = +800)

Caffeine simple main effects	+200 (2,200 – 2,000 = +200)	+800 (3,000 – 2,200 = +800)

Averaging a treatment's simple main effects gives us its overall main effect:

Simple main effect of **Caffeine** in the no-exercise condition	+200
Simple main effect of **Caffeine** in the exercise condition	+800
Average effect (overall main effect) of Caffeine	+1,000/2 = +500

Simple main effect of **Exercise** in the no-caffeine condition	+200
Simple main effect of **Exercise** in the caffeine condition	+800
Average effect (overall main effect) of **Exercise**	1,000/2 = +500

Comparing a treatment's simple main effects tells us whether there is an interaction:
Since the simple main effect for caffeine in the no-exercise conditon (+200) is different than the simple main effect for caffeine in the exercise condition (+800), there is an interaction. In other words, since the effect of exercise is affected by how much caffeine participants consumed, there is an interaction.

• **FIGURE 8-3** •

MAIN EFFECTS FOR CAFFEINE AND EXERCISE, AND AN INTERACTION

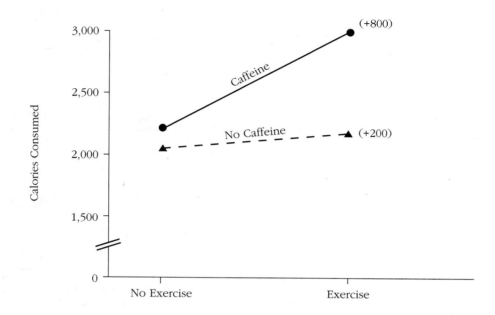

Note: Numbers in parentheses represent the exercise simple main effects. Thus, the simple main effect of exercise was +200 in the no-caffeine condition, but +800 in the caffeine condition.

To see this interaction, look at Figure 8-3. As you can see, the lines are not parallel. They are not parallel because the slope of the caffeine line is much steeper than the slope of the no-caffeine line. That is, the lines are not parallel because the simple main effect of exercise is much stronger in the caffeine condition than in the no-caffeine condition. In other words, the lines are not parallel because there is an exercise × caffeine interaction.

INTERACTION WITHOUT MAIN EFFECTS

You have seen that you can have main effects with interactions, but can you have interactions without main effects? Consider the data in Table 8-11 and Figure 8-4.

From the graph (Figure 8-4), you can see that the lines are not parallel. Instead, the lines actually cross, indicating that exercise has one kind of effect (increasing calorie consumption) in the no-caffeine condition, but an opposite

• **TABLE 8-11** •

NO OVERALL MAIN EFFECTS FOR
CAFFEINE OR EXERCISE WITH AN INTERACTION

	No Exercise	Exercise	Exercise simple main effects
No Caffeine	2,000	2,500	+500 (2,500 − 2,000 = +500)
Caffeine	2,500	2,000	−500 (2,000 − 2,500 = −500)
Caffeine simple main effects	+500 (2,500 − 2,000 = +500)	−500 (2,000 − 2,500 = −500)	

Averaging a treatment's simple main effects gives us its overall main effect:

Simple main effect of **Caffeine** in the no-exercise condition   +500
Simple main effect of **Caffeine** in the exercise condition   −500
Average effect (overall main effect) of **Caffeine**   0/2 = +0

Simple main effect of **Exercise** in the no-caffeine condition   +500
Simple main effect of **Exercise** in the caffeine condition   −500
Average effect (overall main effect) of **Exercise**   0/2 = +0

Comparing a treatment's simple main effects tells us whether there is an interaction:
Since there are very big differences between the two simple main effects for exercise, then there is an interaction. In other words, since the effect of exercise is affected by how much caffeine participants consumed, there is an interaction. Put another way, since the simple main effect for caffeine in the no-exercise condition (+500) is different than the simple main effect for caffeine in the exercise condition (−500), there is an interaction.

---

effect (decreasing calorie consumption) in the caffeine condition. Therefore, you have an interaction.

Note, however, that you do not have a main effect for either caffeine or exercise. On the average, the no-exercise groups consume as much as the exercise groups. Therefore, there isn't an exercise main effect. On the average, the no-caffeine groups consume as much as the caffeine groups (see Table 8-11). Therefore, there isn't a caffeine main effect.

You would say that there is no main effect for either caffeine or exercise. Yet, you would not say that neither caffeine nor exercise has any effect on calories consumed. Instead, you would either say that:

1. Caffeine has an effect, but its effect depends on the level of exercise.

2. Exercise has an effect, but the kind of effect it has depends on the amount of caffeine consumed.

• **FIGURE 8-4** •

No Main Effects for Caffeine or Exercise With an Interaction

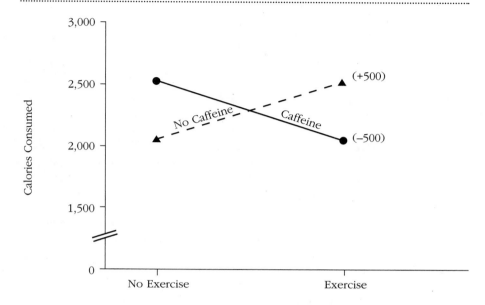

Note: Numbers in parentheses represent exercise simple main effects. Thus, the simple main effect of exercise was +500 in the no-caffeine condition, but –500 in the caffeine condition.

Note that no matter whether you emphasize the effect of caffeine (as in Statement 1) or the effect of exercise (as in Statement 2), you cannot talk about the effect of one variable without talking about the other. That is, as with any interaction, the effect of one variable depends on the other.

ONE MAIN EFFECT AND AN INTERACTION

You have seen that you can have no main effects and an interaction. You have also seen that you can have two main effects and an interaction. Can you also have one main effect and an interaction? Yes. Such a pattern of results is listed in Table 8-12 and graphed in Figure 8-5.

As Table 8-12 reveals, the average effect of varying amount of caffeine is zero. The average effect of varying exercise, on the other hand, is to increase calorie consumption by 250 calories. Note, however, that exercise's effect is uneven. In the no-caffeine condition, exercise increases consumption by 500 calories. But in the caffeine condition, exercise has no effect on calorie consumption. Thus, the effect of exercise differs depending on caffeine level.

• **TABLE 8-12** •

MAIN EFFECT FOR EXERCISE WITH AN INTERACTION

	No Exercise	Exercise	Exercise simple main effects
No Caffeine	2,000	2,500	+500 (2,500 – 2,000 = +500)
Caffeine	2,250	2,250	+0 (2,250 – 2,250 = +0)

Caffeine simple main effects	+250 (2,250 – 2,000 = +250)	–250 (2,250 – 2,500 = –250)

Averaging a treatment's simple main effects gives us its overall main effect:

Simple main effect of **Caffeine** in the no-exercise condition	+250
Simple main effect of **Caffeine** in the exercise condition	–250
Average effect (overall main effect) of **Caffeine**	0/2 = +0

Simple main effect of **Exercise** in the no-caffeine condition	+500
Simple main effect of **Exercise** in the caffeine condition	+0
Average effect (overall main effect) of **Exercise**	500/2 = +250

Comparing a treatment's simple main effects tells us whether there is an interaction:
Since there are very big differences between the two simple main effects for exercise, there is an interaction. In other words, since the effect of exercise is affected by how much caffeine participants consumed, there is an interaction. To look at it another way, since the simple main effect for caffeine in the no-exercise condition (+250) is very different than the simple main effect for caffeine in the exercise condition (–250), there is an interaction.

Figure 8-5 tells the same story. By looking at that figure, you realize there may be an interaction because the lines are not parallel. They are not parallel because the effect of exercise is fairly dramatic in the no-caffeine condition, but nonexistent in the caffeine condition.

Determining the main effects requires a little more mental visualization. If there is a main effect for caffeine, one of the caffeine lines should, on the average, be higher than the other. When one line is always above the other, it is easy to tell whether there seems to be a main effect. In this case, however, the lines cross. Thus, it is hard to tell whether one line is, on the average, above the other. However, if you study the graph carefully, you may see that the midpoint of both lines is at the same spot (2,250). Or, you may realize that the no-caffeine line is below the caffeine line just as often and to just the same extent as it is above the caffeine line. In either case, you would conclude that there is no main effect for caffeine.

• FIGURE 8-5 •

MAIN EFFECTS FOR EXERCISE AND AN INTERACTION

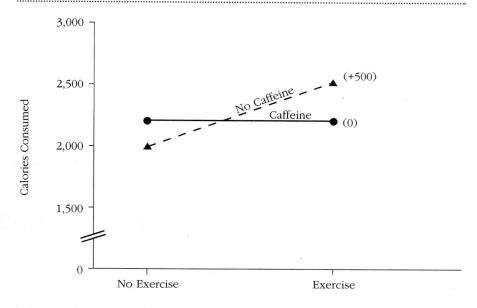

Note: Numbers in parentheses represent exercise simple main effects. Thus, the simple main effect of exercise was +500 in the no-caffeine condition, but 0 in the caffeine condition.

To determine whether there is a main effect for exercise, you could mentally combine the two lines. If you do that, you would "see" that this combined line slopes upward, indicating a main effect for exercise. Failing that, you could reason that because the no-caffeine line slopes upward, and the caffeine line stays straight, the average of the two lines would have to slope upward. Or, you could determine that exercise had an effect by realizing that the right (exercise) side of the graph was higher than the left (no-exercise) side of the graph. Or, if none of these techniques work for you, convert the graph into a table of means. In this case, take Figure 8-5 and see if you can convert it into a table resembling Table 8-12. Once you have your table, you should be able to see that the average for the exercise groups is higher than the average for the no-exercise groups.

NO MAIN EFFECTS AND NO INTERACTION

The last pattern of results you could obtain is to get no statistically significant results. That is, you could fail to find a caffeine effect, fail to find an exercise

• TABLE 8-13 •

NO MAIN EFFECTS AND NO INTERACTION

	No Exercise	Exercise
No Caffeine	2,500	2,500
Caffeine	2,500	2,500

effect, and fail to obtain an interaction between caffeine and exercise. An example of such a dull and dreary set of findings is listed in Table 8-13.

ANALYZING THE RESULTS FROM A 2 × 2 EXPERIMENT

You can now graph and describe the eight possible patterns of results from a 2 × 2 experiment. But how do you analyze your results? How do you know whether a main effect or an interaction is significant?

As you did with the multiple-group experiment, you would use analysis of variance to analyze your data. However, instead of testing for one main effect, you will be testing for two main effects and an interaction. Thus, your ANOVA summary table might look like this:

SOURCE OF VARIANCE	SUM OF SQUARES	DF	MEAN SQUARE	F
Exercise Main Effect (A)	900	1	900	9.00
Caffeine Main Effect (B)	200	1	200	2.00
Interaction (A × B)	100	1	100	1.00
Error Term (within groups)	3,600	36	100	
Total	4,800	39		

WHAT DEGREES OF FREEDOM TELL YOU

Despite the fact that this ANOVA table has two more sources of variance than an ANOVA for the multiple-group experiment described in Chapter 7, most of the rules that apply to the ANOVA table for that design apply to the table for a factorial design (see Box 8-2). In terms of degrees of freedom, the two basic rules that you learned in Chapter 7 will serve you well.

As you may recall, the first rule was that the number of treatment levels is one more than the treatment's degrees of freedom. Since the ANOVA summary table above tells us that the degrees of freedom for exercise is 1, we know that the study used two levels of exercise. Likewise, since the degrees of freedom for

• **BOX 8-2** •

THE MATHEMATICS OF AN ANOVA SUMMARY TABLE FOR BETWEEN-SUBJECTS FACTORIAL DESIGNS

1. Degrees of freedom (*df*) for a main effect equals 1 less than the number of levels of that factor. If there are 3 levels of a factor (low, medium, high), that factor has 2 *df*.

2. Degrees of freedom for an interaction equals the product of the *df* of the factors making up that effect. If you have an interaction between a factor that has 1 *df* and a factor that has 2 *df*, that interaction has 2 *df* (because 1 × 2 = 2).

3. To get the total degrees of freedom, subtract 1 from the number of participants. So, if you have 60 participants, the total degrees of freedom should be 59 (60 − 1).

4. To get the *df* for the error term, determine how many groups you had. Then, subtract the number of groups from the number of participants. In a 2 × 2, you have 4 (2 × 2) groups. Therefore, if you had 60 participants, your *df* error is 56 (60 − 4). If you had a 3 × 2, you would have 6 (3 × 2) groups. So, the *df* error would be 54 (60 − 6).

Another way to get the *df* error is to: (1) add up the *df* for all the main effects and interactions, and then (2) subtract that sum from the total degrees of freedom. Thus, if you had 1 *df* for the first main effect, 1 *df* for the second main effect, 1 *df* for the interaction, the sum of the *df* for your main effects and interactions would be 3 (1 + 1 + 1). You would then subtract that sum from the *df* total. Thus, if the *df* total was 59, your error term would be 56 (59 − 3).

5. To get the mean square for any effect, get the sum of squares for that effect, then divide by that effect's *df*. If an effect's sum of squares was 300, and its *df* was 3, its mean square would be 100 (300/3 = 100). If the effect's sum of squares was 300, and its *df* was 1, its mean square would be 300 (300/1 = 300).

6. To get the *F* for any effect, get its mean square and divide it by the mean square error. If an effect's mean square was 100, and the mean square error was 50, the *F* for that effect would be 2.

caffeine is 1, we know the study used two levels of caffeine. Thus, the ANOVA summary table tells us that the study used a 2 × 2 design.

The second rule was that the total number of participants is one more than the total degrees of freedom. Therefore, the ANOVA table above tells us that there were 40 participants in the experiment (because 39 + 1 = 40).

The only new thing you need to figure out is the degrees of freedom for the interaction term. To calculate the interaction term's degrees of freedom, multiply the degrees of freedom for the main effects making up that interaction. For a 2 × 2 experiment, that would be 1 (*df* for first main effect) × 1 (*df* for second main effect) = 1. For a 2 × 3 experiment, the *df* for the first main effect would be 1 and the *df* for the second main effect would be 2. Therefore, for a

2×3 experiment, the interaction term's degrees of freedom would be 2 (because $1 \times 2 = 2$).

INTERPRETING THE RESULTS OF AN ANOVA TABLE

To determine whether an effect was significant, you compare the F for that effect to the value given in the F table under the appropriate number of degrees of freedom. If your obtained F is larger than the value in the table, the effect is significant.

Generally, you will want to start your inspection of the ANOVA results by seeing if any of your overall main effects are significant. Then, if you have a significant main effect, you will want to know whether this main effect was qualified by an interaction.

Main Effects Without Interactions: It All Adds Up

If the interaction was not significant, your conclusions are simple and straightforward. Having no interactions means there are no "ifs" or "buts" about your main effects. That is, you have not found anything that would lead you to say that the main effect occurs only under certain conditions. For instance, if you have a main effect for caffeine and no interactions, that means that caffeine had the same kind of effect throughout your experiment—no matter what the level of exercise was. In other words, when you don't have interactions, you can just talk about the overall main effects.

Interactions: When Combining Factors Leads to Effects That Differ From the Sum of the Individual Effects

If you find a significant interaction, your results are not as easy to interpret. You can't just talk about one variable's effect without saying that the variable's effect depends on the level of a second variable. Because the effect of one variable is different depending on the level of the second variable, it is misleading to talk only about the effect of one variable. Instead, you have to talk about the effects of combining the two variables. Specifically, you have to talk about how the effect of one variable is moderated by the other variable.

At a more concrete level, having an interaction means that a treatment factor has a different effect on one group of participants than on another. For example, a treatment may be more effective for one group than for another. In our caffeine–exercise example, having an interaction means that caffeine has a different effect depending on the level of exercise the participant received. In other words, the simple main effect of caffeine in the no-exercise condition is different from the simple main effect of caffeine in the exercise condition. Thus, rather than talking about the general, overall main effect, you should talk about the simple main effects that make up the overall main effect.

Before you talk about those simple main effects, you must understand them. The easiest way to understand the pattern of the simple main effects—

and thus understand the interaction—is to graph those simple effects.[4] Because you have a significant interaction, the lines representing these simple main effects will have different slopes, reflecting the fact that the treatment appears to have one effect in one condition, but a different effect in another condition. That is, because you have a significant interaction, the lines in your graph will *not* be parallel.

Closer inspection of these nonparallel lines will tell you what type of interaction you have. As you'll see, it's important to know whether you have an ordinal interaction or a crossover (disordinal) interaction.

Ordinal Interactions: Interaction or Measurement-Induced Mirage?

Suppose that your lines are *not* parallel. However, your lines are sloping in the same direction and do not actually cross. For example, both of the lines may slope upward, but one of the lines has a steeper slope. Or, both of the lines may slope downward, but one has a steeper slope. In either case, you have an **ordinal interaction**.

Ordinal Interactions May Mean That Combining Treatments Multiplies Their Individual Effects

Ordinal interactions suggest that a treatment has a more intense effect in one condition than another. For example, you would find an ordinal interaction if a treatment was more effective for one type of patient than for another. You would also find an ordinal interaction if a teaching strategy helped both shy and outgoing children, but helped outgoing children more. In Figure 8-3, you can see another example of an ordinal interaction: Exercise boosted participants' calorie consumption by only 200 calories in the no-caffeine condition, but it boosted calorie consumption by 800 calories in the caffeine condition.

As Figure 8-3 shows, ordinal interactions may reflect the fact that combining two independent variables produces larger than expected effects. The combination is greater than the sum of its parts.

Ordinal interactions may also reflect the fact that combining treatments is less effective than you would expect from knowing the factors' individual effects. That is, some ordinal interactions result from the combination of treatments being less than the sum of the effects of the individual treatments.

To sum up, some ordinal interactions reflect the fact that a treatment has more of an effect when combined with another treatment. Some ordinal interactions reflect the fact that a treatment has more of an effect when another

---

[4]Interactions suggest that, rather than looking at the overall main effects, you should look at the individual simple main effects. Therefore, one way to understand an interaction is to do statistical analyses on the individual simple main effects. The computations for these tests are relatively simple. However, there are some relatively subtle issues involved in deciding which test to use.

treatment is not around. All ordinal interactions suggest that a factor appears to have more of an effect in one condition than in another condition.

Ordinal Interactions as Measurement-Induced Mirages

We say *appears* to have more of an effect because it is not easy to determine whether a variable had more of a psychological effect in one condition than in another. For example, to state that the difference between 2,200 calories and 2,000 calories is less than the difference between 3,000 calories and 2,200 calories, you must have interval scale data.

Obviously, in this case, you have interval scale data—if you are interested in number of calories consumed. However, if you are using calories consumed as a measure of how hungry people felt, then your measure may not be interval. You may not have a one-to-one correspondence between number of calories consumed and degree of perceived hunger. It may take the same increase in perceived hunger to make a person who normally eats 2,000 calories consume an additional 200 calories as it does to get someone who would normally eat 2,200 calories to eat an additional 800 calories. If it does, then the ordinal interaction is an artifact of your hunger measure yielding ordinal rather than interval data. If you had used an interval scale measure, you would not have obtained an interaction.

To see how you might get an ordinal interaction even when the effect of combining two variables produces nothing more than the sum of their individual effects, consider Figure 8-6. In Figure 8-6a, the lines are not parallel and thus indicate an interaction. Now, look at Figure 8-6b, which is a graph of the same data. In Figure 8-6b, the lines are parallel, indicating no interaction.

Why does one graph yield an interaction whereas the other does not? The first graph yields an interaction because it, like most graphs you have seen, makes the distance between 3 and 4 equal to the distance between 7 and 8. However, by doing this, the author of the graph assumes that the data are interval. Thus, the difference in hunger between those participants who rate their hunger a "3" and those participants who rate their hunger a "4" is depicted as being the same as the difference in hunger between those who rate their hunger a "7" and those who rate their hunger an "8." If this assumption is true, then caffeine makes participants feel hungrier in the exercise condition than it does in the no-exercise condition.

The second graph (8-6b) shows what can happen if we do not buy the assumption that the data are interval. Specifically, the graph shows what happens when the difference in feelings of hunger between rating a "7" and rating an "8" is greater than the difference in hunger between a "3" and "4." In that case, at the psychological level, caffeine's effect on the subjective state of "feeling hungry" is the same in the exercise condition as it is in the no-exercise condition. Thus, even though there is an interaction at the statistical level, there is not an interaction at the psychological level: Caffeine has the same *psychological effect* in both conditions. In other words, seeing that the treatment makes a

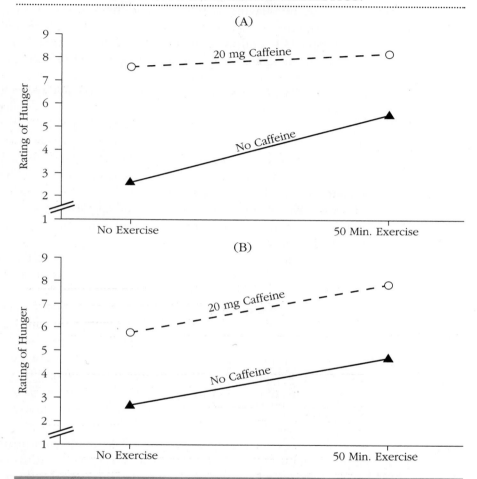

• **FIGURE 8-6** •

HOW AN ORDINAL INTERACTION
MAY NOT BE A TRUE INTERACTION

greater change in participants' scores in one condition doesn't necessarily mean that the treatment makes a greater change in participants' feelings.

When to Suspect That an Ordinal
Interaction May Be Due to Measurement Error

As you have seen, ordinal interactions may be nothing more than an illusion caused by having ordinal, rather than interval, data. Because you can rarely be sure that you have interval data, you should always be cautious when interpreting ordinal interactions. However, you should be especially cautious if you have reason to believe that your data are ordinal.

Ordinal Measures, Like Ranks, May Produce Ordinal Interactions   If your data come from having participants rank items from lowest to highest, then you clearly have ordinal data. You can't say that the difference between something ranked "1" and something ranked "2" is the same as the difference between something ranked "3" and something ranked "4" (see Chapter 4).

A Measure That Is Mostly (But Not Entirely) Interval May Produce Ordinal Interactions   Because ordinal data make ordinal interactions difficult to interpret, you may want to avoid using ordinal measures. Unfortunately, however, avoiding ordinal data is not as easy as avoiding ordinal measures. Even a measure that seems like it should provide interval data may end up providing ordinal data.

To understand how an interval scale measure could produce ordinal data, imagine a typical bathroom scale. Normally, it would provide interval data. However, what if you were measuring football players on it? Your scale would provide interval measurement to those players who weighed less than 250 pounds (or whatever your scale went up to). However, everyone 250 and above would, according to your scale, weigh 250. Thus, you would know that someone who, according to your scale, weighed 250 was heavier than someone weighing 245, but you wouldn't know how much heavier.

Not only would your scale fail you at extremely high weights, it would also fail you at extremely low weights. Thus, if you were weighing the food on football players' plates, your scale would not provide accurate weights.

In technical terminology, your bathroom scale has two weaknesses. First, its *ceiling* (the highest score participants can receive) of 250 pounds is too low to weigh some of the heavier football players. Second, its *floor* (the lowest score participants can receive) of one pound is too high to accurately measure objects less than 1 pound.

The scale's low ceiling could hide the effect of a treatment. For example, suppose the heavy football players are put on a weightlifting program that makes them even heavier. Although the treatment works, the results would not show up on the bathroom scale: The heavy players would, according to that scale, still "weigh" 250 pounds. In technical jargon, your results are misleading because of a **ceiling effect**: the effect of a treatment or combination of treatments is underestimated because the dependent measure is not sensitive to values above a certain level.

The scale's high floor could also hide the effect of a treatment. For example, suppose the football players are rewarded for putting less food on their plates, and the reward system works. However, the researcher measures the amount of food on the plate by using a bathroom scale that has trouble weighing anything under 5 pounds. The measure's high floor makes it look like the players aren't eating less. In technical jargon, our results are misleading because of a **floor ef-**

fect: The effects of the treatment or combination of treatments is underestimated because the dependent measure places too high a floor on what the lowest response can be.

Ceiling and floor effects can make it seem like an effective treatment has no effect. In addition, ceiling and floor effects can make it seem like an effective treatment has a strong effect for one group but no effect for another group.

Let's see how a ceiling effect could make it look like a treatment that is equally effective for two groups is only effective for one of the groups. Let's start by supposing that both light and heavy football players are put on a weightlifting program. Furthermore, suppose that both groups gain 20 pounds. The light football players go from 180 to 200 pounds; the heavy players go from 300 to 320. According to the bathroom scale, the light players gain 20 pounds (180 – 200), but the heavy football players haven't gained a pound. The scale still has them all weighing 250 pounds. In this case, a ceiling effect made it look like weightlifting has more of an effect on light than on heavy players, even though weightlifting's effect is the same for both types of players. That is, due to a ceiling effect, our scale gave us an ordinal interaction when we should not have had one.

Like bathroom scales, psychological scales may be plagued by low ceilings and high floors. Thus, as with extreme scores on our bathroom scale, extreme scores on a psychological measure may be misleading. Some of the low scorers may deserve much lower scores, but the measure is unable to give it to them. In a sense, the "floor" (the lowest score they can receive) is too high. Or, some of the high scorers might, if given a chance, score much higher than the others—but the measure doesn't give them that chance. In such a case, the "ceiling" (the highest score they can receive) is too low.

Thus far, you know that ceiling and floor effects can contaminate your results. If your measure's ceiling is too low, ceiling effects may be contaminating your results. If your measure's floor is too high, floor effects may be contaminating your results. In the next sections, you will learn (1) when to suspect that a ceiling or floor effect is affecting your results and (2) how ceiling and floor effects contaminate your results. Thus, after reading the next section, you will be appropriately cautious when interpreting ordinal interactions.

Ceiling Effects If a group's average scores are quite high, you should suspect that your ordinal interaction may be due to ceiling effects. Ceiling effects occur when the measure does not allow participants to score as high as they should (see Figure 8-7). For example, imagine an extremely easy knowledge test, in which half the class scores 100%. The problem with such a test is that we can't differentiate between the students who knew the material fairly well and the students who knew the material extremely well. The test's "low ceiling" did not allow very knowledgeable students to show that they knew more than the somewhat knowledgeable students.

To see how a ceiling effect can create an ordinal interaction, consider the following experiment. An investigator wants to know how information about a

• **FIGURE 8-7** •

CEILING EFFECTS CAN CAUSE HEADACHES

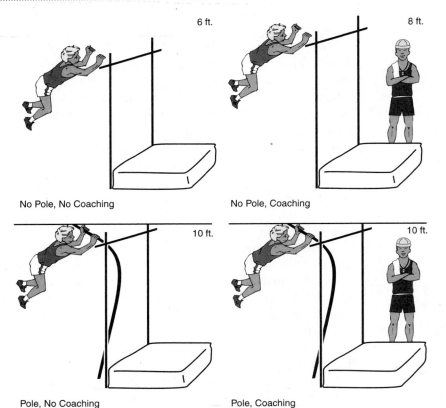

"Headed" for trouble—Coaching doesn't help Larry's performance in the pole vault condition. Maybe if Larry could vault outdoors or in a building with a higher ceiling things would be different.

specific person affects the impressions people form of that person. The investigator uses a 2 (information about a stimulus person's traits [no information versus extremely positive information]) × 2 (information about a stimulus person's behavior [no information versus extremely positive information]) factorial experiment. For the dependent measure, participants rate the stimulus person's character on a three-point scale (1 = below average, 2 = average, 3 = above average).

As you can see from Figure 8-8a, the investigator obtains an ordinal interaction. The interaction suggests that getting information about a specific person's behavior has less of an impact if participants already have information about that person's traits. In fact, the interaction suggests that if participants already know about the stimulus person's traits, information about the person's behavior is worthless.

• **FIGURE 8-8** •

How a Ceiling Effect Can Create an Ordinal Interaction

(a): An ordinal interaction caused by a ceiling effect

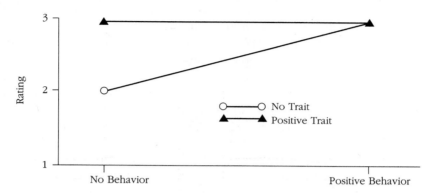

(b): How the same subjects would have scored with a positive "higher ceiling"

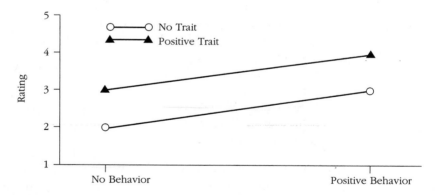

Note: With the higher ceiling, the lines are parallel and the "interaction" disappears.

The problem in interpreting this interaction is that the results could be due to a ceiling effect. That is, even if getting additional favorable information about the stimulus person raises participants' opinions of that person, participants cannot show this increased respect. That is, participants may feel that a person with a favorable trait is a 3 (above average) and a person with both a favorable trait and a favorable behavior is a 4 (well above average)—but they cannot rate the person a 4. The highest rating they can give a person is a 3. The highest rating (above average) on this scale—the ceiling response—is not high enough.

By not allowing participants to rate the stimulus person as high as they wanted to, the investigator did not allow participants to rate the positive trait/positive behavior person higher than either the positive trait/no behavior person or the positive behavior/no trait person. Thus, the investigator's ordinal interaction was due to a ceiling effect. In other words, the interaction is due to the dependent measure placing an artificially low ceiling on how high a response can be. As you can see from Figure 8-8b, "raising the ceiling" would eliminate some ordinal interactions.

Floor Effects   Just as ceiling effects can account for ordinal interactions, so can their opposites—floor effects. For example, suppose the investigator uses the same three-point rating scale as before (1 = below average, 2 = average, 3 = above average). However, instead of using no information and extremely positive information, the investigator uses no information and extremely negative information. The investigator might again obtain an ordinal interaction (see Figure 8-9a). Again, the interaction would indicate that adding behavioral information to trait information has little effect on participants' impressions. This time, however, the interaction could be due to the fact that participants could not rate the stimulus person lower than a "1" (below average). The problem is that the bottom rating—the "floor"—is too high.

By not allowing participants to rate the person as low as they wanted to, the investigator did not allow participants to rate the negative trait/negative behavior stimulus person lower than the negative trait/no behavior person or the negative behavior/no trait person. Thus, the investigator's ordinal interaction was due to a floor effect. As you can see from Figure 8-9b, "lowering the floor" can eliminate some ordinal interactions.

As floor and ceiling effects show, an ordinal interaction may reflect a measurement problem rather than a true interaction. So, be careful when interpreting ordinal interactions.

Crossover (Disordinal) Interactions: When Interactions Really Are Interactions   You do not have to be so careful if you have a crossover interaction. When you have a crossover interaction, as the term "crossover interaction" suggests, the lines in your graph actually cross.

Crossover interactions often indicate that a factor has one kind of effect in one condition and the opposite kind of effect in another condition. For example, you would have a crossover interaction if a therapy that helps patients who have one kind of problem actually hurts patients who have a different kind of problem. In Figure 8-4, you can see another example of a crossover interaction: In the no-caffeine condition, exercise *increases* calorie consumption, but, in the caffeine condition, exercise *decreases* calorie consumption.

Crossover interactions are also called **disordinal interactions**. They are called disordinal interactions because, unlike ordinal interactions, they can't be an artifact of having ordinal, rather than interval, data.

• **FIGURE 8-9** •

HOW A FLOOR EFFECT COULD CAUSE US TO UNDERESTIMATE THE COMBINED EFFECTS OF KNOWING BOTH NEGATIVE TRAITS AND NEGATIVE BEHAVIORS ON THE IMPRESSIONS WE FORM

(a): An ordinal interaction caused by a floor effect

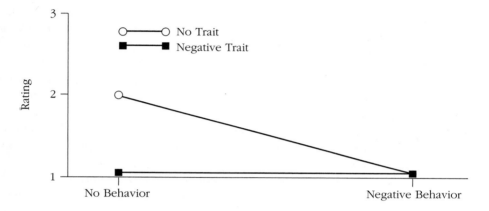

(b): How the same subjects would have scored if there had been a "lower floor"

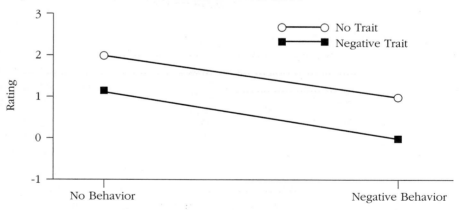

Note: In the second graph, the lines are parallel and the "interaction" disappears.

To understand why disordinal interactions can't be due to having ordinal data, let's imagine a factorial experiment designed to determine the effect of watching exercise videos and monitoring what one eats on physical fitness.

Specifically, middle-aged adult volunteers are assigned to one of four conditions: (1) no video/no diet monitoring, (2) no video/diet monitoring, (3) video/no diet monitoring, and (4) video/diet monitoring. After 6 weeks, fitness is assessed.

The experimenter assesses fitness by having the adults start one block east of First Street and seeing how many blocks the person can run in 10 minutes. Thus, if a person makes it to First Street, he has run one block, if he makes it to Third Street, he gets credit for running three blocks.

Unfortunately, the experimenter did not check to make sure that all the blocks are equal in length. Indeed, as it turns out, the blocks vary considerably in length.

Because some blocks are very short and others are fairly long, the measure provides only ordinal data. For example, we would know that someone who ran eight blocks ran farther than someone who ran six blocks, but we wouldn't know how much farther. We would know one ran two blocks farther, but two blocks might be 100 feet or it might be 10,000 feet. Therefore, if Mary runs eight blocks to Mabel's six, and Sam runs four blocks to Steve's two, we cannot say that Mary outran Mabel by the same distance as Sam outran Steve. Mary may have run 100 feet more than Mabel, but Sam may have run 10,000 feet more than Steve.

How will the use of an ordinal measure hurt the experimenter's ability to interpret the results? The answer to this question depends on the pattern of the results.

If the researcher gets the ordinal interaction depicted in Figure 8-10, there is a problem because the apparent interaction may only be an artifact of having ordinal data. For example, the interaction could be due to the distance between Seventh and Eighth Streets being longer than the distance between Third and Fifth Streets. Thus, if the researcher had used an interval measure (number of feet run), the researcher might not have found an interaction.

If, on the other hand, the researcher gets the disordinal interaction depicted in Figure 8-11, this interaction can't be due to having ordinal data. Even if the blocks are all of different lengths (not at all interval), the fact would remain that the interaction still would reflect the fact that the weight-monitoring was more effective for the people watching the exercise videos than for those not watching the videos. Regardless of the length of the blocks, we know that the difference between being able to make it to Fifth Street versus being able to make it to Seventh Street is smaller than the difference between making it to Third Street versus making it to Eighth Street. (We know this because the distance between Third and Eighth includes the distance between Fifth and Seventh. To walk from Third to Eighth, you have to walk through Fifth and Seventh.)

Why Crossover Interactions Are Easier to Interpret

To reiterate, disordinal interactions are less difficult to interpret than ordinal interactions. Ordinal interactions are difficult to interpret because there are always two possible explanations for an ordinal interaction.

One possible explanation is that the ordinal interaction really represents the fact that combining your two independent variables produces an effect that is dif-

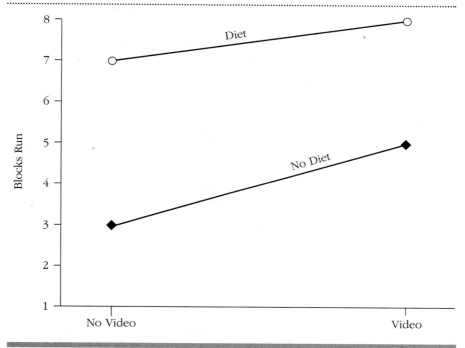

• **FIGURE 8-10** •

AN ORDINAL INTERACTION
BETWEEN DIET AND EXERCISE VIDEOS

ferent from the sum of their individual effects. Specifically, combining the factors really has either less of, or more of, an effect than the sum of their individual effects.

The second possibility is that the apparent interaction is merely an artifact of ordinal scale measurement (see Chapter 4 for a review of scales of measurement). If you had more accurately measured the construct, you would not have found an interaction. Therefore, if you want to say that an ordinal interaction represents a true interaction, you need to establish that you have interval data.

To illustrate the difficulty of interpreting an ordinal interaction, suppose you find that a treatment boosted scores from 15 to 19 in one condition, but from 5 to 8 in the other. At the level of scores, you have an interaction: The treatment increased scores more in one condition than in the other. But what about at the level of psychological reality? Can you say that going from a 15 to a 19 represents more psychological change than going from a 5 to an 8? Only if you have interval or ratio scale data. In other words, with an ordinal interaction, you can only conclude that the variables really interact if you can say that a one-point change in scores at one end of your scale is the same thing (psychologically) as a one-point change at any other part of your scale.

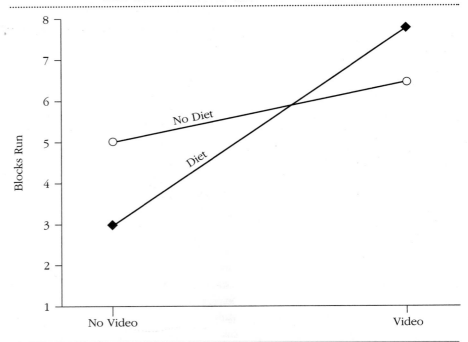

• FIGURE 8-11 •

A DISORDINAL (CROSSOVER) INTERACTION
BETWEEN DIET AND EXERCISE VIDEOS

With crossover (disordinal) interactions, on the other hand, you are not comparing differences between scores on one part of your scale with differences between scores on an entirely different part of your scale. Instead, you are making comparisons between scores that overlap. For example, with a crossover interaction, you might only have to conclude that the psychological difference between 10 and 30 is bigger than a difference between 15 and 19. Because the difference between 10 and 30 includes 15–19, you can conclude that the difference between 10 and 30 is bigger—even if you only have ordinal data. Thus, when you have a crossover (disordinal) interaction, you can conclude that your variables really do interact.

PUTTING THE 2 × 2 TO WORK

You now understand the logic behind the 2 × 2 design. In the next sections, you will see how you can use the 2 × 2 to produce research that is more interesting, has greater construct validity, and has greater external validity than research produced by a simple experiment.

ADDING A REPLICATION FACTOR TO INCREASE GENERALIZABILITY

The generalizability of results from a single simple experiment can always be questioned. Critics ask questions such as, "Would the results have been different if a different experimenter had performed the study?" and "Would the results have been different if a different manipulation had been used?" Often, the researcher's answer to these critics is to do a **systematic replication:** a study that varies from the original only in some minor aspect, such as using different experimenters or different stimulus materials.

For example, Morris (1986) found that students learned more from a lecture presented in a rock-video format than from a conventional lecture. However, Morris only used one lecture and one rock video. Obviously, we would have more confidence in his results if he had used more than one conventional lecture and one rock-video lecture.

Morris would have benefited from doing a 2 × 2 experiment. Because the 2 × 2 factorial design is like doing two simple experiments at once, he could have obtained his original findings and replicated them in a single 2 × 2 experiment. Specifically, in addition to manipulating the factor of presentation type, he could also have manipulated the **replication factor** of **stimulus sets:** the particular stimulus materials shown to two or more groups of participants. Thus, he could have done a 2 (presentation type [conventional lecture versus rock-video format]) × 2 (stimulus sets [material about Shakespeare versus material about economics]) study. Because psychologists often want to show that the manipulation's effect can occur with more than just one particular stimulus set, experimenters routinely include stimulus sets as a replication factor in their experiments.[5]

Stimulus sets are not the only replication factor that researchers use. Some researchers employ more than one experimenter to run the study and then use experimenter as a factor in the design. Some investigators use experimenter as a factor to show the generality of their results. Specifically, they want to show that certain experimenter attributes (gender, attractiveness, status) do not affect the outcome of the experiment.

Other investigators use experimenters as a factor to establish that the experimenters are not intentionally or unintentionally influencing the results. For example, Ranieri and Zeiss (1984) did an experiment in which participants rated their mood by filling out a self-rating form. Ranieri and Zeiss were worried that experimenters might unintentionally influence participants' responses. Therefore, they used three experimenters and randomly assigned participants to experimenter. If they had found that different experimenters achieved differ-

---

[5]Whether traditional, fixed-effects, analysis of variance should be used to analyze such studies is a matter of debate (Clark, 1973; Cohen, 1976; Coleman, 1979; Kenny & Smith, 1980; Richter & Seay, 1987; Wickens & Keppel, 1983; Wike & Church, 1976).

ent patterns of results, they would suspect that the results might be due to experimenter effects rather than to the manipulation itself.

USING AN INTERACTION TO FIND AN EXCEPTION TO THE RULE: LOOKING AT A POTENTIAL MODERATING FACTOR

Thus far, we have discussed instances where the investigator's goal in using the factorial design was to increase the generalizability of the experimental results. Thus, in a study that uses stimulus set as a replication factor, researchers hope that the treatment × stimulus set interaction will not be significant. Similarly, most researchers who use experimenter as a factor hope that there will not be a treatment × experimenter interaction.

Often, however, you may read a research report and say to yourself, "But I bet that would not happen under ___ conditions." In that case, you should do a study in which you essentially repeat the original experiment except that you add what you believe will be a moderating factor that will interact with the treatment.

To see how a moderating factor experiment would work, let's look at a study by Jackson and Williams (1985). Jackson and Williams were aware of the phenomenon of social loafing: Individuals don't work as hard on tasks when they work in groups as when they work alone. Jackson and Williams, however, felt that social loafing would not occur on extremely difficult tasks. Therefore, they did a study, which, like most social-loafing studies, manipulated whether or not participants worked alone or in groups. In addition, they added what they thought would be a moderating factor—whether the task was easy or difficult.

As expected, and as other studies had shown, social loafing occurred. However, social loafing only occurred when the task was easy. When the task was difficult, the reverse of social loafing occurred: Participants worked better in groups than alone. This interaction between task difficulty and number of workers confirmed their hypothesis that task difficulty moderated social loafing (see Figure 8-12).

To better appreciate how you could take advantage of Jackson and Williams's research strategy, let's review what they did. With part of their study, they replicated an existing finding (the social-loafing main effect). With the other part of their study, they tested whether another variable would moderate (interact with) the social-loafing main effect. In other words, their study had one very safe prediction and one risky prediction. Many students like this strategy of being able to propose a single study that will test both a prediction that will probably turn out and a more adventurous prediction. With a moderating factor study, they can have both types of predictions in the same study. By replicating a well-established main effect, they can be fairly confident that they will obtain a significant effect. By looking for a moderating variable that will interact with the main effect, they can try to make a new discovery. You, too, may like this idea of having your cake and eating it, too. Thus, you may find that

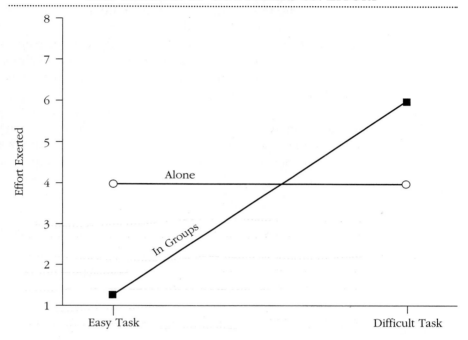

• **FIGURE 8-12** •

INTERACTION BETWEEN TASK DIFFICULTY AND NUMBER OF COWORKERS ON EFFORT

Note: Effort was scored on a 1–7 scale, with higher numbers indicating more effort.

you want to conduct a moderating factor study. (For more tips on designing a moderating factor study, see Chapter 2.)

USING INTERACTIONS TO CREATE NEW RULES

Although we have discussed looking for an interaction to find an exception to an existing rule, some interactions do more than complicate existing rules. Some interactions reveal new rules. Consider Barbara Tversky's (1973) 2 × 2 factorial experiment. She randomly assigned students to one of four conditions:

1. expected a multiple-choice test and received a multiple-choice test
2. expected a multiple-choice test and received an essay test
3. expected an essay test and received a multiple-choice test
4. expected an essay test and received an essay test

She found an interaction between type of test expected and test received. Her interaction showed that participants did better when they got the kind of test they expected. That is, they did better when the test *matched* their expectations (see Figure 8-13).

Similarly, a researcher might find an interaction between mood (happy, sad) at the time of learning and mood (happy, sad) at the time of recall. The interaction might reveal that recall was best when participants were in the same mood at the time of learning as they were at the time of recall. As you can see, the 2 × 2 experiment may be useful for you if you are interested in assessing the effects of *similarity.*

In short, expanding a simple experiment into a 2 × 2 experiment allows you to test more— and more interesting—hypotheses. You can look at the main effect of the factor you would have studied with the simple experiment, the main effect of another factor, and the interaction between those two factors. In

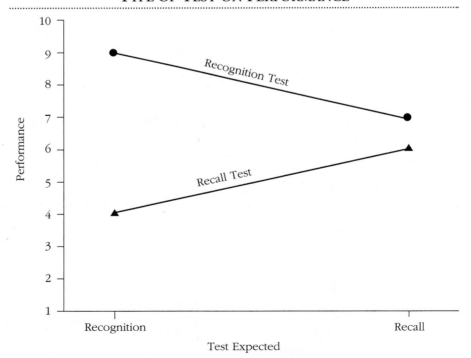

• **FIGURE 8-13** •

THE EFFECT OF EXPECTATIONS AND TYPE OF TEST ON PERFORMANCE

many cases, the hypothesis involving the interaction may be the most interesting. Sometimes, the interaction will suggest important exceptions to the rule that your original factor has a certain effect. Sometimes, the interaction will represent a variable such as similarity.

THE HYBRID DESIGN: A FACTORIAL DESIGN THAT ALLOWS YOU TO STUDY NONEXPERIMENTAL VARIABLES

Rather than converting a simple experiment into a 2 × 2 experiment by adding a second experimental factor, you could convert a simple experiment into a 2 × 2 hybrid design by adding a nonexperimental factor. The nonexperimental factor could be any variable that you cannot randomly assign, such as age, gender, or personality type.

In such a hybrid 2 × 2 design, you could make cause–effect statements about the effects of the experimental factor, but *you could not make any cause–effect statements regarding the nonexperimental factor*. Thus, although the study described in Table 8-14 includes gender of participant as a variable, the study does not allow us to say anything about the effects of a participant's gender.

Why can't you make cause–effect (causal) statements regarding the effects of the participant's gender? Because your two groups may differ in hundreds of ways besides their gender: college major, exercise habits, age, smoking habits, current stress levels, extent to which they cook their own food, and so on. Any one of these differences might be responsible for the difference in behavior between the two groups. Therefore, you cannot legitimately say that gender differences—rather than any of these other differences—are the reason your two groups behaved differently.

To help emphasize that you can only make causal statements about independent variables that you randomly assign, randomly assigned variables are often called "true" independent variables or "strong" independent variables. In contrast, predictor variables that are not randomly assigned are called "weak" independent variables to highlight the fact that you can't determine whether they have an effect.

If you cannot make causal statements about the nonexperimental factor, why would you want to add a nonexperimental variable to your simple experiment? The most obvious and exciting reason is that you are interested in that nonexperimental variable.

To see how adding a nonexperimental variable (age of participant, introvert-extrovert, etc.) can spice up a simple experiment, consider the following simple experiment: Participants are either angered or not angered in a problem-solving task by a confederate who poses as another participant. Later, participants get an opportunity to punish or reward the confederate. Obviously, we would expect participants to punish the confederate more when they had been angered. This simple experiment, in itself, would not be very interesting.

• **TABLE 8-14** •

THE HYBRID DESIGN: A CROSS BETWEEN
AN EXPERIMENT AND A NONEXPERIMENT

	Female	Male	Differences between the group of women and the group of men participating in this study	
No Stress	2,000	3,000	Simple main "effect" of gender in no-stress condition = 1,000	Overall main "effect" of
Stress	*1,500*	*4,000*	Simple main "effect" of gender in stress condition = 2,500	gender = 1,750 ([1,000 + 2,500]/2)

Experimental effects: Effects caused by treatment

Simple main effect of stress for the female group is –500

Simple main effect of stress for the male group is +1,000

Overall main effect of stress is 250
[(–500 +1,000)/2]

Note that the hybrid 2 × 2 design answers two questions that the simple experiment does not:

1. Do the male and female participants differ on the dependent variable? (Answered by the gender main effect.)
2. Is the effect of stress different in our sample of males than in our sample of females? (Answered by the gender by treatment interaction.)

Holmes and Will (1985) added a nonexperimental factor to this study—whether participants were Type A or Type B personalities. (People with Type A personalities are thought to be tense, hostile, and aggressive, whereas people with Type B personalities are thought to be more relaxed and less aggressive.) The results of this study were intriguing: If participants had not been angered, Type A participants were more likely to punish the confederate than Type B participants. However, if participants had been angered, Type A and Type B participants behaved similarly (see Figure 8-14).

Likewise, Hill (1991) could have done a relatively uninteresting simple experiment. He could have determined whether research participants are more likely to want to talk to a stranger if that stranger is supposed to be "warm" than if the stranger supposedly lacks warmth and empathy. The finding that people prefer to affiliate with people who are nice would not have been startling.

Fortunately, Hill conducted a more interesting study by adding another variable: need for affiliation. He found that participants who were high in need for affiliation were very likely to want to interact with an allegedly "warm" stranger, but very unlikely to want to interact with a stranger who allegedly lacked warmth. For low need for affiliation participants, on the other hand, the alleged warmth of the stranger made little difference.

• FIGURE 8-14 •

THE EFFECT OF BEING ANGERED ON THE AGGRESSIVENESS OF TYPE A AND TYPE B PERSONALITY TYPES

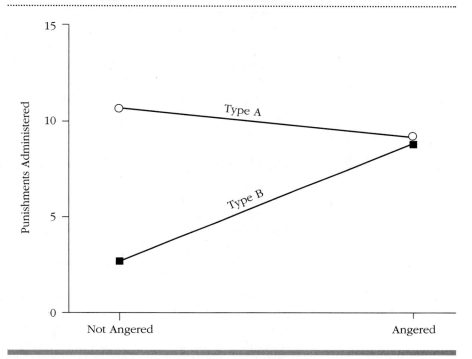

Source: Holmes, D. S., & Will, M. J. (1985). Expression of interpersonal aggression by angered and nonangered persons with the Type A and Type B behavior patterns. *Journal of Personality and Social Psychology, 48,* 723–727.

As you have seen, adding a nonexperimental factor can make a study more interesting. As you will see in the next sections, you can add a nonexperimental variable to a simple experiment for most of the same reasons you would add an experimental variable: to increase the generalizability of the findings, to look for a similarity effect, and to look for a moderating factor.

INCREASING GENERALIZABILITY

You could increase the generalizability of a simple experiment that used only males as participants by using both males and females as participants, and making gender of the participant a factor in your design. This design would allow you to determine whether the effect held for both males and females.

STUDYING EFFECTS OF SIMILARITY

If you were interested in similarity, you might include some participant characteristic (gender, status, etc.) as a factor in your design, while manipulating the comparable experimenter or confederate factor. For example, if you were studying helping behavior, you could use style of dress of the participant (dressed-up/casual) and style of dress of the confederate as factors in your design. You might find this interaction: Dressed-up participants were more likely to help confederates who were dressed-up, but casually dressed participants were more likely to help confederates who were dressed casually. This interaction would suggest that similarity of dress influences helping behavior (see Figure 8-15).

FINDING AN EXCEPTION TO THE RULE

Looking for the effects of similarity is not the only reason you would want to examine interactions involving participant characteristics. As we mentioned earlier, you might look at interactions involving participants to see whether a treatment that works with one type of person is as effective with another type of person. The treatment could be any intervention—from a therapy technique to a teaching style. For example, if you thought that intelligence would be a moderating variable for the effectiveness of computerized instruction, you might use intelligence as a factor in your design. To do this, you would first give your participants an IQ test and then divide them into two groups (above-average intelligence and below-average intelligence). Next, you would randomly

• **FIGURE 8-15** •

AN INTERACTION REPRESENTING
SIMILARITY IN A HYBRID DESIGN

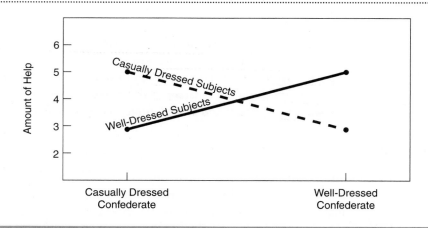

assign the high-intelligence group to condition so that half of them were in computerized instruction and half were in group instruction. You would do the same for the low-intelligence group.

This hybrid study might reveal some interesting findings. For instance, suppose you found that computerized instruction vastly improves learning for low-IQ children, but slightly decreases learning for high-IQ children. If you had only done a simple experiment, you might have found a significant positive effect for the new teaching technique. On that basis, you might have recommended using this technique with all schoolchildren. What a terrible mistake!

Concluding Remarks

In this chapter, you have seen the benefits of using the 2 × 2 experiment. Your awareness of this design opens up new possibilities for research. Just as important, your understanding of this commonly used design increases your ability to read, understand, and evaluate the research of others. Therefore, you now have the ability to discover new paths for research that radiate from the research of others. In the next two chapters, you will refine this ability.

Summary

1. Factorial experiments allow you to look at the effects of more than one independent variable at a time.

2. The simplest factorial experiment is the 2 × 2 ("two by two") experiment.

3. The 2 × 2 allows you to study two independent variables in one experiment and lets you see the effects of combining different levels of your two independent variables.

4. Whenever the effect of combining two independent variables is different from the sum of their individual effects, you have an interaction. In other words, an interaction occurs when one independent variable's effect depends on the level of a second (moderating) variable. For example, the independent variable may have one effect when the second factor is absent and a different effect when the second factor is present.

5. Interactions often indicate that a general rule does not always apply. For example, a treatment × gender interaction indicates that the rule does not apply equally to men and to women.

6. Interactions can most easily be observed by graphing your data. If your two lines aren't parallel, you may have an interaction.

7. If your lines cross, you probably have a crossover (disordinal interaction). A crossover interaction sometimes indicates that a treatment has one effect on one group and the opposite effect on another group. For example, a crossover interaction may mean that a treatment helps one group, but harms the other.

8. If your lines are not parallel, but don't cross, you have an ordinal interaction. Ordinal interactions may be due to a treatment having more of an effect on one group than on another. However, ordinal interactions may be an artifact of having ordinal data. That is, in some cases, if your data had been interval, you would not have obtained an interaction. In other words, even when a treatment has the same psychological effect in all conditions, ordinal data can create the illusion that the treatment has more of an effect in one condition than another.

9. If you have an ordinal interaction, do not rush to conclude that a treatment has more of an effect in some conditions than in others. Instead, ask yourself whether the data were truly interval. For example, ask yourself if ceiling or floor effects could be responsible for the interaction.

10. A significant interaction usually qualifies main effects. Thus, if you find a significant interaction, you can't talk about your main effects without referring to the interaction. If, on the other hand, you don't find a significant interaction, you can just talk about your individual main effects.

11. Sometimes, an interaction represents similarity. For instance, in a 2 (place of learning: basement or top floor) × 2 (place of testing: basement or top floor), an interaction may reveal that it is best to be tested in the *same* place you learned the information.

12. The following summarizes the mathematics of an ANOVA summary table for a factorial design:

Source of Variance (SV)	Sum of Squares (SS)	Degrees of Freedom (DF)	Mean Square (MS)	F
A	SS A	Levels of A − 1	SSA/dfA	MSA/MSE
B	SS B	Levels of B − 1	SSB/df B	MSB/MSE
A × B Interaction	SS (A × B)	df A × df B	SS/df	MS (A × B)/MSE
Error	SSE	Participants − Groups	SSE/df E	
Total		Participants − 1		

13. With the hybrid factorial design, you can look at an experimental factor and a factor that you do not manipulate (personality, gender, age) in the same study. However, because you did not manipulate the nonexperimental factor, you cannot say that you know anything about the effects of your nonexperimental factor.

14. Once you have an idea for a simple experiment, you can easily expand that idea into an idea for a factorial experiment. For example, you could add a replication factor or a personality variable to try to establish the generalizability of your treatment's effect. In that case, you would not be expecting a significant interaction. Alternatively, if you wanted to show that the treatment didn't have the same effect under all circumstances (or for all people), you could add a potential moderating variable. In that case, you would be expecting a significant interaction between the treatment and the factor that you believe will moderate its effect.

Key Terms

factorial experiment: an experiment that examines two or more independent variables (factors) at a time. (p. 260)

simple main effect: the effects of one independent variable at a specific level of a second independent variable. A single, simple main effect could have been obtained merely by doing a simple experiment. The simplest factorial design, the 2×2 experiment, produces four simple main effects. (p. 262)

main effect (overall main effect): the average of a variable's simple main effects: the overall or average effect of an independent variable. (p. 264)

interaction: when the effect of combining two variables is different than the sum of their individual effects. If you need to know how much of one variable participants have received to say what the effect of another variable is, you have an interaction between those two variables. If you have an interaction, then (1) the simple main effect of a variable is different in one condition than in another, and (2) the lines in a graph of your data will not be parallel. (p. 265)

ordinal interaction: reflects the fact that an independent variable seems to have more of an effect under one level of a second independent variable than under another level. If you graph an ordinal interaction, the lines will not be parallel, but they will not cross. It is called an ordinal interaction because the interaction may be due to having ordinal data. That is, despite the existence of an interaction at the statistical level, the independent variable may have the same psychological effect under all levels of the second independent variable. Ordinal interactions may result from ceiling or floor effects. (p. 289)

ceiling effect: the effect of a treatment or combination of treatments is underestimated because the dependent measure cannot distinguish between participants who have somewhat high and those who have very high levels of the construct. The measure puts an artificially low ceiling on how high a participant may score and thus produces ordinal, rather than interval, data. Consequently, a ceiling effect may cause an ordinal interaction. (p. 292)

floor effect: the effect of a treatment or combination of treatments is underestimated because the dependent measure artificially restricts how low scores can be. The measure puts an artificially high floor on how low a participant may score and thus produces ordinal, rather than interval, data. Consequently, a floor effect may cause an ordinal interaction. (p. 292)

crossover (disordinal) interaction: when an independent variable has one kind of effect in the presence of one level of a second independent variable, but a different kind of effect in the presence of a different level of the second independent variable. Examples: Getting closer to someone may increase their attraction to you if you have just complimented them, but may decrease their attraction to you if you have just insulted them. Called a crossover interaction because the lines in a graph will cross. Called a disordinal interaction because it cannot be explained as an artifact of having ordinal, rather than interval, data. (p. 296)

replication factor: a factor sometimes included in a factorial design to see whether an effect replicates (occurs again) under slightly different conditions. For example, suppose an investigator wants to see if a new memory strategy is superior to a conventional one. Instead of having all the participants memorize the same story, the researcher assigns different participants to get different stories. Type of story is the replication factor in the study. The researcher hopes that memory strategy manipulation will have the same effect regardless of which story is used. But, if story type matters (there is an interaction between memory strategy and story type), the researcher might do further research to understand why the strategy was less effective in helping participants remember certain types of stories. (p. 301)

stimulus set: the particular stimulus materials shown to two or more groups of participants. Researchers may use more than one stimulus set in a study so that they can see if the treatment effect replicates across different stimulus sets. In those cases, stimulus sets would be a replication factor. (p. 301)

systematic replication: a study that varies from the original study only in some minor aspect, such as using different stimulus materials. Thus, if you include stimulus set as a factor in your design, your study, in a sense, contains a systematic replication. (p. 301)

Exercises

1. What is the difference between a simple main effect and an overall main effect?
2. What is the difference between an overall main effect and an interaction?
3. Can you have an interaction without a main effect?
4. Below, you see a summary of the means for an experiment looking at the status of speaker and rate of speech on attitude change. Describe the pattern of results in the following table in terms of main effects and interactions. Assume that all differences are statistically significant.

	STATUS OF SPEAKER	
RATE OF SPEECH	LOW STATUS	HIGH STATUS
Slow	10	15
Fast	20	25
	ATTITUDE CHANGE	

5. Following, you see a summary of the means for an experiment looking at the status of speaker and rate of speech on attitude change. Describe the pattern of results in the following table in terms of main effects and interactions. Assume that all differences are statistically significant.

	STATUS OF SPEAKER	
RATE OF SPEECH	LOW STATUS	HIGH STATUS
Slow	10	15
Fast	20	30
	ATTITUDE CHANGE	

6. Half the participants receive a placebo. The other half receive a drug that blocks the effect of endorphins (pain-relieving substances, similar to morphine, that are produced by the brain). Half the placebo group and half the drug group get acupuncture. Then, all participants are asked to rate the pain of various shocks on a 1 (not at all painful) to 10 (very painful) scale. The results are as follows: placebo, no acupuncture group, 7.2; placebo, acupuncture group, 3.3; drug, no acupuncture group, 7.2; drug and acupuncture group, 3.3.
   a. Graph the results.
   b. Describe the results in terms of main effects and interactions (making a table of the data may help).
   c. What conclusions would you draw?

7. Below is an ANOVA summary table of a study looking at the effects of similarity and attractiveness on liking. To answer the following questions, you may wish to consult Box 8-2, as well as the sample ANOVA summary table (Summary point #12).
   a. How many participants were used in the study?
   b. How many levels of similarity were used?
   c. How many levels of attractiveness were used?
   d. Complete the ANOVA table below.

SV	SS	df	MS	F
Similarity (S)	10	1	___	___
Attractiveness (A)	___	2	20	___
$S \times A$ interaction	400	___	200	___
Error	540	54	___	
Total	990	59		

8. A professor does a simple experiment. In that experiment, the professor finds that students who are given lecture notes do better than students who are not given lecture notes. Imagine that you are asked to replicate the professor's simple experiment as a 2 × 2 factorial.
   a. What variable would you add to change the simple experiment into a 2 × 2?
   b. Graph your predictions.
   c. Describe your predictions in terms of main effects and interactions.

9. A lab experiment on motivation yielded the following results:

GROUP	PRODUCTIVITY
No financial bonus, no encouragement	25%
No financial bonus, encouragement	90%
Financial bonus, no encouragement	90%
Financial bonus, encouragement	90%

a. Make a 2 × 2 table of these data.
b. Graph these data (for help with graphing, see page 277).
c. Describe the results in terms of main effects and interactions. Assume that all differences are statistically significant.
d. Interpret the results.

10. A memory researcher looks at the effects of processing time and rehearsal strategy on memory.

GROUP	PERCENT CORRECT
Short exposure, simple strategy	20%
Short exposure, complex strategy	15%
Long exposure, simple strategy	25%
Long exposure, complex strategy	80%

a. Graph these data.
b. Describe the results in terms of main effects and interactions. Assume that all differences are statistically significant.
c. Interpret the results.

11. Suppose a researcher wanted to know whether lecturing was more effective than group discussion for teaching basic facts. Therefore, the researcher did a study and obtained the following results:

SOURCE OF VARIANCE	SS	df	MS	F
Teaching (T)	10	1	10	5
Introversion/Extroversion (I)	20	1	20	10
T × I interaction	50	1	50	25
Error	100	50	2	

a. What does the interaction seem to indicate?
b. Even if there had been no interaction between teaching and extroversion, would there be any value in including the introversion–extroversion variable? Explain.
c. What, if anything, can you conclude about the effects of introversion on learning?

WITHIN-SUBJECTS DESIGNS

OVERVIEW

In Chapters 6, 7, and 8, you learned that you could perform an internally valid experiment by independently and randomly assigning participants to groups. Although you understand the logic of randomly assigning participants to groups, you may still have two basic reservations about between-subjects designs.

First, you may believe that between-subjects designs are wasteful in terms of the number of participants they require. For example, in the simple experiment, the participant is either in the control group or in the experimental group. Clearly, it would seem more efficient if each participant was in both the control group and in the experimental group. One participant would do the job of two.

Second, you may be concerned that between-subject designs are not powerful enough. You may believe that if we use each participant as his or her own control, we could detect differences that would not be detected if we were comparing participants with one another. Your concern is based on the fact that between-subject differences may hide the treatment's effect. For example, suppose you use a simple experiment to examine a treatment that produces a small effect. The treatment's small effect might be discounted as being due to random differences between the two groups. If, on the other hand, we use each participant as his or her own control, the difference that the treatment created between the two conditions could not be dismissed as being due to random differences between the two groups. Consequently, the treatment's effect might be detected and found to be statistically significant.

You are rightfully concerned about the twin weaknesses of between-subjects experiments: They require many participants and have relatively little power. In this chapter, you will learn some alternatives to pure randomized between-subjects designs. These alternatives require fewer participants and often have more power than between-subjects experiments.

Before learning about within-subjects designs, you will learn about a special type of between-subjects design: the matched-pairs design. In the matched-pairs design, you first reduce between-subject differences by matching pairs of participants on a key characteristic. Then, you let random assignment and statistics take care of the effects of the remaining differences between subjects.

Next, you will learn about two main types of within-subjects designs: the randomized within-subjects design and the counterbalanced within-subjects design. In the randomized within-subjects design, you avoid the problem of between-subject differences by using participants as their own controls. Then, you let randomization take care of the effects of the remaining uncontrolled variables. By limiting the variables that randomization has to account for, the pure within-subjects design—like the matched-pairs design—often has impressive power. For all its power, however, the randomized within-subjects design has some serious weaknesses. To build on its power but avoid those weaknesses, many researchers use what they consider a refinement of the randomized within-subjects design—the counterbalanced, within-subjects design.

After learning about the two main types of within-subjects designs, you will learn about mixed designs. Mixed designs have aspects of both between- and within-subjects designs. Specifically, mixed designs are factorial designs in which at least one factor is a between-subjects factor, and at least one factor is a within-subjects factor. In other words, different participants get different levels of the between-subject factor(s), but all participants get all levels of the within-subjects factor(s).

Finally, you will learn how to weigh the tradeoffs involved in choosing among various experimental designs. Thus, by the end of this chapter, you will be better able to choose the best experimental design for your research problem.

THE MATCHED-PAIRS DESIGN

If you do not have enough participants to do a powerful simple experiment, you might use a design, such as a **matched-pairs design,** that requires fewer participants. As you will see, the matched-pairs design combines the best aspects of matching and randomization: It uses matching to reduce the effects of irrelevant variables, and it uses randomization to establish internal validity.

PROCEDURE

In the matched-pairs design, you first measure your participants on a variable that correlates with the dependent measure. For example, if you were measuring memory, your matching variable could be education, IQ, or scores on a memory test. After measuring all your participants on the matching variable, you would form *matched pairs:* pairs of participants who have similar scores on this measure. Thus, if you were doing a memory experiment using a matched-pairs design, you might first give all your participants a memory test. Next, you would rank their scores on this memory test from lowest to highest. Then, you would pair the two highest scorers, the next two highest scorers, and so on. This would give you pairs of participants with similar scores on the memory pretest. Finally, you would randomly assign one member of each pair to the control group and the other member to the experimental group.

CONSIDERATIONS IN USING MATCHED-PAIRS DESIGNS

You now have a general idea of how to conduct a matched-pairs experiment. You also know how it compares to a simple experiment: Unlike a simple experiment, it uses matching; like a simple experiment, it uses random assignment (see Table 9-1). But should you use a matched-pairs experiment instead of a simple experiment? When considering a matched-pairs design, you should consider four questions:

· **TABLE 9-1** ·

COMPARING THE MATCHED DESIGN
WITH THE SIMPLE EXPERIMENT

MATCHED DESIGN	SIMPLE EXPERIMENT
First, *match* participants on key characteristics.	*No matching.*
Then, *randomly assign* each member of the pair to condition.	*Randomly assign* participants to condition.

1. Can you find an effective matching variable?
2. How important is it that you have a powerful design?
3. Will matching harm external validity?
4. Will matching harm construct validity?

Finding an Effective Matching Variable

As we suggested earlier, you can only make effective use of the matched-pairs design if you can create pairs that are very similar to each other. To be more specific, you need to match participants on a variable that correlates strongly with the dependent measure.

How can you match participants on a variable that correlates strongly with the dependent measure? One approach is to match participants on the dependent measure. That is, start your study by giving all the participants the dependent measure task and then match participants based on their scores on that task. Thus, in a memory experiment, participants could be matched based on scores on an earlier memory test; in a maze-running experiment, participants could be matched based on earlier maze-running performance.

If you cannot match on pretest scores, you may have to search the research literature (see Appendix B) to find a matching variable. If you are lucky, you will find matching variables that other researchers have used. More likely, however, you will find out what variables correlate with your dependent measure. Unfortunately, after doing your library research, you may find that (a) there are no variables that have a strong, documented relationship with performance on the dependent measure, or that (b) there are good matching variables, but for ethical or practical reasons you cannot use them.

Power

You want to find an appropriate matching variable so that your study will have adequate **power:** the ability to find differences between conditions. Indeed, the reason you may choose a matched-pairs design is to avoid the problems that plague researchers who use other types of between-subject designs. As you may recall from Chapter 6, researchers who rely exclusively on random assignment to make groups similar lose power because individual differences between participants hide treatment effects. Thus, because participants differ from each other, researchers can't assume that the treatment group and the no-treatment group are identical before the start of the experiment. Consequently, if the groups differ at the end of the experiment, researchers may not know whether this difference is due to the treatment or to the groups being different before the experiment began. In a simple experiment, even a large difference between the treatment and no-treatment groups could be due to random error rather than to treatment.

If matching makes your groups very similar to each other before the experiment begins, then there isn't much random error due to individual differences to hide your treatment effects. Therefore, the same, small difference that would not be statistically significant with a simple experiment may be significant with a matched-pairs design.

How can a matched-pairs design give you more power than a simple experiment? The key, as we mentioned before, is that the matched-pairs design reduces random error, allowing the treatment effect to be seen as statistically significant. Mathematically, the reduced random error results in a larger t-value.

Why would the t-value be larger in a matched-pairs design? The answer lies in the fact that the t-value is the difference between conditions divided by an estimate of random error (the standard error of the difference). So, *with less random error, the* t-*value becomes larger.* For example, if the standard error of the difference for a simple experiment is 6 seconds, then a difference of 6 seconds between conditions would yield a nonsignificant t-value of 1.0 (because 6/6 = 1.0). However, if a matched-pairs design reduced random error so much that the standard error of the difference was only 1.0, then that same difference of 6 seconds would yield a significant t-value of 6.0 (because 6/1 = 6.0). In other words, if matching limits the effects of individual differences, you may be able to find relatively small treatment effects.

But what if matching fails to reduce random error? For example, suppose a researcher matched participants on shoe size. In that case, the t-value will be roughly the same as it would have been in the simple experiment because matching hasn't reduced the amount of random error in the study. In that case, the matched-pairs design would then be *less powerful* than the simple experiment.

To understand why the poor matching leads to a matched-pairs design that is less powerful than a simple experiment, you need to know two facts: (1) Matched-pairs designs have half the degrees of freedom of a same-sized simple experiment, and (2) all other things being equal, fewer degrees of freedom means less power. We'll now take a closer look at these two facts.

By using a matched-pairs design instead of a simple experiment, you lose half your degrees of freedom. You lose half your degrees of freedom because degrees of freedom for a simple experiment equals number of *participants* − 2, but the degrees of freedom for a matched-pairs study equals number of *pairs* − 1. Thus, if you used 20 participants in a simple experiment, you would have 18 degrees of freedom (two fewer than the number of participants). But if you used 20 participants (10 pairs) in a matched-pairs design, you would only have 9 degrees of freedom (one fewer than the number of pairs).

Losing degrees of freedom can cause you to lose power. As you can see by looking at the *t*-table in Appendix E, the fewer degrees of freedom you have, the larger your *t*-value must be to reach significance. For example, with 18 degrees of freedom (what you'd have if you tested 20 participants in a simple experiment), you would only need a *t*-value of 2.101 for your results to be statistically significant at the .05 level. On the other hand, with 9 degrees of freedom (what you'd have if you tested 20 participants [10 pairs of participants] in a matched-pairs experiment), your *t*-value would have to be at least 2.262 to be statistically significant at the .05 level. That is, a difference between your treatment conditions that would have been big enough to be statistically significant if you had used a simple experiment might not be statistically significant with a matched-pairs design in which you matched on a variable that did not correlate with your measure. Thus, if you obtained the same *t*-value with the matched-pairs design as you would have obtained with a simple experiment, then the matched-pairs design cost you power.

If your matching is any good, however, you should not get the same *t*-value with a matched-pairs design as with a simple experiment. Instead, you will almost always get a larger *t*-value with a matched-pairs design because you have reduced a factor that shrinks *t*-values—random error due to differences between participants. Usually, the increase in the size of the *t*-value will more than compensate for the degrees of freedom you will lose. Thus, if you can match participants on a relevant variable, using a matched-pairs design instead of a simple experiment will give you more power.

External Validity

Power is not the only consideration in deciding to use a matched-pairs design. You may use—or avoid—matching for reasons of external validity.

Matched-Pairs Designs May Have Good External Validity   A matched-pairs design may have more external validity than an equally powerful simple experiment. Why? Because unlike the simple experiment, the matched-pairs design can have power without limiting who can be in the experiment.

To obtain adequate power, a researcher using a simple experiment may have to severely restrict the kind of individual who can be in the study. That is, to reduce the degree to which differences between participants create random differences between treatment and no-treatment groups, the experimenter may be forced to use participants who are all very similar. For example, to create a simple experiment that would be as powerful as a matched-pairs design, an experimenter might need to limit participants to male, albino rats between 180–185 days of age. Another researcher might attempt to reduce random error due to individual differences by only allowing middle-class women with IQs between 115–120 to be in the experiment.

With a matched-pairs design, however, you can reduce random differences between the treatment and no-treatment groups without choosing participants who are all alike. Because you can reduce random error by matching up the participants you do have rather than by limiting the kinds of participants you can have, the matched-pairs design may allow you to generalize your results to a broader population.

Matched-Pairs Designs May Have Poor External Validity Matched-pairs designs, however, do not always have better external validity than simple experiments. For example, if participants drop out of the study between the time they are tested on the matching variable and the time they are to perform the experiment, matching will reduce the generalizability of your results. For instance, suppose you start off with 16 matched pairs, but end up with only 10 pairs. In that case, your experiment's external validity is compromised because your results may not apply to individuals resembling the participants who dropped out of your experiment.

Even if participants do not drop out, matching may still harm external validity. That is, you may find that your results only generalize to situations where individuals perform the matching task before getting the treatment.

To illustrate, imagine that an experimenter uses a matched-pairs design to examine the effect of caffeine on anxiety. In that experiment, participants take an anxiety test, then either consume caffeine (the experimental group) or do not (the control group), and then take the anxiety test again. Suppose that the participants receiving caffeine become more anxious than those not receiving caffeine.

Can the investigator generalize her results to people who have not taken an anxiety test before consuming caffeine? No, it may be that caffeine only increases anxiety if it is consumed after taking an anxiety test. For example, taking the anxiety test may make participants so concerned about their level of anxiety that they interpret any increase in arousal as an increase in anxiety. Because of the anxiety test, the arousal produced by caffeine—which might ordinarily be interpreted as invigorating—is interpreted as anxiety.

Construct Validity

In the caffeine study we just discussed, taking the anxiety test before and after the treatment might make participants aware that the experimenter is looking at the effects of a drug on anxiety. The participants' awareness of the hypothesis may harm the study's construct validity.

However, the fact that participants guess the hypothesis does not, by itself, ruin the experiment's construct validity. For instance, if you used a treatment condition and a placebo condition, it does not matter if participants think that taking a pill is supposed to increase anxiety. Since both groups have the same hypothesis ("The pill I took will increase my anxiety"), knowing the hypothesis would not cause the treatment group to differ from the placebo group. Therefore, a significant difference between groups would have to be due to the treatment.

If, on the other hand, your independent variable manipulation has poor construct validity, matching will make your manipulation's weaknesses more damaging. To see how matching can magnify a manipulation's weaknesses, imagine that the caffeine study used an empty control group (nothing was given to the subjects who did not receive the treatment). The experimental group participants fill out an anxiety measure, take a pill, and then fill out another anxiety measure. The experimental group subjects might think that the pill is supposed to increase their anxiety level. This expectation might cause them to be more anxious—or at least, to report being more nervous. The control group subjects, not having been given a pill, would not expect to become more nervous. Consequently, a significant difference between the groups might be due to the two groups acting on different beliefs about what the researchers expected, rather than to any ingredient in the pill.

ANALYSIS OF DATA

We have talked about how matching, by making your study powerful, can help you obtain a significant difference. We have also warned you about external validity and construct validity problems that should make you cautious when interpreting such significant differences. But how do you know whether you have a significant difference?

As we have already suggested, you cannot use a regular, between-subjects t-test. That test compares the overall, average score of the treatment group with the overall, average score of the no-treatment group.

With a matched-pairs design, you need a test that will allow you to compare the score of one member of a matched pair directly with the score of the other member—and to make that comparison for each of your pairs. If you have ratio or interval scale data,[1] you can make those comparisons using the **dependent groups t-test**.[2]

SUMMARY OF THE MATCHED-PAIRS DESIGN

In summary, the matched-pairs design's weaknesses stem from matching (see Table 9-2). If matching alerts participants to the purpose of your experiment, matching may hurt your construct validity. If participants drop out of the experiment between the time they are measured on the matching variable and

---

[1] If you only have ordinal data, you should use the sign test. If you don't know what type of data you have, consult Chapter 4.

[2] To conduct this test, see Appendix F.

• **TABLE 9-2** •

ADVANTAGES AND DISADVANTAGES OF MATCHING

ADVANTAGES	DISADVANTAGES
More power because matching reduces the effects of differences between participants.	Matching makes more work for the researcher.
	Matching may alert participants to the experimental hypothesis.
Power is not bought at the cost of restricting the subject population. Thus, results may, in some cases, be generalized to a wide variety of participants.	Results cannot be generalized to participants who drop out after the matching task.
	The results may not apply to individuals who have not been exposed to the matching task prior to getting the treatment.

the time they are to be given the treatment, matching costs you the ability to generalize your results to the participants who dropped out. Finally, even if participants do not get suspicious and do not drop out, matching still costs you time and energy.

But although matching has its costs, matching offers one big advantage—power without restricting your subject population. Matching makes the matched-pairs design very powerful, while random assignment makes the matched-pairs design internally valid. Because of its power and internal validity, this design is hard to beat when you can only study a few participants.

WITHIN-SUBJECTS (REPEATED MEASURES) DESIGNS

One set of designs that can beat the matched-pairs design, at least in terms of power, are the **within-subjects designs** (also called **repeated-measures designs**). In all within-subjects designs, each subject receives all the levels or types of the treatment that the experimenter administers, and the subject is measured after receiving each level or type of treatment. In the simplest case, each subject would receive only two levels of treatment: no treatment and the treatment. For example, a participant might get no treatment, complete the dependent-measure task, get a treatment, and repeat the dependent-measure task again. The experimenter would estimate the effect of the treatment by comparing how each participant scored after receiving the treatment with how that same participant scored when receiving no treatment.

CONSIDERATIONS IN USING WITHIN-SUBJECTS DESIGNS

You now have a general idea of how a within-subjects (repeated measures) experiment differs from a between-subjects design (for a review, see Table 9-3). But should you use a within-subjects design instead of a between-subjects

---

• **TABLE 9-3** •

COMPARING THREE DESIGNS

	BETWEEN SUBJECTS	MATCHED-PAIRS DESIGN	WITHIN-SUBJECTS
Role of random assignment	Randomly assign participants to treatment conditon.	Randomly assign members of each pair to condition.	Randomly assign to sequence of treatment conditions.
Approach to dealing with the problem that differences between participants may cause differences between the treatment and no-treatment conditions	Allow random assignment and statistics to account for any differences between conditions that could be due to individual differences.	Use matching to reduce the extent to which differences between conditions could be due to individual differences. Then, use random assignment and statistics to deal with the effects of individual differences that were not eliminated by matching.	Avoid the problem of individual differences causing differences between conditions by comparing each participant's performance in one condition with his or her performance in the other condition(s).

---

design? As you will soon see, there is one big reason to use a between-subjects design instead of a within-subjects design: You gain power. However, as you will also soon see, there is one big reason not to switch from a between-subjects design to a within-subjects design: You may lose internal validity because within-subject designs are vulnerable to order effects.

Increased Power

Despite the problems with order effects, the within-subjects design is extremely popular. Perhaps the major reason for the within-subjects design's popularity is power. The within-subjects design increases power in two ways.

The first way is similar to how the matched-pairs design increases power—by reducing random error. As you may recall, the matched-pairs experimenter tries to reduce random error by reducing individual differences. Therefore, the matched-pairs experimenter compares similar participants with one another. Within-subjects experimenters are even more ambitious: They want to eliminate random error due to individual differences. They do not compare one participant with another participant; instead, they compare each participant's score under one condition with that same participant's score under another condition.

The second way the within-subjects design increases power is by increasing the number of observations. The more observations you have, the more random error will tend to balance out; the more random error balances out, the more power you will have. With the designs we have discussed up to now—the between-subjects designs—you can only get one observation per participant. With those designs, the only way you could get more observations was to get more participants. But in a within-subjects experiment, you get at least two scores out of each participant. In the simplest case, your participants serve double duty by being in both the control and experimental conditions. In more complex within-subjects experiments, your participants might do triple, quadruple, or even octuple duty.

Order Effects Harm Internal Validity

As you intuitively realize, the main advantage of within-subjects designs is their impressive power. By comparing each participant with him or herself, even subtle treatment effects may be statistically significant.

However, as you may also intuitively realize, there are problems with comparing participants with themselves. Because participants change from day to day, from hour to hour, and even from minute to minute, a change in a participant may not be due to the treatment. Indeed, as we shall see, how a participant behaves after being exposed to a treatment sometimes depends on when the participant receives the treatment. That is, the order (first or last) in which an event occurs within a sequence of events can be very important. For example, the lecture that might have been scintillating had it been the first lecture you heard that day might be only tolerable if it is your fourth class of the day.

As you have seen, order affects responses. Therefore, if a participant reacts differently to the first treatment than to the last, we have a dilemma: Do we have a treatment effect or an order effect?

To get a better idea of how order effects can complicate within-subjects experiments, let's examine a within-subjects experiment. Specifically, imagine being a participant in a within-subjects experiment where you take a drug, play a video game, take a second drug, and play the video game again.

If you perform differently on the video game the second time around, can the experimenters say that the second drug has a different effect than the first drug? No. The experimenters can't safely make conclusions about the difference between the two drugs because circumstances were different when you took drug 2 than when you took drug 1 (see Table 9-4). In the first trial, before you played the game, you took drug 1. However, in the second trial, before you played the game, you (1) took drug 1, (2) played the video game, and then (3) took drug 2. Put another way, the only treatment you got before you played the video game the first time was drug 1. But before you played the video game the second time, you were exposed to three "treatments": the first drug, playing the video game, and the second drug.

Overview of Four Specific Sources of Order Effects In the next few sections, you will see how being exposed to "treatments" other than the second drug can hurt the study's internal validity. That is, you will see that the variable of order (first trial versus second trial) affects your performance. Specifically, we will look at four nontreatment reasons why you may perform differently on the task after the second treatment:

• TABLE 9-4 •

IN A WITHIN-SUBJECTS DESIGN, THE TREATMENT MAY NOT BE THE ONLY FACTOR BEING MANIPULATED

Events That Occur Before Being Tested

	DRUG 1 CONDITION	DRUG 2 CONDITION
Between-Subjects Experiment	Get Drug 1	Get Drug 2
Within-Subjects Design	Get Drug 1	Get Drug 1 Play Video Game Get Drug 2

---

1. You may do better after the second treatment because you are performing the dependent-measure task a second time. For example, the practice you got on the game after the first drug may help you when you play the game again.

2. You may do worse after the second treatment because you are bored or tired with the dependent-measure task.

3. You may score differently because you are experiencing some delayed or lingering effects of the first treatment.

4. You may have figured out the experimental hypothesis right after you received the second treatment.

To reiterate, by the end of the next few sections, you will understand how the order in which you get a treatment may affect the results. Specifically, you will know why Treatment *A* may appear to have one kind of effect when it comes first, but may appear to have a different kind of effect when it comes second.

Practice Effects   If you perform better after the second treatment than you did after the first treatment, your improvement may simply reflect **practice effects**: You may have learned from the first trial. The first trial, in effect, trained you how to play the video game—although that wasn't the researcher's plan. Not surprisingly, practice effects are common: Participants often perform better as they warm up to the experimental environment and get accustomed to the experimental task. Unfortunately, practice effects may be mistaken for treatment effects.

Fatigue Effects   If your performance is not enhanced by practice, it may decline due to **fatigue effects**.[3] You may do worse on later trials merely because

---

[3]Fatigue effects could be viewed as cases in which performance is hurt by practice; whereas, practice effects could be viewed as cases in which performance is improved by practice.

you are becoming tired or less enthusiastic as the experiment goes on. Unfortunately, a researcher might interpret your fatigue as a treatment effect.

Treatment Carryover Effects   Practice and fatigue effects have nothing to do with any of the treatments participants receive. Often, these effects are simply due to getting more exposure to the dependent-measure task. Thus, in the video game example, performance may improve as you learn the game or worsen as you get bored with the game. However, exposure to the dependent measure is not the only thing that can affect performance in later trials. The effects of a treatment received before the first trial may affect responses in later trials. The effects of an earlier treatment on responses in later trials are called **treatment carryover effects.**

To imagine treatment carryover effects, suppose that on Trial 1, the researcher gave you a tranquilizer. Then, the researcher measured your video game performance. On Trial 2, the researcher gave you alcohol and measured your video game performance. On Trial 3, the researcher gave you a placebo and measured your video game performance. If your performance was the worst in the placebo (no-drug) condition, the researcher might think that your better performance on earlier trials was due to the drugs improving your performance. The researcher, however, could be wrong. Your poor performance in the placebo condition may be due to carryover effects from the previous treatments. During the placebo trial, you may just be starting to feel certain effects of the drugs that you consumed during the earlier trials. Depending on the time between the trials, you may be feeling either "high" or hungover.

Sensitization   In addition to practice, fatigue, and treatment carryover effects, a fourth factor that might cause you to perform differently after the second treatment is **sensitization.** Sensitization occurs if, after getting several different treatments and performing the dependent variable task several times, participants realize (become sensitive to) what the independent and dependent variables are. Consequently, during the latter parts of the experiment, you might guess the experimental hypothesis and play along with it. For example, by the third trial of the video game experiment, you should realize that the experiment had something to do with the effects of drugs on video game performance.

Note that sensitization has two effects. First, it threatens construct validity because participants figure out what the hypothesis is. Second, it threatens internal validity because it makes participants behave differently during the last trial than they did during the first trial.

Review of the Four Sources of Order Effects   You have seen that because of practice, fatigue, carryover, and sensitization, the **sequence** in which participants receive the treatments could affect the results. For example, suppose participants all received the sequence: Treatment *A* first, Treatment *B* second, and Treatment *C* last. Even if none of the treatments had an effect, the effect of **order** (first versus second versus last) might make it look like the treatments had different effects.

For example, suppose practice effects caused participants to do better on the last trial. Because the last trial in our hypothetical study was always Treatment *C*, participants would do best on the trial where they received Treatment *C*. Thus, even if none of the treatments had an effect, the investigator might mistakenly believe that Treatment *C* improves performance.

Fatigue effects, on the other hand, might cause participants to perform the worst on the last treatment condition. Because the last trial was always Treatment *C*, participants would do worst on the trial where they received Treatment *C*. Thus, even if none of the treatments had an effect, the investigator might mistakenly believe that Treatment *C* decreases performance.

Treatment carryover effects might also affect performance on the last trial. For example, if the effect of Treatment *B* is helpful, but delayed, it would help performance on the last trial. If, on the other hand, the effect of Treatment *B* is harmful, but delayed, it will harm performance on the last trial. Thus, even if Treatment *C* has no effect, the investigator might mistakenly believe that Treatment *C* is harmful (if Treatment *B*'s delayed effect is harmful) or that Treatment *C* is helpful (if Treatment *B*'s delayed effect is helpful).

Sensitization might also make it look like Treatment *C* has an effect, even if it does not. The participants were most naïve about the experimental hypothesis when receiving the first treatment (Treatment *A*), least naïve when receiving the last treatment (Treatment *C*). Thus, the ability of the participant to play along with the hypothesis increased as the study went on. Changes in the ability to play along with the hypothesis may create order effects that could masquerade as treatment effects.

DEALING WITH ORDER EFFECTS

You have seen that (1) order effects threaten the internal validity of a within-subjects design and that (2) there are four sources of order effects. Thus, there are four threats to the internal validity of a within-subjects design: practice, fatigue, carryover, and sensitization. As we shall see, there are three steps we can take to reduce the impact of order effects:

1. Minimize each individual threat.
2. Minimize the opportunities for any of these effects to occur.
3. Minimize the chances that an order effect could masquerade as a treatment effect.

Minimizing Each Individual Threat

Perhaps the best place to start to reduce the effect of order is to directly attack the root causes of order effects. Therefore, in the next sections, we will show you how to reduce, one by one, each of the four sources of order effects: practice, fatigue, carryover, and sensitization.

Practice   To minimize the effects of practice, you can give participants extensive practice before the experiment begins. For example, if you are studying maze running and you have the rats run the maze 100 times before you start administering treatments, they've probably learned as much from practice as they can. Therefore, it's unlikely that the rats will benefit greatly from the limited practice they get during the experiment.

Fatigue   You can reduce fatigue effects by making the experiment interesting. In addition, try to make the experiment brief and not too draining.

Carryover   You can reduce carryover effects by lengthening the time between treatments. Allowing adequate time between treatments makes it more likely that the effect of earlier treatments will completely wear off before the participant receives the next treatment. Thus, there will be no treatment carryover. For instance, if you were looking at the effects of drugs on how well rats run a maze, you might space your treatments a week apart (for example, marijuana, wait a week, alcohol, wait a week, placebo).

Sensitization   You can reduce sensitization by preventing participants from noticing that you are varying anything (Greenwald, 1976). For example, suppose you were studying the effects of different levels of full-spectrum light on typing performance. In that case, there would be three ways that you could prevent sensitization. All three ways involve preventing participants from noticing that you were varying the lighting.

First, you could use very similar levels of the treatment in all your conditions. By using slightly different amounts of full-spectrum light, participants may not realize that you are actually varying amount of light.

Second, you could change the level of the treatment so gradually that participants do not notice. For example, if you gave participants a short break in between trials to hand in their typing samples or to go to the restroom, you could change the lighting level watt by watt until it reached the desired level.

Third, you might be able to reduce sensitization effects by using good placebo treatments. That is, rather than using darkness as the control condition, you use light from a normal bulb as the control condition.

A General Strategy for Reducing Order Effects

To this point, we have been limited to giving you some specific steps you could take to reduce practice effects, some steps you could take to reduce fatigue effects, other steps you could take to reduce carryover effects, and still other steps you could take to reduce sensitization (see Table 9-5 for a review). You would probably like one general strategy you could use to reduce several order threats at once.

Fortunately, there is one general strategy you can use to reduce all four causes of order effects—reduce the number of experimental conditions. Having

• **TABLE 9-5** •

ORDER EFFECTS AND HOW TO MINIMIZE THEIR IMPACT

EFFECT	EXAMPLE	WAYS TO REDUCE IMPACT
Practice Effects	Getting better on the task due to being more familiar with the task or the research situation.	Give extensive practice and warm-up prior to introducing treatment.
Fatigue Effects	Getting tired as the study wears on.	Keep study brief, interesting. Use few levels of treatment.
Carryover Effects	Effects of one treatment lasting long enough to affect responses on other trials.	Allow sufficient time between treatments for treatment effect to wear off.
Sensitization	As a result of getting many different levels of the independent variable, the participant—during the latter part of the study—becomes acutely aware of what the treatment is and what the hypothesis is.	Use subtly different levels of treatment. Gradually change treatment levels. Use few treatment levels.

fewer conditions means that there are fewer opportunities for practice, fatigue, carryover, or sensitization to affect your study.

To see how fewer conditions leads to fewer order-effect problems, compare a within-subjects experiment that has 11 conditions with one that has only 2 conditions. In the 11-condition experiment, participants have 10 opportunities to practice on the dependent-measure task before they get the last treatment; in the 2-condition experiment, participants only have one opportunity for practice. The 11-condition participants have 11 conditions to tire them out; 2-condition participants only have 2. In the 11-condition experiment, there are 10 treatments that could carry over to the last trial; in the 2-condition experiment there is only 1. Finally, in the 11-condition experiment, participants have 11 chances to figure out the hypothesis; in the 2-condition experiment, they only have 2 chances.

Mixing up Sequences to Try to Balance out Order Effects: Randomizing and Counterbalancing

Although you can take steps to reduce the impact of order, you can never be sure that you have eliminated its impact. Therefore, if you gave a participant Treatment *A* first and Treatment *B* second, you could not be sure that the difference between the participant's Treatment *A* and Treatment *B* scores was due to a treatment effect. Instead, the difference could simply be due to an order (trials: first versus second) effect. Therefore, if you gave all your participants the treatments in the sequence Treatment *A* first and Treatment *B* second, you could not be sure that the difference between the average of the Treatment *A* scores and the average of the Treatment *B* scores was due to a treatment effect. Instead, the difference could simply be due to an order (trials: first versus second) effect.

To avoid confusing an order (trials) effect for a treatment effect, you should not give each participant the treatments in the same sequence. That is, you should not give all your participants the treatments in this sequence: Treatment *A* first, Treatment *B* second. Instead, some participants should get the treatment sequence: Treatment *A* first, Treatment *B* second; whereas others should get the treatment sequence: Treatment *B* first and then Treatment *A*.

How should you go about making sure that not all participants get the treatment sequence: Treatment *A* first and then Treatment *B*? There are two basic approaches you could use: (1) Randomize the sequence of treatments for each participant, or (2) counterbalance the sequence of treatments. Let's start by examining the first approach: randomizing the sequence of treatments for each participant.

RANDOMIZED WITHIN-SUBJECTS DESIGNS

You can mix up the sequences by randomly determining, for each participant, which treatment they get first, which treatment they get second, and so on. Randomization should ensure that participants get the treatments in different sequences. By using randomization, you have a **randomized within-subjects design.**

The randomized within-subjects design is very similar to the matched-pairs design. In fact, if you conduct both kinds of experiments, you will end up doing very similar things for the same reasons. Although the logic behind both designs is very similar, the two designs' similarities are most apparent when you look at the "nuts and bolts" of carrying out and analyzing the two kinds of experiments.

PROCEDURE

The procedural differences between the two-condition, randomized, within-subjects experiment and matched-pairs experiment stem from a single difference: In the within-subjects experiment, you get a pair of scores from a single participant, whereas in the matched-pairs design, you get a pair of scores from a matched pair of participants. Thus, in the matched-pairs case, each participant only gets one treatment, but in the within-subjects experiment, each participant gets two treatments.

Other than each participant receiving more than one treatment, the two designs are remarkably similar. The matched-pairs researcher randomly determines, for each pair, who will get what treatment. In some pairs, the first member will get Treatment *A,* whereas the second member will get Treatment *B;* in other pairs, the first member will get Treatment *B,* whereas the second member will get Treatment *A.*

The within-subjects researcher randomly determines, for each individual, the sequence of the treatments. For some individuals, the first treatment will be Treatment *A* (and the second treatment will be Treatment *B*); for other individuals, the first treatment will be Treatment *B* (and the second treatment will be Treatment *A*). Whereas the matched-pairs experimenter randomly assigns members of pairs to different treatments, the within-subjects experimenter randomly assigns individual participants to different sequences of treatments.

To see the similarities and differences between the matched-pairs and within-subjects designs, imagine that we are interested in whether observers' judgments about other people are influenced by irrelevant information. Specifically, we want to see whether pseudorelevant information affects whether observers see others as passive or assertive. Therefore, we produce pseudorelevant descriptions (Bill has a 3.2 GPA and is thinking about majoring in psychology) and "clearly irrelevant" descriptions ("Bob found 20 cents in a pay phone in the student union when he went to make a phone call").

In a matched-pairs design, you would match participants—probably based on how assertively they tend to rate people. Then, one member of the pair would read a "pseudorelevant" description while the other read a "clearly irrelevant" description. After reading the information, each participant would rate the assertiveness of the student he read about on a nine-point scale ranging from "very passive" to "very assertive."

In a randomized within-subjects design, on the other hand, each participant would read both "pseudorelevant" and "clearly irrelevant" descriptions. After reading the information, participants would rate the assertiveness of each of these students on a nine-point scale ranging from "very passive" to "very assertive." Thus, each participant would provide data for both the "pseudorelevant" condition and the "clearly irrelevant" condition. The sequence of the descriptions would be randomized. In some of these random sequences, the first description would contain pseudorelevant information whereas in other sequences, the first description would contain clearly irrelevant information.

Hilton and Fein (1989) conducted such a randomized within-subjects experiment and found that participants judged the students about which there was pseudorelevant information as more assertive than those about which there was clearly irrelevant information. Consequently, Hilton and Fein concluded that even irrelevant information affects our judgments about people.

ANALYSIS OF DATA

To analyze data from the two-condition within-subjects design, you can use the same dependent-groups *t*-test that you used to analyze matched-pairs designs.[4] The

---

[4]For more complex within-subjects designs, you would use within-subjects analysis of variance (ANOVA) or multivariate analysis of variance (MANOVA).

only difference is that instead of comparing one member of a pair against the other, you compare each participant with him or herself. Specifically, instead of comparing, for each pair, the member who got one treatment with the member who got the other treatment, you compare, for each participant, the participant when he or she got one treatment with that same participant when he or she got the other treatment. Thus, the dependent-groups *t*-test can also be called the *within-subjects* t-*test*.

SUMMARY OF RANDOMIZED WITHIN-SUBJECTS DESIGNS

As you might expect from two designs that can be analyzed with the same technique, the randomized within-subjects design and the matched-pairs design are very similar. In terms of procedures, the only real difference is that the matched-pairs experimenter randomly assigns members of pairs to treatments; whereas, the randomized within-subjects experimenter randomly assigns individual participants to sequences of treatments.

The two designs share some common strengths. Both designs have impressive power because they reduce the effects of differences between participants. Because of the power of these two designs, both should be seriously considered if participants are scarce.

The randomized within-subjects design, however, has some unique strengths and weaknesses. These strengths and weaknesses stem from the fact that the randomized within-subjects design collects more than one observation per participant (see Table 9-6). Because it uses individual participants (rather than matched pairs) as their own controls, the randomized within-subjects design is more powerful than the matched-pairs design. Because the randomized within-subjects design uses participants as their own controls, it is more useful than the matched-pairs design if you want to generalize your results to real-life situations in which individuals get more than one "treatment." Thus, if you were studying persuasion, you might use a within-subjects design because a person is likely to be exposed to many types of persuasive messages (Greenwald, 1976).

Although there are benefits to collecting more than one observation per participant, there is one big drawback: You have to contend with order effects. To deal with order effects, you can try to minimize the effects of practice, fatigue, carryover, and sensitization. In addition, you can hope that randomization will make it so that each condition comes first about the same number of times as it comes last. That is, you hope that randomization will balance out the sequence of your treatments so that half your participants get one sequence (Treatment *A* first, Treatment *B* second) and half get the other sequence (Treatment *B* first, Treatment *A* second).

COUNTERBALANCED WITHIN-SUBJECTS DESIGNS

Instead of hoping that chance might balance out the sequence of your treatments, why not make sure? That is, why not use a **counterbalanced within-subjects**

• **TABLE 9-6** •

COMPARING THE MATCHED-PAIRS DESIGN WITH THE WITHIN-SUBJECTS DESIGN

MATCHED-PAIRS DESIGN	WITHIN-SUBJECTS DESIGN
Powerful.	More powerful.
Order effects are *not* a problem.	Order effects are a serious problem.
Uses random assignment to balance out differences between participants.	Uses randomization to balance out order effects.
Useful for assessing variables that vary between subjects in real life.	Useful for assessing variables that vary within subjects in real life.

---

design? In a counterbalanced within-subjects design, as in all within-subjects designs, each participant gets more than one treatment. Unlike other within-subjects designs, however, participants are randomly assigned to systematically varying sequences of conditions in a way that ensures that *routine order effects* are balanced out.[5] Thus, if you were studying two levels (*A* and *B*) of a factor, the counterbalanced design would ensure that half your participants got Treatment *A* first and that half got Treatment *B* first. Now that you understand the main objective of counterbalancing, let's look at an example to see how counterbalancing achieves this goal.

PROCEDURE

If you were to use a counterbalanced design to study a two-level factor, you would randomly assign half of your participants to receive Treatment *A* first and Treatment *B* second, while the other half would receive Treatment *B* first and Treatment *A* second. (To see how to use counterbalancing when you have more than two levels of a treatment, see Box 9-1.) By randomly assigning your participants to these counterbalanced sequences, most order effects will be neutralized. For example, if participants tend to do better on the second trial, this will not help Treatment *A* more than Treatment *B* because both occur in the second position equally often.

ADVANTAGES AND DISADVANTAGES OF COUNTERBALANCING

By using a counterbalanced design, you have not merely balanced out routine order effects. You have also added another factor to your design—the between-

---

[5]In football, for example, teams change sides every quarter and this usually balances out the effects of wind. However, if the wind shifts in the fourth quarter, counterbalancing fails to balance out the effects of wind. Similarly, if basketball teams change sides at the end of every half (as in international rules), but a rim gets bent (or fixed) during halftime, counterbalancing has failed to balance out the effects of different baskets.

• **BOX 9-1** •

LATIN SQUARE DESIGNS: THE ABCs
OF COUNTERBALANCING COMPLEX DESIGNS

You have seen an example of the simplest form of counterbalancing in which one group of subjects gets Treatment *A* followed by Treatment *B* (*A–B*) and a second group gets Treatment *B* followed by Treatment *A* (*B–A*). This simple form of counterbalancing is called *A–B, B–A* counterbalancing. Note that even this simple form of counterbalancing accomplishes two goals.

First, it guarantees every condition occurs in every position, equally often. Thus, in *A–B, B–A* counterbalancing, *A* occurs in both the first and last position. The same is true for *B*.

Second, each condition precedes every other condition just as many times as it follows that condition. That is, in *A–B, B–A* counterbalancing, *A* precedes *B* once and follows *B* once. This symmetry is called *balance*.

Although achieving these two objectives of counterbalancing is easy with only two conditions, with more conditions, counterbalancing becomes more complex. For example, with four conditions (*A, B, C, D*) you would have four groups. To determine what order the groups will go through the conditions, you would consult the 4 × 4 Latin Square.

In this 4 × 4 complete Latin Square, Treatment *A* occurs in all four positions (First, Second, Third, and Fourth), as do Treatments,

POSITION

	1	2	3	4
Group 1	*A*	*B*	*D*	*C*
Group 2	*B*	*C*	*A*	*D*
Group 3	*C*	*D*	*B*	*A*
Group 4	*D*	*A*	*C*	*B*

B, C, and *D*. In addition, the square has balance. As you can see from looking at the square, every letter precedes every other letter twice and follows every other letter twice. For example, if you just look at Treatments *A* and *D*, you see that *A* comes before *D* twice (in Groups 1 and 2) and follows *D* twice (in Groups 3 and 4).

Balance is relatively easy to achieve for two, four, six, eight, or even sixteen conditions. But, what if you have three conditions? Immediately you recognize that with a 3 × 3 Latin Square, *A* cannot precede *B* the same number of times as it follows *B*. Condition *A* can either precede *B* twice and follow it once or precede it once and follow it twice. Thus, with an uneven number of conditions, you cannot create a balanced Latin Square.

One approach to achieving balance when you have an uneven number of treatment

(continued)

---

subjects factor of counterbalancing sequence. Adding the factor of counterbalancing sequence has two disadvantages and several advantages.

Disadvantages of Adding a Counterbalancing Factor

A minor disadvantage is that your statistical analysis is now more complex. Rather than using the dependent (within-groups) *t*-test, you now have to use a mixed analysis of variance. This would be a major disadvantage if you had to levels is to add or subtract a level so you have an even number of levels. However, adding a level may greatly increase the number of sequences and groups you need. Subtracting a level, on the other hand, may cause you to lose vital information. Therefore, you may not wish to alter your study to obtain an even number of levels. Fortunately, you can achieve balance with an uneven number of

treatment levels by using two Latin Squares.* For instance, consider the 3 × 3 squares below.

If you randomly assign subjects to six groups, as outlined above, you ensure balance. See for yourself that if you take any two conditions, one condition will precede the other three times and will be preceded by the other condition three times.

	SQUARE 1				SQUARE 2		
	POSITION				POSITION		
	1	2	3		1	2	3
Group 1	*A*	*B*	*C*	Group 4	*C*	*B*	*A*
Group 2	*B*	*C*	*A*	Group 5	*A*	*C*	*B*
Group 3	*C*	*A*	*B*	Group 6	*B*	*A*	*C*

*Another option is to use incomplete Latin Square designs. However, the discussion of incomplete Latin Square designs is beyond the scope of this book.

compute statistics by hand. However, since computers can do these analyses for you, this disadvantage really is minor.

The major disadvantage of adding the two-level between-subjects factor of counterbalancing sequence is that you now need more participants than you did when you were planning to use a pure within-subjects design. You need two groups of participants to determine if the two-level between-subjects factor of counterbalanced sequence has an effect. One of those groups will receive the

A–B sequence, the other will receive the *B–A* sequence. To have enough power to see whether the *A–B* sequence leads to higher average scores than the *B–A* sequence, you will need at least 30 participants in each group. In the pure within-subjects design, on the other hand, we were not comparing one group against another. Thus, in a sense, by going from a pure within-subjects design to a counterbalanced design, you are going from having zero levels of a between-subjects factor to having two levels of a between-subjects factor. As you may recall from our discussion of multiple-group experiments (Chapter 7), the more levels of a between-subjects factor you have, the more participants you need.

Advantages of Using a Counterbalancing Factor

The disadvantage of needing more participants is sometimes offset by being able to discover more effects. With the two-condition, within-subjects experiment, you only obtain a single main effect (the treatment main effect). Thus, you can only find out whether the treatment had an effect. By adding the two-level factor of counterbalancing sequence, you converted the two-condition experiment into a 2 (the within-subjects factor of treatment) × 2 (the between-subjects factor of counterbalancing sequence) experiment.

A big advantage of counterbalancing is that this 2 × 2 experiment gives you more information than the simple two-condition experiment. Specifically, rather than only looking for a single main effect (the within-subjects factor of treatment), you can look for two main effects and an interaction (see Table 9-7). As a result, you find out three things.

First, as was the case with the pure within-subjects design, you can find out whether the treatment had an effect by looking at the treatment main effect. Thus, in the experiment described in Table 9-7, you can look at the treatment main effect to find out whether forming images of words is a more effective memory strategy than making sentences out of the words.

Second, by looking at the counterbalancing sequence main effect, you find out whether the group of participants getting one sequence of treatments (*A–B*) did better than the participants getting the other (*B–A*) sequence. In the experiment described in Table 9-7, the question is, "Did Group 1 (who formed images first and then formed sentences) recall more words than Group 2 (who formed sentences first and then formed images)?"

Third, by looking at the treatment × counterbalancing interaction, you find out whether participants score higher on the first trial or on the second. Looking at the treatment × counterbalancing interaction allows you to detect what some people call a "**trials effect**" and what others call an "**order effect**."

But how can looking at an interaction tell you that participants score differently on the first trial than the second? After all, significant interactions usually indicate exceptions to general rules rather than indicating a general rule such as, "participants do better on the first trial."

The first step to seeing why a significant treatment × counterbalancing interaction tells you that participants score differently on the first trial than on the

---

• **TABLE 9-7** •

A 2 × 2 COUNTERBALANCED DESIGN

....

The first group gets a list of words, is asked to form images of these words, and is asked to recall these words. Then, they get a second list of words, are asked to form a sentence with these words, and are asked to recall the words.

The second group gets a list of words, is asked to form a sentence with these words, and is asked to recall these words. Then, they get a second list of words, are asked to form images of those words, and are asked to recall those words.

GROUP 1

FIRST TASK	SECOND TASK
Form Images	Form Sentences

GROUP 2

FIRST TASK	SECOND TASK
Form Sentences	Form Images

Questions this study can address:
1. Do people recall more when asked to form sentences than when asked to form images?
2. Do Group 1 participants recall more words than Group 2 participants? In other words, is one sequence of learning the two different memory strategies better than the other?
3. Do people do better on the first list of words they see than on the second? That is, does practice help or hurt?

---

second is to imagine such an interaction. Suppose that participants who get Treatment *A first* score highest after receiving Treatment *A, but* participants who get Treatment *B first* score highest after receiving Treatment *B*. At one level, this is an interaction: The rule that participants score highest when receiving Treatment *A* only holds when they receive Treatment *A* first. However, the cause of this interaction is an order (trials) effect: Participants score highest on the first trial.

To get a clearer idea of what a counterbalanced study can tell us, let's look at data from the memory experiment we mentioned earlier. In that experiment, each participant learned one list of words by making a sentence out of the list and learned one list of words by forming mental images. Thus, as would be expected from a within-subjects design, each subject's performance under one treatment condition (sentences) was compared with that same subject's performance under another treatment condition (images).

As would be expected from a simple between-subjects design, participants were randomly assigned to one of two groups. As would be expected from a counterbalanced design, the groups differed in terms of the counterbalanced sequence in which they received the treatments. Half the participants (the group getting the sentence–image sequence) formed sentences for the first list, then formed images to recall the second list. The other half (the group getting the image–sentence sequence) formed images to recall the first list, then formed sentences to recall the second list.

Now that you have a basic understanding of the study's design, let's examine the study's results. To do so, look at both the table of means for that study (Table 9-8) and the analysis of variance summary table (Table 9-9).

By looking at Table 9-9, we see that the main effect for the between-subjects factor of counterbalanced sequence is not significant. As Table 9-8 shows,

---

• **TABLE 9-8** •

TABLE OF MEANS FOR A
COUNTERBALANCED MEMORY EXPERIMENT

Memory Strategy

GROUP'S SEQUENCE	IMAGES	SENTENCES	IMAGES–SENTENCES DIFFERENCE
Group 1 (images 1st, sentences 2nd)	<u>8</u>	<u>6</u>	+2
Group 2 (sentences 1st, images 2nd)	6	8	−2
	14/2 = 7	14/2 = 7	Strategy Main Effect = 0

Counterbalancing Main Effect = 0

> On the average, participants in both groups remembered a total of 14 words (8 in one condition, 6 in another)

Strategy Effect = 0

> Average recalled in image condition was 7 ([<u>8</u> + 6]/2).

> Average recalled in sentence condition was 7([<u>6</u> + 8]/2).

Order Effect = +2

> Participants remember the first list best.

> They averaged 8 words on the first list, 6 on the second.

> The order (first vs. second) effect is revealed by an *interaction* involving counterbalancing *group* and rehearsal *strategy.*

> That is, Group 1 did better in the image condition (<u>8</u> to <u>6</u>), but Group 2 did better in the sentence condition (8 to 6).

• **TABLE 9-9** •

ANOVA SUMMARY TABLE FOR A COUNTERBALANCED DESIGN

Analysis of Variance Table

SOURCE	SS	df	MS	F	p
Group Sequence (counterbalancing)	0	1	0	0	n.s.*
Error Term for Between-Subjects Factor	44	22	2		
Memory Strategy	0	1	0	0	n.s.
Interaction Between Memory Strategy and Group Sequence (effect of order— 1st versus 2nd list)	10	1	10	10	p < .01
Within-Subjects Error Term	23	23	1.0		

*n.s. is abbreviation for not statistically significant

Note: "*p*" values in an ANOVA summary table indicate the probability that the researchers could get differences between their conditions that were this big even if the variables were not related. That is, the *p* values tell you the probability that the difference between the groups could occur due to chance alone. Thus, the smaller the *p* value, the less likely the results are due only to chance—and the more likely that the variables really are related.

members of both groups recalled, on the average, a total of 14 words in the course of the experiment. Participants getting the treatment sequence *A–B* did not, on the average, recall more words than participants getting the sequence *B–A*.

Next, we see that the within-subjects factor of the memory strategy factor was also not significant. Because participants recalled the same number of words in the imagery condition (7) as they did in the sentence condition (7), we have no evidence that one strategy is superior to the other. Thus, there is no treatment effect.

Finally, we have a significant interaction of memory strategy and group sequence. By looking at Table 9-8, we see that this interaction is caused by the fact that Group 1 (which gets images first) recalled more words in the imagery condition whereas Group 2 (which gets sentences first) recalled more words in the sentences condition. In other words, participants do better on the first list than on the second.

What does this order (trials) effect mean? If the researchers were not careful in their selection of lists, the order effect could merely reflect the first list being made up of words that were easier to recall than the second list. The researchers, however, should not have made that mistake.[6] Therefore, if the experiment were properly conducted, the order effect must reflect either the effects of practice, fatigue, treatment carryover, or sensitization. In this case, it probably reflects the fact that the practice participants get on the first list hurts their memory for the second list. This negative practice effect is not considered a nuisance by psychologists. On the contrary, this negative practice effect is one of the most important and most widely investigated facts of memory—proactive interference.

Now that you understand the three effects (two main effects and the treatment × counterbalancing interaction) that you can find with a 2 × 2 counterbalanced design, let's look at an experiment where the researcher is interested in all three effects. Suppose that Mary Jones, a politician, produces two commercials: an emotional commercial and a rational commercial. She hires a psychologist to find out which commercial is most effective so she'll know which one to give more airtime. The researcher uses a counterbalanced design to address the question (see Table 9-10).

By looking at the treatment main effect, the researcher is able to answer the original question, "Which ad is more effective?" By looking at the counterbal-

---

• TABLE 9-10 •

EFFECTS REVEALED BY A 2 × 2 COUNTERBALANCED DESIGN

GROUP 1

FIRST AD	SECOND AD
EMOTIONAL AD	RATIONAL AD

GROUP 2

FIRST AD	SECOND AD
RATIONAL AD	EMOTIONAL AD

Questions Addressed by the Design:

1. Is the rational ad more effective than the emotional ad? (Main effect of the within-subjects factor of type of ad)

2. Is it better to show the emotional ad and then the rational ad or the rational ad and then the emotional ad? (Main effect of the between-subjects factor of counterbalancing sequence)

3. Are attitudes more favorable to the candidate after seeing the second ad than after seeing the first? (Ad by counterbalancing interaction)

---

[6]There are at least three ways to avoid this mistake: (1) Extensively pretest the lists to make sure that both are equally memorable, (2) consult the literature to find lists that are equally memorable, and (3) counterbalance lists so that, across participants, each list occurred equally often under each instructional condition. The third approach is probably the best.

ancing sequence main effect, the researcher is able to find out whether one sequence of showing the ads is better than another. He is able to answer the question, "Should we show the emotional ad first and then the rational ad or should we show the ads in the opposite sequence?" Finally, by looking at the ad by counterbalancing interaction, the researcher is able to determine if there is an order (trials) effect. He is able to answer the question, "Are participants more favorable toward the candidate after they've seen the second ad?" Obviously, he would expect that voters would rate the candidate higher after seeing the second ad than they did after seeing the first ad.

Let's suppose that all three effects were statistically significant and the means were as follows:

	TYPE OF AD	
	EMOTIONAL AD	**RATIONAL AD**
Group 1: (Emotional–Rational sequence)	<u>4</u>	6
Group 2: (Rational–Emotional sequence)	8	7

Note: Scores are rating of the candidate on a 1 (strongly disapprove of) to 9 (strongly approve of) scale.

As you can see from comparing the two ad columns, the rational ad is slightly more effective than the emotional ad. That is, the treatment main effect suggests that, on the average, the rational ad is more effective than the emotional ad. As you can see from comparing the two groups, Group 2 likes the candidate more than Group 1. The between-groups counterbalancing sequence main effect suggests that it would be better to present the ads in the Rational–Emotional sequence than in the Emotional–Rational sequence.

The table doesn't make it as easy to see the order effect. To see whether participants liked the candidate better after the second trial than after the first, this table makes you interpret the treatment × counterbalancing interaction. To help you find the order effect in this table, we have underlined the mean for the ad that each group saw first. Thus, we underlined 4 because Group 1 saw the emotional ad first, and we underlined 7 because Group 2 saw the rational ad first. By recognizing that 4 + 7 is less than 8 + 6, you could determine that scores were lower on the first trial than on the second. To better see the order effect, you should rearrange the table so that the columns represent "Order" rather than "Type of Ad." Your new table would look like this:

	ORDER OF ADS	
	FIRST AD	**SECOND AD**
Group 1: (Emotional–Rational sequence)	<u>4</u>	6
Group 2: (Rational–Emotional sequence)	7	8

As you can see from this table, the order effect reveals that people like the candidate more after the second ad. The ads *do* build on each other.

It's possible, however, that the consultant may not have obtained an order effect. For example, suppose the consultant obtained the following pattern of results:

	TYPE OF AD	
	EMOTIONAL AD	RATIONAL AD
Group 1: Emotional–Rational sequence)	<u>5</u>	6
Group 2: (Rational–Emotional sequence)	5	<u>6</u>

In this case, the rational ad is more effective than the emotional ad for both Group 1 participants (who get the rational ad last) and Group 2 participants (who get the rational ad first). Thus, there is no treatment by counterbalancing interaction. Since there is no treatment $\times$ counterbalancing interaction, there is no order effect. However, an easier way to see that there was no order effect would be to create the table below:

	ORDER OF ADS	
	FIRST AD	SECOND AD
Group 1: Emotional–Rational sequence)	<u>5</u>	6
Group 2: (Rational–Emotional sequence)	<u>6</u>	5

With these data, the consultant would probably decide to just use the rational ad.

Instead of obtaining no order effect, the consultant could have obtained an order effect such that people always rated the candidate worse after the second ad. For example, suppose the consultant obtained the following results:

	ORDER OF ADS	
	FIRST AD	SECOND AD
Group 1: (Emotional–Rational sequence)	<u>5</u>	4
Group 2: (Rational–Emotional sequence)	<u>6</u>	4

If the consultant obtained these results, he would take a long, hard look at the ads. It may be that both ads are making people dislike the candidate, or it may be that the combination of these two ads does not work. Seeing both ads may reduce liking for the candidate by making her seem inconsistent. For example, one ad may suggest that she supports increased military spending while the other may suggest that she opposes increased military spending.

CONCLUSIONS ABOUT COUNTERBALANCED WITHIN-SUBJECTS DESIGNS

As you can see from this last example, the counterbalanced design does more than balance out routine order effects. It also tells you about the impact of both trials (order: first versus second) and sequence. Therefore, you should use counterbalanced designs when:

1. You want to make sure that routine order effects are balanced out.
2. You are interested in sequence effects.
3. You are interested in order (trials) effects.

You will usually want to balance out order effects because you don't want order effects to destroy your study's internal validity. That is, you want a significant treatment difference between your treatment conditions to be due to the treatment, rather than to order effects.

You will often be interested in **sequence effects** because real life is often a sequence of treatments (Greenwald, 1976). That is, most of us are not assigned to receive either praise or criticism; to see either ads for a candidate or against a candidate; to experience only success or failure, pleasure or pain, and so on. Instead, we receive both praise and criticism, see ads for and against a candidate, and experience both success and failure. Counterbalanced designs allow us to understand the effects of receiving different sequences of these "treatments."

You will probably be most interested in sequence effects when you can control the sequence in which a series of events will occur. There are probably many situations in which you may ask yourself, "If I do these tasks in one sequence, will that lead to a better overall outcome than if I do these tasks in a different sequence?" For instance, would it be better to eat and then exercise—or to exercise and then eat? Would it be better to meditate and then study—or to study and then meditate? Or, if you are going to compliment and criticize a friend, would you be better off to criticize, then praise—or to praise, then criticize? To find out about these sequence effects, you would use a counterbalanced design and then look at the main effect for the between-subjects factor of counterbalancing sequence.

Order (trials) effects, on the other hand, will probably interest you if you can control whether a particular event will be first or last in a series of events. Thus, you might be interested in using a counterbalanced design to find out whether it's best to be the first or the last person interviewed for a job. Or, suppose you want to do well in one particular course (research design, of course). Then, you might like to know whether you'd do better in that particular course if it were the first subject you studied or if it were the last course for which you studied. To find out about these order effects, you'd use a counterbalanced design and look at the treatment $\times$ counterbalancing interaction.

CHOOSING DESIGNS

If you want to compare two levels of an independent variable, you have several designs you can use: matched pairs, within-subjects designs, counterbalanced designs, and the simple between-subjects design. To help you choose among these designs, we will briefly summarize the ideal situation for using each design.

CHOOSING DESIGNS: THE TWO-CONDITIONS CASE

The matched-groups design is ideal when:

1. You can readily obtain participants' scores on the matching variable without arousing their suspicions about the purpose of the experiment.
2. The matching variable correlates highly with the dependent measure.
3. Participants are scarce.

The pure within-subjects design is ideal when:

1. Sensitization, practice, fatigue, or carryover effects are not problems.
2. You want a powerful design.
3. Participants are hard to get.
4. You want to generalize your results to real-life situations, and in real life, individuals tend to be exposed to both levels of the treatment.

The 2 × 2 counterbalanced design is ideal when:

1. You want to balance out the effects of order, or you are interested in learning the nature of any order or sequence effects.
2. You have enough participants to meet the requirement of a counterbalanced design.
3. You are not concerned that being exposed to both treatment levels will alert participants to the purpose of the experiment.

The simple experiment is ideal when:

1. You think fatigue, practice, sensitization, or carryover effects could affect the results.
2. You have access to a relatively large number of participants.
3. You want to generalize your results to real-life situations, and in real life, individuals tend to receive either one treatment or the other, but not both.

CHOOSING DESIGNS: WHEN YOU HAVE MORE THAN ONE INDEPENDENT VARIABLE

Thus far, we have discussed how to choose a design when you are studying the effects of a single variable (see Table 9-11). Often, however, you may want to investigate the effects of two or more variables.

In that case, you would appear to have three choices: a between-subjects factorial design, a within-subjects factorial design, and a counterbalanced design. However, counterbalancing becomes less attractive—especially for the beginning researcher—as the design becomes more complicated. Thus, as a general rule, beginning researchers who plan on manipulating two independent variables usually are choosing between a two-factor within-subjects design and a two-factor between-subjects design.

Using a Within-Subjects Factorial Design

You should use a pure within-subjects design if:

1. You can handle the statistics (you will have to use within-subjects analysis of variance or multivariate analysis of variance).
2. Sensitization, practice, fatigue, and carryover effects are not problems.
3. You are concerned about power.
4. In real-life situations, people are exposed to all your different combinations of treatments.

Using a Between-Subjects Factorial Design

On the other hand, you should use a between-subjects design if:

1. You are worried about the statistics of a complex within-subjects design.
2. You are worried that order effects would destroy the internal validity of a within-subjects design.
3. You are not worried about power.
4. In real-life situations, people are exposed to either one combination of treatments or another.

Using a Mixed Design

Sometimes, however, you will find it difficult to choose between a completely within-subjects design and a completely between-subjects design. For example, consider the following two cases.

Case 1: You are studying the effects of brain lesions and practice on how well rats run mazes. On the one hand, you do not want to use a completely within-subjects design because you consider brain damage to occur "between subjects" in real life (because some individuals suffer brain

• **TABLE 9-11** •

IDEAL SITUATIONS FOR DIFFERENT DESIGNS

SIMPLE EXPERIMENT	MATCHED GROUPS	WITHIN SUBJECTS	COUNTERBALANCED DESIGN
Participants are plentiful.	Participants are very scarce.	Participants are very scarce.	Participants are somewhat scarce.
Order effects could be a problem.	Order effects could be a problem.	Order effects are not a problem.	Want to assess order effects or order effects can be balanced out.
Power isn't vital.	Power is vital.	Power is vital.	Power is vital.
In real life, people usually only get one or the other treatment, rarely get both.	In real life, people usually only get one or the other treatment, rarely get both.	In real life, people usually get both treatments, rarely get only one or the other.	In real life, people usually get both treatments, rarely get only one or the other.
Multiple exposure to dependent measure will tip participants off about hypothesis.	Exposure to matching variable will *not* tip participants off about hypothesis.	Multiple exposure to dependent measure will *not* tip participants off about hypothesis.	Multiple exposure to dependent measure will *not* tip participants off about hypothesis.
Exposure to different levels of the independent variable will tip participants off about hypothesis.	Exposure to different levels of the independent variable will tip participants off about hypothesis.	Exposure to different levels of the independent variable will *not* tip participants off about hypothesis.	Exposure to different levels of the independent variable will *not* tip participants off about hypothesis.
	Matching variable is easy to collect and correlates highly with the dependent measure.		

damage, and others do not). On the other hand, you do not want to use a completely between-subjects design because you think that practice occurs "within subjects" in real life (because all individuals get practice and, over time, the amount of practice an individual gets increases).

Case 2: You are studying the effects of subliminal messages and marijuana on creativity. You expect that if subliminal messages have any effect, it will be so small that only a within-subjects design could detect it. However, you feel that oral ingestion of marijuana should not be studied in a within-subjects design because of huge carryover effects (see Table 9-12).

• **TABLE 9-12** •

IDEAL SITUATIONS FOR MAKING A FACTOR BETWEEN OR WITHIN

Should a Factor Be a Between-Subjects Factor or a Within-Subjects Factor?

MAKE FACTOR BETWEEN SUBJECTS	MAKE FACTOR WITHIN SUBJECTS
Order effects pose problems.	Order effects are not a problem.
Lack of power is *not* a concern.	Lack of power is a serious concern.
You want to generalize the results to situations where participants receive either one treatment or another.	You want to generalize the results to situations where participants receive all levels of the treatment.

Fortunately, in these cases, you are not forced to choose between a totally within-subjects factorial and a totally between-subjects factorial. As you know from our discussion of counterbalanced designs, you can do a study in which one variable is between and one is within. Such designs are called **mixed designs** and are analyzed using a mixed analysis of variance.

In the two cases we just discussed, the mixed design is an ideal solution. For example, in Case 1, we could make brain lesion a between-subjects variable by randomly assigning half the participants to get lesions and half not. That way we do not have to worry about carryover effects. We could make practice a within-subjects variable by having each participant run the maze three times. Consequently, we have the power to detect subtle differences due to practice (see Table 9-13 and Figure 9-1).

Note that in this lesion experiment, the interesting statistical effects might have little to do with the two main effects. That is, we would not be terribly

• **TABLE 9-13** •

ANALYSIS OF VARIANCE SUMMARY TABLE FOR A MIXED DESIGN

Source of Variance	df	SS	MS	F	p
Brain Lesion	1	51.0	*51.0*	*10.0*	.0068
Between-Subjects Error	14	72.4	*5.1*		
Trials	2	26.6	13.3	11.1	.0003
Lesions × Trials	2	13.7	6.8	5.7	.0083
Within-Subjects Error	28	33.6	*1.2*		

Note: The mean square error for the within-subjects term is much smaller than the between-subjects error term (1.2 to 5.1), giving the design tremendous power for detecting within-subjects effects. This table corresponds to the graph in Figure 9-1.

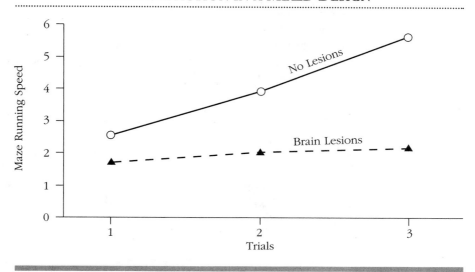

• **FIGURE 9-1** •

AN INTERACTION IN A MIXED DESIGN

surprised to find a main effect for lesion, telling us that the brain-lesioned rats performed worse.[7] Nor would we be surprised to find a main effect for practice, telling us that participants improve with practice. However, we would be interested in knowing about the practice × lesion interaction. A significant practice × lesion interaction would tell us that one group of rats was benefiting from practice more than another. In this case, as you can see from Figure 9-1, it is the non-lesion group that is benefiting most from practice.

Similarly, we could investigate the hypotheses in Case 2 using a mixed design. We would randomly assign participants so that half ingested marijuana and half did not. This random assignment would allow us to avoid carryover effects. Then, we would expose all participants to a variety of subliminal messages. Some of these would be designed to encourage creativity, some of these messages would be neutral. By comparing the average overall creativity scores from the marijuana group to that of the no-marijuana group, we could assess the effect of marijuana. By comparing participants' scores following the "creative" subliminal messages to their scores following "neutral" subliminal messages, we could detect even rather subtle effects of subliminal messages. Finally, by looking at the interaction

---

[7]The lesion main effect would be especially unsurprising if our control group didn't get any surgery. However, such empty control groups are rare. Typically, the control group would be a "sham lesion" control group that got brain surgery and was treated the same as the treatment group except that, instead of being injected with a chemical that would destroy (lesion) part of the brain, they would be injected with a harmless saline solution.

between marijuana and messages, we could determine whether the marijuana group was more influenced by the subliminal messages.

In both Case 1 and in Case 2, the mixed design is the ideal solution for two reasons. First, the mixed design allows you to examine the effects of two independent variables and their interaction. Second, instead of trading off the needs of one variable for the needs of another variable, you are able to give both variables the design they need. Because of its versatility, the mixed design is one of the most popular experimental designs.

Concluding Remarks

You are now familiar with most of the basic experimental designs. You know what they are, how to perform them, how to analyze them, and how to choose among them. Therefore, your comfort level while reading research should be improving. In the next chapter, you will further refine your ability to read and interpret research.

Summary

1. The matched-pairs design uses matching to reduce the effects of random differences between participants and uses random assignment and statistics to account for the remaining effects of random error. Because of random assignment, the matched-pairs design has internal validity. Because of matching, the matched-pairs design has power.

2. Because the matched-pairs design gives you power without limiting the kind of participant you can use, you may be able to generalize your results to a broader population than if you had used a simple experiment.

3. The matched-pairs design's weaknesses stem from matching: Matching may sensitize participants to your hypothesis and participants may drop out of the study between the time of the matching and the time the experiment is performed.

4. Within-subjects designs are also known as repeated-measures designs.

5. The two-condition, within-subjects design gives you two scores per participant.

6. The within-subjects design increases power by eliminating random error due to individual differences and by increasing the number of observations that you obtain from each participant.

7. Both the matched-pairs design and the two-condition, pure within-subjects design can be analyzed by the dependent groups *t*-test. Complex within-subjects designs require more complex analyses. Specifically, they should be analyzed by within-subjects analysis of variance (ANOVA) or by multivariate analysis of variance (MANOVA).

8. Because of practice effects, fatigue effects, carryover effects, and sensitization, the order in which a participant gets the treatments may affect the results.

9. To reduce the effects of order, you should randomly determine the sequence in which each participant will get the treatments or use a counterbalanced design.

10. In the counterbalanced design, participants are randomly assigned to systematically varying sequences of conditions to ensure that routine order effects are balanced out.

11. **Order effects** are different from sequence effects.

12. *Order effects* refer to whether participants respond differently on one trial (e.g., the first) than on some other trial (e.g., the last). Order is a within-subjects factor in a counterbalanced design. Order effects can be detected by looking at the treatment $\times$ counterbalancing sequence interaction.

13. *Sequence effects* refer to whether participants respond differently to getting a series of treatments in one sequence than getting the treatments in a different sequence. For example, the group of participants who get the treatments arranged in the sequence Treatment *A,* then Treatment *B* may have higher overall average scores than the group of participants who get the treatments arranged in the sequence Treatment *B,* then Treatment *A.* Sequence is a between-subjects factor.

14. A counterbalanced design allows you to assess the effect of (1) the treatment, (2) receiving different counterbalanced sequences of treatments, and (3) order (whether participants respond differently on the first trial than on the last).

15. Because you must include the between-subjects factor of counterbalancing in your analyses, counterbalanced designs require more participants than pure within-subjects designs.

16. If you want to compare two levels of an independent variable, you can use a matched-pairs design, a within-subjects design, a counterbalanced design, or a simple between-subjects design.

17. Mixed designs have both a within- and a between-subjects factor. Counterbalanced designs are one form of a mixed design.

18. Mixed designs should be analyzed by using a mixed analysis of variance.

Key Terms

matched-pairs design: an experimental design in which the participants are paired off by matching them on some variable assumed to be correlated with the dependent variable. Then, for each matched pair, one member is randomly assigned to one treatment condition, whereas the other is assigned to the other treatment condition (or to a control condition). This design usually has more power than a simple between-groups experiment. (p. 317)

dependent groups *t*-test (also called **within-subjects *t*-test):** a statistical test for analyzing matched-pairs designs or within-subjects designs that use only two levels of the treatment. (p. 322)

repeated-measures design: see **within-subjects design.**

within-subjects design: an experimental design in which each participant is tested under more than one level of the independent variable. Because each participant is measured more than once (for example, after receiving Treatment *A*, then after receiving Treatment *B*), this design is also called a repeated-measures design. In a within-subjects (repeated-measures) design, a participant may receive Treatment *A* first, Treatment *B* second, and so on. (p. 323)

randomized within-subjects design: to make sure that not every participant receives a treatment series in the same sequence, within-subjects researchers may randomly determine which treatment comes first, which comes second, and so on. In other words, participants all get the same treatments, but they receive different sequences of treatments. (p. 331)

order: the position in a sequence (first, second, third, etc.) in which a treatment occurs. (p. 327)

order effects (trial effects): a big problem with within-subjects designs. The order in which the participant receives a treatment (first, second, etc.) will affect how participants behave. Order effects may be due to practice effects, fatigue effects, carryover effects, or sensitization. Do not confuse with sequence effects. (p. 337)

practice effects: after doing the dependent-measure task several times, a participant's performance may improve. In a within-subjects design, this improvement might be incorrectly attributed to having received a treatment. (p. 326)

fatigue effects: decreased performance on the dependent measure due to being tired or less enthusiastic as the experiment continues. In a within-subjects design, this decrease in performance might be incorrectly attributed to a treatment. Fatigue effects could be considered negative practice effects. (p. 326)

carryover effects (also called **treatment carryover effects):** the effects of a treatment administered earlier in the experiment persist so long that they are present even while participants are receiving additional treatments. Carryover effects create problems for within-subjects designs because you may believe that the participant's behavior is due to the treatment just administered when, in reality, the behavior is due to the lingering effects of a treatment administered some time earlier. (p. 327)

sensitization: after getting several different treatments and performing the dependent-variable task several times, participants in a within-subjects design may realize (become sensitive to) what the hypothesis is. Consequently, a participant in a within-subjects design may behave very differently during the last trial of the experiment (now that the participant knows what the experiment is about) than the participant did in the early trials (when the participant was naïve). (p. 327)

counterbalanced within-subjects designs: designs that give participants the treatments in systematically different sequences. These designs balance out routine order effects. (p. 333)

sequence effects (do not confuse with **order effects**): if participants who receive one sequence of treatments score differently than those participants who receive the treatments in a different sequence, there is a sequence effect. (p. 344)

mixed design: a design that has at least one within-subjects factor and one between-subjects factor. Counterbalanced designs are a type of mixed design. (p. 348)

power: the ability to find statistically significant results when variables are related. Within-subjects designs are popular because of their power. (p. 318)

Exercises

1. What feature of the matched-pairs design makes it an internally valid design?

2. What feature of the matched-pairs design makes it a powerful design?

3. A researcher uses a simple between-subjects experiment involving 10 participants to examine the effects of memory strategy (repetition versus imagery) on memory. Do you think the researcher will find a significant effect? Why or why not? What design would you recommend?

4. If the researcher had used a matched-pairs study involving 10 participants, would the study have more power? Why? How many degrees of freedom would the researcher have? What type of matching task would you suggest? Why?

5. An investigator wants to find out whether hearing jokes will allow a person to persevere longer on a frustrating task. The researcher matches participants based on their reaction to a frustrating task. Of the 30 original participants, 5 quit the study after going through the "frustration pretest." Beyond the ethical problems, what problems are there in using a matched-pairs design in this situation?

6. What problems would there be in using a within-subjects design to study the "humor-perseverance" study (discussed in question 5)? Would a counterbalanced design solve these problems? Why or why not?

7. Why are within-subjects designs more powerful than matched-pairs designs?

8. Two researchers hypothesize that spatial problems will be solved more quickly when the problems are presented to participants' left visual fields than when stimuli are presented to participants' right visual fields. (They reason that messages seen in the left visual field go directly to the right brain, which is often assumed to be better at processing spatial information.) Conversely, they believe verbal tasks will be performed more quickly

when stimuli are presented to participants' right visual fields than when the tasks are presented to participants' left visual fields. What design would you recommend? Why?

9. A student hypothesizes that alcohol level will affect sense of humor. Specifically, the student has two hypotheses. First, the more people drink, the more they will laugh at slapstick humor. Second, the more people drink, the less they will laugh at other forms of humor. What design would you recommend the student use? Why?

10. In a study using a mixed design, one Mean Square Error is 12, the other Mean Square Error is 4. Which Mean Square Error is probably the between-subjects error term? Why?

11. You want to determine whether caffeine, a snack, or a brief walk has a more beneficial effect on mood. What design would you use? Why?

12. Imagine that a student, using a counterbalanced design, compares the taste of orange juice with the taste of milk. Match the following findings to the statistical effect.

___ Individuals liked the first fluid they consumed better than the second thing they drank.	a. Treatment main effect
___ The group drinking milk and then orange juice had higher average liking ratings than the group drinking orange juice and then drinking milk.	b. Counterbalancing main effect
___ Orange juice is better liked than milk.	c. Treatment × Counterbalancing interaction

READING AND EVALUATING RESEARCH

It's not what you don't know that's the problem. It's what you know that just ain't so.
—**WILL ROGERS**

OVERVIEW

In this chapter, you will learn how to benefit from reading other people's research. You will start by learning how to make sense of a research article. Then, you will learn how to spot flaws and limitations in research. Finally, you will learn how you can get research ideas by reading research. Thus, the aim of this chapter is to make you an intelligent consumer and producer of research.

READING FOR UNDERSTANDING

You wouldn't find a "how to" manual about how to fix a Volkswagen very useful unless you were reading it while you were fixing a Volkswagen. Similarly, you will find this "how to read an article" chapter little more than a review of what you already know, unless you read it while you are reading an article. Therefore, before you go on to the next section, get an article.

CHOOSING AN ARTICLE

Do not get just any article. To repeat, don't just read the first article you come across! Because critically evaluating means actively applying what you have learned about research design, get an article that will motivate you to apply what you know about research design. That is, choose an article that uses a design with which you are familiar and that deals with an area that you find interesting.

To start your quest for such an article, you could:

1. Look at sections of texts that you find particularly interesting and look up the articles they reference. For example, you might want to look up a study referenced in this textbook, such as the study by Wilson and Schooler (1991) on when thinking about why we like something hurts our ability to know how much we like it.
2. Consult Appendix B: Searching the Literature to learn how to search for articles by a topic that interests you or by a researcher whose work interests you.
3. Skim the table of contents of current journals.

Your first clue to whether an article is interesting is its title. Usually, the title identifies the key variables in the study. For example, in articles describing an experiment, the independent variable(s) and the dependent variable may be in the title. In some cases, the title may hint at what the hypothesis was or even what the main findings were.

Once you find an article that has an interesting title, the next step is to read a brief, one-paragraph summary of that article. This one-paragraph summary of the research's purpose, methodology, and results is called the **abstract.**

Even if you don't have the original article, you can read its abstract—provided you have access to one of the resources described in Appendix B, such as *Psychological Abstracts* or PsycLit® (the computerized version of *Psychological Abstracts*). If you have the original article, the only problem in finding the abstract is that it is usually not labeled. To find the abstract, turn to the article's first page. Right under the title, you will see a paragraph that stands apart from the rest of the article. Although unlabeled, this one-paragraph summary of the study is called the abstract.[1]

READING THE ABSTRACT

By reading the abstract, you should get a general sense of what the researchers' hypotheses were, how they tried to test those hypotheses, and whether the results supported those hypotheses. But most importantly, you will get an idea about whether you want to read the article. To reiterate, you will probably not want to read the first article that you find. Indeed, when we have students analyze an article, we find that the students who look at more than five abstracts before choosing an article are the happiest with their articles. The unhappiest students are those who read the first article they find.

READING THE INTRODUCTION

Once you find an article that has an interesting title and abstract, you are ready to start reading the rest of the article. For the beginning student, the best place to start reading an article is at the beginning. Although unlabeled, the beginning of the article is called the **introduction.** The introduction is the most difficult, most time consuming, and most important part of the article to understand. You must understand the introduction because it is where the authors tell you:

1. how they came up with the hypothesis, including reasons why they think the hypothesis will be supported
2. reasons why the hypothesis might not be correct
3. why the hypothesis is important
4. why the authors' way of testing the hypothesis is the best way to test the hypothesis (see Figure 10-1)

One way of thinking of the introduction is as a commercial for the article. The authors try to sell you on the importance of their research. They may try

---

[1]Some older articles do not have an abstract but do contain a summary placed at the end of the article.

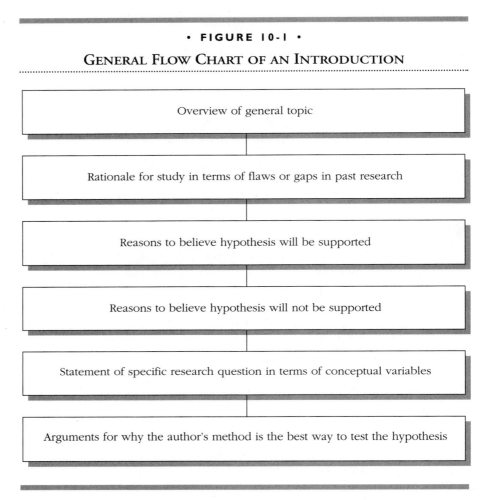

• **FIGURE 10-1** •

GENERAL FLOW CHART OF AN INTRODUCTION

Overview of general topic

Rationale for study in terms of flaws or gaps in past research

Reasons to believe hypothesis will be supported

Reasons to believe hypothesis will not be supported

Statement of specific research question in terms of conceptual variables

Arguments for why the author's method is the best way to test the hypothesis

to sell you on their study by claiming that, relative to previous research ("our competitor's brands"), their methodology is "clearly superior."

Sometimes they argue that their methodology is superior because their study has better construct validity. For example, they may argue that they use a more valid measure, a more valid manipulation, or a better way of preventing participants and experimenters from biasing the results. Sometimes they argue that their study has more internal validity because they have used random assignment to make sure that their results are not due to nontreatment factors. Sometimes they argue that their study has more external validity because they are using random sampling, a broader range of participants, or more naturalistic settings. Sometimes they argue that their study has more power because they are using a more sensitive design, more reliable measures, or more participants.

If they don't try to sell you on the methodological superiority of their study, they may try to sell you on their study by telling you that, relative to previous hypotheses, their hypothesis is "new and improved." In other words, they will try to say that their study has a special ingredient that other studies don't have. Thus, they will try to get you to say, "It's incredible that people have done all this other, related research, but not tested this hypothesis! Why didn't anyone else think of this?" Generally, they are trying to excite you about a study that extends existing research by:

1. using a different sample than previous research (women versus men)
2. looking at a different behavior (manner of walking instead of facial expression, gambling rather than bar-pressing)
3. looking at a variable, such as experience, ability, or motivation, that might moderate or alter a previously discovered relationship
4. looking at cognitive (feelings of being overwhelmed) or physiological (blood pressure) variables that may mediate a previously discovered relationship
5. testing a competing explanation for a treatment's effect (evolution versus cultural)
6. attempting to reconcile the fact that studies have produced apparently conflicting results

A second way of looking at the introduction is as a preview to the rest of the article. The authors start by giving you a general overview of the research area. Next, the authors give you the rationale for the study. Usually, the rationale is either that the research fills a gap in past research or that it fixes a flaw in past research. Then, the authors explicitly state the research question. Finally, the authors may explain why their method for testing the hypothesis is the best way (see Figure 10-1). For example, they may justify their choice of design, their choice of measures, and their choice of participants. Consequently, if you understand the introduction, you should be able to anticipate what will be said in the rest of the article.

Unfortunately, understanding the introduction is not always easy. The main reason the introduction may be hard for you to understand is that the authors are not writing it with you in mind. Instead, they are writing it to other experts in the field. Their belief that the reader is an expert has two important consequences for how they write up their research. First, because they assume that the reader is an expert in the field, they do not think that they have to give in-depth descriptions of the published articles they discuss. In fact, authors often assume that just mentioning the authors and the year of work (for instance, Miller & Smudgekins, 2000) will make the reader instantly recall the essentials of that article. Second, because they assume that the reader is an expert, they do not think they have to define the field's concepts and theories.

Because you are not an expert in the field, the authors' failure to describe studies and define concepts may make it difficult to understand what they are trying to say. Fortunately, you can compensate for not having the background the authors think you have by doing two things. First, read the abstracts of the articles that the authors mention. Second, look up unfamiliar terms or theories in a textbook. If you can't find the term in a textbook, consult the sources listed in Table 10-1.

To encourage yourself to look up all relevant terms and theories, make a photocopy of your article. On the photocopy, use a yellow highlighter to mark any terms or concepts you do not understand (Brewer, 1990). Then, do some background reading and reread the introduction. As you reread the article, highlight any terms or concepts you do not understand with a pink marker. Do some more background reading to get a better understanding of those terms. Then, reread the introduction using a green marker to highlight terms you still do not understand.

By the third time you go through the introduction, you should see much less green than yellow, visually demonstrating that you are making progress. However, even if you know all the individual terms, how do you know that you understand the introduction? One test is to try to describe the logic behind the hypothesis in your own words. A more rigorous test is to design a study to test the hypothesis and then describe the impact of those results for current theory and further research.

To reiterate, do not simply skim the introduction and then move on to the method section. The first time through the introduction, ask yourself two questions:

• TABLE 10-1 •

DECIPHERING JOURNAL ARTICLES

Even experts may need to read a journal article several times to understand it fully. One way to help discipline yourself—and to show that you are making progress—is to photocopy the article. Next, highlight any terms or concepts that you do not understand. The highlighting shows you what you don't understand (if you highlight the entire article, maybe you should find another article). Once you identify the terms that you don't understand, decipher those terms by using one of the techniques listed below.

TO DECIPHER HIGHLIGHTED TERMS

Consult an introductory psychology text.

Consult an advanced psychology text.

Consult a psychological dictionary or encyclopedia.

Consult a professor.

Consult general sources such as *Psychological Science, Psychological Bulletin, Annual Review, and American Psychologist*—to better understand key theories.

Consult other articles that were referenced in the article.

Consult our Web site (http://www.researchmethods.com)

1. What concepts do I need to look up?
2. What references do I need to read?

Then, after doing your background reading, reread the introduction. Do not move on to the method section until you can answer these six questions:

1. What variables are they interested in?
2. What is the hypothesis involving these variables? (What is being studied?)
3. Why does the prediction make sense?
4. Why is the authors' study a reasonable way to test this hypothesis?
5. Does the study correct a weakness in previous research? If so, what was that weakness? Where did others go wrong?
6. Does the study fill a gap in previous research? If so, what was that gap? What did others overlook?

READING THE METHOD SECTION

After you are clear about what predictions are being made, why those predictions are being made, and why the study provides a good test of those predictions, read the method section. That is, once you know why the authors did their research, you are ready to find out what they did.

In the **method section,** the authors will tell you what was done in terms of:

1. who the participants were and how they were selected
2. what measures and equipment were used
3. what the researchers said and did to the participants

An efficient way to tell you about each of these three aspects of the method is to devote a section to each aspect. Therefore, many method sections are subdivided into these three subsections: participants, apparatus, and procedure.

Not all method sections are divided into these three subsections. Some have more. For example, some method sections also have an overview subsection or a design subsection.

You are most likely to see an overview subsection when the article reports several studies, all of which use basically the same procedure. By using an overview section, the author of a four-experiment paper can describe the aspects of the method that are the same for all four studies once, rather than repeating those details in all four method sections. You may also see brief overview subsections for method sections that are long or detailed. With such method sections, the authors fear that the reader would lose the forest for the trees without an overview section.

You may sometimes see a separate design subsection For example, the design subsection might tell you whether the design was a between-subjects design, a within-subjects design (often referred to as a repeated-measures design), or a mixed design. However, authors do not need to include a separate design section. Instead, they may put information about the design in the participants section, in some other section, or even leave design information out of the method section entirely.

Just as authors often do not include a design subsection, authors often do not include either a materials or an apparatus section. Instead, they may incorporate information about the apparatus or materials in the procedure section.

In short, there is no one rule for how many subsections a method section should have. Many will have only two: a participants section and a procedure section. Others may have an overview section, a participants and design section, a procedure section, and a dependent-measures section. Other method sections will use still different formats.

Regardless of its structure, the method section should be the easiest section of the article to understand for two reasons. First, the only thing the method section is trying to do is to tell you what happened in the study—who the participants were, how many participants there were, and how they were treated. The authors should make it very easy for you to imagine what it would be like to be a participant in the study. Indeed, some of the really good procedure sections almost make you feel like you are watching a video, shot from the participants' perspective, of what happened in the study.

Second, the method section should be easy to understand because the introduction should have foreshadowed how the authors planned to test the hypothesis.[2] Therefore, the only trouble you may have in understanding a method section is if you are unfamiliar with some task (for example, a Stroop task) or piece of equipment (such as a tachistoscope) that the researchers used.

What should you do if you run into an unfamiliar task or measure? If you run into unfamiliar apparatus, look up that apparatus in the index of either an advanced textbook or a laboratory equipment catalog. If that fails, ask your professor. If you run into an unfamiliar measure, find a source that describes the measure in detail. Such a source should be referenced in the original article's bibliography. If it is not, look up the measure in the index of one or more textbooks. If that fails, look up the concept the measure is claiming to assess in *Psychological Abstracts*. The *Abstracts* should lead you to an article that will describe the measure. If you still cannot find a description of the apparatus or measure, you may be able to find what you need through our Web page (http://www.researchmethods.com).

---

[2]We do not mean to say that all method sections are easy to read. We mean that authors should be able to write a clear, understandable method section. Unfortunately, authors sometimes do not write coherent method sections. Therefore, if you do not understand a method section, it is probably not your fault. It is the fault of the author and editor. In such cases, we have found that professors are more than happy to help you translate a poorly written method section.

After reading the method section, take a few minutes to think about what it would have been like to be a participant in each of the study's conditions. Then, think about what it would have been like to be the researcher.

Do not go on to the results section until you understand what happened well enough that you could act out the roles of both researcher and participant. More specifically, do not go on to the results section until you can answer these four questions:

1. What were the participants like (species, gender, age), and how did they come to be in the study?
2. What was done to the participants?
3. What tasks or actions did the participants perform?
4. What was the design?

READING THE RESULTS SECTION

Now, turn to the results section of the article you selected to find out what happened. Just like a sports box score tells you how your team did, the **results section** tells you how the hypotheses did.

Like a box score, the results section tells you more than whether the hypothesis "won." You probably could have told whether the hypothesis was supported just from reading the article's title, just like you could tell whether your team won merely from reading the headline. The results section, like the box score, provides a more in-depth analysis of the results.

Of course, there are many differences between box scores and results sections. One difference is that authors of box scores do not have to explain what the numbers in the box scores mean. Most fans know what the player had to do to get his score. That is, any baseball fan knows that a "1" in the "HR" column means that the batter hit one home run. But in a study, what does it mean that the participants averaged a "6"? The meaning of a "6" would depend on the study. Therefore, at the beginning of the results section (if they did not do so in the method section), the authors will briefly explain how they got the numbers that they later put into the statistical analysis. That is, they will describe how they scored participants' responses. Often, the scoring process is fairly straightforward. For example, researchers may say, "The data were the number of correctly recalled words."

Occasionally, computing a score for each participant involves a little more work. For example, in one study, researchers were looking at whether participants believed a person to be normal or mentally ill (Hilton & von Hippel, 1990). To measure these beliefs, the researchers had participants answer two questions. First, participants answered either "yes" or "no" to a question about whether the person had a mental illness. Then, researchers had participants rate, on a one-to-nine scale, how confident participants were of their decision.

How did the researchers turn these two responses into a single score? To quote the authors:

> In creating this scale, a value of –1 was assigned to "no" responses and a value of +1 was assigned to "yes" responses. The confidence ratings were then multiplied by these numbers. All ratings were then converted to a positive scale by adding 10 to the product. This transformation led to a scale in which 1 indicates a high degree of confidence that the person is normal and 19 represents a high degree of confidence that the person is pathological.

Do not just glance at the brief section describing the scores to be used. Before leaving that section, be sure you know what a low score indicates and what a high score indicates. If you do not understand what the numbers being analyzed represent, you will not be able to understand the results of analyses based on those numbers.

After explaining how they got the scores for each participant, the authors may explain how those scores were analyzed. For example, they may write, "The prison sentence the participant recommended was divided by the maximum prison sentence that the participant could have recommended to obtain a score on the dependent measure. These scores were then subjected to a 2 (attractiveness) × 3 (type of crime) between subjects analysis of variance (ANOVA)."

Both the kind and the number of analyses will depend on the study. Depending on the study, the authors will usually report anywhere from one to four kinds of results.

Basic Descriptive Statistics

The first kind of analysis that may be reported—but often is not— is an analysis focusing on basic, descriptive statistics. That is, the authors may summarize the sample's scores on one or more measures. Typically, they will describe the average score using the mean (which they will abbreviate as M), the range of scores (or the standard deviation, abbreviated SD), and the degree to which the scores were normally distributed. For instance, they may report that: "Overall, recall was fairly good ($\underline{M} = 12.89$, $\underline{SD} = 2.68$) and recall scores were normally distributed."

Knowing that the data are normally distributed is useful because many statistical tests, such as the t-test and ANOVA, assume that data are normally distributed. If the data are not normally distributed, the researcher has two choices. First, the researcher can decide not to use those tests. Second, the researcher may be able to perform some mathematical operation (transformation) on the scores to get a more normal distribution (see Figure 10-2). Occasionally, this mathematical operation is relatively simple. For instance, rather than analyze how much *time* it took participants to scan a word, a researcher may analyze the scanning *speed*. The time-to-speed transformation involves inverting the time scores. Thus, a scanning time of half a second per word may become a speed of 2 words per second (2/1.)

• FIGURE 10-2 •

HOW TRANSFORMING SCORES CAN CAUSE
SCORES TO BECOME NORMALLY DISTRIBUTED

Many statistical tests assume that your data are normally distributed. If the assumption of normality is violated, the conclusions from the statistical test may be misleading. However, your data might not be normally distributed. For example, you might get data like the reaction time scores below.

(a) Before transformation

Distribution of Time It Took Participants to React

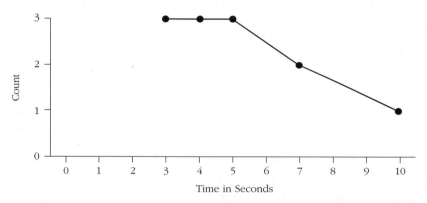

Fortunately, such "non-normally" distributed data can often be transformed into data that are normally distributed. For example, the graph below represents the same data as the graph above. The only difference is that the data above are reaction times, whereas the data below are reaction speeds.

(b) After transformation

Speed at Which Participants Reacted

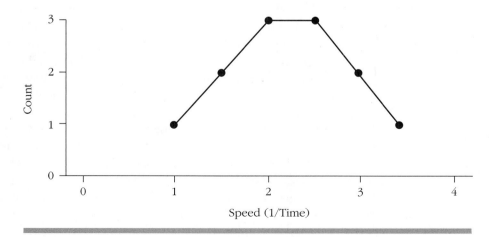

If a new measure is used, the authors may report evidence of the measure's reliability or internal consistency. For example, if a scale was internally consistent, they might report that the scale had a "coefficient alpha of .91." Similarly, they may report that: "Inter-rater reliability was extremely high ($r = .98$)."

Results of the Manipulation Checks

The next type of results that may be reported would be in a section that describes the results of the manipulation check. Usually, these results will be statistically significant and unsurprising. For example, if a study manipulates attractiveness of defendant, the researchers might report that: "Participants rated the attractive defendant ($M = 6.2$ on a 1–7 scale) as significantly more attractive than the unattractive defendant ($M = 1.8$), $F(1,44) = 11.56$, $p < .01$." Once they've shown you that they manipulated the factor they said they manipulated, they are ready to discuss the effects of that factor.

Results Relating to Hypotheses

The next findings the authors would discuss are the findings that every author discusses—those that relate to the hypotheses. The authors try to connect the results to the hypotheses so that the reader can easily tell how the hypotheses fared. For example, if the hypothesis was that attractive defendants would receive lighter sentences than unattractive defendants, then the author would report what the data said about this hypothesis:

> The hypothesis that attractive defendants would receive lighter sentences was not supported. Attractive defendants received an average sentence of 6.1 years whereas the average sentence for the unattractive defendants was 6.2 years. This difference was not significant, $\underline{F}(1,32) = 1.00$, ns.

Other Significant Results

After reporting results relating to the hypotheses (whether or not the results are statistically significant), authors will dutifully report any other statistically significant results. Even if the results are unwanted and make no sense to the investigator, significant results must be reported. Therefore, you may read things like: "There was an unanticipated interaction between attractiveness and type of crime. Unattractive defendants received heavier sentences for violent crimes whereas attractive defendants received heavier sentences for nonviolent crimes, $F(1,32) = 18.62$, $p < .05$." Or, you may read: "There was also a significant four-way interaction between attractiveness of defendant, age of defendant, sex of defendant, and type of crime. This interaction was uninterpretable." Typically, these results will be presented last: Although the author is obligated to report these unexpected and unwelcomed findings, the author is not obligated to emphasize them.

Conclusions About Reading the Results Section

In conclusion, depending on the statistics involved, reading the results section may be difficult. The first time through the results section, you may not understand everything. However, before moving on to the discussion section, you should be able to answer these five questions:

1. What are the scores they are putting into the analysis?
2. What are the average scores for the different groups? Which types of participants score higher? Lower?
3. Do I understand all the tables and figures that contain descriptive statistics, such as tables of means, percentages, correlations, and so on?
4. What type of statistical analysis did the authors use?
5. Do the results appear to support the authors' hypotheses? Why or why not?

READING THE DISCUSSION

Finally, read the **discussion.** The relationship between the discussion and the results section is not that different from the relationship between a sports article and the box score. The article about the game reiterates key points from the box score, but focuses on putting the game in a larger context—what the team's performance means for the team's playoff hopes, the team's place in history, or even for the league itself. Similarly, the discussion section relates your results to the real world, theory, and future research. That is, whereas the results section analyzes the results in relationship to the hypothesis, the discussion section interprets the results in light of the bigger picture.

The discussion should hold few surprises. In fact, before reading the discussion, you could probably write a reasonable outline of it. All you would have to do is to:

1. Jot down the main findings.
2. Relate these findings to the introduction.
3. Speculate about the reasons for any surprising results.

Because many discussion sections follow this three-step formula, the discussion is mostly a reiteration of the highlights of the introduction and results sections. If the authors get the results they expect, the focus of these highlights will be on the consistency between the introduction and the results. If, on the other hand, the results are unexpected, the discussion section will attempt to reconcile the introduction and results sections. After discussing the relationship between the introduction and the results, the authors will provide some general conclusions about the significance of their research and offer suggestions for future research. Consequently, by the time you finish the discussion section, you should be able to answer these five questions:

1. How well do the authors think the results matched their predictions?
2. How do they explain any discrepancies between their results and their predictions?
3. Do the authors admit that their study was flawed or limited in any way? If so, how?
4. What additional studies, if any, do the authors recommend?
5. What are the authors' main conclusions?

DEVELOPING RESEARCH IDEAS FROM EXISTING RESEARCH

Once you understand the article, you can take advantage of what you have learned in previous chapters to question the article's conclusions. For example, you can question the study's power as well as its internal, external, and construct validity.

As you can see from Box 10-1, there are many questions you can ask of any study. But what good is this questioning? Questioning a study pays off in at least two ways.

First, because you become aware of the study's limitations, you avoid the mistake of believing that something has been proven to be true when it has not. Consequently, you are less likely to act on the basis of misinformation. Acting on the basis of bad information will often be bad for you—as a consumer, you may buy the wrong product; as a citizen, you may support the wrong policies. As you assume more power and responsibility, acting on the basis of misinformation may often harm others. Thus, the executive acting on wrong information may bankrupt the company. Similarly, a therapist using an ineffective or harmful treatment may harm many people.

Second, because you are aware that no single study answers every question, you realize that additional studies should be done. In other words, a common result of asking questions about research is that you end up designing additional studies that will either document, destroy, or build on the previous research. Thus, familiarity with research breeds more research.

THE DIRECT REPLICATION

Whenever you read a study, one obvious research idea always comes to mind—repeat the study. That is, do a **direct replication.**

One reason to do a direct replication is to develop research skills. Many professors—in chemistry, biology, and physics, as well as in psychology—have their students repeat studies to help students develop research skills.

But, from a research standpoint, isn't repeating a study fruitless? Isn't it inevitable that you will get the same results the author reported? Not necessarily—especially if there was an error in the original study. Unfortunately, there

Ch #10
368-
379

• BOX 10-1 •

QUESTIONS TO ASK OF A STUDY

....

Questions About Construct Validity

1. Was the manipulation valid?
   a. Is the manipulation consistent with definitions of the construct that is allegedly being manipulated?
   b. Did the researchers use a manipulation check to see how participants interpreted the manipulation?
   c. Are *more* or *better* control conditions needed? (The control condition[s] and the experimental condition[s] should be identical except for those aspects directly related to the construct being manipulated.)

2. Was the measure valid?
   a. Was it reliable?
   b. Was it objectively scored?
   c. Did research show that it correlated with other measures of that same construct?
   d. Did research show that it was uncorrelated with measures of unrelated constructs?
   e. Was the measure consistent with accepted definitions of the construct?

3. Could the researchers have biased the study's results?
   a. Were researchers "blind"?
   b. Did the lack of standardization make it easy for researchers to bias the results?

4. Could participants have figured out the hypothesis?
   a. Could participants have learned about the study from former participants?
   b. Were participants experienced enough to figure out the hypothesis (for instance, senior psychology majors who had participated in several studies)?
   c. Was the hypothesis a fairly easy one to figure out?
   d. Was an empty control group used?

   e. Did the researcher fail to make the study a double-blind study?
   f. Were any procedures used that might sensitize participants to the hypothesis (matching on dependent variable, a within-subjects design, etc.)?
   g. Was it obvious to participants what was being measured? (For example, did participants fill out a self-report scale?)
   h. Did the study lack *experimental realism:* the ability to psychologically involve participants in the task so that they would not merely be playing the role of cooperative participant?
   i. Did the researchers fail to have an effective "cover story" that disguised the true purpose of the study?

Questions About External Validity

1. Would results apply to the average person?
   a. Were participants human?
   b. Were participants distinct in any way?
   c. Were the participants too homogeneous? That is, were there certain types of individuals (women, minorities) who were not included in the study?
   d. Was the dropout rate high—or high among certain groups (for example, the elderly)? If so, the results only apply to those who would stay in the study.
   e. Is there any specific reason to suspect that the results would not apply to a different group of participants?

2. Would the results generalize to different settings? Can you pinpoint a difference between the research setting and a real-life setting and give a specific reason why
(continued)

• BOX 10-1 (CONTINUED) •

QUESTIONS TO ASK OF A STUDY

this difference would prevent the results from applying to real life?

3. Would the results generalize to different levels of the treatment variable?
   a. What levels of the treatment variable were included?
   b. What levels of the treatment variable were not used?
   c. How many levels of the treatment variable were used?

Questions About Internal Validity

1. Was an experimental design used?
   a. Was the treatment manipulated? (Otherwise, the alleged effect may have occurred before the alleged cause.)
   b. Was the influence of nontreatment factors dealt with in at least one of the following three ways?
      (1) Those factors were kept constant.
      (2) Randomization was used to allow the researcher to statistically account for those variables.
      (3) Counterbalancing was used to balance out the effects of those variables.

2. Was independence established and maintained?

3. Did more participants drop out of the treatment group than the control group?

4. Was a within-subjects design used, even though order effects posed a serious threat?

Questions About Power

1. If null results were obtained, ask:
   a. Were measures sensitive enough?
   b. Was the study sufficiently standardized? That is, did lack of standard-

ization and lack of control over the testing environment create so much error variance that the treatment effect was overlooked?
   c. Were enough participants used?
   d. Did conditions differ enough on the treatment/predictor variable?
   e. Were participants homogeneous enough—or did between-subject differences hide the treatment effect?
   f. Was the design sensitive enough? For example, perhaps the researchers should have used a within-subjects design instead of a between-subjects design.
   g. Could the null results be due to a floor or ceiling effect?

Questions About Statistical Analyses

1. Do the data meet the assumptions of the statistical test?
   a. If they did an independent-groups t-test, did they have independent observations and at least interval scale data?
   b. If they used a matched-pairs design and had interval scale data, did they use the dependent-groups t-test?

2. Are they running a high risk of making a Type 1 error?
   a. Are they doing multiple statistical tests without correcting for the fact that their reported significance level is only valid if they are doing a single test? For example, if they use a .05 (5%) significance level, but do 100 tests, 5 tests could turn out significant by chance alone.
   b. Are they using fairly liberal significance levels? For example, are they using a .13 or .25 level rather than a .05 level? *(continued)*

3. Were the appropriate follow-up tests done so that the right conditions are being compared?
   a. In a multiple-condition experiment, did they claim that particular groups differed from each other without doing a post hoc test (or planned comparison) to determine which groups were significantly different from each other?
   b. In a multiple-condition experiment, did they claim to know that the relationship between variables was linear, cubic, or quadratic without doing a trend analysis to verify whether that particular linear, cubic, or quadratic trend was statistically significant?

4. Did they accurately interpret the results of their statistical analyses?
   a. Did they fail to realize that an ordinal interaction may merely be the result of a floor or ceiling effect?
   b. Did they represent differences between means as real, even though the results were not statistically significant?

are at least three reasons why the results reported in the original study may be misleading: fraud, Type 1 errors, and Type 2 errors.

Suspicion of Fraud

Although fraud is very unusual, it does occur. Some cheat for personal fame. Others cheat because they believe their ideas are right, even though their results fail to reach the $p <. 05$ level of significance.

Since thousands of researchers want to be published and since many are under great pressure to publish, why is cheating so unusual? Cheating is unusual because the would-be cheat knows that others may replicate the study. If these replications don't get the results the cheat reported, the credibility of the cheat and of the original study would be questioned. Thus, the threat of direct replication keeps would-be cheats in line. Some scientists, however, worry that science's fraud detectors are not as effective as they once were because people are not doing replications as often as they once did (Broad & Wade, 1982).

Suspicion of Type 1 Errors

Although fraud is one reason that some findings in the literature are probably inaccurate (Broad & Wade, 1982), perhaps more common sources of nonreplicable findings are Type 1 and Type 2 errors. As you may remember from Chapter 6, Type 1 errors are statistical "false alarms." That is, the variables are not really related, even though the statistical test suggested that they were. Type 2 errors, on the other hand, occur when the statistical test fails to detect that the variables really are related. Partly because of psychologists' concerns about Type 1 and Type 2 errors, some journals solicit and accept studies that replicate—or fail to replicate—previously published research.

To understand how the original study's results may have been significant because of a Type 1 error, imagine that you are a crusty journal editor who only allows simple experiments that are significant at the $p = .05$ level to be published in your journal. If you accept an article, the chances are only about 5 in 100 that the article will contain a Type 1 error (the error of mistakenly declaring that a chance difference is a real difference). Thus, you are appropriately cautious. But what happens once you publish 100 articles? Then, you may have published five articles that have Type 1 errors.

In fact, you may have many more Type 1 errors than that. How? Because people do not send you nonsignificant results. They may have done the same experiment eight different times, but it only came out significant the eighth time. Thus, they only send you the results of the eighth replication. Or, if 20 different teams of investigators do basically the same experiment, only the team that gets significant results (the team with the Type 1 error) will submit their study to your journal.

To illustrate that people tend to only send in significant results, let's look at an actual example. While serving as editor for the *Journal of Personality and Social Psychology,* Anthony Greenwald received an article that found a significant effect for ESP. Since Dr. Greenwald was aware that many other researchers had done ESP experiments that had not obtained significant results, he asked for a replication. The authors could not replicate their results. Thus, the original study was not published because the original results were probably the result of a Type 1 error.

Suspicion of Type 2 Errors

Just as studies that find significant effects may be victimized by Type 1 errors, studies that fail to find significant effects may be victimized by Type 2 errors. Indeed, there are reasons to expect that Type 2 errors may be even more common than Type 1 errors. Realize that, in a typical study, the chance of a Type 1 error is usually about 5%. However, in most studies, the chance of a Type 2 error is much higher. To give you an idea of how much higher, Jacob Cohen, who has championed planning studies with adequate power, wants psychologists to set the chance of a Type 2 error at about 20%. Thus, even if researchers would live up to Dr. Cohen's relatively high standards, the risk of making a Type 2 error in a study would be at least four times higher than the risk of making a Type 1 error!

Few researchers, however, conduct studies that come close to Cohen's standards. For example, Cohen (1990) reports that, even in some highly esteemed journals, the studies published are ones that ran more than a 50% chance of making a Type 2 error. Similarly, when reviewing the literature on the link between attributions and depression, Robins (1988) found that only 8 of 87 published analyses had the level of power that Cohen recommends. No wonder some studies found relationships between attributions and depression whereas others did not! Thus, when a study fails to find a significant effect, do not assume that a direct replication would also fail to find a significant effect. Repeating the study may yield statistically significant results.

THE SYSTEMATIC REPLICATION

Rather than merely repeating the study, you could do a **systematic replication:** a study that varies in some systematic way from the original study. Generally, systematic replications fall into two categories.

First, the systematic replication refines the design or methodology of the previous study. For example, the systematic replication may use more participants, more standardized procedures, or more objective methods of coding behavior than the original research.

Second, the person doing the systematic replication may make different tradeoffs than the original researcher. That is, whereas the original researcher sacrificed construct validity to get power, the person doing the replication may sacrifice power to get construct validity.

You now know what a systematic replication is, but why should you do one? There are two basic reasons.

First, as we suggested earlier, you might do a systematic replication for any of the reasons you would do a direct replication. That is, because the systematic replication is similar to the original study, the systematic replication, like the direct replication, can help verify that the results reported by the original author are not due to a Type 1 error, a Type 2 error, or to fraud.

Second, you might do a systematic replication to make new discoveries. The systematic replication may uncover new information because it will either do things differently or do things better than the original study. Because you can always make different tradeoffs than the original researcher and because most studies can be improved, you can almost always do a useful systematic replication.

In the next few sections, we will show you how to design a useful systematic replication. Specifically, we will show you how to design systematic replications that have more power, more external validity, or more construct validity than the original. We will begin by showing you how to change the original study to create a systematic replication that has more power than the original.

Improving Power by Tightening up the Design

As we suggested earlier, if a study obtains null results, you may want to repeat the study, but add a few minor refinements to increase power (see Table 10-2). You might improve power by increasing standardization. For example, you might have researchers follow a very detailed script, or have a computer present the stimuli. You might improve power by using more participants than the original study and choosing participants who were more homogeneous than those used in the original study. Alternatively, you might increase power by using a more sensitive measure or by using more extreme levels of the treatment variable. Finally, you might replicate the original study using a more sensitive design. For instance, if the authors used a simple experiment and found no effect for a certain memory strategy on words recalled, you might replicate the experiment

· **TABLE 10-2** ·

HOW TO DEVISE A SYSTEMATIC REPLICATION
THAT WILL HAVE MORE POWER THAN THE ORIGINAL STUDY

1. Improve standardization of procedures.
2. Use more participants.
3. Use more homogeneous participants.
4. Use more extreme levels of treatment or predictor variables.
5. Use a more sensitive dependent measure.
6. Use a more powerful design. For example, replicate a pure between-groups experiment as a within-subjects experiment.

with a matched-pairs design (matching participants on IQ), or with a repeated-measures (within-subjects) design.

Improving External Validity

If the original study had adequate power, this power may have come at the expense of other valued characteristics (see Table 10-3), such as external validity. To illustrate, let's look at two cases where attempts to help power hurt the generalizability of the results.

In the first case, a researcher is worried that individual differences among the participants will hide the treatment effect. Therefore, the researcher tries to reduce individual differences by choosing a group of individuals who are all fairly similar. The researcher knows that using a homogeneous group of participants will tend to boost power. However, choosing a group of homogeneous participants will decrease the extent to which the results can be generalized to other kinds of participants. What applies to this particular group of participants (for example, white, middle-class, first-year college students between the ages of 18 and 19) may not apply to other groups of people (for instance, the poor, the uneducated, or the elderly).

In the second case, a researcher is worried that random, real-life events would create so much error variance that it would hide the treatment effect. Therefore, to reduce error variance, the researcher performs the study in a lab rather than in the field. The problem is that we do not know whether the results would generalize outside of this artificial environment.

To increase a study's generalizability, there are at least four things you can do (see Table 10-4). To help you visualize these four possibilities, suppose that some students performed a lab experiment at their college to examine the effects of defendant attractiveness.

First, you can systematically vary the kinds of participants used. If the study used all male participants, you might use all female participants.

• **T A B L E   1 0 - 3** •

TRADEOFFS INVOLVING POWER

	STEPS THAT INCREASE POWER
POWER versus CONSTRUCT VALIDITY	Using empty control group, not controlling for placebo effects.
	Using sensitive measure, despite its vulnerability to self-report biases.
	Using a within-subjects design despite serious sensitization problems.
	Using a matched-pairs design despite the fact that matching alerts participants to the hypothesis.
POWER versus EXTERNAL VALIDITY	Using a restricted sample of participants to reduce random error due to subject differences.
	Using a simple, controlled environment to reduce random error due to uncontrolled situational variables.
	Using a within-subjects design even though—in real life—individuals rarely receive more than one level of the treatment.
	Maximizing the number of participants per group by decreasing the number of groups. That is, you may choose to do a simple experiment rather than multilevel or factorial experiment. Consequently, the degree to which the results generalize to various levels of treatment or across different factors is hard to assess.
POWER versus INTERNAL VALIDITY	Using a within-subjects design even when carryover, fatigue, and practice effects are likely.
	Increasing risk of Type 1 error to increase power.

Second, you can change a lab experiment into a field experiment. For example, suppose that the defendant study used college students as participants. By moving the defendant study to the field, you might be able to use real jurors as participants rather than college students.

Third, you can use different levels of the independent variable to see whether the effects will generalize to different levels of the independent variable. In the defendant study, researchers may have only compared attractive versus unattractive defendants. Therefore, you might replicate the study to see whether extremely attractive defendants have an advantage over moderately attractive defendants.

Fourth, you can wait a while before collecting the dependent measure to see whether the effect lasts. Often, researchers measure the dependent variable almost immediately after the participant gets the treatment to maximize their chances of obtaining a significant effect. Researchers are afraid that the effect will wear off if they wait. However, in real life, there may be a gap between treatment and opportunity to act.

• TABLE 10-4 •

HOW TO DEVISE A SYSTEMATIC REPLICATION THAT WILL HAVE MORE EXTERNAL VALIDITY THAN THE ORIGINAL STUDY

1. Use more heterogeneous group of participants or use a participant group (for instance, females) that was not represented in the original study.
2. Repeat as a field study.
3. Use more levels of the independent or predictor variable.
4. Delay measurement of the dependent variable to see if the treatment effect persists over time.

Improving Construct Validity

Finally, you might do a systematic replication to improve a study's construct validity. Often, you can make some minor changes that will reduce the threat of hypothesis-guessing (see Table 10-5).

To illustrate, imagine a two-group experiment where one group gets caffeine (in a cola), whereas the other group gets nothing. You might want to replace this empty control group with a placebo treatment (a caffeine-free cola). Or, you might keep the empty control group, but add a treatment condition in which participants get a very small amount of caffeine. This will give you three levels of the treatment variable. If both treatment conditions differ from the control group, but do not differ from one another, you might suspect that participant and experimenter expectancies were responsible for the treatment effect.

Admittedly, it is not easy to find simple, two-group experiments. Major journals rarely publish such studies. However, you can easily find many designs that use only two levels of a given treatment variable. Major journals frequently publish 2×2 and 2×3 designs. Therefore, you can easily use the strategy of improving a study by using three, rather than two, levels of a treatment variable. For example, you could replicate a 2×2 study as a 3×2 or even as a 3×3.

• TABLE 10-5 •

HOW TO DEVISE A SYSTEMATIC REPLICATION THAT WILL HAVE MORE CONSTRUCT VALIDITY THAN THE ORIGINAL STUDY

1. Replace an empty control group with a placebo treatment group.
2. Use more than two levels of the independent variable.
3. Alter the study so that it is a double-blind study.
4. Add a cover story or improve the existing cover story.
5. Replicate it as a field study.

Besides adding levels of the independent variable, there are three other minor alterations you can do to make it harder for participants to figure out the hypothesis. First, you could replicate the study, making it a double-blind experiment. Second, you could mislead the participants regarding the purposes of the study by giving them a clever cover story. Third, you could do the study in the field: If participants do not know they are in a study, they probably will not guess the hypothesis.

In short, the systematic replication accomplishes everything a direct replication does and more. By making some slight modifications in the study, you can improve the original study's power, external validity, or construct validity.

THE CONCEPTUAL REPLICATION

Suppose you think there were problems with the original study's construct validity. However, you believe that these problems cannot be solved by making minor procedural changes. Then, you should perform a **conceptual replication:** a study that is based on the original study, but uses different methods to better assess the true relationships between the variables. In a conceptual replication, you might use a different manipulation or a different measure.

Because there is no such thing as a perfect measure or manipulation, virtually every study's construct validity can be questioned. Since the validity of a finding is increased when the same basic result is found using other measures or manipulations, virtually any study can benefit from conceptual replication. Therefore, you should have little trouble finding a study you wish to conceptually replicate.

There are a variety of ways to design a conceptual replication (see Table 10-6). For example, you could use a different way of manipulating the treatment variable. The more manipulations of a construct that find the same effect, the more confident we can be that the construct actually has that effect. Indeed, you might use

---

• TABLE 10-6 •

HOW TO DEVISE A CONCEPTUAL REPLICATION THAT WILL HAVE MORE CONSTRUCT VALIDITY THAN THE ORIGINAL STUDY

1. Use a different manipulation of the treatment variable and add a manipulation check.

2. Use a different dependent measure. One that:

   a. is less vulnerable to social desirability biases and demand characteristics, such as:

      (1) a measure of overt behavior (actual helping rather than reports of willingness to help).

      (2) a measure that is unobtrusive (how far people sit from each other, rather than reports of how much they like each other).

   b. is closer to accepted definitions of the construct.

two or three manipulations of your treatment variable and use the type of manipulation as a factor in your design. For instance, suppose a study used photos of a particular woman dressed in either a "masculine" or "feminine" manner to manipulate the variable "masculine versus feminine style." You might use the original experiment's photos for one set of conditions, but also add two other conditions that use your own photos. Then, your statistical analysis would tell you whether your manipulation had a different impact than the original study's manipulation.

Of course, you are not limited to using the same type of manipulation as the original study. Thus, instead of manipulating "masculine" versus "feminine" by dress, you might manipulate "masculine" versus "feminine" by voice (masculine-sounding versus feminine-sounding voices).

Although varying the treatment variable for variety's sake is worthwhile, changing the manipulation to make it better is even more worthwhile. One way of improving a treatment manipulation is to make it more consistent with the definition of the construct. Thus, in our previous example, you might feel that the original picture manipulated "fashion sense" rather than "masculine/feminine style." Therefore, your manipulation might involve two photos: one photo of a woman who was fashionably dressed in a feminine way, one of a woman who was fashionably dressed in a masculine manner. You might also want a manipulation check to get more evidence as to the validity of the manipulation. Thus, you might ask participants to rate the "masculine" and "feminine" photos in terms of attractiveness, fashion sense, and masculinity–femininity.

Because no manipulation is perfect, replicating a study using a different treatment manipulation is valuable. Similarly, because no measure is perfect, replicating a study using a different measure is valuable. Often, you can increase the construct validity of a study by replacing a self-report measure with a behavioral measure. Thus, if the study uses a rating scale measure of "willingness to help," you might replicate the study by actually giving participants an opportunity to help. By using a behavioral measure, your study may be less vulnerable to demand characteristics and self-report biases.

THE VALUE OF REPLICATIONS

Replications are important to advancing psychology as a science. Direct replications are essential for guaranteeing that the science of psychology is rooted in solid, documented fact. Systematic replications are essential for making psychology a science that applies to all people. Conceptual replications are essential for making psychology a science that can make accurate statements about constructs. That is, conceptual replications help us go beyond talking about the relationship of specific procedures with scores on specific measures to knowing about the relationships between broad, universal constructs such as stress and mental health.

In addition to replicating previous research, systematic and conceptual replications extend previous research. Consider, for a moment, the conceptual replication that uses a better measure of the dependent variable or the systematic replication that shows the finding occurs in real-world settings. Such conceptual and systematic replications can transcend the original research.

EXTENDING RESEARCH

Systematic and conceptual replications are not the only ways to extend published research. Of the many other ways to extend published research (see Table 10-7), let's briefly discuss the two easiest.

First, you could both replicate and extend research by repeating the original study while adding a variable that you think might moderate the observed effect. For instance, if you think that being attractive would hurt a defendant if the defendant had already been convicted of another crime, you might add the factor of whether or not the defendant had been previously convicted of a crime.

• TABLE 10-7 •

EXTENDING RESEARCH

1. Replicate the research, but add a factor (subject or situational variable) that may moderate the effect. That is, pin down under what situations and for whom the effect is most powerful.

2. Conduct studies suggested by authors in their discussion section.

3. Look for variables that may mediate the relationship. That is, look for cognitive or physiological mechanisms that may be the underlying causes of the effect.

4. Look for related treatments that might have similar effects. For example, if additional time to rehearse is assumed to improve memory by promoting the use of more effective rehearsal strategies, consider other variables that should promote the use of more effective rehearsal strategies, such as training in the use of effective rehearsal strategies.

5. See if the effects last. For example, many persuasion and memory studies only look at short-term effects.

6. Instead of using a measure of a general construct, use a measure that will tap a specific aspect of that construct. This focused measure will allow you to pinpoint exactly what the treatment's effect is. For example, if the original study used a general measure of memory, replicating the study with a measure that could pinpoint what aspect of memory (encoding, storage, or retrieval) was being affected would allow a more precise understanding of what happened.

7. If the study involves basic (nonapplied) research, see if the finding can be applied to a practical situation. For example, can a memory effect demonstrated in the lab be used to help students on academic probation?

8. If the study describes a correlational relationship between two variables, do an experiment to determine if one variable causes the other. For example, after finding out that teams wearing black were more likely to be penalized, the authors of this textbook's sample paper (Appendix D) did an experiment to find out if wearing black causes one to be more violent.

9. Do a study to test a competing explanation for the study's results. For example, if the researchers argue that people wearing black are more likely to be violent, you might argue that there is an alternative explanation: People wearing black are more likely to be *perceived* as violent.

Second, you could extend the research by doing the follow-up studies that the authors suggest in their discussion section. Sometimes, the authors will clearly suggest follow-up studies, even going so far as to have a subheading in discussion titled "Directions for Future Research." At other times, you will have to find the paragraph where they talk about the limitations of the research. Thus, if they say that a limitation of the study was that it covered only a short period of time, they are suggesting a replication involving a longer period of time. If they say that a limitation was that they used self-report measures, they are suggesting a replication using other types of measures.

In short, much of the work done by scientists is a reaction to reading other scientists' work. Sometimes, the reaction is excitement: The researcher thinks the authors are on to something special, so the researcher follows up on that work. Sometimes, the reaction is anger: The researcher thinks that the authors are wrong, so the researcher designs a study to prove them wrong. Regardless, the outcome is the same: The publication of an article not only communicates information, but it also creates new questions. As a result of scientists reacting to each others' work, science progresses.

Concluding Remarks

After reading this chapter, you can be one of the scientists who reacts to another's work and helps science progress. You not only know how to criticize research, but also how to improve it. Thus, every time you read an article, you should get at least one research idea.

Summary

1. Not all articles are equally easy and interesting to read. Therefore, if you are given an assignment to read any article, you should look at several articles before committing to one.

2. Reading the title and the abstract can help you choose an article that you will want to read.

3. The abstract is a short, one-paragraph summary of the article. In journals, the abstract is the paragraph immediately following the authors' names and affiliations.

4. In the article's introduction, the authors tell you what the hypothesis is, why it is important, and justify their method of testing it.

5. To understand the introduction, you may need to refer to theory and previous research.

6. The method section tells you who the participants were, how many participants there were, and how they were treated.

7. In the results section, authors should report any results relating to their hypotheses and any statistically significant results.

8. The discussion section either reiterates the introduction and results sections or tries to reconcile the introduction and results sections.

9. When you critique the introduction, question whether (1) testing the hypothesis is vital, (2) the hypothesis follows logically from theory or past research, and (3) the authors have found the best way to test the hypothesis.

10. When you critique the method section, question the construct validity of the measures and manipulations, and ask how easy it would have been for participants to have played along with the hypothesis.

11. When you look at the results section, question any null results. The failure to find a significant result may be due to the study failing to have enough power.

12. In the discussion section, question the authors' interpretation of the results, try to explain results that the authors have failed to explain, find a way to test your explanation, and note any weaknesses that the authors concede.

13. The possibility of Type 1 error, Type 2 error, or fraud may justify doing a direct replication.

14. You can do a systematic replication to improve power, external validity, or construct validity.

15. Conceptual replications are mandated when problems with a study's construct validity cannot be fixed by minor changes.

16. Replications are vital for the advancement of psychology as a science.

17. Reading research should stimulate research ideas.

Key Terms

Psychological Abstracts: a useful resource that contains abstracts from a wide variety of journals. The *Abstracts* can be searched by year of publication, topic of article, or author. (p. 357)

abstract: a short, one-paragraph summary of a research proposal or article. The abstract should not be more than 120 words long. It comes before the introduction. (p. 357)

introduction: the part of the article that occurs right after the abstract. In the introduction, the authors tell you what their hypothesis is, why their hypothesis makes sense, how their study fits in with previous research, and why their study is worth doing. (p. 357)

method section: the part of the article immediately following the introduction. Whereas the introduction explains *why* the study was done, the method section describes *what* was done. For example, it will tell you what design was used, what the researchers said to the participants, what measures and equipment were used, how many participants were studied, and how they were selected. The method section could also be viewed as a "how we did it" section. The method section is often subdivided into three subsections: participants, apparatus, and procedure. (p. 361)

results section: the part of the article immediately following the method section that reports selected statistical results and relates those results to the hypotheses. From reading this section, you should know whether the results supported the hypothesis. (p. 363)

discussion: the part of the article immediately following the results section that interprets the results. For example, the discussion section may explain the importance of the findings and suggest research projects that could be done to follow up on the study. (p. 367)

direct replication: a later copy of the original study. Direct replications are useful for establishing that the findings of the original study are reliable. (p. 368)

systematic replication: a study that varies from the original study only in some minor aspect. For example, a systematic replication may use more participants, more standardized procedures, more levels of the independent variable, or a more realistic setting than the original study. (p. 373)

conceptual replication: a study that is based on the original study, but uses different methods to better assess the true relationships between the treatment and dependent variables. In a conceptual replication, you might use a different manipulation or a different measure. The conceptual replication is the most sophisticated kind of replication. (p. 377)

Exercises

1. Find an article to critique. If you are having trouble finding an article, consult Appendix B (Searching the Literature) or use the article in Appendix D. Using Box 10-1, critique the article you selected.
2. What are the major weaknesses of the article?
3. Design a direct replication of the study you critiqued. Do you think your replication would yield the same results as the original? Why or why not?
4. Design a systematic replication based on the study you critiqued. Describe your study. Why is your systematic replication an improvement over the original study?
5. Design a conceptual replication based on the study you critiqued. Describe your study. Why is your conceptual replication an improvement over the original study?

SINGLE-*n* DESIGNS AND QUASI-EXPERIMENTS

Real life is messy.
—ANONYMOUS

OVERVIEW

To this point, we have shown you only one way to infer causality—by using random assignment. In this chapter, you will learn about efforts to infer causality without the benefit of random assignment.

We will begin by reviewing how randomized experiments meet the requirements for establishing causality. Then, you will examine two types of designs that attempt to meet these requirements without random assignment: single-*n* designs and quasi-experiments.

In short, after reading this chapter, you should be well prepared to design a study to determine whether a real-life treatment causes an effect. Specifically, you will know a variety of designs that can be used to infer causality, as well as the advantages and disadvantages of these designs.

INFERRING CAUSALITY IN RANDOMIZED EXPERIMENTS

Whether you use a randomized experiment or any other design, you must satisfy three criteria if you are to infer that one variable (smiling at others) causes a change in another variable (others helping you). Specifically, you must establish

1. covariation (that there is a relationship between changes in the treatment and changes in behavior)
2. temporal precedence (that changes in the treatment occur before changes in behavior)
3. that the change in behavior is *not* due to something other than the treatment

ESTABLISHING COVARIATION

Before you can show that the treatment causes a change in behavior, you must first establish **covariation**: that changes in the treatment are accompanied by changes in the behavior. Therefore, to show that smiling causes people to help you, you must prove that people are more helpful to you when you smile than when you do not.

In the randomized experiment, you would establish covariation by seeing whether the amount of help you received when you smiled was greater than when you did not smile. If the average amount of helping was the same in both groups, then you would not have covariation. Because you would not have covariation (variations in smiling would not correspond with variations in helping), you would not conclude that the treatment had an effect. If, on the other hand, you received more help in the smiling condition than in the no-smile condition, then you would have covariation.

ESTABLISHING TEMPORAL PRECEDENCE

Establishing covariation, by itself, does not establish causality. You must also establish **temporal precedence**: that the treatment comes before the change in behavior. In other words, you must show that you smile at others before they help out. Otherwise, it may be that you react with a smile after people help you. Without temporal precedence, you can't determine which variable is the cause and which is the effect.

In a randomized experiment, you automatically establish that the cause comes before the change in behavior (temporal precedence) by manipulating the independent variable. You always present the independent variable (smiling) before you present the dependent measure task (giving participants an opportunity to help).

BATTLING SPURIOUSNESS

In addition to establishing temporal precedence, you must show that the covariation you observed could only be due to the treatment. Ideally, you would do this by showing that the treatment is the only thing that varies, that everything else is constant. Therefore, to show that your smiling causes others to help you, you must show that everything—except for your smiling—is the same during the times that you smile and the times that you do not smile.

The Value of Battling Spuriousness

It's difficult to prove that the only difference between the times when you get help and times when you don't is your smile. But without such proof, you can't say that your smiling causes people to be more helpful. Why not? Because you might be smiling more when the weather is nice or when you are with your friends. These same conditions (being with friends, nice weather) may be the reason you are getting help—your smile may have nothing to do with it. If you cannot be sure that everything else was the same, then the relationship between smiling and helpfulness may be **spurious**: due to other variables.

Battling Spuriousness Without Keeping All Nontreatment Variables Constant

In the randomized experiment, you do not keep everything—except for the treatment variable—constant. There are some nontreatment variables, such as individual differences, that you can't control. There may be other nontreatment variables that you choose not to control. For example, you may decide to do your experiment in a real-world setting where you can't keep temperature, noise, and other factors constant.

How do you deal with these nontreatment variables that aren't being controlled? You use random assignment so that these uncontrolled variables are now random variables. There are two advantages of converting nontreatment variables into random variables: (1) Random variables should not influence one group significantly more than another, and (2) statistics can be used to subtract out the effects of random variables.

Random Variables Affect All Groups (Almost) Equally   One advantage of random assignment is that the nontreatment variables should not substantially affect one group more than the other. Random assignment should spread those variables more or less equally into each of your groups, just like an electric mixer should distribute ingredients fairly equally to both sides of the bowl. Your conditions will be equivalent except for the effects of the independent variable and the chance impact of random variables. Therefore, as a result of random assignment, only random variables stand in the way of keeping irrelevant variables constant.

Statistics Can Help You Estimate the Effects of Random Variables   If you could remove those random variables, you would be able to keep everything constant. By keeping the nontreatment variables constant, you could isolate the treatment as the cause of the change in behavior. Unfortunately, in the randomized experiment, you cannot keep nontreatment variables constant, and you cannot remove them. However, you can use statistics to estimate their effects: If the difference between groups is much greater than the estimated effects of random error, the results are declared "statistically significant."

If you find a statistically significant effect for your treatment variable, you can argue that your treatment variable causes a change in scores on the dependent measure. However, you may be wrong. Even with statistics, you can't perfectly estimate the effects of random variables 100% of the time. If you underestimate the effects of random variables in your study, then you may falsely label a chance difference as a treatment effect. That is, you may make a Type 1 error.

Fortunately, before you do the study, you establish what your chances are of making a Type 1 error. Usually, most investigators make the chances of committing a Type 1 error fairly remote. Specifically, most investigators set the probability of mistaking chance variation as a genuine treatment effect at less than 5 in 100 ($p < .05$).

SINGLE-*n* DESIGNS

Like experimental designs, single-*n* designs establish that the cause comes before the effect (temporal precedence) by manipulating the treatment variable *before* presenting the dependent measure task. Thus, the experimenter would smile at the participant before giving the participant an opportunity to help. Like experimental designs, single-*n* designs establish covariation by comparing the different treatment conditions (comparing the amount of help received in the smiling versus no-smiling conditions). However, unlike experimental designs, single-*n* designs do not rely on randomization and statistical tests to rule out spuriousness (the effects of nontreatment factors).

Instead, the single-*n* design strives to keep nontreatment factors constant. That is, rather than letting nontreatment variables vary and then statistically accounting for the effects of those variables, single-*n* researchers try to take nontreatment variables out of the equation. The objective is to isolate the treatment's effect by stopping nontreatment factors from varying (see Table 11-1).

KEEPING NONTREATMENT FACTORS CONSTANT: THE A–B DESIGN

To understand how single-*n* researchers keep nontreatment factors constant, let's examine the simplest **single-*n* design**, the *A–B* design. In the ***A–B* design**, as in all single-*n* designs, the researcher studies a single participant. The researcher makes sure that the participant's behavior on the dependent measure task occurs at a consistent rate. Thus, if we were studying the effects of rewards on how often a chicken pecked at a bar, we would first make sure the chicken was pecking at a constant rate. The process of ensuring that the behavior occurs at a steady, consistent rate is called establishing a **stable baseline**. This first step is designated as *A*. Next, the researcher introduces the treatment. The researcher then compares posttreatment behavior (*B*) with baseline (*A*).

• TABLE 11-1 •

HOW DIFFERENT DESIGNS INFER CAUSALITY

REQUIREMENT	RANDOMIZED EXPERIMENTS	A–B SINGLE-N DESIGN
TEMPORAL PRECEDENCE (Treatment came before changes in scores)	Introduce treatment *before* there is a change in the dependent variable	Introduce treatment *before* there is a change in the dependent variable
COVARIATION (Different treatment conditions score differently on measure)	Observing difference between treatment and control conditions	Observing difference between conditions *A* (baseline) and *B* (posttreatment behavior)
ACCOUNTING FOR IRRELEVANT VARIABLES (Determining that the change in behavior is not due to nontreatment factors)	1. Independent random assignment to make sure all irrelevant factors vary randomly rather than systematically 2. Then, use statistics to account for effects of these random factors. If the difference between groups is greater than would be expected as a result of these random factors, the difference is assumed to be the effect of the one non-random, systematically varied factor: the treatment.	1. Eliminate between-subject variables by using only one participant 2. Control relevant environmental factors. Demonstrate that those factors have been controlled by establishing a stable baseline. Then, introduce treatment. If change occurs, that change is assumed to be due to the treatment.

As with all single-*n* designs, the *A–B* design strives to keep everything but the treatment constant. Specifically, the *A–B* design tries to make sure that differences between the conditions are not due to either of the two basic types of nontreatment variability: (1) between-subject variability unrelated to the treatment and (2) within-subject variability unrelated to the treatment.

As with all single-*n* designs, the *A–B* design makes sure that between-subject variability can't cause the difference between treatment conditions. The difference between scores in the *A* condition and the *B* condition can't possibly be due to the subject in *A* being a different subject than the subject in *B* (differences between subjects) because the subject in *A* was the same individual who was in the *B* condition.

Within-subject variability, however, is a problem. An individual's moods and behaviors may naturally vary from moment to moment. Thus, in a sense, the same subject could be a different subject during the *A* phase of the study than during the *B* phase. In other words, even without the treatment, a subject may vary. How does the single-*n* researcher know that the treatment is responsible for the change in the participant's behavior?

The single-*n* researcher is confident that the difference between no-treatment and treatment conditions is not due to random within-subject variability because she has established a stable baseline. The **baseline** shows that the subject's behavior is not varying.

But how does a single-*n* researcher obtain a stable baseline? After all, behavior is variable. To obtain a stable baseline, the single-*n* researcher must control all relevant environmental variables. That is, the single-*n* researcher strives to hold constant all those variables that might affect the participant's responses.

If the researcher does not know what the relevant variables are, the researcher tries to keep the participant's environment as constant as possible. For example, the researcher might perform the study under highly controlled conditions in a soundproof laboratory.

If the researcher knows what the relevant variables are, then the researcher only needs to control those variables. Thus, if a researcher knew that parental praise was the only relevant variable in increasing studying behavior, the researcher would only need to control that one variable. The researcher, however, usually does not know which variables can be safely ignored. Psychology has not advanced to the state where we can catalog what variables affect and don't affect every possible response.

After attempting to control variables, the researcher checks whether she has succeeded by looking at the baseline. If the baseline is not stable, the researcher continues to control variables until the behavior becomes stable.

But what if a researcher cannot achieve a stable baseline? Then, the researcher planning to use an *A–B* design has a problem: Changes in behavior that occur after the treatment are introduced may be due to something other than the treatment. In other words, the researcher probably wouldn't know whether the change in behavior is due to normal fluctuations in the participant's behavior or due to treatment effects.

However, there is still hope for the researcher who can't achieve a stable baseline. For example, as you can see from Figure 11-1, *A–B* researchers can make a convincing case that the results are not due to normal baseline fluctuations if the participants' behavior changes dramatically after the treatment is introduced.

Although it is difficult to achieve a stable baseline, we should point out that single-*n* researchers often do achieve a stable baseline. They are especially successful when they put a simple organism in a simple environment and have it perform a simple behavior. Thus, it is relatively easy to achieve a stable baseline if you have a pigeon in a Skinner box pecking at a disk.

To this point, you have seen how the single-*n* researcher using an *A–B* design can hold individual difference variables and relevant environmental variables constant. But how does the researcher know that the difference between conditions is not due to **maturation**: natural biological changes in the organism, such as those due to development or fatigue?

The single-*n* researcher may limit maturation by choosing an organism that she knows won't mature substantially during the course of the study. Thus, she might use a pigeon or a rat because the extent of their maturation as it relates to certain tasks (bar pressing and pecking) is well documented.

Or, as you will soon see, the researcher may use a design that will allow her to account for maturation. But before looking at a design that accounts for maturation, let's look at an example of the *A–B* design.

In an early study of the effects of psychoactive drugs, Donald Blough (1957) wanted to study the impact of LSD on a pigeon's visual perception. His first step was to place the pigeon in a highly controlled environment—a Skinner box—equipped with a light that illuminated a spot on the stimulus panel.

By varying the intensity of the light, Blough could make the spot easier— or more difficult—to see. On the wall of the Skinner box were two disks—"1" and "2." As an index of visual threshold, the pigeon was conditioned to peck at disk "1" when the spot was visible and to peck at disk "2" when the spot was not visible.

Before Blough began to manipulate his independent variable (LSD), he had to make sure that no other variables were influencing the pigeon's behavior. To do this, he had to keep all the relevant variables in the pigeon's environment constant. Therefore, he placed the pigeon in the Skinner box and carefully observed the pigeon's behavior. If he had succeeded in eliminating all nontreatment variables, the pigeon's behavior would be relatively stable—the relationship between pecking and illumination would be constant. If he had failed, he would observe fluctuations in the pigeon's behavior (for example, erratic increases and decreases in pecking).

Once the pigeon's behavior was stable, Blough was ready to introduce the independent variable, LSD. After administering the LSD, Blough compared the pigeon's behavior after the treatment (*B*), to its behavior before the treatment

• FIGURE 11-1 •

A BEHAVIOR MODIFICATION PROGRAM APPEARS
TO REDUCE A CLIENT'S CIGARETTE SMOKING

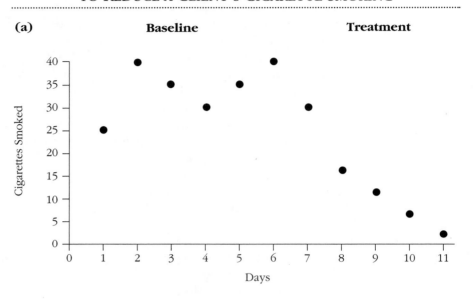

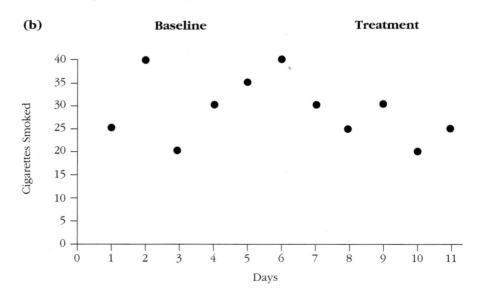

Note: The data from the participant in Figure 11-1a strongly suggest that the treatment (begun on Day 7) had an effect. The data from the participant in Figure 11-1b, on the other hand, might be due to normal fluctuations in the participant's behavior rather than to the treatment.

(*A*). Blough found that after taking the LSD, the pigeon experienced decreased visual ability. Specifically, the pigeons pecked at disk "2" (cannot see spot) under a level of illumination that—prior to treatment—always led to a peck at disk "1." Because Blough had ensured that nontreatment variables were not influencing the pigeon's behavior, he concluded that the LSD was the sole cause of the decrease in visual ability.

Blough's study was exceptional because he knew that the pigeon's behavior on this task normally wouldn't change much over time. However, in studies with other kinds of participants or tasks, the researcher would not know whether participants would change, develop, or learn over a period of time. Therefore, most researchers are not so confident that they have controlled all the important variables. On the contrary, they know that two potentially important nontreatment variables have changed from measurement at baseline (*A*) to measurement after administering the treatment (*B*).

First, because the posttest occurs after the pretest, participants have had more practice on the task when performing the posttest than they had when performing the pretest. Thus, their performance may have improved as a result of **testing:** the effects of doing the dependent measure task on subsequent performance on that task. For example, the practice a participant gets doing the task during the *A* phase may help the participant do better during the *B* phase.

Second, because the posttest occurs after the pretest, time has passed from pretest to posttest. Consequently, changes from pretest to posttest may be due to *maturation*. That is, the participant's behavior may have changed over time as a result of fatigue, boredom, or development.

VARIATIONS ON THE *A–B* DESIGN

Because psychologists want to know that their results are due to the treatment rather than to testing or maturation, single-*n* researchers rarely use the *A–B* design. Instead, they use variations on the *A–B* design such as the reversal design, psychophysical designs, and the multiple-baseline design.

The Reversal Design: Giving and Taking Away

In the **reversal design,** also known as the *A–B–A* **design,** the researcher measures behavior (*A*), then administers the treatment and measures behavior (*B*), and then withdraws the treatment and measures behavior again (*A*).

To see why the *A–B–A* design is superior to the *A–B* design, consider one in a series of classic single-*n* designs that first demonstrated that behavior modification was an effective therapy for mental patients (Ayllon & Azrin, 1968). Ted Ayllon and Nathan Azrin worked with a group of psychotics in a mental hospital to see if a token economy was an effective way of increasing socially appropriate behavior. In a typical study, Ayllon and Azrin first identified an appropriate behavior (for instance, feeding oneself). Next, the researchers observed how often a certain patient performed that behavior. This phase of collecting baseline data for a patient could be labeled *A*. They then attempted to reinforce that behavior with a "token." Like money, the token could be exchanged for desirable outcomes such as candy, movies, social interaction, or privacy. Thus, during the treatment phase (labeled *B*), Ayllon and Azrin gave the patient tokens for each instance of the socially appropriate behavior and measured the behavior. They found that the patient performed more socially appropriate behaviors after the tokens were introduced. Great! A token economy increases socially appropriate behavior. Right?

If Ayllon and Azrin's study had ended here, you could not be confident about that conclusion. Remember, with an *A–B* design, you don't know whether a change in behavior is due to maturation, testing, or the treatment.

Fortunately, Ayllon and Azrin expanded the *A–B* design to an *A–B–A* design by stopping the treatment while continuing to observe their patient's behavior. After removing the treatment, the incidence of socially appropriate behavior decreased. Consequently, Ayllon and Azrin were able to determine that the treatment (tokens) increased socially appropriate behavior.

If, after withdrawing the treatment, socially appropriate behavior had continued to increase, they would not have concluded that the increase in socially appropriate behavior was due to the treatment. Instead, they would have concluded that the increase could be due to maturation or testing.

We should point out that the results were not quite as neat as we described. Admittedly, they found that socially appropriate behavior increased when they introduced the tokens and decreased when they stopped giving out tokens. Removing the tokens, however, did not cause the behavior to fall back all the way to baseline levels. Instead, the behavior fell back to near-baseline levels.

If tokens caused the effect, shouldn't their withdrawal cause the behavior to fall to baseline rather than near baseline? Admittedly, if the dependent measure (the rate of socially appropriate behavior) returned to baseline level, it would help make the case that the treatment had an effect. However, most behaviors won't return to baseline after you withdraw the treatment because of:

1. maturation effects
2. testing effects
3. **carryover effects:** the treatment's effects persisting even after the treatment has been removed

Because of these three effects, you might be willing to say that the treatment had an effect, even if the behavior did not return to baseline. For example, you might be willing to say that the treatment had an effect if the participant's behavior was substantially different during treatment phase (*B*) than during either the pretreatment (*A*) and posttreatment (*A*) conditions (see Figure 11-2).

You would probably feel comfortable claiming that the treatment had an effect if treatment behavior is substantially different from both pretreatment and posttreatment behavior. You might feel especially comfortable if posttreat-

• **FIGURE 11-2** •

RESULTS FROM *A–B–A* DESIGN: NUMBER OF VIOLENT ACTS PERFORMED BY JIM DURING THE NO-PUNISHMENT AND "TIME-OUT" PUNISHMENT PHASES

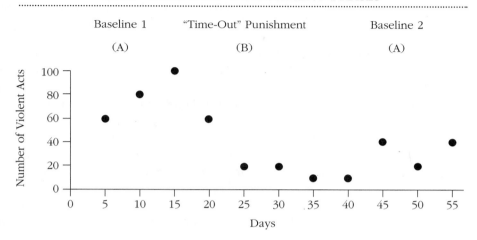

Note: Even though posttreatment violence did not revert back to pretreatment levels, a strong case can still be made that the time-out punishment reduced the violent behavior.

ment behavior returned to pretreatment baseline levels. Unfortunately, even though you might feel comfortable making such cause–effect claims, your claims of a treatment effect could be wrong.

How could you be wrong? You could be wrong if the effects of practice and/or maturation are cyclical. For instance, suppose performance was affected by menstrual cycles. Thus, performance might be good during the pretreatment phase (before menstruation), poor during the treatment phase (during menstruation), and good during the posttreatment phase (after menstruation). Although such an unsteady effect of maturation or testing would be unlikely, it's possible.[1]

To rule out the possibility that apparent treatment effects are due to some simple cyclical pattern involving either maturation or practice, you might extend the *A–B–A* design. For example, you might make it an *A–B–A–B* design. Ayllon and Azrin did this, and found that reintroduction of the token rewards led to an increase in the socially appropriate behavior.

---

[1]A similar problem could result if the individual you studied regularly went through periods of depression followed by periods of normal mood followed by depression (cyclical depression).

Expanding beyond even the *A–B–A–B* design allows you to rule out the possibility of an even more complicated maturational or practice cycle. The more you expand the design, the less likely that maturation or practice would increase performance every time the treatment is introduced, but never increase performance when the control condition occurs. Thus, it would be very hard to describe a cycle of maturation and practice effects that could mimic treatment effects in an *A–B–A–B–A–B–A–B–A–B–A–B–A–B* design.

Psychophysical Designs

Psychophysical designs extend the *A–B–A–B–A* design. In psychophysical designs, participants are asked to judge stimuli. For example, they may be asked to rate whether one light is brighter than another, one weight is heavier than another, or one picture is more attractive than another. The idea is to see how variations in the stimulus relate to variations in judgments. Because the dependent variable is psychological judgment and the independent variable is often some variation of a stimulus's physical characteristic (loudness, intensity, etc.), the name *psychophysics* is appropriate.

Since a participant can make psychophysical judgments quickly, a participant in a psychophysical experiment will be asked to make many judgments. Indeed, in a few exceptional cases, participants have been asked to make 67,000 judgments!

With so many judgments, you might worry about maturation effects. For example, participants might get tired as the research session goes on—and on.

In addition, you might be concerned about treatment carryover effects. Specifically, you might worry that earlier stimuli may affect ratings of later stimuli. For instance, suppose you were rating how heavy you thought a 50-pound weight was. If the last 10 weights you had judged were all about 100 pounds, you might tend to rate 50 pounds as light. However, if the last 10 weights had all been around 10 pounds, you might tend to rate 50 pounds as heavy. Similarly, if you were judging how wealthy a person making $50,000 was, your rating would be affected by whether the previous people you had judged had been multimillionaires or poverty stricken (Wedell & Parducci, 1988).

To deal with these order effects, researchers may use three techniques. Surprisingly, all three of these strategies were suggested by one of the earliest pioneers in psychophysics—Gustav Fechner.

First, researchers usually have participants rate each stimulus more than once. If the same stimulus receives different ratings when it is presented at different times, then researchers know there are order effects.

Second, researchers average the ratings that the stimulus receives. Their hope is that although a single rating of the stimulus may be inflated (or deflated) because of order effects, the average of several ratings won't be. That is, if half the ratings of the stimulus were inflated by order effects and half were deflated, the average of those ratings would not be affected. Taking the average would allow the order effects to balance out. However, if the average is going to balance out order effects, the researcher can't present the stimuli in the same sequence each time. For example, if Stimulus *A* is presented before Stimulus *B* both times, the average rating of both *A* and *B* may still reflect an order effect. Thus, if a participant's ratings get harsher as the study goes on, the average of Stimulus *A* would tend to be higher than the average of Stimulus *B*. Fortunately, Fechner's third tip helps us balance out order effects.

Third, Fechner recommended that researchers randomize the order in which stimuli are presented and/or they counterbalance the order in which they present the stimuli. Randomization makes it unlikely that Stimulus *A* will always come before Stimulus *B*; counterbalancing guarantees that Stimulus *A* will not always come before Stimulus *B*. Specifically, in counterbalancing, researchers present Stimulus *A* before Stimulus *B* half the time; the other half of the time Stimulus *B* comes before Stimulus *A*.

In summary, maturation, testing, and carryover may cause order effects. To deal with the order effects caused by maturation, testing, and carryover, psychophysical designs use three techniques:

1. multiple ratings
2. averaging
3. randomizing/counterbalancing

The Multiple-Baseline Design

Another single-*n* design that rules out the effects of maturation, testing, and carryover is the multiple-baseline design. In a typical **multiple-baseline design**, you would collect baselines for several key behaviors. For example, you might collect baselines for a child making her bed, putting her toys away, washing her hands, and vacuuming her room. Then, you would reinforce one of those key behaviors. If the behavior being reinforced (putting her toys away) increases, you would suspect that reinforcement is causing the behavior to increase.

But the effects might be due to the child becoming more mature or to some other nontreatment effect. To see whether the child's improvement in behavior is due to maturation or some other nontreatment factor, you would look at her performance on the other tasks. If those tasks are still being performed at baseline level, then nontreatment factors such as maturation and testing are not improving performance on those tasks. Since maturation and testing are not increasing the other behaviors, maturation and testing probably are not increasing the particular behavior you decided to reinforce. Therefore, you would be relatively confident that the improvement in putting toys away was due to reinforcement.

To be even more confident that the reinforcement is causing the change in behavior, you would reinforce a second behavior (washing hands) and compare it against the other nonreinforced behaviors. You would continue the process until you had reinforced all the behaviors. You would hope to find that when you reinforced hand washing, hand washing increased—but that no other behavior increased. Similarly, when you reinforced tooth brushing, you would hope tooth brushing—and only tooth brushing—increased. If increases in behavior coincided perfectly with reinforcement, you would be very confident that reinforcement was responsible for the increases in behavior (see Figure 11-3).

EVALUATION OF SINGLE-*n* DESIGNS

You have now examined some of the more popular single-*n* designs. Before leaving these designs, let's see how they stand up on three important criteria: internal, construct, and external validity.

Internal Validity

The single-*n* researcher uses a variety of strategies to achieve internal validity. Like the physicist, the single-*n* researcher keeps many relevant variables constant. The single-*n* researcher holds individual difference variables constant by studying a single participant and may hold environmental variables constant by placing that participant in a highly controlled environment. For example, the single-*n* researcher may study a single rat pressing a bar inside a soundproof Skinner box.

Like the within-subjects researcher (see Chapter 9), the single-*n* researcher must worry that the changes in the participant's behavior could be due to the participant naturally changing over time (maturation) or to the participant getting practice on the dependent measure task (testing). Not surprisingly, within-subjects and single-*n* researchers may adapt similar strategies to deal with the threats of maturation and testing.

Both within-subjects and single-*n* researchers may try to rule out maturation by keeping their study so short that there is not enough time for maturation to occur. Both may try to reduce the effects of testing by giving participants extensive practice on the task prior to beginning the study. By giving extensive practice on the task before introducing the treatment, both within-subjects and single-*n* researchers reduce the likelihood that participants will benefit from any additional practice they get during the research study.

You don't have to take the single-*n* researchers' word that participants got enough practice. By showing that the response rate is stable before the treatment is introduced (the stable baseline), single-*n* researchers show that neither the practice nor anything else is causing the participant to improve during the latter part of the pretreatment phase.

Like the within-subjects experimenter, the single-*n* experimenter must be concerned about treatment carryover effects. Because of carryover, investigators using an *A–B–A* design frequently find that participants do not return to the original baseline. These carryover problems multiply when you use more levels of the independent variable and/or when you use more than one independent variable. Because carryover effects are a serious concern, most single-*n* researchers minimize carryover's complications by doing studies that have only two

• **FIGURE 11-3** •

HYPOTHETICAL DATA FROM A MULTIPLE-BASELINE DESIGN

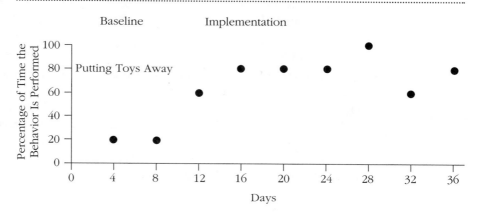

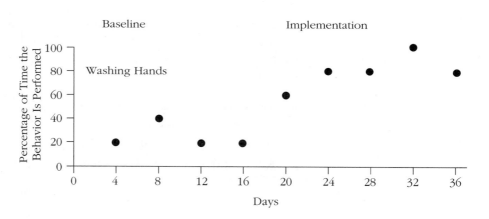

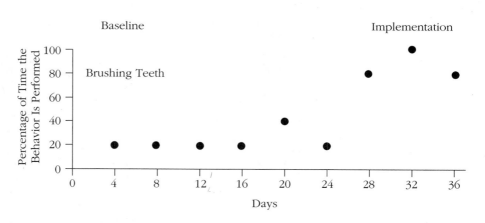

levels of a single independent variable. That is, rather than use an *A–B–C–D–E–F–G–G–F–E–D–C–B–A* design, most single-*n* researchers only use *A–B–A–B* designs. However, as you will soon see, internal validity concerns are not the only reason for simpler designs. Construct validity concerns also lead to choosing simpler designs.

Construct Validity

Although there are similarities between the single-*n* researcher and the within-subjects researcher in how they deal with internal validity concerns, the two researchers have even more in common when they attack threats to construct validity (see Table 11-2). For both researchers, sensitization (participants figuring out the hypothesis because they have been exposed to several levels of the treatment) poses a serious problem, and both researchers use the same solution. Specifically, both try to reduce the effects of sensitization by:

1. using placebo treatments
2. using very few levels of treatment
3. making the difference between the treatment conditions so subtle that participants don't realize that anything has changed (such as gradually varying the loudness of a stimulus)

• TABLE 11-2 •

SIMILARITIES BETWEEN WITHIN-SUBJECTS EXPERIMENTS AND SINGLE-*N* DESIGNS

PROBLEM	SINGLE-*N* EXPERIMENT	WITHIN-SUBJECTS DESIGN
Practice effects may harm internal validity.	Give extensive practice before introducing treatment.	Give extensive practice before introducing treatment.
Fatigue or maturation may harm internal validity.	Keep study brief.	Keep study brief.
Assorted order effects may harm internal validity.	Counterbalance sequence.	Counterbalance sequence and randomly assign participants to different sequences.
Carryover effects may harm internal validity.	Use few levels and few variables. Wait a long time between treatments.	Use few levels and few variables. Wait a long time between treatments.
Participants may learn what the study is about (sensitization), thus harming construct validity.	1. Placebo treatments 2. Few levels of treatment 3. Gradually increase or decrease intensity of treatment or use very similar levels.	1. Placebo treatments 2. Few levels of treatments 3. Gradually increase or decrease intensity of treatment or use very similar levels.

External Validity

You may be satisfied with both the single-*n* design's internal validity and its construct validity. But what about its external validity?

At first glance, the single-*n* design seems to have less external validity than other designs. How can the results from one participant be generalized to others? Furthermore, how can the results from a design conducted in such a highly controlled setting be generalized to other settings? Although it seems that other designs must have more external validity than the single-*n* design, things are not always as they seem.

Whether you use one participant or 1,000 participants, you can only infer that your results will apply to individuals who weren't in your study. In other words, to generalize the results of any study, you must *assume* that no other individual-difference variables interact with your treatment to reverse or negate its effects. There are at least two main reasons why single-*n* researchers can frequently justify this assumption.

First, single-*n* researchers often replicate their studies. That is, they examine the effects of their treatment on several individuals. By demonstrating that the treatment has the same effect on each individual, they provide some evidence that the effect generalizes across individuals.

Second, single-*n* researchers often investigate fundamental processes that are well understood and known to occur in all organisms. The results of such studies can be generalized to other members of the same species. Thus, the results of psychophysical and operant-conditioning designs performed on a single member of a species can often be generalized to other members of that species.

Similarly, the results of a design conducted under highly controlled conditions can be generalized to other settings, especially when the single-*n* design investigates universal phenomena that are relatively unaffected by setting (such as sensation). Even when single-*n* investigators cannot generalize their results to all settings, their detailed knowledge of the phenomena may allow them to be specific about the extent to which their results can be generalized to different settings.

CONCLUSIONS ABOUT SINGLE-*n* DESIGNS

We have evaluated the single-*n* design in terms of internal, construct, and external validity. Overall, single-*n* designs, although not possessing the internal validity of a true, randomized experiment, have some internal validity. Generally, single-*n* designs can have adequate construct validity. Thus, often the decision about whether to use a single-*n* design comes down to external validity concerns. Single-*n* designs are most useful under two circumstances: (1) when external validity is not a goal and (2) when external validity is not a problem.

In applied situations, external validity may not be a goal. That is, you may only be interested in the causes of one individual's behavior. For example, suppose you were trying to change your own behavior or the behavior of a family pet. Or, suppose a therapist is treating a patient and wants to see if the treatment is having a measurable effect on that particular patient. In all these cases, the single-*n* design would be the best way to evaluate the effect of the treatment.

In some situations, generalizing the results from one participant to a larger group may be acceptable. For example, suppose that you want to make statements about fundamental, universal processes that we understand fairly well. Then, according to single-*n* researchers, you should use a single-*n* design. After all, it would be wasteful to study many participants if the treatment has the same effect on everyone. Because all people tend to respond similarly to reinforcements, the single-*n* design is commonly used in behavior-modification research. Similarly, because everyone seems to respond similarly to psychophysical manipulations, the single-*n* design is also a popular alternative to the randomized experiment in psychophysical research.

QUASI-EXPERIMENTS

Another popular alternative to the randomized experiment is the **quasi-experiment.** Like true experiments, quasi-experiments involve administering a treatment. However, unlike in true experiments, participants are not randomly assigned to treatment (Cook & Campbell, 1979).

Ideally, researchers would always make sure that participants were randomly assigned to condition. That way, researchers could determine the treatment's effects. Researchers, however, do not run the world.

People who do run the world usually won't relinquish their power and control to researchers. They want to decide who gets which treatment, rather than letting researchers use random assignment to determine who gets which treatment. Judges usually like to decide what sentence to give, rather than leaving it up to random assignment. Parents may not allow their children to be randomly assigned to watch violent television or to not receive instruction on how to use a computer. Bosses often want to choose who gets training. Cable companies may want to decide who to serve based on geography and income rather than on random assignment.

Even when money and power aren't issues, some people object that random assignment is not fair. On the one hand, this argument seems absurd. What could be fairer than allowing everyone who wants a treatment an equal chance at it? On the other hand, a good case can be made that the treatment should be given to the people who are the most needy or the most qualified.

Regardless of the reason, researchers often are unable to get the powers that be to randomly assign participants to condition. Thus, when evaluating the effects of many real-world treatments—from therapy, to training programs, to introducing new technology to social programs—quasi-experimental designs are often the researcher's best option.

Because quasi-experimental designs are so useful for assessing the effects of real-life treatments, we will devote the rest of this chapter to these designs. We will begin by discussing the general logic behind quasi-experimental designs. Then, we will take a more detailed look at some popular quasi-experimental designs.

THE PROBLEM: ACCOUNTING FOR NONTREATMENT FACTORS

Like experiments, quasi-experiments manipulate a treatment. Therefore, like experiments, quasi-experiments establish temporal precedence by establishing that the treatment comes before the change in behavior. Also like experiments, quasi-experiments assess covariation by comparing treatment versus nontreatment conditions. However, unlike experiments, quasi-experiments do not randomize the effects of nontreatment factors. Therefore, unlike experimenters, quasi-experimenters cannot randomize the effects of nontreatment factors and then statistically control for those random effects. Furthermore, unlike single-n researchers, quasi-experimenters cannot control for nontreatment factors by keeping those factors constant.

Identifying Nontreatment Factors: The Value of Campbell and Stanley's Spurious Eight

The challenge in quasi-experiments is to rule out the effects of nontreatment variables without either the aid of random assignment or the ability to control nontreatment variables. The first step in meeting this challenge is to identify all the variables other than your treatment that might account for the change in participants' scores. Once you have identified those nontreatment factors, you will try to demonstrate that those nontreatment factors did not account for the change in participants' scores. After you have ruled out all those nontreatment factors, you can argue that your treatment caused the effect.

To identify all the nontreatment factors that might account for the relationship between the treatment and the change in scores is a tall order. Fortunately, however, Campbell and Stanley (1963) discovered that all possible nontreatment factors fall into eight categories. More specifically, as we discussed in Chapter 5, Campbell and Stanley discovered that there are eight threats to internal validity:

1. **maturation:** apparent treatment effects that are really due to natural biological changes—from changes due to growing and developing to changes due to becoming more tired or more hungry.

2. **testing:** apparent treatment effects that are really due to participants having learned from the pretest. For example, practice on the pretest may improve performance on the posttest.

3. **history:** apparent treatment effects that are really due to events in the outside world that are unrelated to the treatment.

4. **instrumentation:** apparent treatment effects that are really due to changes in the measuring instrument. For example, the researcher may use a revised version of the measure on the retest.

5. **regression (regression toward the mean, statistical regression)**: apparent treatment effects that are really due to regression toward the mean (the tendency for participants who receive extreme scores on the pretest to receive less extreme scores on the posttest).

6. **mortality**: apparent treatment effects that are really due to participants dropping out of the study. For instance, suppose that participants who would score poorly drop out of the treatment condition, but not out of the no-treatment condition. In that case, the treatment group would score higher than the no-treatment group, even if the treatment had no effect.

7. **selection**: differences between groups that are not due to the treatment, but to the groups being different from each other before the study started.

8. **selection-maturation interaction**: differences between two groups who scored similarly on the pretest that are due to the groups naturally growing apart. In other words, just because two groups scored similarly at the beginning of the study, you cannot assume that they would have scored identically at the end of the study.

As you will soon see, the eight threats to validity fall into three general categories. First, there are those environmental and physiological events—other than the treatment—that cause individuals to change. Second, there are errors in measurement that cause changes in participants' scores. Third, there are problems related to the fact that treatment and no-treatment groups—because different individuals are in the two groups—may differ from each other even when the treatment has no effect.

Three Reasons Individuals Change Even Without Treatment   The first three threats to validity—maturation, testing, and history—include all the nontreatment factors that can cause individual participants to change. The first two—maturation and testing—are threats we talked about in terms of the single-*n* design. That is, we were concerned that changes in an *A–B* design might be due to testing (the participant learning from doing the dependent measure task several times). We were also concerned about maturation (any changes in the participant's internal, physiological environment, such as changes due to growing old or hungry). However, because we could (in the single-*n* design) keep the outside environment constant, we did not concern ourselves with history (any nontreatment changes in the external environment).

How Measurement Errors Can Look Like a Treatment Effect   The next two threats, instrumentation and statistical regression, can cause participants in the treatment conditions to have different scores than they did in the no-treatment condition even though the participants themselves have not changed. With instrumentation, participants are tested with one measuring instrument in one condition and a different measuring instrument in another condition. No wonder their scores are different.

Statistical regression is harder to spot. To understand statistical regression (also called *regression* and *regression toward the mean*), remember that most scores contain some random error. Usually, this is not a problem because random error tends to balance out to zero. That is, random error pushes some scores upward, others downward, but the net effect on the overall average score is zero.

But what if we only select those participants whose scores have been pushed way up by random error? When we retest them, their scores will go down. Their scores going down might fool us into thinking they had really changed. In fact, all that has happened is that random error isn't going to push all these scores up again (just as lightning is unlikely to strike the same place twice). Instead, this second time, random error will push some up, some down, and have almost no effect on the remaining scores.

You might wonder how we would select scores that have been pushed up by random error. One way is to select extreme scores. For example, if we select only those people who got 100% on an exam, we know that random error did not decrease their scores. However, random error (lucky guesses, scorer failing to see a question that was missed) could have increased those scores. Thus, if we give these people a test again, their scores are likely to go down. This tendency for extreme scorers to score less extremely when they are retested is called *regression toward the mean*.

Regression toward the mean is a powerful effect. Whether watching a baseball player on a hitting streak (or in a hitting slump), watching the economy, or observing a patient, you will find that extreme events tend to revert back to more-normal levels.

To this point, we have talked about factors that could change an individual's scores. We explained that a participant in the treatment condition may change for reasons having nothing to do with the treatment (maturation, testing, history). We have also talked about how an individual's score can change, even though the individual doesn't really change (instrumentation, regression). In some cases, these changes in individual participants' scores could cause a treatment group to score differently from a no-treatment group.

Three Differences Between Treatment and No-Treatment Groups That Have Nothing to Do With the Treatment   However, even when the individual scores are accurate and unaffected by treatment-irrelevant influences, the treatment group may differ from the no-treatment group for reasons having nothing to do with the treatment. That is, the treatment and no-treatment groups may differ because the participants in the treatment group have different characteristics than those in the no- treatment group. Basically, there are three treatment-irrelevant factors that could cause participants in the treatment condition to systematically differ from participants in the no-treatment condition: mortality, selection, and selection-maturation.

With mortality, for example, your poor performers may have dropped out of the treatment condition. As a result, your treatment condition scores would be higher than your no-treatment condition scores—even if your treatment had no effect.

With selection, you are comparing groups that were different before the study began. As the saying goes, "that's not fair—you're comparing apples and oranges." Since your treatment group started out being very different from your no-treatment group, the differences between your group's scores at the end of the study may not be due to the treatment. Therefore, you shouldn't conclude that the difference in scores between your two groups is due to the treatment.

Unfortunately, even if you selected two groups who scored similarly on your measure before you introduced the treatment, you can't conclude that they would have scored similarly at the end of the study. Why not? Because of selection-maturation interactions: Groups that scored similarly in the pretest may naturally mature at different rates.

Using Logic to Combat the Spurious Eight

Once you have identified the threats to internal validity, you must determine which threats are automatically ruled out by the design and which threats you can eliminate through logic (see Table 11-3). Quasi-experimental designs differ in their ability to automatically rule out these threats. Some rule out most of these threats; some rule out only a few. Yet, even with a quasi-experimental design that automatically rules out only a few of these threats, you may occasionally be able to infer causality.

To illustrate the potential usefulness of quasi-experimental designs, we will start by looking at a design that most people would not even consider to be in the same class as a quasi-experimental design: the **pretest–posttest design.** The pretest–posttest design is very similar to the single-*n* A–B design. As the name suggests, you test one group of participants, administer a treatment, and then retest them.

This design does not rule out many threats automatically; hence, its low status as a design. However, because you are comparing individuals against themselves, it does automatically rule out selection and selection-maturation interactions.

Although the pretest–posttest design does not automatically rule out mortality, instrumentation, regression, maturation, history, and testing, you may still be able to rule out these threats. If nobody dropped out of your study, mortality is not a problem. If you were careful enough to use the same measure and administer it in the same way, instrumentation is not a problem. If there were only a few minutes between the pretest and posttest, then history is unlikely.

If there were only a few minutes between pretest and posttest, maturation is also unlikely. About the only maturation that could occur in a short period of time would be boredom or fatigue. If performance was better on the posttest than on the pretest, then you could rule out boredom and fatigue—and thus maturation.

You might even be able to rule out regression. The key to ruling out regression is to realize that regression occurs when extreme pretest scores that were

• **TABLE 11-3** •

STEPS QUASI-EXPERIMENTERS MAY TAKE TO MINIMIZE THREATS TO INTERNAL VALIDITY

THREATS	PRECAUTIONS
History	Isolate participants from external events during the course of the study.
Maturation	Conduct the study in a short period of time to minimize the opportunities for maturation. Use participants who are maturing at slow rates.
Testing	Only test participants once. Give participants extensive practice on task prior to collecting data so that they won't benefit substantially from practice they obtain during the study. Know what testing effects are (from past data) and subtract out those effects. Use different versions of same test to decrease the testing effect.
Instrumentation	Administer same measure, the same way, every time.
Mortality	Use rewards, innocuous treatments, and brief treatments to keep participants from dropping out of the study. Use placebo treatments or subtly different levels of the treatment so that participants won't be more likely to drop out of the treatment condition. Make sure participants understand instructions so that participants aren't thrown out for failing to follow directions.
Regression	Don't choose participants on basis of extreme scores. Use reliable measures.
Selection	Match on all relevant variables. Don't use designs that involve comparing one group of participants with another.
Selection Interactions	Match on all relevant variables, not just on pretest scores. In addition, use tips from earlier in this table to reduce the effects of variables—such as history and maturation—that might interact with selection. In other words, reducing the role of maturation will also tend to reduce selection by maturation interactions.

inflated (or deflated) by random error revert back to more-average scores on the retest. Therefore, to rule out regression, you need to make the case that random error had not inflated (or deflated) pretest scores. There are two main arguments you could use to make that case. First, you could argue that your measure was so reliable (so free of random error) that random error would have little impact on pretest scores. Second, you could argue that the participants in the study did not have pretest scores that were extreme. If their scores weren't extremely different from the average score for their group, there is little reason for the scores to regress back toward the mean.

Thus far, in this particular study, you have been able to rule out every threat except testing—and you might even be able to rule out testing. For instance, if participants did not know they had been observed (you used an unobtrusive measure), testing should not be a problem. Or, if you used a standardized test, you might know how much people tend to improve when they take the test the second time. If your participants improved substantially more than people typically improve upon retesting, you could rule out the testing effect as the explanation for your results.

As you have seen, the pretest–posttest design, by itself, has poor internal validity because it automatically eliminates only a few threats to internal validity. However, as you have seen, you may be able to use your wits to rule out the remaining threats and thereby infer causality (see Table 11-4 for a review). Furthermore, as you will soon see, by extending the pretest–posttest design, you can create a quasi-experimental design that eliminates most threats to internal validity—the time-series design.

TIME-SERIES DESIGNS

Like the pretest–posttest design, the **time-series design** tests and retests the same participants. However, unlike the pretest–posttest design, the time-series design does not use a single pretest and a single posttest. Instead, the time-series design uses several pretests and posttests. Thus, you could call time-series designs "pre–pre–pre–pre–post–post–post–post" designs.

• TABLE 11-4 •

HOW TO DEAL WITH THE THREATS TO INTERNAL VALIDITY IF YOU MUST USE A PRETEST–POSTTEST DESIGN

THREAT	HOW TO DEAL WITH IT
Selection	Automatically eliminated since participants are tested against themselves.
Selection by Maturation	Automatically eliminated since participants are tested against themselves.
Mortality	Not a problem if participants don't drop out. Conduct study over short period of time and use an undemanding treatment.
Instrumentation	Standardize the way you administer the measure.
Regression	Do not select participants based on extreme scores. Use a reliable measure.
Maturation	Minimize the time between pretest and posttest.
History	Minimize the time between pretest and posttest.
Testing	Use an unobtrusive measure. Have data from previous studies about how much participants' scores tend to change from test to retest.

To illustrate the differences between the pretest–posttest design and the time-series design, suppose you are interested in seeing if a professor's disclosures about her problems with learning material affects how students evaluate her. Let's start by examining how you would use a pretest–posttest design to find the effect of such disclosures.

With a pretest–posttest design, you would have a class evaluate the professor before she tells them about her problems with learning material. Then, you would have them rate her after she discloses her problems. If you observed a difference between pretest and posttest ratings, you would be tempted to say that the difference was due to the disclosure. However, the difference in ratings might really be due to history, maturation, testing, mortality, instrumentation, or regression. Because you have no idea of how much of an effect history, maturation, testing, mortality, and instrumentation may have had, you cannot tell if you had a treatment effect.

Estimating the Effects of Threats to Validity With a Time-Series Design

What if you extended the pretest–posttest design? That is, what if you had students rate the professor after every lecture for the entire term, even though the professor would not disclose her problems with learning material until the fifth week? Then, you would have a time-series design.

What do you gain by all these pretests? From plotting the average ratings for each lecture, you know how much of an effect maturation, testing, instrumentation, and mortality tend to have (see Table 11-5). In other words, when you observe changes from pretest to pretest, you know those changes are not due to the treatment. Instead, those differences must be due to maturation, testing, history, instrumentation, or mortality. For example, suppose ratings steadily improve at a rate of .2 points per week during the 5-week, predisclosure period. If you then found an increase of .2 points from Week 5 (when the professor made the disclosures about her problems) to Week 6, you would not attribute that increase to the disclosures. Instead, you would view such a difference as being due to the effects of history, maturation, mortality, testing, or instrumentation. If, on the other hand, you found a much greater increase in ratings from Week 5 to Week 6 than you found between any other 2 consecutive weeks, you would conclude that the professor's disclosures about her problems with learning material improved her student evaluations (see Figure 11-4).

Problems in Estimating Effects of Nontreatment Factors

Unfortunately, that conclusion could be wrong. Your conclusion is valid only if you can correctly estimate the effects of history, maturation, mortality, testing, and instrumentation during the time that the treatment was administered. On the surface, it seems safe to assume that you can estimate the effects of those variables. After all, for the pretest period, you know what the effects of those variables were. Thus, you may feel safe assuming that the effects of those variables were the same during the treatment period as they were during the pretest period. This

• **TABLE 11-5** •

HOW PRETEST-POSTTEST DESIGNS AND TIME-SERIES DESIGNS STACK UP IN TERMS OF DEALING WITH CAMPBELL AND STANLEY'S THREATS TO INTERNAL VALIDITY

Type of Design

THREAT TO VALIDITY	PRETEST-POSTTEST DESIGN	TIME-SERIES DESIGN
Selection	Automatically eliminated	Automatically eliminated
Selection × Maturation Interactions	Automatically eliminated	Automatically eliminated
Mortality	Through logic and careful planning, this threat can be eliminated.	Through logic and careful planning, this threat can be eliminated.
Instrumentation	Through logic and careful planning, this threat can be eliminated.	Through logic and careful planning, this threat can be eliminated.
Maturation	Problem!	Often, you will be able to estimate the extent to which differences between your groups could be due to maturation.
History	Problem!	Problem!
Regression	Problem!	You should be able to determine whether regression is a plausible explanation for the difference between conditions.

assumption, however, is only correct if the effects of history, maturation, mortality, instrumentation, and testing are relatively consistent over time. In other words, your conclusions about the treatment's effect could be wrong if there is a sudden change in any one of these nontreatment factors (see Table 11-6).

Unfortunately, sudden changes in these nontreatment factors are possible. As you will see, history and regression tend to produce sudden changes, and the effects of testing, instrumentation, mortality, and maturation are not always slow and consistent across time.

History To see how history could produce a sudden change, imagine just some of the many specific events that could affect performance on the posttest. For instance, ratings of the professor might change as a result of students getting the midterm back, the professor becoming ill, the professor reading a book on teaching, and so on. Unlike the single-*n* design, the time-series design does not control all these history effects. Indeed, you could argue that the time-series design's

• FIGURE 11-4 •

TWO VERY DIFFERENT PATTERNS OF RESULTS IN A TIME-SERIES DESIGN IN WHICH THE TREATMENT WAS INTRODUCED AFTER THE FIFTH WEEK

(a): Little evidence of a treatment effect

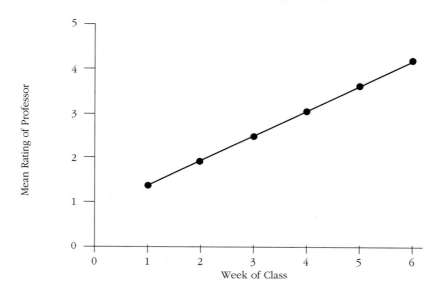

(b): Evidence of a treatment effect

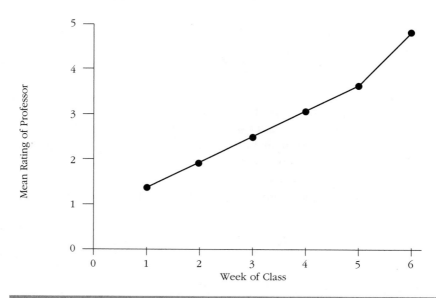

• **TABLE 11-6** •

Threats to Time-Series Designs

History!

Regression

Inconsistent effects

    Inconsistent instrumentation effects

    Inconsistent mortality effects

    Inconsistent testing effects

    Inconsistent maturation effects

lack of control over history, and thus its vulnerability to history, prevents it from reaching experimental-design status.

Although *history is the one threat to which the time-series is extremely vulnerable*, you can try to reduce its effects. One strategy is to have a very short interval between testing sessions. With an extremely short interval, you give history fewer opportunities to have an effect.

In addition to reducing the effects of history, you can also try to do a better job of estimating its effects. Since intimately knowing the past should enhance your ability to predict the future, you might collect an extensive baseline. Ideally, you would collect baseline data for several years. This baseline will help you identify any historical events or patterns that tend to repeat themselves regularly. For instance, your baseline would alert you to cyclical patterns in student evaluations, such as students being very positive toward the professor during the first 2 weeks of the term, more negative toward the professor after the midterm examination, then becoming more favorable during the last week of the term. Thus, consulting your baseline data would prevent you from mistaking these cyclical fluctuations for a treatment effect.

Regression   Like the effects of history, regression effects will not change steadily from week to week. After all, regression is due to chance measurement error, and chance measurement error will not change steadily and predictably from week to week. Therefore, you cannot use a time-series design to measure regression's effect. However, you *can* use time-series designs to determine if regression is a likely explanation for your results. Specifically, you should suspect regression if:

1. The ratings immediately before the treatment are extremely high or extremely low relative to the previous ratings.

2. The posttreatment ratings, although very different from the most immediate pretreatment level, are not substantially different from earlier pretreatment ratings.

Inconsistent Effects From Threats That Are Often Consistent   As we have discussed, the effects of history and regression can almost be expected to be inconsistent. On the other hand, the effects of instrumentation, mortality, testing, and maturation tend to be consistent. Unfortunately, as you will see, the effects of instrumentation, mortality, testing, and maturation are not always consistent.

Inconsistent Instrumentation Effects   Suppose you administered the same rating scale in the same way for the first 5 weeks. Your measurements from Weeks 1 through 5 would not be affected by instrumentation. There was no instrumentation effect. As a result, your estimate for the amount of change to expect between Week 5 and Week 6 would not include any effect for instrumentation. However, suppose that you ran out of copies of the original rating scale during Week 6 and decided, while you were going to the trouble to run off more copies, that you would make some minor corrections to the form. Consequently, you handed out a refined version of your rating scale during Week 6—the same week the professor started telling her class about her problems with learning material. In that case, you might have an instrumentation effect that could not have been estimated based upon the previous weeks' data. Therefore, you might mistake an instrumentation effect for a treatment effect.

Inconsistent Mortality Effects   Similarly, if mortality does not follow a consistent pattern, you might mistake mortality's effects for treatment effects. For example, suppose that the last week to drop the course was the same week the professor started to tell the class about her problems. In that case, a disproportionate number of students who did not like the professor might drop out during that week. Consequently, the professor's ratings might improve because of mortality rather than because of her disclosures.

   Note that if the students who didn't like the professor dropped the class at a consistent rate, the time-series design would allow us to discount the mortality effect. In other words, if mortality was gradually causing an increase in ratings during Weeks 1 through 5, and this trend continued into Week 6, you would not mistake a mortality effect for a treatment effect. However, if there is a sudden rash of mortality during Week 6 (as dissatisfied students drop the class just before the deadline), then mortality will have more of an effect than the data from Weeks 1 through 5 would lead you to expect. Consequently, you could mistake this inconsistent mortality effect for a treatment effect.

Inconsistent Testing Effects   In the study we've been discussing, the effect of testing should be gradual and consistent. However, the effect of testing will not be consistent in every study. For example, in some studies, participants might develop insight into the task. As a result of discovering the rule behind the task, their performance may increase dramatically.

Inconsistent testing effects are not limited to situations in which participants are aware of having an insight. That is, practice does *not* always produce steady, continuous improvement. As you know from experience, after weeks of practice or study with little to show for it, you may suddenly improve greatly.

Inconsistent Maturation Effects   Similarly, maturation's effect may sometimes be discontinuous. For instance, suppose you measure young children every 3 months on a motor abilities test. Then, you expose them to an enriched environment and measure them again. Certainly, you will see a dramatic change, but is this change due to the treatment? Or, is it due to the children jumping to a more advanced developmental stage (for example, learning to walk)?

Unfortunately, you cannot escape sudden, sporadic maturation by studying adults. Even in our teacher evaluation study, participants might mature at an inconsistent rate. That is, first-year students might grow up quickly after getting their first exams back, or students might suddenly develop insight into the professor's lecturing style. If this sudden development occurred the same week the professor started to disclose her problems with learning material, maturation could masquerade as a treatment effect.

Eliminating, Rather Than Estimating, Threats to Validity

In short, although the time-series design can rule out certain threats to validity by estimating the effects of those threats (see Table 11-7), there are certain effects that it cannot accurately estimate. Therefore, when using a time-series design, do not focus so much on estimating the impact of the threats to validity that you don't try to eliminate those threats. For example, try to eliminate the threat of instrumentation by using the same measuring instrument each time and administering it the same way. In our student evaluation study, we would give students the same rating scales and the same instructions each time.

Likewise, try to eliminate mortality. Thus, if you had students sign their rating sheets, you could eliminate mortality by only analyzing data from students who had perfect attendance.

If you can't eliminate a threat, at least try to reduce its effects. Try to reduce the effects of both maturation and history by keeping the interval between pretest and posttest short. Minimize the likelihood of regression occurring by choosing the time that you will administer the treatment well in advance—don't administer the treatment as an immediate reaction to extremely low ratings.

Variations on the Traditional Time-Series Design

Now that you are familiar with the basic logic behind the time-series design, you are ready to see how it can be extended. One simple way of extending a time-series design is to increase the number of pretest and posttest measurements you take. There are two advantages to increasing the number of pretest and posttest measurements you take.

• TABLE 11-7 •

HOW THE TIME-SERIES DESIGN DEALS WITH THREATS TO INTERNAL VALIDITY

THREAT	APPROACH
Selection	Automatically eliminated because testing and retesting the same participants.
Selection by Maturation	Automatically eliminated because testing and retesting the same participants.
Instrumentation	If effects are constant, effects can be estimated. In addition, try to use the same instrument in the same way every time.
Mortality	If effects are constant, effects can be estimated. In addition, if no participants drop out, mortality is not a problem.
Testing	If effects are constant, effects can be estimated.
Maturation	If effects are constant, effects can be estimated. In addition, study slowly maturing participants or make sure that time between the last pretest and the posttest is very brief.
Regression	Regression is unlikely if ratings prior to introducing the treatment were not extreme and did not differ greatly from previous ratings. Use a reliable measure.
History	Try to collect extensive pretest data to predict history's effects. In addition, you may try to make sure that: 1. Time between the last pretest and the posttest is brief. 2. Participants are isolated from outside events.

First, the more measurements you take, the more accurate you should be at estimating the combined effects of maturation, history, mortality, testing, and instrumentation. Thus, you are less likely to mistake these effects for a treatment effect.

Second, the more measurements you have, the less likely it is that an unusual history, maturation, mortality, testing, or instrumentation effect would influence only the measurement taken after you administered the treatment. To illustrate the advantages of having more measurements, suppose you only measure student reactions on the fifth, sixth, and seventh weeks. You administer the treatment between the sixth and seventh weeks. Would it be an unusual coincidence if history, maturation, mortality, testing, or maturation had more of an effect between the sixth and seventh weeks than between the fifth and sixth weeks? No. Consequently, any of these threats to validity might easily imitate a treatment effect. However, what if you had students evaluate the teacher from Week 1 to Week 12? Then, it would be quite a coincidence for a threat to have an extraordinarily large effect between the sixth (the same week you gave the treatment) and seventh weeks, but not have such an effect between any of the other weeks.

Reversal Time-Series Designs   In addition to taking more measurements, you can extend your time-series design by administering and withdrawing the treatment. That is, you can imitate the single-*n* researcher's reversal design.

For example, you might pretest, administer the treatment, posttest, withdraw the treatment, and test again. You might even withdraw and introduce the treatment several times.

To see the beauty of this *reversal time-series design*, imagine that you were able to get increases each time the professor tells her class about her problems with learning material, then decreases when she stops talking about her problems, followed by increases when the professor again tells her class about her studying woes. With that pattern of results, you would be very confident that the disclosures made a difference.

Despite the elegance of the reversal design, ethical and construct validity problems may prevent you from using it. The ethical problems are the most serious: In some situations, you cannot ethically withdraw the treatment after you have administered it (for example, psychotherapy, reinforcement for wearing seatbelts).

The construct validity problems can also be serious. Specifically, withdrawing and re-administering the treatment may alert participants to your hypothesis. Consequently, your results may be due to participants guessing the hypothesis and playing along.

To prevent participants from guessing the hypothesis or becoming resentful when you withdraw the treatment, use placebo treatments or multiple levels of the treatment. Thus, if you were to use this design for your student evaluations study, you might have a placebo condition in which the professor discloses innocuous facts about studying experiences. Alternatively, you might use several levels of disclosure ranging from innocuous to intimate.

Two-Group Time-Series Design   A final way of extending the time-series design is to collect time-series data on two groups. One group, the control group, would not get the treatment. The advantage of using a control group is that it allows you to rule out certain history effects. In your disclosure study, the control group might be another section of the same professor's class. If, after the treatment was administered, the ratings went down only in the treatment group, you could rule out general history effects (midterm blues, spring fever) as an explanation of the results.

However, you can't rule out every history effect because the two classes may have different histories. For example, the professor may have gotten mad at one class and not the other.

THE NONEQUIVALENT CONTROL-GROUP DESIGN

You do not have to use a time-series design. For example, rather than using a two-group time-series design, you could simply: (1) Give one group the treatment, then (2) measure both groups. Such a study would be called a **nonequiv-**

alent control-group design. Essentially, the nonequivalent control-group design is the simple experiment without random assignment.

Because of the nonequivalent control-group design's similarity to the simple experiment, it has many of the simple experiment's strengths. For example, because every participant is only tested once, the nonequivalent control-group design, like the simple experiment, is not vulnerable to maturation, testing, or instrumentation. Furthermore, because of the control group, the nonequivalent group design, like the simple experiment, can usually deal with the effects of history, maturation, and mortality.

The Nonequivalent Control-Group Design
Is Extremely Vulnerable to Selection

But because this design does not use random assignment, the control and treatment groups are not equivalent. Since the control and treatment groups are not equivalent, comparing them may be like comparing apples and oranges. That is, with the nonequivalent control-group design, *the threat of selection is serious.*

Why Matching Doesn't Make Groups Equal

To address the selection threat, some investigators match participants. Investigators' attempts to make the nonequivalent control group equivalent to the treatment group may include trying to make sure that each participant in the control group is identical in several key respects to a participant in the treatment group. Or, investigators may try to make sure that groups have the same average scores on key variables. Sometimes participants or groups are matched on a few background variables (age, gender, IQ) that are expected to correlate with task performance. Sometimes participants are matched on actual task performance (pretest scores).

Although you might think that matching would succeed at making the nonequivalent control group equivalent to the treatment group, realize two important points about matched participants:

1. Matched participants/groups are only matched on a few variables rather than on every variable.
2. Matched participants/groups are not matched on characteristics directly, but on imperfect measures of those characteristics.

You Can't Match on Everything   Just because two groups are matched on a few variables, you shouldn't think that they are matched on all variables. They aren't. The unmatched variables may cause the two groups to score differently on the dependent measure (see Table 11-8). For instance, suppose you decide to use a nonequivalent group design to test your hypothesis about the effect of self-disclosing problems with learning material. To make the two classes similar, you match the classes on IQ scores, grade-point average, proportion of psychology majors, proportion of females and males, and proportion of sophomores, juniors, and seniors. However, you have not matched them in terms of interest in going on to graduate school, number of times they had taken classes from this professor before, and a few hundred other variables that might affect their ratings of the professor. Unfortunately, these unmatched variables, rather than the treatment, may be responsible for the difference between your treatment and control groups.

Since investigators realize that they cannot match participants on every single factor that may influence task performance, some investigators try to match participants on task performance (pretest scores). Yet, even when groups are matched on pretest scores, unmatched variables can cause the groups to score differently on the posttest. Just because two groups of students start out with the same enthusiasm for a course, you cannot be sure that they will end the term with the same enthusiasm. For example, one group may end the term with more enthusiasm because that group began the course with a clearer understanding of what the course would be like, what the tests would be like, and how much work was involved. Consequently, although both groups might rate the professor the same at first, the groups may differ after they get the first exam back. For instance, because the naïve group had misconceptions about what the professor's exams would be like, they may rate the professor more harshly than the experienced group.

Although this change in student attitudes toward the professor might appear to be a treatment effect, it is not. Instead, the difference between the two

• **TABLE 11-8** •

How Two Nonequivalent Control-Group Designs Stack up in Terms of Dealing With Threats to Internal Validity

	TYPE OF NONEQUIVALENT CONTROL GROUP	
THREAT TO VALIDITY	**UNMATCHED**	**MATCHED**
Selection	Big problem!	Problem
Selection × Maturation	Problem	Problem
Regression	Not a problem	Big problem!
Mortality	Should not be a problem	Should not be a problem
Instrumentation	Should not be a problem	Should not be a problem
Maturation	Automatically eliminated by the design	Automatically eliminated by the design
Testing	Automatically eliminated by the design	Automatically eliminated by the design
History	Automatically eliminated by the design	Automatically eliminated by the design

groups is due to the fact that participants changed over time in different ways because of variables on which they were not matched. Technically, there was a selection by maturation interaction. Because of interactions between selection and other variables, even matching on pretest scores does not free you from selection problems.

What can be done about interactions between selection and other variables? One approach is to assume that nature prefers simple, direct main effects to complex interactions. Thus, if an effect could be due to either a treatment main effect or an interaction between selection and maturation, assume that the effect is a simple treatment main effect. Be aware, of course, that your assumption could be wrong.

If you want to go beyond merely assuming that selection interactions are unlikely, you can make them less likely. One way to make selection interactions less likely is to make the groups similar on as many selection variables as possible. That is, not only can you match the groups on pretest scores, but also on other variables. With such matching, there would be fewer variables on which the groups differed and, therefore, fewer selection variables to interact with maturation. Hence, you would reduce the chance of selection-maturation interactions occurring.

You have seen one way to reduce interactions between selection variables and maturation—reduce differences between groups that might contribute to selection. The other way to reduce interactions between selection and maturation is to reduce opportunities for maturation. After all, if neither group can mature, then you won't have a selection-maturation interaction. Therefore, to reduce the potential for a selection by maturation interaction, you may decide to present the posttest as soon after the pretest as possible.

You Match on Measures of Variables—Not on Variables   As you have seen, failing to match on every relevant variable sets you up for selection-maturation interactions. Failing to match on every relevant variable, however, is not the only problem with matching. Another problem with matching is that participants must be matched on observed scores, rather than on true scores.

Unfortunately, observed scores are not the same as true scores. Observed scores are merely imperfect reflections of true scores because observed scores are contaminated by measurement error. As a result of this measurement error, two groups might appear to be similar on certain variables, although they are actually very different on those variables.

How can participants score the same on a measure of a variable, but actually be very different in terms of that variable? To see how, suppose a researcher wanted to examine the effect of a drug on treating clinical depression. The practitioner/researcher has received approval and patients' permissions to give the drug to the 10 clinically depressed patients at her small psychiatric facility. However, she realizes that if the participants improve after getting the drug, it proves nothing. Maybe the patients would get better anyway. She wants to have a comparison group that does not get the drug. After getting a phone call asking her to give a guest lecture at a nearby college, she gets an idea. She could use some college students as her comparison group. After testing hundreds of students, she obtains a group of 10 college students who score the same on the depression scale as her group of 10 mental patients.

But are the two groups equal in terms of depression? Probably not. The college student participants' scores are extremely depressed relative to the average college student. The fact that the participants' scores are extremely different from the mean (average) sets up regression toward the mean.

Regression toward the mean occurs because extreme scores tend to have an extreme amount of random error. Thus, when the students are tested again, their scores will be less extreme because their scores will not be as dramatically swayed by random error. That is, on the posttest, the college student participants will probably score more like average college students—less depressed. Thus, because of the regression toward the mean phenomenon, it may appear that the drug hurts recovery from depression.

How can you stop from mistaking such a regression effect for a treatment effect? One approach is to reduce regression. As we mentioned earlier, there are two ways to reduce the potential for regression effects. First, because regression takes advantage of random measurement error, you can reduce regression by using a measure that is relatively free of random measurement error: a reliable measure. Second, because extreme scores tend to be more influenced by random error than less extreme scores, don't select participants who have extreme pretest scores.

A trickier approach to combat regression is to obtain results that regression cannot account for. In our depression example, regression would tend to make it look like the college students had improved more than the mental patients. Thus, if you found that college students improved more than mental patients, your results might be due to regression. However, if you found the opposite results— mental patients improving in mood more than college students—regression would not be an explanation for your results. Thus, one approach to eliminating regression is to get results exactly opposite from what regression would predict.

Unfortunately, there is no way to guarantee that your treatment's effect will push scores in exactly the opposite direction of where regression would push scores. Furthermore, even if the treatment effect goes against the regression effect, regression effect may cancel or even overwhelm the treatment effect. That is, even though your treatment had a positive effect, the treatment group's scores—because of regression—may still decline. When regression and selection by maturation are both pushing scores in the opposite direction of the treatment, the effect of even a moderately effective treatment may be hidden.

To illustrate how regression and selection by maturation can hide a treatment's effect, consider research attempting to determine the effects of social programs. Sometimes researchers try to find the effect of a social program by matching a group of individuals who participate in the program with individuals who are not eligible. For example, researchers compared children who participated in "Head

Start" with an upper-income group of children who had the same test scores. Unfortunately, this often meant selecting a group of upper-income children whose test scores were extremely low compared to their upper-income peers. Consequently, on retesting, these scores regressed back up toward the mean of upper-income children. Because of this regression toward the mean effect, scores in the no-treatment group increased more than scores in the "Head Start" group.

Not only was regression a problem, but there was also the potential for a selection by maturation interaction—especially for studies that looked for long-term effects of "Head Start." That is, even if the groups started out the same, the upper-income group, because of superior health, nutrition, and schools, might mature academically at a faster rate than the disadvantaged group. Thus, not surprisingly, some early studies of "Head Start" that failed to take regression and selection by maturation into account made it look like "Head Start" harmed, rather than helped, children. Thus, as you can see, matching is far from the perfect solution that it first appears to be (see Table 11-9). Therefore, the nonequivalent control-group design is a flawed way of establishing that a treatment has an effect.

CONCLUSIONS ABOUT QUASI-EXPERIMENTAL DESIGNS

Unfortunately, all quasi-experimental designs are flawed methods of establishing that a treatment caused an effect. Although quasi-experiments ensure temporal precedence and assess covariation, quasi-experiments do not automatically rule out the effects of nontreatment factors. As a result, quasi-experimenters use a variety of tactics to compensate for the limitations of their designs.

Quasi-experimenters may combine two quasi-experimental designs, using one design to cover for another's weaknesses. For example, they may use a time-series design to rule out selection biases and then use a nonequivalent control-group design to rule out history effects.

Quasi-experimenters may also identify a specific threat to their study's internal validity and then take specific steps to minimize that threat (for a review,

---

• **TABLE 11-9** •

PROBLEMS WITH TRYING TO
MAKE GROUPS EQUIVALENT BY MATCHING

PROBLEM	IMPLICATION
You cannot match on all variables.	Selection by maturation interactions possible.
You cannot match on true scores. Instead, you have to match on observed scores, which are not totally accurate.	Regression effects possible.

see Table 11-3). For instance, they may eliminate instrumentation biases by administering the same measure, the same way, every time.

Finally, they may eliminate some threats by arguing that the particular threat is not a likely explanation for the effect. That is, they may argue that mortality was low and therefore not a threat or that pretest scores were not extreme and so regression was not a problem.

When arguing that nontreatment factors are unlikely explanations for their results, quasi-experimenters often invoke the law of parsimony. The **law of parsimony** is the assumption that the simplest explanation is the most likely. Thus, the time-series researcher argues that the simplest assumption to make is that the effects of maturation, instrumentation, testing, and mortality are consistent over time. Therefore, a dramatic change after introducing the treatment should not be viewed as a complex, unexpected maturation effect, but as a simple, straightforward treatment effect.

Clearly, the quasi-experimenter's job is a difficult one, requiring much creativity and effort. But there are rewards. Quasi-experimenters can often study the effects of treatments that couldn't be studied with conventional experimental designs. For example, quasi-experimenters can study treatments that could not—or should not—be randomly assigned. Thus, quasi-experimenters can study the effects of disasters, new laws, new technology, and new social programs. Furthermore, because quasi-experimenters often study real-world treatments, their studies sometimes have more external validity than traditional experimental designs.

Concluding Remarks

Quasi-experiments, single-*n* designs, and the methods described in the last few chapters are extremely useful—*if you want to infer that a treatment causes an effect.* But what if you don't want to infer causality? What if you want to describe or predict behavior? Then, you will want to use one of the methods discussed in the next two chapters.

Summary

1. To infer that a treatment causes an effect, you must show that changes in the amount of the treatment are accompanied by changes in participants' behavior (covariation), that changes in the treatment come before changes in the behavior (temporal precedence), and that nothing other than the treatment is responsible for the change in behavior (the change is not due to spuriousness).

2. By comparing treatment and nontreatment conditions, you can see if the cause and the effect covary.

3. When you manipulate the treatment, you make sure that the treatment comes before the change in behavior, thereby establishing temporal precedence.

4. Randomization is an effective way of ruling out the likelihood that non-treatment factors may be responsible for the change in behavior.

5. Like randomized experiments, single-n designs manipulate the treatment to ensure temporal precedence and compare conditions to assess covariation.

6. Single-n researchers try to identify the important, nontreatment variables. Once those variables are identified, they try to keep those variables constant. That is, they try to stop those variables from varying in their study.

7. Single-n researchers prevent individual difference variables from varying within their study by limiting their study to examining a single participant. That is, differences between subjects (between-subject variability) cannot make the treatment condition score higher than the control condition because the subject in the treatment condition is the same subject that is in the control condition.

8. Single-n researchers often keep environmental variables constant by keeping the participant in a highly controlled environment.

9. The A–B–A reversal design and the multiple-baseline design are used by single-n researchers to rule out the effects of maturation and testing.

10. When it comes to construct validity, the single-n researcher and the within-subjects researcher use very similar approaches. To prevent participants from figuring out the hypothesis, both researchers may use: (1) few levels of the independent variable, (2) placebo treatments, and/or (3) gradual variations in the levels of the independent variable.

11. Unlike single-n researchers, quasi-experimenters cannot keep relevant nontreatment factors from varying.

12. Quasi-experimenters must explicitly rule out the eight threats to internal validity: history, maturation, testing, instrumentation, mortality, regression, selection, and selection by maturation interactions.

13. Instrumentation can be ruled out by using the same measure, the same way, every time.

14. By definition, mortality will not be a threat to your study's internal validity if you can keep participants from dropping out of your study.

15. You can probably rule out regression if participants were not chosen on the basis of their extreme scores or if your measuring instrument is extremely reliable.

16. The time-series design is very similar to the A–B single-n design. The main differences are that the time-series design: (1) studies more participants; (2) does not control the variables necessary to establish a stable baseline; and (3) doesn't isolate participants from history the way the single-n design does. Because the time-series design cannot control nontreatment, environmental events (history), the time-series' Achilles' heel is history.

17. The nonequivalent control-group design resembles the simple experiment. However, because participants are not randomly assigned to groups, selection is a serious problem in the nonequivalent control-group design.

18. Although quasi-experimental designs are not as good as experimental designs for inferring causality, they are more versatile.

Key Terms

temporal precedence: changes in the suspected cause occur before changes in behavior. Because causes come before effects, researchers trying to establish causality must establish temporal precedence. Experimental designs establish temporal precedence by manipulating the treatment variable. (p. 385)

covariation: changes in the treatment are accompanied by changes in the behavior. To establish causality, you must establish covariation. (p. 384)

spurious: when the covariation observed between two variables is not due to the variables influencing each other, but because both are being influenced by some third variable. For example, the relationship between ice cream sales and assaults in New York is spurious—not because it does not exist (it does!)—but because ice cream does not cause increased assaults, and assaults do not cause increased ice cream sales. Instead, high temperatures probably cause both increased assaults and ice cream sales. Beware of spuriousness whenever you look at research that does not use an experimental design. (p. 385)

single-*n* designs: designs that try to establish causality by studying a single participant and arguing that the covariation between treatment and changes in behavior could not be due to anything other than the treatment. A key to this approach is preventing factors other than the treatment from varying. (p. 387)

baseline: the participant's behavior on the task prior to receiving the treatment. (p. 388)

stable baseline: when the participant's behavior, prior to receiving the treatment, is consistent. To establish a stable baseline, the researcher may have to keep many factors constant. If the researcher establishes a stable baseline and then is able to change the behavior after administering the treatment, the researcher can make the case that the treatment caused the effect. (p. 387)

A–B design: the simplest single-*n* design, consisting of measuring the participant's behavior at baseline (*A*) and then measuring the participant after the participant has received the treatment (*B*). (p. 387)

A–B–A reversal design: a single-*n* design in which baseline measurements are made of the target behavior (*A*), then a treatment is administered and the participant's behavior is recorded (*B*), and then the treatment is removed and the target behavior is measured again (*A*). The *A–B–A* design makes a more convincing case for the treatment's effect than the *A–B* design. (p. 391)

carryover effects: the effects of a treatment condition persist into later conditions. Because of carryover, investigators using an *A–B–A* design frequently find that the participant's behavior does not return to the original baseline. The possibilities for carryover effects increase dramatically when you use more levels of the independent variable and/or when you use more than one independent variable. Because carryover effects are a serious concern, many single-n researchers minimize carryover's complications by doing experiments that use only two levels of a single independent variable. (p. 392)

multiple-baseline design: a single-n design in which the researcher studies several behaviors at a time. The researcher collects a baseline on these different behaviors. The researcher then introduces a treatment to try to modify one of the behaviors. The researcher hopes that the treatment will change the selected behavior, but that the other behaviors will stay at baseline. Next, the researcher tries to modify the second behavior and so on. For example, a manager might collect baseline data on employee absenteeism, tardiness, and cleanliness. Then, the manager would reward cleanliness while continuing to collect data on all three variables. Then, the manager would reward punctuality, and so on. (p. 395)

history: events in the environment—other than the treatment—that have changed. Differences between conditions that are believed to be due to treatment may sometimes be due to history. (p. 401)

instrumentation: differences between conditions being due to differences in how the conditions were measured. If, for example, the actual measurement instrument used in the pretest was different than the measure used in the posttest (or the way the instrument was administered changed from pretest to posttest), you should be concerned about instrumentation. (p. 401)

testing: participants score differently on the posttest as a result of what they learned from taking the pretest. Practice effects could be considered a type of testing effect. (p. 391)

maturation: changes in the participant that naturally occur over time. Physiological changes such as fatigue, growth, and development are common sources of maturation. (p. 389)

mortality: differences between conditions are due to participants dropping out of the study. (p. 402)

selection: treatment and no-treatment groups were different at the end of the study because the groups differed before the treatment was administered. (p. 402)

selection-maturation interaction: treatment and no-treatment groups, although similar at one point, would have grown apart (developed differently) even if no treatment had been administered. That is, the effect of maturation is different for one group than another. (p. 402)

regression toward the mean (also known as regression and statistical regression): one reason we don't know an individual's true score on a variable is that measurements are affected by random error. Averaged over all scores, random error has no net effect. That is, although random error pushes some individuals' scores up higher than their true scores, it pushes other individuals' scores down. However, if we only select participants with extremely high scores, we are selecting—for the most part—only those pretest scores that random error increased (if it had decreased them, those scores wouldn't be so high). If we retest these individuals, their retest scores will be lower because random error will probably not push all of their scores up two times in a row. Consequently, these participants' retest scores will be less extreme. That is, their scores will revert back to more average levels. In other words, their retest scores will regress toward the mean. Likewise, if you select participants based on their having extremely low pretest scores, you will find that the scores of those participants will tend to be not as low on the posttest. (p. 402)

quasi-experiment: a study that resembles an experiment except that random assignment played no role in determining which participants got which level of treatment. Quasi-experiments have less internal validity than experiments. The time-series design and the nonequivalent control-group design are considered quasi-experimental designs. (p. 400)

pretest–posttest design: a before–after design in which each participant is given the pretest, administered the treatment, then given the posttest. The pretest–posttest design is not vulnerable to selection and selection by maturation interactions. It is, however, extremely vulnerable to history, maturation, and testing effects. The pretest-posttest design is does not have enough internal validity to be considered an experimental design. In fact, because of its poor internal validity, it is usually not even considered to be a quasi-experimental design. (p. 404)

time-series design: a quasi-experimental design in which a series of observations is taken from a group of participants over time before and after they receive treatment. Collecting a series of observations on each participant allows the researcher to estimate the extent to which the participant's behavior tends to change. Thus, the researcher is in a good position to see whether the changes that occur after the treatment is introduced are greater than the changes that normally occur. Because the time-series design is in a better position to estimate the effects of many potential threats to internal validity, it is an improvement over the pretest–posttest design. However, it is still extremely vulnerable to history effects. (p. 406)

nonequivalent control-group design: a quasi-experimental design that, like a simple experiment, has a treatment group and a no-treatment comparison group. However, unlike the simple experiment, random assignment does not determine which subjects get the treatment and which do not. Having a comparison group is better than not having one, but if the comparison group was not really equivalent to the treatment group at the start of the study, you may be comparing apples with oranges. Thus, you may mistakenly believe that the treatment had an effect when it did not. In other words, selection is a serious threat to the validity of the nonequivalent control-group design. (p. 414).

law of parsimony: the assumption that the simplest explanation is the most likely. Quasi-experimenters often argue that their results are more parsimoniously explained by the treatment having an effect than by some cyclical effect of some other variable or than by a selection by maturation interaction. (p. 420)

Exercises

1. Suppose that the means for the treatment and no-treatment conditions are the same. If so, which requirement of establishing causality has not been met?

2. If the study does not manipulate the treatment, which requirement of establishing causality will be difficult to meet?

3. If participants are not randomly assigned to condition, which requirement for establishing causality will be almost impossible to meet?

4. Compare and contrast how single-*n* designs and randomized experiments account for nontreatment factors.

5. What arguments can you make for generalizing results from the single-*n* design?

6. How do the *A–B* design and the pretest–posttest design differ in terms of:
   a. Procedure?
   b. Internal validity?

7. How does the single-*n* researcher's *A–B–A* design differ from the quasi-experimenter's reversal time-series design in terms of:
   a. Procedure?
   b. Internal validity?

8. Design a quasi-experiment that looks at the effects of a course on simulating parenthood, including an assignment that involves taking care of an egg, on changing the expectations of junior-high school students about parenting. What kind of design would you use? Why?

9. An ad depicts a student who has improved his grade-point average from 2.0 to 3.2 after a stint in the military. Consider Campbell and Stanley's "spurious eight." Is the military the only possible explanation for the improvement?

10. According to one study, holding students back a grade harmed students. The evidence: Students who had been held back a grade did much worse in school than students who had not been held back.
    a. Does this evidence prove that holding students back harms their performance? Why or why not?
    b. If you were a researcher hired by the Department of Education to test the assertion that holding students back harms them, what design would you use? Why?

INTRODUCTION TO DESCRIPTIVE METHODS

Summary
Key Terms
Exercises

The invalid assumption that correlation implies cause is probably among the two or three most serious and common errors of human reasoning.
—STEPHEN JAY GOULD, *THE MISMEASURE OF MAN* (1981), P. 242

OVERVIEW

In this chapter, you will be introduced to descriptive research. Descriptive research is relatively straightforward because to describe behavior, all you need to do is measure variables.

In fact, at the most primitive level of describing behavior, you only have to measure a single variable, such as counting how many times something happens. Thus, the earliest research on "date rape" involved finding out how frequently women were raped by their dates.

At a more sophisticated level of description, you would measure your original variable and several other variables to see if they are related. Thus, research on date rape evolved from testing hypotheses about the number of date rapes to testing hypotheses about variables that might be associated with being a date rapist or victim. For example, researchers studied whether date rapists exhibited aggressive tendencies prior to raping their victim and whether certain situations, such as blind dates, were more likely to lead to a date rape.

As you can see, descriptive research quickly progresses from describing a single variable to describing relationships among variables. Almost as soon as researchers had estimated the number of date rapes, they were finding factors that related to date rape. Because descriptive research almost always involves determining how variables *covary*, or how variables *relate* to one another, descriptive research methods are also called *correlational* methods.

USES AND LIMITATIONS OF DESCRIPTIVE METHODS

When you use descriptive methods, you gain the ability to test hypotheses about virtually any variable in virtually any situation. For example, you can use descriptive methods even when you can't manipulate variables. You can use descriptive methods even when you can neither control irrelevant variables nor account for their effects. In short, if your hypothesis is that two or more variables are related, descriptive methods give you the flexibility to test that hypothesis.

DESCRIPTIVE RESEARCH AND CAUSALITY

But this flexibility comes at a cost. Without being able to manipulate variables and account for the effects of irrelevant variables, you cannot legitimately make cause–effect statements. As a result, you cannot determine the reason for the relationships you find. Thus, if you find a relationship between low self-esteem and people who have been raped, you cannot say *why* low self-esteem and rape are related. Certainly, you cannot say that low self-esteem causes one to be raped.

Why Descriptive Methods Can't Test Causal Hypotheses

Why not? There are two reasons.

First, because you do not know that rape victims had low self-esteem *before* they were raped. It may be that prior to being raped, rape victims had high self-esteem but that rape lowered self-esteem. Instead of low self-esteem being the cause of rape, it may be an effect of rape.

Second, you haven't controlled for, or accounted for, other variables that might be responsible for the relationship between self-esteem and rape. Many factors might lead both to having low self-esteem and to being raped. For example, being short may lead to low self-esteem as well as decreasing one's ability to fight off an attacker. Or, having a low income may lead to low self-esteem and also make one more vulnerable to rape—if low-income people live in more-dangerous neighborhoods (see Figure 12-1).

To repeat a very important point, correlational methods do not have internal validity, so they do not allow you to make cause–effect statements. When you use a correlational method to find a relationship between two variables, you do not know whether the relationship is due to (1) changes in the first variable causing changes in the second variable; (2) changes in the second variable causing changes in the first variable; or (3) a third variable causing the changes in both variables.

How Descriptive Methods Can Stimulate Causal Hypotheses

Although correlational methods do not allow you to infer causality, they may stimulate causal hypotheses. As you can see from Table 12-1, there are two ways that correlational methods may stimulate causal hypotheses.

First, if you find a relationship between two variables, you may want to do an experiment to determine whether the relationship is a causal relationship. For instance, knowing that there was a correlation between smoking and lung cancer led to experiments that tested whether smoking caused lung cancer.

Second, even if you know that the two factors do not directly influence each other, you may try to find out what causes them to be statistically related. That is, you may try to find out what third factor accounts for their relationship. For example, suppose you find that, in general, students who study more have lower grade-point averages. This finding may suggest the following idea: Perhaps some students are using study strategies that are both time consuming and ineffective. This idea may lead you to do experiments to test whether some

• FIGURE 12-1 •

THREE BASIC POSSIBILITIES FOR AN OBSERVED RELATIONSHIP

1. The "first" factor causes a change in the "second" factor.

2. The "second" factor causes a change in the "first" factor.

3. Some "third" factor could cause a change in both the "first" and "second" factors.

3 a.

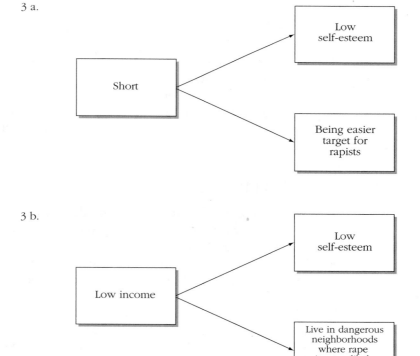

3 b.

Note that there are many "third" factors that might account for the relationship. We have listed only two (height and income).

• TABLE 12-1 •

GENERATING CAUSAL HYPOTHESES FROM CORRELATIONAL DATA

For each correlational finding listed below, develop an experimental hypothesis.

1. Listeners of country music tend to be more depressed than people who listen to other types of music.
2. There is a correlation between attendance and good grades.
3. Attractive people earn higher salaries than less-attractive people.
4. In restaurants, large groups tend to leave lower tips (in terms of percentage of bill) than individuals.
5. Teams that wear black uniforms are penalized more often than other teams.
6. People report being more often persuaded by newspaper editorials than by television editorials.
7. Students report that they would be less likely to cheat if professors walked around the class more during exams.
8. Students who take notes in outline form get better grades than those who don't.

study strategies are more effective than others. Alternatively, if you think the relationship is due to poorer students being slower and poorer readers, you might design an experiment to see if training in reading skills improves grades.

In summary, descriptive research does not allow you to infer causality (see Table 12-2). However, descriptive research may stimulate experimental research that will allow you to infer causality: Once you use a *descriptive* design to find out *what* happens, you can use an *experimental* design to try to find out *why* it happens.

DESCRIPTION FOR DESCRIPTION'S SAKE

By hinting at possible causal relationships, descriptive research can indirectly help psychologists achieve two goals of psychology—explaining behavior and controlling behavior. But the main purpose of descriptive research is to achieve another important goal of psychology—describing behavior.

But is description really an important scientific goal? Yes, in fact, description is a major goal of every science. What is chemistry's famed periodic table but a description of the elements? What is biology's system of classifying plants and animals into Kingdom, Phylum, Genus, and Species but a way of describing living organisms? What is astronomy's mapping of the stars but a description of outer space? What is science but systematic observation and measurement? Thus, one reason psychologists value descriptive methods is because description is the cornerstone of science. Besides, psychologists, like everyone else, want to be able to describe what people think, feel, and do.

• **TABLE 12-2** •

QUESTIONS THAT MUST BE ANSWERED TO ESTABLISH THAT TWO VARIABLES ARE CAUSALLY RELATED

Is there a relationship between the two variables in the sample?

Did the researchers accurately measure the two variables?

Did the researchers accurately record the two variables?

Did the researchers accurately perceive the degree to which the variables were related?

If the variables are related in the sample, are the variables related in the population?

Is the sample a random sample of the population?

Even if the sample is a random sample of the population, is the sample large enough—and the relationship strong enough—that we can be confident that the relationship really occurs in the population?

If the variables are related, did the predictor variable cause changes in the criterion?

Is it possible that the "criterion" variable caused changes in the predictor variable? In other words, is our "cause" really the effect?

Do we know which variable came first?

Do we have data that suggest to us which came first? For example, high school records might provide information about self-esteem before being victimized. If there is no difference between victims' and nonvictims' self-esteem before the attack, we would be more confident that the attacks came before the lowered self-esteem.

Can we logically rule out the possibility that one variable preceded the other? For example, if height and being a victim were correlated, we can make a good case that the person's height was established before he or she was attacked. (Posture might be affected, but we would rely on accurate measurement to correct for this.)

Is it possible that a third variable could be responsible for the relationship? That is, neither variable may directly influence (cause) the other. Instead, the two variables might be statistically related because they are both effects of some other variable. For example, increases in assaults and ice cream consumption may both be consequences of heat.

Were all other variables kept constant or randomized? (This only happens in experimental designs.)

Does the researcher know what the potential third variables are? If so, the researcher may be able to statistically control for those variables. However, it is virtually impossible to know and measure every potential third variable.

DESCRIPTION FOR PREDICTION'S SAKE

Psychologists also like descriptive methods because knowing what *is* happening helps us predict what *will* happen. In the case of suicide, for example, psychologists discovered that certain signals (giving away precious possessions, abrupt changes in personality) were associated with suicide. Consequently, psychologists now realize that people sending out those signals are more likely to attempt suicide than people not behaving that way.

WHY WE NEED SCIENCE TO DESCRIBE BEHAVIOR

Certainly, describing behavior is an important goal of psychology. But do we need to use scientific methods to describe what's all around us? Yes! Intuition alone cannot achieve all four steps necessary to accurately describe behavior:

1. Objectively measure variables.
2. Keep track of these measurements.
3. Use these measurements to accurately determine the degree to which variables are related.
4. Accurately infer that the observed pattern of results reflects what typically happens (see Figure 12-2).

Indeed, intuition alone fails at each of these steps. Thus, as you will soon see, we need science to measure variables, keep track of those measurements, determine the degree to which variables are related, and to accurately infer the extent to which the observed pattern of results reflects what typically happens.

WE NEED SCIENTIFIC MEASUREMENT

We need scientific methods to accurately measure the variables we want to measure. As you saw in Chapter 3, reliable and valid measurement of psychological variables is not automatic. If you are to observe psychological variables in a systematic, objective, and unbiased way, you must use scientific methods. Imagine

---

• **FIGURE 12-2** •

STEPS INVOLVED IN DETERMINING THAT THERE REALLY IS A RELATIONSHIP BETWEEN TWO VARIABLES

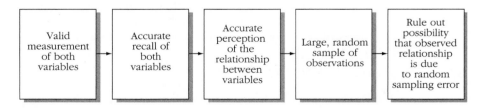

Note: People who draw conclusions based on their own personal experience could be making mistakes at every single one of these stages.

Do you know anyone who executes all 5 steps correctly?
Probably not. Indeed, even some scientific studies fail to execute all 5 steps correctly.

using intuition to measure a person's level of motivation, intelligence, or some other psychological variable!

WE NEED SYSTEMATIC, SCIENTIFIC RECORD-KEEPING

Even if you could intuitively get accurate measurements of psychological variables, you could not rely on your memory to keep track of your observations. Your memory can fool you, especially when it comes to estimating how often things occur. For example, our memories may fool us into believing that more people die from plane crashes than actually do and that more words start with "r" than have "r" as their third letter (Myers, 1999). Therefore, if you are to describe behavior accurately, you need to record your observations systematically so that your conclusions are not biased by memory's selectivity.

WE NEED OBJECTIVE WAYS TO DETERMINE IF VARIABLES ARE RELATED

Obviously, if you're poor at keeping track of observations of one variable, you are going to be even worse at keeping track of two variables—plus the relationship between them. Therefore, you cannot rely on your judgment to determine whether two things are related.

People are so eager to see relationships that they sometimes "see" variables as being related, even when those variables are not related. In several experiments on illusory correlation (Chapman & Chapman, 1967; Ward & Jenkins, 1965), researchers showed participants some data that did not follow any pattern and that did not indicate any relationship among variables. Remarkably, participants usually "found" patterns in these patternless data and "found" relationships (**illusory correlations**) between the unrelated variables.

Out of the lab, we know that people "see" systematic patterns in the stock market, even though the stock market behaves in an essentially random fashion (Shefrin & Statman, 1986). Similarly, many people believe that the interview is an invaluable selection device, even though research shows that interviews have virtually no validity (Schultz & Schultz, 1990; Dawes, 1994).

Even when there is a relationship between two variables, the relationship people "see" between two variables may be exactly opposite of the relationship that exists. For example, basketball players and coaches swear (both literally and figuratively) that if a player makes a shot, that player will be more likely to make the next shot. However, as Gilovich, Vallone, and Tversky (1985) have discovered, a shooter is less likely to make the next shot if he has made the previous shot. Similarly, many people are aware of the famed "*Sports Illustrated* jinx"— the "fact" that a team or person on the cover of *Sports Illustrated* will perform worse from then on. The belief in the "jinx" is so strong that many fans hate to see their favorite team on the magazine's cover. But fans needn't fear—the truth is that players and teams tend to do better after appearing on the cover of *Sports Illustrated*.

Of course, sports fans are not the only ones to misperceive relationships. Many bosses and parents swear that rewarding people doesn't work while punishing them does, even though research shows that rewards are more effective than punishments. Many students swear that cramming for exams is more effective than studying consistently, even though research contradicts this claim. In short, because people may misperceive the relationship between variables, we need to do research to determine the real relationship between variables.

WE NEED SCIENTIFIC METHODS TO GENERALIZE FROM EXPERIENCE

Even if you accurately describe your own experience, how can you generalize the results of that experience? After all, your experience is based on a limited and small sample of behavior.

One problem with small samples is that they may cause you to overlook a real relationship. Thus, it's not surprising that one man wrote to "Dear Abby" to inform her that lung cancer and smoking were not related: He knew many smokers and none had lung cancer.

Another problem with small samples is that the relationship that exists in the sample may not reflect what typically happens in the population. Thus, our experiences may represent the exception rather than the rule. That is, the relationship you observe may simply be due to a coincidence. For example, if we go by some people's experiences, playing the lottery is a financially profitable thing to do.

As you have seen, even if you accurately observe a pattern in your experiences, you must take one additional step—determining whether that pattern is simply a coincidence. But how can you intuitively determine the likelihood that a pattern of results is due to a coincidence?

To discount the role of coincidence, you need to do two things. First, you need to have a reasonably large and random sample of behavior. Second, you need to use probability theory to determine the likelihood that your results are due to random error. Thus, even if you were an intuitive statistician, you would still face one big question: What's to say that your experience is a large, random sample of behavior? Your experience may be a small and biased sample of behavior. Results from such biased samples are apt to be wrong. For example, several years ago, George Bush beat Michael Dukakis by one of the biggest margins in the history of U. S. presidential elections. However, right up to election eve, some ardent Dukakis supporters thought that Dukakis would beat George Bush. Why? Because everybody they knew was voting for Dukakis.

In summary, generalizations based on personal experience are often wrong. These informal generalizations are error prone because they (1) are based on small or biased samples and (2) are based on the assumption that what happens in one's experience happens in all cases. To avoid these problems, researchers who make generalizations about how people typically act or think (1) study a large, random sample and then (2) use statistics to determine how likely it is that the pattern observed in the sample holds in the population.

CONCLUSIONS ABOUT THE NEED FOR DESCRIPTIVE RESEARCH

As you can see, we need descriptive research if we are to accurately describe and predict what people think, feel, or do. Fortunately, descriptive research is relatively easy to do. To describe how two variables are related, you need to get a representative sample of behavior, accurately measure both variables, and then objectively assess the association between those variables. The bottom line in doing descriptive research is getting accurate measurements from a representative sample.

The key to getting a representative sample is to get a large and random sample. But how can you get accurate measurements from a large and random sample?

SOURCES OF DATA

In the next few sections, we'll look at several ways to get measurements. We'll start by examining ways of making use of data that have already been collected, then we'll move to collecting our own data.

DATA YOU PREVIOUSLY COLLECTED

One possible source of data for descriptive research is data that you have already collected. For example, you may have done an experiment looking at the effects of time pressure on performance on a verbal task. At the time you did the study, you may not have cared about the age, gender, personality type, or other personal characteristics of your participants. For testing your experimental hypothesis (that the treatment had an effect), these individual difference variables were irrelevant. However, like saving money for a rainy day, you collected this information anyway.

After the experiment is over, you might want to go back and look for relationships between these "irrelevant" variables and task performance. This kind of research is called **ex post facto research:** research done after the fact.

External Validity

Suppose your ex post facto research revealed that women did better than men on the verbal task. Although this finding is interesting, you should be careful about generalizing your results. Unless the males and females in your study are a random sample drawn from the entire population of males and females, you cannot say that females do better at this verbal task than males do. Your effect may simply be due to sampling males of average intelligence and females of above average intelligence. This sampling bias could easily occur, especially if your school was one that had higher admissions standards for women than for men. (Some schools did this when they switched from being all-women colleges to coeducational institutions.)

You could have a bit more confidence that your results were not due to sampling error if you had also included a mathematical task and found that although the women did better than the men on the verbal task, men did better on the mathematical task. If, in this case, your results are due to sampling error, they aren't due to simply having sampled women who are above average in intelligence. Instead, your sampling error would have to be due to something rather strange such as sampling women who were better than the average woman in verbal ability and who were worse than the average woman in mathematical ability. Although such a sampling bias is still possible, it is not as likely as having merely sampled women who are above average in intelligence. Therefore, with this pattern of results, you would be a little more confident that your results were not due to sampling error.

Construct Validity

Even if you could show that your results are not due to sampling error, you could not automatically conclude that women had greater verbal ability than men. To make this claim, you would have to show that your measure was a valid measure of verbal ability and that the measure was just as valid for men as it was for women. That is, you would have to show that your measure wasn't biased against men (for example, using vocabulary terms relating primarily to different colors, women's fashions, and ballet).

Internal Validity

Through careful random sampling and choice of measures, you might be able to claim that women had better verbal ability than men. However, you could not say why women had superior verbal ability. As you'll recall, correlational methods are not useful for inferring causality. Therefore, you could not say whether the difference in men's and women's verbal ability was due to inborn differences between men and women or due to differences in how men and women are socialized.

Conclusions About Ex Post Facto Research

In summary, ex post facto research takes advantage of data you have already collected. Therefore, the quantity and quality of ex post facto research depends on the quantity and quality of data you collect during the original study. The more information you collect about your participants' personal characteristics, the more ex post facto hypotheses you can examine. The more valid your measures, the more construct validity your conclusions will have. The more representative your sample of participants, the more external validity your results will have. Therefore, if you are doing a study, and there's any possibility that you will do ex post facto research, you should prepare for that possibility by using a random sample of participants and/or collecting a lot of data about each participant's personal characteristics.

ARCHIVAL DATA

Rather than use data that you have collected, you can use **archival data:** data that someone else has already collected. Basically, there are two kinds of archival data—coded data and uncoded data.

Collected and Coded Data

Coded data are data that have been collected and tabulated by others. Market researchers, news organizations, behavioral scientists, and government research-ers are all collecting and tabulating data. How much data? To give you some idea, more than 5,000 Americans are surveyed every day—and surveys are just one way that these researchers collect data.

If you can get access to archival research, you can often look at data that you could never have collected yourself. Unfortunately, many of these data you never would have wanted to collect because they were collected and coded in a way that is inappropriate for your research problem.

Collected but Uncoded Data

If you are willing to code data yourself, but you do not want to collect your own data, you can use the second kind of archival data—data that have been recorded, but are uncoded. You can find a large amount and a large variety of such data. For example, records of behavior include letters to the editor, tran-scripts of congressional hearings, videotapes of television talk shows, baseball statistics, comments made on Internet discussion groups, and ads in the per-sonal columns for a dating partner.

The primary advantage of using records of behavior is that the basic data have already been collected for you. All you have to do is code them—and you can code them as best suits your needs.

Content Analysis: Objectively Coding the Uncoded   The disadvantage of this kind of data is that you have to code them. That is, you have to convert these videotapes or transcripts into a form that you can meaningfully and objectively analyze. To succeed at this task, use **content analysis.**

Content analysis has been used to categorize a wide range of free re-sponses—from determining whether a threatening letter is really from a terror-ist to determining whether someone's response to an ambiguous picture shows that they have a high need for achievement. In content analysis, you code be-havior according to whether it belongs to a certain category (aggressive, sexist, superstitious, etc.).

To successfully use content analysis, you must first carefully define your coding categories. To define these categories, you should do a review of the re-search to find out how others have coded those categories. If you can't borrow or adapt one of their coding schemes, you might decide to do a ministudy just to get an idea of the types of behavior you will be coding. Seeing the types of behavior you will be coding should help you choose and define the categories you will use to code the data.

After you have defined your categories, you should provide examples of behavior that would fit into each of your categories. Then, train your raters to use these categories.

The primary aim in content analysis is to define your categories as objectively as possible. Some researchers define their categories so objectively that all the coder has to do is count the number of times certain words come up. For example, to get an indication of America's mood, a researcher might count the number of times words like "war," "fight," and so on appear in *The New York Times*. These word-counting schemes are so easy to use that even a computer can do them. In fact, researchers have invented a computer program that can tell genuine suicide notes from fake ones (Stone, Dunphy, Smith, & Ogilvie, 1966). Thus, objective coding can be simple and valid.

Is Objective Coding Valid?   Unfortunately, objective criteria are not always so valid. To get totally objective criteria, you often have to ignore the context—yet the meaning of behavior often depends on the context. For example, you might use the number of times the word "war" appears in the paper as a measure of how eager we are for war. This method would be objective, but what if the newspaper was merely reporting wars in other countries? Or, what if the newspaper was full of editorials urging us to "avoid war," no matter what the cost? In that case, our measure would be objective, but invalid.

Indeed, context is so important that completely objective scoring criteria of certain variables is virtually impossible. For example, whether a remark is sarcastic, humorous, or sexist may depend more on when, where, and how the statement is made than on what is said. However, despite the difficulties of objectively and accurately coding archival data, researchers often have successfully developed highly objective ways of coding archival data.

An Example of Archival Research

To get a clearer picture of both the advantages and disadvantages of archival research, suppose that you wanted to know if people were more superstitious when they were worried about the economy. As your measure of concern about the economy, you use government statistics on unemployment. As your measure of how superstitious people are, you have the computer count the number of key words such as "magic," "superstition," and "voodoo" that appear in local newspapers and then divide this number by the total number of words in the newspaper. This would give you the percentage of superstitious words in local newspapers.

Internal Validity

Once you had your measures of both economic concern and of superstitiousness, you would correlate the two. Suppose you found that the higher the unemployment rate is, the more superstitious words were used in the newspaper. Because you have done a correlational study, you cannot say why the two variables are related. That is, you do not know whether:

1. The economy caused people to become superstitious.
2. Superstitious beliefs caused the downfall of the economy.
3. Some other factor (bad weather ruining crops) is responsible for both an increase in superstitious beliefs and a decline in the economy.

Construct Validity

In addition to the internal validity problems that you have any time you use correlational data, you have several construct validity problems specific to archival data. You are using measures of a construct, not because they are the best, but because they are the only measures that someone else bothered to collect. Although you are using unemployment records as an index of how insecure people felt about the economy, you would have preferred to ask people how they felt about the economy. To the degree that the relationship between how many people were unemployed and how people felt about the economy is questionable, your measure's construct validity is questionable.

Even if there is a strong relationship between unemployment and concerns about the economy, your measure may still lack construct validity because it may not accurately assess unemployment. It may have poor construct validity because of **instrumentation bias**: changes in scores due to changes in the measuring instrument. In this case, instrumentation bias would occur if the criteria for who is considered unemployed changed over time. Sometimes, this change in criteria is planned and is formally announced. For example, the government may change the definition from "being unemployed" to "being unemployed and showing documentation that he or she looks for three jobs every week." Other times, the change may not be announced. For instance, computerization and unemployment compensation make current unemployment statistics more complete than they were in the early 1900s. Or, because the people who would collect unemployment statistics—social workers and other government workers—are sometimes laid off during hard economic times, unemployment statistics might be less complete during periods of high unemployment. Or, more sinisterly, politicians may distort unemployment data to make things seem better than they are.

Like the construct validity of your measure of unemployment, the construct validity of your measure of superstition is questionable. Is the number of times superstitious terms are mentioned in newspapers a good index of superstition? Perhaps these articles sell papers, and major newspapers only stoop to using these articles when sales are very low. It would probably be better to have results of some nationwide survey that questioned people directly about their superstitious beliefs. However, your measure has one advantage over the poll—it is **nonreactive**: Collecting it does not change participants' behavior.

External Validity

Because you can collect so much data so easily, your results should have good external validity. In some cases, your results may apply to millions of people because you have data from millions of people. For example, you can easily get unemployment statistics for the entire United States. Furthermore, because you can collect data for a period of years rather than for just the immediate present, you should be able to generalize your results across time.

The Limits of Aggregate Data

Gaining access to group data (for instance, the unemployment rate for the entire United States for 1931) is convenient and may aid external validity. However, as psychologists, we are interested in what individuals do. Therefore, we want individual data. Consequently, even if we find that there is a correlation between unemployment for the nation as a whole and superstition for the nation as a whole, we are still troubled because we do not know which *individuals* are superstitious. Are the individuals who are unemployed the ones who are superstitious? Or, are the superstitious ones the people whose friends have been laid off? Or, do the rich become superstitious? With aggregate data, we can't say.

Conclusions About Archival Research

By using archival data, you can gain access to a great deal of data that you did not have to collect. Having access to these data may allow you to test hypotheses you would otherwise be unable or unwilling to test. Furthermore, because these data often summarize the behavior of thousands of people, your results may have impressive external validity.

Unfortunately, relying on others to collect data has its drawbacks. You may find that others used measures that have less construct validity than the measures you would have used. You may find that others did not collect the data as carefully and as consistently as you would have. You may find that you have data about groups, but no data about individuals. You will almost always find that the data were collected by people who were not asking the question you want to answer. As a result of these problems with archival data, you may decide that the best way to get data that will answer your questions is to collect your own data.

OBSERVATION

One way to collect your own data is through observation. As the name implies, observation involves watching (observing) behavior.

Observation can be incorporated into many research methods. For example, an experimenter manipulating a drug could use observation to collect the dependent measure. Thus, a researcher studying rats, rather than having a machine record each rat's behavior, might himself observe and categorize each rat's behavior. Similarly, a researcher studying humans, rather than collecting the dependent measure by having a participant fill out a questionnaire, may herself observe and categorize each participant's behavior.

Observation is also of interest for its own sake. Describing behavior is a vital concern of every field of psychology. Developmental psychologists use observation to describe child–parent interactions, social psychologists to describe cults, clinical psychologists to describe abnormal behavior, counseling psychologists to describe human sexual behavior, and comparative psychologists to describe animal behavior.

Types of Observational Research

Observation can be done in the laboratory. However, many researchers want to observe real-world behavior. Basically, there are two approaches to observing real-world behavior: naturalistic observation and participant observation.

In **naturalistic observation,** you try to observe the participants in a natural setting *unobtrusively:* without letting them know you are observing them. Often, naturalistic observation involves keeping your distance—both physically and psychologically.

In **participant observation,** on the other hand, you actively interact with your participants. In a sense, you become "one of them."

Both types of observation can lead to ethical problems. Naturalistic observation may involve spying on your participants. Often, it involves collecting data without participants' informed consent. Participant observation, on the other hand, may involve infiltrating a group and collecting data without the participants' informed consent. Because the participant observer has more effect on participants, most people consider participant observation to present more ethical problems than naturalistic observation.

But which method provides more valid data? Not everyone agrees on the answer to this question. Advocates of participant observation claim that you get more "inside" information by using participant observation.

Advocates of naturalistic observation counter that the information you get through participant observation may be tainted. As a participant, you are in a position to influence (bias) what your participants do. Furthermore, as an active participant, you may be unable to sit back and record behavior as it occurs. Instead, you may have to rely on your (faulty) memory of what happened.

Problems With Observation

Whether you use participant or naturalistic observation, you face two major problems. First, if participants know they are being watched, they may not behave in their normal, characteristic way. Second, even if participants act "natural," you may fail to objectively record their behavior. That is, your personality and motives may affect what things you ignore and how you interpret those things you do pay attention to.

Effects of the Observer on the Observed   There are two basic strategies you can use to minimize the degree to which you change behavior by observing it.

First, you can observe participants unobtrusively (without letting them know you are observing them). For example, you might want to observe participants through a one-way mirror.

If you cannot be unobtrusive, you may try the second strategy—become less noticeable. There are two basic strategies for becoming less noticeable. First, you can observe participants from a distance, hoping that they will ignore you. Second, you can let participants become familiar with you, hoping that they will eventually get used to you. Once participants are used to you, they may forget that you are there and revert back to normal behavior.

Difficulties in Objectively Coding Behavior   While you are observing behavior, you will also be recording it. As was the case with archival data, one problem with observation is that different observers may code the same behavior differently. As was the case with archival data, the solution is to develop a coding scheme. You need to:

1. Define your categories in terms of specific target behaviors.
2. Develop a check sheet to mark off each time a target behavior is exhibited.
3. Train and motivate raters to use your check sheet.

Training and motivating your raters are even more important in observational research than in archival research for two reasons. First, in observational research, the rater not only codes the data, but also collects the data. Second, in observational research, there usually are no permanent records of data. Because there are no permanent records, unmotivated or disorganized raters do not get a second chance to rate a behavior they missed: There is no instant replay. Furthermore, because there are no permanent records, you cannot check or correct a rater's work.

We have shown you why training is so important. But how do you train people? Training observers should involve at least three steps. First, you should spell out what each category means, giving both a definition of each category and some examples of behaviors that belong and do not belong in each category. Second, you should have raters judge several videotapes, then you should tell them why their ratings are right or wrong. Third, you should continue the training until each rater is at least 90% accurate.

Conclusions About Observation

In conclusion, observation can be a powerful technique for finding out what people do. However, observers may let you down by changing the behavior of the individuals they are observing or by letting their biases affect what they record.

TESTS

If you do not want to rely on observers, you may decide to use tests. Tests are especially useful if you want to measure ability, knowledge, or personality variables. For instance, you might correlate scores on an extroversion test with scores on a happiness test.

External Validity

As was the case with ex post facto research, the external validity of a study that uses tests depends on the representativeness of the sample. You cannot generalize your results to a population unless you have a random sample of that population. Therefore, you cannot say that women score more extroverted on an extroversion test than men unless you have a random sample of all men and women. Similarly, you cannot say that extroverts are happier than introverts unless you have a random sample of all introverts and extroverts.

Internal Validity

As is the case with all correlational research, if you find a relationship between test scores, that relationship is not necessarily a causal relationship. For example, if extroverts are happier than introverts, we don't know whether extroversion causes happiness, happiness causes extroversion, or some other factor (supportive parents, social skills, etc.) causes both extroversion and happiness.

The fact that correlation does not prove causation is important to keep in mind. Without an understanding of this concept, you may mistake circumstantial evidence for proof. For example, certain authors try to show a genetic basis for some characteristic (career preferences, schizophrenia, introversion, etc.) by showing that identical twins score similarly on a test of a particular trait. However, identical twins could be similar on the trait because they share a similar environment or because they have influenced one another.

Conclusions About Using Tests

By using tests, you can take advantage of measures that other people have spent years developing. As a result, construct validity is usually less of a problem than if you had devised your own measures. Furthermore, tests are often easier to use than other measures. Because of these advantages, tests are often used in experimental as well as nonexperimental research. However, when tests are used in nonexperimental research, this research has the same weaknesses as other correlational research: It doesn't allow you to establish causality and the generalizability of your results will only be as good as the representativeness of your sample (to compare different descriptive designs, see Table 12-3).

DESCRIBING DATA FROM CORRELATIONAL STUDIES

Once you have coded your data, you want to compile and summarize them. You want to know what your data "look like."

You may start by describing participants' scores on key variables. Often, describing those scores will involve calculating the average score and an index of

• **TABLE 12-3** •

COMPARING DIFFERENT CORRELATIONAL METHODS

VALIDITY	EX POST FACTO	ARCHIVAL	OBSERVATION	TESTS
Internal validity	Poor	Poor	Poor	Poor
Construct validity	Fair	Fair to poor	Fair to poor	Fair to good
Objective—Avoids observer bias	Good	May be good	May be poor	Good
Nonreactive—Avoids subject bias	Often a problem	Often good	Can be poor	Reactive—But steps taken to control for subject biases
Operational definition fits definition of construct	Fair to good	Often poor	Fair	Good
External validity				
Ease of getting a large, representative sample	Depends on original study	May be easy	Difficult	May be easy

the degree to which scores vary from the mean or from each other. For example, you might report that the mean score on the personality test was 78 and the *range* (the highest score minus the lowest score) was 50. Or, instead of reporting the range, you might report the standard deviation (an index of the extent to which individual scores differ from the mean). Thus, you might say that the mean was 78 and the standard deviation was 10.

Usually, however, you will want to do more than describe how participants scored on individual measures. Instead, you will want to know how participants' scores on one measure relate to their scores on some other measure. To describe these relationships between variables, you should graph your data and compute correlation coefficients.

GRAPHING DATA

Usually, one of the first things you should do after collecting your scores is to graph them. Start by labeling the *x*-axis (the line that goes straight across the page) with the name of your predictor variable. More specifically, go a few spaces below the bottom of the graph and then write the name of your predictor variable. Next, label the other axis, the *y*-axis (the vertical line on the left side of the graph), with the name of your criterion/dependent variable. Then, plot each observation.

• **FIGURE 12-3** •

THE BEGINNING OF A SCATTERPLOT

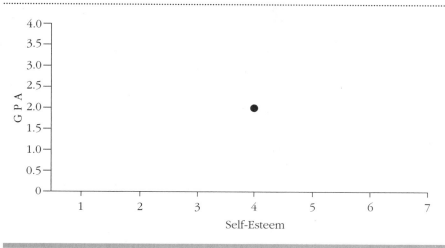

For example, suppose we were looking at the relationship between self-esteem and grade-point average (GPA). More specifically, suppose we were trying to see whether we could use self-esteem to predict grade-point average. Figure 12-3 shows the beginning of such a graph. As you can see, we have plotted the score of our first participant, a student who has a score of 4 on the self-esteem scale and a 2.0 GPA. As we plot more and more of our data, the points will be scattered throughout the graph. Not surprisingly then, our graph will be called a **scatterplot.** There are four basic relationships that the scatterplot could reveal.

A Positive Relationship

First, the scatterplot could reveal a pattern like the one shown in Figure 12-4. The figure indicates that the higher one's self-esteem, the higher one's grade-point average is likely to be. Put another way, the lower one's self-esteem, the lower one's grade-point average will be. This kind of relationship indicates a positive correlation between the variables. One common example of a **positive correlation** is the relationship between height and weight: The taller you are, the more you are likely to weigh.

A Negative Relationship

Second, the scatterplot could reveal a pattern like the one shown in Figure 12-5, where the higher one's self-esteem, the lower one's grade-point average. Put another way, the less self-esteem one has, the higher one's grade-point average.

• FIGURE 12-4 •

A Scatterplot Revealing a Positive Correlation

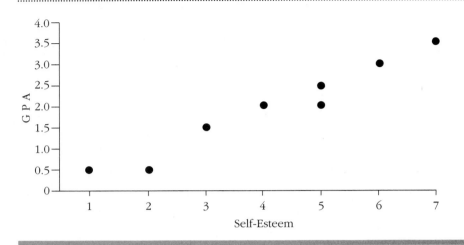

This relationship indicates a **negative correlation** between the variables. Many variables are negatively (*inversely*) related. One common example of a negative correlation is the relationship between exercise and weight: The more you exercise, the less you tend to weigh.

• FIGURE 12-5 •

A Scatterplot Revealing a Negative Correlation

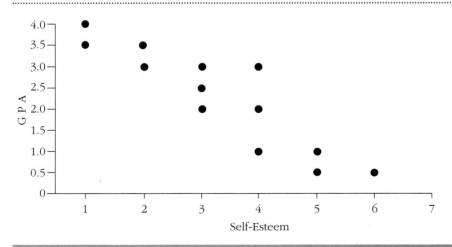

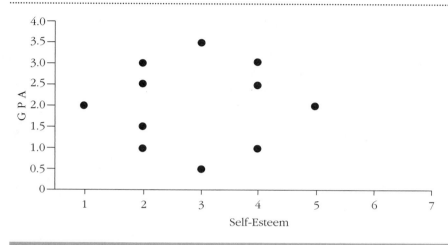

• FIGURE 12-6 •

A SCATTERPLOT REVEALING A ZERO CORRELATION

No Relationship

Third, the scatterplot might reveal that there is no relationship between self-esteem and grade-point average. This pattern, which reflects a **zero correlation** between the two variables, is depicted in Figure 12-6.

A Nonlinear Relationship

Fourth, you could have a nonlinear relationship between self-esteem and grade-point average (GPA). As you can see from Figure 12-7, in a complex, nonlinear relationship, the relationship between self-esteem and GPA may vary, depending on the level of the variables. Thus, in the low ranges of self-esteem, self-esteem may be positively correlated with GPA, but in the high ranges, self-esteem may be negatively correlated with GPA. Such a pattern could emerge in any situation in which a low amount of a variable could be too little, a medium amount of a variable could be just right, and a high level of the variable could be too much. For example, with too little motivation, performance may be poor; with a moderate amount of motivation, performance could be good; and with too much motivation, performance might be poor.

CORRELATION COEFFICIENTS

Although a graph gives a good picture of your data, you may want to summarize your data with a single number: a **correlation coefficient.** The kind of

• **FIGURE 12-7** •

A SCATTERPLOT REVEALING A NONLINEAR RELATIONSHIP

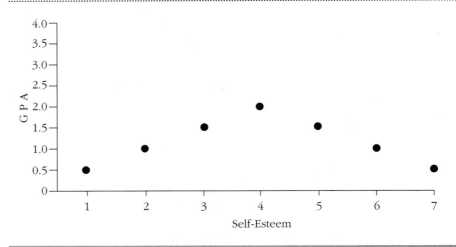

correlation coefficient you use will depend on the nature of your data (see Table 12-4). Probably, you will use the most commonly calculated correlation coefficient—the Pearson r.

The Pearson r, like most correlation coefficients, ranges from −1 to +1. More importantly, like all correlation coefficients, the Pearson r summarizes the relationship described in a scatterplot with a single number.

As you will soon see, the Pearson r should be consistent with the data in your scatterplot. If your scatterplot indicates a positive correlation between the two variables, your correlation coefficient should also be positive. If the scatterplot indicates that your variables are not related, then your correlation coefficient should be near zero. Finally, if your variables are negatively correlated (inversely related), then the correlation coefficient should be negative.

The Logic Behind the Pearson r

If you want to compute a Pearson r, you can use a computer, a calculator, or the formula described in Appendix F. At this point, however, we do not want you to focus on how to compute the Pearson r. Instead, we want you to focus on understanding the logic behind the Pearson r. Basically, there are two ways to think about that logic: (1) in terms of the definition of correlation and (2) in terms of a scatterplot of the data.

As you know, the correlation coefficient is a number that describes the relationship between two variables. If the variables are positively correlated, then, when one variable is above average, the other is usually above average. In addition, when one variable is below average, the other tends to be below average. If

• TABLE 12-4 •

DIFFERENT KINDS OF CORRELATION COEFFICIENTS

In reading the literature, you may come across correlation coefficients other than the Pearson r. In addition, you may be called on to compute correlations other than the Pearson r. This table should help you understand the distinctions among these different coefficients.

NAME OF COEFFICIENT	LEVEL OF MEASUREMENT REQUIRED	EXAMPLE	DATA ENTERED
Pearson r	Both variables must be at least interval.	Height with weight	Actual scores
Point biserial	One variable is interval, the other nominal.	Weight with gender	Actual scores for the interval variable, 0 or 1 for the nominal variable
Spearman's rho	Ordinal data	High school rank with military rank	Ranks
Phi coefficient	Nominal data	Race with learning style	0's and 1's. Zero if the participant is not a member of a category, 1 if the participant is a member of that category.

Although this table focuses on the differences between these correlation coefficients, these coefficients share commonalities. For example, all of them yield coefficient between −1 (a perfect negative correlation) and +1 (a perfect positive correlation). Furthermore, as Cohen and Cohen (1983, pp. 38–39) point out, the Pearson r, the point biserial, the phi coefficient, and Spearman's rho can all be computed using the same formula. That formula is the formula for the Pearson r (see Appendix F). The difference in calculating them comes from what data are entered into that formula (see right-hand column of the table). For example, if you were calculating Spearman's rho, you would not enter participants' actual scores into the formula. Instead, you would convert those scores to ranks and then enter those ranks into the formula.

the variables are negatively correlated, the reverse happens: When one is above average, the other is usually below average.

To see how the Pearson r mathematically matches that description, suppose that we have the scores of 20 students on two variables—how well they learned definitions of certain words and how well they pick up on nonverbal cues.[1] To see if student learning is correlated with sensitivity to nonverbal cues, we convert those scores in the following way. If a student scores below the average in terms of recalling the definitions, the student gets a negative score on learning

---

[1]For a published example of a Pearson r calculated on these two variables see Bernieri, F. J. (1990). Interpersonal sensitivity in teaching interactions. *Personality and Social Psychology Bulletin, 17,* 98–103.

(a score of −1). If the student recalls more than the average student in the study, then the participant gets a positive score (a score of +1). We do the same thing for the students' scores on reading nonverbal cues: A score of −1 indicates the participant is below average, a score of +1 indicates the participant is above average.

Next, we multiply each participant's learning score times his or her sensitivity score. For example, if someone is above average in both learning and sensitivity to nonverbal cues, we multiply +1 × +1. If someone is below average in both definitions learned and nonverbal sensitivity, we multiply −1 × −1. In both cases, the product of the multiplication will be +1. However, if someone is below average in definitions learned (−1) and above average in nonverbal sensitivity (+1), the product for that person would be −1. Note that we could consider each of these products as an association score: When for a given individual, definitions learned and nonverbal sensitivity are positively associated, the product is +1; when for a given individual, definitions learned and nonverbal sensitivity are negatively associated, the product is −1. By adding up the results of these 20 multiplications (the 20 association scores) and then dividing this total by 20 (the number of research participants), we will end up with a number between −1 and +1.

This number will be positive if there is a positive correlation between amount learned and nonverbal sensitivity. That is, people who are high in both amount learned and nonverbal sensitivity will contribute +1's (because +1 × +1 = +1), as will people who are low in both amount learned and nonverbal sensitivity (because −1 × −1 = +1). Therefore, if the variables are positively correlated for most people, most of these products (their association scores) will be +1's. Consequently, the total of everyone's association scores will be positive. Furthermore, the greater the percentage of people who are either high on both variables or low on both variables, the closer the average of all these scores will be to +1. Thus, if we had the data below, the average of these scores (our "correlation index") would be 1.00.

	Sensitivity to Nonverbal Cues	
WORDS LEARNED	BELOW AVERAGE (−1)	ABOVE AVERAGE (+1)
Below Average (−1)	10	0
Above Average (+1)	0	10

Conversely, if participants who are above average on one variable (+1) are usually below average on the other variable (−1), we will end up with a negative correlation. We would end up with a negative correlation because most scores would be −1 (because +1 × −1 = −1). Indeed, if everyone who is high on one variable is low on the other, as is the case in the data below, everyone's score would be −1. Consequently, the average of these scores (our "correlation index") would be −1.

Sensitivity to Nonverbal Cues

WORDS LEARNED	BELOW AVERAGE (–1)	ABOVE AVERAGE (+1)
Below Average (–1)	0	10
Above Average (+1)	10	0

Finally, consider the case below in which there is no relationship between the variables.

Sensitivity to Nonverbal Cues

WORDS LEARNED	BELOW AVERAGE (–1)	ABOVE AVERAGE (+1)
Below Average (–1)	5	5
Above Average (+1)	5	5

In this case, half (five) of the participants who are above the average in non-verbal sensitivity are also above average in amount learned. These five participants are contributing +1's. However, half (five) of the participants who are above average in nonverbal sensitivity are below average on amount learned. These five participants are contributing –1's. In other words, half the participants who are above average in nonverbal sensitivity are contributing a +1 (because +1 $\times$ +1 = +1), whereas half are contributing a –1 (because +1 $\times$ –1 = –1). The five +1's and the five –1's cancel each other out, summing to 0.

What about the 10 participants who score below average in nonverbal sensitivity? Half (five) of the participants who are below average on nonverbal sensitivity are also below average on amount learned. Those five contribute +1's. However, half (five) of the participants who are below the average on nonverbal sensitivity are above average on amount learned. Those five contribute –1's. In short, five of the participants who are below average in nonverbal sensitivity are each contributing a +1 (because –1 $\times$ –1 = +1), whereas five are each contributing a –1 (because –1 $\times$ +1 = –1). The +1's and the –1's cancel each other out, summing to 0.

Let's review the situation in which the two variables are unrelated in our sample of 20 participants. In that case, the sum of the contributions of the 10 participants who scored above average in nonverbal sensitivity was zero. The sum of the contributions of the 10 participants who scored below average in nonverbal sensitivity was also zero. Consequently, our coefficient will end up being 0.

Mathematically, the Pearson r is a little more complicated than what we have described. However, if you understand our description, you understand the basic logic behind the Pearson r.

We have discussed how the Pearson r produces a number that is consistent with a verbal description of the data. Now, we will show how the Pearson r produces a number that is consistent with a graph of the data.

Pearson r could be estimated by drawing a straight line through the points in your scatterplot. If the line slopes upward, the correlation is positive. If the line slopes upward and every single point in your scatterplot fits on that line, you have a perfect correlation of +1.00. Usually, however, there are points that are not on the line. For each point that is not on the line, the correlation coefficient is made closer to zero by subtracting a value from the coefficient. The farther the point is from the line, the larger the value that is subtracted. Once all the misfit points are accounted for, you end up with the correlation coefficient.

If the line that fits the points slopes downward, the correlation is negative. If every single point fits on that line, you have a perfect negative relationship; thus, your correlation coefficient equals –1.00. However, perfect negative relationships are rare. Therefore, many points probably are not on that line. For each point that is not on the line, the correlation coefficient is made closer to zero by adding a value to the coefficient. The farther the point is from the line, the larger the value that is added. After all the misfit points are accounted for, you end up with the correlation coefficient.

As we have just discussed, the correlation coefficient describes how well the points on the scatterplot fit a straight *line*. That is, the correlation coefficient describes the nature of the *linear* relationship between your variables. But what if the relationship between your variables is not described by a straight line, but by some other type of curved line? For example, suppose the relationship between your variables was *nonlinear*, like the nonlinear relationship depicted in Figure 12-7.

The fact that the correlation coefficient examines only the degree to which variables are linearly related is not as severe a drawback as you may think. Why? First, totally nonlinear relationships among variables are rare. Second, even if you encounter a nonlinear relationship, you would know that you had such a relationship by looking at your scatterplot. That is, you would notice that the points on your scatterplot fit a nonlinear pattern, such as a u-shaped curve.

Squaring the Pearson *r:* The Coefficient of Determination

The sign of the correlation coefficient tells you the kind of relationship you have (positive or negative). However, you may want to know not only what kind of relationship you have, but how strong this relationship is.

The strength of the relationship is revealed by how far the correlation coefficient is from zero. The farther the correlation coefficient is from zero, the stronger the relationship. In other words, the strength of the relationship has nothing to do with the sign of the correlation coefficient. To better understand this point, you must realize that to find out how closely two variables are associated, many scientists square the correlation coefficient. If they had a +.8 correlation, they would get +.64—just as they would if they had a correlation of –.8. Squaring the correlation coefficient not only gets rid of the sign, but yields the **coefficient of determination.**

The coefficient of determination tells the degree to which knowing a participant's score on one variable helps you know (determine) the participant's score on the other variable. The coefficient of determination can range from 0 (knowing participants' scores on one variable is absolutely no help in guessing what their scores on the other variable will be) to +1.00 (if you know participants' scores on one variable, you will know exactly what their scores are on the other variable).

So, if you have a correlation of +1, you have a coefficient of determination of 1.00 (because +1 × +1 = 1.00). This means that if you know one variable, you can predict the other one with 100% accuracy. The same would be true if you had a correlation coefficient of −1 (because −1 × −1 = 1.00).

Essentially, the coefficient of determination tells you the amount of scatter in your scatterplot. If the coefficient of determination is near 1, there is little scatter in your scatterplot. If you draw a straight line through your scatterplot, most of the points would be on or near that line. If, on the other hand, the coefficient of determination is near zero, there is a lot of scatter in your scatterplot. If you draw a straight line through the scatterplot of that data, very few of the points will be close to your straight line.[2]

SUMMARY OF DESCRIBING CORRELATIONAL DATA

You now have two ways to summarize data from a correlational study. First, you can visually summarize your data with a scatterplot. Second, you can use two numbers that summarize the essence of your scatterplot: the correlation coefficient and the coefficient of determination.

MAKING INFERENCES FROM CORRELATIONAL DATA

Occasionally, you may only want to know what happened in a particular sample. If you only want to describe the relationship between self-esteem and grade-point average in one particular class during one particular term, scatterplots and correlation coefficients are all you need.

Most of the time, however, you are interested in generalizing the results obtained in a limited sample to a larger population. You know what happened in this sample, but you want to know what would happen in other samples.

To generalize your results to a larger population, you first need a random sample of that population. If you want to generalize results based on observing a few students in your class to all the students in your class, then the participants you examine should be a random sample of class members. If you want to generalize the results based on measuring a few people to all Americans, you

---

[2]There are two cases where you can have a zero correlation and yet draw a line through all the points: (1) when the line goes straight up, or (2) when the line goes straight across. However, you could only draw such lines if there was no variability in scores for one of the variables. In our self-esteem and grade-point average example, you would have a zero correlation if all your participants scored a 5 on the self-esteem measure (producing a line of points going straight up) as well as if all your participants had a 3.0 grade-point average (producing a line of points going straight across your scatterplot).

must have measured a random sample of Americans. If you want to generalize results based on observing two rats for an hour a day to all the times that the rats are awake, then the times you observe the rats must be a random sample from the rats' waking hours.[3]

Of course, random samples are not perfect samples. Even with a random sample, you are going to have sampling error. For example, suppose you studied a random sample of sophomores at your school and found a correlation of −.30 between grade-point average and self-esteem. Clearly, you found a negative correlation in your random sample. However, you can't say that if you had studied all sophomores at your school, you would have obtained a negative correlation coefficient.

To convince yourself that what happens in a sample does not necessarily mirror what happens in the population, you could conduct the following study. Find three people. Have each person flip a coin one time. Record each person's height and the number of "heads" (0 or 1) the person flipped. Do this for 10 different "samples" of three individuals. Then graph each sample individually. Some of your graphs will reveal a positive correlation, even though there really is no relationship between a person's height and how many "heads" he will flip. Similarly, some of your graphs will reveal a negative correlation, even though there really is no relationship between a person's height and how many "heads" they will flip. Thus, the relationship observed in a sample may not hold in the population.

ANALYSES BASED ON CORRELATION COEFFICIENTS

As you have seen, even if the two variables are not related, they will appear to be related in some samples. That is, *a relationship that exists in a particular sample may not exist in the population.* Consequently, if you observe a relationship, you will want to know if you have observed a real pattern that is characteristic of the population—or if the relationship you observe is just a mirage caused by random sampling error alone.

Fortunately, there is a way to determine whether what is true of your sample is true of the population: Use inferential statistics. Inferential statistics will allow you to determine how likely it is that the relationship you saw in your sample could be due to random error. Specifically, inferential statistics allow you to ask the question: "If there is no relationship between these variables in the population, how likely is it that I would get a correlation coefficient this large in this particular random sample?"

---

[3]Many researchers do not randomly sample from a population, but they still generalize their results. How? They argue that their sample could be considered a random sample of an unknown population. Then, they use statistics to determine whether the results are due to sampling error or whether the results hold in the larger population. If their results are statistically significant, they argue the results hold in this unspecified population. (The "unspecified population" might be "participants I would study at my institution.") Although you might see some problems with generalizing to an unspecified population, researchers argue that significant results indicate that if they repeated the study, they would probably obtain the same pattern of results.

If the answer to this question is "not very likely," then you can be relatively confident that the correlation coefficient in the population is not zero. Therefore, you would conclude that the variables are related. To use proper terminology, you would conclude that your correlation coefficient is significantly different from zero (see Figure 12-8).

Precisely which test you use to determine if a correlation coefficient is statistically different from zero depends on which kind of correlation coefficient you have (see Table 12-4). However, regardless of which test you use, the test will determine how unlikely it is that your sample's correlation coefficient came from a population where the coefficient between those variables was zero. To determine if your correlation coefficient comes from such a population, the test will take advantage of two facts about samples from populations where the correlation is zero.

First, if the population correlation coefficient is zero, the sample's correlation coefficient will tend to be near zero. Consequently, *the farther the sample's correlation coefficient is from zero, the less likely the population coefficient is zero.* Thus, a correlation coefficient of .8 is more likely to be significantly different from zero than a correlation coefficient of .2.

Second, if the variables are not related in the population, the larger the sample, the closer its correlation coefficient will be to zero. Therefore, *the larger the sample, the more likely that a nonzero correlation coefficient indicates that the variables really are related in the population.* Thus, a correlation coefficient of .30 is more likely to be significantly different from zero if it comes from a sample of 100 observations than if it comes from a sample of 10 observations.

Thus far, we have discussed the most popular statistical test involving correlation coefficients: Determining if the coefficient is significantly different from zero. Significant results allow the researcher to conclude that the two variables are related. However, you are not limited to asking if the correlation between your variables is different from zero. By using other types of statistical tests, you could also ask the following questions:

• FIGURE 12-8 •

Necessary Conditions for
Producing Generalizable Results

Random sample of a population	+	Statistical significance	=	Results that generalize to that population

1. Is the correlation between self-esteem and GPA higher among women than among men?

2. Is the correlation between self-esteem and GPA greater than the correlation between impulsivity and GPA?

3. In the population, is the correlation between self-esteem and GPA fairly strong? For example, rather than asking if the correlation is different from zero, you might ask if it is greater than .60.

Although these questions are interesting, showing you how to answer them is beyond the scope of this book. If you wish to ask these kinds of questions, consult Cohen & Cohen's (1983) book on correlational analysis.

ANALYSES NOT INVOLVING CORRELATION COEFFICIENTS

You do not have to use correlation coefficients to analyze data from correlational research. That is, if you are trying to see whether there is a relationship between gender and scores on a self-esteem test, you do not have to calculate the correlation between gender and self-esteem scores. Instead, you could get the average (mean) self-esteem score for men and the average (mean) score for women. You could then compare the differences between means, using a *t*-test or an analysis of variance (ANOVA).

The t-Test

Doing a *t*-test to see if the differences between the group means is greater than zero is very similar to seeing if the correlation between the variables is greater than zero (see Box 12-1). In both cases, a significant result would indicate that, for the population from which you randomly sampled, gender and self-esteem are related.

Doing a Median Split to Set up the *t*-Test   To do a *t*-test, you need two groups. But what if you don't have two groups? For example, what if you have a bunch of people's self-esteem scores and their grade-point averages? In that case, you could create two groups by dividing your participants into high scorers or low scorers depending on their test score. Then, you would compare the GPA of high scorers (participants with above-average self-esteem) with the GPA for low scorers (participants with below-average self-esteem). The procedure of dividing participants into two groups depending on whether they scored above or below the **median** (the middle score) is called a **median split.**

Doing a median split and then conducting a *t*-test is a common way of analyzing correlational data. You will frequently encounter such analyses in published articles.

The Case Against Doing a Median Split   However, rather than doing a median split and then computing a *t*-test, you should simply determine whether the correlation is statistically significant (see Table 12-5). Why? Because using a

• BOX 12-1 •

THE SIMILARITIES BETWEEN A T-TEST, AN F-TEST, AND A TEST TO DETERMINE IF A CORRELATION COEFFICIENT IS SIGNIFICANTLY ABOVE ZERO

When you only have two groups, doing a t-test, an F-test, and an analysis of correlation is the same. Thus, in the simple experiment, the three procedures are quite similar. In all three cases, you are seeing if there is a relationship between the treatment and the dependent variable. That is, in all three cases you would be looking to see if the treatment and the dependent variable covary.

The only difference is in how you measure the extent to which the treatment and dependent measure covary. In the t-test, you use the difference between means of the two groups as your measure of covariation; in the F-test, you use a variance between means of the two groups as the measure of covariation; and in testing the significance of a correlation, you use the correlation between the treatment and the dependent variable as the measure of covariation. Consequently, regardless of which technique you use to analyze the results of a simple experiment, significant results will allow you to make cause–effect statements. Furthermore, regardless of which technique you use to analyze the results of a correlational study, significant results will not allow you to make cause–effect statements.

To show you that the three analyses are the same, we have done these three analyses of the same data. The results of these analyses are:

T-TEST ANALYSIS

Group:	N	Mean
Group 1	59	9.429
Group 2	58	8.938

Standard error of the difference = .565

$$t = \frac{9.429 - 8.938}{.565} = \frac{.491}{.565} = .87$$

df:	t-Value	Probability*
115	.87	.3859

*Probability (often abbreviated as p) refers to the chances of finding a relationship in your sample that is as large as the one you found if the two variables are really unrelated in the population. Thus, the smaller p is, the less likely it is that the relationship observed in your sample is just a fluke. In other words, the smaller p is, the more likely it is that the variables really are related in the population.

ANALYSIS OF VARIANCE

SOURCE	DF	SUM OF SQUARES	MS	F VALUE	PROBA-BILITY
Treatment	1	4.155	4.155	.758	.3859
Error	115	630.768	5.485		

CORRELATIONAL ANALYSIS

COUNT:	R:	Probability
117	.081	.3859**

**Note that the probability (p) value is exactly the same, no matter what the analysis. That is, our p is .3859 whether we do a t-test, F-test, or a correlational analysis. The t that led to this probability value is 0.87, just as it was when we calculated the t between group means. However, since we were testing a correlation, we used a different formula. Applying that formula (which you can find in Appendix F) to our data, led to the following computations:

$$t = \frac{.081 * \text{square root of } 115}{\text{square root of } .993} = \frac{.868}{.996} = 0.87$$

t-test based on median splits reduces your ability to find relationships (Cohen, 1990). You are less able to find relationships because you have less information with which to work. Put another way, you have less ability to find differences

• **TABLE 12-5** •

ADVANTAGES AND DISADVANTAGES OF USING A *T*-TEST BASED ON A MEDIAN SPLIT TO ANALYZE RESULTS OF CORRELATIONAL RESEARCH

ADVANTAGES	DISADVANTAGES
The *t*-test is a convenient way to analyze data.	Before you can do a *t*-test you may have to recode scores based on median split.
	"Convenience" of the *t*-test may cost you power. You have less power than correlational analysis because you are not using actual scores. Instead, you are using much less detailed information. That is, instead of using a participant's actual score, you are recording only whether the score is in the top half or bottom half of distribution.
Familiar, conventional way to analyze data.	Because it is a conventional way to analyze *experimental* data, some may *falsely* conclude that significant results indicate that one variable causes the other.

because you are recoding data in a way that hides differences. That is, instead of using participants' specific scores, you are using the median split to lump together all the participants who scored above average. Thus, a participant who scores 1 point above average gets the same score—as far as the analysis is concerned—as a participant who scores 50 points above average. Similarly, you are lumping together everyone who scored below average, despite the differences in their scores. In a sense, you are deliberately throwing away information about participants' actual scores.

Not surprisingly, some researchers object to this waste. For example, Cohen (1990) argues that researchers should not lose power and information by "mutilating" variables. Instead of "throwing away" the information regarding a participant's specific score by doing a median split, Cohen believes that researchers should do correlational analyses that use participants' actual scores.

Analysis of Variance (ANOVA)

Rather than breaking your participants down into two groups (top half, bottom half), you might decide to break your participants into three or more groups. You could then compare the different groups by doing an analysis of variance (ANOVA).

With a multiple-group ANOVA, your analysis includes more detail about participants' scores than if you just did a *t*-test. For instance, rather than coding that a participant scored in the top half, you might code that the participant scored in the top fourth. Because you have more information about participants' scores, you may have more power (see Table 12-6).

As you may realize, this argument for using a multiple-group ANOVA is not particularly strong. If you want more information about participants' scores, you would be better off using a correlational analysis that will allow you to use everyone's precise score. So why use ANOVA instead of a correlational analysis? Usually, because you want to do one of two types of analyses.[4]

First, you might use an ANOVA to determine if the relationship between your variables is nonlinear. For example, an ANOVA might find that the group with moderately high self-esteem got better grades than the groups with very high or very low self-esteem.

Second, you could use ANOVA to examine the relationships among three or more variables. That is, you could look at two or more predictors at one time. For example, with ANOVA, you could look at how self-esteem and gender together predict grade-point average. Specifically, an ANOVA would allow you to compare the grade-point averages of: (1) women with low self-esteem,

---

• **TABLE 12-6** •

TESTS THAT USE MORE INFORMATION HAVE MORE POWER

The more detailed the information we put into an analysis, the more information we get out. Put another way, the finer the distinctions made between participants in the data plugged into the analysis, the finer the distinctions that will be pulled out. Thus, the *t*-test that only looks to see if the participant is above or below the median has very little power. An *F*-test that divides scores into low, medium, or high would have more power. An *F*-test that divided scores into very low, low, medium, high, and very high would have even more power. However, the analysis that would have the most power is the one that would use each individual's actual score—the test to see if the correlation coefficient is above zero.

STATISTICAL TEST	AMOUNT OF INFORMATION OBTAINED FROM INDIVIDUAL SCORES	POWER OF THE TEST
Two-group *t*-test	Very little—only look to see whether the score is above or below the median.	Very low
Three-level ANOVA	Little—look to see whether the score was low, medium, or high.	Low
Test for significance of the correlation	Much—use actual scores.	High

---

[4]Although these analyses could also be done using sophisticated correlational analyses, most researchers are more familiar with how to do these analyses using ANOVA.

• TABLE 12-7 •

ADVANTAGES AND DISADVANTAGES OF USING ANOVA
TO ANALYZE THE RESULTS FROM A CORRELATIONAL STUDY

ADVANTAGES	DISADVANTAGES
Allows you to perform a variety of analyses fairly easily.	You have less power than testing the statistical correlation coefficient because ANOVA doesn't use actual scores. Instead, it uses much less detailed information. For example, if you use a two-level ANOVA, you are only recording whether the score is in the top half or the bottom half of the distribution.
1. You can do more than look at the simple relationships between two variables. Instead, you can look at the relationship among three or more variables at once. 2. You could determine whether the relationship between variables is nonlinear.	
You can minimize the problem of losing detail by dividing scores into more groups. That is, you are not limited to just comparing the top half vs. the bottom half. Instead, you could compare the top fifth, vs. the second fifth, vs. the third fifth, vs. the fourth fifth, vs. the bottom fifth. Because you would be entering more detailed information into your analysis, you would have reasonable power.	However, you still do not have as much detail and power as if you had used participants' actual scores.
Convenient way to analyze data.	It may not be so convenient if you have an unequal number of participants in each group. In that case, you would have what is called an unbalanced ANOVA. Many computer programs can't accurately compute statistics for an unbalanced ANOVA.
Familiar way to analyze data.	Because it is a conventional way to analyze experimental data, people may falsely conclude that significant results mean that one variable causes changes in the other.

---

(2) women with high self-esteem, (3) men with low self-esteem, and (4) men with high self-esteem. By doing this analysis, you might find that high self-esteem is related to high grade-point averages for women, but that high self-esteem is related to low grade-point averages for men. (See Table 12-7 for a summary of the advantages and disadvantages of using ANOVA to analyze the results of correlational research.)

INTERPRETING SIGNIFICANT RESULTS

No matter what statistical tests you use, remember what a statistically significant result means (see Table 12-8). It means that the relationship you observed is prob-

• TABLE 12-8 •

THE DIFFERENT MEANINGS OF STATISTICAL SIGNIFICANCE

QUESTION ASKED ABOUT A STATISTICALLY SIGNIFICANT RESULT	CORRELATIONAL STUDY	EXPERIMENT
Are the variables related?	Yes	Yes
Do we know whether the predictor variable caused changes in the criterion variable?	No. We do not know which variable changed first. (Our "cause" may really be an effect.)	Yes. The experimental design guaranteed that the treatment came before the change in the dependent variable.
	In addition, changes in both the predictor variable and the criterion variable could be due to some third factor.	The experimental design also guaranteed that the treatment was the only systematic difference between treatment conditions. Thus, the relationship between the variables could not be due to some third factor.

ably not due to random error. Instead, the relationship you observed in the sample probably also exists in the population from which you randomly sampled.

Significant Results Do Not Allow You to Make Cause–Effect Statements

Keep in mind that statistical significance does not mean that the variables are causally related. As we said earlier in this chapter, to infer causality, you must do much more than establish that your variables are statistically related. For example, to infer that self-esteem caused low grade-point averages, you would have to show not only that self-esteem and grade-point average are related, but also that:

1. The low self-esteem students had low self-esteem before they got low grades, whereas the high self-esteem students had high self-esteem before they got high grades.
2. No other differences between your high and low self-esteem individuals could account for this relationship (there were no differences between groups in terms of parental encouragement, IQ, ability to delay gratification, etc.).

Significant Results May Be Type 1 Errors

As we've seen, significant results in correlational research do not mean that changes in one variable caused a change in the other. At best, significant results only mean that both variables are correlated. However, all too often, significant results don't even prove that two variables are correlated.

To understand why they don't, suppose that a researcher is trying to determine whether two variables are correlated. The researcher uses the conventional $p < .05$ significance level. Suppose further that, in reality, the variables aren't correlated. What are the chances that the researcher will obtain significant results? You might be tempted to say "about 5%." You would be correct—if the researcher had only conducted one statistical test. However, because correlational data are often easy to obtain, some researchers correlate hundreds of variables with hundreds of other variables. If they do hundreds of statistical tests, many of these tests will be significant by chance alone.[5] Put another way, if the researcher uses a $p = .05$ level of significance and does 100 tests, the researcher should expect to obtain 5 significant results, even if none of the variables were related. The moral: If you aren't careful, disciplined, and ethical, you will "find" relationships that are really statistical errors. Therefore, we urge you to resist temptation to have the computer calculate every possible correlation coefficient and then pick out the ones that are significant. Instead, decide which correlation coefficients relate to your hypotheses and test to see if those correlation coefficients differ from zero.

If you are doing more than one statistical test, there are at least two things you can do to avoid mistaking a coincidence for a correlation. One option is to make your significance level more conservative than the traditional $p = .05$ level. Instead, use a $p < .01$ or even a $p < .001$ level. A second option is to repeat your study with another random sample of participants to see if the correlation coefficients that were significantly different from zero with the first group are still significant with a second group.

INTERPRETING NULL RESULTS

If your results are not statistically significant, it means that you failed to show that any correlations you observed were due to anything other than random error. It does not mean your variables are not related—it only means that you have failed to establish that they were related. If there is a relationship, why would you fail to find it? There are four main reasons.

First, you may not have had enough observations. Even if you observed a fairly strong relationship in your sample, it's hard to say that your observed relationship is not a fluke unless your sample is big enough.

Second, your variables may be related in a nonlinear way. Having a nonlinear relationship is a problem because your statistical tests are most sensitive to detecting straight line (linear) relationships. Fortunately, you can easily tell whether you have a nonlinear relationship by looking at a scatterplot of your data. If you can draw a straight line through the points of your scatterplot, you don't have a nonlinear relationship. If, on the other hand, a graph of your data

---

[5]Unless they use a sophisticated multivariate statistical test that controls for making multiple comparisons.

revealed a nonlinear relationship, such as a definite u-shaped curve, you would know that a conventional correlation coefficient underestimates the strength of the relationship between your variables.

Third, you may have failed to find a significant relationship because of **restriction of range:** You sampled from a population in which everyone is similar on one of the variables. Restriction of range is a problem because, to say that both variables vary together, you need both variables to vary. If both variables don't vary, you end up with correlations of zero. For example, suppose you were looking at the relationship between IQ and grade-point average, but everyone in your sample scored between 125 and 130 on the IQ test. In this case, the correlation between IQ and grade-point average would be pretty small. Consequently, the correlation might not be significant; however, if your participants' IQs had ranged from 85 to 185, you would probably have a sizable and statistically significant correlation between IQ and GPA.

Fourth, you may fail to find a significant relationship because you had insensitive measures. An insensitive measure, by preventing you from seeing how one variable varies, also prevents you from seeing how that variable covaries with another variable.

Concluding Remarks

In this chapter, you have been introduced to the logic of descriptive research. However, you have not learned about the most common method of doing descriptive research: asking questions. Therefore, the next chapter is devoted to showing you how to conduct surveys.

Summary

1. Descriptive research allows you to describe behavior accurately. The key to descriptive research is to measure and record your variables accurately using a representative sample.

2. Although descriptive research cannot tell you whether one variable causes changes in another, it may suggest cause–effect (causal) hypotheses that you could test in an experiment.

3. Description is an important goal of science. Description also paves the way for prediction.

4. Ex post facto research uses data that you collected before you came up with your hypothesis.

5. Archival research uses data collected and sometimes coded by someone else.

6. With both ex post facto and archival research, data may not have been measured, collected, or coded in a way appropriate for testing your hypothesis.

7. Observational methods are used in both correlational and experimental research.

8. In both naturalistic observation and participant observation, the researcher must be careful that the observer does not affect the observed and that coding is objective.

9. Using pre-existing, validated tests in your correlational research may increase the construct validity of your study. As with all research, the external validity of testing research depends on the representativeness of your sample.

10. Using a scatterplot to graph your correlational data will tell you the direction of the relationship (positive or negative) and give you an idea of the strength of the relationship.

11. Correlational coefficients give you one number that represents the direction of the relationship (positive or negative). These numbers range from -1.00 to $+1.00$.

12. A positive correlation between two variables indicates that if a participant scores high on one of the variables, the participant will probably also score high on the other.

13. A negative correlation between two variables indicates that if a participant scores high on one of the variables, the participant will probably score low on the other variable.

14. A zero correlation between two variables indicates there is no relationship between how a participant scores on one variable and how that participant will score on another variable. The further a correlation coefficient is away from zero, the stronger the relationship. Thus, a $-.4$ correlation is stronger than a $+.3$.

15. By squaring the correlation coefficient, you get the coefficient of determination, which tells you the strength of the relationship between two variables. The coefficient of determination can range from 0 (no relationship) to 1 (perfect relationship). Note that both a $+1$ and a -1 correlation coefficient would translate into a coefficient of determination of 1.

16. If your results are based on a random sample, you may want to use inferential statistics to analyze your data.

17. Remember, statistical significance only means that your results can be generalized to the population from which you randomly sampled. Statistical significance does *not* mean that you have found a cause–effect relationship.

18. Beware of doing too many tests of significance. Remember, if you do 100 tests and use a .05 level of significance, 5 of those tests might be significant by chance alone.

19. You may obtain null results even though your variables are related. Common culprits are insufficient number of observations, nonlinear relationships, restriction of range, and insensitive measures.

Key Terms

ex post facto research: when a researcher goes back, after the research has been completed, looking to test hypotheses that were not formulated prior to the beginning of the study. (p. 435)

archival data: data from existing records and public archives. (p. 437)

instrumentation bias: apparent changes in participants that are really due to changes in the measuring instrument. A real problem in archival research because the way records are kept may change over time. For example, unemployment statistics are difficult to interpret because the government has changed its definition of unemployment. (p. 439)

content analysis: a way to categorize a wide range of open-ended (unrestricted) responses. Content analysis schemes have been used to code the frequency of violence on certain television shows and are often used to code archival data. (p. 437)

nonreactive: measurements that are taken without changing the participant's behavior. Researchers in both participant and naturalistic observation try to be nonreactive, but both often fail. (p. 439)

participant observation: an observation procedure in which the observer participates with those being observed. The observer becomes "one of them." Some worry that, in participant observation, the observer may change the behavior of the people being observed. (p. 441)

naturalistic observation: a technique of observing events as they occur in their natural setting—without participating in those events. Advocates believe that naturalistic observation has more external validity than lab observation. In addition, they hope that naturalistic observation will be less reactive than either participant observation or lab observation. (p. 441)

scatterplot: a graph made by plotting the scores of individuals on two variables (for instance, plotting each participant's height and weight). By looking at this graph, you should get an idea of what kind of correlation (positive, negative, zero) exists between the two variables. (p. 445)

positive correlation: a relationship between two variables in which the two variables tend to change in the same direction—when one increases, the other tends to increase. (For example, height and weight: The taller one is, the more one tends to weigh; the less tall one is, the less one tends to weigh.) (p. 445)

negative correlation: a relationship between two variables in which the two variables tend to change in opposite directions—when one is high or increases, the other tends to be low or decrease. An example of this inverse relationship between two variables would be happiness and depression: The more happy one is, the less depressed one is. (p. 446)

zero correlation: when there doesn't appear to be a linear relationship between two variables. For practical purposes, any correlation between −.10 and +.10 may be considered so small as to be nonexistent. (p. 447)

illusory correlation: when there is really no relationship (a zero correlation) between two variables, but people perceive that the variables are related. (p. 433)

correlation coefficient: a number that can vary from −1.00 to +1.00. The sign of the correlation coefficient indicates the kind of relationship that exists between two variables (positive or negative). The correlation coefficient also indicates the strength of the relationship. Specifically, the closer the correlation coefficient is to 0, the weaker the relationship; the farther from 0 (regardless of the sign), the stronger the relationship. (p. 447)

coefficient of determination: the square of the correlation coefficient; tells the degree to which knowing one variable helps to know another. Can range from 0 (knowing a participant's score on one variable tells you absolutely nothing about the participant's score on the second variable) to 1.00 (knowing a participant's score on one variable tells you exactly what the participant's score on the second variable was). Note that the sign of the correlation coefficient (whether it is positive or negative) has absolutely no effect on the coefficient of determination. (p. 452)

restriction of range: to observe a sizable correlation between two variables, both must be allowed to vary widely (if one variable does not vary, the variables cannot vary together). Occasionally, investigators fail to find a relationship between variables because they study one or both variables only over a highly restricted range. For example, saying that weight has nothing to do with playing offensive line in the NFL on the basis of your finding that great offensive tackles do not weigh much more than poor offensive tackles. Problem: You only compared people who ranged in weight from 315 to 330 pounds. (p. 463)

median: if you arrange all the scores from lowest to highest, the middle score will be the median. (p. 456)

median split: the procedure of dividing participants into two groups ("highs" and "lows") based on whether they score above or below the median. (p. 456)

Exercises

1. Steinberg and Dornbusch (1991) find that there is a positive correlation between class-cutting and hours of week adolescents work. In addition, they find a negative correlation between grade-point average and number of hours worked.
   a. Describe, in your own words, what the relationship is between class-cutting and hours of week that adolescents work.
   b. Describe, in your own words, what the relationship is between grade-point average and hours of week that adolescents work.
   c. What conclusions can you draw about the *effects* of work? Why?
   d. If you had been analyzing their data, what analysis would you use? Why?

2. Steinberg and Dornbusch (1991) also reported that the correlation between hours of employment and interest in school was statistically significant. Specifically, they reported that $r(3,989) = -.06$, $p < .001$. [Note that the $r(3,989)$ means that they had 3,989 participants in their study.] Interpret this finding.

3. Brown (1991) found that a measure of aerobic fitness correlated +.28 with a self-report measure of how much people exercised. He also found that the measure of aerobic fitness correlated −.41 with resting heart rate. Is resting heart rate or self-report of exercise more closely related to the aerobic fitness measure?

4. In the same study, gender was coded as 1 = male, 2 = female. The correlation between gender and aerobic fitness was −.58, which was statistically significant at the $p < .01$ level.

   a. In this study, were men or women more fit?

   b. What would the correlation have been if gender had been coded as 1 = female and 2 = male?

   c. From the information we have given you, can you conclude that one gender tends to be more aerobically fit than the other? Why or why not?

5. Suppose you wanted to see if men differed from women in terms of the self-descriptions they put in personal ads. How would you get your sample of ads? How would you code your ads? That is, what would your content analysis scheme look like?

6. A physician looked at 26 instances of crib death in a certain town. The physician found that some of these deaths were due to parents suffocating their children. As a result, the physician concluded that most crib deaths in this country are not due to problems in brain development, but to parental abuse and neglect. What problems do you have with the physician's conclusions?

7. A study began by looking at how a sample of 5-year-olds were treated by their parents. Then, 36 years later, when the participants were 41-year-olds, the study looked the degree to which these individuals were socially accomplished. The investigators then looked at the relationship between childrearing practices when the child was 5 and how socially accomplished the person was at 41 (Franz, McClelland, & Weinberger, 1991). They concluded that having a warm and affectionate father or mother was significantly associated with "adult social accomplishment."

   a. What advantages does this prospective study have over a study that asks 41-year-olds to reflect back on their childhood?

   b. How would you measure "adult social accomplishment"?

   c. How would you measure "parental warmth"? Why?

   d. Assume, for the moment, that the study clearly established a relationship between parenting practices and adult social accomplishment. Could we then conclude that parenting practices account for (cause) adult social accomplishment? Why or why not?

   e. Imagine that they had failed to find a significant relationship between the variables of "adult social accomplishment" and parental warmth. What might have caused their results to fail to reach significance?

CHAPTER 13

SURVEY RESEARCH

A fool can ask more questions in an hour than a wise man can answer in seven years.
—ENGLISH PROVERB

....

OVERVIEW

If you want to know *why* people do what they do or think what they think, you should use an *experimental* design. If, on the other hand, you want to know *what* people are thinking, feeling, or doing, you should use a *nonexperimental* design, such as a **survey research** design.

Successful survey design means meeting three objectives. First, you must know what your research hypotheses are so that you know what you want to measure. Second, your questionnaire, test, or interview must accurately measure the thoughts, feelings, or behaviors that you want to measure. Third, you must be able to generalize your results to a certain, specific group. This group, called a **population,** could be anything from all U.S. citizens to all employees at a local company.

Because there are three main aspects of survey research, there are three main ways that survey research can go wrong.

First, survey research may be flawed because the researchers did not know what they wanted to find out. If you don't know what you're looking for, you probably won't find it. Instead, you will probably be overwhelmed by irrelevant data.

Second, survey research may be flawed because the questionnaire, test, or interview measure has poor construct validity. The measure will have poor construct validity if:

1. The questions are unclear or confusing.
2. The questions demand knowledge that participants don't have.
3. The questions, by hinting at the answer the researcher wants to hear, invite participants to lie.
4. The researcher misinterprets or miscodes participants' answers.

Third, survey research may have little external validity because the people who were questioned did not represent the target population. For example, the results of a survey research study will have little external validity if the sample of people surveyed was biased or too small.

As you can see, there is more to survey research than asking a bunch of people some questions that you jotted down. Instead, survey research, like all research, requires careful planning. You have to determine whether the survey design is appropriate for your research problem. Then, you have to decide what questions you are going to ask, why you are going to ask those questions, to whom you are going to ask those questions, how you are going to ask those questions, and how you are going to analyze the answers to those questions.

Unfortunately, few people engage in the careful planning necessary to conduct sound survey research. Consequently, even though the survey is by far the most commonly used research method, it is also the most commonly abused. By reading this chapter, you can become one of the relatively few people who conduct sound and ethical survey research.

QUESTIONS TO ASK BEFORE DOING SURVEY RESEARCH

The most obvious—but least asked—question in survey research is, "Should I use a survey?" To answer this question correctly, you must answer these five questions:

1. What are my hypotheses?
2. Will I know what to do with the data after the survey is finished?
3. Am I interested only in describing and predicting behavior, or do I want to make cause–effect statements?
4. Can I trust respondents' answers?
5. Do my results apply only to those people who responded to the survey, or do the results apply to a larger group?

WHAT IS YOUR HYPOTHESIS?

The first question to ask is, "What is my hypothesis?" Since good research begins with a good hypothesis, you might think that everyone would ask this question. Unfortunately, many inexperienced researchers try to write their survey questions without clear research questions. What they haven't learned is that you can't ask pertinent questions if you don't know what you want to ask. Therefore, before you write your first survey question, make sure you have a clear hypothesis on which to base your questions.

Do Your Questions Relate to Your Hypothesis?

Having a hypothesis doesn't do you much good unless you are disciplined enough to focus your questions on that hypothesis. In other words, if you don't focus your questions on your hypothesis, you may end up with an overwhelming amount of data—and still not find out what you wanted to know. For example, the now-defunct United States Football League (USFL) spent millions of dollars on surveys to find out whether they should be a spring or fall league. Despite the fact that it took more than 20 books to summarize the survey results, the surveys did not answer the research question (*USA Today*, 1984). So don't be seduced by how easy it is to ask a question. Instead, ask questions that address the purpose of your research.

We take two steps to make sure that we ask useful questions. First, we determine what analyses we plan to do *before* we administer the questionnaire. You can do this yourself by constructing a table like Table 13-1, which is the table we used to help develop the survey displayed in Box 13-1. If we don't plan

• **TABLE 13-1** •

TABLE TO DETERMINE VALUE OF INCLUDING QUESTIONS FROM BOX 13-1 IN THE FINAL SURVEY

QUESTION NUMBER	PURPOSE(S) OF QUESTION	PREDICTIONS REGARDING QUESTION	ANALYSES TO TEST PREDICTION
1	1. Qualify 2. See if sample reflects population.	Percent of instructors in sample will be the same as in the population.	Compare percentages of sample at each rank with school's report of percentages of total faculty at each rank.
2–3	1. Find out computer use without using a leading question.	1. Average computer use will be less than 5 hours per week. 2. Computer users will be more sympathetic to students. 3. Male faculty members use computers more than female faculty. 4. Younger faculty will use computers more than older faculty.	1. Compute mean and confidence intervals. 2. Correlate question 3 with the sum of questions 6–11. (Graph data to see if there is a curvilinear relationship.) 3. Correlate this question with question 16. 4. Correlate this question with question 15.
4–5	Engage respondent/aid transition to next section.		
6–11	Scale to measure attitudes toward students.	1. Faculty will have positive attitudes toward students. 2. See predictions made under questions 2–3.	1. Compute average and confidence intervals for question 11 and for sum of scale. See if the mean is significantly above the midpoint. 2. See analyses described under 2–3.
12–16	See if sample reflects population.	Sample will reflect the population.	Compare sample's characteristics against the university's data on faculty.

• **BOX 13-1** •

SAMPLE TELEPHONE SURVEY

Hello, my name is ____. I am conducting a survey for my Research Design Class at Bromo Tech. Your name was drawn as a part of a random sample of university faculty. I would greatly appreciate it if you would answer a few questions about your job and your use of computers. The survey should take only 5 minutes. Will you help me?

1. **What is your position at Bromo Tech?** (read as an open-ended question)

   ____ Instructor

   ____ Assistant Professor

   ____ Associate Professor

   ____ Professor

   ____ Other (If other, terminate interview)

2. **Do you use computers?**

   ____ Yes

   ____ No (put "0" in slot for question 3, and skip to 4)

3. **How many hours a week do you estimate you use computers?** (read as open-ended question)

   ____ (Write hours, then check ✔ the appropriate box. If exact hours are not given, read categories and check appropriate box)

   ____ < 1 hour

   ____ 2–4 hours

   ____ 5–9 hours

   ____ 10–14 hours

   ____ 15–19 hours

   ____ > 20 hours

Please indicate how much you agree or disagree with the following statements. State whether you strongly agree, agree, disagree, strongly disagree, or are undecided.

4. **Computers have made the job of the average professor less stressful.**

   SA   A   U   D   SD

5. **Computers have made the average student's life less stressful.**

   SA   A   U   D   SD

6. **College is stressful for students.**

   SA   A   U   D   SD

7. **Colleges need to spend more time on students' emotional development.**

   SA   A   U   D   SD

8. **Colleges need to spend more time on students' physical development.**

   SA   A   U   D   SD

9. **College students should be allowed to postpone tests when they are sick.**

   SA   A   U   D   SD

10. **College students work hard on their studies.**

    SA   A   U   D   SD

11. **I like college students.**

    SA   A   U   D   SD

(continued)

---

on doing any analyses involving responses to a specific question and the question serves no other purpose, we get rid of that question.

Second, with the remaining questions, we imagine participants responding in a variety of ways. For example, we may graph the results we predict and results that are completely opposite of what we would predict. If we find that no pattern

• BOX 13-1 •
SAMPLE TELEPHONE SURVEY *(continued)*

Demographics

Finally, I have just a few more questions to insure that we get opinions from a variety of people.

12. **How long have you been teaching at Bromo Tech?***

____ (Write years, then check ✔ the appropriate box. If exact years are not given, read categories and check appropriate box)

  ____ 0–4 years

  ____ 5–9 years

  ____ 10–14 years

  ____ 15–19 years

  ____ 20 or more years

13. **What department do you teach in?**

  ____ Anthropology

  ____ Art

  ____ Biology

  ____ Business

  ____ Chemistry

  ____ English

  ____ History

  ____ Math

  ____ Physical Education

  ____ Physics

  ____ Political Science

  ____ Psychology

  ____ Sociology

  ____ Other _____

14. **What is the highest academic degree you have earned?**

  ____ B.A./B.S.

  ____ M.A./M.D.

  ____ Ph.D./Ed.D.

  ____ Other _____

15. **How old are you?**

____ (Write age, then check ✔ the appropriate box. If exact years not given, read categories and check appropriate box)

  ____ < 25

  ____ 26–34

  ____ 35–44

  ____ 45–54

  ____ 55–64

  ____ > 65

  ____ refused

Thank you for your help.

Note: Complete the following after the interview is finished. Do not ask this question.

16. Gender (Don't ask)

  ____ Male

  ____ Female

*Questions 12–15 can be read as open-ended questions.

of answers to a question would give us useful information, we eliminate that question. For example, we may find that, no matter how participants answer the question, it won't disprove any of our hypotheses. Or, if we are doing a survey for an organization, we may find that, no matter how participants answer a certain question, it wouldn't change how that organization runs its business.

Do You Have a Cause–Effect Hypothesis?

If your questions focus on the research hypothesis, your survey will be able to address your research question—if you are trying to describe a group's opinions. In other words, if you want to find out how many people have a certain characteristic or support a certain position, a survey can answer that type of question. For example, a social worker may do a survey to find out what percentage of adolescents in the community have contemplated suicide. Similarly, a politician may do a survey to find out what percentage of the voters in her district support a certain position.

At a more advanced level of description, a researcher may use surveys to develop a detailed profile of certain groups. You might use surveys to develop a list of differences between those who try to commit suicide and those who don't; those who support gun control and those who don't; those who use computers versus those who don't, and so on.

Alternatively, you might want to determine what people's intentions are so that you can predict their behavior. For example, news organizations do surveys to predict how people will vote in an election, and market researchers do surveys to find out what products people plan to buy.

As we have discussed, the survey is a useful tool for finding out what people think. However, the survey is not a useful tool for finding out *why* people do what they do. Like all nonexperimental designs, the survey design does not allow you to establish causality. Therefore, if you have a cause–effect hypothesis, do not use a survey.

To illustrate why you cannot make causal inferences from a survey design, let's imagine that you find that professors are more sympathetic toward students than administrators are. In that case, you cannot say that being an administrator causes people to have less sympathy for students. It could be that professors who didn't like students became administrators. Or, it could be that some other factor (like being bossy), causes one to be an administrator and that factor is also associated with having less sympathy toward students.

Unfortunately, even some students who realize the weaknesses of nonexperimental methods still want to use survey methods to establish causality. They argue that all they have to do to establish causality is ask people why they behaved in a certain manner. The problem: Although respondents can give reasons for their behavior, these reasons may not be accurate. For example, Nisbett and Wilson (1977) demonstrated that if participants are shown a row of television sets, participants will prefer the TV farthest to the right. Yet, when asked why they preferred the TV on the right, nobody says, "I like it because it's on the right."

CAN SELF-REPORT PROVIDE ACCURATE ANSWERS?

Nisbett and Wilson's research illustrates a general problem with questioning people: People's answers may not reflect the truth. There are numerous reasons why people's self-reports may be inaccurate. However, these reasons fit into four general categories:

1. Participants never knew, and never will know, the answer to your question.
2. Participants no longer remember the information needed to correctly answer your question.
3. Participants do not yet know the correct answer to your question.
4. Participants know the correct answer to your question, but they don't give you the correct answer.

Are You Asking People to Tell More Than They Know?

As we have discussed, when you ask people why they did something, they don't know. People do not know why they do everything they do or feel everything they feel. For example, people may not know why they like (or dislike) broccoli, why they call "heads" more often than "tails," why they usually wake up right before their alarm goes off, or why they find some comedians funnier than others. From your own experiences, you can probably think of examples that clearly showed that you did not know everything that every system and cell of your more than 100 billion neuron brain was doing. The bottom line: Although asking people questions about why they behave the way they do is interesting, you can't accept their answers at face value.

Are You Asking More Than Participants Can (Accurately) Remember?

As Nisbett and Wilson's study showed, when people do not know the real cause, they make up a reason—and they believe that reason. Similarly, even though people have forgotten certain facts, they may still think they remember. For example, obese people tend to under-report what they have eaten and students tend to over-report how much they study. Both groups are surprised when they actually record their behavior (Williams & Long, 1983).

Because memory is error-prone, you should be very careful when interpreting responses that place heavy demands on participants' memories. If you aren't skeptical about the meaning of those responses, be assured that your critics will be. Indeed, one of the most commonly heard criticisms of research is that "the results are questionable because they are based on **retrospective self-reports** (participants' statements about what they remembered)."

Are You Asking Participants to Look Into a Crystal Ball?

As bad as people are at remembering the past, they can be even worse about predicting the future. Thus, asking people "What would you do in _____ situation?" may make for interesting conversation, but the answers will often have little to do with what people would actually do if they were put in that situation (Sherman, 1980). For example, most people claim that, if they were in a conformity experiment, they would not conform. Thus, if we relied on what people told us they would do in a certain situation, virtually none of the participants in the classic conformity experiments would conform. In reality, however, 60–80% of participants conform. For example, nearly two-thirds of Milgram's participants went along with an experimenter's orders to give high-intensity shocks to another person (Milgram, 1974).

If Participants Know, Will They Tell?

To this point, we have discussed cases where participants aren't giving you the right answer because they don't know the right answer. However, even when participants know the right answer, they may not share that answer with you because they want to impress you, they want to please you, or they don't want to think about the question.

Social Desirability Bias   Sometimes, participants will give you the answer that will impress you the most. For example, to impress you, they may exaggerate the amount of money they give to charity. In other words, the **social desirability bias** is a problem. Participants are most likely to commit the social desirability bias when the survey is not anonymous and the question is extremely personal ("Have you cheated on your spouse?").

Obeying Demand Characteristics   Sometimes participants will give you the answer they think you want to hear. Their behavior may be very similar to yours when, after having a lousy meal, the server asks you, "Was everything okay?" In such a case, rather than telling the server everything was lousy and ruining his day, you say what you think he wants to hear—"Yes, everything was okay." In technical terms, you are **obeying the demand characteristics** of the situation.

Following Response Sets   Rather than think about what answer you want, participants may not give their answers any serious thought. Instead, they may respond in a certain, set way, regardless of what the question says. Some may "strongly agree" with every statement. In technical terms, they are following a "yea-saying" **response set.** Some may "strongly disagree" with every statement. They would be following a "nay-saying" response set. Others may always choose the "neutral" response—the central tendency response set.

TO WHOM WILL YOUR RESULTS APPLY?

Even if you have a good set of questions that are all focused on your hypotheses, and you can get accurate answers to those questions, your work is probably not done. Usually, you want to generalize your results beyond the people who responded to your survey. For example, you might survey a couple of classes at your university, not because you want to know what the people in those particular classes think, but because you think those classes are a representative sample of your college as a whole. But are they? Unfortunately, they probably aren't.

For example, if you selected a first-year English course because "everybody has to take it," your sample may fail to represent seniors and those first-year students taking remedial writing courses. As you will see, obtaining an unbiased sample is difficult.

Even if you start out with an unbiased sample, by the end of the study your sample may become biased. Why? People often fail or refuse to respond to a questionnaire. In fact, if you do a mail survey, don't be surprised if only 10% of your sample returns the survey. Is this 10% typical of your population? Probably not. It's very likely that these participants feel more strongly about the issue than nonrespondents. Consequently, **nonresponse bias** is one of the most serious threats to the survey design's external validity.

CONCLUSIONS ABOUT THE ADVANTAGES AND DISADVANTAGES OF SURVEY RESEARCH

A survey can be a relatively inexpensive way to get information about people's attitudes, beliefs, and behaviors. With a survey, you can collect a lot of information on a large sample in a short period of time.

Although surveys can be valuable, recognize that they may have poor construct validity and external validity and that they will have poor internal validity. If participants' self-reports are inaccurate, your survey will have poor construct validity. If your sample is biased, your survey will have poor external validity. Finally, no matter what you do, your survey will not allow you to know why something happened. That is, if you want to know what causes a certain effect, don't use a survey design.

THE ADVANTAGES AND DISADVANTAGES OF DIFFERENT SURVEY INSTRUMENTS

If you decide that a survey is the best approach for your research question, then you need to decide what type of survey instrument you are going to use. Basically, you can choose from two types of survey instruments: (1) **questionnaire**-type surveys in which participants read the questions and then write their responses, and (2) interview surveys in which participants hear the questions and speak their responses.

WRITTEN INSTRUMENTS

If you are considering a questionnaire-type survey, you have essentially three options: self-administered questionnaires, investigator-administered questionnaires, and psychological tests. In this section, we will discuss the advantages and disadvantages of these three written instruments.

Self-Administered Questionnaires

A **self-administered questionnaire,** as the name suggests, is filled out by participants in the absence of an investigator. Behavioral scientists, as well as manufacturers, special-interest groups, and magazine publishers, all use self-administered questionnaires. You probably have seen some of these questionnaires in your mail, on the Internet, at restaurant tables, and in magazines.

Self-administered questionnaires have two main advantages. First, self-administered questionnaires are easily distributed to a large number of people. Second, self-administered questionnaires often allow anonymity. Allowing respondents to be anonymous may be important if you want honest answers to highly personal questions.

Using a self-administered questionnaire can be a cheap and easy way to get data. However, there are at least two major drawbacks to this method.

First, surveys that rely on self-administered questionnaires usually have a low return rate. Since the few individuals who return the questionnaire may not be typical of the people you tried to survey, you may have a biased sample. In other words, nonresponse bias is a serious problem with self-administered questionnaires.

Second, because the researcher and the respondent are not interacting, problems with the questionnaire can't be corrected. Thus, if the survey contains an ambiguous question, the researcher can't help the respondent understand the question. For example, suppose we ask people to rate the degree to which they agree with the statement, "College students work hard." One respondent might think this question refers to a job a student might hold down in addition to school. Another respondent might interpret this to mean, "students work hard at their studies." Because respondent and researcher are not interacting, the researcher will have no idea that these two respondents are, in a sense, answering two different questions.

Investigator-Administered Questionnaires

To avoid the problems with the self-administered questionnaire, some researchers use the investigator-administered questionnaire. The investigator-administered questionnaire is filled out in the presence of a researcher.

Investigator-administered questionnaires share many of the advantages of the self-administered questionnaire. With both types of measures, many respondents can be surveyed at the same time. With both types of measures, surveys can be conducted in a variety of locations, including the lab, the street, in class, over the phone, and at respondents' homes.

A major advantage of having an investigator present is that the investigator can clarify questions for the respondent. In addition, the investigator's presence encourages participants to respond. As a result, surveys that use investigator-administered questionnaires have a higher response rate than surveys using self-administered questionnaires.

Unfortunately, the investigator's presence may do more than just increase response rates. The investigator-administered questionnaire may reduce perceived anonymity. Because respondents feel their answers are less anonymous, respondents may be less open and honest.

Psychological Tests: Borrowing From the Best

An extremely refined form of the investigator-administered questionnaire is the psychological test. Whereas questionnaires are often developed in a matter of days or hours, psychological tests are painstakingly developed over months, even decades. Nevertheless, the distinction between questionnaires and tests is sometimes blurred.

One reason there is not always a clear-cut difference between questionnaires and tests is that questionnaires often incorporate questions from psychological tests. For example, in a study of people's concern about body weight, Pliner, Chaiken, and Flett (1990) incorporated two psychological tests into their questionnaire: Garner and Garfinkel's (1979) Eating Attitudes Test (EAT) and Janis and Field's (1959) Feeling of Social Inadequacy Scale.

Even if you do not include a test as part of your questionnaire, try to make your questionnaire as "test-like" as possible. To make your questionnaire as valid as a test, try to follow these six steps:

1. Pretest your questionnaire.

2. Standardize the way you administer the questionnaire.

3. Score answers as objectively as possible. For example, use "objective" items (such as multiple-choice questions) that do not require the person scoring the test to interpret the participant's response. In addition, develop a detailed scoring key for those responses that do require the scorer to interpret responses. Finally, don't let scorers know the identity of the respondent. For example, if the hypothesis is that male respondents will be more aggressive, do not let coders know whether the respondent is male or female.

4. Balance out the effects of response-set biases, such as "yea" saying (always agreeing) and "nay" saying (always disagreeing) by re-asking the same question in a variety of ways. For example, you might ask, "How much do you like the President?" as well as, "How much do you dislike the President?"

5. Make a case for your measure's reliability. For example, resurvey respondents a month later to see if they score similarly both times. Finding a strong positive correlation between the two times of measurement will suggest that scores reflect some stable characteristic rather than random error.

6. Make a case for your measure's validity by correlating it with measures that do not depend on self-report. For example, Steinberg and Dornbusch

(1991) justified using self-reported grade-point average (GPA) rather than actual grade-point average by establishing that previous research had shown that school-reported and self-reported GPA were highly correlated.

Written Instruments: A Summary

To review, an investigator-administered survey is generally better than a self-administered survey because administering the survey gives you higher response rates and more control over how the questionnaire is administered. If you follow our six additional steps to make your questionnaire more like a test, your questionnaire may have construct validity approximating that of a psychological test.

INTERVIEWS

At one level, there is very little difference between the questionnaire and the **interview.** In both cases, the investigator is interested in participants' responses to questions. However, in an interview, rather than having respondents read the questions and write down their responses, the interviewer orally asks respondents a series of questions and also records responses. As subtle as these differences seem to be, they have important consequences.

One important consequence is that interviews are more time consuming than questionnaires. The main reason interviews are more time consuming is because you should not interview more than one person at a time.

Why shouldn't you interview several people at a time in a group interview? If you did interview more than one person at a time, each individual's response would not be independent. Instead, what one participant said might depend on what other participants had already said. In other words, participants might go along with the group rather than disclosing their true opinions.

Because interviews are more time consuming than questionnaires, they are also more expensive than questionnaires. However, some researchers think interviews are worth the extra expense.

Advantages of Interviews

What does the added expense of the interview buy you? Basically, the expense buys you more interaction with the participant. Because of this interaction, you can clarify questions the respondents don't understand. You can follow up on ambiguous or interesting responses—a tremendous asset in exploratory studies in which you have not yet identified all the important variables. Finally, this personal touch may increase your response rate.

Two Methodological Disadvantages of Interviews

Unfortunately, the personal nature of the interview creates two major problems. First, there is the problem of **interviewer bias:** The interviewer may influence respondents' responses by verbally or nonverbally encouraging and rewarding "correct" answers.

Second, participants may try to impress the interviewer. As a result, participants may, rather than telling the truth, give socially desirable responses that would make the interviewer like them or think well of them. Thus, answers may be tainted by the social desirability bias.

Advantages of Telephone Interviews

Psychologists have found that the telephone interview is less affected by interviewer bias and social desirability bias than the personal interview. Furthermore, the telephone interview may have fewer problems with sampling bias and nonresponse bias than other survey methods.

Because the telephone interviewer can't see the respondents, the interviewer cannot bias respondents' responses via subtle visual cues. Furthermore, by monitoring and tape-recording all the interviews, you can discourage interviewers from saying anything that might bias respondents' responses. For example, you could prevent interviewers from changing the wording or order of questions or from giving more favorable verbal feedback for expected answers.

The telephone survey also appears to reduce the effects of subject biases such as the social desirability bias and obeying demand characteristics by giving participants a greater feeling of anonymity (Groves & Kahn, 1979). This feeling of anonymity is also partly responsible for the fact that telephone surveys sometimes have a higher response rate than personal interviews. Thus, thanks to anonymity, the telephone survey may be less vulnerable to both nonresponse bias and subject biases than other survey methods.

The telephone survey also reduces sampling bias by making it easy to get a representative sample. If you have a list of your population's phone numbers, you can randomly select numbers from that list. If you don't, you may be able to get a random sample of your population by *random digit dialing:* randomly selecting numbers from all possible numbers that have the area code and the three-number prefixes that you are interested in. Note, however, that with random digit dialing, you call a lot of fax numbers and disconnected or unused numbers.

Thus far, we have discussed two basic advantages of telephone interviews. First, partly because there are no visual, nonverbal cues, the telephone survey is superior to the personal interview for reducing subject biases and interviewer biases. Second, because it is easy to get a random sample and because nonresponse bias is less of a problem than other methods, the telephone survey gives you the best sample of any survey method. However, the main reason for the popularity of the telephone interview is practicality: The telephone survey is more convenient, less time consuming, and cheaper than the personal interview.

Disadvantages of Telephone Interviews

Although there are many advantages to using the telephone interview, you should be aware of its limitations. First, as with any survey method, there is the possibility of sampling bias. Even if you followed proper random sampling techniques, telephone interviews are limited to those households with phones. Although this limitation may not seem serious, you should be aware that not everyone has a telephone—and many people have unlisted numbers.

Second, as with any survey method, nonresponse bias can be a problem. Some people will, after screening their calls through an answering machine or through "Caller ID," choose not to respond to your survey. Indeed, one study reported that 25% of men between the ages of 25 and 34 screen all their calls (Honomichl, 1990). Even when a person does answer the phone, he or she may refuse to answer your questions. In fact, some people get very angry when they receive a phone call regarding a telephone survey. The authors have been yelled at on more than one occasion by people who believe that telephone interviews are a violation of their privacy.

Third, telephone surveys limit you to asking very simple and short questions. Rather than answering your questions, participants' attention may be focused on the television show they are watching, the ice cream that is melting, or the baby who is crying.

Fourth, by using the telephone survey, you limit yourself to only learning what participants tell you. You can't see anything for yourself. Thus, if you want to know what race the respondent is, you must ask. Not only can't you see the respondent or the respondent's environment, but the respondent knows you can't. Therefore, a 70-year-old bachelor living in a shack could tell you he's a 35-year-old millionaire with a wife and five kids. He knows you have no easy way of verifying his fable.

How to Conduct a Telephone Survey

After weighing the pros and cons, you've decided to conduct a telephone survey. How do you go about it?

Your first step is to determine what population you wish to sample and figure out a way of getting all of their phone numbers. Often, your population is conveniently represented in a telephone book, membership directory, or campus directory. Once you obtain the telephone numbers, you are ready to draw a random sample from your population. (Later in this chapter, you will learn how to draw a random sample.)

When you draw your sample, pull more names than you actually plan to survey. You won't be able to reach everyone that you attempt to phone, so you'll need some alternate names. Usually, we draw 25% more names than we actually plan on interviewing.

Next, you do what any good survey researcher would do. That is, as you'll see in the next section ("Planning a Survey"), (1) you will decide whether to ask your questions as essay questions, multiple-choice questions, or use some other format; (2) you will edit your questions; and (3) you will put your questions in a logical order.

After editing your questions and putting them in the right order, you will further refine your survey. Start by having a friend read the survey to you.

Often, you will find that some of your questions don't "sound" right. Edit them so they sound better. Then, conduct some practice telephone interviews. For example, interview a friend on the phone. As a result of the practice interviews, you may find that you need to refine your questions further to make them sound more understandable. Much of this editing will involve making the questions shorter.

Once you've made sure your questions are short and concise, concentrate on keeping your voice clear and slow. Try not to let your tone of voice signal that you want participants to give certain answers. Tape yourself reading the questions and play it back. Is your voice hinting at the answer you want participants to give? If not, you're ready to begin calling participants.

If you get a busy signal or a phone isn't answered, try again later. As a general rule, you should phone a person 6–8 times at different times of the day before replacing him with an alternate name or number.

When you do reach a person, identify yourself and ask for the person on the list. As with any study, informed consent is a necessary ingredient. Therefore, after you identify yourself, give a brief description of what the survey is about and ask the person if she or he is willing to participate. Then, ask the questions slowly and clearly. Be prepared to repeat and clarify questions.

Once the survey is completed, thank your respondents. Then volunteer to answer any questions they have. Often, you may give participants the option of being mailed a summary of the survey results.

PLANNING A SURVEY

Before conducting a telephone survey—or any other type of survey—you need to do some careful planning. In this section, we will take you through the necessary steps in developing and executing your survey.

DECIDING ON A RESEARCH QUESTION

As with all psychological research, the first step in designing a survey is to have a clear research question. You need a hypothesis to guide you if you are to develop a cohesive and useful set of survey questions. Writing a survey without a hypothesis to unify it is like writing a story without a plot: In the end, all you have is a set of disjointed facts that tell you nothing.

Not only do you want a clear research question, you want an important one. Therefore, before you write your first survey question, justify why your research question is important. That is, you should be able to answer at least one of these questions:

1. What information will the survey provide?
2. What practical implications could the survey results have?

CHOOSING THE FORMAT OF YOUR QUESTIONS

You've decided that your research question is appropriate. In addition, you've also decided what kind of survey instrument (questionnaire or interview) will give you the best information. Now, you are ready to decide what types of questions to use.

Fixed-Alternative Questions

In a **fixed-alternative** question, you give participants the question and a choice of several answers. Their job is to pick the appropriate alternative.

Actually, there are a variety of fixed-alternative formats. For example, true–false and multiple-choice questions are fixed-alternative items, as are items that require people to choose a number on a rating scale.

Nominal-dichotomous   Sometimes, fixed-alternative questions ask respondents to tell the researcher whether they belong to a certain category. For example, participants may be asked to classify (categorize) themselves according to gender, race, or religion. These types of questions, which essentially ask people whether they have a certain quality, yield nominal data.

Dichotomous questions—questions that allow only two responses (usually yes or no)—also give you qualitative data. That is, they ask whether a person has a given quality. Often, respondents are asked whether they are a member or nonmember of a category (for instance, "Are you employed?" or "Are you married?").

Sometimes, several dichotomous questions are asked at once. Take the question: "Are you African American, Hispanic, Asian, or Caucasian (non-Hispanic)?" Note that this question could be rephrased as several dichotomous questions: "Are you African American?" (yes or no), "Are you Hispanic?" (yes or no), and so on. The information is still dichotomous—either participants claim to belong to a category or they don't. Consequently, the information you get from these questions is still categorical, qualitative information. If you code African American as a "1," Hispanic as "2," and so on, there is no logical order to your numbers. Higher numbers would not stand for having more of a quality. In other words, different numbers stand for different types (different qualities) rather than for different amounts (quantities).

The fact that **nominal-dichotomous** items present participants with only two—usually very different—options has at least two advantages. First, respondents often find it easier to decide between two choices (such as, "Are you for or against animal research?"), than between 13 (for example, "Rate how favorably you feel toward animal research on a 13-point scale."). Second, when there are only two very different options, respondents and investigators should have similar interpretations of the options. Therefore, a well-constructed dichotomous item can provide reliable and valid data.

Although there are advantages to offering only two choices, there are also disadvantages. One disadvantage of nominal-dichotomous items is that some respondents will think that their viewpoint is not represented by the two alternatives given. To illustrate this point, consider the following question:

"Do you think abortion should continue to be legal in the United States?" Yes or No?

How would people who are ambivalent toward abortion respond? How would people who are fervently opposed to legalized abortion feel about not being allowed to express the depth of their feelings?

If you have artificially limited your respondents to two alternatives, your respondents may not be the only ones irritated by the fact that your alternatives prevent them from accurately expressing their opinions. You should be annoyed, as well—because by depriving yourself of information about subtle differences among respondents, you deprive yourself of **power:** the ability to find relationships among variables.

Likert-Type and Interval Items   One way to give yourself power is to use Likert-type items. **Likert-type items** typically ask participants to respond to a statement by checking "strongly disagree" (scored a "1"), "disagree" (scored a "2"), "undecided" ("3"), "agree" ("4"), or "strongly agree" ("5").

Traditionally, most psychologists have assumed that a participant who "strongly agrees" (a "5") and a participant who merely "agrees" (a "4") differ by as much, in terms of how they feel, as a participant who is "undecided" (a "3") differs from someone who "disagrees" (a "2"). Both participants differed by the same distance on the scale (one point), and so both supposedly differed by the same amount psychologically. In other words, Likert-type scales are assumed to yield interval data. With interval data, differences between ratings correspond perfectly to differences in mental feelings. Questions 4 through 11 in Box 13-1 are examples of Likert-type, interval-scale items.

Likert-type items are extremely useful in questionnaire construction. Whereas dichotomous items allow respondents to only agree or disagree, Likert-type items give respondents the freedom to strongly agree, agree, be neutral, disagree, or strongly disagree. Thus, Likert-type items yield more information than nominal-dichotomous items. Furthermore, because Likert-type items yield interval data, responses to Likert-type items can be analyzed by more powerful statistical tests than nominal-dichotomous items.

The major disadvantage of Likert-type items is that respondents may resist the fixed-alternative nature of the question. One approach to this problem is to have a "Don't Know" option. That way, respondents won't feel forced into an answer that doesn't reflect their true position. In an interview, you can often get around the problem by reading the question as if it were an open-ended question. Then, you would simply record the answer under the appropriate alternative. As you can see, many of the questions in Box 13-1 could be read like open-ended items.

Using Likert-Type Items to Create Summated Scores   If you have several Likert-type items that are designed to measure the same variable (such as liking for students), you can sum (add up) each respondent's answers to all those questions to get a total score for each respondent on that variable. For example, consider Questions 6–11 in Box 13-1. For each of those questions, a "5" indicates a high degree of liking for students, whereas a "1" indicates a low level of liking for students. Therefore, you might add (*sum*) the answers (*scores*) for each of those questions to produce a **summated score** for student liking. Thus, suppose you obtained the following pattern of responses from one professor:

Question 6 = 1 (strongly disagree)
Question 7 = 2 (disagree)
Question 8 = 1 (strongly disagree)
Question 9 = 3 (undecided)
Question 10 = 1 (strongly disagree)
Question 11 = 2 (disagree)

Then, the summated score (total score for liking students) would be 10 (because $1 + 2 + 1 + 3 + 1 + 2 = 10$).

There are two statistical advantages to using summated scores. First, just as a 50-question multiple-choice test is more reliable than a one-question test, a score based on several questions is more reliable than a score based on a single question. Second, analyses are often simpler for summated scores. If we summed the responses for questions 6–11 in Box 13-1, we could compare computer users and non-computer users on "student liking" by doing one *t*-test. Without a summated score, you would have to perform six separate *t*-tests, and then correct the *t*-test for the effects of having done multiple analyses.[1]

Conclusions About Fixed-Alternative Items   Fixed-alternative questions can be used to ask the respondent how much of a quality he has. For example, a question might ask, "How much do you agree or disagree with the following statement?" (The fixed alternatives could be strongly agree, agree, disagree, strongly disagree.) Or, the question might ask how much of a certain behavior the person did. For instance, "How many days a week do you study (a. 0, b. 1, c. 2, d. 3, e. 4, f. 5, g. 6, h. 7)?" If asked the right way, these "how many"and "how much" questions can yield interval data.

Unfortunately, many of these "how much" and "how many" questions are *not* asked the right way. Consequently, they do not yield interval data. For example, when asking respondents about their grade-point averages, some re-

---

[1]Or, you could use more complex analysis such as multivariate analysis of variance (MANOVA).

searchers make 1 = 0.00–0.99, 2 = 1.0–1.69, 3 = 1.7–2.29, 4 = 2.3–2.7, 5 = 2.8–4.0. Note that the response options do not cover equal intervals. The interval covered by option "4" is .4, whereas the range of GPAs covered by option "5" is 1.2. Because there aren't equal intervals between response options, averaging respondents' responses is meaningless.

A better choice of options would be 1 = 0.00–0.99, 2 = 1.00–1.99, 3 = 2.00–2.99, and 4 = 3.00–4.00. However, probably the best thing to do would be to leave the fixed-response format and just ask participants the open-ended question, "What is your grade-point average?"

Open-Ended Questions

Before discussing other situations in which you might want to use **open-ended questions,** let's contrast the two types of questions. Whereas fixed-response items resemble multiple-choice items, open-ended questions resemble short-answer or essay questions. Rather than having respondents choose among several researcher-determined response options, participants are free to respond in their own words. This format gives respondents more freedom about how they answer questions than fixed-alternative and scaled items. There are two main advantages to letting participants respond in their own words.

First, you avoid putting words in participants' mouths. To illustrate how fixed alternatives may influence participants, when asked "What is the most important thing for children to prepare them for life?" almost two-thirds of respondents chose the alternative "To think for themselves." However, when the question was asked as an open-ended question, fewer than 1 in 20 respondents gave a response like "to think for themselves" (Schwarz, 1999).

Second, you can find out the beliefs and opinions behind the respondents' answers to the fixed-alternative questions. In some cases, open-ended questions may reveal that there are no beliefs or opinions behind a participant's answers to the fixed-alternative questions. That is, you might find that although the respondent is dutifully checking and circling responses, the respondent really doesn't know anything about the topic. Without open-ended questions, you might not realize that the respondent was making uninformed ratings. In other cases, asking open-ended questions allows you to discover that respondents making the same ratings have different opinions and beliefs. For example, consider two professors who respond to Question 11 in Box 13-1, "I like college students" with "undecided." Open-ended questions may allow you to discover that one professor circles "undecided" because he is new to the college and doesn't know, whereas the other professor circles "undecided" because she has mixed feelings about students. Without asking open-ended questions, you would not have known that these two respondents have different reasons for giving the same response.

Although there are two main advantages to letting respondents answer in their own words, there are also two main disadvantages.

First, open-ended questions place greater demands on participants. Because of the difficulty of generating their own responses, participants will often skip open-ended questions.

Second, answers to open-ended questions are difficult to score. Answers may be so varied that you won't see an obvious way to code them. If you aren't careful, the coding strategy you finally adopt will be arbitrary. To help you come up with a logical and systematic method of coding open-ended questions, try to come up with a content analysis scheme (see Chapter 12) before you start collecting data.

Once you have done a content analysis, you may convert the information from your open-ended questions into nominal or interval data where appropriate. For example, if you coded answers in terms of how aggressive an image was judged to be, you would analyze these quantitative data as interval data. If you coded responses in terms of whether or not ideas about loyalty were mentioned, you would analyze these qualitative, categorical data as nominal data.

CHOOSING THE FORMAT OF YOUR SURVEY

If you use an interview, in addition to deciding the format of your questions, you also need to determine the format of your interview. In this section, we will discuss the three basic interview formats: structured, semistructured, and unstructured.

Structured

The **structured interview** is the kind most often used in psychological research. In a structured interview, all respondents are asked a standard list of questions in a standard order.

In many structured interviews, all respondents are asked a standard list of fixed-alternative items in a standard order. The structured format ensures that each participant is asked the same questions. By using a standard list of questions, you reduce the risk of interviewer bias—and, by using fixed-alternative questions, you obtain easily interpretable responses.

Semistructured

A **semistructured interview** is constructed around a core of standard questions. However, unlike the structured interview, the interviewer may expand on any question in order to explore a given response in greater depth.

Like the structured interview, the semistructured interview tells you how respondents answered the standard questions. In addition, the semistructured interview allows the investigator to ask additional questions to follow up on any interesting or unexpected answers to the standard questions.

Unfortunately, the advantage of being able to follow up on questions is usually outweighed by two major disadvantages. First, data from the follow-up questions are hard to interpret because different participants are asked different questions. One can't compare how Participant 1 and Participant 2 answered follow-up Question 6c if Participant 1 was the only person asked that follow-up question.

Second, the answers from the standard questions are also hard to interpret because the standard questions were not asked in the same standard way to all participants. Participant 1 might have answered Question 2 right after Question 1, whereas Participant 2 did not answer Question 2 until first answering 10 minutes of follow-up questions. Those follow-up questions might shape the answers to Question 2 (Schwarz, 1999). Thus, in giving the interviewer more freedom to follow up answers, you may be giving the interviewer more freedom to bias the results. In other words, by deciding which answers to probe and how to probe them, the interviewer may affect what participants say in response to the standard questions.

Given the disadvantages of the semistructured interview, when should it be used? Perhaps the best time to use it is when you are conducting a preliminary pilot (exploratory) study so that you can better formulate your research question. For example, you may know that there are a few questions you want to ask, but you also know that you "don't really know enough to know what to ask." The standard questions give you some interpretable data, from which you may be able to get some tentative answers to the specific questions you do have. From the answers to the follow-up questions, you may get some ideas for other questions you could ask.

In short, if you do not yet know enough about your respondents or a certain topic area to create a good structured interview, you may want to first conduct a semistructured interview. What you learn from the results of that interview may enable you to generate a good structured interview or questionnaire.

Unstructured

Unstructured interviews are very popular in the media, in the analyst's office, and with inexperienced researchers. In the unstructured interview, interviewers have objectives that they believe can be best met without an imposed structure. Therefore, there isn't a set of standard questions. The interviewer is free to ask what she wants, how she wants to, and the respondent is free to answer how he pleases. Without standardization, the information is extremely vulnerable to interviewer bias and is usually too disorganized for analysis.

Because of these problems, the unstructured interview is best used as an exploratory device. As a research tool for reaping meaningful and accurate information, the unstructured survey is limited. As a tool for a beginning researcher like yourself, the unstructured interview is virtually worthless.

EDITING QUESTIONS: NINE MISTAKES TO AVOID

By now, you have probably decided that you will use either a structured interview or a questionnaire. Having decided on the general format of your survey, it's time to focus on your questions. Although asking questions is a part of everyday life, asking good survey questions is not. Therefore, in this section, you will learn how to avoid nine mistakes people often make when writing questions.

1. Avoid Leading Questions

Remember, your aim is to get accurate information, not to get agreement with your beliefs. Therefore, don't ask **leading questions**: questions that clearly *lead* participants to the answer you want. For example, don't ask the question: "You disapprove of the biased, horrible way that television news covers the abortion issue, don't you?" Instead ask, "Do you approve or disapprove of the way television news shows cover the abortion issue?"

2. Avoid Questions That Are Loaded With Social Desirability

Don't ask questions that have a socially correct answer, such as, "Do you donate money to student causes?" Generally, the answers to such questions cannot be trusted because participants will respond with the socially desirable answer. Such questions may also contaminate participants' responses to subsequent questions because such questions may arouse respondents' suspicions. For instance, the respondent may think, "They said there were no right or wrong answers. They said they just wanted my opinion. But obviously, there are right and wrong answers to this survey." Or, the respondent may think, "They know I would give that answer. Anyone would give that answer. This survey is starting to feel like one of those 'surveys' used by people who try to sell you something. What are they trying to sell?"

3. Avoid Double-Barreled Questions

You wouldn't think of asking a respondent more than one question at the same time. But that's exactly what happens when you ask a **double-barreled question**: more than one question packed into a single question, such as: "How much do you agree with the following statement: 'Colleges need to spend more time on students' emotional *and* physical development'?" The responses to this question are uninterpretable because you don't know whether participants were responding to the first statement, "Colleges need to spend more time on students' emotional development," the second statement, "Colleges need to spend more time on students' physical development," or both statements.

As you can see, the conjunction *and* allowed this question to be double-barreled. Almost all double-barreled questions are joined by "and" or some other conjunction. So when looking over your questions, look suspiciously at all "ands," "ors," "nors," and "buts."

4. Avoid Long Questions

Short questions are less likely to be double-barreled. Furthermore, short questions are easier to understand. A useful guideline is to keep most of your questions under 10 words and all your questions under 20 words.

5. Avoid Negations

The appearance of a negation, such as "no" or "not," in a questionnaire item increases the possibility of misinterpretation. Furthermore, it takes more time to process and interpret a negation than a positively stated item. To illustrate, compare the next two statements: "Do you not like it when students don't study?" versus "Do you like it when students study?"

6. Avoid Irrelevant Questions

Be sensitive to the relevancy of a questionnaire item for your population and your research question. For example, "Do you eat fondue?" is irrelevant to the research question, "Are professors who use computers more sympathetic to students?"

Although there are many obvious reasons for not including irrelevant questions, the most important reason is that irrelevant questions annoy respondents. If you ask an irrelevant question, many respondents will conclude that you are either incompetent or disrespectful. Since they have lost respect for you, they will be less likely to give accurate answers to the rest of your questions. In fact, they may even refuse to continue with the survey.

7. Avoid Poorly Worded Response Options

From your experiences with multiple-choice tests, you are keenly aware that the response options are part of the question. The options you choose will affect the answers that participants give (Schwarz, 1999). Not only should you carefully consider the wording of each option, but you should also carefully consider how many options you will include.

As a general rule, the more options, the greater your ability to detect subtle differences between participants. According to this rule, if you use a 1–7 scale, you may find differences that you would have failed to find if you had used a 1–3 scale.

However, like most rules, this one has exceptions. If you give participants too many options, participants may be overwhelmed. Likewise, if the options are too similar, participants may be confused. The easiest way to determine how many options are appropriate is to pretest your questions.

8. Avoid Big Words

Your task is not to impress respondents with your command of vocabulary and technical jargon. Instead, your task is to make sure respondents understand you; therefore, use simple words and avoid jargon.

9. Avoid Words and Terms That May Be Misinterpreted

There are three steps you can take to make sure that participants know exactly what you are talking about.

First, avoid slang terms. Slang terms often have different meanings to different groups. Thus, if you want to know people's attitudes toward marijuana, use the word "marijuana" rather than a slang term like "dope." "Dope" may be interpreted as meaning marijuana, heroin, or all drugs.

Second, be specific. If you want to know whether your respondents like college students, don't ask, "How do you feel about students?" Instead, ask, "Do you like college students?"

Third, pretest the questions. Often, the only way to find out that a question or term will be misinterpreted is by asking people what they think the question means. For example, through extensive pretesting, you might find that a seemingly straightforward question such as, "Should Pittsburgh increase coke production?" may be interpreted in at least five different ways:

1. Should Pittsburgh increase cocaine production?
2. Should Pittsburgh increase coal production?
3. Should Pittsburgh increase steel production?
4. Should Pittsburgh increase soft drink production?
5. Should Pittsburgh increase Coca-Cola production?

To repeat, even if you carefully evaluate and edit each question, there are some problems that you can only discover by having people try to answer your questions. Therefore, *pretesting questions is one of the most important steps in developing questions.*

SEQUENCING QUESTIONS

Once you have edited and pretested your questions, you need to decide in what order to ask them. Ordering questions is important because the sequence of questions can influence results (Krosnick & Schuman, 1988). To appropriately sequence questions, follow these five rules:

1. Put innocuous questions first, personal questions last.
2. Qualify early.
3. Be aware of response sets.
4. Keep similar questions together.
5. Put demographic questions last.

1. Put Innocuous Questions First, Personal Questions Last

Participants are often tense or anxious at the beginning of a survey. They don't know what to expect. They don't know whether they should continue the survey. The questions you ask at the beginning of the survey set the tone for the rest of the survey. Thus, if the first question is extremely personal, participants may decide to withdraw from the survey. Even if they don't withdraw, they will be very defensive throughout the survey. If, on the other hand, your initial questions are innocuous, participants may relax and feel comfortable enough to respond frankly to personal questions.[2]

Putting the most-sensitive questions at the end of your survey will not only increase the number of candid responses, it will also yield more data. To illustrate, suppose that you have a 20-item survey in which all but one of the questions are relatively innocuous. If you put the sensitive item first, respondents may quit the survey immediately. Because this item was the first question you asked, you have gathered no information whatsoever. If, on the other hand, you put the sensitive item last, respondents may still quit. But even though they've quit, you still have their responses to 19 of the 20 questions.

2. Qualify Early

If people must meet certain qualifications to be asked certain questions, find out if your participant has those qualifications before asking her those questions. In other words, don't ask people questions that don't apply to them. There is no need to waste their time—and yours—by collecting useless information. Participants don't like saying, "no, doesn't apply" repeatedly.

The survey in Box 13-1 begins with a simple qualifying question: "What is your position at Bromo Tech?" This question establishes the presence of two qualifications for the survey: (1) that the person is a professor; and (2) the person teaches at Bromo Tech. If people don't meet these qualifications, the survey is terminated at the start of the interview, not at the end. This saves time and energy.

3. Be Aware of Response Sets

If all your questions have the same response options, some participants may lock onto one of those options. For example, if each question has the alternatives, "Strongly Agree, Agree, Neutral, Disagree, Strongly Disagree," some respondents may circle the option "neutral" for every question. By always checking the neutral option, they can get the questionnaire over with as soon as possible.

To avoid the neutral response set, you may want to eliminate the neutral option. Unfortunately, the neutral response set isn't the only response bias. As we mentioned earlier, there are a variety of response sets, including the "yea-saying" (always agreeing) and the "nay-saying" (always disagreeing) biases.

One of the most common ways of dealing with response sets is to alternate the way you phrase the questions. You might ask respondents to strongly agree, agree, disagree, or strongly disagree to the statement, "Most students work hard on their studies." Then, later in the questionnaire, you could ask them to

---

[2]Not everyone agrees with this rule. For example, Dillman (1978) suggests that surveys should start with questions that hook the respondent's interest. If you are having trouble getting people to participate in your survey, you might consider Dillman's advice. However, we have found that by carefully explaining the purpose of the survey before administering it (in accordance with the principle of informed consent), participants will conscientiously answer questions.

strongly agree, agree, disagree, or strongly disagree with the statement, "Most students are lazy when it comes to their studies."

4. Keep Similar Questions Together

There are three reasons why you get more accurate responses when you keep related questions together.

First, your participants will perceive the survey to be organized and professional. Therefore, they will take the survey seriously.

Second, participants will be less likely to misunderstand your questions. You minimize the problem of participants thinking that you are asking about one thing when you are really asking about another topic.

Third, since you ask all the related questions together, participants are already thinking about the topic before you ask the question. Since they are already thinking about the topic, they can respond quickly and accurately. If respondents aren't thinking about the topic before you ask the question, it may take some respondents awhile to think of the answer to the question. At best, this makes for some long pauses. At worst, respondents will avoid long pauses by saying they don't know or by making up an answer.

5. Put Demographic Questions Last

In addition to writing items that directly address your research question, you should ask some questions that will reveal your sample's **demographics**: characteristics, such as age, gender, and education level. Thus, in our survey of college professors (see Box 13-1), we asked four demographic questions (Questions 12–15).

By comparing our sample's responses to these demographic questions with the population's demographics, we can see how representative our sample is. For example, we can look in the college catalog or go to the personnel office to find out what percentage of the population we are interested in (all teachers at Bromo Tech) is male. Then, we can compare our sample demographics to these population demographics. If we found that 75% of the faculty was male, but that only 25% of our sample was male, we would know that our sample wasn't representative of the faculty.

Note that we, like most researchers, put the demographic questions last (Questions 12–15). We put our demographic questions last for two reasons. First, respondents are initially suspicious of questions that do not clearly relate to the purpose of the survey. Second, people seem increasingly reluctant to provide demographic data. To reduce suspiciousness and increase openness, we try to put our respondents at ease before we ask demographic questions.

PUTTING THE FINAL TOUCHES ON YOUR SURVEY INSTRUMENT

You've written your questions, carefully sequenced them, and pretested them. Now, you should carefully proofread and pretest your questionnaire to make sure that it is accurate, easy to read, and easy to score.

Obviously, participants are more likely to take your research seriously if your questionnaire looks professional. Therefore, your final copy of the questionnaire should be free of smudges and spelling errors. The spaces between questions should be uniform.

Even though the questionnaire is neatly typed, certain key words may have been scrambled and omitted. At best, these scrambled or missing words could cause embarrassment. At worst, they would cause you to lose data. Therefore, not only should you proofread the questionnaire to ensure that the form of the questionnaire looks professional, but you should also pretest the questionnaire to ensure that the content is professional.

Once you have thoroughly checked and rechecked both the form and the content of the questionnaire, you should fill out the questionnaire and then code your own responses. After coding your responses, you should consider ways of making coding easier. Basically, there are three strategies you can use to facilitate coding:

1. Put the answer blocks in the left margin. This will allow you to score each page quickly because you can go straight down the page without shifting your gaze from left to right and without having to filter out extraneous information (see Box 13-1).

2. Have respondents put their answers on an answer sheet. With an answer sheet, you don't have to look through and around questions to find the answers. The answer sheet is an especially good idea when your questionnaire is more than one page long, because the answer sheet saves you the trouble of turning pages.

3. Have participants put their responses on a coding sheet that can be scored by computer. Computer scoring is more accurate than hand scoring. Besides, since computers like dull, time-consuming tasks, why not let them code responses?

CHOOSING A SAMPLING STRATEGY

Once you have decided what questions you will ask and how you will ask them, you need to decide whom you will ask. To decide whom you will ask, you first have to decide exactly what population you want to study. If your population is extremely small (all art history teachers at your school), you may decide to survey every member of your population. Usually, however, your population is so large that you can't easily survey everyone. Therefore, instead of surveying the entire population, you will survey a sample of people from that population. Whether you acquire your sample by random sampling, stratified random sampling, convenience sampling, or quota sampling, your goal is to get a sample that is representative of your population.

Random Sampling

In **random sampling,** each member of the population has an equal chance of being selected. Furthermore, the selection of respondents is independent. In other words, the selection of a given person has no influence on the selection or exclusion of other members of the population from the sample.

Obtaining a Random Sample   To select a random sample for a survey, you would first identify every member of your population. Next, you would go to a random numbers table and use that table to assign each member of the population a random number. Then, you would rank each member from lowest to highest based on the size of his or her random number. Thus, if a person were assigned the random number 00000, that person would be the first person on the list, whereas a person assigned the number 99999 would be the last person on the list. You would select your sample by selecting names from the beginning of this list until you got the sample size you needed. Thus, if you needed 100 respondents, you would select the first 100 names on the list.

As you can imagine, random sampling can be very time consuming. First, you have to identify every member of the population. That can be a chore, depending on your population. If you are interested in a student sample, then a trip to the registrar's office might yield a list of all currently enrolled students. In fact, most schools can generate a computerized random sample of students for you. If you are interested in sampling a community, the local telephone book is a good place to start. Or, if you are willing to spend the money, you can buy census tapes from the government or from marketing research firms.

After you've identified the population, you have to assign random numbers to your respondents. Just the first step—assigning random numbers to all members of a population—can be cumbersome and time consuming. Imagine assigning 1,000,000 random numbers to names! But after that's done, you still have to order the names based on these random numbers to determine whom you will sample. Fortunately, computers can eliminate many of the headaches of random sampling—especially if you can find a computer file or database that has the names of everybody in your population.

Despite the hassles involved with random sampling, researchers willingly use it because random sampling allows them to generalize the results of one study to a larger population. To be more specific, you can use inferential statistics to infer the characteristics of a population from a random sample of that population.

Determining an Appropriate Sample Size   As you know, your random sample may differ from the population by chance. That is, although your population may have 51% females, your random sample may have 49% females. You also know that you can reduce random sampling error by increasing your sample size. In other words, a sample of 10,000 will tend to reflect the population more accurately than a sample of 10. However, surveying 10,000 people may cost more time and energy than the added accuracy it buys. To determine how many people you will need to randomly sample, consult Table 13-2.

Stratified Random Sampling

What if you can't afford to survey as many people as Table 13-2 says you need? Then, if you use pure random sampling, random sampling error may cause your sample to be less representative than you would like. With pure random sampling, the only defense you have against random sampling error is a large sample size. With **stratified random sampling,** on the other hand, you don't leave the representativeness of your sample entirely to chance. Instead, you make sure that the sample is similar to the population in certain respects. For example, if you know that the population is 75% male and 25% female, you make sure your sample is 75% male and 25% female. You would accomplish this goal by dividing your population (stratum) into two subpopulations, or substrata. One substratum would consist of male members of the population, the other substratum

---

• TABLE 13-2 •

REQUIRED SAMPLE SIZE AS A FUNCTION OF POPULATION SIZE AND DESIRED ACCURACY (WITHIN 5%, 3%, OR 1%) AT THE 95% CONFIDENCE LEVEL

	SAMPLING ERROR		
SIZE OF THE POPULATION	5%	3%	1%
50	44	48	50
100	79	92	99
200	132	169	196
500	217	343	476
1,000	278	521	907
2,000	322	705	1,661
5,000	357	894	3,311
10,000	370	982	4,950
20,000	377	1,033	6,578
50,000	381	1,066	8,195
100,000	383	1,077	8,926
1,000,000	384	1,088	9,706
100,000,000	384	1,089	9,800

Example of how this table works: If you are sampling from a population that consists of 50 people and you want to be 95% confident that your results will be within 5% of the true percentage in the population, you need to randomly sample 44 people.

Note: Table provided by David Van Amburg of MarketSource, Inc.

would consist of female members. Next, you would decide on how many respondents you would sample from each substratum (for example, 75 from the male stratum, 25 from the female stratum). Finally, you would draw random samples from each substratum, following the same basic procedures you used in random sampling. The only difference is that you are collecting two samples from two substrata, rather than one sample from the main population.

By using stratified random sampling, you have all the advantages of random sampling, but you don't need to sample nearly as many people. Thus, thanks to stratified sampling, the Gallup Poll can predict the outcome of U.S. presidential elections based on samples of only 300 people. Furthermore, a stratified random sample ensures that your sample matches the population on certain key variables.

Convenience Sampling

In **convenience sampling,** you simply sample people who are easy to survey. Convenience surveys are very common. Newspapers ask people to mail their responses to a survey question, and radio stations ask people to call in their reactions to a question. Even television stations have gotten into the act, asking people to call one number if they are in favor of a position on an issue and another number if they are opposed to that position.

To see how you would get a convenience sample, suppose that you were given one week to get 1,000 responses to a questionnaire. What would you do? You might go to areas where you would expect to find lots of people, such as a shopping mall. Or, you might ask your professors if you could do a survey in their classes. Or, you might put an ad in the newspaper, offering people money if they would respond to a questionnaire.

In conclusion, you can use convenience sampling techniques to get a relatively large sample quickly. Unfortunately, you do not know whether the sample represents your population. Your best bet is that it does *not*. In fact, if your respondents are actively volunteering to be in your survey, you can bet that your sample is extremely biased. People who call in to radio shows, write letters in response to questions in the newspaper, or respond to ads asking for people to be in a survey do not represent a significant portion of the population: people without the time or desire to respond to such surveys.

Quota Sampling

Quota sampling is designed to make your convenience sample more representative of the population. Like stratified random sampling, quota sampling is designed to guarantee that your sample matched the population on certain characteristics. For instance, you might make sure that 25% of your sample was female, or that 20% of your sample was Hispanic.

Unlike stratified random sampling, however, quota sampling doesn't involve random sampling. Consequently, even though you met your quotas, your sample may not reflect the population at all. For example, you may meet your

20% quota of Hispanics by hanging around a hotel where there is a convention of high-school Spanish teachers; obviously, the Hispanics in your survey would not be representative of the Hispanics in your community.

Conclusions About Sampling Techniques

To get samples that represent your population, we recommend that you use either random sampling or stratified random sampling. However, even if you start off with a perfect sample, you will not end up with a perfect sample because respondents have the last say about whether they will be in the sample. That is, you can try to question participants, but they may choose not to answer you. As a result, your sample will not represent members of the population who choose not to respond. In other words, even if your sample is not affected by sampling bias, it will probably be affected by nonresponse bias.

There are two things you can do about the bias caused by nonresponse. First, you can get your response rate so high that nonresponse is not a big problem. For example, by using brief telephone surveys, some investigators obtain response rates of 97% or better.

Second, keep detailed records on the people who refused. If possible, unobtrusively record their gender, race, and estimated age. By knowing who is dropping out of your sample, you may know to whom your results don't apply.

ADMINISTERING THE SURVEY

You have your survey questions. You've carefully sequenced your questions, and you've determined your sampling technique. You have had your study approved by your professor and any appropriate ethical review committees. Now it's time for you to actually administer your survey. Basically, you are going to follow the same advice you received for administering experiments, quasi-experiments, and other correlational studies. That is, you must follow APA's ethical guidelines (APA, 1992) and you must conduct yourself professionally during every step of the survey (see Appendixes A and C).

For example, participants should always be greeted. If participants can't be greeted in person (as with a mail questionnaire) then the questionnaire should always be accompanied by a cover letter—a written greeting. In this written greeting, you should introduce yourself, explain the nature of your study, and request the participant's help—just as you would if you were greeting the participant in person.

Participants should always be given clear instructions. As with any other study, an important part of these instructions is making it clear that participation is entirely voluntary. In an interview, the instructions are oral. In a questionnaire, they are written. However, if an investigator is administering the questionnaire, any written instructions can be backed up with oral ones.

After participants complete the survey, they should be thanked and debriefed about the purpose of the survey. At the end of a mail questionnaire, you should thank your participants, give them any additional instructions, and give them the opportunity to be debriefed. For example, you might write, "Please mail your questionnaire in the enclosed envelope. To find out more about the survey, put a check mark in the upper left-hand corner of the questionnaire and we will send you a summary of the results once the data have been analyzed. If you wish to talk to me about the study, please call me at 1-800-555-5555. Thank you for your participation."

Finally, as in all studies, you should be careful to ensure your participants' confidentiality. This means that you should not only be careful when collecting data (for example, by using a cover page and spreading participants out so that they do not see each other's responses), but also when storing and disposing of data (see Appendixes A and C).

ANALYZING SURVEY DATA

Once you have collected your survey data, you need to analyze them. In this section, we will show you how to summarize and make inferences from your data.

SUMMARIZING DATA

The first step in analyzing survey data is to determine what data are relevant to your hypotheses. Once you know what data you want, you need to summarize those data. How you summarize your data will depend on what kind of data you have.

The type of data you have will depend on the type of questions you ask. When you ask rating-scale questions or when you ask people to quantify their behavior ("How many hours a week do you use a computer?"), then you probably can assume that your data are interval-scale data. If you ask questions that people have to answer either "yes" or "no" ("Do you use a computer?" "Do you like students?"), or questions that call on people to classify themselves ("Are you male or female?"), then you have nominal data.

Summarizing Interval Data

If you simply want to know the typical response to an interval-scale question, ("On the average, how many hours do people in the sample use computers?"), then you only need to calculate the mean for that question. More often, however, you will be interested in the relationship between the answer to one question with the answers to other questions. That is, you probably will be interested in the relationship between two or more variables. If you are interested in such a relationship, you will usually want to construct tables of means that reflect that relationship.

Summarizing Relationships Between Pairs of Variables   In our survey example, we expected that there would be a relationship between computer use and sympathy for students. Therefore, we compared computer users' average sympathy for students with non-computer users' average sympathy for students (see Table 13-3). In addition, as you can tell from Table 13-3, we were also interested in seeing whether male or female professors were more sympathetic to students. To supplement your tables of means, you may want to compute a correlation coefficient (the Pearson r) to get an idea of the strength of the relationship between your two variables.

Describing Complex Relationships Among Three or More Variables   Once you have looked at relationships between pairs of variables (for example, computer use and sympathy; gender and sympathy; gender and computer use), you may want to see how three or more variables are related. The easiest way to compare three or more variables is to construct a table of means, as we have

---

• TABLE 13-3 •

TABLE OF MEANS AND INTERACTIONS

TABLE OF MEANS FOR COMPUTER USAGE ON QUESTION 11:

"I Like College Students"

Computer Usage

Yes	No
4.0	3.0

Average score on a 1 (strongly disagree) to 5 (strongly agree) scale.

TABLE OF MEANS FOR GENDER ON QUESTION 11:

"I Like College Students"

Gender

MALE	FEMALE
3.25	3.75

Average score on a 1 (strongly disagree) to 5 (strongly agree) scale.

INTERACTION FOR GENDER BY COMPUTER USAGE ON QUESTION 11:

"I Like College Students"

Computer Usage

Gender	Yes	No
MALE	3.5	3.0
FEMALE	4.5	3.0

Average score on a 1 (strongly disagree) to 5 (strongly agree) scale.

done at the bottom of Table 13-3. As you can see, this 2 × 2 table of means allows us to look at how both computer use and gender are related to sympathy.

Summarizing Ordinal and Nominal Data

If your data are not interval-scale data, don't summarize your data by computing means. For example, if you code 1 = male, 2 = female, do not say that "the mean sex in my study was 1.41."

Similarly, if you are having participants rank several choices, do not say that the mean rank for Option *B* was 2.2. To understand why not, imagine that five people were ranking three options. All five people ranked Option *A* as second best (the rankings were "2–2–2–2–2") whereas two ranked Option *B* best, and three ranked Option *B* third best (the rankings were "1–1–3–3–3"). The mean rank for Option *A* is 2.0; the mean rank for Option *B* is 2.2 (Semon, 1990). Thus, according to the mean, *A* is assumed to be better liked (because it is closest to the average rank of 1.0, which would mean first choice).

The mean, however, is misleading. The mean gives the edge to *A* because the mean assumes that the difference between being a second choice and being a third choice is the same as the difference between being a first choice and being a second choice. As you know, this is not the case. There is usually a considerable drop-off between a person's favorite and her second choice, but not such a great difference between their second and third choices (Semon, 1990). For example, you may find an enormous drop-off between your liking of your favorite opposite-sex friend and your second best opposite-sex friend or between your favorite football team and your second favorite football team.

To go back to our example of Options *A* and *B,* recall that *A*'s average rank was better than *B*'s. However, because two people ranked *B* best and nobody ranked *A* first, we could argue that Option *B* was more liked (Semon, 1990). The moral of this example: If you do not have interval data, do not use means to summarize your data. Instead, use frequencies or percentages.

Summarizing Relationships Between Pairs of Variables   To look at relationships among nominal variables, use tables of either percentages or frequencies to compare different groups' responses. As you can see from Table 13-4, these tables can help you visualize similarities and differences between groups.

If you want to compute a measure to quantify how closely two nominal variables are related, you can calculate a correlational coefficient called the *phi coefficient* (see Appendix F). Like most correlation coefficients, phi ranges from −1 (perfect negative correlation) to +1 (perfect positive correlation).

Describing Complex Relationships Among Three or More Variables   If you want to look at how three or more variables are related, do not use the phi coefficient. Instead, construct tables of frequencies, as we have done in Table 13-4. These two 2 × 2 tables of frequencies do for our ordinal data what the 2 × 2 table of means did for our interval data—allow us to look at three variables at once.

• **TABLE 13-4** •

TABLES OF NOMINAL DATA

COMPUTER USE BY GENDER

Use Computers?	Gender	
	Male	Female
Yes	(A) 20	(B) 15
No	(C) 55	(D) 10

The Relationships Among Computer Use, Gender, and Academic Department

Use Computers	Gender			Use Computers	Gender	
	Male	Female			Male	Female
Yes	10	10		Yes	20	20
No	80	0		No	40	20
Physical Sciences Professors				**Social Sciences Professors**		

USING INFERENTIAL STATISTICS

In addition to using descriptive statistics to describe the characteristics of your sample, you may wish to use inferential statistics. Inferential statistics may allow you to generalize the results of your sample to the population it represents. There are two main reasons why you might want to use inferential statistics.

First, you might want to use inferential statistics to estimate certain **parameters** (characteristics of the population) such as the population mean for how much time professors spend using computers. Thus, if you wanted to use the average amount of time professors in your sample said they used computers to estimate the average amount of time all Bromo Tech professors spend using computers, you would be using **parameter estimation.**

Second, you might want to determine whether the relationship you found between two or more variables would hold in the population. For example, you might want to determine whether using computers and grade-point average are related in the population. Because you are deciding whether to reject the null hypothesis (that the variables are *not* related in the population), this use of inferential statistics is called **hypothesis testing.**

Parameter Estimation With Interval Data

As we just mentioned, one reason for using inferential statistics would be to estimate population parameters. For example, from our survey of computer usage and student sympathy, we might want to estimate one parameter: the amount of sympathy the average professor at our school has for students.

Our best guess of the amount of sympathy the average professor at our school has for students is the average amount of sympathy the average professor in our sample has for students. However, the average for our sample may differ from the average in the population. Therefore, it is often useful to establish a range in which the population mean is likely to fall. For example, you may want to establish a **95% confidence interval:** a range in which you can be 95% sure that the population mean falls.

You can establish 95% confidence intervals for any population mean from the sample mean, if you know the **standard error of the mean.** (If you don't have a computer or calculator that will compute the standard error of the mean for you, see Appendix F.) You establish the lower limit of your confidence interval by subtracting two standard errors from the sample mean. Then, you establish the upper limit of your confidence interval by adding two standard errors to the sample mean. Thus, if the average sympathy rating for all the professors in our sample was 3.0 and the standard error was .5, we could be 95% confident that the true population mean is somewhere between 2.0 and 4.0.

Hypothesis Testing With Interval Data

You can also use statistics to see if there are significant differences between groups. That is, we might want to know if the differences we observe in our sample also apply to the population at large.

Testing Relationships Between Two Variables   Through a *t*-test (see Appendix F), we could test whether the differences in sympathy we observed between computer users and non-computer users were too large to be due to sampling error and thus probably represented a true difference.

The *t*-test between means is not the only way to determine whether there is a relationship between computer usage and student sympathy. We could also determine whether a relationship exists between computer usage and student sympathy by determining whether the correlation coefficient between those two variables was significant. (To do this test, consult Appendix F).

If you were comparing more than one pair of variables, you could do several *t*-tests or test the significance of several correlations. In either case, you should correct for doing more than a single statistical test by using a more stringent significance level than the conventional .05 level. For example, if you looked at 5 comparisons, you might use the .01 level; if you looked at 50 comparisons, you might use the .001 level.

To understand why you should correct for doing multiple tests, imagine that you are betting on coin flips. You win if you get a heads. If you flip a coin once, it's fair to say that there's a 50% chance of getting a "heads." However, if you flip a coin three times and declare victory if any of those flips come up "heads," then it's not fair to claim that you only had a 50% chance of winning.

Similarly, a .05 significance level means that you only have a 5% chance of getting those results by chance alone. This false alarm rate of .05 only applies if you were doing one test. If you are doing 100 tests and none of your variables are related, then it would not be unusual for you to get 5 false alarms (because .05 $\times$ 100 = 5).

Testing Relationships Among More Than Two Variables   Suppose you wanted to look at more than two variables at once. For example, suppose you wanted to explore the relationship between computer usage, gender, and sympathy summarized in Table 13-3. In such cases, you might use analysis of variance (ANOVA). If you perform multiple ANOVAs, you should correct your significance level for the number of ANOVAs you computed, just as you would if you computed multiple t-tests.

Analysis of variance is not the only—or even the most common—way to examine complex relationships among interval-scale variables. Factor analysis, multivariate analysis of variance, and multiple regression are all techniques that are commonly used to analyze survey research data. However, these statistical techniques are beyond the scope of this book.

Using Inferential Statistics With Nominal Data

Just as inferential statistics can be applied to interval data, they can be applied to nominal data. Indeed, if you do research as part of your job, you will probably be more likely to do parameter estimation and hypothesis testing with nominal data than with interval data.

Parameter Estimation With Nominal Data   You might start by doing some basic parameter estimation such as estimating the percentage of people who have some characteristic. If you used random sampling and chose your sample size according to the first column of Table 13-2, you can be 95% confident that your sample percentages are within 5% of the population's percentages. Thus, if you found that 35% of your participants were female, you would be 95% confident that 30–40% of your population was female.

Hypothesis Testing With Nominal Data   After estimating the percentages of the population that had certain characteristics, you might go on to look for differences between groups. In that case, you would use significance tests to determine whether differences between sample percentages reflect differences in population percentages. For example, in your sample, you may find that more men than women use computers. Is that a relationship that holds in your population—or is that pattern due to random sampling error? To find out, you would use a statistical test. But instead of using a t-test, as you would with interval data, you would use the **chi-square** test (see Appendix F).

If you are performing more than one chi-square test, you should correct for the number of analyses performed. That is, just as with the t-test, you should raise your significance level to compensate for doing multiple analyses. Thus, if you are comparing five chi-squares, you should use a .01 significance level rather than a .05 significance level.

Concluding Remarks

In this chapter, you learned the essence of good survey research. Early in the chapter, you were introduced to the applications and limitations of survey research. You saw the advantages and disadvantages of different survey formats, as well as the strengths and weaknesses of different kinds of questions. After learning how to write a survey, you learned how to administer, score, and analyze survey data. Thus, if you apply what you have learned in this chapter, you can become a skilled survey researcher.

Summary

1. Surveys can help you describe what people are thinking, feeling, or doing.

2. Surveys allow you to gather information from a large sample with less effort and expense than most other data-gathering techniques.

3. In a survey, it is important to ask only relevant questions.

4. Don't accept respondents' answers as truth. People don't always tell the truth or even know what the "truth" is.

5. Surveys yield only correlational data. You cannot draw cause–effect conclusions from correlational data.

6. There are two main drawbacks to self-administered questionnaires: (1) They have a low return rate, and (2) respondents may misinterpret questions.

7. Investigator-administered questionnaires have a higher response rate than self-administered questionnaires.

8. Interviews are especially useful for exploratory studies. However, interviews are expensive, and the interviewer may bias participants' responses.

9. Telephone surveys have higher response rates, are easier to administer, and offer greater anonymity than personal interviews.

10. Your first step in survey research is to have a hypothesis.

11. There are three basic question formats: nominal-dichotomous, Likert-type, and open-ended.

12. Structured surveys are more useful than unstructured.

13. In survey research, you want to ask the right people the right questions.

14. To ask the "right people," you need a representative sample. To get a representative sample, you must first know what your population (the group that you want to generalize to) is. Once you know your population, you can get a representative sample by using either random or stratified random sampling.

15. To ask good questions, (1) make sure they relate to your hypotheses; (2) edit them so they are short, clear, and unbiased; and (3) pretest them.

16. Careful attention should be placed on sequencing questions. Keep similar questions together and put personal questions last.

17. Be aware of response biases, such as a tendency of participants to agree with statements or the tendency to answer questions in a way that puts the participant in a positive light.

18. Spending a little time deciding how to code your questionnaire before you administer it can save a great deal of time later on.

19. Both random and stratified random sampling allow you to make statistical inferences from your data.

20. Participants in survey research should be treated with the same respect as human participants in any other kind of study.

Key Terms

survey research: a nonexperimental design in which you design a questionnaire, test, or interview *and* administer it to either the group you are interested in or to a sample of that group. This nonexperimental design can be useful for describing what people are thinking, feeling, or doing.

Note that using a questionnaire, test, or interview in your study does not mean that you are doing survey research. For example, in experimental research, you may estimate the effect of a treatment by administering a questionnaire, test, or interview after administering the treatment manipulation. Many experiments use questionnaires, tests, and interviews rather than observation to measure participants' responses. (p. 469)

population: everyone to whom you want to generalize your results. Depending on your goals, a population could be everyone who votes in the presidential election, everyone at your school, or everyone who spends more than $100 a year on videos. Because you usually don't have the time to survey everyone in your population, you will usually survey a sample of those individuals. (p. 469)

convenience sampling: choosing to include people in your sample simply because they are convenient to survey. It is hard to generalize the results accurately from a study that used convenience sampling. (p. 498)

quota sampling: making sure you get the desired number of (meet your quotas for) certain types of people (certain age groups, minorities, etc.). This method does not involve random sampling and usually gives you a less representative sample than random sampling would. It may, however, be an improvement over convenience sampling. (p. 498)

random sampling: a sample that has been randomly selected from a population. If you want to generalize your results, random sampling is better than both quota sampling and convenience sampling. (p. 496)

stratified random sampling: like quota sampling, a strategy for ensuring that the proportion of certain subgroups (e.g., men and women) is the same in the sample as it is in the population. However, it goes beyond quota sampling because it involves random sampling. For example, if the population of interest was 75% women and 25% men, you might obtain a list of all the women and randomly sample 75 from that list. Then, you would obtain a list of all the men in that population and randomly sample 25 from that list. Stratified random sampling has all the advantages of random sampling with even greater accuracy. Thus, a relatively small stratified random sample may more accurately represent the population than a larger, nonstratified random sample. (p. 497)

nonresponse bias: the problem caused by people who were in your sample refusing to participate in your study. Nonresponse bias is one of the most serious threats to a survey design's external validity. (p. 477)

demographics: characteristics of an individual or group, such as gender, age, and social class. If you know the demographics of the population, you can compare those to the demographics of your sample. A big discrepancy would indicate sampling bias or nonresponse bias. (p. 494)

double-barreled question: a single questionnaire item that actually (because of a word like "and") contains at least two questions. Responses to a double-barreled question are difficult to interpret. For example, if someone responds, "No," to the question, "Are you hungry and thirsty?" we do not know whether he is hungry, but not thirsty; not hungry, but thirsty; or neither hungry nor thirsty. (p. 490)

leading question: a question that leads respondents to the answer the researcher wants (such as, "You like this book, don't you?"). (p. 490)

obeying demand characteristics: if participants know how the researcher wants them to act, some will act that way regardless of their true feelings. That is, some participants want to give the researcher the results that will support the researcher's hypothesis. A leading question shows participants what the demand characteristics are for that question. (p. 476)

social desirability bias: rather than giving accurate answers, participants may give answers that make them look good. For example, they may overstate the extent to which they help others out and understate the extent to which they lose their temper. (p. 476)

response set: pattern of responding to questions that is independent of the particular question's content (for instance, a participant might always check "agree" no matter what the statement is). (p. 476)

retrospective self-report: participants telling you what they said, did, or believed in the past. In addition to problems with ordinary self-report (response sets, giving the answer that a leading question suggests, etc.), retrospective self-report is vulnerable to memory biases. Thus, retrospective self-reports should *not* be accepted at face value. (p. 475)

fixed-alternative items: items on a test or questionnaire in which a person must choose an answer from among a few specified alternatives. Multiple-choice, true–false, and rating-scale questions are all fixed-alternative items. (p. 484)

open-ended items: questions that do not provide fixed-response alternatives. Essay and fill-in-the-blank questions are open-ended. (p. 487)

nominal-dichotomous items: items that lead to concluding that the participant belongs to a certain category or has a certain quality. Data from qualitative items cannot be scored in terms of saying that one participant has more of a certain quality than another. Questions asking about gender and group membership are nominal items. Data from nominal items are analyzed differently than data from Likert-type items. (p. 484)

Likert-type items: items that typically ask participants whether they strongly agree, agree, are neutral, disagree, or strongly disagree with a certain statement. Psychologists often assume that Likert-type items produce interval data. (p. 485)

summated scores: when you have several Likert-type questions that all tap the same dimension (such as attitude toward democracy), you could add up (sum) each participant's responses from the different questions to get an overall (summated) score. (p. 486)

parameters: characteristics of populations—not samples. For example, the mean of a sample is *not* a parameter, but the mean of the entire population *is* a parameter. (p. 503)

parameter estimation: using measurements obtained from a sample to estimate the true characteristics of the entire population. You might use your sample mean to estimate the population mean. (p. 503)

standard error of the mean: an index of the degree to which random error may cause the sample mean to be an inaccurate estimate of the population mean. (p. 504)

95% confidence interval: the range in which, given a sample mean, the true population mean would fall 95% of the time. Often, the 95% confidence interval extends from two standard errors of the mean below the sample mean to two standard errors of the mean above the sample mean. (p. 504)

hypothesis testing: the use of inferential statistics to determine if the relationship found between two or more variables in a particular sample holds true in the population. (p. 503)

power: the ability to find relationships among variables. If your study has little power, hypothesis testing will probably not be productive. (p. 485)

chi square: a statistical test used to do hypothesis testing on nominal data (data from nominal items). If data were interval, you would probably use a *t*-test instead. (p. 505)

questionnaire: a survey that respondents read. (p. 477)

self-administered questionnaire: a questionnaire filled out in the absence of an investigator. (p. 478)

interview: a survey in which the researcher orally asks questions. (p. 480)

interviewer bias: when the interviewer influences participant's responses. For example, the interviewer might verbally or nonverbally reward the participant for giving responses that support the hypothesis. Or, the interviewer might adopt a more enthusiastic tone of voice when reading the desired response than when reading the less desired response. (p. 480)

unstructured interview: when the interviewer has no standard set of questions that he or she asks each participant. The unstructured survey is a virtually worthless approach if the goal is to collect scientifically valid data. (p. 489)

semistructured interview: an interview constructed around a core of standard questions; however, the interviewer may expand on any question in order to explore a given response in greater depth. (p. 488)

structured interview: an interview in which all respondents are asked a standard list of questions in a standard order. For collecting valid data, the structured survey is superior to the semistructured and unstructured surveys. (p. 488)

Exercises

1. Develop a hypothesis that can be tested by administering a survey.
2. Is a survey the best way to test your hypothesis? Why?
3. Is an interview or a questionnaire the best way to test your hypothesis? Why?
4. For the three basic question formats, list their advantages and disadvantages in the grid below.

QUESTION FORMAT	ADVANTAGES	DISADVANTAGES
Nominal-dichotomous		
Likert-type		
Open-ended		

5. Write three nominal-dichotomous questions that might help you test your hypothesis.
6. Write three Likert-type questions that might help you test your hypothesis.
7. Write three open-ended questions that might help you test your hypothesis.
8. Edit your questions using the points presented in this chapter.
9. Why can you make statistical inferences from data obtained from a random sample?

CHAPTER 14

PUTTING IT ALL TOGETHER: WRITING RESEARCH PROPOSALS AND REPORTS

It takes less time to do a thing right than it does to explain why you did it wrong.
—HENRY WADSWORTH LONGFELLOW

OVERVIEW

Your research should be carefully planned before you test your first participant. Without such planning, you may fail to have a clear hypothesis, or you may fail to test your hypothesis properly. In short, poor planning leads to poor execution.

Poor execution can lead to unethical research. At best, it wastes participants' time; at worst, it harms participants. Therefore, the purpose of this chapter is to help you avoid unethical research by showing you how to plan and report the results of your study. If you follow our advice, your research should be humane, valid, and meaningful.

AIDS TO DEVELOPING YOUR IDEA

In this section, you will learn about two major research tools: the research journal and the research proposal. Many scientists regard the research journal and the research proposal as essential to the development and implementation of sound, ethical research.

THE RESEARCH JOURNAL

We recommend that you keep a **research journal:** a diary of your research ideas and your research experiences. Keeping a journal will help you in at least three ways. First, you won't have to rely on memory to explain why and how you did what you did. Second, writing to yourself helps you think through design decisions. Third, a research journal can help you prepare your research proposal.

Since the journal is for your eyes only, it does not have to be neatly typed and free of grammatical errors. What's in the journal is much more important than how it is written.

What should you put in your journal? Every idea you have about your research project. At the beginning of the research process, when you're trying to develop a research hypothesis, use your research journal for brainstorming. Write down any research ideas that you think of, and indicate what stimulated each idea. When you decide on a given idea, explain why you decided on that particular research idea. When reading related research, summarize and critique it in your journal. Remember to write down the authors, year, title, and publisher for each source. This information will come in very handy when you write your research proposal. In short, whenever you have an insight, find a relevant piece of information, or make a design decision, record it in your journal.

To use the information in your journal, you will have to organize it. One key to effective organization is to write down only one idea per page. Another key is to rewrite or rearrange your entries every couple of days. Your goal in rearranging entries should be to put them in an order that makes sense to you.

For example, your first section may deal with potential hypotheses, your second section may deal with ideas related to the introduction section of your paper, and your third section may deal with methods and procedures.

THE RESEARCH PROPOSAL

Like the research journal, the purpose of the research proposal is to help you think through each step of your research project. In addition, the research proposal will also let others (such as friends and professors) think through your research plan so that they can give advice that will improve your study. By writing the proposal, you will have the opportunity to try out ideas and explore alternatives without harming a single participant. In other words, the process of writing the proposal will help you make intelligent and ethical research decisions.

Although the research proposal builds on the research journal, the research proposal is much more formal than the journal. When you write the proposal, you will have to go through several drafts. The result of this writing and rewriting will be a proposal that is not only clear, but also conforms in content, style, and organization to the guidelines given in the *Publication Manual of the American Psychological Association* (1994).

We want to emphasize that it is not enough to have good ideas. You must present them in a way that people will receive them. History is full of examples of people who had good ideas but got little credit because they expressed them poorly. Conversely, some people have become famous more for how well they expressed their ideas than for the originality of their ideas.

If you write using APA (American Psychological Association) style, you will have a better chance of expressing your ideas well. Think of APA format as a kind of language that makes it easier for professionals in the psychology field to communicate with one another.

If, on the other hand, you fail to write a research proposal or article that conforms to APA format, most professors will judge the content of your proposal more harshly. They will feel that if you cannot follow that format, you are incapable of doing good research.

To reiterate, following APA format is important. Indeed, one of the best-known professors of research design, Dr. Charles Brewer, cites learning APA format as one of the most important things students learn from his design class (Brewer, 1990).

As we have stressed, following APA style will help you communicate the content of your proposal. However, before you worry about how to communicate your content clearly, you need to have content: Style without substance is worthless. The substance of your proposal will be your statements regarding:

1. why your general topic is important
2. what your hypothesis is
3. how your hypothesis is consistent with theory or past research

4. how your study fits in with existing research
5. how you define and operationalize your variables
6. who your participants will be
7. what procedures you will follow
8. how you will analyze your data
9. what implications you hope your results will have for theory, future research, or real life

Thus, there is considerable overlap between the substance of the research proposal and the substance of the final research report. To be more specific, the introduction and the method sections you write for your research proposal should be highly polished drafts of the introduction and method sections of your final report. Furthermore, parts of the research proposal will serve as rough drafts of the abstract, results, and discussion sections of your final report. In short, writing the research proposal lays the groundwork for both the study and the final report.

WRITING THE RESEARCH PROPOSAL

Now that you know what a research proposal is, it's time for you to begin writing one. We will first show you how to write the introduction.

GENERAL STRATEGIES FOR WRITING THE INTRODUCTION

The purpose of the **introduction** is to demonstrate to your readers that you have read the relevant research and thoroughly understand your research question. Once you have articulated the reasoning behind your hypothesis, you will explain your general strategy for testing the hypothesis. After reading the introduction, your reader should know:

1. why your research area is important
2. why your prediction makes sense
3. what your hypothesis is
4. why your study is the best way to test the hypothesis

Establishing the Importance of Your Study

To persuade people that your study is important and interesting, you must first let them know exactly what you are studying. You must define your concepts. Once you've explained what your concepts are, then you can explain why the concepts are important. In this section, we will discuss three common strategies for establishing the importance of concepts:

1. prevalence: presenting statistical or other evidence of how often people encounter the basic principle or topic

2. relevance: presenting a case study or other arguments to illustrate how the concept has significant implications for real life

3. precedence: demonstrating that the concept has captured the interest of other researchers

Demonstrate the Concept's Prevalence   One strategy for showing that your study is important is to show that your general topic area is a common part of real life. Sometimes, authors boldly assert that the phenomenon they are studying is common. For example, authors may write "_____ is a part of everyday life" or "People are bombarded with _____."

Rather than asserting "Most people have experienced _____," you might document the prevalence of the concept by presenting statistical evidence. Thus, if you were studying widowhood, you might present statistics on the percentage of people who are widowed. In the absence of statistics, you could use quotations from influential people or organizations (for example, the American Psychological Association) to stress the prevalence of your concept.

Demonstrate the Concept's Relevance to Real Life   Rather than emphasizing the concept's prevalence, you might emphasize its relevance. For example, you might stress the practical problems that might be solved by understanding the concept. Alternatively, you might demonstrate the problem's relevance by presenting a real-life example of your concept in action. Giving an example of the concept is a very good way to both define the concept and provide a vivid picture of its importance at the same time.

Demonstrate Historical Precedence   Finally, you might show that there is a historical precedence for your study. You could emphasize the great minds that have pondered the concept you will study, the number of people through the ages who have tried to understand the behavior, or the length of time that people have pondered the concept. Generally, you will also want to show that the research topic has—or should have—been important to both researchers and theorists.

The Literature Review

One way of establishing historical precedence is to summarize research done on the topic. In addition to helping the reader understand your research question, citing research shows the reader that the field considers your general research area important. That is, if the field did not consider these concepts important, investigators would not be researching these areas, and their findings would not be published. Thus, it is not uncommon for introductions to include statements such as, "The focus of research for the past 20 years . . ." or "Historically, research has emphasized . . ."

However, even if you do not use the literature review to establish the importance of the general concepts, you will still want to write a literature review. To reiterate, *all introductions should contain a literature review.*

The literature review shows how your particular research study fits in with existing work. In other words, although there are several ways to show that the general concepts are important, there is only one way to show that your particular research study is important—the literature review.

Goals of the Literature Review   Because the literature review is designed to "sell" your particular study, you need to do more than merely summarize previous work. You must also use the summary to set the stage for your study. You will set the stage for your study by either (1) showing that your study corrects a weakness in previous research; or (2) showing that your work builds on and extends the work of previous researchers.

As you can see, you have to set the stage for your research by showing that existing research is in some way deficient or not extensive enough. That is, you need to make the reader feel that there is a need for more research.

Deciding Which Research to Summarize   We have addressed the goals of the literature review. You know why you should review the literature. Now, let's talk about what you will review. When citing research, review several older, classic works as well as recent research (see Appendix B about how to find articles to review). Critiquing—rather than merely summarizing—these articles will show that you have thought about what you have read. By critiquing a number of articles, you will establish that you have done your homework.

Although critiquing these journal articles may establish you as a scholar, realize that your goal is not simply to establish your credibility. Instead, your primary goal is to show how your study follows from existing research.

You may find that these two goals (establishing your expertise versus showing that your study follows from existing research) conflict. On the one hand, you want to establish that you know what you are talking about. Therefore, you may feel that you should cite all research ever done in the field. On the other hand, you want to use the literature review to set up your research study. Consequently, you want to cite and analyze only those studies that bear directly on your study. There are two things you can do to address the apparent conflict between these two goals.

First, realize that your main goal is to set up your study. Thus, you will be offering in-depth critiques of only those studies that directly apply to your study.

Second, realize that introductions begin by talking about the general area and then start to focus on the specific research question. Thus, you should cite classic research that establishes the importance of your general topic. However, if those classic findings are only indirectly related to your work, then you should probably only cite them in your first paragraph.

Not knowing what to include in a literature review is one of the two main problems students have in writing the literature review. The other problem is that their literature review often seems disorganized.

To help organize your literature review, please follow the next bit of advice. Before you start writing, group together the studies that seem to have something in common. Thus, if you have summaries of all your studies on large index cards, you might find that you have the following four piles of cards:

1. a pile that emphasizes the importance of the general concept
2. a pile that deals with problems with previous research
3. a pile that deals with reasons to believe that your hypothesis will not be supported
4. a pile that deals with reasons to believe that your hypothesis would be supported

Alternatively, you may find that you have three piles:

1. a pile that deals with how to measure your outcome variable
2. a pile that deals with studies that obtained a certain finding
3. a pile that deals with studies that obtained the opposite finding

Regardless of the specific content of your piles, the fact that you have piles shows that you have some way of organizing the studies. Now, you have to convert those organized piles into an organized literature review. Your first step is to turn each pile into a paragraph.

To help convert these piles into meaningful paragraphs, write a sentence summarizing what all the cards have in common. Each pile's sentence could be the topic sentence for a paragraph, with the rest of the pile providing evidence and citations for the statements made in that sentence (Kuehn, 1989).

Once you have finished a draft of your literature review, reread it. This literature review should do more than evaluate other people's work; it should also set the stage for your study. For example, the measure you praise will be in your study; the manipulation you attack will not. Furthermore, just from reading your literature review, a very astute reader could guess what your hypothesis is and how you plan to test it.

However, you won't make people guess the rationale for your hypothesis and for your study. After summarizing the relevant research, spell out the reasoning that led to your hypothesis. Spell out your reasoning so carefully and explicitly that your readers will know what your hypothesis is before you actually state it.

Stating Your Hypothesis

Even though your readers may have guessed your hypothesis, leave nothing to chance: *State your hypothesis*! To emphasize a point that can't be emphasized enough, state your hypothesis boldly and clearly so that readers can't miss it. Let them know what your study is about by writing, "The hypothesis is . . ."

When you state your hypothesis, be sensitive to whether you'll be testing it with an experiment or a correlational study. Only with an experiment may you use the word "cause." ("A sedentary lifestyle causes depression.") If you don't plan on directly manipulating your predictor variable, you have a correlational study—you can test only whether two or more variables are related. ("A sedentary lifestyle is related to depression.")

Review of the Basic Elements of an Introduction

We have given you some general advice about how to write an introduction. You have seen the importance of clearly defining your concepts, critically summarizing research, carefully explaining the reasoning behind your hypothesis, and explicitly stating your hypothesis. Because of the importance of summarizing research, explaining the reasoning behind hypotheses, and explicitly stating hypotheses, you are probably not surprised to find that some authors include subheadings such as "Overview of Past Research," "Theoretical Background," and "Hypotheses" in their introductions. Although you do not need to include such subheadings, you should outline your introduction, and your outline should incorporate headings such as "Overview of Past Research," and "Hypotheses."

SPECIFIC STRATEGIES FOR WRITING INTRODUCTION SECTIONS FOR DIFFERENT TYPES OF STUDIES

Thus far, you have been given only general advice because the specific way you will justify your study will depend on the kind of study you are doing. In the next section, you will learn how to justify six common types of studies:

1. exploratory
2. direct replication
3. systematic replication
4. conceptual replication
5. replication and extension
6. theory-testing study

The Exploratory Study

In introducing an **exploratory study**—a study investigating a new area of research—you must take special care to justify your study, your hypothesis, and your procedures. You must compensate for the fact that your reader will not have any background knowledge about this new research area.

New Is Not Enough   To justify an exploratory study, you can't use one of the most common strategies in introductions: the strategy of stating that your research area is important because it has inspired a lot of research. It hasn't—that's why your study is an exploratory study. To justify an exploratory study, don't merely state that your research question has been ignored. Convince your readers that your research question deserves top priority. Let them think it is a tragedy that your research question has been overlooked. Make them believe this wrong must be righted to help psychology advance as a science.

One approach you can use to justify your exploratory study is to discuss hypothetical or real-life cases that could be solved or understood by answering your research question. For example, consider how Latane and Darley (1968) opened their pioneering work on helping behavior. They did say that helping behavior had not been extensively investigated. However, they did not stop there. Instead, they referred to the case of murder victim Kitty Genovese. Ms. Genovese was brutally attacked for more than half an hour in the presence of more than 30 witnesses—none of whom intervened. Thus, Latane and Darley effectively convinced readers that understanding why people fail to help is an important research area.

To reiterate, your first step in justifying an exploratory study is to show that the area is important. Once you have convinced your readers that the research area is important, you can further excite them by emphasizing that you are exploring new frontiers, going where no investigators have gone before.

Spell Out Your Reasoning   In an exploratory study, as in all studies, you must spell out the rationale for your hypothesis. Since you are studying an unexplored dimension, you must give your readers the background to understand your predictions. Therefore, be extremely thorough in explaining the logic behind your predictions—even if you think your predictions are just common sense. Not everyone will share your common sense.

How do you explain the logic behind commonsense predictions? Even commonsense predictions can often be justified by theory or research on related variables. For example, suppose you are interested in seeing how low-sensation seekers and high-sensation seekers differ in their reactions to stress. You might argue that your hypothesis is consistent with arousal theory—the theory that we all have an ideal level of arousal (Berlyne, 1971). That is, you might argue that high-sensation seekers like stress because it raises their arousal up to the optimal level, whereas low-sensation seekers hate stress because it raises their arousal beyond the optimal level.

In addition to—or instead of—using theory to support your hypothesis, you could use research on related concepts. Thus, in our example, you might start by arguing that introversion–extroversion and sensation-seeking are related concepts. Then, you might argue that because introversion and sensation-seeking are related, and because stress has different effects on introverts and extroverts, stress should also have different effects on low-sensation seekers versus high-sensation seekers.

Defend Your Procedures   In addition to explaining your predictions, you may have to take special care in explaining your procedures. That is, you may be studying variables that have never been studied before. In that case, you can't tell the reader that you are using well-accepted measures and manipulations with which the reader is familiar. Instead, you may have to invent your own measures and manipulations. Therefore, you will need to explain, either here or in the method section, why your manipulations and measures are valid.

The Direct Replication

Rather than doing a completely original exploratory study, you may decide to do the opposite. That is, you may decide to do a **direct replication:** a repetition of an original study. Before doing a direct replication, you must be very clear about why you are repeating the study. If you are not careful, the reader may think you performed the study before you realized that someone else had done your study. Even if you do spell out why you repeated the study, some journal reviewers will find the fact that you did a direct replication a legitimate reason to reject the paper for publication (Fiske & Fogg, 1990). However, there is a two-pronged strategy you can use to persuade people that your study is worth doing.

Document the Original Study's Importance   First, to justify a direct replication, you should show that the original study was important. To establish the study's importance, discuss its impact on psychology. To get some objective statistics about the number of times the study has been cited, you can use the *Social Science Citation Index* described in Appendix B.

Explain Why the Results Might Not Replicate   After establishing the study's importance, try to convince your readers that the study's results might not replicate. There are basically four arguments you can make in support of the idea that the findings won't replicate:

1. The findings appear to contradict other published work.
2. The original study may be a Type 1 error.
3. The original study may be a Type 2 error.
4. People or times have changed so much from when the original study was performed that a replication would produce different results.

Perhaps the strongest argument you can make for replicating the study is to show that the findings appear to contradict other published work. The more you can make the case that other findings directly contradict the finding, the stronger the case for a replication.

If you can also make a good argument that the statistically significant result in the original study could be the result of a Type 1 error, your case for replicating the study could be even stronger. Thus, if you also showed that the original study had a fairly high risk of making a Type 1 error, you would have a strong case for replicating the study.

But what if the original study reported null results? If the original study reported null results, then you could argue that random error or poor execution of the study may have hidden real differences. That is, you could argue that the null results were due to a Type 2 error. If the original study's findings seem to conflict with several other published papers that *did* find a significant relationship between those variables, you have a compelling rationale for replicating the study.

If you can't reasonably argue that the original results are due to either a Type 1 or Type 2 error, you still might be able to justify a direct replication on the grounds that the study would come out differently today. For example, you might want to replicate a conformity study because you feel that people are no longer as conforming as they were when the original study was conducted. Regardless of what approach you take, you must present a compelling rationale for any study that is merely a rerun of another study.

The Systematic Replication

Rather than repeating the study, you might conduct a **systematic replication:** a study that makes a minor modification in the original study. As such, the systematic replication accomplishes everything the direct replication does and more. Therefore, every reason for doing a direct replication is also a reason for doing a systematic replication. In addition, you can justify a systematic replication by showing that modifying the procedures would improve the original study's power, construct validity, or external validity.

Improved Power   If you thought the original study's null results were due to Type 2 error, you might make a minor change in procedure to improve power. For example, you might use more participants, more extreme levels of the predictor/independent variable, or a more accurate way of measuring participants' responses (for instance, a more accurate stopwatch) than the original study used.

Improved Construct Validity   You might also want to modify the original study if you thought that the original study's results were biased by demand characteristics. Thus, you might repeat the study using a double-blind procedure to reduce subject and researcher bias.

Improved External Validity   If you are systematically replicating a study to improve external validity, you should explain why you suspect that the results may not generalize to different stimulus materials, levels of the treatment variable, or participants. Even if it seems obvious to you why a study done on rats might not apply to humans, why a study done on college students might not apply to factory workers, why a study done on men might not apply to women, or why the results wouldn't hold if different levels of the treatment were used, spell out your reasons for suspecting that the results wouldn't generalize.

The Conceptual Replication

Most of the reasons for conducting a systematic replication are also relevant for introducing and justifying a **conceptual replication:** a study that is based on the original, but uses different methods to better assess the true relationships between the variables being studied. In addition, the conceptual replication has several other unique selling points, depending on how you changed the original study.

Using a Different Measure   Your conceptual replication might differ because you used a way of measuring the dependent variable that differed from what the original authors did. In that case, you should show that your measure is more reliable, sensitive, or valid than the original measure. To make the case for your measure, you may want to cite other studies that used your measure. As in the legal arena, precedent carries weight in psychology. If someone else published a study using a given measure, the measure automatically gains some credibility.

Using a Different Manipulation   Instead of trying to use a different measure of a construct, you might want to use a different manipulation of a construct. For example, if one researcher induced stress in participants by suggesting that they would get painful electric shocks, you might decide to replicate the study, but induce stress by giving participants a very short period of time to do certain mathematical problems. If you use a different treatment manipulation, you should start by defining the variable you are trying to manipulate. Next, you should discuss weaknesses of previous manipulations. Then, show why your manipulation avoids these weaknesses. Conclude by showing that your manipulation is consistent with definitions of the concept you are trying to manipulate.

Using a Different Design   If you are changing the original study's design, explain why. If you are replicating a between-subjects design using a within-subjects (repeated measures) design to improve power, tell your readers. If you are converting a within-subjects design to a between-subjects design because you feel participants will be less likely to guess the hypothesis in a between-subjects design, tell your readers. Your readers will not instantaneously realize the advantages of using a different design.

The Replication and Extension

Your study may go beyond a conceptual replication to looking at additional factors or measures. In that event, your introduction would not only contain everything a conceptual replication would, but also a rationale for the additional factors or measures.

Rationale for Additional Factors   For example, suppose the original author found that people loaf when "working" in groups. You might think of a situation (for example, a group in which all members were good friends) where social loafing wouldn't occur. Thus, you might include friendship as a factor in your design. Be sure to justify your reasoning for including the factor, defend your manipulation of that factor, and state your predictions regarding the factor.

Rationale for Additional Dependent Measures   Instead of adding a predictor/independent variable to a study, you might add a criterion/dependent measure. Your purpose would be to discover how the treatment produces the effect. In other words, you are trying to show that a certain mental or physiological reaction is both (1) triggered by the treatment and (2) the mediating mechanism by which the treatment has its effect on behavior.

How would you go about finding out the invisible processes underlying an observable effect? In a social-loafing experiment, you might collect measures of participants' perceptions of others to find out the cognitive processes responsible for social loafing (such as perceptions that their efforts are not being noticed). Or, you might monitor arousal levels in an attempt to discover the physiological reasons for social loafing (for example, lower physiological arousal in a group setting). However, even if you found that working in a group reduced arousal or changed perceptions, you could not say that these changes, in turn, caused the loafing.

Not surprisingly then, the tricky part about writing an introduction to a "process" study is to persuade your readers that you really are measuring the underlying causes of a phenomenon. You must do more than merely show that these processes occur before the phenomenon. These processes could be incidental side effects of the treatment. For instance, a fever may appear before you get ill—and may intensify as you get ill—but a fever doesn't cause you to be ill. It's a side effect of your illness. In the same way, a mental or physiological event may accompany a change in behavior, but not be the cause of that behavioral change.

Not surprisingly then, critics will usually not accept evidence that the treatment had certain effects on a physiological or mental process as proof that the treatment works by altering that process. Instead, the proof they want is more direct: Show that the treatment doesn't work the same way when you alter the process (Sigall & Mills, 1998).

To show how clever some of these experiments can be, pretend that you and a friend are participants in the following experiment (Steele, Southwick, & Critchlow, 1981). You are asked to write an essay favoring a big tuition increase. According to dissonance theory, you will feel unpleasant tension after writing this essay. To reduce this tension, you will then tend to be less opposed to tuition increases. As dissonance theory would predict, you now are less opposed to tuition increases. But did you change your attitudes as a way to reduce that unpleasant tension? To find out, let's look at your friend's reaction. Your friend did not experience the unpleasant tension for long because, after writing the essay, she drank alcohol, supposedly as part of a study on judging beverages. Furthermore, she did not change her views about tuition increases. By using alcohol to reduce the tension caused by writing the essay, Steele and his colleagues were able to reduce the effect of the treatment (the essay). This study provides strong evidence that having people write counterattitudinal essays has its effect by creating unpleasant tension that people try to reduce.

In summary, you can extend an existing study by adding measures or manipulations. Such extensions may provide insights into how a treatment has its effect. When proposing such a study, remember that you must (1) justify why you are adding the measure or manipulation, and (2) explain your predictions regarding the additional measure or manipulation.

The Theory-Testing Study

If you are testing a prediction from a theory, there's good news and bad news. The good news is that you won't have to spend much effort justifying your study's importance. Almost everyone assumes that testing a theory is important.

The bad news is that not everyone will agree that your predictions follow from the theory. To protect yourself, you must clearly spell out how your predictions follow from theory. By being clear, everyone will follow your logic, and some may even agree with it.

WRITING THE METHOD SECTION

You have reviewed the literature, developed a hypothesis, decided how to measure your variables, and stated your reasons for testing your hypothesis. Your preliminary work, however, is still not done. You must now decide exactly what specific actions you will take. In other words, although you probably have decided on the general design (for example, a simple experiment), your plan is not complete until each detail of your study has been thought through and written down.

In your journal, specify exactly what procedures you will follow. For example, what instructions will participants be given? Who will administer the treatment? Where? Will participants be run in groups or individually? How should the researcher interact with participants? Although your answers must be accountable to issues of validity, your paramount concern must always be ethics. You do not have the right to harm another.

Once you have thoroughly thought out each step of your study, you are ready to write the **method section**[1] of your proposal. The method section is the "how" section—here you will explain exactly how you plan to conduct your study. However, keep in mind that—just like the introduction—the method section is written on two levels. As you will recall, at one level, the introduction

---

[1]Don't irritate your professor by making the mistake of labeling your "method" section as the "methods" section.

summarizes existing research. But, at another level, the introduction sells the need for your study by pointing out deficiencies in existing research. Similarly, on one level, the method section tells the reader what you are going to do. However, at another level, it sells the reader on the idea that what you plan to do is the correct thing to do.

Although the introduction may have already set this section up by pointing out which participants should be studied, which measures should be used, and what variables should be controlled for, do not hesitate to remind your reader again of the wise design choices you have made. Thus, in the method section, you may mention that your measure is valid, that your manipulation is widely accepted, or that you are doing something a certain way to reduce demand characteristics, researcher biases, random error, or some other problem.

In short, selling the value of a research strategy is a neverending job. If possible, you should sell your strategy in each of the method section's subsections.

The method must include two subsections: a participants section and a procedure section. However, a method section may include other subsections such as overview, design, apparatus, materials, manipulations, and dependent measures subsections.

Participants

In the participants section, you will describe the general characteristics of your participants. State how many participants you plan to have, how many will be male, how many will be female, their ages, how you plan to obtain or recruit them. In addition, include any other relevant information (like what strain of rat). You should also indicate whether they will be tested individually or in groups. If they will be tested in groups, you should state the size of the groups. If you plan to exclude data from some participants, state the precise criteria for exclusion (such as scores above 16 on a depression inventory).

The participants section is written in a straightforward and somewhat mechanical fashion. In fact, it is so mechanical that you can often use the following as a guideline.[2]

---

[2]As an anonymous reviewer pointed out, you should be aware of two serious problems with finding parts of articles that convey approximately what you want to say. First, you may end up committing **plagiarism**: using someone else's words, thoughts, or work without giving proper credit. Plagiarism is considered a serious act of academic dishonesty. Indeed, at some institutions, students convicted of plagiarism are expelled. Furthermore, concerns about plagiarism are no longer limited to colleges and universities. More and more, the world economy is based on information. Thus, more and more, businesses and individuals are concerned about the theft of ideas (intellectual property). Therefore, if you quote someone's work, use quotation marks; and if you paraphrase or in any sense borrow an idea from a source, cite that source. Second, you will rarely find a section that says exactly what you want to say. So, rarely copy things word for word. For example, do not copy this participants section word for word. Instead, create an original participants subsection that best describes how participants will be recruited and assigned in your study.

Participants

The participants will be 80 introductory psychology students (52 men and 28 women) from Clarion University who will be given extra credit for their participation. Participants will be run individually and will be randomly assigned to experimental condition.

Design (Optional)

The design section is also easy to write. Merely describe the design of your study. For an experiment, state the number of levels for each independent variable and whether the independent variable is a between-subjects variable or a within-subjects variable. Then, state the dependent variable. For example, you might write that "The design is a 2 (source expertise: nonexpert/expert) × 2 (information type: unimportant/important) between-subjects design. The dependent measure is memory for the presented information."

Apparatus and Materials (Optional)

In the apparatus and materials section, describe the equipment and materials you plan to use. This includes laboratory equipment, tests, computers, and so on.

If you plan to use equipment made by a company, list the brand name and the model of the product. If you designed your equipment, briefly describe it. You need to give enough detail so that readers will have a general idea of what it looks like. In the appendix, include a photo or diagram of your apparatus.

If you used a test or questionnaire, reference the source of the test and give at least one example of a typical item. This gives readers a feel for what the participants will see. In the appendix, include a copy of your test or questionnaire.

Procedure

As the name suggests, your procedure section will be a summary of what you actually are going to do. However, contrary to what the name suggests, the focus is on what happens to participants. Readers should be able to visualize what it would be like to be a participant in your study. Note how the sample paper (Appendix D) does a good job of showing what *happens from the participants' perspective.*

Like the authors of the sample paper, you can make it easy for readers to make a movie in their head of what happened to participants by using the following methods:

1. Start with what first happened to the participants and continue in chronological order, so that the last part of the procedure deals with the last thing that happens to participants.
2. Keep the focus on participants by making the word "participants" the subject of most sentences. That is, most sentences should deal with what participants do or see.

Besides not putting the focus on participants, beginning authors have trouble figuring out what to put in and what to leave out of the procedure section. Thus, a common question is, "How much detail should I include?" To help you answer this question, we offer five suggestions.

First, be sure to include enough information so that the reader will understand how you operationalized your independent and dependent variables. To help the reader understand your independent variable manipulation, don't forget to include key elements of instructions to participants, especially instructions that are different for the experimental group than they are for the control group. To make sure the reader knows what the dependent variable was, you might choose to be very direct. For example, you might explictly state: "The dependent measure was . . ."

Second, include any methodological wrinkles that you feel are critical to the study's internal, external, or construct validity. For example, if you used a placebo treatment or double-blind procedures, tell the reader that you did so.

Third, read the procedure sections of several related studies and mimic their style—but avoid plagiarism. Reading these sections will help you understand how much detail to include.

Fourth, leave out most of the "behind the scenes" details about events that participants don't see. Thus, don't include information about who did what, such as "Tom randomly assigned people to group." Similarly, don't say "We made the booklets by cutting sheets of paper in half, typing them up on a computer, and then using a copier."

Finally, don't worry if your procedure section seems too brief. You can include your complete protocol in the appendix of your proposal.

WRITING THE RESULTS SECTION

In a proposal, you may not have a results section. After all, there are no results. Thus, your professor may advise you to replace the results section with a "Design and Data Analysis" section or even skip the section entirely.

If you do have a results, data analysis, or related section, the main goal is to show that you would know how to code and analyze participants' responses. As was the case with the method section, your goal is not only to tell the reader what you are going to do, but also to sell the reader on the idea that you are doing the right thing. Thus, it is important to be clear about not only what analysis you are going to do, but why. Ideally, your proposal should answer four questions:

1. What data will be analyzed? That is, how will a participant's response be converted into a score?

2. What statistical test will be used on those scores?

3. Why can that statistical test be used? Thus, you might show that the data meet the assumptions of the statistical test or you might cite a text or article that supports the use of the test under these conditions.

4. Why should the analysis be done? Usually, you will remind the reader of the hypothesis you want to test. To emphasize the value of the analysis, you may want to describe what results of that analysis would support your hypothesis and what outcomes would not. You might even—with your professor's permission— plug in imaginary outcomes of your study to give the reader a concrete example of how your proposed analyses will help test your hypotheses.

To illustrate how a results section might accomplish these goals, consult the following sample results section:

Results

I will sum participants' responses to the two altruism items to come up with an altruism score for each participant that will range from 2 (very low to 10 (very high). Such scores are assumed to be interval (Winer, 1972). Consequently, those scores will then be subjected to a 2×2 between-subjects analysis of variance.

I hypothesize that mood will affect altruism. If the results turn out as I predict, positive-mood participants will score significantly higher on my altruism scale than negative-mood participants. This significant main effect would indicate support for the hypothesis that mood influences altruism. Furthermore, I also predict a significant mood by arousal interaction. Analyses of simple main effects will show that negative-mood participants who are in the high-arousal condition will score lower on altruism than negative-mood participants in the low-arousal condition. In contrast, positive-mood participants in the high-arousal condition will score higher on altruism than positive-mood participants in the low-arousal condition.

As you can see, the results section clearly shows the reader what data will be put into the analysis, what analyses will be done, and what results from the analyses will support the hypotheses.

WRITING THE DISCUSSION SECTION

Once you have decided how you will analyze your data, you are ready to discuss how you will interpret them. By referring back to both the literature you discussed in the introduction and the arguments you made in the introduction, you should be able to address two key questions:

1. What would be the implications for interpreting existing theory and research if your hypothesis is supported?

2. What would be the implications if the results don't support your hypothesis?

In addition to addressing these two key questions, the **discussion** is the place to present the limitations of your study, to speculate about what research should be done to follow up on your study, and to discuss the practical implications of your study.

Writing the discussion section of the proposal is difficult because you do not know how the study will turn out. Probably the easiest thing to do is to imagine that your study turned out as you expected. In that case, your discussion can be primarily a rehash of the introduction.

To be more specific, your discussion should probably devote a paragraph to at least four of the following six points:

1. relating the predicted results to the hypothesis ("Consistent with our predictions, . . .")

2. relating the predicted results to previous research and theory discussed in the introduction ("This study joins others in showing . . ." or "The findings are consistent with ___ theory.")

3. discussing the limitations of the study ("However, the current research is only correlational so we cannot say whether our variables are causally related" or "The results may not generalize to non-college students.")

4. discussing future research that would build on the present study ("Future research might consider testing the generality of this effect.")

5. discussing practical implications of the research findings

6. stressing the importance of remembering or building on the study's major findings ("To summarize, we found that the effectiveness of rewards depended on the participant's personality. This finding suggests that teachers should not use salient rewards on intrinsically motivated students. Furthermore, in light of these findings, learned industriousness theory must be revised. In short, this research takes an enormous step toward understanding creativity.")

Almost all authors devote the first paragraph of the discussion to the first of these six points. In fact, you will often see the first sentence of the discussion have both the words "support" and "hypothesis" in it. Most authors explicitly address at least four of these six points. Indeed, you will sometimes find discussion sections with subheadings such as "Comparisons With Previous Research," "Suggestions for Future Research," "Implications," and "Concluding Remarks."

Do you need to have a separate paragraph for all six of these paragraphs? No. Usually, the content and organization of your discussion will be fine as long as you:

1. Connect your discussion to your introduction.

2. Explain how your study will contribute to existing knowledge.

3. Outline it.

PUTTING ON THE FRONT AND BACK

You've written the introduction, method, results, and discussion sections. Now it's time to return to the beginning of your proposal. Specifically, it's time to type the title page and the abstract.

Title and Title Page

The title is the first thing readers will see. Your title should be simple, direct, honest, and informative. Ideally, your title should be a brief statement about the relationship between your predictor/independent and criterion/dependent variables.

Avoid being too cute or obscure. If there is some catchy saying or title that you must include, use a colon to add this extra title to the simpler title. Such a title might be, "The Effect of Eating Sugar on Anxiety: A Bittersweet Dilemma."

The title should appear centered on a separate piece of paper. One double-spaced line below the title, center your name. For more information about typing and formatting the title page, see Box 14-1.

The title should also appear, centered, at the top of the first page of your introduction. Thus, in the introduction, the title takes the place of the heading "Introduction."

Abstract

Once they've read your title, readers will continue to the next section—the **abstract.** In your abstract, you will give them a short, one-paragraph summary of your research proposal.

Jolley, Murray, and Keller (1992) describe six basic sentences that are included in most abstracts. The first sentence describes the general research topic (for example, "Love is a common topic in popular music"). The order of the next five sentences often varies. However, there should be a sentence that gives the number of participants and their treatment ("Sixteen participants will listen to love ballads for one hour, while 16 control participants will sit in a quiet room for one hour"). In another sentence, you should explain how you plan to collect the dependent measure ("Participants will fill out the Reuben Love–Like Scale 10 minutes after receiving the treatment"). You should have a sentence that spells out the hypothesis ("It is hypothesized that listening to love ballads will raise scores on the Love–Like Scale"). The last sentence will not be in your proposal, but will be in your final research report. In that sentence, you'll describe the main results—the results that relate to your hypothesis.

In addition to these six sentences, you should end your abstract with a sentence or two about the implications of your results. This miniature version of your discussion section might read something like, "The implications for ____ theory are discussed," or "The results are discussed in light of previous studies."

References

Now that you have the title and abstract written, it's time to write your reference list. To help you organize your references, we suggest you write each

• BOX 14-1 •

FORMAT CHECKLIST

Title Page

- ☑ 1. Is there a separate title page?
- ☑ 2. At the top right-hand corner do you have:
  - ☑ 2.1. a short, two- or three-word "mini-title" of your paper? This "mini-title" must be the first two or three words of your title.
  - ☑ 2.2. the number "1," indicating that it is page 1? You have two options about where to place page numbers. The "1" could be on the same line as the mini-title, just five spaces to the right of it (flush right). Or, you could put the page number flush right and one double-spaced line below the mini-title.
- ☑ 3. One double-spaced line below the short title and the page number, do you have a line that:
  - ☑ 3.1. starts at the left margin (about an inch from the left edge of the page)?
  - ☑ 3.2. begins with the words "Running head:" followed by a short (two to six words) phrase that describes your paper's topic? Note: The running head is *not* the same as the mini-title.
- ☑ 4. Is the two-to-six-word running head in all-capital letters?
- ☑ 5. Is the title centered? Is it one double-spaced line below the running head? Are the first letters of each word (except for words like "and" and "of") capitalized?
- ☑ 6. Is the title simple and to the point? Does it include the names of the relevant variables (in an experiment, the independent and dependent variables;

in a correlational study, the predictor and criterion variables)?
- ☑ 7. Is your name (first name, *middle initial,* and last name):
  - ☑ 7.1. one double-spaced line below the title?
  - ☑ 7.2. centered?
- ☑ 8. Is your institution's affiliation:
  - ☑ 8.1. one double-spaced line below your name?
  - ☑ 8.2. centered?

Abstract

- ☑ 1. Is it on its own separate page?
- ☑ 2. Do you have the number "2," indicating that it is page 2, at the top right-hand corner. (The "2" could either be five spaces to the right of the mini-title or flush right and one double-spaced line below the mini-title.)
- ☑ 3. Is the heading "Abstract" centered at the top of the page?
- ☑ 4. Is the text one double-spaced line below the heading?
- ☑ 5. Is it fewer than 120 words?
- ☑ 6. Is it a single paragraph?
- ☑ 7. Is the beginning of the abstract not indented? That is, the entire abstract (other than the title "Abstract") should look like a single block, with all lines beginning at the left margin.

Introduction

- ☑ 1. Does it begin on a separate page (page 3)?
- ☑ 2. Is the title of the article centered at the top of the first page of the introduction?
- ☑ 3. Did you remember that the introduction is *not* labeled? If you have the heading "Introduction," delete it.
- ☑ 4. When citing sources, did you avoid footnotes? Citations should be in parentheses.

(continued)

• BOX 14-1 •

FORMAT CHECKLIST *(continued)*

If you mention the authors in the sentence, simply put the date in parentheses. For example, "Jolley and Mitchell (1996) argued that . . ." If the authors' names are not part of the sentence, put their names and the date in parentheses. Separate the names from the dates with a comma. For example, "Some have argued that . . . (Jolley & Mitchell, 1996)."

☑ 5. If you are citing several articles within one set of parentheses, are the articles listed in alphabetical order? Did you separate the articles with a semicolon? For example, (Brickner, 1980; Jolley, 2000; Mitchell, 2001; Ostrom, 1965; Pusateri, 1995; Williams, 1992).

☑ 6. If you are discussing a paper with three or more authors, did you mention all the authors the first time you cited that paper? After you have referred to all the authors, you can—in subsequent citations—use the first author's last name, followed immediately (with no comma) by "et al." (for example, Glick et al., 1996).

☑ 7. Did you cite all your sources? Even when you don't quote them, you must still cite them. To reiterate, if you summarize or paraphrase a work, it must be cited!

Method Section

☑ 1. Is it written in the past tense?

☑ 2. Is the heading "Method" both centered and one double-spaced line below the last line of the introduction?

☑ 3. Is the word "Participants" one double-spaced line below "Method"?

☑ 4. Is the label "Participants" on the left margin and underlined?

☑ 5. Does the text for the participants section begin one double-spaced line below the "Participants" heading?

☑ 6. If you started a sentence with a number (such as, "Twenty undergraduates served as participants,"), did you spell out the number? Note: You can say: "Participants were 20 undergraduates," but you cannot say "20 undergraduates were participants." Instead, you must say "Twenty undergraduates were participants."

☑ 7. Is the word "Procedure" on the left margin and underlined?

☑ 8. Is it one double-spaced line below the last line of the previous section?

☑ 9. Does the text for the procedure section start on the line below the "Procedure" heading?

☑10. If you used standard laboratory equipment, did you identify the manufacturer and model number?

Results Section

☑ 1. Does it immediately follow the method section? (Don't skip to a new page.)

☑ 2. Is the title "Results" centered? Is it one double-spaced line below the last line of the method section?

☑ 3. Is it written in the past tense?

☑ 4. Are all statistics and probability values underlined?
   Right: . . . $\underline{t}$ = 9.08, $\underline{p}$ < .05.
   Wrong: . . . t = 9.08, p < .05.

☑ 5. When you report the result of a statistical test, did you give the statistic, the degrees of freedom for the test, the value of the statistic, and the level of significance (the *p* value)? The format, *except for the spacing*, should follow that shown below:

• BOX 14-1 •

FORMAT CHECKLIST *(continued)*

STATISTIC	*DF*	NUMERICAL VALUE OF THE TEST	PROBABILITY
F	(2,46) =	3.85,	p < .05
t	(24) =	3.0,	p < .001
r	=	.71,	p < .01

Note that you need to underline the statistic (F, t, r, etc.) and the "p." Also note that, in your report, you won't leave the spaces that are included in the table. Thus, in text, you would write F (2,46) = 3.85, p < .05.

- [✓] 6. If you have tables, do you refer to those tables in the text of your paper (such as, "As Table 1 indicates . . .")? Are tables numbered sequentially as they appear in the text of your paper?
- [✓] 7. Are all tables and graphs located at the very end of your report—after the references? Is each one on a separate page?
- [✓] 8. Have you referred to all graphs as figures ("Figure" 1, not "Graph" 1)? Did you label both the *x* and *y* axes? Did you give each graph an informative heading?
- [✓] 9. Is everything in each table double-spaced?
- [✓] 10. Do the tables comply with the format illustrated at right?

Discussion

- [✓] 1. Is the title "Discussion" centered? Is it one double-spaced line below the last line of the results section?
- [✓] 2. Did you use the same rules for citing sources as you did in the introduction (see Points 4–7 of the "Introduction" checklist)?
- [✓] 3. Did you avoid footnotes?
- [✓] 4. Did you cite any source from which you got ideas—even if you did not directly quote that source? If you have

Table 1

Pearson Product Moment Correlation for Self-Esteem

Group	Body Concept	
	Attractiveness	Fitness
Female	.65***	.50**
Male	.35*	.70***

*p < .05, **p < .01, ***p < .001

Table 2

Analysis of Variance: Exercise and Self-Esteem

Source	SS	df	MS	F
Between (Treatment)	499.41	2	249.71	9.75
Within (Error)	145.76	57	2.56	

any doubt about whether you should cite a source, then cite it!

References

- [✓] 1. Does your reference section start on a separate page?
- [✓] 2. Is the word "References" at the top of the page, centered?
- [✓] 3. Is everything double-spaced?
- [✓] 4. Are your references listed in alphabetical order (according to the last name of the first author)?
- [✓] 5. Is the first line of every reference indented five spaces?
- [✓] 6. If a reference takes up more than one line, are the additional lines of that reference *not* indented?
- [✓] 7. Does each individual reference start with the authors' last names and initials, followed by the year of publication (in parentheses) and then a period?
- [✓] 8. Are the titles of all books underlined?
- [✓] 9. Are the titles of all journals underlined?
- [✓] 10. Are the volume numbers of every journal underlined?

• BOX 14-1 •

FORMAT CHECKLIST *(continued)*

☑ 11. Did you avoid underlining the titles of journal articles?

☑ 12. When citing journal articles, did you avoid the word "pages" and the abbreviation "pp."?

☑ 13. Does every individual reference end with a period?

☑ 14. Are all the references in this section also cited in your paper? If not, you will have to add some citations to the body of your paper—or delete the reference.

☑ 15. Are all the sources cited in your paper also listed in this section? If not, you will have to add those sources to your references.

☑ 16. Are all sources you used both referenced and cited? If not, you may be guilty of plagiarism.

General Format

☑ 1. Is everything double spaced? Nothing should be single spaced!

☑ 2. Are the first two or three words of the title and the page number at the top, right-hand corner of every page?

☑ 3. Did you start every paragraph by indenting five spaces? (One exception: Don't indent the abstract.)

☑ 4. Have you avoided sexist and racist language?

☑ 5. Have you avoided passive sentences as much as possible?

☑ 6. Is the paper's appearance professional (no typos, neatly typed, etc.)?

☑ 7. Do not hyphenate words at the end of a line.

☑ 8. Do not have narrow margins. You should be able to take a ruler and find that there is nothing but white space within 1 inch from any edge of any page.

☑ 9. Are all main headings (Abstract, Method, Results, Discussion, References, etc.) centered, but *not* underlined? Are only the first letters of words in these headings capitalized?

☑ 10. Are all subheadings (Participants, Procedure, etc.) flush left (not indented) and underlined? Are only the first letters of words in these subheadings capitalized?

☑ 11. Be sure that you have not included anyone's first name or affiliation in your paper (except for the title page).

☑ 12. Be sure that you have given proper credit for any ideas, words, or quotes that you obtained from other sources.

---

reference on an index card and alphabetize the cards. If you have more than one reference for an author, put the cards for that author in chronological order (from oldest to most recent). By writing references on cards before you type them up, you reduce the chances of making two common errors: (1) not including all your references (which can lead to charges of plagiarism), and (2) not typing all your references in alphabetical order.

Once you have your references organized, you need to put them in APA style. The easiest way to get your references in APA style is to use the reference section of the sample paper (Appendix D) as a model. Thus, if you need to write the reference for a journal article with two authors, follow the example of the first reference.

One problem with using any model is that you may think you are doing what the model is doing, but you really aren't. To make sure that you are closely following the model in the sample paper, check your references page against the reference checklist in Box 14-1.

WRITING THE RESEARCH REPORT

If you wrote a research proposal, much of the work on your research report already has been done. Essentially, your research proposal was the first draft of your research report. The next few pages will help you convert that first draft into a polished, complete research report.

WHAT STAYS THE SAME OR CHANGES VERY LITTLE

The title page, introduction, and references from your proposal can be transferred to your research report without any changes. You will, however, need to make three changes in the method section.

First, you will need to change the method section to reflect any changes you made in how you conducted the study. Generally, the procedures you initially proposed are not the ones you end up following. Sometimes, after reading your proposal, your professor will ask you to make some modifications. Sometimes an ethics committee may mandate some changes. Often, after testing out your procedures on a few participants, you will make some changes so that the actual study will run more smoothly.

Second, you probably will have to make some minor changes in the participants section. Prior to running the study, you can rarely anticipate who your participants will be and how many you will have to exclude.

Third, you need to rewrite the method section in the past tense. In the proposal, you told people what you were going to do; in the report, you tell them what you did.

Like your method section, your abstract needs only minor modifications. Specifically, you need to add a sentence to describe the main results.

In contrast to the other sections, the results and discussion sections cannot always be transferred to the final report. Instead, you often will have to revise these sections extensively before you can put them in your final report.

Because these sections change the most from proposal to final report, the rest of this chapter will be devoted to these two sections.

WRITING THE RESULTS SECTION

There are two main purposes of the **results section:** (1) to show the reader that you competently analyzed the data, and (2) to tell the reader what you found. To accomplish these goals, you will report anywhere from one to five kinds of results:

1. results describing the distribution of participants' scores
2. results supporting the validity of your measure
3. results of the manipulation check
4. results relating to your hypothesis
5. other statistically significant results

Results Describing the Distribution of Scores

At the beginning of your results section, you might include a section that describes the distribution of scores on your dependent variable. Thus, you might give the mean and the standard deviation (or range) of scores.[3] For example, you might report that, "The scores on the measure were normally distributed ($M = 75$, range = 50–100)."

Most authors do not include a section that describes the distribution of scores. If you do include such a section, it probably will be for one of the following five reasons:

1. to make a case that the sample is representative of some population by showing either that the scores are very similar to the population's distribution of scores or that the scores were not unusually extreme
2. to argue that their data meet the assumptions of the statistical tests by showing that the scores were normally distributed or that the different groups had the same variances
3. to show that their data had to be transformed or that the data could not be analyzed by a certain statistical test because the data were not normally distributed
4. to argue that there should be no problems due to ceiling effects, floor effects, or restriction of range because there was a wide range of scores and those scores were normally distributed
5. to emphasize descriptive statistics that are of interest in their own right, as would be the case if reporting the percentage of the sample who had attempted suicide

Results Supporting the Measure's Validity

Like the section describing the distribution of scores, the section supporting the measure's validity often is omitted. If you are using an accepted, validated measure, you probably will omit this section. If you choose to include this section, you probably will stress the results that emphasize the measure's

1. test–retest or alternate-forms reliability, indicating that the measure is not unduly influenced by random error as shown by the fact that participants get the same score from one day to the next

---

[3]If the data are not normally distributed, you may want to provide a graph of the raw scores.

2. interobserver reliability, indicating that the measure is objectively scored because different observers give the participants the same scores

3. internal consistency, indicating that the items of a test or subscale are all measuring the same thing because the items correlate with each other. If a test is internally consistent, people who scored high on a characteristic according to one question on the test also tended to score high on that characteristic according to other questions on the test.

Results of the Manipulation Check

If you used a manipulation check, you should put these findings near the beginning of the results section. Although these results usually will be statistically significant and unsurprising, it is important to demonstrate that you manipulated what you said you would manipulate. Thus, reporting the outcome of your manipulation check is a good lead into discussing results relating to your hypothesis. That is, once you have shown the reader that you manipulated the variable you planned to manipulate, the reader is ready to know whether that variable produced the effects you expected.

Results Relating to Your Hypothesis

Your results section may not describe the distribution of scores, provide evidence for the validity of the measure, or describe the results of a manipulation check. However, your results section must describe the results relating to the hypothesis. In writing the results section, your main goal should always be to make it very easy for your readers to tell how the hypothesis did.

To make it easy for readers to tell how the hypothesis fared, tell your readers what the hypothesis was and whether it was supported. Then, clearly link the results to the hypothesis. For example, if your hypothesis was that people who own cats are less likely to hit their children, report what the data said about this hypothesis: "The hypothesis that people who own cats would be significantly less likely to hit their children was supported. Cat owners hit their children on the average 2.3 times a month per child, whereas people who did not own cats hit their children on the average 4.6 times, $F(1,64) = 18.2$, $p < .05$."

Other Significant Results

After reporting results relating to your hypothesis (whether or not the results were significant), you should report any other statistically significant results. Even if the results are unwanted and make no sense to you, significant results must be reported. Therefore you might report: "There was an unanticipated relationship between gender of the child and cat ownership. Girls were more likely to own cats, $F(1,64) = 20.1$, $p < .05$."

Tips on Writing the Results Section

Now you are familiar with the general parts of the results section, but how do you write one? To write a good results section, you need to realize that the goal of the results section is to help the reader understand what you found. There are three things you can do to help your reader understand what your results mean: (1) Go slowly, (2) explain what you are doing, and (3) focus on the hypothesis.

Tip 1: Start Off Simple   Sometimes, beginning writers lose their audience at the very beginning of the results section. To avoid that problem, start out slowly. You might begin the results section by simply explaining what the scores meant. Your goal would be to give the reader some sense as to what a participant who had a low score did differently than a person getting a high score.

What if the meaning of the scores is too obvious? Or, what if you explained how scores were computed in the method section? Then, you might start the results section with a simple analysis. For example, you might discuss results relating to the degree to which the different coders coded the data similarly. Or, you might discuss other results which should be fairly predictable and fairly easy to understand, such as the results of the manipulation check.

When discussing a set of analyses, start off by discussing simple or general findings and then move to more specific or complex tests. For example, report main effects before interactions and report the results of the overall F-test before talking about the results of more specific follow-up tests.

Tip 2: Don't Report Results—Analyze Them   Do not, however, merely report results. That is, do not, in effect, shove the results of the computer printout in the reader's face and say "Here, see if you can make sense of this!" Instead, follow our second tip, which is to give the reader your *analysis* of the results.

Your analysis will not include every statistic the computer generated. Instead, you will give the reader only those statistics that make a point.

In addition to giving the reader an analysis only if the analysis makes a point, you will tell the reader what the point is. The reader should not be left wondering, "Why is she telling me this?" For example, if you are doing an analysis to see whether your manipulation check worked, you will let the reader know by writing something like, "As a check on our attractiveness manipulation, we conducted a t-test on participants' ratings of the pictures. As predicted, the attractive ($M = 7.2$) pictures were rated as more attractive than the unattractive ($M = 2.1$) pictures, $t(28) = 81.2$, $p < .05$." To further help the reader realize the purpose of the analysis, you might even label that subsection "Attractiveness Manipulation Check."

Tip 3: Focus on the Hypothesis   The third, and most important tip, is to ask the question, "After reading the results section, will the reader know whether the results supported the hypothesis?" One way to determine if your results section achieves this goal is to ask a friend to read your results section. See if your friend can answer these five questions:

1. What was the hypothesis?
2. Was the hypothesis supported?

3. What statistical test was used to find this out?

4. What were the results of that test (value of the statistic and the **probability value:** the chances of obtaining this pattern of results if only chance were at work)?

5. Do the averages (or some other summary statistic, such as means, percentages, or correlation coefficients) help you understand whether the prediction was supported? If not, would a table or graph make things clearer?

By focusing on helping the reader understand whether the results supported the hypothesis, you will end up doing many of the things that we suggested above. You will leave out information that is irrelevant and distracting to the reader. You will include all information that helps the reader understand the results section such as what the scores mean, why the analysis is being done, and what the analysis shows.

Conclusions About Writing the Results Section

In short, you should try to make your results section as clear and understandable as possible. If you focus your results section on your hypothesis and have empathy for your reader, you should be able to write an understandable and useful results section.

WRITING THE DISCUSSION SECTION

If the results matched your predictions, the discussion section you wrote for your proposal might work as the discussion section for the final report. However, there are two reasons why the discussion section you wrote for your proposal probably will have to be substantially modified. First, it is unlikely that you will get exactly the results you expected. Second, during the course of conducting the research or writing the paper, you probably will think of problems or implications that you did not think of when you wrote your proposal.

As you revise the discussion section, be sure that you:

1. Briefly review the research question or hypothesis.

2. Briefly summarize the results, relating them to the hypothesis.

3. Interpret the results in light of the arguments made in your introduction.

4. Acknowledge alternative explanations for your results, trying to dismiss these alternatives, if possible.

5. Discuss unexpected findings and speculate on possible reasons for them.

6. Discuss, in general terms, future research. What would you do if you were to follow up on this research (assume an unlimited budget)? Follow-up research might focus on improving the methodology of your study, exploring unexpected findings, trying to rule out alternative theoretical explanations for your findings, testing the generality of your findings, looking for practical implications of the findings, looking for

variables that might have similar effects, or looking for mental or physiological factors that mediate the observed relationship.

7. Discuss the practical or theoretical implications of your findings.

Once you have written your discussion section, you are nearly finished. However, as with most papers, you will need to write several drafts before you have a polished paper. To help you edit your paper so that it conforms to APA format, check your "next-to-final draft" against the checklist in Box 14-1. In addition, *make sure that your paper matches the style of the model paper in Appendix D.*

Concluding Remarks

Well, you've done it! If you carefully followed the advice in this book, you should have just completed a carefully planned, meaningful, and ethical research project. Congratulations and best wishes for your continued success as a researcher!

Summary

1. The research journal and proposal will help you plan and conduct ethical and valid research.

2. The research proposal is more formal than the research journal and should conform to the *Publication Manual of the American Psychological Association* (1994).

3. In the introduction of your proposal, you need to summarize and critique relevant research. This critique should set up the reasons you think that your hypothesis: (a) will be supported, (b) should be tested, and (c) should be tested the way you are going to test it.

4. In the introduction, state your hypothesis, explain why your predictions make sense, and explain why your study will provide a valid test of your hypothesis.

5. Before writing the method section, you should carefully plan out each step of your study.

6. Once you have planned out every detail of your study, you should formalize your plan in the method, results, and discussion sections in your proposal.

7. The method section is the "how" section in which you explain how you plan to conduct your study and why you are going to do it that way.

8. In the proposal's results section, you will discuss how you plan to analyze your results.

9. In the discussion section, you will explore the implications of your anticipated research findings for theory, future research, or real life.

10. Once you finish the body of the proposal, write the abstract (a brief summary of the proposal), the title page, and the reference section. Much of your final report will be based on your proposal—provided you wrote a good proposal.

11. The title page, introduction, and reference sections of your proposal can be transferred directly to your final report. After you change the method section to the past tense, it may also be transferred (with only minor modifications) to the final report.

12. Try to make the results section as understandable as possible. Tell the reader what you are trying to find out by doing the analysis, and then tell the reader what you actually did find out from doing the analysis.

13. In the results section, be sure to stress whether the results supported or failed to support your hypothesis.

14. In the discussion section, summarize the main findings of your study and relate these to the points you made in the introduction.

15. Writing involves a great deal of rewriting.

16. Do not plagiarize! Keep notes about what you read so that you can cite it. Realize that even if you didn't quote a source, you still have to cite it if you borrowed from it or got some ideas from it.

Key Terms

plagiarism: using someone else's words, thoughts, or work without giving proper credit. Plagiarism is considered a serious act of academic dishonesty. Indeed, at some institutions, students convicted of plagiarism are expelled. Furthermore, concerns about plagiarism are no longer limited to colleges and universities. More and more, the world economy is based on information. Thus, more and more, businesses and individuals are concerned about the theft of ideas (intellectual property). Therefore, if you quote someone's work, use quotation marks; and if you paraphrase or in any sense borrow an idea from a source, cite that source. (p. 525)

abstract: a short, one-paragraph summary of a research proposal or article. The abstract must not exceed 120 words. It comes before the introduction. (p. 530)

introduction: after the abstract comes the introduction to the study. In the introduction, the authors tell you what their hypothesis is, why their hypothesis makes sense, how their study fits in with previous research, and why their study is worth doing. (p. 514)

method section: the part of the article immediately following the introduction. Whereas the introduction explains *why* the study was done, the method section describes *what* was done. For example, it will tell you what design was used, what the researchers said to the participants, what measures and equipment were used, how many participants were studied, and how they were selected. The method section could also be viewed as a "what we did" section. The method section is usually subdivided into at least two subsections: participants and procedure. (p. 524)

results section: the part of the article, immediately following the method section, that reports statistical results and relates those results to the hypotheses. From reading this section, you should know if the results supported the hypothesis. (p. 535)

discussion: the part of the article, immediately following the results section, that discusses the research findings and the study in a broader context and suggests research projects that could be done to follow up on the study. (p. 529)

research journal: a diary of your research ideas and your research experiences. The research journal can be a useful resource when it comes time to write the research proposal. (p. 512)

exploratory study: a study investigating an entirely new area of research. Unlike replications, an exploratory study does not follow directly from an existing study. (p. 518)

direct replication, exact replication: a copy of the original study. Direct replications are useful for establishing that the findings of the original study are reliable. (p. 520)

systematic replication: a study that varies from the original study only in some minor aspect. For example, a systematic replication may use more participants, more standardized procedures, more levels of the independent variable, or a more realistic setting than the original study. (p. 521)

conceptual replication: a study that is based on the original study, but uses different methods to better assess the true relationships between the variables examined in the original study. In a conceptual replication, you might use a different manipulation or a different measure. The conceptual replication is the most sophisticated kind of replication. (p. 522)

probability value (*p* value): the chances of obtaining a certain pattern of results if there really is no relationship between the variables. (p. 539)

APPENDIXES

APPENDIX A

ETHICS

Throughout this text, we have mentioned the importance of conducting research in an ethical manner. Therefore, you may wonder why we have an appendix on ethics. The main reason is so that you can have quick access to APA's ethical guidelines governing research.

HUMAN RESEARCH

Although we have included APA's guidelines on human research in this appendix, we will first highlight the main principles. The first thing a researcher should do is to try to foresee the risks to the people who would participate in the study. Knowing the risks can help in devising safeguards, in deciding whether the study should be conducted, and in letting participants decide whether to participate.

If there are any risks to participants, the researcher should seek out the advice of others to determine whether the study should be done. (As a student researcher, you should do this even if you think the study involves virtually no risk.) That is, the researcher should ask other researchers. In addition, researchers are often required by federal law or by their institution to submit their research to their department's ethics committee or the institution's Internal Review Board. (Your professor will tell you which committee[s] you have to deal with.) In consulting other people, the researcher may end up filling out a form like the one in Box A-1.

The point of consulting others is twofold. First, consulting others will help you look at alternatives. That is, others will ask the question: "Are there ways of answering the research question that would put participants at less risk?" Second, consulting with others may help you decide whether to do the study at all. Other people may see risks you did not see, or they may be more objective than you when it comes to weighing the risks to the participants against the potential gain. As a result of seeing and weighing the risks, your professor or an ethics committee may demand that the study not be done.

• BOX A-1 •
SAMPLE ETHICAL REVIEW FORM

Title:

Researcher:

1. Main hypothesis to be tested or brief statement of the problem to be investigated:

2. Will extra credit be given to students who participate in the project?

   Yes   No

3. Will participants include anyone other than students from our school?

   Yes   No

4. Will participants include children under 18, adults who are not legally competent, mentally handicapped, physically handicapped, prisoners, or pregnant women?

   Yes   No

   If yes, circle group or groups.

5. Will participants be video/audio taped?

   Yes   No

6. Will anyone other than the researchers be able to find out how an individual participant responded (are participants' responses coded in such a way that others could identify a particular participant's responses)?

   Yes   No

7. Does the research deal with sensitive aspects of participants' behavior such as illegal conduct, drug use (including alcohol), or sexual behavior?

   Yes   No

8. Are participants free to withdraw at any time without penalty?

   Yes   No

9. Are there any deceptive elements to the study?

   Yes   No

10. Will participants be exposed to any psychological stress such as fatigue, assault on values, or threats to self-esteem?

    Yes   No

11. Will participants be exposed to physical stress (electric shock, cold temperatures, etc.)?

    Yes   No

Attach the following:

1. Draft of the method section: Describe, in detail, the methodology of your study (essentially, how will the study be conducted from start to finish, as far as human participants are concerned?). Be specific about any manipulations used and any measurement instruments involved.

2. Copies of questionnaires, surveys, tests, or other paper-and-pencil measures to be used in the study.

3. Informed consent form.

Even if the research is approved by a review board, the bottom line is that the investigator is still the one person who is responsible for any harm done to the participants. To help minimize this harm, the researcher should have participants sign an informed consent form (see Box A-2) prior to participating in the study. The form should stress:

1. any foreseeable risks or discomforts that might cause the participant to decide not to participate

2. that the participant's participation is totally voluntary

3. that the participant can quit the study at any time, without giving a reason, and without any penalty

4. that the participant's responses will be confidential (if responses won't be confidential, this should be explained)

To ensure confidentiality, you might keep participants' responses anonymous: Don't have them put their names on the answer sheet. If you must have their names, use code numbers. Store the data with the code numbers in one place; store the names and the code numbers in a different place.

After the participant has filled out the consent form and participated in your study, you should debrief the participant. During this *debriefing*, you should:

1. Correct any misconceptions that were planted by the researchers.

2. Try to detect and remove any harm that may have been produced by the study.

3. Give a summary of the study in nontechnical terms (many departments believe this summary should be both written and oral, the written part

---

• BOX A-2 •

SAMPLE INFORMED CONSENT FORM

I have been informed that the study in which I have been asked to participate is investigating personnel decision making. I have also been informed that I will be asked to read personnel files of two job applicants and then asked to decide which of the two individuals I would be more likely to hire. I also understand that I will be asked to justify my decision. Furthermore, I understand that the study will take about 30 minutes of my time. I understand that the responses I give will be kept confidential. Although the researchers may write up the results of this study, my name will never be used.

I understand that I can withdraw from the study at any time without any problems. That is, if I choose to withdraw, I will receive full credit for participating. Furthermore, I understand that if participating becomes too stressful, I should withdraw from the study.

I understand that, after I have finished the study, the researcher will gladly answer any questions I might have. If I have any questions after that, I should feel free to call

Dr. _____ at

_____

Name (printed) _____.

I have read this statement and have had all my questions answered. Therefore, I give my written consent to participate in this investigation.

Signature _____ Date _____

Signature of person obtaining consent

_____ Date _____

being about one full page typed, describing the hypotheses, why the procedures were used, and why the study was important).

4. Provide participants an opportunity to ask whatever questions they may have (some departments want you to provide a number for participants to call so research participants can ask follow-up questions).

5. Thank the participant for participating.

6. Explain why deception was necessary (if deception was used).

Debriefing is a good time to assess the degree to which you and your co-investigators are conducting the study in an ethical manner. To do so, ask participants to complete an anonymous questionnaire that assesses their perceptions of the study. Such a questionnaire might include the following questions:

1. Could you quit the study at any time?

2. Were you given enough information to decide whether you wanted to participate? If not, what should you have been told before you took part in the study?

3. What was the purpose of this research?

4. Were you treated with respect?

5. Was the researcher polite?

6. Did you have all your questions answered?

7. Were you deceived in any way? If so, did the researcher provide justification for the deception? Are you satisfied with that justification? Why or why not?

8. Did you experience more discomfort than you would in your day-to-day activities? If so, did the researcher provide sufficient justification for discomfort? What caused this discomfort?

9. Do you think your responses will be kept confidential?

As you can see, the ideal study would not involve stress or deception. Participants would choose whether to participate only after reading an accurate description of the study. After the study was done, all data would be kept entirely confidential, and participants would be completely debriefed.

The ethical principles, however, recognize that studies may be ethical even though the studies may involve unpleasantness of some kind, may involve deception, may have participants participate without the benefit of informed consent, or may be done without completely debriefing participants. However, when such guidelines as informed consent and complete debriefing are violated, it can be for only one of two reasons.

First, the potential benefits of the study must justify such a violation—and an outside committee, rather than the researcher, should make the judgment. However, even if an impartial committee agrees that the benefits outweigh the costs, alternatives to the study must be considered.

Second, the guidelines may be violated if upholding one guideline means harming the participant. For example, suppose that a participant's response was bizarre and unusual. Telling a participant that his behavior was bizarre might meet the guideline of giving a complete debriefing. However, such a disclosure might upset the participant. For a closer look at ethical guidelines for human research, see Box A-3.

ANIMAL RESEARCH

Conducting animal research in an ethical manner is vital. Unethical treatment of animals is inhumane and, in many cases, illegal. However, we have not spent much time on ethics in animal research for two basic reasons. First, the basic concepts that govern human research also govern animal research. For example, in animal research, as in human research, pain and discomfort should be minimized. Likewise, in both human and animal research any study that inflicts stress must be justifiable on the basis that: (1) The study is likely to produce some benefit that outweighs the risks, and (2) there is no other way to get that potential benefit.

Second, because humane treatment of animals is so important, APA has taken the following three steps to almost guarantee that you cannot do animal research without knowing APA's ethical standards:

1. If you conduct research with animal participants, you must be trained in the humane care, handling, and maintenance of animals.
2. As a student, you cannot conduct research with animals unless you are supervised by someone who is well trained in both animal research and in how to handle, care for, and maintain animals.
3. A copy of the ethical guidelines relating to animal research must be posted in the animal lab.

Because you will be shown how to take care of the animals, because you will be supervised, and because the guidelines will be right in the lab, you probably will not violate ethical principles out of ignorance. However, since violating ethical procedures in animal research may violate federal law, you should be very careful.

If you are conducting research with animals, you should consult APA's ethical guidelines for animal research at the end of this appendix (see Box A-4). In addition, you should work closely with your research supervisor. Finally, figure out some strategy so that you do not forget to take care of your animal. Unless you have a routine or a system, it is easy to forget to check on your animal during the weekend. However, animals need food, water, gentle handling, and a clean living environment *every single day.*

• BOX A-3 •

The American Psychological Association's Principles Covering the Treatment of Human Participants

1.14 Avoiding Harm

Psychologists take reasonable steps to avoid harming their patients or clients, research participants, students, and others with whom they work, and to minimize harm where it is foreseeable and unavoidable.

6.06 Planning Research

(a) Psychologists design, conduct, and report research in accordance with recognized standards of scientific competence and ethical research.

(b) Psychologists plan their research so as to minimize the possibility that results will be misleading.

(c) In planning research, psychologists consider its ethical acceptability under the Ethics Code. If an ethical issue is unclear, psychologists seek to resolve the issue through consultation with institutional review boards, animal care and use committees, peer consultations, or other proper mechanisms.

(d) Psychologists take reasonable steps to implement appropriate protections for the rights and welfare of human participants, other persons affected by the research, and the welfare of animal subjects.

6.07 Responsibility

(a) Psychologists conduct research competently and with due concern for the dignity and welfare of the participants.

(b) Psychologists are responsible for the ethical conduct of research conducted by them or by others under their supervision or control.

(c) Researchers and assistants are permitted to perform only those tasks for which they are appropriately trained and prepared.

(d) As part of the process of development and implementation of research projects, psychologists consult those with expertise concerning any special population under investigation or most likely to be affected.

6.08 Compliance With Law and Standards

Psychologists plan and conduct research in a manner consistent with federal and state law and regulations, as well as professional standards governing the conduct of research, and particularly those standards governing research with human participants and animal subjects.

6.09 Institutional Approval

Psychologists obtain from host institutions or organizations appropriate approval prior to conducting research, and they provide accurate information about their research proposals. They conduct the research in accordance with the approved research protocol.

6.10 Research Responsibilities

Prior to conducting research (except research involving only anonymous surveys, naturalistic observations, or similar research), psychologists enter into an agreement with participants that clarifies the nature of the research and the responsibilities of each party.

6.11 Informed Consent to Research

(a) Psychologists use language that is reasonably understandable to research participants in obtaining their appropriate

(continued)

informed consent (except as provided in Standard 6.12, Dispensing With Informed Consent). Such informed consent is appropriately documented.

(b) Using language that is reasonably understandable to participants, psychologists inform participants of the nature of the research; they inform participants that they are free to participate or to decline to participate or to withdraw from the research; they explain the foreseeable consequences of declining or withdrawing; they inform participants of significant factors that may be expected to influence their willingness to participate (such as risks, discomfort, adverse effects, or limitations on confidentiality, except as provided in Standard 6.15, Deception in Research); and they explain other aspects about which the prospective participants inquire.

(c) When psychologists conduct research with individuals such as students or subordinates, psychologists take special care to protect the prospective participants from adverse consequences of declining or withdrawing from participation.

(d) When research participation is a course requirement or opportunity for extra credit, the prospective participant is given the choice of equitable alternative activities.

(e) For persons who are legally incapable of giving informed consent, psychologists nevertheless (1) provide an appropriate explanation, (2) obtain the participant's assent, and (3) obtain appropriate permission from a legally authorized person, if such substitute consent is permitted by law.

6.12 Dispensing With Informed Consent

Before determining that planned research (such as research involving only anonymous questionnaires, naturalistic observations, or certain kinds of archival research) does not require the informed consent of research participants, psychologists consider applicable regulations and institutional review board requirements, and they consult with colleagues as appropriate.

6.13 Informed Consent in Research Filming or Recording

Psychologists obtain informed consent from research participants prior to filming or recording them in any form, unless the research involves simply naturalistic observations in public places and it is not anticipated that the recording will be used in a manner that could cause personal identification or harm.

6.14 Offering Inducements for Research Participants

(a) In offering professional services as an inducement to obtain research participants, psychologists make clear the nature of the services, as well as the risks, obligations, and limitations. (See also Standard 1.18, Barter [With Patients or Clients].)

(b) Psychologists do not offer excessive or inappropriate financial or other inducements to obtain research participants, particularly when it might tend to coerce participation.

6.15 Deception in Research

(a) Psychologists do not conduct a study involving deception unless they have determined that the use of deceptive techniques is justified by the study's prospective scientific, educational, or applied value and that equally effective alternative procedures that do not use deception are not feasible.

(b) Psychologists never deceive research participants about significant aspects that would affect their willingness to participate, such as physical risks, discomfort, or unpleasant emotional experiences.

(c) Any other deception that is an integral feature of the design and conduct of an experiment must be explained to participants as early as is feasible, preferably at the conclusion of their participation, but no later than at the conclusion of the research. (See also Standard 6.18, Providing Participants With Information About the Study.)

6.16 Sharing and Utilizing Data

Psychologists inform research participants of their anticipated sharing or further use of personally identifiable research data and of the possibility of unanticipated future uses.

6.17 Minimizing Invasiveness

In conducting research, psychologists interfere with the participants or milieu from which data are collected only in a manner that is warranted by an appropriate research design and that is consistent with psychologists' roles as scientific investigators.

6.18 Providing Participants With Information About the Study

(a) Psychologists provide a prompt opportunity for participants to obtain appropriate information about the nature, results, and conclusions of the research; and psychologists attempt to correct any misconceptions that participants may have.

(b) If scientific or humane values justify delaying or withholding this informa-

tion, psychologists take reasonable measures to reduce the risk of harm.

6.19 Honoring Commitments

Psychologists take reasonable measures to honor all commitments they have made to research participants.

5.02 Maintaining Confidentiality

Psychologists have a primary obligation and take reasonable precautions to respect the confidentiality rights of those with whom they work or consult, recognizing that confidentiality may be established by law, institutional rules, or professional or scientific relationships. (See also Standard 6.26, Professional Reviewers.)

5.03 Minimizing Intrusions on Privacy

(a) In order to minimize intrusions on privacy, psychologists include in written and oral reports, consultations, and the like, only information germane to the purpose for which the communication is made.

(b) Psychologists discuss confidential information obtained in clinical or consulting relationships, or evaluate data concerning patients, individual or organizational clients, students, research participants, supervisees, and employees, only for appropriate scientific or professional purposes and only with persons clearly concerned with such matters.

5.04 Maintenance of Records

Psychologists maintain appropriate confidentiality in creating, storing, accessing, transferring, and disposing of records under their control, whether these are written, automated, or in any other medium. Psychologists maintain and dispose of records in accordance with law and in a manner that permits compliance with the requirements of this Ethics Code.

(continued)

• BOX A-3 (CONTINUED) •

THE AMERICAN PSYCHOLOGICAL ASSOCIATION'S PRINCIPLES
COVERING THE TREATMENT OF HUMAN PARTICIPANTS

6.21 Reporting of Results

(a) Psychologists do not fabricate data or falsify results in their publications.

(b) If psychologists discover significant errors in their published data, they take reasonable steps to correct such errors in a correction, retraction, erratum, or other appropriate publication means.

6.22 Plagiarism

Psychologists do not present substantial portions or elements of another's work or data as their own, even if the other work or data source is cited occasionally.

SOURCE: Ethical Principles of Psychologists and Code of Conduct (1992). *American Psychologist, 47,* 1597–1611. Reprinted with the kind permission of the American Psychological Association.

• BOX A-4 •

GUIDELINES FOR ETHICAL CONDUCT IN
THE CARE AND USE OF ANIMALS

I. Justification of the Research

A. Research should be undertaken with a clear scientific purpose. There should be a reasonable expectation that the research will a) increase knowledge of the processes underlying the evolution, development, maintenance, alteration, control, or biological significance of behavior; b) determine the replicability and generality of prior research; c) increase understanding of the species under study; or d) provide results that benefit the health or welfare of humans or other animals.

B. The scientific purpose of the research should be of sufficient potential significance to justify the use of animals. Psychologists should act on the assumption that procedures that would produce pain in humans will also do so in other animals.

C. The species chosen for study should be best suited to answer the question(s) posed. The psychologist should always consider the possibility of using other species, nonanimal alternatives, or procedures that minimize the number of animals in research, and should be familiar with the appropriate literature.

D. Research on animals may not be conducted until the protocol has been reviewed by an appropriate animal care committee, for example, an institutional animal care and use committee (IACUC), to ensure that the procedures are appropriate and humane.

E. The psychologist should monitor the research and the animals' welfare throughout the course of an investigation to ensure continued justification for the research.

II. Personnel

A. Psychologists should ensure that personnel involved in their research with animals be familiar with these guidelines.

B. Animal use procedures must conform with federal regulations regarding personnel, supervision, record keeping, and veterinary care.[1]

C. Behavior is both the focus of study of many experiments as well as a primary source of information about an animal's health and well-being. It is therefore necessary that psychologists and their assistants be informed about the behavioral characteristics of their animal subjects so as to be aware of normal, species-specific behaviors and unusual behaviors that could forewarn of health problems.

D. Psychologists should ensure that all individuals who use animals under their supervision receive explicit instruction in experimental methods and in the care, maintenance, and handling of the species being studied. Responsibilities and activities of all individuals dealing with animals should be consistent with their respective competencies, training, and experience in either the laboratory or the field setting.

III. Care and Housing of Animals

The concept of psychological well-being of animals is of current concern and debate and is included in Federal Regulations (United States Department of Agriculture [USDA], 1991). As a scientific and professional organization, APA recognizes the complexities of defining psychological well-being.

Procedures appropriate for a particular species may be inappropriate for others. Hence, APA does not presently stipulate specific guidelines regarding the maintenance of psychological well-being of research animals. Psychologists familiar with the species should be best qualified professionally to judge measures such as enrichment to maintain or improve psychological well-being of those species.

A. The facilities housing animals should meet or exceed current regulations and guidelines (USDA, 1990, 1991) and are required to be inspected twice a year (USDA, 1989).

B. All procedures carried out on animals are to be reviewed by a local animal-care committee to ensure that the procedures are appropriate and humane.

The committee should have representation from within the institution and from the local community. In the event that it is not possible to constitute an appropriate local animal-care committee, psychologists are encouraged to seek advice from a corresponding committee of a cooperative institution.

C. Responsibilities for the conditions under which animals are kept, both within and outside of the context of active experimentation or teaching, rests with the psychologist under the supervision of the animal-care committee (where required by federal regulations) and with individuals appointed by the institution to oversee animal care. Animals are to be provided with humane care and healthful conditions during their stay in the facility. In addition to the federal requirements to provide for the psychological well-being of nonhuman primates used in research, psychologists are encouraged to consider

(continued)

---

[1]U. S. Department of Agriculture. (1989, August 21). Animal welfare; Final rules. Federal Register. U. S. Department of Agriculture. (1990, July 16). Animal welfare; Guinea pigs, hamsters, and rabbits. Federal Register. U. S. Department of Agriculture. (1991, February 15). Animal welfare; Standards; Final rule. Federal Register.

• BOX A-4 (CONTINUED) •

GUIDELINES FOR ETHICAL CONDUCT IN THE CARE AND USE OF ANIMALS

enriching the environments of their laboratory animals and should keep abreast of literature on well-being and enrichment for the species with which they work.

IV. Acquisition of Animals

A. Animals not bred in the psychologist's facility are to be acquired lawfully. The USDA and local ordinances should be consulted for information regarding regulations and approved suppliers.

B. Psychologists should make every effort to ensure that those responsible for transporting the animals to the facility provide adequate food, water, ventilation, space, and impose no unnecessary stress on the animals.

C. Animals taken from the wild should be trapped in a humane manner and in accordance with applicable federal, state, and local regulations.

D. Endangered species or taxa should be used only with full attention to required permits and ethical concerns. Information and permit applications can be obtained from:

Fish and Wildlife Service
Office of Management Authority
U. S. Dept. of the Interior
4401 N. Fairfax Dr., Rm. 432
Arlington, VA 22043
703-358-2104
Similar caution should be used in work with threatened species or taxa.

V. Experimental Procedures

Humane consideration for the well-being of the animal should be incorporated into the de-

sign and conduct of all procedures involving animals, while keeping in mind the primary goal of experimental procedures—the acquisition of sound, replicable data. The conduct of all procedures is governed by Guideline I.

A. Behavioral studies that involve no aversive stimulation to, or overt sign of distress from, the animal are acceptable. These include observational and other noninvasive forms of data collection.

B. When alternative behavioral procedures are available, those that minimize discomfort to the animal should be used. When using aversive conditions, psychologists should adjust the parameters of stimulation to levels that appear minimal, though compatible with the aims of the research. Psychologists are encouraged to test painful stimuli on themselves, whenever reasonable. Whenever consistent with the goals of the research, consideration should be given to providing the animals with control of the potentially aversive stimulation.

C. Procedures in which the animal is anesthetized and insensitive to pain throughout the procedure and is euthanized before regaining consciousness are generally acceptable.

D. Procedures involving more than momentary or slight aversive stimulation, which is not relieved by medication or other acceptable methods, should be undertaken only when the objectives of the research cannot be achieved by other methods.

E. Experimental procedures that require prolonged aversive conditions or produce tissue damage or metabolic disturbances require greater justification and surveillance. These include prolonged exposure to extreme environmental conditions, experimentally induced prey killing, or infliction of physical trauma or tissue damage. An animal observed to be in a state of severe distress or chronic pain that cannot be alleviated and is not essential to the purposes of the research should be euthanized immediately.

F. Procedures that use restraint must conform to federal regulations and guidelines.

G. Procedures involving the use of paralytic agents without reduction in pain sensation require particular prudence and humane concern. Use of muscle relaxants or paralytics alone during surgery, without general anesthesia, is unacceptable and should be avoided.

H. Surgical procedures, because of their invasive nature, require close supervision and attention to humane considerations by the psychologist. Aseptic (methods that minimize risks of infection) techniques must be used on laboratory animals whenever possible.

1. All surgical procedures and anesthetization should be conducted under the direct supervision of a person who is competent in the use of the procedures.

2. If the surgical procedure is likely to cause greater discomfort than that attending anesthetization, and unless there is specific justification for acting otherwise, animals should be maintained under anesthesia until the procedure is ended.

3. Sound postoperative monitoring and care, which may include the use of analgesics and antibiotics, should

be provided to minimize discomfort and to prevent infection and other untoward consequences of the procedure.

4. Animals cannot be subjected to successive surgical procedures unless these are required by the nature of the research, the nature of the surgery, or for the well-being of the animal. Multiple surgeries on the same animal must receive special approval from the animal-care committee.

I. When the use of an animal is no longer required by an experimental protocol or procedure, in order to minimize the number of animals used in research, alternative uses of the animals should be considered. Such uses should be compatible with the goals of research and the welfare of the animal. Care should be taken that such an action does not expose the animal to multiple surgeries.

J. The return of wild-caught animals to the field can carry substantial risks, both to the formerly captive animals and to the ecosystem. Animals reared in the laboratory should not be released because, in most cases, they cannot survive, or they may survive by disrupting the natural ecology.

K. When euthanasia appears to be the appropriate alternative, either as a requirement of the research or because it constitutes the most humane form of disposition of an animal at the conclusion of the research:

1. Euthanasia shall be accomplished in a humane manner, appropriate for the species, and in such a way as to ensure immediate death, and in accordance with procedures outlined in the latest version of the American

---

• BOX A-4 (CONTINUED) •

GUIDELINES FOR ETHICAL CONDUCT IN THE CARE AND USE OF ANIMALS

Veterinary Medical Association (AVMA) Panel on Euthanasia.[2]

2. Disposal of euthanized animals should be accomplished in a manner that is in accord with all relevant legislation, consistent with health, environmental, and aesthetic concerns, and approved by the animal-care committee. No animal shall be discarded until its death is verified.

VI. Field Research

Field research, because of its potential to damage sensitive ecosystems and ethologies, should be subject to animal-care committee approval. Field research, if strictly observational, may not require animal-care committee approval (USDA, 1989, pg. 36126).

A. Psychologists conducting field research should disturb their populations as little as possible—consistent with the goals of the research. Every effort should be made to minimize potential harmful effects of the study on the population and on other plant and animal species in the area.

B. Research conducted in populated areas should be done with respect for the property and privacy of the inhabitants of the area.

C. Particular justification is required for the study of endangered species. Such research on endangered species should not be conducted unless animal-care committee approval has been obtained and all requisite permits are obtained (see IVD).

SOURCE: *Guidelines for Ethical Conduct in the Care and Use of Animals* (1996). Reprinted with the kind permission of the American Psychological Association.

[2]Write to: AVMA, 1931 N. Meacham Road, Suite 100, Schaumburg, IL 60173, or call (708) 925-8070

SEARCHING THE LITERATURE (ELECTRONICALLY AND THE OLD-FASHIONED WAY)

Library research is a necessary and useful component of any research project. Library research can help you come up with your basic research question, refine that question into a hypothesis, and inform you about research and theories that relate to your hypothesis.

Once you have refined and justified your hypothesis, a literature review can help you design your study. Specifically, a thorough search through your library's resources can help by directing your attention to measures and manipulations that other researchers have found fruitful.

To some students, conducting a literature search means doing a computer search. However, to conduct a literature review, there are eight basic steps you can take—and seven of those do not involve computer searches. Specifically, you could:

1. Consult books.
   a. Consult introductory psychology texts.
   b. Consult specialized texts (texts on your general topic [such as memory]). These texts may target juniors, seniors, or even graduate students.
   c. Consult books or chapters written for experts in the field. You may be able to find these texts by:
      1. looking at *Books in Print*
      2. looking at *PsycBooks: Books & Chapters in Psychology,* a set of volumes especially designed to help psychologists locate recent books and chapters that are relevant to their specific interest area
      3. looking at the *Annual Review of Psychology*
      4. consulting the card catalog or browsing through the "BF" section of your library

2. Track down articles referenced in those books. Note: Older, bound issues of journals may be in different parts of the library than newer issues.

3. Read those articles and their reference sections. Then, track down the research cited in those articles.

4. To see if the authors have done more-recent research, look them up in the author index of *Psychological Abstracts* or in the *Social Science Index* (both are located in the reference section of your library).

5. Look up your topic in the subject index of *Psychological Abstracts*.

6. See what recent articles have referenced your key articles by consulting the *Social Science Citation Index* (located in the reference section of your library).

7. Scan current issues of journals that are general in scope (*Psychological Bulletin, American Psychologist, Psychological Science, PsychScans, Current Contents*).

8. Identify key terms (often, with the assistance of a reference librarian and the *Psychological Thesaurus*) that will allow you to search the literature by taking advantage of the library's access to electronic databases.

The first three steps of the literature search (looking at books and the articles they cite) are fairly straightforward. The remaining steps are not. Therefore, the rest of this appendix is devoted to making those steps more manageable.

PSYCHOLOGICAL ABSTRACTS

Many people start their literature search with the *Psychological Abstracts*. The *Psychological Abstracts* include brief (fewer than 120 words) summaries of a wide range of work in psychology and related fields. To get a sense of what a rich resource the *Abstracts* are, consider that they summarize articles from hundreds of journals, as well as summarize books and doctoral dissertations.

The inclusiveness of the *Abstracts* means that they probably include any relevant article you might want. However, the inclusiveness also poses a problem: How do you find the articles you want from among the thousands of articles summarized in the *Abstracts*? Reading the *Abstracts* from cover to cover is not a practical option. Fortunately, because the *Abstracts* are well organized, it is fairly easy to get all the information you need.

SEARCHING BY SUBJECT

Since the *Abstracts* are organized and indexed by topic, the first step is to decide what topics you want to look up. At the very least, you will want to look up your dependent measure and the general topic you are investigating.

USING THE THESAURUS

At best, looking under these topics will probably cause you to miss some important references. At worst, looking under these topics might give you no references. Why? Because psychologists may have used other names for the topics and concepts you wish to research. To find out about those other terms, look at the *Psychological Thesaurus.* The thesaurus will tell you other terms under which your criterion variable might be listed. For example, "self" is also called identity, personality, and ego. Because the *Psychological Thesaurus* is so useful for searching the *Abstracts,* it usually will be located with the *Abstracts.*

Once you have consulted the thesaurus (and perhaps also talked to a reference librarian), you should be armed with key terms that will guide a productive search. At that point, you are ready to tackle the *Abstracts.*

CURRENT ISSUES OF *PSYCHOLOGICAL ABSTRACTS*

If you are trying to find current references, locate the *Abstracts* issues over the past year. The abstracts published during the year will be found in several softbound issues that share the same volume number. For example, all of the issues published in 1996 are classified as Volume 83.

Once you have rounded up all the issues for the year, the rest of your job is simple. Look up your terms in the subject index in the back of each issue. The index will give you the *numbers* of the abstracts relating to that term. For example, if next to your term you saw "1029," that would tell you that the abstract is number 1029, the 1,029th abstract of that volume. (Each abstract has a number. Like page numbers, abstract numbers go in order. Thus, 1,000 is right after *Abstract* number 999 and right before number 1,001. At first, you might think it would be better to give page numbers rather than abstract numbers. However, abstract numbers are more useful because there could be 20 abstracts on a single page. Thus, the numbers tell you exactly where to look. Consequently, after using the abstracts for just a few minutes, you will appreciate the value of using the abstract's specific number.)

After reading the numbers of all the potentially important abstracts from the index, go back through the issue locating those abstracts. The only hassle is that since each monthly index covers only that issue, you will have to look up your terms several times. That is, you have to look up "self" in the January issue index as well as in the March issue.

HARDBOUND ISSUES

To help people avoid the hassle of looking up the same term again and again, most libraries bind together the previous years' issues. Specifically, they bind all the issues of the *Abstracts* that bear the same volume number. For example, all of the issues published in 1996 are probably bound together with a hardbound cover and labeled Volume 83. However, they do not bind the indexes with the *Abstracts*. Instead, the subject and author indexes are bound separately. Thus, there are three "books" for each year: a subject index, an author index, and a volume containing the actual abstracts. In other words, for each of the hardbound volumes there is a hardbound subject index and a hardbound author index. The indexes will have the same volume number as the *Abstracts* to which they refer. Consequently, the 1996 Abstracts, the 1996 subject index, and the 1996 author index are all labeled Volume 83.

In short, if you want to locate references for previous years, find the hardbound indexes that correspond to the years in which you are interested. Look up your terms in the subject indexes. When you find a listing for one of your terms, write down both the volume number of the index and the abstract numbers. Then, go to that volume of the *Abstracts*.

Looking up References by Author

If you know the names of investigators who have done research relating to your study, you may want to see if they have done more-recent work. In that case, look up their names in a recent volume's author index.

Browsing Through the Abstracts

In a given volume, all abstracts that are on the same topic are located together. Thus, once you find an abstract that addresses your topic, look at the surrounding abstracts.

Finding the Original Resource

After reading an abstract of the study, you will have a good idea whether you want to read the original source. If so, you will find a reference for the original publication with the abstract. Go to your library's catalog files to locate the original source. If your library doesn't own it, ask the library if you can get it through interlibrary loan.

SOCIAL SCIENCES INDEX

A source that is like the *Abstracts*—but even more inclusive—is the *Social Sciences Index*. This index is a comprehensive source for journal references in all the social sciences. In addition to psychology, such fields as anthropology, sociology, social work, and geography are included. Since psychologists are not the only people who conduct behavioral research, *Social Sciences Index* can help you locate useful references published in nonpsychological journals.

Like *Psychological Abstracts*, several issues are published each year. Like the *Abstracts*, the issues for a particular year are identified by the same volume number and bound together in hardback. Finally, like the *Abstracts*, the most recent indexes will probably be in several softbound issues, each bearing the same volume number.

Unlike the *Abstracts,* the *Social Sciences Index* does not summarize the studies it cites. Thus, it is more like the indexes to the *Abstracts* than the *Abstracts* themselves. Indeed, if you combined the subject and author indexes of the *Abstracts*—and kept everything in alphabetical order—this combined index would resemble the *Social Sciences Index.*

In short, there are five points to keep in mind about the *Social Sciences Index:*

1. You can search it by author and topic.
2. If you search it by topic, consult the *Psychological Thesaurus* to be sure that you are using the appropriate term(s) for your topic.
3. It contains citations to work in psychology and to fields other than psychology.
4. It does not provide summaries of the articles it references.
5. It is simpler to use than *Psychological Abstracts.*

....

SOCIAL SCIENCE CITATION INDEX

Unlike the *Social Sciences Index,* the *Social Science Citation Index (SSCI)* gives you three different ways to locate references. You can find references by topic, by who wrote it, and by who referenced (cited) it. The *Social Science Citation Index* is able to do this because it consists of three separate but related indexes: a subject index, author index, and citation index. Each index covers the same journal articles. They all index more than 70,000 articles that appear in more than 2,000 journals. The difference is in how they index those articles.

The fact that they all cover the same articles has two important implications. First, you can start your search using any of the indexes. Where you start will probably depend on what you already know. If you only know the topic, you will use the subject index. If you know a researcher who does work in this area, you may start with the author index. If you know of a classic study in your area, you may want to find articles that cite that study. Therefore, you would start your search in the citation index.

Second, you may get information in one index that will give you leads that you can follow up in another index. For instance, in searching the subject index, you may repeatedly find the name of a certain author. Therefore, you may choose to look up that author in the author index.

The Permuterm Subject Index

The *Social Science Citation Index* refers to its subject index as the Permuterm Subject Index (PSI). In the PSI, every major word or phrase from the title of an article is paired with every other major word in that title. The goal is to develop word pairs that indicate what the study is about. For example, if an article were titled "Sex differences in the effect of television viewing on aggression" the article would be indexed under "Sex Differences and Aggression"; "Sex Differences and Television Viewing"; and "Television Viewing and Aggression." These permuted (arranged in all possible ways) pairs are alphabetically listed as two-level indexing entries and linked to the names of the authors who used them in the titles of their articles. For example, an entry in the PSI might look like this:

AGGRESSION	
SEX DIFFERENCES	ERON M
TELEVISION VIEWING	BUNKER A
SEX DIFFERENCES	
AGGRESSION	ERON M
TELEVISION VIEWING	MUTIN SS
TELEVISION VIEWING	
AGGRESSION	BUNKER A
SEX DIFFERENCES	MUTIN SS

Thus, the PSI tells you that during the period indexed, the authors Bunker and Mutin used the words shown opposite their name ("Television Viewing and Aggression" and "Television Viewing and Sex Differences," respectively).

To use PSI, simply think of words and word pairs that are likely to appear in the titles of articles related to your study. By looking up these words, you will discover the names of authors who have used the words in the titles of their articles. Once you find the names of authors, look them up in the Source Index.

The Source Index

The Source Index is a straightforward author index for the articles covered each year. For each article indexed, you are given the language it is written in (if it isn't English), its title, authors, journal, volume number, page numbers, year, the number of references cited in the article, and the journal issue number. In addition, beginning with the May–August 1974 issue, the references contained in each indexed article are listed. To facilitate reprint requests and other correspondence, a mailing address is often provided for each first author. Below is a sample entry:

BUNKER, A
    THE RELATIONSHIP OF AGGRESSION AND TV VIEWING
     J APPL PSY 25 09 87 20R N3
     CTR FOR REHABILITATIVE CHANGE, CENTER AVENUE
      NEW MEXICO, MEXICO

As the entry's third line reveals, the entry comes from an article published in the *Journal of Applied Psychology*, volume 25. It begins on page 9, was published in 1987, has 20 references, and is in issue number 3.

The Citation Index

The final index included in the *Social Science Citation Index* is the Citation Index. This index looks at what references authors cite in their paper. The Citation Index is based on two related assumptions. First, if a paper cites an article, then the paper is on the same topic as the older (cited) reference. Second, papers that refer to (cite) the same article usually address the same topic. For example, many of the papers that cite an article on the effects of chlorpromazine on the sexual behavior of rats probably investigate the effects of drugs on the sexual behavior of rats.

To start a search in the Citation Index, look up the name of an author who published material relevant to your topic. If anything the author has written was cited during the indexing period, the names of the publications that were cited will be listed. This feature is useful in at least two ways. First, if you are not completely familiar with the author's work, you may find out about other interesting articles by that author. Second, if nobody cited the paper you are interested in, you will know instantly because the article will not appear.

If the article you are interested in was cited, the Citation Index will include the name of that article. Next to the article name will be the names of the authors who cited the publication. Now that you know who referenced the publication, you need to find out in which journal and in which article they referenced it. To do this, look up their names in the Source Index.

In summary, the *Social Sciences Citation Index* allows you to do at least three basic types of searches. If you know of a classic study in your area of research, you can do a citation search. If you do not know of an earlier, relevant paper, you can do a search by looking up the variables you are studying: a permuterm (subject) search. Finally, when you know the name of a researcher who has recently published on your topic (or learn of such a person as a result of a permuterm or citation search), do an author search.

CURRENT CONTENTS

In contrast to the sources we described earlier, *Current Contents* is very easy to use. *Current Contents* simply lists the tables of contents for several journals. Since you can often figure out whether an article is relevant to your topic from its title, this reference can be very useful. Thus, by looking at titles you can determine which articles you want to find and read. Although you might prefer that the articles be organized by topic rather than by journal, you will soon find that most journals cover only certain topics. That is, if you are looking for a measure of aggression, you would not look at the contents for *The Journal of Memory and Cognition*. To get a better idea of what journals you should scan, see Table B-1.

• **TABLE B-1** •

A LOOK AT SELECTED JOURNALS

JOURNAL	RELEVANCE TO YOU
Psychological Bulletin	Publishes articles that review existing work on either a research area or a research/statistical technique.
Psychological Review	Publishes work that compares and criticizes existing theories.
American Psychologist	Publishes theoretical articles, review articles, and empirical articles. Although articles are often written by distinguished scholars, they are written to a broad audience and are thus relatively easy to understand.
Psychological Science	Publishes theoretical articles, review articles, and empirical articles. Although articles are often written by distinguished scholars, they are written to a fairly broad audience and are thus relatively easy to understand. You may find the articles slightly harder to understand than those in the *American Psychologist.*
Contemporary Psychology	Reviews of recent books. Easy to read. Covers a wide range of topics.
Psychological Abstracts	Presents brief summaries of most published articles in psychology. Good browsing or reference tool. The abstracts are indexed by both author and topic.
PsychScan	Like *Psychological Abstracts,* contains summaries of recent articles. There are six different *PsychScans* for six different content areas: (1) developmental, (2) clinical, (3) learning disorders and mental retardation, (4) applied psychology, (5) applied experimental and engineering, and (6) psychoanalysis.
American Journal of Psychology	Primarily original research in basic psychological science. Not as competitive as *JEP* (see below).
Journals of Experimental Psychology (JEP)	Usually original experimental studies concerning basic mechanisms of perception, learning, motivation, and performance. Four different journals: *JEP: General* *JEP: Animal Behavior Processes* *JEP: Learning, Memory, and Cognition* *JEP: Human Perception and Performance*
Behavioral Neuroscience	Emphasizes biological basis of behavior. Because of the interdisciplinary nature of the journal, you may find some of the articles hard to understand if you do not have a background in chemistry and endocrinology.
Journal of Comparative Psychology	Articles may include both laboratory and field observation of species. Emphasis is on relating findings to the theory of evolution.
Bulletin of the Psychonomic Society	Articles cover any area of general experimental psychology. Good source of short articles describing relatively simple studies. Articles do not undergo peer review.
Memory and Cognition	A good source of articles in human experimental psychology. See also *Cognitive Science, Cognitive Psychology,* and *Journal of Experimental Psychology: Learning, Memory, and Cognition.*

• TABLE B-1 (CONTINUED) •
A LOOK AT SELECTED JOURNALS

JOURNAL	RELEVANCE TO YOU
Journal of Applied Behavior Analysis	Articles reporting a sizable effect on an important behavior, usually employing a single-participant design.
Psychological Record	Articles discussing theory or reporting experiments. Average article is relatively brief.
Psychological Reports	Articles in general psychology. Good source of brief articles.
Journal of Consulting and Clinical Psychology	Wide range of articles and brief reports dealing with theory and research in counseling. Some use of the case study method.
Psychological Assessment: A Journal of Consulting and Clinical Psychology	Studies assessing the validity of a variety of tests and measures.
Journal of Counseling Psychology	Publishes research articles evaluating the effectiveness of counseling, studies on the effectiveness of selecting and training counselors, theoretical articles, and other articles relating to counseling.
Journal of Abnormal Psychology	Occasionally reports experimental studies on humans or animals related to emotion or pathology; some studies that test hypotheses derived from psychological theories.
Psychology and Aging	Research reporting on physiological and behavioral aspects of aging during older adulthood. Fairly easy to read.
Developmental Psychology	Primarily research relating to development. See also *Child Development, Merrill Palmer Quarterly, Psychology and Aging.* In addition, can track down related work by consulting *PsychScan/Developmental.*
Journal of Educational Psychology	Research and theoretical articles relating to teaching and learning. Fairly easy to read.
American Education Research Journal	Research in education. Single study papers are accepted.
Journal of Applied Psychology	Reports research relating to industry, government, health, education, consumer affairs, and other applied areas.
Journal of Personality and Social Psychology	Contains three sections: (1) attitudes and social cognition, (2) interpersonal relations and group processes, and (3) personality and individual differences. Primarily reports articles involving several studies or fairly complex designs. Discussions may suggest follow-up studies that could be performed.
Journal of Experimental Social Psychology	Almost all articles report the results of experiments.
Journal of Social Psychology	Source of fairly simple studies.
Personality and Social Psychology Bulletin	Contains short articles that are often easy to understand.
Representative Research in Social Psychology	One of the few journals to publish studies that have nonsignificant results.

COMPUTER SEARCHES

The quickest way to locate references may be to do a computer search.[1] Whereas it might take you hours to search through all the resources we discussed in this appendix to find the references you need, computer searches can condense that time into minutes. For example, you can use either PsycINFO or PsycLIT to quickly search most journals in psychology and you can use the ERIC database to search a wide range of research relating to educational psychology.

One way that computer searches save you time is by allowing you to do searches for groups of terms rather than merely searching for individual terms. For example, if your topic is aggression in food-deprived monkeys, the computer will find only those references that concern "aggression" in "food-deprived" "monkeys." If you were using a non-computerized abstract or index, you could look up only one (two at the most) of these variables at a time. Thus, if you looked up "aggression," you would have to read through all the references concerning aggression in humans, rats, birds, and lions to find ones that dealt with monkeys. You would then have to sort through all the scattered monkey listings to find "food-deprived" monkeys.

Although computer searches can save time, you will save time only if you have some knowledge about how to conduct a computer search. If you are having trouble with your computer search, Table B-2, which has tips for dealing with common problems, may help. You may also want to consult the text's Web page (http://www.researchmethods.com). If you need more help than Table B-2 or the Web page can provide, ask your reference librarian for help.

---

[1]Computers are not always faster. In some library assignments we have used, students have taken almost twice as long to complete them when using computers. Problems like waiting for a computer, waiting to access the Internet, not searching the right term, and not having access to a database that includes the journals you need can substantially slow down—or completely disrupt—a computer search.

• TABLE B-2 •

USING THE COMPUTER TO FIND REFERENCES: TIPS FOR USING PSYC LIT, PSYCHINFO, ERIC, AND RELATED TOOLS

PROBLEM	POSSIBLE SOLUTION
Not finding enough references	1. Find other names for your key concept. For example, brain storm, use the thesaurus (or press key labeled F9) or consult with a reference librarian.
	2. Use the term "or" to look for articles that contain any of the terms you are looking for.
	3. Use the stem of the term you are interested in followed by an asterisk (*). This will give you all articles that have this root word as a stem. Thus, doing teen* will get you articles that mention "teen," "teens," "teen-age," and "teenagers."
	4. If you are using an author search, check the index (F5) to make sure (1) that you have the author's name spelled correctly, and (2) that the author doesn't use more than one way of presenting his or her name (with or without middle initial, etc.).
Finding too many references	1. Use the "and" command to make sure that the reference has to satisfy several criteria before it is captured by your search. For example, you might search "death and English in la" to get only those articles that are both on death and in English. Often, you will want "and" between the predictor and criterion variables you are searching for.
	2. If you find that you are getting articles that have your keyword in the abstract, but don't have anything to do with your concepts, narrow your search by making sure that you get only articles that someone else has described as pertaining to your topic. To do this, add "in de" to your key word. Thus, instead of searching for "recall," you might search for "recall in de."
	3. If you find that many of the "wrong references" you get are calling up a certain term, you could add "and not __ (that irrelevant term)" to your search. Or, if the search keeps giving you articles from a journal that your library doesn't have, you could add "and not child-development in jn." Or, if you didn't want any animal research references, you could add "and not animal in po."
	4. You could limit your search to only the most recent year ("and 2001 in py").
	5. If you only want literature reviews, include "and literature-review in de." If you want to exclude literature reviews, include "and not literature-review in de."

APPENDIX C

CONDUCTING A STUDY

PLANNING YOUR PROCEDURES

You have reviewed the literature, developed a hypothesis, operationalized your variables, and given sound reasons for testing your hypothesis. However, your preliminary work is still not done. You must now decide exactly what specific actions you will take. In other words, although you probably have decided on the general design (such as a simple experiment or a 2×2), your plan is not complete until each detail has been thought through and written down.

You should write down *exactly* what procedures you will follow. For example, what instructions, word for word, will participants be given? Who will administer the treatment? Where? Will participants be run in groups or individually? In answering these questions, you must take into account issues of validity. However, your paramount concern must always be ethics. You do not have the right to harm another.

ETHICAL CONSIDERATIONS: HUMAN RESEARCH

Ethics should be the foundation of your research plan. Therefore, you should read Appendix A (Ethics) before conducting a study.

In addition to reading Appendix A, you must be extremely careful not to harm your participants. Ideally, your participants should feel just as well when they leave the study as they did when they began the study. Unfortunately, even in the most innocuous studies, protecting your participants from discomfort is much easier said than done.

Weighing the Risks

Realize that any experience may be traumatic to some participants. Trauma can occur from things you would never think of as being traumatic. Because any study has risks and because you won't know all of the risks, *don't run a single participant without your professor's permission.*

To begin to sensitize yourself to the risks involved in your proposed study, list the 10 worst things that could possibly happen to participants. If you are using human participants, be aware that not all participants will react in the same way. Some may experience trauma because the study triggers some painful memory. Some participants may feel bad because they think they did poorly. Other participants may feel bad because they think their behavior ruined your study. Realize that some of your participants may be mentally unbalanced and any attack on their self-esteem might lead to disastrous consequences. Because participants are often fragile, you should list some serious consequences in your worst-case scenario.

Reducing Risks

Because any study has the potential for harm, the possibility of severe consequences doesn't mean that your professor won't allow you to do the study. However, you and your professor should think about ways to minimize the risks.

Screening Participants One method of minimizing risks is to screen out "vulnerable participants." For instance, if there is any reason to believe that your study may increase heart rate or blood pressure, you may want to make sure that only people in good health participate in your study. If your study might harm people with low self-esteem, you may want to use only well-adjusted participants who have high levels of self-esteem. Therefore, you might give a measure of self-esteem to potential participants to eliminate those with low self-esteem.

Informed Consent Not only should you screen participants, but you should also let participants screen themselves. That is, participants should be volunteers who give their *informed consent:* They should know what the study is about before volunteering for it.

How informed is informed consent? Very informed, when it comes to telling participants about any unpleasant aspect of the study. If participants are going to get shocked or exposed to loud noises or extreme cold, they should be informed of this before they volunteer. Consequently, if your study does involve unpleasantness, you may have difficulty getting participants to volunteer.

Informed consent is considerably less informed when it comes to more innocuous aspects of the study. After all, the study would be ruined if participants knew everything that would happen (and why it happened) before it happened. So, although participants are usually told the truth, they are not always told the whole truth. For example, a memory experiment's description would mention that participants have to memorize words, but might omit the fact that the researcher is looking at the order in which facts are recalled or that there is a surprise recall of all the lists at the end of the study.

Because participants are not fully informed about your study, there may be some things about it that they dislike. For example, suppose a participant finds the task too difficult or finds it upsetting to try the surprise recall task. What can you do?

One protection against these unexpected problems is to make sure participants understand that they can quit the study at any time. So, before the participants begin your study, tell them that if they find any aspect of the study uncomfortable, they can and *should* escape this discomfort by quitting the study. Assure them that it is their duty to quit if they experience discomfort and that they will still get full credit.

Modifying the Study

You have seen that you can minimize ethical problems by letting participants know what they are in for and by letting participants gracefully withdraw from the study. You should also minimize harm by making your study as humane as possible. You can make your study more ethical by reducing the strength of your treatment manipulation, carefully selecting stimulus materials, and by being a conscientious researcher.

Reducing the Treatment Strength   Although using extreme levels of your predictor variable may help you get a significant change in the criterion variable, extreme levels may harm your participants. For example, 24 hours of food deprivation is more likely to cause hunger than 12 hours. However, 24 hours of deprivation is more stressful to the participant. If you plan an unpleasant manipulation, remember your participants' welfare and minimize the unpleasant consequences as much as possible. Consider using levels of the predictor variable that are less severe than you originally intended.

Modifying Stimulus Materials   By modifying your stimulus materials, you may be able to prevent them from triggering unpleasant memories. For instance, if you were interested in the effects of caffeine on memory for prose, you wouldn't want the prose passage to cover some topic like death, divorce, alcoholic parents, or rape. Instead, you would want to use a passage covering a less traumatic topic such as sports. If the sports article referred to someone's death or hospitalization, you might want to delete that section of the article.

The Conscientious Researcher

Often, it's not the study that causes ethical problems, it's the researcher's arrogance. For example, an arrogant researcher may rush through research sessions providing only superficial explanations and almost no time for questions and feedback. Although we know of a few participants who were hurt as a direct result of a research manipulation, we know of many more who were hurt because the researcher treated them like dirt. To ensure that you are sensitive, courteous, and respectful to all of your human participants, you should do two things.

First, when scheduling your research sessions, make sure you leave a 10-minute gap between the end of one session and the beginning of the next session. Some investigators feel that, like a physician, they should efficiently schedule people one after another. Their "efficiency" results in participants having to wait for the investigator, the investigator having to rush through the formalities of greeting participants, or—even worse—the investigator rushing through debriefing. Thus, the "efficient" investigator, like the efficient physician, is seen as unconcerned. Although this conduct does not become physicians, it's intolerable for psychological researchers! After a research participant has given an hour of his or her time, you should be more than willing to answer any questions the participant has. Furthermore, if you rush through greeting or debriefing each participant, the participants will see you as uncaring. Consequently, they will be less likely to tell you about any psychological discomfort they felt and less likely to accept any aid you might offer. Thus, the first step is to walk, rather than to run, participants through your study.

Second, give the participants power. That is, allow participants to rate your study on a scale such as the one in Table C-1. Give each participant's rating sheet to your instructor. Following this simple procedure helps you to be a conscientious and courteous researcher.

Debriefing

Although you should try to anticipate and prevent every possible bad reaction a participant may have to being in your study, you won't be successful. Inevitably, your procedures will still cause some unpleasantness. After the study is over, you should try to remove this unpleasantness by informing participants about the study, reassuring them that their reactions were normal, and expressing your appreciation for their participation.

You should also listen to participants and be sensitive to any unexpected, unpleasant reactions to your study. By being a good listener, you should be able to undo any damage you have unwittingly done. This process of informing

---

• TABLE C-1 •

SAMPLE DEBRIEFING RATING SCALE*

Being a participant in psychology studies should provide you with a firsthand look at research. On the scale below, please indicate how valuable or worthless you found being in today's study by circling a number from +3 to –3.

WORTHLESS	–3	–2	–1	+1	+2	+3	VALUABLE

If you wish to explain your rating or to make comments on this study, either positive or negative, please do so below.

Note: This scale is a slightly modified version of a scale that has been used at Ohio State University.
* For more detailed information on debriefing scales and procedures, please see Appendix A.

your participants about the study and removing any harm done is called *debriefing*. Occasionally, ordinary debriefing will not undo the harm caused to the research participant. In those cases, there are several steps you may take to alleviate distress. For participants who are upset with their responses, you should ask them whether they want you to destroy their data. Participants whom you cannot calm down you should take to talk with a professor, counselor, or friend—even if this means canceling a research session you had scheduled.

In summary, you should be very concerned about ethics. Since ethics involves weighing the costs of the study against the potential benefits, you should do everything you can to minimize the risk of participants becoming uncomfortable. If, despite your efforts, a participant experiences discomfort, you should try to reduce that discomfort during debriefing.

ETHICAL CONSIDERATIONS: ANIMAL RESEARCH

With animal participants, you incur the same responsibilities that you did with human participants—you must protect animal participants from undue stress and discomfort. In many ways, you have even more responsibility to animal participants because they depend on you for their mere existence. You must keep them fed, clean, warm, and comfortable—24 hours a day. To fulfill your responsibility to animal participants, you must follow APA's guidelines for proper housing, food and water, and handling (see Appendix A).

Furthermore, because your animal participants do not have the power to give their informed consent, nor the power to quit the study, you must carefully question the value of your study. Ask yourself and your professor this question: "Is the potential knowledge gained from the study worth the cost to the animals?" Finally, if you must euthanize (kill) your animal participants at the end of your study, follow APA's guidelines to ensure that this is done in the most humane way.

MAXIMIZE THE BENEFITS: THE OTHER SIDE OF THE ETHICS COIN

We have discussed ways of minimizing harm to participants. However, minimizing harm is not enough to ensure that your study is ethical. For your study to be ethical, the potential benefits must be greater than the potential harm. Thus, an extremely harmless study can be unethical if the study has no potential benefits. So, just as you owe it to your participants to reduce potential harm, you owe it to your participants to maximize the potential benefits of your study. You maximize that potential by making sure your study provides accurate information. To provide accurate information, your study needs to have power and validity.

Power Is Knowledge

One of the most serious obstacles to obtaining accurate information is lack of power. Remember, null results don't prove the null hypothesis. They only make people wonder about the study's power. There is no point in doing a study that is so powerless that it will lead to inconclusive, null results.

To have power, you should use a strong manipulation, a sensitive dependent measure, well-standardized procedures, a sensitive design, and enough participants.

Sample Size: There's Power in Numbers   Perhaps your most important obstacle to finding a significant effect is a lack of participants. As a general rule, you should have at least 16 participants in each group.[1] However, the number of participants you need in each group will be affected by the sensitivity of your design, the heterogeneity of your participants, the number of observations you get from each participant, the size of the difference you expect to find between conditions, and the sensitivity of your dependent measure.

If you have a within-subjects design, a reliable and sensitive dependent variable, and expect a rather large difference between your conditions, you may be able to use fewer than 16 participants per group. If, on the other hand, you are using a simple, between-subjects design, heterogeneous participants, a manipulation that may have little effect, and a relatively insensitive dependent measure, you may want at least 100 participants per condition.

Hunting for Participants

How are you going to get all the volunteer participants you need to conduct a powerful study? The threat of death is not ethical.

The Draft   Some researchers rely on "captive" samples. For example, many colleges "volunteer" students in introductory psychology courses for the research draft. In fact, most of the research strength of modern psychology has been built using this research draft. If your school has such a draft, count yourself among the blessed. All you have to do is ask your professor how to become a recruiter.

Enlisting Volunteers   If your school does not have a draft, an effective way of getting participants is to ask professors to request volunteers from their classes. Many professors will gladly do this. Some will even give volunteers extra credit as an incentive for participating in your study.

---

[1] The more participants, the more power. Indeed, some (Cohen, 1990) would consider 64 participants per group to be a reasonable minimum. We have talked about minimums. Are there maximums? Could you have a design that was too powerful? Some would argue that, in some cases, researchers use so many participants that even the smallest of effects, no matter how practically and theoretically insignificant, would be statistically significant. However, having a design that is too powerful is rarely a problem for novice researchers.

Non-College Samples   But what if you don't want to use college students in your study? For example, suppose you want to study children or retirees? Or, suppose you agree with the skeptics who claim that results from studies done on college students cannot be applied to "normal people." Then, you would look beyond college classrooms for participants. A note of caution: You may find that getting real-world participants takes as much work and creativity as planning your study.

Children   If you want to study children, you may be able to take advantage of the "captive" audience approach. After all, most children have to go to school. However, obtaining access to those children may turn into a nightmare of red tape. You will have to obtain permission from all or many of the following: the school board, the superintendent, principal, teacher, parent, child, your professor, and university. If you are going to get these permissions in time for your study, you'll need to plan ahead—and be very lucky.

Adults   Finding adult participants can be even more challenging than finding children. For example, one of your textbook's authors wanted an adult population for her doctoral dissertation. Her first thought was to contact a major company and gain access to its employees. This tactic failed. Next, she tried to run a newspaper ad asking for volunteers. One newspaper refused to print it. Another would only run it in the "Personal" section. Thus, her appeal for participants appeared with ads for astrological advice, massage services, and people wanting dates. Although a few "volunteers" called, most wanted either a date or an obscene conversation. We do not recommend newspaper ads—especially if your goal is to get a representative sample of the adult population.

Older Adults   The authors have had greater success recruiting elderly participants. Nutrition centers, retirement communities, friendship networks, and nursing homes have been fruitful sources of participants. In addition, we recommend the "grandmother connection": having an older relative or friend introduce you to other prospective participants.

Summary

Finding human participants will take planning, perseverance, and luck. Once you contact prospective participants, you should explain your study to them and have them sign a permission form. The permission form will protect both you and your participants. Basically, it states that you have explained the study to the volunteers and that they agree to participate (see Table C-2). If minors are participating in your study, you need to have separate forms for both the participants and their parents.

Animal Participants   Our experiences with recruiting human participants might have increased your enthusiasm for animal research. In many ways, ani-

---

• TABLE C-2 •

SAMPLE INFORMED-CONSENT FORM

Students taking PSY 455, Research Design, are investigating the effects of noise and sleep deprivation on anxiety.

If you participate in this study, you will be deprived of sleep for two nights and exposed to common city noise for one hour. During that hour, you will be asked to fill out two questionnaires, and your pulse and blood pressure will be measured several times.

You will be asked to spend two nights in a special dorm room so that your sleep can be monitored. In addition, it will take 90 minutes for the noise treatment and measures to be completed.

You will receive $20 for participating in the study.

Physical injury, psychological injury, or deception are not part of this study. In addition, all your responses and answers will be held confidential. No one other than the investigators will see information about your particular responses.

Any questions you have regarding this project should be addressed to the investigators or to Dr. _____, faculty supervisor.

If you agree to participate in this study, please sign the following statement.

- -

I have read the above Consent Form and understand the proposed project. I consent to participate in this study. I understand that I can quit the study at any time. Finally, I will be paid $20 whether or not I complete the study.

_____   _____

Signature   Date

---

mals are better participants than humans. You don't have to worry about permission slips, extra credit, or obscene phone calls. Consult with your instructor about obtaining animals for your research. Often, schools have rat colonies or purchase animals for student research.

Reducing Threats to Construct Validity

After ensuring that your study has adequate power, we would like to be able to tell you that you can take it easy and relax. Unfortunately, however, you can't relax. Power is not your only concern when conducting psychological research. You must also ensure that the construct validity of your results is not destroyed by (1) researchers failing to conduct your study in an objective, standardized way, or (2) participants reacting to how they think you want them to react to the treatment, rather than reacting to the treatment itself.

Researcher Effects   If you use more than one investigator, you may be able to detect researcher effects by including the researcher as a factor in your design. In other words, randomly assign participants to both a condition and to a researcher. For example, if you have two treatment conditions (*A* and *B*) and two researchers (1 and 2), you would have four conditions: (1) *A*1, (2) *B*1, (3) *A*2, and (4) *B2*. After having Researcher 1 run conditions 1 and 2 and Researcher 2 run conditions 3 and 4, you could do an analysis of variance (ANOVA) using researcher as a factor to see whether different researchers got different results.[2]

Using ANOVA to detect researcher effects can be useful. However, there are at least two reasons why using ANOVA may not eliminate researcher effects. First, this statistical approach will only tell you if one researcher is getting different results than other researchers. If all your researchers are biased, you may not get a significant researcher effect. (Besides, if you are the only researcher, you can't use researcher as a factor in an ANOVA.) Second, and more importantly, detecting researcher effects is not the same as preventing researcher effects.

To prevent researcher effects, you must address the three major causes of researchers failing to conduct studies in an objective and standardized manner. What are these causes? First, researchers may not know how to behave because the procedures for how the researchers should conduct the study have not been spelled out. Second, researchers may not follow those procedures. Third, the researchers may strongly expect participants to behave in certain ways.

Loose-Protocol Effect: The Importance of Developing a Protocol   Often, the researchers aren't behaving in an objective and standardized way because of the *loose-protocol effect:* The instructions aren't detailed enough. Fortunately, the loose-protocol effect can avoided.

Before you start your study, carefully plan everything out. As a first step, you should write out a set of instructions that chronicles the exact procedure for each participant. These procedures should be so specific that by reading and following your instructions, another person could run your participants the same way you do.

To make your instructions specific, you might want to write a computer program based on these instructions. Since computers don't assume anything, writing such a program forces you to spell out everything down to the last detail. If you can't program, just write the script as if a robot were to administer the study. Write out each step, including the actual words that researchers will say to the participants. The use of such a script will help standardize your procedures, thus reducing threats to validity.

Once you have a detailed draft of your protocol, give it a test run. For example, to ensure that you are as specific as you think you are, pretend to be a participant and have several different people run you through the study using *only* your instructions. See how the different individuals behave. This may give you clues as to how to tighten up your procedures. In addition, you should run several practice participants. Notice whether you change procedures in some subtle way across participants. If so, adjust your instructions to get rid of this variability.

---

[2]You may want to consult with your professor as to the type of ANOVA you should use. There is some debate as to whether conventional ANOVA should be performed or a "random effects" model should be used.

• TABLE C-3 •
PROTOCOL CHECKLIST

How will you manipulate your treatment variables?

How will you measure your dependent (criterion) variables?

How many participants will you need?

Do you have your professor's permission to conduct the study?

Do you have a suitable place to run your participants?

How will you get your participants?

If you are using animals, how will they be cared for?

What will you do with your animals after the study?

If you are using human participants, how will you make your sign-up sheets available to potential participants?

Have you included a description of the study (including how long it takes) on the sign-up sheet?

Will participants be rewarded for volunteering to be in your study (such as money or extra credit)?

If you are conducting an experiment, how will you assign participants to condition?

Have you written out a detailed research protocol?

If you are using human participants, have you developed a consent form?

If you are using human participants, have you written out the oral instructions you will give your participants?

If you are using human participants, have you written out what you will say during debriefing?

If volunteers are college students seeking extra credit, how will you notify professors about which students participated?

Will you inform participants about the outcome of your study? How?

At the end of your test runs, you should have a detailed set of instructions that you and any co-investigator can follow to the letter. To double-check your protocol, see Table C-3.

Inspiring the Troops to Avoid Researcher Effects   Unfortunately, even if you write out your *protocol* (procedures) in detail, you or your co-investigators may still fail to follow that protocol. To avoid the *researcher failure-to-follow-protocol effect,* you need to make sure: (1) that all investigators know the procedures, and (2) that everyone is motivated to follow the procedures.

To make sure investigators learn the procedures, you should hold training sessions. Supervise investigators while they practice the procedures on each other and on practice participants.

Once researchers know the right way to run the study, the key is to make sure that they are motivated to run the study the same way every time. To increase researchers' motivation to be consistent, you might have them work in pairs. While one researcher runs the participants, the other will listen in through an intercom or watch through a one-way mirror. You may even wish to record research sessions.

If your researchers still have trouble following procedures, you may need to automate your study. For instance, you might use a computer to present instructions, administer the treatment, or collect the dependent measure. Computers have the reputation for following instructions to the letter, so using a computer may help standardize your procedures. Of course, computers aren't the only machines that can help you. Some of the machines that could help you give instructions and present stimuli include automated slide projectors, tape recorders, and videotape players. Countless other devices can be used to record your data accurately, from electronic timers and counters to noise-level meters.

Researcher-Expectancy Effect   The final source of researcher bias is the *researcher-expectancy effect:* Researchers' expectations are affecting the results. You can take three steps to prevent the researcher-expectancy effect:

1. Be very specific about how investigators are to conduct themselves. Remember, researcher expectancies probably affect the results by changing the investigator's behavior rather than by causing the investigator to send a telepathic message to the participants.

2. Don't let the investigators know the hypothesis.

3. Don't let investigators know what condition the participant is in—making the investigator "*blind.*" Although making investigators blind is easiest in drug experiments where participants take either a placebo or the real drug, you can make investigators blind in nondrug experiments.

For example, if you present stimuli in booklets, you can design your booklets so that booklets for different conditions look very similar. In that way, an investigator running a group of participants might not know what condition each participant is in. For some studies, you may be able to use a second investigator who does nothing except collect the dependent measure. This second investigator could easily be kept in the dark as to what condition the participant was in.

Review of Researcher Effects   Whether you are the only investigator or one of a team of investigators, researcher effects may bias your results. Therefore, you should always try to prevent the loose-protocol effect, the failure-to-follow-protocol effect, and the researcher-expectancy effect.

Participant Effects

Unfortunately, in psychological research, you must be aware not only of researcher effects, but also of *participant effects:* Participants may see through the study and try to play along with what the investigator wants. Fortunately, there are various ways of preventing participants' expectancies from biasing your results.

Preventing Participants' Expectancies For starters, you might make your researcher blind to reduce the chance that the participant will get any ideas from the researcher. Thus, the techniques for reducing research effects that we just discussed may also reduce the effects of participants' expectancies.

In addition, you may also be able to prevent participants' expectancies by skillfully choosing your research design. In experimental investigations, for example, you might use a between-subjects design rather than a within-subjects design because participants who are exposed to only one treatment condition are less likely to guess the hypothesis than participants who are exposed to all treatment conditions.

Placebo Treatments Another design trick you can use to reduce the impact of participants' expectancies is to use placebo treatments. Placebo treatments prevent participants from knowing that they are in the "no-treatment" condition. Therefore, if you have comparison condition(s), use placebo treatment(s) rather than no-treatment condition(s). That way, all groups think they are receiving the treatment. Thus, any treatment effect you find will not be due to participants changing their behavior because they expect the treatment to have an effect.

Unobtrusive Recording Participants are less likely to know the hypothesis if they don't know what you are measuring. Obviously, if they don't even know they are being observed—as in some field studies—they won't know what you are measuring. Thus, if your hypothesis is an obvious one, you might try to do a field study.

Although field studies lend themselves to unobtrusive recording, unobtrusive recording can even occur in a laboratory study. That is, participants will assume that if you are not in the room with them, you are not observing them. However, thanks to one-way mirrors and intercoms, you can monitor participants' behavior from the next room.

Unobtrusive Measures Even if the participant knows you are watching, the participant doesn't have to know what you are watching. That is, you can use unobtrusive measures. For example, you might put the participant in front of a computer and ask the participant to type an essay. Although the participant thinks you are measuring the essay's quality, you could have the computer programmed to monitor speed of typing, time between paragraphs, number of errors made, and times a section was rewritten. In addition, you might also have tape-recorded and videotaped the participant, monitoring his or her facial expressions, number of vocalizations, and loudness of vocalizations.

Experimental Realism   Rather than trying to obscure or confuse participants as to the purpose of the study, you might try to prevent participants from thinking about the purpose of the study. How? By designing a study that has a high degree of research realism: a study that involves participants in the task. Experimental realism means that participants aren't constantly saying to themselves: "What does the researcher really want me to do?" or "If I were a typical person, how would I behave in this situation?" Note that experimental realism doesn't mean the study is like real life; it means that participants are engrossed in the task. In this age of video games, even a fairly artificial task can be very high in experimental realism.

ETHICS SUMMARY

Before now, you might have been surprised to see experimental realism and other strategies for reducing participant effects in a section on ethics. However, you now know that planning an ethical study involves taking into account many factors. Not only must you ensure the safety of your participants, but you must also demonstrate the validity of your methods. To avoid overlooking an important ethical consideration, consult Table C-4, Appendix A, and your professor.

BEYOND THE PROPOSAL: THE PILOT STUDY

Even after you have carefully designed your study, modified it based on comments from your instructor, and been given your professor's go-ahead to run it, you may still want to run several participants (friends, family members, other members of the class) just for practice. By running practice participants, you'll get some of the "bugs" out of your study. Specifically, by running and debriefing practice participants, you will discover:

1. whether participants perceived your manipulation the way you intended
2. whether you can perform the study the same way every time or whether you need to spell out your procedures in more detail
3. whether you are providing the right amount of time for each of the research tasks and whether you are allowing enough time in between tasks
4. whether your instructions were clear
5. whether your cover story was believable
6. whether you need to revise your stimulus materials
7. how participants like the study
8. how long it takes you to run and debrief a participant

In short, running practice participants helps you to fine-tune your study. Because running practice participants is so useful, many professional investiga-

• TABLE C-4 •

RESEARCH WITH HUMAN PARTICIPANTS: AN ETHICS CHECKLIST

Is a physically unpleasant stimulus going to be used in your study? If so:

1. Is this fact clearly stated
   a. on the sign-up sheet?
   b. on the consent form?

2. Have you considered alternatives that would be less unpleasant?

3. Have you limited the intensity of this stimulus?

4. Have you taken steps to reduce potential harm to your participants caused by a physically unpleasant stimulus?

Are you going to use stress of some sort (such as sense of insecurity or failure, assault upon values, fatigue, or sleep deprivation) in your study? If so:

1. Is this fact clearly stated
   a. on the sign-up sheet?
   b. on the consent form?

2. Have you considered alternatives that would be less stressful?

3. Have you limited the intensity of this stimulus?

4. Have you taken steps to reduce potential harm to your participants caused by a psychologically unpleasant stimulus?

What will you do if participants exhibit signs of harm (for instance, crying, disoriented behavior)?

Are you prepared to describe the purpose and nature of your study to your participants during debriefing?

Will you use deception in your study? If so, what will you tell participants during debriefing?

Are you aware that participants can quit your study at any time? If a participant does drop out, will you give your participants credit for participating? Is this fact stated on the informed consent form? Is this fact part of your instructions to the participants?

What educational gain do you think participants will obtain from participating in your study?

How will you ensure the confidentiality of each participant's data?

tors run enough practice participants to constitute a small study—what researchers call a *pilot study*.

CONDUCTING THE ACTUAL STUDY

The dress rehearsal is over. Final changes in your proposal have been made. Now you are ready for the real thing—you are ready to "run" your study! This section will show you how.

ESTABLISHING RAPPORT

As you may imagine, some of your prospective participants may be apprehensive about the study. Participants often aren't sure whether they are in the right place, or even whether the researcher is a Dr. Frankenstein.

To put your participants at ease, let them know they are in the right place, and be courteous. You should be both friendly and businesslike. The expert investigator greets the participant warmly, pays close attention to the participant, and seems concerned that the participant knows what will happen in the study. The expert investigator is obviously concerned that each participant is treated humanely and that the study is done professionally.

Being professional doesn't hurt how participants view you. Why? First, most participants like knowing that they are involved in something important. Second, some will view your professionalism as a way of showing that you value their time—which you should.

So, how can you exude a professional manner? Some novice investigators think that they appear professional when they act aloof and unconcerned. Nothing could be less professional. Participants are very turned off by a disinterested attitude. They feel that you don't care about the study and that you don't care about them.

To appear professional, you should be neatly dressed, enthusiastic, well-organized, and prompt. "Prompt" may be an understatement. You should be ready and waiting for your participants at least 10 minutes before the study is scheduled to begin. Once your participants arrive, concentrate exclusively on the job at hand. Never ask a participant to wait a few minutes while you socialize with friends.

What do you lose by being a "professional" investigator? Problem participants. If you seem enthusiastic and professional, your participants will also become involved in doing your study—even if the tasks are relatively boring. Thus, if you are professional in your manner and attitude, you will probably not even have to ask the participants to refrain from chatting throughout the study. Similarly, if you are professional, participants will stop asking questions about the study if you say, "I'll explain the purpose at the end of the study."

After you have established rapport, you need to give your participants instructions. To get participants to follow instructions to the letter, you might:

1. Be repetitive.

2. Have participants read the instructions.

3. Orally paraphrase those instructions.

4. Run participants individually.

5. Invite participants to ask questions.

6. Have participants demonstrate that they understand the instructions by quizzing them or by giving them a practice trial before beginning the study.

Once the study has begun, try to follow the procedure to the letter. Consistently following the same procedures improves power and reduces the possibility of bias. Therefore, don't let participants change your behavior by reinforcing or punishing you. For instance, imagine you are investigating *long-term memory*. You want to expose participants to information and then see what they can write down. However, if you do this, participants may be writing down information that is in *short-term memory*. Thus, you would not be assessing long-term memory. Therefore, you add a counting backwards task that should virtually eliminate all of the information from short-term memory. Specifically, in your memory study, participants are exposed to information, are supposed to count backwards from a number like 781 by 3's for 20 seconds, and then are asked to recall the information. Ideally, their recall will represent only what they have in long-term memory. Unfortunately, many participants will find the counting task unpleasant, embarrassing, or simply an unwanted nuisance. Consequently, some participants will thank you for telling them they can stop; others will plead nonverbally for you to stop. Clearly, you cannot let any of these strategies stop you from making them count backwards for the full 20 seconds. If you vary your procedures from participant to participant based on each participant's individual whims, your study will have questionable validity.

DEBRIEFING

Once the study is over, you should debrief your participants. In debriefing, you should first try to find out whether the participants suspected the hypothesis. Simply ask participants what they thought the study was about. Then, explain the purpose of your study.

If you deceived your participants, you need to make sure they are not upset about the deception. You also need to make sure that they understand why deception was necessary. Participants should leave the study appreciating the fact that there was one and only one reason you employed deception: It was the only way to get good information about an important issue.

Making sure participants accept your rationale for deception is crucial for three reasons. First, you don't want your participants to feel humiliated or angry. Second, if they get mad, they may not only be mad at you, but also at psychologists in general. Perhaps that anger or humiliation will stop them from visiting a psychologist when they need help. Third, the unhappy participant may spread the word about your deception, ruining your chances of deceiving other participants.

After explaining the purpose of the study, you should answer any questions the participants have. Although answering questions may sometimes seem like a waste of time, you owe it to your participants. They gave you their time, now it's your turn.

After participants' questions and doubts have been dealt with, give them an opportunity to rate how valuable they felt the study was. These ratings (1) encourage you to be courteous to your participants; (2) let you know whether your study is more traumatic than you originally thought; and (3) make participants feel that you respect them because you value their opinions.

After the rating, you should assure participants that their responses during the study will be kept confidential. Tell them that no one but you will know their responses. Then, ask the participants not to talk about the study because it is still in progress. For example, you might ask them not to talk about the study until next week. Finally, you should thank your participants, escort them back to the waiting area, and say goodbye.

PROTECTING DATA: CONFIDENTIALITY

You might think that once a participant leaves the study, your responsibilities to that participant end. Wrong! You are still responsible for guaranteeing the participant's privacy. Knowledge about a given participant is between you (the investigator) and the participant—*no one else.* Never violate this confidentiality. To ensure confidentiality, you should take the following precautions:

1. Assign each participant a number. When you refer to a given participant, always use the assigned number—never that participant's name.
2. Never store a participant's name and data in a computer—this could be a computer hacker's delight.
3. If you have participants write their names on booklets, tear off and destroy the cover of the booklet after you have analyzed the data.
4. Store a list of participants and their numbers in one place and the data with the participants' numbers on it in another place.
5. Watch your mouth. There is rarely a reason to talk casually about a participant's behavior. Even if you don't mention any names, other people may guess or think they have guessed the identity of your participant. We realize that it is hard to keep a secret. But to talk freely about someone who participated in your study is to betray a trust. Furthermore, keeping secrets will, for many of you, be an important part of your professional role: Therapists, researchers, consultants, lawyers, and physicians all must keep their clients' behaviors confidential.

SAMPLE RESEARCH PAPER

Adapted from Frank, M. G., & Gilovich, T. (1988). The dark side of self- and social-perception: Black uniforms and aggression in professional sports. *Journal of Personality and Social Psychology, 54,* 74–85. Used with the kind permission of Mark Frank, Thomas Gilovich, and the American Psychological Association.

Running head: BLACK UNIFORMS AND AGGRESSION

The Dark Side of Self Perception:

Black Uniforms and Aggression

Mark G. Frank and Thomas Gilovich

Cornell University

Abstract

Black is viewed as the color of evil and death in virtually
all cultures. With this association in mind, we were
interested in whether a cue as subtle as the color of a
person's clothing might have a significant impact on the
wearer's behavior. To test this possibility, we performed a
laboratory experiment to determine whether wearing a black
uniform can increase a person's inclination to engage in
aggressive behavior. We found that participants who wore
black uniforms showed a marked increase in intended
aggression relative to those wearing white uniforms. Our
discussion focuses on the theoretical implications of these
data for an understanding of the variable, or "situated,"
nature of the self.

The Dark Side of Self Perception:

Black Uniforms and Aggression

A convenient feature of the traditional American Western film was the ease of which the viewer could distinguish the good guys from the bad guys: The bad guys wore the black hats. Of course, film directors did not invent this connection between black and evil, but built upon an existing association that extends deep into our culture and language. When a terrible thing happens on a given day, we refer to it as a "black day," as when the Depression was ushered in by the infamous "Black Thursday." We can hurt ourselves by "blackening" our reputation or be hurt by others by being "blacklisted," or "blackballed," or "blackmailed" (Williams, 1964). When the Chicago White Sox deliberately lost the 1919 World Series as part of a betting scheme, they became known as the Chicago Black Sox, and to this day the "dark" chapter in American sports history is known as the Black Sox Scandal. In a similar vein, Muhammed Ali has observed that we refer to white cake as "angel food cake" and dark cake as "devil's food cake."

These anecdotes concerning people's negative associations to the color black are reinforced by the research literature on color meanings. In one representative experiment, groups of college students and seventh graders who were asked to make semantic differential rating of colors were found to associate black with evil, death, and badness (Williams & McMurty, 1970). Moreover, this association between black and evil is not strictly an American or Western phenomenon, because college students in Germany, Denmark, Hong Kong, and India (Williams, Moreland, &

Underwood, 1970) and Ndembu tribesmen in Central Africa (Turner, 1967) all report that the color black connoted evil and death. Thus, Adams and Osgood (1973) concluded that black is seen, in virtually all cultures, as the color of evil and death.

The intriguing question is whether these associations influence people's behavior in important ways. For example, does wearing black clothing lead the wearer to actually act more aggressively?

This possibility is suggested by studies on anonymity and "deindividuation" which show that a person's clothing can affect the amount of aggression he or she expresses. In one study, female participants in a "learning" experiment were asked to deliver shocks to another participant whenever she made a mistake. Under the pretense of minimizing individual identities, one half of the participants wore nurses uniforms (a prosocial cue), and the other half wore outfits resembling Ku Klux Klan uniforms (an antisocial cue). As predicted, participants who wore nurses uniforms delivered less shock to the "learner" than did participants who wore the Ku Klux Klan uniforms, which demonstrates that the cues inherent in certain clothes can influence the wearer's aggressive behavior (Johnson & Downing, 1979).

Although such studies are suggestive, they involve rather contrived situations that raise troubling questions of experimental demand. Accordingly, we decided to seek parallel evidence for a link between clothing cues and aggressiveness by examining the effect of a much more subtle cue, the color of a person's uniform.

There are a couple of difficulties that confront any attempt to test whether wearing a black uniform tends to make a person more aggressive. First, any such test is fraught with the usual ethical problems involved in all research on human aggression. Second, since black is associated with violence, observers may be biased when judging the behavior of participants wearing black. The usual solution to these twin problems is to use some version of the bogus shock paradigm (Buss, 1961). However, we chose not to use this procedure because of the difficulty in finding participants who--given the publicity of Milgram's (1965, 1974) work--would not view the proceedings with extreme suspicion.

Our solution to these problems was to collect "behavioroid" data (Carlsmith, Ellsworth, & Aronson, 1976) in the form of the participants' intended aggressive behavior. Volunteers for an experiment on competition were led to believe that they would be vying against other participants in several competitive events. They were also led to believe that they could exercise some control over which events they were to participate in by selecting their 5 most preferred events from a list of 12. The 12 events varied in the amount of aggressiveness they called for, allowing us to use participants' choices as a measure of their reading to engage in aggressive action. By means of a suitable cover story, we elicited participants' choices twice: once individually when wearing their usual clothes, and later as a team of 3 wearing black or white jerseys. We hypothesized that wearing black jerseys would induce participants to view themselves as more mean and aggressive and thus would produce more of a "group shift" toward aggressive choices by participants wearing black jerseys than by those wearing white (Drabman & Thomas, 1977; Jaffe, Shapir, & Yinon, 1981; Jaffe & Yinnon, 1979).

Method

Overview

Participants participated in groups of 3 in an experiment ostensibly on the "psychology of competition." Each group was told that they would be competing against another team of 3 on a series of five games of everyone's choosing. To find out their preferences, they were asked to individually rank order 5 activities from a group of 12. After making their choices, the participants were outfitted in either white or black uniforms in the guise of facilitating team identity. Then, while the experimenter was supposedly administering instructions to the other team, the 3 participants were told to discuss their individual choices and to decide as a group on the rank ordering of the five activities they would like to include in the competition. This second ranking allowed us to assess whether the participants would choose more aggressive games as a group after donning black uniforms than after putting on white uniforms. Finally, as an auxiliary measure of aggression, participants were administered a brief version of Murray's (1943) Thematic Apperception Test (TAT) to assess their level of aggressive ideation.

Participants

The participants were 72 male students from Cornell University who were paid $3 for their participation. They were run in groups of 3, with the members of each group unacquainted with one another.

Procedure

As the participants reported for the experiment they were brought together in one room and led to believe that another group of participants was assembling in a different room. Participants were told that:

> You will be competing, as a team, on a series of five games against another group of three participants who are waiting in the next room. I matched the two teams for size as you came in, so the contests should be fair. This study is designed to mimic real-life competition as closely as possible...[and so]...we want you to choose the games you want to play.

Participants were then given a list of descriptions of 12 games and were asked to indicate, individually, which games they would like to play. They were asked to choose 5 of the 12 games and to rank order those 5. After reminding the participants not to discuss their choices with one another, the experimenter left the room, ostensibly to elicit the choices of the other team.

Upon his return, the experimenter collected the participants' individual choices and stated that "now I would like you to make a group decision as to which games you will play, because many times people's preferences are so divergent that we need to use a group choice to serve as a tie-breaker when deciding on which games to play." The experimenter further explained that "to make the experiment more like real-world competition and to build team cohesion, I would like you to put these uniforms on over your shirts. From now on you will be referred to as the black [white] team." The participants were then given black or white uniforms with silver duct-tape numerals (7,8, and 11) on the backs.

The experimenter once again left the room to allow the participants to make their group choices and then returned after 5 minutes. He then explained,

> Now that I have everyone's individual and team selections, I will go and set up the five games that received the most votes. While I am doing this, I want you to complete a standard psychological task to get all of you in the same state of mind before we start.

Participants were asked to write a brief story about a scene depicted in a TAT card (Card 18 BM from Murray's, 1943, original series). Participants were given 4 minutes to write a story based on the following questions: (a) what is happening in the picture? (b) what is being thought by the characters in the picture? (c) what has led up to this picture? and (d) what will happen to the characters in the picture?

After 4 minutes the experimenter returned, collected the TAT protocols, and thoroughly debriefed the participants. All participants seemed surprised (and many disappointed) to learn that the experiment was over. The debriefing interview also made it clear that none of the participants had entertained the possibility that the color of the uniforms might have been the focus of the experiment.

Dependent Measures

The primary measure in this experiment was the level of aggressiveness involved in the games participants wanted to include in the competition. A group of 30 participants had earlier rated a set of descriptions of 20 games in terms of how much aggressiveness they involved. The 12 games that had received the most consistent ratings and that represented a wide spectrum of aggressiveness were then used as the stimulus set in this experiment. These 12 games were ranked in terms of these aggressiveness ratings and assigned point values consistent with their ranks, from the most aggressive (12, 11, and 10 points for "chicken fights," "dart gun duel," and "burnout," respectively) to the least aggressive (1, 2, and 3 points for "basket shooting," "block stacking," and "putting contest," respectively). Participants were asked to choose the five games that they wanted to include in the competition and to rank order their five choices in terms of preference. To get an overall measure of the aggressiveness of each participant's preferences, we multiplied the point value of his first choice by 5, his second choice by 4, and so forth, and then added these five products. When comparing the choices made by the participants individually (without uniforms), we compared the average individual choices of the 3 participants with their group choice.

The second dependent measure in this experiment was participants' responses to the TAT card. Participants' TAT stories were scored on a 5-point aggressiveness scale (Feshbach, 1955). Stories devoid of aggression received a score of 1, those with a

little indirect aggression a score of 2, those with considerable
indirect or a little direct aggression a 3, those with direct
physical aggression a 4, and those with graphic violence a 5.
These ratings were made by two judges who were unaware of the
participants' condition. The judges' ratings were in perfect
agreement on 47% of the stories and were within one point on
another 48%.

Results

The mean levels of aggressiveness in participants' individual
and group choices are presented in Table 1. As expected, there was
no difference in participants' individual choices across the two
groups (MS = 113.4 vs. 113.5), because they were not wearing
different-colored uniforms at the time these choices were made.
However, the participants who donned black uniforms subsequently
chose more aggressive games (mean change in aggressiveness =
16.8), whereas those who put on white uniforms showed no such
shift (mean change = 2.4). A 2 X 2 mixed between/within ANOVA of
participants' choices yielded a significant interaction between
uniform color and individual/group choice $F(1,22) = 6.14$, $p<.05$,
indicating that the pattern of choices made by participants in
black uniforms was different from that of those wearing white.
Wearing black uniforms induced participants to seek out more
aggressive activities, matched-pairs $t(11) = 3.21$, $p<.01$; wearing
white uniforms did not, matched-pairs $t(11) = 1.00$, ns.

The participants who wore black uniforms also tended to
express more aggressive ideation (M = 3.20) in their TAT

stories than did participants wearing white uniforms ($\underline{M}$ =
2.89), although this difference was not significant, $\underline{t}$<1.

Discussion

The results of this experiment support the hypothesis
that wearing a black uniform can increase a person's
inclination to engage in aggressive behavior. Participants
who wore black uniforms showed a marked increase in intended
aggression relative to those wearing white uniforms.

It should be noted, however, that our demonstration
involved only intended aggression. It did not involve actual
aggression. It would have been interesting to have allowed
our participants to compete against one another in their
chosen activities and seen whether those in black jerseys
performed more aggressively. We refrained from doing so
because of ethical and methodological difficulties (i.e., the
difficulty of objectively measuring aggression, especially
given that observers tend to be biased toward viewing people
wearing black uniforms as being more aggressive).
Nevertheless, the results of this experiment make the
important point that in a competitive setting at least,
merely donning a black uniform can increase a person's
willingness to seek out opportunities for aggression. If the
wearing of a black uniform can have such an effect in the
laboratory, there is every reason to believe that it would
have even stronger effects on the playing field (or rink),
where many forms of aggression are considered acceptable
behavior.

One question raised by this research concerns the generality of the effect of uniform color on aggression. It is very unlikely that donning any black uniform in any situation would make a person more inclined to act aggressively. We do not believe, for example, that the black garments worn by Catholic clergymen or Hassidic Jews don't make them any more aggressive than their secular peers. Rather, it would seem to be the case that the semantic link between the color black and evil and aggressiveness would be particularly salient in domains that already possess overtones of competition, confrontation, and physical aggression.

With this in mind, any speculation about other domains in which analogous effects might be obtained should center on those areas that also possess inherent elements of force and confrontation. The actions of uniformed police officers and prison guards may be one such area. Is it the case, in other words, that the color of the uniforms worn by such individuals influences the amount of aggressiveness they exhibit in performing their duties? This intriguing possibility could readily be tested by examining archival indicators of aggression and violence involving police officers and prison guards, such as charges of police brutality and assaults on police officers (Mauro, 1984). These analyses could involve both cross-sectional comparisons of police departments (or prisons) with different-colored uniforms, as well as longitudinal comparisons within departments that have changed uniform colors. We should point out, however, that we strongly doubt whether there are any police departments or penal institutions in this country that issue black uniforms to their personnel, possibly out of implicit recognition of this article's central thesis. Nevertheless, the uniforms of police officers and prison guards do vary in color a great deal, from dark blue to light khaki. Thus, one might still expect to find an effect of uniform color on aggressiveness if the subsequent research alluded to above indicates that the uniform effect we have documented is indeed more than a simple dichotomous difference between black and nonblack uniforms.

Perhaps the most important question raised by this research concerns the exact mechanisms by which the color of a uniform might affect the behavior of the wearer. Our own explanation for this phenomenon centers upon the implicit demands on one's behavior generated by wearing a particular kind of uniform. To wear a certain uniform is to assume a particular identity, an identity that not only elicits a certain response from others but also compels a particular pattern of behavior from the wearer (Stone, 1962). Wearing an athletic uniform, for example, thrusts one into the role of athlete, and leads one to "try on" the image that such a role conveys. When the uniform is that of a football or hockey player, part of that image--and therefore part of what one "becomes"--involves toughness, aggressiveness, and "machismo." These elements are particularly salient when the color of one's uniform is black. Just as observers see those in black uniforms as tough, mean, and aggressive, so too does the person wearing that uniform (Bem, 1972). Having inferred such an identity, the person then remains true to the image by acting more aggressively in certain prescribed contexts.

More broadly construed, then, our results serve as a reminder of the flexible or "situated" nature of the self (Alexander & Knight, 1971; Goffman, 1959; Mead, 1934; Stone, 1962). Different situations, different roles, and even different uniforms can induce us to try on different identities. Around those who are socially subdued or shy, we become a vivacious extrovert; around true socialites, we may retreat into the more reserved role of resident intellectual. In the presence of family members, we play the role of learned scholar granted us by our advanced degrees; in the company of Nobel laureates, we think of ourselves less as scientists and more as amateur musicians, devoted fathers and mothers, or fun-loving globetrotters. Some of these identities that we try to adopt do not suit us, and they are abandoned. This sustains our belief that personalities are stable and reassures us that at our core lies a "true" self. To a surprising degree, however, the identities we are led to adopt do indeed fit, and we continue to play them out in the appropriate circumstances. Perhaps the best evidence for this claim is the existence of identity conflict, such as that experienced by college students who bring their roommates home to meet their parents. This is often a disconcerting experience for many students because they cannot figure out how they should behave or "who they should be"--with their parents they are one person and with their friends they are someone else entirely.

The present investigation demonstrates how a seemingly trivial environmental variable, the color of one's uniform, can induce such a shift in a person's identity. This is not to suggest, however, that in other contexts the direction of causality might not be reversed. The black uniforms worn by gangs like the Hell's Angels, for example, are no doubt deliberately chosen precisely because they convey the desired malevolent image. Thus, as in the world portrayed in the typical American Western, it may be that many inherently evil characters choose to wear black. However, the present investigation makes it clear that in certain contexts at least, some people become the bad guys because they wear black.

References

Adams, F. M., & Osgood, C. E. (1973). A cross-cultural study of the affective meanings of color. <u>Journal of Cross-Cultural Psychology, 4,</u> 135-156.

Alexander, C. N., & Knight, G. (1971). Situated identities and social psychological experimentation. <u>Sociometry, 34,</u> 65-82.

Bem, D. J. (1972). Self-perception theory. In L. Berkowitz (Ed.), <u>Advances in experimental social psychology</u> (Vol.6, pp.1-62). New York: Academic Press.

Carlsmith, J. M., Ellsworth, P. C., & Aronson, E. (1976). <u>Methods of research in social psychology.</u> Reading, MA: Addison-Wesley.

Drabman, R. S., & Thomas, M. H. (1977). Children's imitation of aggressive and prosocial behavior when viewing alone and in pairs. <u>Journal of Communication, 27,</u> 199-205.

Feshbach, S. (1955). The drive-reducing function of fantasy behavior. <u>Journal of Abnormal and Social Psychology, 50,</u> 3-11.

Goffman, E. (1959). <u>The presentation of self in everyday life.</u> New York:Doubleday.

Jaffe, Y., Shapir, N., & Yinon, Y. (1981). Aggression and its escalation. <u>Journal of Cross-Cultural Psychology, 12,</u> 21-36.

Johnson, R. D. & Downing, L. L. (1979). Deindividuation and valence of cues: Effects of prosocial and antisocial behavior. *Journal of Personality and Social Psychology, 37,* 1532-1538.

Mauro, R. (1984). The constable's new clothes: Effects of uniforms on perceptions and problems of police officers. *Journal of Applied Social Psychology,14,* 42-56.

Mead, G. H. (1934). *Mind, self, and society.* Chicago: University of Chicago Press.

Milgram, S. (1965). Some conditions of obedience and disobedience to authority. *Human Relations, 18,* 57-76.

Milgram, S. (1974). *Obedience to authority.* New York: Harper.

Murray, H. A. (1943). *Thematic Apperception Test Manual.* Cambridge, MA: Harvard University Press.

Stone, G. P. (1962). Appearance and the self. In A. M. Rose (Ed.), *Human behavior and social process* (pp.86-118). Boston: Houghton Mifflin.

Turner, V. (1967). *The forest of symbols: Aspects of Ndembu ritual.* Ithaca, NY: Cornell University Press.

Williams, J. E. (1964). Connotations of color names among Negroes and Caucasians. *Perceptual and Motor Skills, 18,* 721-731.

Williams, J. E., & McMurty, C. A. (1970). Color connotations among Caucasian 7th graders and college students. *Perceptual and Motor Skills, 30,* 701-713.

Williams, J. E., Moreland, J. K., & Underwood, W. I. (1970). Connotations of color names in the U.S., Europe, and Asia. <u>Journal of Social Psychology, 82,</u> 3-14.

Table 1

Mean Level of Aggressiveness Contained in Participants'

Chosen Activities as a Function of Uniform Condition

	Mean individual choice (without uniforms)		Group choice (with uniforms)		Change in aggression	
Uniform color	M	SD	M	SD	M	SD
White	113.4	23.9	115.8	25.4	+2.4	8.5
Black	113.5	18.4	130.3	22.9	+16.8	18.1

STATISTICS AND RANDOM NUMBERS TABLES

DIRECTIONS FOR USING TABLE E-1

Find the row that has the same number of degrees of freedom that your study had (for the simple experiment, that row will have a number that is two less than the number of participants you had). Then, unless you have a one-tailed test, read across until you find the column corresponding to your level of significance. The number in that cell will be the critical value of t for your study. To be statistically significant, the absolute value of t that you obtain from your study must be greater than the value you found in the table. For example, suppose $df = 40$ and $p < .05$ (two-tailed test). In that case, to be statistically significant, the absolute value of the t you calculated must be greater than 2.021.

DIRECTIONS FOR USING TABLE E-2

Find the row that has the same number of degrees of freedom that your study had (To calculate your df, subtract one from the number of columns in your chi-square, then subtract one from the number of rows, and then multiply those results together. Thus, with a 2×2 chi-square, you would have 1 df [because 1 $\times$ 1 = 1], and with a 3×2 chi-square, you would have 2 df [because 2 $\times$ 1 = 2]). Then, unless you have a one-tailed test, look across until you find the column corresponding to your level of significance. The number in that cell will be the critical value of chi-square for your study. To be statistically significant, your chi-square value must be greater than the value you found in the table. For example, if $df = 1$ and your significance level is $p < .05$, then your chi-square value must be greater than 3.84146.

• TABLE E-I •

CRITICAL VALUES OF T

Level of Significance for Two-Tailed t-Test

DF	.10	.05	.02	.01
1	6.314	12.706	31.821	63.657
2	2.920	4.303	6.965	9.925
3	2.353	3.182	4.541	5.841
4	2.132	2.776	3.747	4.604
5	2.015	2.571	3.365	4.032
6	1.943	2.447	3.143	3.707
7	1.895	2.365	2.998	3.499
8	1.860	2.306	2.896	3.355
9	1.833	2.262	2.821	3.250
10	1.812	2.228	2.764	3.169
11	1.796	2.201	2.718	3.106
12	1.782	2.179	2.681	3.055
13	1.771	2.160	2.650	3.012
14	1.761	2.145	2.624	2.977
15	1.753	2.131	2.602	2.947
16	1.746	2.120	2.583	2.921
17	1.740	2.110	2.567	2.898
18	1.734	2.101	2.552	2.878
19	1.729	2.093	2.539	2.861
20	1.725	2.086	2.528	2.845
21	1.721	2.080	2.518	2.831
22	1.717	2.074	2.508	2.819
23	1.714	2.069	2.500	2.807
24	1.711	2.064	2.492	2.797
25	1.708	2.060	2.485	2.787
26	1.706	2.056	2.479	2.779
27	1.703	2.052	2.473	2.771
28	1.701	2.048	2.467	2.763
29	1.699	2.045	2.462	2.756
30	1.697	2.042	2.457	2.750
40	1.684	2.021	2.423	2.704
60	1.671	2.000	2.390	2.660
120	1.658	1.980	2.358	2.617
∞	1.645	1.960	2.326	2.576

• TABLE E-2 •

CRITICAL VALUES FOR CHI-SQUARE TESTS

Level of Significance

DF	.10	.05	.01	.001
1	2.70554	3.84146	6.63490	10.828
2	4.60517	5.99147	9.21034	13.816
3	6.25139	7.81473	11.3449	16.266
4	7.77944	9.48773	13.2767	18.467
5	9.23635	11.0705	15.0863	20.515
6	10.6446	12.5916	18.5476	
7	12.0170	14.0671	18.4753	24.322
8	13.3616	15.5073	20.0902	26.125
9	14.6837	16.9190	21.6660	27.877
10	15.9871	18.3070	23.2093	29.588
11	17.2750	19.6751	24.7250	31.264
12	18.5494	21.0261	26.2170	32.909
13	19.8119	22.3621	27.6883	34.528
14	21.0642	23.6848	29.1413	36.123
15	22.3072	24.9958	30.5779	37.697
16	23.5418	26.2962	31.9999	39.252
17	24.7690	27.5871	33.4087	40.790
18	25.9894	28.8693	34.8053	42.312
19	27.2036	30.1435	36.1908	43.820
20	28.4120	31.4104	37.5662	45.315
21	29.6151	32.6705	38.9321	46.797
22	30.8133	33.9244	40.2894	48.268
23	32.0069	35.1725	41.6384	49.728
24	33.1963	36.4151	42.9798	51.179
25	34.3816	37.6525	44.3141	52.620
26	35.5631	38.8852	45.6417	54.052
27	36.7412	40.1133	46.9630	55.476
28	37.9159	41.3372	48.2782	56.892
29	39.0875	42.5569	49.5879	58.302
30	40.2560	43.7729	50.8922	59.703
40	51.8050	55.7585	63.6907	73.402
50	63.1671	67.5048	76.1539	86.661
60	74.3970	79.0819	88.3794	99.607
70	85.5271	90.5312	100.425	112.317
80	96.5782	101.879	112.329	124.839
90	107.565	113.145	124.116	137.208
100	118.498	124.342	135.807	149.449

DIRECTIONS FOR USING TABLE E-3

Look up the degrees of freedom for the effect (the first df) and the error term (the second df). Thus, if you had 1 df for the effect and 25 for the error term, you would look for the effect under the column labeled "1" for the row labeled "25." There, you would find the critical value 4.24. To be statistically significant at the $p < .05$ level, your obtained F would have to be greater than 4.24.

• TABLE E-3 •

CRITICAL VALUES OF F for $p < .05$

1ST DF / 2ND DF	1	2	3	4	5	6	7	8	9	10
1	161.4	199.5	215.7	224.6	230.2	234.0	236.8	238.9	240.5	241.9
2	18.51	19.00	19.16	19.25	19.30	19.33	19.35	19.37	19.38	19.40
3	10.13	9.55	9.28	9.12	9.01	8.94	8.89	8.85	8.81	8.79
4	7.71	6.94	6.59	6.39	6.26	6.16	6.09	6.04	6.00	5.96
5	6.61	5.79	5.41	5.19	5.05	4.95	4.88	4.82	4.77	4.74
6	5.99	5.14	4.76	4.53	4.39	4.28	4.21	4.15	4.10	4.06
7	5.59	4.74	4.35	4.12	3.97	3.87	3.79	3.73	3.68	3.64
8	5.32	4.46	4.07	3.84	3.69	3.58	3.50	3.44	3.39	3.35
9	5.12	4.26	3.86	3.63	3.48	3.37	3.29	3.23	3.18	3.14
10	4.96	4.10	3.71	3.48	3.33	3.22	3.14	3.07	3.02	2.98
11	4.84	3.98	3.59	3.36	3.20	3.09	3.01	2.95	2.90	2.85
12	4.75	3.89	3.49	3.26	3.11	3.00	2.91	2.85	2.80	2.75
13	4.67	3.81	3.41	3.18	3.03	2.92	2.83	2.77	2.71	2.67
14	4.60	3.74	3.34	3.11	2.96	2.85	2.76	2.70	2.65	2.60
15	4.54	3.68	3.29	3.06	2.90	2.79	2.71	2.64	2.59	2.54
16	4.49	3.63	3.24	3.01	2.85	2.74	2.66	2.59	2.54	2.49
17	4.45	3.59	3.20	2.96	2.81	2.70	2.61	2.55	2.49	2.45
18	4.41	3.55	3.16	2.93	2.77	2.66	2.58	2.51	2.46	2.41
19	4.38	3.52	3.13	2.90	2.74	2.63	2.54	2.48	2.42	2.38
20	4.35	3.49	3.10	2.87	2.71	2.60	2.51	2.45	2.39	2.35
21	4.32	3.47	3.07	2.84	2.68	2.57	2.49	2.42	2.37	2.32
22	4.30	3.44	3.05	2.82	2.66	2.55	2.46	2.40	2.34	2.30
23	4.28	3.42	3.03	2.80	2.64	2.53	2.44	2.37	2.32	2.27
24	4.26	3.40	3.01	2.78	2.62	2.51	2.42	2.36	2.30	2.25
25	4.24	3.39	2.99	2.76	2.60	2.49	2.40	2.34	2.28	2.24
26	4.23	3.37	2.98	2.74	2.59	2.47	2.39	2.32	2.27	2.22
27	4.21	3.35	2.96	2.73	2.57	2.46	2.37	2.31	2.25	2.20
28	4.20	3.34	2.95	2.71	2.56	2.45	2.36	2.29	2.24	2.19
29	4.18	3.33	2.93	2.70	2.55	2.43	2.35	2.28	2.22	2.18
30	4.17	3.32	2.92	2.69	2.53	2.42	2.33	2.27	2.21	2.16
40	4.08	3.23	2.84	2.61	2.45	2.34	2.25	2.18	2.12	2.08
60	4.00	3.15	2.76	2.53	2.37	2.25	2.17	2.10	2.04	1.99
120	3.92	3.07	2.68	2.45	2.29	2.17	2.09	2.02	1.96	1.91
∞	3.84	3.00	2.60	2.37	2.21	2.10	2.01	1.94	1.88	1.83

CRITICAL VALUES OF F for $p < .025$

1ST DF / 2ND DF	1	2	3	4	5	6	7	8	9	10	12	15	20	24	30
1	647.8	799.5	864.2	899.6	921.8	937.1	948.2	956.7	963.3	968.6	976.7	984.9	993.1	997.2	1001
2	38.51	39.00	39.17	39.25	39.30	39.33	39.36	39.37	39.39	39.40	39.41	39.43	39.45	39.46	39.46
3	17.44	16.04	15.44	15.10	14.88	14.73	14.62	14.54	14.47	14.42	14.34	14.25	14.17	14.12	14.08
4	12.22	10.65	9.98	9.60	9.36	9.20	9.07	8.98	8.90	8.84	8.75	8.66	8.56	8.51	8.46
5	10.01	8.43	7.76	7.39	7.15	6.98	6.85	6.76	6.68	6.62	6.52	6.43	6.33	6.28	6.23
6	8.81	7.26	6.60	6.23	5.99	5.82	5.70	5.60	5.52	5.46	5.37	5.27	5.17	5.12	5.07
7	8.07	6.54	5.89	5.52	5.29	5.12	4.99	4.90	4.82	4.76	4.67	4.57	4.47	4.42	4.36
8	7.57	6.06	5.42	5.05	4.82	4.65	4.53	4.43	4.36	4.30	4.20	4.10	4.00	3.95	3.89
9	7.21	5.71	5.08	4.72	4.48	4.32	4.20	4.10	4.03	3.96	3.87	3.77	3.67	3.61	3.56
10	6.94	5.46	4.83	4.47	4.24	4.07	3.95	3.85	3.78	3.72	3.62	3.52	3.42	3.37	3.31
11	6.72	5.26	4.63	4.28	4.04	3.88	3.76	3.66	3.59	3.53	3.43	3.33	3.23	3.17	3.12
12	6.55	5.10	4.47	4.12	3.89	3.73	3.61	3.51	3.44	3.37	3.28	3.18	3.07	3.02	2.96
13	6.41	4.97	4.35	4.00	3.77	3.60	3.48	3.39	3.31	3.25	3.15	3.05	2.95	2.89	2.84
14	6.30	4.86	4.24	3.89	3.66	3.50	3.38	3.29	3.21	3.15	3.05	2.95	2.84	2.79	2.73
15	6.20	4.77	4.15	3.80	3.58	3.41	3.29	3.20	3.12	3.06	2.96	2.86	2.76	2.70	2.64
16	6.12	4.69	4.08	3.73	3.50	3.34	3.22	3.12	3.05	2.99	2.89	2.79	2.68	2.63	2.57
17	6.04	4.62	4.01	3.66	3.44	3.28	3.16	3.06	2.98	2.92	2.82	2.72	2.62	2.56	2.50
18	5.98	4.56	3.95	3.61	3.38	3.22	3.10	3.01	2.93	2.87	2.77	2.67	2.56	2.50	2.44
19	5.92	4.51	3.90	3.56	3.33	3.17	3.05	2.96	2.88	2.82	2.72	2.62	2.51	2.45	2.39
20	5.87	4.46	3.86	3.51	3.29	3.13	3.01	2.91	2.84	2.77	2.68	2.57	2.46	2.41	2.35
21	5.83	4.42	3.82	3.48	3.25	3.09	2.97	2.87	2.80	2.73	2.64	2.53	2.42	2.37	2.31
22	5.79	4.38	3.78	3.44	3.22	3.05	2.93	2.84	2.76	2.70	2.60	2.50	2.39	2.33	2.27
23	5.75	4.35	3.75	3.41	3.18	3.02	2.90	2.81	2.73	2.67	2.57	2.47	2.36	2.30	2.24
24	5.72	4.32	3.72	3.38	3.15	2.99	2.87	2.78	2.70	2.64	2.54	2.44	2.33	2.27	2.21
25	5.69	4.29	3.69	3.35	3.13	2.97	2.85	2.75	2.68	2.61	2.51	2.41	2.36	2.24	2.18
26	5.66	4.27	3.67	3.33	3.10	2.94	2.82	2.73	2.65	2.59	2.49	2.39	2.28	2.22	2.16
27	5.63	4.24	3.65	3.31	3.08	2.92	2.80	2.71	2.63	2.57	2.47	2.36	2.25	2.19	2.13
28	5.61	4.22	3.63	3.29	3.06	2.90	2.78	2.69	2.61	2.55	2.45	2.34	2.23	2.17	2.11
29	5.59	4.20	3.61	3.27	3.04	2.88	2.76	2.67	2.59	2.53	2.43	2.32	2.21	2.15	2.09
30	5.57	4.18	3.59	3.25	3.03	2.87	2.75	2.65	2.57	2.51	2.41	2.31	2.20	2.14	2.07
40	5.42	4.05	3.46	3.13	2.90	2.74	2.62	2.53	2.45	2.39	2.29	2.18	2.07	2.01	1.94
60	5.29	3.93	3.34	3.01	2.79	2.63	2.51	2.41	2.33	2.27	2.17	2.06	1.94	1.88	1.82
120	5.15	3.80	3.23	2.89	2.67	2.52	2.39	2.30	2.22	2.16	2.05	1.94	1.82	1.76	1.69
∞	5.02	3.69	3.12	2.79	2.57	2.41	2.29	2.19	2.11	2.05	1.94	1.83	1.71	1.64	1.57

CRITICAL VALUES OF F for $p < .01$

1ST DF / 2ND DF	1	2	3	4	5	6	7	8	9	10	12	15	20	24	30
1	4052	4999.5	5403	5625	5764	5859	5928	5982	6022	6056	6106	6157	6209	6235	6261
2	98.50	99.00	99.17	99.25	99.30	99.33	99.36	99.37	99.39	99.40	99.42	99.43	99.45	99.46	99.47
3	34.12	30.82	29.46	28.71	28.24	27.91	27.67	27.49	27.35	27.23	27.05	26.87	26.69	26.60	26.50
4	21.20	18.00	16.69	15.98	15.52	15.21	14.98	14.80	14.66	14.55	14.37	14.20	14.02	13.93	13.84
5	16.26	13.27	12.06	11.39	10.97	10.67	10.46	10.29	10.16	10.05	9.89	9.72	9.55	9.47	9.38
6	13.75	10.92	9.78	9.15	8.75	8.47	8.26	8.10	7.98	7.87	7.72	7.56	7.40	7.31	7.23
7	12.25	9.55	8.45	7.85	7.46	7.19	6.99	6.84	6.72	6.62	6.47	6.31	6.16	6.07	5.99
8	11.26	8.65	7.59	7.01	6.63	6.37	6.18	6.03	5.91	5.81	5.67	5.52	5.36	5.28	5.20
9	10.56	8.02	6.99	6.42	6.06	5.80	5.61	5.47	5.35	5.26	5.11	4.96	4.81	4.73	4.65

• TABLE E-3 (CONTINUED) •

CRITICAL VALUES OF F for $p < .01$

1ST DF / 2ND DF	1	2	3	4	5	6	7	8	9	10	12	15	20	24	30
10	10.04	7.56	6.55	5.99	5.64	5.39	5.20	5.06	4.94	4.85	4.71	4.56	4.41	4.33	4.25
11	9.65	7.21	6.22	5.67	5.32	5.07	4.89	4.74	4.63	4.54	4.40	4.25	4.10	4.02	3.94
12	9.33	6.93	5.95	5.41	5.06	4.82	4.64	4.50	4.39	4.30	4.16	4.01	3.86	3.78	3.70
13	9.07	6.70	5.74	5.21	4.86	4.62	4.44	4.30	4.19	4.10	3.96	3.82	3.66	3.59	3.51
14	8.86	6.51	5.56	5.04	4.69	4.46	4.28	4.14	4.03	3.94	3.80	3.66	3.51	3.43	3.35
15	8.68	6.36	5.42	4.89	4.56	4.32	4.14	4.00	3.89	3.80	3.67	3.52	3.37	3.29	3.21
16	8.53	6.23	5.29	4.77	4.44	4.20	4.03	3.89	3.78	3.69	3.55	3.41	3.26	3.18	3.10
17	8.40	6.11	5.18	4.67	4.34	4.10	3.93	3.79	3.68	3.59	3.46	3.31	3.16	3.08	3.00
18	8.29	6.01	5.09	4.58	4.25	4.01	3.84	3.71	3.60	3.51	3.37	3.23	3.08	3.00	2.92
19	8.18	5.93	5.01	4.50	4.17	3.94	3.77	3.63	3.52	3.43	3.30	3.15	3.00	2.92	2.84
20	8.10	5.85	4.94	4.43	4.10	3.87	3.70	3.56	3.46	3.37	3.23	3.09	2.94	2.86	2.78
21	8.02	5.78	4.87	4.37	4.04	3.81	3.64	3.51	3.40	3.31	3.17	3.03	2.88	2.80	2.72
22	7.95	5.72	4.82	4.31	3.99	3.76	3.59	3.45	3.35	3.26	3.12	2.98	2.83	2.75	2.67
23	7.88	5.66	4.76	4.26	3.94	3.71	3.54	3.41	3.30	3.21	3.07	2.93	2.78	2.70	2.62
24	7.82	5.61	4.72	4.22	3.90	3.67	3.50	3.36	3.26	3.17	3.03	2.89	2.74	2.66	2.58
25	7.77	5.57	4.68	4.18	3.85	3.63	3.46	3.32	3.22	3.13	2.99	2.85	2.70	2.62	2.54
26	7.72	5.53	4.64	4.14	3.82	3.59	3.42	3.29	3.18	3.09	2.96	2.81	2.66	2.58	2.50
27	7.68	5.49	4.60	4.11	3.78	3.56	3.39	3.26	3.15	3.06	2.93	2.78	2.63	2.55	2.47
28	7.64	5.45	4.57	4.07	3.75	3.53	3.36	3.23	3.12	3.03	2.90	2.75	2.60	2.52	2.44
29	7.60	5.42	4.54	4.04	3.73	3.50	3.33	3.20	3.09	3.00	2.87	2.73	2.57	2.49	2.41
30	7.56	5.39	4.51	4.02	3.70	3.47	3.30	3.17	3.07	2.98	2.84	2.70	2.55	2.47	2.39
40	7.31	5.18	4.31	3.83	3.51	3.29	3.12	2.99	2.89	2.80	2.66	2.52	2.37	2.29	2.20
60	7.08	4.98	4.13	3.65	3.34	3.12	2.95	2.82	2.72	2.63	2.50	2.35	2.20	2.12	2.03
120	6.85	4.79	3.95	3.48	3.17	2.96	2.79	2.66	2.56	2.47	2.34	2.19	2.03	1.95	1.86
∞	6.63	4.61	3.78	3.32	3.02	2.80	2.64	2.51	2.41	2.32	2.18	2.04	1.88	1.79	1.70

SOURCE: This table is abridged from Table 18 of the *Biometrika Tables for Statisticians* (Vol. 1, 3rd ed.) by E. S. Pearson and H. O. Hartley (Eds.), 1970, New York: Cambridge University Press. Used with the kind permission of the Biometrika trustees.

USING TABLE E-4 TO COMPUTE TREND ANALYSES

Suppose you had the following significant effect for sugar on aggression.

	DF	SS	MS	F
Sugar Main Effect	2	126.95	63.47	6.35
Error Term	21	210.00	10.00	

How would you compute a trend analysis for this data? In other words, how would you calculate an F-ratio for the linear and quadratic effects so that you could complete the following ANOVA table?

	DF	SS	MS	F
Sugar Main Effect	2	126.95	63.47	6.35
Linear Component	1			
Quadratic Component	1			
Error Term	21	210.00	10.00	

Before you generate an *F*-ratio, you must have a sum of squares. To compute the sum of squares for a trend, you must first get the sum of the scores for each condition. One way to get the sum of scores for a condition is to add up (sum) all the scores for that condition. Another way to get the sum of scores for each condition is to multiply each condition's average by the number of scores making up each average. Thus, if one condition's mean was 10 and there were 8 scores making up that mean, the sum for that condition would be 10×8 which is 80.

Next, arrange these totals, starting with the total for the group that received the smallest amount of the treatment and ending with the total for the group that received the highest amount of the treatment. That is, place the sum for the condition connected with the lowest level of the independent variable first, the sum for the condition with the next highest level of the independent variable next, and so on. In our example, you would order your sums like so:

TOTAL NUMBER OF VIOLENT INSTANCES PER CONDITION

AMOUNT OF SUGAR	TOTAL NUMBER OF VIOLENT INSTANCES
0 mg	10.0
50 mg	50.0
100 mg	12.0

Now, you are ready to consult the tables of orthogonal polynomials in Table E-4. Because this example involves three conditions, you would look for the three-condition table. The table reads:

THREE-CONDITION CASE

	TREND	
	1 (LINEAR)	**2** (QUADRATIC)
CONDITION 1	−1	1
CONDITION 2	0	−2
CONDITION 3	1	1
WEIGHTING FACTOR	2	6

To get the numerator for the sum of squares for the linear trend, multiply the sum for the lowest level of the independent variable by the first value in the "Linear" column of the table for the three-condition case (−1), the second sum by the second value in the "Linear" column of the table (0), and the third sum by the third value in the "Linear" column of the table (+1). Next, get a sum by adding these three products together. Then, square that sum. So, for the sugar example we just described, you would do the following calculations:

$$[(-1 \times 10) + (0 \times 50) + (1 \times 12)]^2$$

or

$$(-10 + 0 + 12)^2$$

or

$$(2)^2$$

or

$$4$$

To get the denominator for the sum of squares, multiply the weighting factor for the linear trend (2) by the number of observations in each condition. Because there were eight observations in each condition, the denominator would be 16 (2×8). The sum of squares linear would be the numerator (4) divided by the denominator (16), which equals .25.

Once you have computed the sum of squares for the linear trend, the rest is easy. All you have to do is compute F-ratio by dividing the mean square linear by the mean square error and then see if that result is significant.

Calculating the mean square linear involves dividing the sum of squares linear by the degrees of freedom linear. Because the degrees of freedom for any trend is always 1.00, you could divide your sum of squares (.25) by 1.00 and get .25. Or, you could simply remember that a trend's mean square is always the same as its sum of squares.

Getting the mean square error is also easy: Just find the mean square error in the printout that was used to test the overall main effect. In this example, that would be 10.0.

So, to get the F-value for this linear comparison, you would divide the mean square for the comparison (.25) by the mean square error used on the overall main effect (10.0). Thus, the F would be .25/10, or .025. Because the F is below 1.00, this result is obviously not significant.

But how large would the F have had to be to be significant? That depends on how many trends you were analyzing. If you had decided to look only at the linear trend, the significant F at the .05 level would have to exceed the value in the F-table for 1 degree of freedom (the df for any trend) and 21 degrees of freedom, the df for the error term. That value is 4.32.

However, if you are going to analyze more than one trend, you must correct for the number of Fs you are going to compute. The correction is simple: You divide the significance level you want (say .05), by the number of trends you will test. In this example, you are computing two Fs. Therefore, you should use the the critical value of F for the significance level of .05/2 which is .025. So, rather than look in an F-table listing the critical values of F for $p < .05$, you would look in an F-table listing the critical values of F for $p < .025$. In this example, you would only declare a trend significant at the .05 level if the F for that trend exceeds the critical value for $F(1,21)$ at the .025 level: 5.83.

Obviously, the F for the linear component, $F(1,21) = .025$, falls far short of the critical value of 5.83. But what about the quadratic component? To determine whether the quadratic component is significant, you would follow the same steps as before. The only difference is that you would look at the "Quadratic" column of the table for the three-condition case instead of the "Linear" column.

Thus, you would first multiply the treatment sums by the constants listed in the "Quadratic" column, add them together, and square that sum. In other words,

$$((1 \times 10) + (-2 \times 50) + (1 \times 12))^2$$

or

$$(10 + (-100) + 12)^2$$

or

$$(-78)^2$$

or

$$6084$$

Then, you would divide 6084 by 8 (the number of observations in each condition) $\times$ 6 (the weighting factor for the quadratic effect). So, SS quadratic is $6084/(8 \times 6) = 6084/48 = 126.7$, as is the MS quadratic (SS (126.7)/df(1) = MS (126.7)).

To get the F, you would divide the MS quadratic by MS error. Therefore, the F would be $126.7/10 = 12.67$. As before, the critical value for the comparison is the F-value for the .025 significance level with 1 and 21 degrees of freedom: 5.83. Because our F of 12.67 exceeds the critical value of 5.83, we have a statistically significant quadratic trend.

So, our complete ANOVA table, including the linear and quadratic components, would be as follows:

	DF	SS	MS	F
Sugar Main Effect	2	126.95	63.47	6.35*
Linear	1	0.25	0.25	0.02
Quadratic	1	126.70	126.70	12.67*
Error Term	21	210.00	10.00	

*Significant at .05 level.

From looking at the table, you see that if you add up the degrees of freedom for all the trends involved in the sugar main effect (1 + 1), you get the total df for the main effect (2). More importantly, note that if you add up the sum of squares for the components (126.70 + .25), you get the sum of squares for the overall effect (126.95). This fact gives you a way to check your work. Specifically, if the total of the sums of squares for all the components does not add up to the sum of squares for the overall effect, you have made a mistake.

• TABLE E-4 •

COEFFICIENTS OF ORTHOGONAL POLYNOMIALS

CONDITION	3-Condition Case Trend		4-Condition Case Trend			5-Condition Case Trend			
	1	2	1	2	3	1	2	3	4
	(LIN)	(QUAD)	(LIN)	(QUAD)	(CUBIC)	(LIN)	(QUAD)	(CUBIC)	
1	−1	1	−3	1	−1	−2	2	−1	1
2	0	−2	−1	−1	3	−1	−1	2	−4
3	1	1	1	−1	−3	0	−2	0	6
4			3	1	1	1	−1	−2	−4
5						2	2	1	1
Weighting Factor	2	6	20	4	20	10	14	10	70

CONDITION	6-Condition Case Trend					7-Condition Case Trend					
	1	2	3	4	5	1	2	3	4	5	6
	(LIN)	(QUAD)	(CUBIC)			(LIN)	(QUAD)	(CUBIC)			
1	−5	5	−5	1	−1	−3	5	−1	3	−1	1
2	−3	−1	7	−3	5	−2	0	1	−7	4	−6
3	−1	−4	4	2	−10	−1	−3	1	1	−5	15
4	1	−4	−4	2	10	0	−4	0	6	0	−20
5	3	−1	−7	−3	−5	1	−3	−1	1	5	15
6	5	5	5	1	1	2	0	−1	−7	−4	−6
7						3	5	1	3	1	1
Weighting Factor	70	84	180	28	252	28	84	6	154	84	924

SOURCE: This table is adapted from Table VII of *Statistics* (pp. 662–664) by W. L. Hays, 1981, New York: Holt, Rinehart and Winston. Copyright (c) 1982 by Holt, Rinehart and Winston, Inc. Adapted by permission.

USING TABLE E-5 TO COMPUTE POST HOC TESTS

Post hoc tests, such as the Tukey test, can be used after finding a significant main effect for a multilevel factor. These tests help determine which conditions are significantly different from one another.

To see how you could use table E-5 to compute post hoc tests, suppose that an investigator uses 24 subjects (8 in each group) to examine the effect of color (blue, green, or yellow) on mood. As you can see from the following table, the investigator's ANOVA table reveals a significant effect of color.

SOURCE	SUM OF SQUARES	DEGREES OF FREEDOM	MEAN SQUARE	F
Color	64	2	32.0	4.0*
Error	168	21	8.0	

*Significant at .05 level.

The means for the three color conditions are:

BLUE	GREEN	YELLOW
10.0	5.0	8.0

Now, the question is "Which conditions differ from one another?" Does yellow cause a different mood than green? Does blue cause a different mood than yellow? To find out, we need to do a post hoc test. For this example, we will do the Tukey test.

The formula for the Tukey test is

$$\frac{\text{Mean 1} - \text{Mean 2}}{\sqrt{(\text{MSE} \times 1/\text{number of observations per condition})}}$$

Because the mean square error is 8 (see original ANOVA table) and there are eight subjects in each group, the denominator in this example will always be:

$$\sqrt{(8 \times 1/8)}$$

or

$$\sqrt{8/8}$$

or

$$\sqrt{1}$$

or

$$1$$

The numerator will change, depending on what means you are comparing. Thus, if you are comparing blue and green, the numerator would be $10 - 5$ or 5. So, to see whether the blue and green conditions differ significantly, you would do the following calculations.

$$\frac{\underset{\text{(blue mean)} \ \text{(green mean)}}{10.0 \ - \ 5.0}}{\sqrt{(8 \times 1/8)}} = \frac{5.0}{\sqrt{1}} = \frac{5.0}{1.0} = 5.0$$

To find out whether 5.0 is significant, go to Table E-5 and look at the column labeled "3" because you have three means you are comparing. Then, go down and look at row 21 because you have 21 degrees of freedom in your error term (as you can see by looking at the original ANOVA table). The value in that table is 3.57. This is the critical value that you will use in all your comparisons. If your Tukey statistic for a pair of means is larger than this critical value, there is a significant difference between conditions. Because 5.0 is greater than 3.57, your result is significant at the .05 level.

But, do blue and yellow differ? To find out, compute the Tukey statistic.

$$\frac{10.0 - 8.0}{\sqrt{(8 \times 1/8)}} = \frac{2.0}{\sqrt{1}} = \frac{2.0}{1.0} = 2.0$$

Because 2.0 is less than our critical value of 3.57, the difference between blue and yellow is not statistically significant at the .05 level.

Do yellow and green differ?

$$\frac{8.0 - 5.0}{\sqrt{(8 \times 1/8)}} = \frac{3.0}{\sqrt{1}} = \frac{3.0}{1.0} = 3.0$$

Because 3.0 is less than our critical value of 3.57, the difference between yellow and green is not statistically significant at the .05 level.

• **TABLE E-5** •

CRITICAL VALUES FOR THE TUKEY TEST
AT THE .05 LEVEL OF SIGNIFICANCE

Number of Means

DF ERROR	2	3	4	5	6	7	8	9
10	3.15	3.88	4.33	4.65	4.91	5.12	5.30	5.46
11	3.11	3.82	4.26	4.57	4.82	5.03	5.20	5.35
12	3.08	3.77	4.20	4.51	4.75	4.95	5.12	5.27
13	3.06	3.73	4.15	4.45	4.69	4.88	5.05	5.19
14	3.03	3.70	4.11	4.41	4.64	4.83	4.99	5.13
15	3.01	3.67	4.08	4.37	4.59	4.78	4.94	5.08
16	3.00	3.65	4.05	4.33	4.56	4.74	4.90	5.03
17	2.98	3.63	4.02	4.30	4.52	4.70	4.86	4.99
18	2.97	3.61	4.00	4.28	4.49	4.67	4.82	4.96
19	2.96	3.59	3.98	4.25	4.47	4.65	4.79	4.92
20	2.95	3.58	3.96	4.23	4.45	4.62	4.77	4.90
21	2.95	3.57	3.95	4.22	4.43	4.60	4.75	4.88
30	2.89	3.49	3.85	4.10	4.30	4.46	4.60	4.72
40	2.86	3.44	3.79	4.04	4.23	4.39	4.52	4.63
60	2.83	3.40	3.74	3.98	4.16	4.31	4.44	4.55
120	2.80	3.36	3.68	3.92	4.10	4.24	4.36	4.47
∞	2.77	3.31	3.63	3.86	4.03	4.17	4.29	4.39

SOURCE: This table is abridged from Table 29 of the *Biometrika Tables for Statisticians* (Vol. 1, 3rd ed.) by E. S. Pearson and H. O. Hartley (Eds.), 1970, New York: Cambridge University Press. Used with the kind permission of the Biometrika Trustees.

DIRECTIONS FOR USING TABLE E-6

If you are doing an experiment, you can use Table E-6 to randomly assign participants to treatment condition. If you are doing a survey, you can use Table E-6 to generate a random sample.

RANDOMLY ASSIGNING PARTICIPANTS TO GROUPS IN AN EXPERIMENT

STEP 1: Across the top of a piece of paper, write down your conditions. Under each condition, draw a line for each participant you will need. In this example, we had three conditions and needed 12 participants.

GROUP 1	GROUP 2	GROUP 3
_____	_____	_____
_____	_____	_____
_____	_____	_____
_____	_____	_____

STEP 2: Turn to Table E-6. Roll a die to determine which column in the table you will start at.

STEP 3: Assign the first number in the column to the first space under Group 1, the second number to the second space, and so on. When you have filled the spaces for Group 1, put the next number under the first space under Group 2. Similarly, when you fill all the spaces under Group 2, place the next number in the first space under Group 3.

GROUP 1	GROUP 2	GROUP 3
12	20	63
39	*3*	64
53	37	95
29	*1*	18

STEP 4: Assign the first person who participates in your study to the condition with the lowest random number. The second participant will be in the condition with the second lowest random number, and so on. Thus, in this example, your first two participants would be in Group 2 and your third participant would be in Group 1.

USING TABLE E-6 TO GET A RANDOM SAMPLE

STEP 1: Determine how large your sample will be.

STEP 2: Get a list of your population and put a line next to each individual's name.

STEP 3: Turn to Table E-6. Roll a die to determine which column in the table you will start at.

STEP 4: Assign the first number in the column to the first name on your list, the second number to the second space, and so on.

STEP 5: Put your participants in order based on their random number. Thus, the individual with the lowest random number next to his or her name would be the first on the list, the individual with the second lowest random number would be the second, and so on.

STEP 6: Go down the list to get your sample. If your sample will be 50, pick the first 50 individuals on the list. If it is 100, pick the first 100 individuals on the list.

• TABLE E-6 •

TABLE OF RANDOM NUMBERS

5	28	80	31	99	77	39	23	69	0	15	49	100	2	22	64	73	92	53
29	71	48	4	87	32	17	90	89	9	99	34	58	8	61	73	98	48	89
90	94	19	80	70	36	2	17	48	63	82	39	85	26	65	27	81	69	83
62	66	48	74	86	6	66	41	15	65	6	41	85	57	84	64	70	39	64
67	54	3	54	23	40	25	95	93	55	59	46	77	55	49	82	26	8	87
75	27	62	15	81	36	22	26	69	42	44	91	55	0	84	48	68	65	5
70	19	7	100	94	53	81	76	73	40	22	58	49	42	96	18	66	89	8
75	7	9	20	58	92	41	42	79	26	91	44	63	87	45	21	23	15	6
55	70	10	23	25	73	91	72	29	47	93	58	21	75	80	52	9	12	36
83	42	62	53	55	12	11	54	19	2	45	43	67	13	5	74	30	93	11
94	20	76	23	65	72	55	27	44	19	10	72	50	67	83	18	67	22	49
51	10	72	9	59	47	66	32	17	6	75	8	54	22	37	3	46	83	95
99	50	22	2	92	9	98	9	40	23	34	8	63	58	49	31	70	39	83
9	12	3	23	2	0	82	75	36	63	71	19	78	26	66	63	16	75	7
20	40	50	29	51	82	81	47	73	69	74	100	80	37	14	67	1	90	92
90	92	54	52	74	0	88	71	45	49	38	54	80	2	85	42	75	47	20
25	6	92	30	19	31	22	41	0	22	79	87	84	61	6	19	67	97	60
13	12	94	76	29	61	50	67	29	76	27	70	97	16	83	88	100	22	48
91	77	51	3	92	85	46	22	0	58	84	64	87	93	94	94	13	98	41
29	12	39	35	32	47	30	81	40	32	37	8	48	81	50	77	18	39	7
43	96	86	14	91	24	22	85	16	51	42	37	41	100	94	76	45	50	67
57	44	72	45	87	21	7	29	26	82	69	99	10	39	76	29	11	17	85
63	10	10	76	7	75	19	91	2	31	45	94	54	72	10	48	52	7	12
34	28	11	95	4	82	51	7	69	53	93	36	81	66	93	88	15	73	54

SOURCE: This table is taken from the random numbers table in Appendix D of *Foundations of Behavioral Research,* 3rd ed. (pp. 642–643) by F. N. Kerlinger, 1986, New York: Holt, Rinehart and Winston. Copyright (c) 1986 by Holt, Rinehart and Winston. Reprinted by permission.

INTRODUCTION TO STATISTICS

....

CHOOSING THE CORRECT ANALYSIS

To analyze statistical data correctly, you must choose the correct statistical test. The test you should use if you have interval data is not the same test you should use if you have nominal data. The test you should use if you are comparing each participant with himself or herself is not the same test you should use if you are comparing one group to another group. The test that would work if you only had two conditions may not work if you are comparing more than two conditions. In other words, there are at least three factors you should take into consideration when choosing a statistical test: (1) the scale of measurement that your measure provides (see Chapter 4); (2) the type of comparison you are making (within-subjects or between-subjects); and (3) the number of conditions you have. In the next three sections, we will show you how to take each of these three factors into account so that you can choose the right analysis for your study.

SCALES OF MEASUREMENT

Often, the type of test depends on what type of data you have. That is, you will do one kind of test if you have nominal data, but another kind of test if you have interval data. This fact is summarized in the following table:

SCALE OF MEASUREMENT	EXAMPLE	SUMMARY STATISTIC (AVERAGE)	MEASURE OF CORRELATION	TYPICAL STATISTICAL ANALYSIS
Nominal	When numbers represent categories, such as 1 = Democrat, 2 = Republican, 3 = Independent	Mode (most common score) or simply describe the percentage of participants in each category	Phi coefficient	Chi-square
Ordinal	Ranks	Median (middle score)	Spearman's rho	Mann-Whitney (if testing two groups), Kruskal-Wallis (if testing more than two groups), Friedman test (if using within-subjects design)
Interval	Rating scales	Mean	Pearson r	t-test, ANOVA
Ratio	Height, magnitude estimation	Mean	Pearson r	t-test, ANOVA

WITHIN-SUBJECTS VERSUS BETWEEN-SUBJECTS DESIGNS

Another factor that determines which statistics you should use is whether you are using a within-subjects design (comparing each participant with himself or herself) or a between-subjects design. For example, if you were using a within-subjects design, you should **not** use a between-subjects ANOVA. Nor should you use an independent-groups t-test. Instead, you should use either a dependent-groups t-test or a within-subjects ANOVA.

NUMBER OF CONDITIONS

Finally, you must also consider the number of conditions you are comparing. If you are only comparing two conditions, you can use a *t*-test. If you are comparing more than two conditions, you cannot use a *t*-test. Instead, you would use ANOVA (if you have interval or ratio data).

These facts are summarized in the following table:

TYPE OF DATA	NUMBER OF CONDITIONS	
	TWO	MORE THAN TWO
Nominal, between-subjects	Chi-square	Chi-square
Nominal, within-subjects or matched pairs	McNemar Test	Cochran Q Test
Ordinal, between-subjects	Mann-Whitney Test	Kruskal-Wallis Test
Ordinal, within-subjects or matched pairs	Wilcoxon Matched Pair	Friedman Test
Interval/Ratio, between-subjects	Independent-groups *t*-test or between-subjects ANOVA	Between-subjects ANOVA
Interval/Ratio, within-subjects or matched subjects	Dependent *t*-test or within-subjects ANOVA	Within-subjects ANOVA

PERFORMING THE CORRECT ANALYSIS: AN OVERVIEW OF THE REST OF THIS APPENDIX

If you refer to the information we just discussed, you will choose the right analysis. But how do you conduct it? In the rest of this appendix, we will discuss the logic and computations behind the most commonly used statistical techniques.

We will begin by discussing the independent-groups *t*-test. Learning about the *t*-test will not only teach you about one of the most commonly used statistical techniques, but it will also give you the foundation for understanding other statistical techniques. We will then discuss the most common technique for analyzing the results of an experiment that has more than two groups: ANOVA. We will finish our discussion of techniques typically used by students to analyze data from experiments with a description of the dependent *t*-test.

After talking about techniques commonly used in experiments, we will discuss techniques commonly used with correlational data. We will begin by talking about how to compute the Pearson *r*. Then, we will show you how to find out if a Pearson *r* in your sample indicates that the two variables are really related in the population. Following this discussion of techniques that are commonly used when you have interval data, we show you how to do comparable analyses when you have nominal data. Finally, we discuss the logic behind a correlational analysis that is in almost one in six journal articles—factor analysis (Reis & Stiller, 1992).

....

ANALYZING DATA FROM THE SIMPLE, TWO-GROUP EXPERIMENT: THE INDEPENDENT-GROUPS *t*-TEST

To use the independent-groups *t*-test,

1. You must have two groups.
2. Your observations must be independent.
3. Each of your groups should have approximately the same variance.
4. Your scores should be normally distributed.
5. You should be able to assume that your data are either interval or ratio.

As long as your data meet these assumptions, then you can use the *t*-test to analyze your data. Thus, the *t*-test can be used to look at differences on a measure between men and women, computer users versus nonusers, or any two independent groups. However, the most common use of the *t*-test is to analyze the results of a simple (two-group, between-subjects) experiment.

To understand why you can use the *t*-test to analyze the results of a simple experiment, remember why you did the simple experiment. You did it to find out whether the treatment would have an effect on a unique population—all the individuals who participated in your experiment. More specifically, you wanted to know the answer to the hypothetical question: "If I had put all my participants in the experimental condition, would they have scored differently than if I had put all of them in the control condition?" To answer this question, you need to know the averages of two populations:

Average of Population 1: what the average score on the dependent measure would have been if all your participants had been in the control group

Average of Population 2: what the average score on the dependent measure would have been if all your participants had been in the experimental group

Unfortunately, you cannot measure both of these populations. If you put all your participants in the control condition, then you won't know how they would have scored in the experimental condition. If, on the other hand, you put all your participants in the experimental condition, you won't know how they would have scored in the control condition.

ESTIMATING WHAT YOU WANT TO KNOW

Because you cannot directly get the population averages you want, you do the next best thing—you estimate them. You can estimate them because—thanks to independent random assignment—you divided all your participants (your population of participants) into two random samples. That is, you started the experiment with two random samples from your original population of participants. Those two samples were the control group and the experimental group.

The average score of the random sample of your participants who received the treatment (the experimental group) is an estimate of what the average score would have been if all your participants received the treatment. The average score of the random sample of participants who received no treatment (the control group) is an estimate of what the average score would have been if all of your participants had been in the control condition.

Calculating Sample Means

Even though only half your participants were in the experimental group, you will assume that the experimental group is a fair sample of your entire population of participants. Thus, the experimental group's average score should be a reasonably good estimate of what the average score would have been if all your participants had been in the experimental group. Similarly, you will assume that the control group's average score is a fairly good estimate of what the average score would have been if all your participants had been in the control group. Therefore, the first step in analyzing your data will be to calculate the average score for each group. Usually, the average you will calculate is the *mean:* the result of adding up all the scores and then dividing by the number of scores.

Comparing Sample Means

Once you have your two sample means, you can compare them. Before talking about how to compare them, let's understand why we are comparing the means. We are comparing the sample means because we know that, before the treatment was administered, both groups represented a random sample of the population consisting of every subject who participated in the study. Thus, at the end of the experiment—if the treatment had no effect—the control and experimental groups would both still be random samples from that population.

As you know, two random samples from the same population will be similar to each other. For example, two random samples of the entire population of New York City should be similar to each other, two random samples from the entire population of students at your school should be similar to each other, and two random samples from the entire group of participants who participated in your study should be similar to each other. Thus, if the treatment has no effect, at the end of the experiment, the experimental and control groups should be similar to each other.

Because random samples of the same population should be similar, you might think all we need to do is subtract the control group mean from the experimental group mean to find the effect. But such is not the case: Even if the treatment has no effect, the means for the control group and experimental group will rarely be identical. To illustrate, suppose that Dr. N. Ept made a serious mistake while trying to do a double-blind study. Specifically, although Dr. N. Ept succeeded in not letting his assistants know whether the participants were getting the real treatment or a placebo, his study was ruined because all the participants got the placebo. In other words, both groups ended up being random samples of the same population—participants who did not get the treatment. Even in such a case, the two groups may have very different means.

Dr. N. Ept's study illustrates an important point: Even if groups are random samples of the same population, they may still differ because of random sampling error. You are aware of random sampling error from reading about public opinion polls that admit to a certain degree of sampling error or from reading about two polls of the same population that produced slightly different results.

In summary, some random samples will not be representative of their parent population. Because of the possibility that a sample may be strongly affected by random sampling error, your sample means may differ even if the real, parent population means do not.

INFERENTIAL STATISTICS: JUDGING THE ACCURACY OF YOUR ESTIMATES

We have told you that random error can throw off your estimates of population means. Because of random error, the treatment group mean is an imperfect estimate of what would have happened if all the participants had received the treatment. Because of random error, the control group mean is an imperfect estimate of what would have happened if none of the participants had received the treatment. Thus, the difference between your experimental group mean and control group mean could be due to random error; in other words, finding a difference doesn't prove that you have a treatment effect.

If the difference between your group means could be due to random error, how can you determine whether a difference between the sample means is due to the treatment? You need to know how much of a difference random error could make. If the actual difference between your group means was much bigger than the difference that chance could make, then you could conclude that the treatment had an effect.

Estimating the Accuracy of Individual Sample Means

How can you determine if the difference between your sample means is too large to be due to random error? Knowing the accuracy of each of your individual sample means should help. For example, suppose you knew the control group mean was within one point of its true population mean. Furthermore, suppose you knew that the experimental group mean was also within one point of its real population mean. In other words, you knew that: (1) the estimate for what the mean would be if everybody had been in the control group was not off by more than one point, and that (2) the estimate for what the mean would be if everyone had been in the experimental group was also not off by more than one point.

If you knew all that, and if your control group mean differed from your experimental group mean by 20 points, then you would know that your two sample means represent different population means. In other words, you could assume that if all your participants had been given the treatment, they would have scored differently than if they had all been deprived of the treatment.

If, on the other hand, the two group means had differed by less than one point, the difference between the groups could easily be due to random error. In that case, you would not be able to conclude that the treatment had an effect.

Consider Population Variability: The Value of the Standard Deviation   You have seen that a key to determining whether your treatment had an effect is to determine how accurately your two sample means reflect their population means. But how can you determine how closely each of your sample means are to their population means? One factor that affects how well a mean based on a random sample of the population reflects the population mean is the amount of variability in the population. If there is no variability in the population, then all scores in the population will be the same as the mean. Consequently, there would be no sampling error. For example, if everyone in the population scored a five, the population mean would be five, and the mean of every random sample would also be five. Thus, since all Roman Catholic cardinals hold very similar positions on the morality of abortion, almost any sample of Roman Catholic cardinals you took would accurately reflect the views of Roman Catholic cardinals on that issue.

If, on the other hand, scores in a population vary considerably (for example, ranging anywhere from 0 to 1,000), then independent random samples from that population could be extremely inaccurate. For instance, even if the population mean was 500, you might get sample means ranging from 0 to 1,000. Thus, two sample means from such a heterogeneous population could be very different.

To recap, you have seen that the variability of scores in a population affects how accurately individual samples will reflect that population. Because the extent of the variability of scores in the population influences the extent to which we have random sampling error, it would be nice to have an index of the variability of scores within a population.

The ideal index of the population's variability is the population's *standard deviation:* a measure of the extent to which individual scores deviate from the population mean. Unfortunately, to get that index, you have to know the population mean (for the control condition, the average of the scores if all the participants had been in the control condition; for the experimental condition, the average of the scores if all the participants had been in the experimental condition). Obviously, you don't know the population mean for either the control or experimental condition—that's what you are trying to find out!

Although you cannot calculate the population standard deviation, you can estimate it by looking at the variability of scores within your samples. In fact, by following the steps in Box F-1, you can estimate what the standard deviation would have been if everyone had been in the control group (by looking at

---

• BOX F-I •

HOW TO COMPUTE A STANDARD DEVIATION

Assume we have four scores (108, 104, 104, 104) from a population. We could estimate the population's standard deviation by going through the following steps.

STEP 1:	STEP 2:	STEP 3:
Calculate the mean (*M*).	Subtract scores from mean (105) to get differences.	Square differences.
108	−105 = +3	$(+3)^2 = +9$
104	−105 = −1	$(-1)^2 = +1$
104	−105 = −1	$(-1)^2 = +1$
104	−105 = −1	$(-1)^2 = \underline{+1}$
420 = Total		SS = 12

Mean = 420/4 = 105

STEP 4: Add (sum) the squared differences obtained in step 3 to get sum of squared differences, otherwise known as sum of squares. Sum of squares is often abbreviated as (*SS*). SUM OF SQUARES (*SS*) = 12.

STEP 5: Get variance by dividing *SS* (which was 12) by one less than the number of scores (4 − 1 = 3). This division yields a variance of 4 (because 12/3 = 4).

STEP 6: Get the standard deviation by taking the square root of variance. Because the variance is 4, the standard deviation is 2 (because the square root of 4 is 2).

For those preferring formulas:

$S = \sqrt{(\sum X - M)^2 / N - 1}$ where *X* stands for the individual scores, *M* is the sample mean, *S* is the estimate of the population's standard deviation, and *N* is the number of scores.

---

variability within the control group) and what the standard deviation would have been if all your participants had been in the experimental group (by looking at variability within the experimental group).

One reason the standard deviation is a particularly valuable index of variability is that many populations can be completely described simply by knowing the standard deviation and the mean. You probably already know that the mean is valuable for describing many populations. You know that, for many populations, most scores will be near the mean and that as many scores will be above the mean as will be below the mean.

What you may not know is that, for many populations, you can specify precisely what percentage of scores will be within a certain number of standard deviations of the mean. For instance, you can say that 68% of the scores will be within one standard deviation of the mean, 95% will be within two standard deviations of the mean, and 99% of the scores will be within three standard deviations of the mean. If a population's scores are spread out (distributed) in this manner, the population is said to be *normally distributed.*

As the term "normally distributed" suggests, many populations are normally distributed—from test scores to the heights of American women. Because normally distributed populations are common, graphing the distribution of scores in a population will often produce a *normal curve*: a bell-shaped, symmetrical curve that has its center at the mean (see Figure F-1).

It's convenient to summarize an entire distribution of scores with just two numbers: the mean, which gives you the center of a normal distribution; and the standard deviation, which gives you an index of the width of the distribution. It's comforting to know that 68% of the scores will be within one standard deviation of the mean, that 95% of the scores will be within two standard deviations of the mean, and that virtually all the scores will be within three standard deviations of the mean.

But the standard deviation has more uses than merely describing a population. You could use the standard deviation to make inferences about the population mean. For example, suppose you don't know the population's mean, but you know that the distribution is normally distributed and that its standard deviation is three. Then, you don't need much data to make certain inferences about that population. Specifically, you know that if you randomly selected a single score from that population, there would be a 68% chance that the population mean would be within three points (one standard deviation) of that score and a 95% chance that the population mean would be within six points (two standard deviations) of that score.

• **FIGURE F-1** •

THE NORMAL CURVE

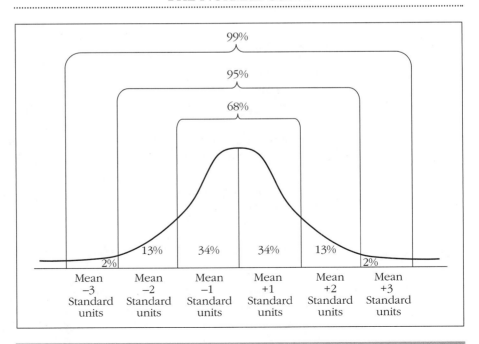

Consider Sample Size: The Role of the Standard Error   Of course, to estimate your control group's population mean, you would not use just one score. Instead, you would use the control group mean. Intuitively, you realize that using a sample mean based on several scores will give you a better estimate of the population mean than using a single score.

You also realize that using a sample mean based on many scores is better than using a sample mean based on a few scores. In other words, the bigger your independent random sample, the better your random sample will tend to reflect the population. Consequently, the bigger your sample, the closer its mean should be to the population mean.

To reiterate, the accuracy of your sample mean depends on how many scores you use to calculate that mean. However, the standard deviation does not take into account how many scores the sample mean is based on. The standard deviation will be the same whether the sample mean is based on 2 scores or 2,000. Because the standard deviation does not take into account sample size, the standard deviation is not a good index of your sample mean's accuracy.

A good index of the degree to which a sample mean may differ from its population mean must include both factors that influence the accuracy of a sample mean, namely:

1. population variability (the less population variability, the more accurate the sample mean will tend to be)
2. sample size (the larger the sample, the more accurate the sample mean will tend to be)

Not surprisingly, both of these factors are included in the formula for the standard error of the estimate of the population mean: an index of the degree to which random error may cause a sample mean to be an inaccurate estimate of its population mean.

The standard error (of the estimate of the population mean) equals the

$$\frac{\text{standard deviation (a measure of population variability)}}{\text{the square root of the number of participants (an index of sample size)}}$$

Thus, if the standard deviation were 40 and you had 4 people in your sample, the standard error would be:

$$\frac{40}{\sqrt{4}} = \frac{40}{2} = 20$$

Note that dividing by the square root of the sample size means that the bigger the sample size, the smaller the standard error. Thus, the formula reflects the fact that you have less random sampling error with larger samples. Consequently, in the example above, if you had used 100 participants instead of 4, your standard error would have shrunk from 20 ($40/\sqrt{4}$) to 4 ($40/\sqrt{100}$).

What does the standard error tell you? Clearly, the larger the standard error, the more likely a sample mean will misrepresent the population mean. But does this random error contaminate all samples equally or does it heavily infest some samples while leaving others untouched? Ideally, you would like to know precisely how random error is distributed across various samples. You want to know what percentage of samples will be substantially tainted by random error so that you know what chance your sample mean has of being accurate.

Using the Standard Error   Fortunately, you can know how sample means are distributed. As a result of drawing numerous independent random samples from a normally distributed population and plotting the means of each sample, statisticians have shown that the distribution of sample means is normally distributed. Most (68%) of the sample means will be within one standard error of the population mean, 95% will be within two standard errors of the population mean, and 99% will be within three standard errors of the population mean. Therefore, if your standard error is 1.0, you know that there's a 68% chance that the true population mean is within 1.0 points of your sample mean, a 95% chance that the population mean is within 2.0 points of your sample mean, and a 99% chance that the population mean is within 3.0 points of your sample mean.

When you can assume that the population is normally distributed, you can estimate how close your sample mean is to the true population mean. You do this by taking advantage of the fact that sample means from normally distributed populations will follow a very well-defined distribution: the normal distribution. But what if the underlying population isn't normally distributed?

Even then, as the *central limit theorem* states, the distribution of sample means will be normally distributed—if your samples are large enough (30 or more participants). To understand why the central limit theorem works, realize that if you take numerous large random samples from the same population, your sample means will differ from one another for only one reason—random error. Because random error is normally distributed, your distribution of sample means will be normally distributed—regardless of the shape of the underlying population. Consequently, if you take a large random sample from any population, you can use the normal curve to estimate how closely your sample mean reflects the population mean.

Estimating Accuracy of Your Estimate of the Difference Between Population Means

Because you know that sample means are normally distributed, you can determine how likely it is that a sample mean is within a certain distance of its population mean. But in the simple experiment, you are not trying to find a certain population mean. Instead, you are trying to find out whether two population means differ. As we mentioned earlier, you want to know whether there was a difference between two hypothetical population means: (1) what the mean score would have been if all your participants had been in the control group, and (2) what the mean score would have been if all your participants had been in the experimental group. Put another way, you are asking the question: "If all the participants had received the treatment, would they have scored differently than if they had all been in the control group?"

Because you want to know whether the treatment made a difference, your focus is not on the individual sample means, but on the difference between the two means. Therefore, you would like to know how differences between sample means (drawn from the same population) are distributed.

How the Differences Between Means Are Distributed: The Large Sample Case   Fortunately, statisticians know how differences between sample means drawn from the same population are distributed. Statisticians have repeated the following steps thousands of times:

1. Take two random samples from the same population.
2. Calculate the means of the two samples (Group 1 and Group 2).
3. Subtract the Group 1 mean from the Group 2 mean to get the difference between Group 1 and Group 2.

From this work, statisticians have established three basic facts about the distribution of differences between sample means drawn from the same population.

First, if you subtracted the Group 1 mean from the Group 2 mean an infinite number of times, the average of all these differences would equal zero. This is because, in the long run, random error averages out to zero. Because random error averages out to zero, the mean of all the Group 1 means would be the true population mean—as would the mean of all the Group 2 means. Since the Group 1 means and the Group 2 means both average out to the same number, the average difference between them would be zero.

Second, the distribution of differences would be normally distributed. This makes sense because: (1) The only way random samples from the same population can differ is because of random error, and (2) random error is normally distributed.

Third, the standard unit of variability for the distribution of differences between means is neither the standard deviation nor the standard error. Instead, it is the standard error of the difference between means.

The standard error of the difference *between* means is larger than the standard error *of* the mean. This fact shouldn't surprise you. After all, the difference between sample means is influenced by the random error that affects the control group mean *and* by the random error that affects the experimental group mean. In other words, sample means from the same population could differ because the first sample mean was inaccurate, because the second sample mean was inaccurate, or because both were inaccurate.

The formula for the standard error of the difference between means reflects the fact that this standard error is the result of measuring two unstable estimates. Specifically, the formula is:

$$\sqrt{\frac{s_1^2}{N_1} + \frac{s_2^2}{N_2}}$$

where s_1 is the estimate of the population standard deviation for Group 1 and s_2 is the estimate of the population standard deviation for Group 2, N_1 is the number of participants in Group 1, and N_2 is the number of participants in Group 2.

We know that with large enough samples, the distribution of differences between means would be normally distributed. Thus, if the standard error of the difference was 1.0, we would know that: (1) 68% of the time, the true difference would be within one point of the difference we observed; (2) 95% of the time, the true difference would be within two points of the difference we observed; and (3) 99% of the time, the true difference would be within three points of the difference we observed. Therefore, if our two sample means (the control group mean and the experimental group mean) differed by more than three points, we would be confident that the treatment had an effect. In other words, we would be confident that the groups were samples from populations that had different means: If all the participants had received the treatment, their mean score would be different than if they had all been in the control condition.

If, however, we observed a difference of 1.0, we realize that such a difference might well reflect random error, rather than the groups coming from different populations. That is, with a difference of 1.0 and a standard error of the difference of 1.0, we could not disprove the null hypothesis. In other words, we would not be able to conclude that the treatment had an effect.

How Differences Are Distributed: The Small Sample Case   Although the distribution of differences would be normally distributed if you used large enough samples, your particular experiment probably will not use enough participants. Therefore, you must rely on a more conservative distribution, especially designed for small samples: the t-distribution.

Actually, the t-distribution is a family of distributions. The member of the t-distribution family that you use depends on the sample size. That is, with a sample size of 10, you will use a different t-distribution than with a sample size of 11.

The larger your sample size, the more the t-distribution will be shaped like the normal distribution. The smaller your sample size, the more spread out your t-distribution will be (see Figure F-2). Thus, with small samples, a difference between means of more than two standard errors of the difference might not be statistically significant (whereas such a difference would be significant with a large sample).

• **FIGURE F-2** •

WITH LARGER SAMPLES, *T*-DISTRIBUTIONS APPROXIMATE THE NORMAL CURVE

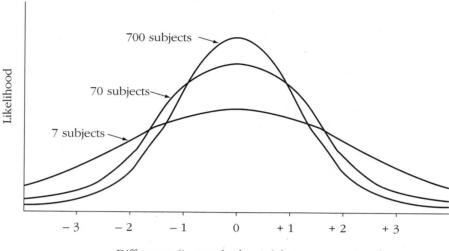

Difference (in standard units) between means of
two random samples from the same population

Although the particular *t*-distribution you use depends on sample size, you do not determine which particular *t*-distribution to use by counting how many participants you have. Instead, you determine how many degrees of freedom (*df*) you have.

To calculate your degrees of freedom, simply subtract 2 from the number of participants in your experiment. For example, if you had 32 participants, your *df* would be 30 (because 32 − 2 = 30).

Executing the *t*-Test

You now understand that the difference between your experimental group mean and control group mean could be due to random error. You also realize that to estimate the chances that a difference between means could be due to random error, you need to do two things.

First, you need to compare the difference between the means to the standard error of the difference. In other words, you need to find out how far apart—*in terms of standard errors of the difference*—the two group means are.

Second, you need to use a *t*-distribution to figure out how likely it is that two means could differ by that many standard errors of the difference. The particular *t*-distribution you will use depends on your degrees of freedom.

Now that you understand the basic logic behind the t-test, you're ready to do one. Start by subtracting the means of your two groups. Then, divide this difference by the standard error of the difference (see Box F-2). The number you will get is called a t-ratio. Thus, t = Difference between means/standard error of the difference. Less technically, the t-ratio is simply the difference between your sample means divided by an index of random error.

Once you have your t-ratio and your degrees of freedom, refer to a t-table to see whether your t-ratio is significant. Specifically, you would look under the row corresponding to your degrees of freedom. As we mentioned before, the degrees of freedom are two fewer than the number of participants. Thus, if you studied 32 participants, you would look at the t-table in Appendix E under the row labeled 30 *df.*

When comparing the t-ratio you calculated to the value in the table, act like your t-ratio is positive. That is, even if you have a negative t-ratio, treat it as if it is a positive t-ratio. In other words, take the absolute value of your t-ratio.

If the absolute value of your t-ratio is not bigger than the number in the table, then your results are not statistically significant at the $p < .05$ level. If, on the other hand, the absolute value of your t-ratio is bigger than the number in the table, then your results are statistically significant at the $p < .05$ level.

If your results are statistically significant at the $p < .05$ level, there's less than a 5% chance that the difference between your groups is solely due to chance. Consequently, you can be reasonably sure that your treatment had an effect. You might report your results as follows: "As predicted, the experimental group's mean recall (8.12) was significantly higher than the control group's (4.66), $t(30) = 3.10$, $p < .05$."

• BOX F-2 •

CALCULATING THE BETWEEN-SUBJECTS T-TEST FOR EQUAL-SIZED GROUPS

$$t = \frac{\text{Group 1 Mean} - \text{Group 2 Mean}}{\text{Standard Error of the Difference}}$$

And where the standard error of the difference can be calculated in either of the following 2 ways:

1.
$$\sqrt{\frac{S_1^2}{N_1} + \frac{S_2^2}{N_2}}$$

Where S_1 = standard deviation of Group 1 (see Box F-1), S_2 = standard deviation of Group 2, N_1 equals number of participants in Group 1, and N_2 equals number of participants in Group 2.

2.
$$\sqrt{\frac{\text{SS Group 1} + \text{SS Group 2}}{N - 2} \times (1/N_1 + 1/N_2)}$$

Where SS equals the sum of squares (see Box F-1), N_1 equals the number of participants in Group 1, N_2 equals the number of participants in Group 2, and N equals the total number of participants.

ANOVA: ANALYZING DATA FROM A MULTIPLE-GROUP EXPERIMENT

To analyze data from a multiple-group experiment, most researchers use analysis of variance. To use analysis of variance, as was the case with the *t*-test:

1. Your observations must be independent.
2. Each of your groups should have approximately the same variance.
3. Your scores should be normally distributed.
4. You should be able to assume that your data are either interval or ratio.

In analysis of variance, you set up the *F-ratio:* a ratio of the between-groups variance to the within-groups variance. Or, to use proper terminology, you set up a ratio of Mean Square Between (*MSB*) to Mean Square Within (*MSW*).

To calculate Mean Square Within groups, you must first calculate the sum of squares for each group. You must subtract each score from its group mean, square each of those differences, and then add up all those squared differences. If you had the following three groups, your first calculations would be as follows:

	GROUP 1	GROUP 2	GROUP 3
	5	6	14
	4	5	12
	3	4	10
Group Mean	4	5	12

Sum of Squares Within for Group 1:

$$(5 - 4)^2 + (4 - 4)^2 + (3 - 4)^2 =$$
$$(1)^2 + (0)^2 + (-1)^2 =$$
$$1 + 0 + 1 = 2$$

Sum of Squares Within for Group 2:

$$(6 - 5)^2 + (5 - 5)^2 + (4 - 5)^2 =$$
$$(1)^2 + (0)^2 + (-1)^2 =$$
$$1 + 0 + 1 = 2$$

Sum of Squares Within for Group 3:

$$(14 - 12)^2 + (12 - 12)^2 + (10 - 12)^2 =$$
$$(2)^2 + (0)^2 + (-2)^2 =$$
$$4 + 0 + 4 = 8$$

To get the sum of squares within groups, you add all of these sums of squares together (2 + 2 + 8 = **12**).

To get the mean square within groups, you divide the sum of squares within groups (SSW) by the within-groups' degrees of freedom. In a multiple-group experiment, the within-groups' degrees of freedom equals the number of participants – number of groups. Since you had 9 participants and 3 groups, your within-groups' degrees of freedom is 6 (because 9 – 3 = 6). In this case, because your sum of squares within is 12 and your within-groups degrees of freedom is 6, your MSW is 2 (12/6).

To get the mean square between groups, calculate the variance of the group means as follows:

Calculate mean of group means (4 + 5 + 12)/3 = 21/3 = 7.

Subtract each group mean from the overall mean and square each difference:

$$4 - 7 = -3; \ -3 \text{ squared} = 9$$
$$5 - 7 = -2; \ -2 \text{ squared} = 4$$
$$12 - 7 = 5; \ 5 \text{ squared} = 25$$

Add up all these squared differences (25 + 9 + 4 = 38).

Divide this term by one less than the number of groups. Since you have three groups, divide by two.

So, your variance among groups is 19 (38/2 = 19).

To transform your variance among groups to a mean square between, multiply it by the number of participants in each group. In this case, you have three participants per group, so you multiply 19 $\times$ 3 and get 57.

Your F-ratio is the ratio of mean square between (MSB) to mean square within (MSW). In this case, your MSB is 57 and your MSW is 2. Therefore, your F-ratio is 57/2 or 28.5.

Thus, at this point, your ANOVA summary table would look like this:

SOURCE OF VARIANCE	SUM OF SQUARES	DEGREES OF FREEDOM	MEAN SQUARE	F-RATIO
Treatment	?	?	57	28.5
Error	12	6	2	

To fill in the rest of the table, you need to know the sum of squares treatment and the degrees of freedom for the treatment. The degrees of freedom for the treatment are one less than the number of groups. Since you have 3 groups, your df for the treatment is 2. To get the sum of squares for the treatment, simply multiply the df for the treatment by the mean square for the treatment (2 $\times$ 57 = 114).

Thus, your completed ANOVA summary table would look like this:

SOURCE OF VARIANCE	SUM OF SQUARES	DEGREES OF FREEDOM	MEAN SQUARE	F-RATIO
Treatment	114	2	57	28.5
Error	12	6	2	

To determine whether the F of 28.5 is significant at the $p < .05$ level, you would look in the F table (Appendix E, Table E-3) for the critical F value for 2 degrees of freedom in the numerator and 6 degrees of freedom in the denominator. If 28.5 is larger than that value, the results would be statistically significant.

ANALYZING DATA FROM THE SIMPLE, TWO-CONDITION, WITHIN-SUBJECTS EXPERIMENT (OR THE MATCHED-PAIRS DESIGN): THE DEPENDENT T-TEST

If you are comparing two conditions (treatment and no treatment), but your observations are not independent, you cannot use the independent-groups t-test. Your treatment and no-treatment scores would not be independent if they both came from the same subject (as in a within-subjects design). Nor would they be independent if you used a matched-pairs design.

If you are using a two-condition, within-subjects design (or a matched-pairs design) and you have interval data, you could analyze your data with a dependent-groups (within-subjects) t-test. There are seven steps to this analysis.

STEP 1: For each matched pair (in the matched-pairs design) or for each participant (in the two-condition, within-subjects design), subtract the Condition 2 score from the Condition 1 score.

PAIR OR PARTICIPANT	CONDITION 1 SCORE	CONDITION 2 SCORE	DIFFERENCE
1	3	2	1
2	4	3	1
3	5	4	1
4	2	1	1
5	3	2	1
6	5	2	3
7	5	2	3
8	4	3	1
9	3	4	−1
10	5	6	−1

STEP 2: Sum up the differences between each pair of scores, then divide by the number of pairs of scores to get the average difference.

$$\text{SUM OF DIFFERENCES} = 10$$
$$\text{AVERAGE DIFFERENCE} = 10/10 = 1$$

STEP 3: Calculate the variance for the differences by subtracting each difference from the average difference. Square each of those differences, sum them up, and divide by one less than the number of pairs of scores.

PAIR OR PARTICIPANT	AVERAGE DIFFERENCE (*AD*)	OBSERVED DIFFERENCE (*D*)	*AD–D*	*AD–D* SQUARED
1	1	1	0	0
2	1	1	0	0
3	1	1	0	0
4	1	1	0	0
5	1	1	0	0
6	1	3	–2	4
7	1	3	–2	4
8	1	1	0	0
9	1	–1	2	4
10	1	–1	2	4

TOTAL SUM OF SQUARES = 16
VARIANCE OF DIFFERENCES = 16/9 = 1.77

STEP 4: Take the square root of the variance of the differences to get the standard deviation of the differences.

$$\text{Standard deviation of the differences} = \sqrt{1.77} = 1.33$$

STEP 5: Get the standard error of the difference by dividing the standard deviation of the differences by the square root of the number of pairs of scores.

$$\frac{1.33}{\sqrt{10}} = .42$$

STEP 6: Set up the *t*-ratio by dividing the average difference by the standard error of the difference.

$$t = \frac{1}{.42} = 2.38$$

STEP 7: Calculate the degrees of freedom by subtracting 1 from the number of pairs of scores. In this example, since we have 10 pairs of scores, we have 9 degrees of freedom. Then, compare your obtained *t*-value to the *t*-value needed to be statistically significant. That value is listed in Table E-1 of Appendix E. In this case, the *t*-value needed to be significant at the .05 level with 9 degrees of freedom is 2.262. Because our value (2.380) is higher than that, our results are statistically significant at the $p < .05$ level.

CORRELATIONAL ANALYSES

If you are examining the relationship between scores on two or more variables, you may decide to use a correlational analysis. The type of analysis you use will depend not only on your goals, but also on whether your data are at least interval scale.

If you want to describe your data—and you have interval data—you would probably compute a Pearson *r*. If, on the other hand, your data are ordinal, you may choose to describe the relationship between your variables using a phi coefficient.

If you want to make inferences about whether a relationship exists in the population, the type of test you should use depends on your data. If you have interval data, you should determine whether the Pearson *r* between the variables is significantly different from zero. If, on the other hand, you have nominal data, you should do a chi-square test.

In the next few sections, we will show you how to perform these tests. We will then conclude by discussing the basic logic behind one of the most commonly reported statistical techniques: factor analysis.

THE PEARSON *r*

If two variables are related, you can describe that relationship with a scatterplot. However, if both variables are interval-scale variables, you will probably also want to know what the Pearson *r* correlation coefficient is between the two variables.

The formula for the Pearson *r* is:

$$\frac{\Sigma XY - ((\Sigma X * \Sigma Y)/N)}{N * sd\ x * sd\ y}$$

where: ΣX = the sum of all the scores on the first variable, ΣY = the sum of all the scores on the second variable, ΣXY = multiplying each pair of scores together and then adding up all those products, N = number of participants, $sd\ x$ = standard deviation of the x scores (the first set of scores), and $sd\ y$ = standard deviation of the y scores (the second set of scores).

This formula for the Pearson *r* makes sense once you realize three important facts:

1. The formula must produce an index of the degree to which two variables (which we will denote as X and Y) vary together.

2. The formula must produce positive numbers when the variables are positively correlated, negative numbers when the variables are inversely related, and the number zero when the variables are unrelated.

3. The formula must produce numbers between −1 and +1. That is, the formula can't produce numbers above +1 (or below −1), no matter how many scores there are and no matter how large those scores may be.

Because the Pearson r is an index of the degree to which two variables vary together, each pair of scores is multiplied together. Specifically, the X member of each pair is multiplied by the Y member of the pair. We then add up all these $X * Y$ products.

However, correlation coefficients may be negative. Indeed, if X and Y are inversely related, Pearson r should indicate that by being negative. But if X and Y are both always positive (height and salary), how can we obtain a negative number? If both variables are always positive, we would obviously never get a negative number if all we did was multiplied X times Y for each pair of scores and then added up those products. Thus, there must be more to the formula for correlation coefficients than just adding up all the XY products.

How can we obtain a negative number if X and Y are both always positive? To allow ourselves to get negative numbers when the variables are negatively (inversely) related, we subtract a number from the sum of the XY products. That number is an estimate of what the sum of all the XY products would have been if the two sets of scores were completely unrelated. Thus, if the variables are positively related, subtracting this estimate will still leave us with a positive number. If the variables are not related, subtracting this estimate will leave us with zero. If the variables are inversely related, subtracting this estimate from the actual product of $X * Y$ will result in a negative number.

To this point, we have a formula that can produce positive and negative numbers. The formula does not, however, meet our final criterion for the correlation coefficient: Coefficients must always be between -1 and $+1$. The numbers produced by our incomplete version of the correlation formula might be far outside of the -1 to $+1$ range, especially if:

1. We have many pairs of scores.
2. The scores are extremely spread out.

The more XY pairs there are, the more scores there will be to add up and the larger the total will tend to be. Similarly, the more spread out the scores, the more extreme the products of the scores can be. For example, if scores range from 1 to 5 on both variables, the individual XY products cannot be greater than 25 (because $5 * 5 = 25$). However, if the scores on both variables can range from 1 to 10, the XY products can be as large as 100 ($10 * 10$).

You have seen that our incomplete formula would produce "correlation co-efficients" that would be far outside the -1 to $+1$ boundaries of conventional correlation coefficients. More importantly, the correlation coefficients would be influenced by two factors that have nothing to do with the extent to which two variables are related to each other: the number of pairs and the variability (spread) of the distributions. Therefore, we need to add one more step to our formula. Specifically, we need to take the number we have obtained so far and divide it by an index composed of (1) the number of XY pairs, (2) a measure of the variability of the X scores (the first set of scores), and (3) a measure of the variability of the Y scores (the second set of scores).

By adding this final step, you now have a formula that will produce a correlation coefficient that will range between −1 and +1, regardless of whether you compute a correlation based on 5 pairs or 5,000 and regardless of whether participants' raw scores range from 1.5 to 1.6 or from 200 to 200,000.

Thus, as we stated before, one formula for the Pearson r is:

$$\frac{\Sigma XY - ((\Sigma X * \Sigma Y)/N)}{N * sd\,x * sd\,y}$$

where N = number of participants, $sd\,x$ = standard deviation of the x scores (the first set of scores), and $sd\,y$ = standard deviation of the y scores (the second set of scores).

To see this formula in action, imagine that you collected data from five students at your school on self-esteem (X) and grade-point average (Y). Furthermore, assume that self-esteem and grade-point average are interval-scale variables. To see if the variables were related, you would use the following steps to compute a Pearson r.

STEP 1: List each pair of scores in the following manner:

	Score for X	Score for Y	X Times Y
First pair of scores	1	1	1
Second pair of scores	2	2	4
Third pair of scores	3	2	6
Fourth pair of scores	4	4	16
Fifth pair of scores	5	3	15

STEP 2: Sum the scores in each column. 15 12 **42**

STEP 3: Calculate the means for variables X and Y.

$$15/5 = 3 \qquad\qquad 12/5 = 2.4$$

(Mean of X)   (Mean of Y)

STEP 4: Calculate the Sum of Squares (SS) for variables X and Y.

$$
\begin{array}{cc}
(X - \bar{X})^2 & (Y - \bar{Y})^2 \\
(1 - 3)^2 & (1 - 2.4)^2 \\
(2 - 3)^2 & (2 - 2.4)^2 \\
(3 - 3)^2 & (2 - 2.4)^2 \\
(4 - 3)^2 & (4 - 2.4)^2 \\
(5 - 3)^2 & (3 - 2.4)^2 \\
\mathbf{10} & \mathbf{5.2}
\end{array}
$$

STEP 5: Calculate the variance for X and Y (Variance = SS/N).

$$10/5 = 2.0 \qquad\qquad 5.2/5 = 1.04$$

STEP 6: Calculate the standard deviations for X and Y (sd = square root of the variance).

$$\sqrt{2.0} = 1.41 \qquad\qquad \sqrt{1.04} = 1.02$$

STEP 7: Multiply the sum of X by the sum of Y. Then, divide by the number of pairs.

$$(15 * 12)/5 = 180/5 = 36$$

STEP 8: Subtract the result that we calculated in Step 7 (36) from the sum of $X * Y$ that we calculated in Step 1 (42).

$$42 - 36 = 6$$

STEP 9: Divide the result (6) by the number of pairs times the standard deviation of X times the standard deviation of Y.

$$6/(5 * 1.41 * 1.02) = .83$$

HOW TO DETERMINE THE SIGNIFICANCE OF A PEARSON r

You may want to determine whether the Pearson r in the sample data means that the two variables are related in the population. For example, suppose you collected self-esteem and grade-point average data from a random sample of students at your school. In that case, you could use your sample data to determine whether there is a relationship between self-esteem and grade-point average for the entire school. All you would have to do would be to determine whether the observed Pearson r is significantly different from zero by following the steps listed below. In this case let's suppose that $r = +.58$ and there were five participants.

STEP 1: Compute a t-value, using the formula:

$$t = \frac{r * \sqrt{(N-2)}}{\sqrt{([1 - (r * r)]}}$$

r = the Pearson r and N = number of participants

Note that, all other things being equal, the bigger N is, the bigger t will be. Also, note that the bigger r is, the bigger t will tend to be. Not only does a larger r increase the size of the numerator, but it shrinks the size of the denominator. In other words, the larger the relationship and the more participants you have, the greater the chance of finding a statistically significant result.

$$t = \frac{.58 * \sqrt{(5 - 2)}}{\sqrt{1 - (.58 * .58)}}$$

$$t = \frac{.58 * 1.73}{\sqrt{1 - .34}}$$

$$t = \frac{1.00}{.81} = 1.23$$

STEP 2: After computing the t-value, look the value up in the t-table (Table E-1 in Appendix E) under 3 degrees of freedom ($N - 2$) for the .05 level of significance. That value is 3.182. Because 1.23 does not reach that value, you would conclude that the correlation coefficient was not significantly greater than zero.

COMPUTING A 2 × 2 CHI-SQUARE AND THE PHI COEFFICIENT

Calculating the Pearson r is a good way to describe the relationship between two interval-scale variables in your sample. Similarly, testing whether a Pearson r is statistically significant is a good way to determine if the results in the sample would hold for the population.

But what if you do not have interval data? Even if you only have nominal data, you can conduct similar types of analyses using the chi-square and the phi coefficient.

Suppose you asked men and women whether they believed homosexuals deserved the same employment opportunities as heterosexuals. If you wanted to know whether there was a gender difference in their responses, you could find out by calculating a chi-square using the following steps.

STEP 1: Set up a table like the one below.

	FEMALE	MALE	TOTAL
YES	A	B	
NO	C	D	
			(N) = Total Number of participants

STEP 2: Replace the letter A with the number of women who said "yes." Replace the letter B with the number of men who said "yes."

Replace the letter C with the number of women who said "no."

Replace the letter D with the number of men who said "no."

Replace N with the total number of participants.

By the end of this process, your table might look like the one below:

	FEMALE	MALE	TOTAL
YES	20	15	35
NO	55	10	65
TOTALS	75	25	(N) 100

STEP 3: Multiply the number in the B square by the number in the C square. Then, multiply the number in the A square by the number in the D square. For the data above, that would be:

$$B * C = 15 * 55 = 825$$
$$A * D = 20 * 10 = 200$$

STEP 4: Plug in the appropriate numbers in the following formula:

$$X^2 = \frac{N(B*C - A*D)^2}{(A + B) * (C + D) * (A + C) * (B + D)}$$

$$X^2 = \frac{100(825 - 200)^2}{35 * 65 * 75 * 25}$$

$$X^2 = \frac{100 * 390625}{4265625} = \frac{39062500}{4265625} = 9.16$$

STEP 5: Turn to the Chi-Square Table (Table E-2 in Appendix E) and find the row corresponding to 1 degrees of freedom. (For a 2×2, your degrees of freedom will always be 1 because *df* equals the number of rows minus 1, times the number of columns minus 1).

STEP 6: Determine whether your chi-square is one-tailed or two-tailed. If you predicted only that the groups would differ, then you have a two-tailed test. For example, if you only predicted that there would be a difference between the genders in views toward homosexuals' employment rights, you have a two-tailed test. If, on the other hand, you predicted which group would score higher than the other, then you have a one-tailed test. Thus, if you predicted that men were less likely to think homosexuals should have equal employment opportunities, then you have a one-tailed test.

STEP 7: If you have a two-tailed test with a value of 3.84 or more, your test is significant at the .05 level. Our value of 7.937 exceeds that value, so our test would be significant at the .05 level.

To compute the phi coefficient, use the following formula:

$$\frac{B*C - A*D}{\sqrt{(A + B) * (C + D) * (A + C) * (B + D)}}$$

In this case,

$$\frac{825 - 200}{\sqrt{4265625}} = .30$$

INTRODUCTION TO FACTOR ANALYSIS

We have shown you how researchers can use correlational analyses to (1) describe the relationship between two variables (with the Pearson r or the phi coefficient) and (2) determine whether two variables that were related in a sample are also related in the population (testing to see whether the Pearson r is statistically different from 0 or using the chi-square test). However, we have not shown you a very common use of correlational analyses: to help assess the validity of a measure.

To see how correlational analyses can help assess the quality of a measure, suppose you want to measure love, and you think that love has two different dimensions (sexual attraction and willingness to sacrifice for the other). Furthermore, you believe that these dimensions are relatively independent. For example, you believe that a person could be high on sexual attraction, but low on willingness to sacrifice—and vice-versa.

One approach would be to make up a love scale that had two different subscales. If your two subscales are really measuring two different things, then:

1. A participant's answers to each question in the first subscale should correlate (correspond, agree) with each other.
2. A participant's answers to each question in the second subscale should correlate with each other.
3. A participant's score on the first subscale should not correlate highly with that participant's scores on the second subscale.

That is, all the responses to items related to sexual attraction should correlate with one another, and all the responses to items related to sacrifice should correlate with one another. However, the sexual attraction items should not correlate highly with the sacrifice items.

A more sophisticated and extremely common approach to determining whether the items on a test correlate with each other is to do a factor analysis (Reis & Stiller, 1992). We can define *factor analysis* as a statistical technique designed to divide the many questions on a test into as few coherent groups as possible. Put another way, rather than explaining how participants answer the test by talking about how participants answer each individual question, factor analysis tries to explain participants' patterns of answers in terms of a smaller number of underlying hypothetical factors.

The logic behind factor analysis is fairly straightforward. We assume that if participants' answers to one group of questions correlate with each other, then those questions all measure the same factor. For example, imagine that we have a 10-item test. In that test, participants answered the first six questions similarly: If we know how they answered one of those questions, we can make a reasonable prediction about how they answered the other five. Similarly, their responses to the last four items were highly correlated. However, their responses to the first six questions did not correlate very well with their answers to the last four questions. In such a case, factor analysis would say that because the test seems to be composed of two groups of items, the test measures two factors. In technical terminology, the first six items of the test would load on one factor, the last four items would load on another factor. Each question's *factor loading* tells us the degree to which it appears to be measuring a given factor.

Factor loadings, like correlation coefficients, can range from −1 to +1. Ideally, questions designed to measure a certain factor would have a factor loading of 1.0. However, because of unreliability and other measurement error, a question's factor loadings will usually be well below 1.0. Indeed, a factor loading of +.7 is considered very high and some researchers are happy if a question has a factor loading above +.3.

You have seen that factor analysis tries to find out how many factors are being measured by a test and how well individual questions measure those factors. But what results would you want to obtain from a factor analysis of your love scale? In the case of your love scale, you would hope for two outcomes.

First, you would hope that the factor analysis supported the view that there were two different factors being measured by the test. You would be disappointed if the factor analysis reported that, based on participants' responses, your test seemed to be composed of three types of items. If the factor analysis supports the view that there are two factors, you might be able to report something like, "the two-factor solution accounts for a large amount (at least 60%) of the variability in participants' responses."

Second, you would hope that the factor analysis found that the items that you thought made up the sexual attraction subscale all corresponded to one factor and the items that made up the sacrifice subscale all corresponded to another factor. In technical terminology, you would hope that all the sexual attraction items loaded on one factor, and all the sacrifice items loaded on a different factor. Specifically, because factor loadings are like a correlation between the test question and the factor, you would want all your sexual attraction items to have high loadings (above .5) on the factor you want to label sexual attraction and near zero loadings on the factor that you want to label sacrifice. Conversely, you would want all your sacrifice items to have very low factor loadings on the factor that you want to label sexual attraction and high loadings on the factor you want to label sacrifice.

GLOSSARY

A–B **design** The simplest single-*n* design, consisting of measuring the participant's behavior at baseline (*A*) and then measuring the participant after the participant has received the treatment (*B*).

A–B–A **reversal design** A single-subject or small-*n* design in which baseline measurements are made of the target behavior (*A*), then an experimental treatment is given (*B*), and the target behavior is measured again (*A*). The *A–B–A* design makes a more convincing case for the treatment's effect than the *A–B* design.

Abstract A short (fewer than 120 words), one-page summary of a research proposal or article.

Analysis of variance (ANOVA) A statistical test for analyzing data from experiments. Especially useful if the experiment has more than one independent variable or more than two levels of an independent variable.

Archival data Data from existing records and public archives.

Baseline The participant's behavior on the task before receiving the treatment. A measure of the dependent variable as it occurs without the experimental manipulation. Used as a standard of comparison in single-subject and small-*n* designs.

Between-groups variance (mean square treatment, mean square between) An index of the degree to which group means differ. An index of the combined effects of random error and treatment. This quantity is compared to the within-groups variance in ANOVA. It is the top half of the *F*-ratio. If the treatment has no effect, the between-groups variance should be roughly the same as the within-groups variance. If the treatment has an effect, the between-groups variance should be larger than the within-groups variance.

Bias Systematic errors that can push the scores in a given direction. Bias may lead to "finding" the results that the researcher wanted.

Blind A strategy of making the participant or researcher unaware of what condition the participant is in.

Blind observer An observer who is unaware of the participant's characteristics and situation. Using blind observers reduces observer bias.

Carryover effects (also called *treatment carryover*) The effects of a treatment administered earlier in the experiment persist so long that they are present even while participants are receiving additional treatments. Often a problem with single-subject and within-subjects designs because you do not know whether the participant's behavior is due to the treatment just administered or to a lingering effect of a treatment administered some time ago.

Ceiling effect The effect of treatment(s) is underestimated because the dependent measure is not sensitive to psychological states above a certain level. The measure puts an artificially low ceiling on how high a participant may score.

Central limit theorem If numerous large samples (30 or more scores) from the same population are taken, and you plot the mean for each of these samples, your plot would resemble a normal curve—even if the population from which you took those samples was not normally distributed.

Chi square (X^2) A statistical test you can use to determine whether two or more variables are related. Best used when you have nominal data.

Coefficient of determination The square of the correlation coefficient; tells the degree to which knowing one variable helps to know another. Can range from 0 (knowing a participant's score on one variable tells you absolutely nothing about the participant's score on the second variable) to 1.00 (knowing a participant's score on one variable tells you exactly what the participant's score on the second variable was).

Conceptual replication A study that is based on the original study, but uses different methods to assess the true relationships between the treatment and dependent variables better. In a conceptual replication, you might use a different manipulation or a different measure.

Confounding variables Variables, other than the independent variable, that may be responsible for the differences between your conditions. There are two types of confounding variables: ones that are manipulation irrelevant and ones that are the result of the manipulation. Confounding variables that are irrelevant to the treatment manipulation threaten internal validity. For example, the difference between groups may be due to one group being older than the other rather than to the treatment. Random assignment can control for the effects of those confounding variables. Confounding variables that are produced by the treatment manipulation hurt the construct validity of the study. They hurt the construct validity because even though we may know that the treatment manipulation had an effect, we don't know what it was about the treatment manipulation that had the effect. For example, we may know that an "exercise" manipulation increases happiness (internal validity), but not know whether the "exercise" manipulation worked because people exercised more, got more encouragement, had a more structured routine, practiced setting and achieving goals, or met new friends. In such a case, construct validity is harmed because we don't know how properly to label the "exercise" manipulation.

Construct A mental state that cannot be directly observed or manipulated with our present technology, such as love, intelligence, hunger, and aggression.

Construct validity The degree to which a study, test, or manipulation measures and/or manipulates what the researcher claims it does. For example, a test claiming to measure aggressiveness would not have construct validity if it really measured assertiveness.

Content analysis A method used to categorize a wide range of open-ended (unrestricted) responses. Content analysis schemes have been used to code the frequency of violence on certain television shows and are often used to code archival data.

Content validity The extent to which a measure represents a balanced and adequate sampling of relevant dimensions, knowledge, and skills. In many measures and tests, participants are asked a few questions from a large body of knowledge. A test has content validity if its content is a fair sample of the larger body of knowledge. Students hope that their psychology tests have content validity.

Control group Participants who are randomly assigned to *not* receive the experimental treatment. These participants are compared to the treatment group to determine whether the treatment had an effect.

Convenience sampling Choosing to include people in your sample simply because they are easy (convenient) to survey. It is hard to generalize the results accurately from a study that used convenience sampling.

Convergent validity Validity demonstrated by showing that the measure correlates with other measures of the construct.

Correlation coefficient A number that can vary from −1.00 to +1.00 and indicates the kind of relationship that exists between two variables (positive or negative as indicated by the sign of the correlation coefficient) and the strength of the relationship (indicated by the extent to which the coefficient differs from 0). Positive correlations indicate that the variables tend to go in the same direction (if a participant is low on one variable, the participant will tend to be low on the other). Negative correlations indicate that the variables tend to head in opposite directions (if a participant is low on one, the participant will tend to be high on the other).

Counterbalanced within-subjects designs Designs that give participants the treatments in different sequences. These designs balance out routine order effects.

Counterbalancing Any technique used to control order effects by distributing order effects across treatment conditions. Typically, it involves giving different participants the treatments in systematically different sequences in an attempt to balance out order effects.

Covariation Changes in the treatment are accompanied by changes in the behavior. To establish causality, you must establish covariation.

Crossover (disordinal) interaction When an independent variable has one kind of effect in the presence of one level of a second independent variable, but a different kind of effect in the presence of a different level of the second independent variable. Examples: Getting closer to people may increase their attraction to you if you have just complimented them, but may decrease their attraction to you if you have just insulted them. Called a *crossover interaction* because the lines in a graph will cross. Called *disordinal interaction* because it cannot be explained by having ordinal rather than interval data.

Curvilinear relationship A relationship between an independent and dependent variable that is graphically represented by a curved line.

Debriefing Giving participants the details of a study at the end of their participation. Proper debriefing is one of the researcher's most serious obligations.

Degrees of freedom (*df*) An index of sample size. In the simple experiment, the *df* for your error term will always be two less than the number of participants.

Demand characteristics Characteristics of the study that suggest to the participant how the researcher wants the participant to behave.

Demographics Characteristics of a group, such as gender, age, social class.

Dependent-groups *t*-test A statistical test used with interval or ratio data to test differences between two conditions on a single dependent variable. Differs from the between-groups *t*-test in that it is only to be used when you are getting two scores from each participant (within-subjects design) or when you are using a matched-pairs design.

Dependent variable The factor that the experimenter predicts is affected by the independent variable: The participant's response that the experimenter is measuring.

Direct replication Repeating a study as exactly as possible, usually to determine whether or not the same results will be obtained. Direct replications are useful for establishing that the findings of the original study are reliable.

Discriminant validity When a measure does not correlate highly with a measure of a different construct. Example: A violence measure might have a degree of discriminant validity if it does not correlate with the measures of assertiveness, social desirability, and independence.

Discussion The part of the article, immediately following the results section, that discusses the research findings and the study in a broader context and suggests research projects that could be done to follow up on the study.

Disordinal interaction See *crossover interaction*.

Double-barreled question A statement that contains more than one question. Responses to a double-barreled question are difficult to interpret. For example, if someone responds, "No," to the question "Are you hungry and thirsty?" we do not know whether he is hungry, but not thirsty; not hungry, but thirsty; or neither hungry nor thirsty.

Double-blind A strategy for improving construct validity that involves making sure that neither the partici-

pant nor the person who has direct contact with the participant knows what type of treatment the participant has received.

Empty control group A group that does not get any kind of treatment. The group gets nothing, not even a placebo. Usually, because of participant and experimenter biases that may result from such a group, you will want to avoid using an empty control group.

Environmental manipulation A manipulation that involves changing the participant's environment rather than giving the participant different instructions.

Ethical Conforming to the American Psychological Association's principles of what is morally correct behavior. To learn more about these guidelines and standards, see Appendix A.

Experimental group Participants who are randomly assigned to receive the treatment.

Experimental hypothesis A prediction that the treatment will cause an effect.

Experimental (research) realism When a study engages the participant so much that the participant is not merely playing a role (helpful participant, good person).

Experimenter bias Experimenters being more attentive to participants in the treatment group or giving different nonverbal cues to treatment group participants than to other participants. When experimenter bias is present, differences between groups may be due to the experimenter rather than to the treatment.

Exploratory study A study investigating (exploring) a new area of research. Unlike replications, an exploratory study does not follow directly from an existing study.

Ex post facto research When a researcher goes back, after the research has been completed, looking to test hypotheses that were not formulated prior to the beginning of the study. The researcher is trying to take advantage of hindsight. Often an attempt to salvage something out of a study that did not turn out as planned.

External validity The degree to which the results of a study can be generalized to other participants, settings, and times.

Extraneous factors Factors other than the treatment. If we cannot control or account for extraneous variables, we can't conclude that the treatment had an effect. That is, we will not have internal validity.

F-ratio Analysis of variance (ANOVA) yields an *F*-ratio for each main effect and interaction. In between subjects experiments, the *F*-ratio is a ratio of between-groups variance to within-groups variance. If the treatment has no effect, *F* will tend to be close to 1.0.

Face validity The extent to which a measure looks, on the face of it, to be valid. Face validity has nothing to do with actual, scientific validity. That is, a test could have face validity and not real validity or could have real validity, but not face validity. However, for practical/political reasons, you may decide to consider face validity when comparing measures.

Factor analysis A statistical technique designed to explain the variability in several questions in terms of a smaller number of underlying hypothetical factors.

Factorial experiment An experiment that examines two or more independent variables (factors) at a time.

Factor loading Tells us the degree to which a given question appears to be measuring a certain factor. Factor loadings, like correlation coefficients, can range from −1 to +1.

Failure-to-follow-protocol effect Contamination caused when investigators deviate from the study's "script."

Fatigue effects Decreased performance on a task due to being tired or less enthusiastic as a study continues. In a within-subjects design, this decrease in performance might be incorrectly attributed to a treatment.

Field experiment An experiment performed in a non-laboratory setting.

Fixed-alternative items Items on a test or questionnaire in which a person must choose an answer from among a few specified alternatives. Multiple-choice, true–false, and rating-scale questions are all fixed-alternative items.

Floor effect The effects of treatment(s) are underestimated because the dependent measure artificially restricts how low scores can be.

Functional relationship The shape of a relationship. Depending on the functional relationship between the independent and dependent variable, a graph of the relationship might look like a straight line or might look like a u, an s, or some other shape.

Grand mean The mean of all the scores in a study. Sometimes used when doing the calculations for an ANOVA.

Hawthorne Effect When the treatment group changes their behavior not because of the treatment itself, but because they know they are getting special treatment.

History Events in the environment—other than the treatment—that have changed. Differences between conditions that may seem to be due to the treatment may really be due to history.

Hypothesis A testable prediction about the relationship between two or more variables.

Hypothesis-guessing When participants alter their behavior to conform to their guess as to what the research hypothesis is. Hypothesis-guessing can be a serious threat to construct validity, especially if participants guess right.

Hypothesis testing The use of inferential statistics to determine if the relationship found between two or more variables in a particular sample holds true in the population.

Hypothetical construct See *construct.*

Illusory correlation When there is really no relationship (a zero correlation) between two variables, but people perceive that the variables are related.

Independence Factors are independent when they are not causally or correlationally linked. Independence is a key assumption of most statistical tests. In the simple experiment, observations must be independent. That is, what one participant does should have no influence on what another participant does and what happens to one participant should not influence what happens to another participant. Individually assigning participants to the treatment or no-treatment condition and individually testing each participant are ways to achieve independence.

Independent random assignment Randomly determining for each individual participant which condition he will be in. For example, you might flip a coin for each participant to determine to what group he will be assigned.

Independent variable The variable being manipulated by the experimenter. Participants are assigned to a level of independent variable by independent random assignment.

Inferential statistics Procedures for determining the reliability and generalizability of a particular research finding.

Informed consent If participants agree to take part in a study after they have been told what is going to happen to them, you have their informed consent.

Instructional manipulation Manipulating the treatment by giving written or oral instructions.

Instrumentation bias The way participants were measured changed from pretest to posttest. In instrumentation bias, the actual measuring instrument changes or the way it is administered changes. Sometimes people may think they have a treatment effect when they really have an instrumentation effect.

Interaction When you need to know how much of one variable participants have received to say what the effect of another variable is, you have an interaction between those two variables. If you graph the results from an experiment that has two or more independent variables, and the lines you draw between your points are not parallel, you may have an interaction.

Internal consistency The degree to which each question on a scale correlates with the other questions. Internal consistency is high if answers to each item correlate highly with answers to all other items.

Internal validity The degree to which a study establishes that a factor causes a difference in behavior. If a study lacks internal validity, the researcher may falsely believe that a factor causes an effect when it really doesn't.

Interobserver (judge) agreement The percentage of times the raters agree.

Interobserver reliability An index of the degree to which different raters give the same behavior similar ratings.

Interval-scale data Data that give you numbers that can be meaningfully ordered along a scale (from lowest to highest) and in which equal numerical intervals represent equal psychological intervals. That is, the difference between scoring a "2" and a "1" and the difference between scoring a "7" and a "6" are the same not only in terms of scores (both are a difference of 1), but also in terms of the actual psychological characteristic being measured. Interval scale measures allow us to compare participants in terms of how much of a quality participants have—and in terms of how much more of a quality one group may have than another.

Interview A survey in which the researcher orally asks questions.

Interviewer bias When the interviewer influences participant's responses. For example, the interviewer might verbally or nonverbally reward the participant for giving responses that support the hypothesis.

Introduction The part of the article that occurs right after the abstract. In the introduction, the authors tell you what their hypothesis is, why their hypothesis makes sense, how their study fits in with previous research, and why their study is worth doing.

Known-groups technique A way of making the case for your measure's convergent validity that involves seeing whether groups known to differ on the characteristic you are trying to measure also differ on your measure (for example, ministers should differ from atheists on an alleged measure of religiosity).

Leading question Questions structured to lead respondents to the answer the researcher wants (such as, "You like this book, don't you?").

Levels of an independent variable When the treatment variable is given in different amounts, these different amounts are called *levels*. In the simple experiment, you only have two levels of the independent variable.

Level of significance The risk the researcher takes of making a Type 1 error. With a .05 level of significance, the researcher takes a 5-in-100 chance of declaring the results significant when the variables are not related.

Likert-type items Items that typically ask participants whether they strongly agree, agree, are neutral, disagree, or strongly disagree with a certain statement. These items are assumed to yield interval data.

Linear relationship A relationship between an independent and dependent variable that is graphically represented by a straight line.

Loose-protocol effect Variations in procedure because the written procedures (the protocol) is not detailed enough. These variations in procedure may result in researcher bias.

Main effect (overall main effect) The overall or average effect of an independent variable.

Manipulation check A question or set of questions designed to determine whether participants perceived the manipulation in the way that the researcher intended.

Matched-pairs design An experimental design in which the participants are paired off by matching them on some variable assumed to be correlated with the dependent variable. Then, for each matched pair, one member is randomly assigned to one treatment condition, the other gets the other treatment condition. This design usually has more power than a simple, between-groups experiment.

Matching Choosing your groups so that they are similar (they match) on certain characteristics. Matching reduces, but does not eliminate, the threat of selection bias.

Maturation Changes in participants due to natural growth or development. A researcher may think that the treatment had an effect, when the difference in behavior is really due to maturation.

Mean An average calculated by adding up all the scores and then dividing by the number of scores.

Median If you arrange all the scores from lowest to highest, the middle score will be the median.

Median split The procedure of dividing participants into two groups ("highs" and "lows") based on whether they score above or below the median.

Mediating variable Variables inside the individual (such as thoughts, feelings, or physiological responses) that come between a stimulus and a response. In other words, the stimulus has its effect because it causes changes in mediating variables which, in turn, cause changes in behavior.

Method section The part of the article immediately following the introduction. Whereas the introduction explains *why* the study was done, the method section describes *what* was done. For example, it will tell you what design was used, what the researchers said to the participants, what measures and equipment were used, how many participants were studied, and how participants were selected. The method section could also be viewed as a "how we did it" section. The method section is usually subdivided into at least two subsections: participants and procedure.

Mixed designs An experimental design that has at least one within-subjects factor and one between-subjects factor.

Moderator variables Variables that can intensify, weaken, or reverse the effects of another variable. For example, the effect of wearing perfume may be moderated by gender: If you are a woman, wearing perfume may make you more liked; if you are a man, wearing perfume may make you less liked.

Mortality (attrition) Participants dropping out of a study before the study is completed. Sometimes, differences between conditions may be due to participants dropping out of the study rather than to the treatment.

Multiple-baseline design A single-subject or small-*n* design in which different behaviors receive baseline periods of varying lengths prior to the introduction of the treatment variable. Often, the goal is to show that the behavior being rewarded changes, whereas the other behaviors stay the same until they too are reinforced.

Mundane realism Extent to which the research setting or task resembles real life.

Naturalistic observation A technique of observing events as they occur in their natural setting.

Negative correlation An inverse relationship between two variables (such as number of suicide attempts and happiness).

Nominal-scale data Qualitative data; different scores do not represent different amounts of a characteristic (quantity). Instead, they represent different kinds of characteristics (qualities, types, or categories). Because larger numbers do not represent more of a quality than smaller numbers, nominal-scale measurement is considered the lowest level of measurement.

Nonequivalent control-group design A quasi-experimental design that, like a simple experiment, has a treatment group and a no-treatment comparison group. However, unlike the simple experiment, random assignment does not determine which participants get the treatment and which do not.

Nonlinear relationship See *curvilinear relationship*.

Nonreactive measures Measurements that are taken without changing the participant's behavior; also referred to as *unobtrusive measures*.

Nonresponse bias The problem caused by people who were in your sample refusing to participate in your study. Nonresponse bias is one of the most serious threats to a survey design's external validity.

Nonsignificant results See *null results*.

Normal curve A bell-shaped, symmetrical curve that has its center at the mean.

Normal distribution If the way the scores are distributed follows the normal curve, scores are said to be normally distributed. For example, a population is said to be normally distributed if 68% of the scores are within one standard deviation of the mean, 95% are within two standard deviations of the mean, and 99% of the scores are within three standard deviations of the mean. Many statistical tests, including the *t*-test, assume that sample means are normally distributed.

Null hypothesis The hypothesis that there is no relationship between two or more variables. The null hypothesis can be disproven, but it cannot be proven.

Null results (nonsignificant results) Results that fail to disconfirm the null hypothesis; results that fail to provide convincing evidence that the factors are related. Null results are inconclusive because the failure to find a relationship could be due to your design lacking the power to find the relationship. In other words, many null results are Type 2 errors.

Observer bias Bias created by the observer seeing what the observer wants or expects to see.

Open-ended items Questions that do not provide fixed response alternatives. Essay and fill-in-the-blank questions are open-ended.

Operational definition A publicly observable way to measure or manipulate a variable; a "recipe" for how you are going to measure or manipulate your factors.

Order The place in a sequence (first, second, third, etc.) when a treatment occurs.

Order effects A big problem with within-subjects designs. The order in which the participant receives a treatment (first, second, etc.) will affect how participants behave.

Ordinal-scale data Numbers that can be meaningfully ordered from lowest to highest. With ordinal data, you know a participant with a high score has more of a characteristic than a participant with a low score. But you do not know how much more. For example, with ranked data, you know the top-ranked student has a higher score than the second-ranked student, but how much higher? You do not know if you only have ranked data. Furthermore, someone with a rank of one might be way ahead of the second-ranked scorer, but the number two scorer may be only slightly ahead of the number three scorer.

Ordinal interaction Reflects the fact that an independent variable *seems* to have more of an effect under one level of a second independent variable than under another level. If you graph an ordinal interaction, the lines will not be parallel, but they will not cross. Called an ordinal interaction because the interaction, the failure of the lines to be parallel, may be an illusion resulting from having ordinal data.

Parameter estimation The use of inferential statistics to estimate certain characteristics of the population (parameters) from a sample of that population.

Parameters Measurements describing populations; often inferred from statistics, which are measurements describing a sample.

Parsimony Explaining a broad range of phenomena with only a few principles.

Participant observation An observation procedure in which the observer participates with those being observed. The observer becomes "one of them."

Phi coefficient A correlation coefficient to be used when both variables are measured on the nominal scale.

Placebo treatment A fake treatment that we know has no effect, except through the power of suggestion. It allows experimenters to see if the treatment has an effect beyond that of suggestion. For example, in medical experiments, participants who are given pills that do not contain a drug may be compared to participants who are given pills that contain the new drug.

Population The entire group that you are interested in. You can estimate the characteristics of a population by taking large random samples from that population.

Positive correlation A relationship between two variables where the two variables tend to vary together—when one increases, the other tends to increase. (For example, height and weight: The taller one is, the more one tends to weigh; the shorter one is, the less one tends to weigh.)

Post hoc test Usually refers to a statistical test that has been performed after an ANOVA has obtained a significant effect for a factor. Because the ANOVA only says that at least two of the groups differ from one another, post hoc tests are performed to find out which groups differ from one another.

Post hoc trend analysis A type of post hoc test designed to determine whether a linear or curvilinear relationship is statistically significant (reliable).

Power The ability to find differences or, put another way, the ability to avoid making Type 2 errors. The ability to find significant differences when differences truly exist.

Practice effects The change in a score on a test (usually a gain) resulting from previous practice with the test. In a within-subjects design, this improvement might be incorrectly attributed to receiving a treatment.

Pretest–posttest design A before–after design in which each participant is given the pretest, administered the treatment, then given the posttest.

Probability value, *p* value The chances of obtaining a certain pattern of results if there really is no relationship between the variables.

Psychological Abstracts A useful resource that contains abstracts from a wide variety of journals. The *Abstracts* can be searched by year of publication, topic of article, or author. For more about the *Abstracts,* see Appendix B.

Psychological construct A mental state that can't be directly observed or manipulated, such as love, intelligence, hunger, feeling warm, and aggression.

Quasi-experiment A study that resembles an experiment except that random assignment played no role in determining which participants got which level of treatment. Usually, quasi-experiments have less internal validity than experiments.

Questionnaire A written survey instrument.

Quota sampling Making sure you get the desired number of (meet your quotas for) certain types of people (certain age groups, minorities, etc.). This method does not involve random sampling and usually gives you a less representative sample than random sampling would. It may, however, be an improvement over convenience sampling.

Random assignment In random assignment, you divide your participants into different groups. Each subgroup starts off as a random sample of the same larger group. Because all the subgroups come from the same parent population, all the subgroups are similar to each other at the start of the study. However, because the subgroups are assigned to different treatments, the subgroups may differ from each other by the end of the experiment. Random assignment to experimental condition is what allows the simple experiment, the multiple-group experiment, and the factorial experiment to have internal validity. Note that random assignment is not the same as random sampling and does nothing for a study's external validity.

Random error Variations in scores due to unsystematic, chance factors.

Random sampling A sample that has been randomly selected from a population. If you randomly select enough participants, those participants will usually be fairly representative of the entire population. That is, your random sample will reflect its population. Often, random sampling is used to maximize a study's external validity. Note that random sampling—unlike random assignment—does not promote internal validity.

Randomized within-subjects design As in all within-subjects designs, all participants receive more than one level or type of treatment. However, to make sure that not every participant receives the series of treatments in the same sequence, the researcher randomly determines which treatment comes first, which comes second, and so on. In other words, participants all get the same treatments, but they receive different sequences of treatments.

Ratio-scale data The highest form of measurement. With ratio-scale numbers, the difference between any two consecutive numbers is the same (see *interval scale*). But in addition to having interval-scale properties, in ratio-scale measurement, a zero score means the total absence of a quality. (Thus, Fahrenheit is not a ratio-scale measure of temperature because 0 degrees Fahrenheit does not mean there is no temperature.) If you have ratio-scale numbers, you can meaningfully form ratios between scores. If IQ scores were ratio (they are not; very few measurements in psychology are), you could say that someone with a 60 IQ was twice as smart as someone with a 30 IQ (a ratio of 2 to 1). Furthermore, you could say that someone with a 0 IQ had absolutely no intelligence whatsoever.

Regression The tendency for scores that are extremely unusual to revert back to more-normal levels on the retest. If participants are chosen because their scores were extreme, these extreme scores may be loaded with extreme amounts of random measurement error. On retesting, participants are bound to get more-normal scores as random measurement error abates to more-normal levels. This regression effect could be mistaken for a treatment effect.

Regression to the mean See *regression*.

Reliability A general term, often referring to the degree to which a participant would get the same score if retested (test–retest reliability). Reliability can, however, refer to the degree to which scores are free from random error. A measure can be reliable, but not valid. However, a measure cannot be valid if it is not also reliable.

Repeated-measures design See *within-subjects design*.

Replicable Repeatable. A skeptical researcher should be able to repeat another researcher's study and obtain the same pattern of results.

Replication factor A factor sometimes included in a factorial design to see whether an effect replicates (occurs again) under slightly different conditions. For example, a researcher may decide to use stimulus set as a replication factor. In that case, the goal would be to see if the treatment has the same effect when different stimulus materials are used.

Research journal A relatively informal notebook in which you jot down your research ideas and observations. The research journal can be a useful resource when it comes time to write the research proposal. Note: Despite the fact that they sound similar, the term "research journal" is not similar to the term "scientific journal." The term "scientific journal" is used to distinguish journals from magazines. In contrast to magazines, scientific journals tend (1) not to have ads for popular products, (2) not to have full-page color pictures, (3) to have articles that follow APA format (having abstract, introduction, method, results, discussion, and reference sections), and (4) to have articles that have been peer-reviewed.

Research realism A study that involves the participant so that the participant is less likely to play a role during the study.

Researcher effect Ideally, you hope that the results from a study would be the same no matter who was conducting it. However, it is possible that the results may be affected by the researcher. If the researcher is affecting the results, there is a researcher effect.

Researcher expectancy effect When a researcher's expectations affect the results. This is a type of researcher bias.

Response set Habitual way of responding on a test or survey that is independent of a particular test item (for instance, a participant might always check "agree" no matter what the statement is).

Restriction of range To observe a sizable correlation between two variables, both must be allowed to vary widely (if one variable does not vary, the variables cannot vary together). Occasionally, investigators fail to find a relationship between variables because they only study one or both variables over a highly restricted range. Example: comparing NFL offensive linemen and saying that weight has nothing to do with playing offensive line in the NFL on the basis of your finding that great offensive tackles do not weigh much more than poor offensive tackles. Problem: You only compared people who ranged in weight from 315 to 330.

Results section The part of an article, immediately following the method section, that reports statistical results and relates those results to the hypotheses. From reading this section, you should know whether the results supported the hypotheses.

Retrospective self-report Participants telling you what they said, did, or believed in the past. In addition to problems with ordinary self-report (response sets, giving the answer that a leading question suggests, etc.), retrospective self-report is vulnerable to memory biases. Thus, retrospective self-reports should *not* be accepted at face value.

Sampling (inferential) statistics The science of inferring the characteristics of a population from a sample.

Scatterplot A graph made by plotting the scores of individuals on two variables (for example, each participant's height and weight). By looking at this graph, you should get an idea of what kind of relationship (positive, negative, zero) exists between the two variables.

Selection bias Apparent treatment effects being due to comparing groups that differed even before the treatment was administered (comparing apples with oranges).

Selection by maturation interaction Treatment and no-treatment groups, although similar at one point, would have grown apart (developed differently) even if no treatment had been administered.

Self-administered questionnaire A questionnaire filled out in the absence of an investigator.

Semistructured interview An interview constructed around a core of standard questions; however, the interviewer may expand on any question in order to explore a given response in greater depth.

Sensitivity The degree to which a measure is capable of distinguishing between participants who have different amounts of a construct or who do more of a certain behavior.

Sensitization After getting several different treatments and performing the dependent variable task several times, participants may realize (become sensitive to) what the hypothesis is. Sensitization is a problem in within-subjects designs.

Sequence effects Participants who receive one sequence of treatments score differently than those participants who receive the same treatments in a different sequence when you have a sequence effect.

Simple experiment A study in which participants are independently and randomly assigned to one of two groups, usually to either a treatment group or to a no-treatment group. It is the easiest way to establish that a treatment causes an effect.

Simple main effect The effects of one independent variable at a specific level of a second independent variable. The simple main effect could have been obtained merely by doing a simple experiment.

Single-blind To reduce either subject biases or researcher biases, you might use a single-blind experiment in which either the participant (if you are most concerned about subject bias) or the person running participants (if you are more concerned about researcher bias) is unaware of who is receiving what level of the treatment. If you are concerned about both subject and researcher bias, then you should probably use a double-blind study.

Single-*n* designs See *single-subject designs*.

Single-subject designs Designs that try to establish causality by studying a single participant and arguing that the covariation between treatment and changes in behavior could not be due to anything other than the treatment. A key to this approach is to prevent factors other than the treatment from varying. Single-*n* designs are common in operant conditioning and psychophysical research. See also *A–B design, A–B–A reversal design, multiple-baseline design*.

Social desirability A bias resulting from participants giving responses that make them look good rather than giving honest responses.

Spurious When the covariation observed between two variables is not due to the variables influencing each other, but because both are being influenced by some third variable. For example, the relationship between ice cream sales and assaults in New York is spurious—not because it does not exist (it does!)—but because ice cream does not cause assaults, and assaults do not cause ice cream sales. Instead, high temperatures probably cause both increased assaults and ice cream sales. Beware of spuriousness whenever you look at research that does not use an experimental design.

Stable baseline When the participant's behavior, prior to receiving the treatment, is consistent. Single-*n* experimenters try to establish a stable baseline.

Standard deviation A measure of the extent to which individual scores deviate from the population mean. The more scores vary from each other, the larger the standard deviation will tend to be. If, on the other hand, all the scores are the same as the mean, the standard deviation would be zero.

Standard error of the difference An index of the degree to which random sampling error may cause two sample means representing the same populations to differ. In the simple experiment, if we are to find a treatment effect, the difference between our experimental-group mean and control-group mean will usually be at least twice as big as the standard error of the difference. To find out the exact ratio between our observed difference and the standard error of the difference, we conduct a *t*-test.

Standard error of the mean An index of the degree to which random error may cause the sample mean to be an inaccurate estimate of the population mean. The standard error will be small when the standard deviation is small, and the sample mean is based on many scores.

Standardization Treating each participant in the same (standard) way. Standardization can reduce both bias and random error.

Statistical regression See *regression.*

Statistical significance When a statistical test says that the relationship we have observed is probably not due to chance alone, we say that the results are statistically significant. In other words, because the relationship is probably not due to chance, we conclude that there probably is a real relationship between our variables.

Stimulus set The particular stimulus materials that are shown to two or more groups of participants. Researchers may use more than one stimulus set in a study so that they can see if the treatment effect replicates across different stimulus sets. In those cases, stimulus sets would be a replication factor.

Stooges Confederates who pretend to be participants, but are actually the researcher's assistants. The use of stooges raises ethical questions.

Stratified random sampling Making sure that the sample is similar to the population in certain respects (for instance, percentage of men and women) and then randomly sampling from these groups (strata). Has all the advantages of random sampling with even greater accuracy.

Straw theory An oversimplified version of an existing theory. Opponents of a theory may present and attack a straw version of that theory, but claim they have attacked the theory itself.

Structured interview An interview in which all respondents are asked a standard list of questions in a standard order.

Subject bias (subject effects) Ways the participant can bias the results (guessing the hypothesis and playing along, giving the socially correct response, etc.).

Summated scores When you have several Likert-type questions that all tap the same dimension (such as attitude toward democracy), you can add up each participant's responses to those questions to get an overall, total (summated) score.

Survey design A nonexperimental design useful for describing how people think, feel, or behave. The key is to design a valid questionnaire, test, or interview and administer it to a representative sample of the group you are interested in.

Systematic replication A study that varies from the original study only in some minor aspect. For example, a systematic replication may use more participants, more standardized procedures, more levels of the independent variable, or a more realistic setting than the original study.

t-**test** The most common way of analyzing data from a simple experiment. It involves computing a ratio between two things: (1) the difference between your group means, and (2) the standard error of the difference (an index of the degree to which group means could differ by chance alone). If the difference you observe is more than three times bigger than the difference that could be expected by chance, then your results are probably statistically significant. We can only say "probably" because the exact ratio that you need for statistical significance depends on your level of significance and on how many participants you have.

Temporal precedence The causal factor comes before the change in behavior. Because causes must come before effects, researchers trying to establish causality must establish that the factor alleged to be the cause was introduced before the behavior changed (temporal precedence).

Testing Participants score differently on the posttest as a result of what they learned from taking the pretest. Occasionally, people may think the participants' behavior changed because of the treatment when it really changed due to testing.

Test–retest reliability A way of assessing the amount of random error in a measure by administering the measure to participants at two different times and then correlating their results. If the measure is free of random error, scores on the retest should be highly correlated with scores on the original test.

Time-series design A quasi-experimental design in which a series of observations are taken from a group of participants before and after they receive treatment. Because it uses many times of measurement, it is an improvement over the pretest–posttest design. However, it is still extremely vulnerable to history effects.

Trend analysis See *post hoc trend analysis*.

Type 1 error Rejecting the null hypothesis when it is in fact true. In other words, declaring a difference statistically significant when the difference is really due to chance.

Type 2 error Failure to reject the null hypothesis when it is in fact false. In other words, failing to find a relationship between your variables when there really is a relationship between them.

Unobtrusive measurement Recording a particular behavior without the participant knowing you are measuring that behavior. Unobtrusive measurement reduces subject biases such as social desirability bias and obeying demand characteristics.

Unstructured interview When the interviewer has no standard set of questions that he or she asks each participant—virtually worthless approach for collecting scientifically valid data.

Within-groups variance (mean square within, mean square error, error variance) An estimate of the amount of random error in your data. The bottom half of the F-ratio in a between-subjects analysis of variance.

Within-subjects design An experimental design in which each participant is tested under more than one level of the independent variable. The sequence in which the participants receive the treatments is usually randomly determined. See also *randomized within-subjects design* and *counterbalanced within-subjects designs*.

Zero correlation When there doesn't appear to be a linear relationship between two variables. For practical purposes, any correlation between −.10 and +.10 may be considered so small as to be nonexistent.

REFERENCES

Abelson, R. P. (1995). *Statistics as principled argument.* Mahwah, NJ: Erlbaum.

Alexander, C. N., Langer, E. J., Newman, R. I., Chandler, H. M., & Davies, J. L. (1989). Transcendental meditation, mindfulness, and longevity: An experimental study with the elderly. *Journal of Personality and Social Psychology, 57,* 950–964.

Allen, J. B., Schnyer, R. N., & Hitt, S. K. (1998). The efficacy of acupuncture in the treatment of major depression in women. *Psychological Science, 9,* 397–401.

American Psychological Association. (1982). *Ethical principles in the conduct of research with human behavior.* Washington, DC: Author.

American Psychological Association. (1992). Ethical principles of psychologists and code of conduct. *American Psychologist, 47,* 1597–1611.

American Psychological Association. (1994). *Publication manual of the American Psychological Association* (4th ed.). Washington, DC: Author.

American Psychological Association. (1996). *Guidelines for ethical conduct in the care and use of animals.* Washington, DC: Author.

American Psychological Association. (1996). *Task force on statistical inference initial report.* Washington, DC: Author.

Antill, J. K. (1983). Sex role complementarity versus similarity in married couples. *Journal of Personality and Social Psychology, 45,* 145–155.

Aronson, E. (1990). Applying social psychology to desegregation and energy conservation. *Personality and Social Psychology Bulletin, 16,* 118–131.

Aronson, E., & Carlsmith, J. M. (1968). Experimentation in social psychology. In G. Lindzey & E. Aronson (Eds.), *Handbook of social psychology* (2nd ed., pp. 1–79). Reading, MA: Addison–Wesley.

Ayllon, T., & Azrin, N. H. (1968). *The token economy: A motivational system for therapy and rehabilitation.* New York: Appleton-Century-Crofts.

Banaji, M. R., & Crowder, R. G. (1989). The bankruptcy of everyday memory. *American Psychologist, 44,* 1185–1193.

Berlyne, D. E. (1971). *Conflict, arousal, and curiosity.* New York: McGraw-Hill.

Bernieri, F. J. (1991). Interpersonal sensitivity in teaching interactions. *Personality and Social Psychology Bulletin, 17,* 98–103.

Berscheid, E., Dion, K., Walster, E., & Walster, G. W. (1971). Physical attractiveness and dating choice: A test of the matching hypothesis. *Journal of Experimental Social Psychology, 7,* 173–189.

Blough, D. S. (1957). Effect of lysergic acid diethylamide on absolute visual threshold in the pigeon. *Science, 126,* 304–305.

Brewer, C. L. (1990). *Teaching research methods: Three decades of pleasure and pain.* Presentation at the 98th Annual Convention of the American Psychological Association, Boston.

Broad, W. J., & Wade, N. (1982). Science's faulty fraud detectors. *Psychology Today, 16,* 50–57.

Brown, J. D. (1991). Staying fit and staying well: Physical fitness as a moderator of life stress. *Journal of Personality and Social Psychology, 60,* 555–561.

Burke, J. (1978). *Connections.* Boston: Little, Brown.

Burke, J. (1985). *The day the university changed.* Boston: Little, Brown.

Buss, D. M. (1994). *The evolution of desire.* New York: Basic Books.

Byrne, D. (1971). *The attraction paradigm.* New York: Academic Press.

Campbell, D. T., & Stanley, J. C. (1963). *Experimental and quasi-experimental designs for research.* Chicago: Rand McNally.

Chapman, L. J., & Chapman, P. J. (1967). Genesis of popular but erroneous psychodiagnostic observations. *Journal of Abnormal Psychology, 72,* 193–204.

Clark, H. H. (1973). The language-as-fixed-effect fallacy: A critique of language statistics in psychological research. *Journal of Verbal Learning and Verbal Behavior, 12,* 335–359.

Cohen, J. (1976). Discussion of Wike and Church's comments. *Journal of Verbal Learning and Verbal Behavior, 15,* 262–262.

Cohen, J. (1990). Things I have learned (so far). *American Psychologist, 45,* 1304–1312.

Cohen, J., & and Cohen, P. (1983). *Applied multiple regression/correlation analysis for the behavioral science.* Hillsdale, NJ: Erlbaum.

Coile, D. C., & Miller, N. E. (1984). How radical animal activists try to mislead humane people. *American Psychologist, 39,* 700–701.

Coleman, E. B. (1979). Generalization effects vs. random effects. *Journal of Verbal Learning and Verbal Behavior, 18,* 243–256.

Coles, C. D. (1993). Saying "goodbye" to the "crack baby." *Neurotoxicology and Teratology, 15,* 290–292.

Cook, T. D., & Campbell, D. T. (1979). *Quasi-experimentation: Design and analysis for field settings.* Chicago: Rand McNally.

Custer, S. (1985). *The impact of backward masking.* Presented at the Thirteenth Annual Western Pennsylvania Undergraduate Psychology Conference in Clarion, Pennsylvania.

Dawes, R. M. (1994). *A house of cards: Psychology and psychotherapy built on myth.* New York: Free Press.

Dawkins, R. (1998). *Unweaving the rainbow: Science, delusion, and the appetite for wonder.* Boston: Houghton Mifflin.

Dillman, D. A. (1978). *Mail and telephone surveys: The total design method.* New York: John Wiley and Sons.

Dillon, K. (1990). Generating research ideas; or, that's salada tea. . . . *High School Psychology Teacher, 21,* 6–7.

Edwards, T. (1990, July 23). Marketing grads told to take a reality check. *AMA News,* p. 9.

Field, T. (1993). The therapeutic effects of touch. In G. C. Brannigan, & M. R. Merrens (Eds.), *The undaunted psychologist: Adventures in research.* New York: McGraw-Hill.

Fiske, D. W., & Fogg, L. (1990). But the reviewers are making different criticisms of my paper! Diversity and uniqueness in reviewer comments. *American Psychologist, 45,* 591–598.

Forer, B. R. (1949). The fallacy of personal validation: A classroom demonstration of gullibility. *Journal of Abnormal and Social Psychology, 44,* 118–123.

Frank, M. G., & Gilovich, T. (1988). The dark side of self- and other perceptions: Black uniforms and aggression in professional sports. *Journal of Personality and Social Psychology, 54,* 74–85.

Franz, C. E., McClelland, D. C., & Weinberger, J. (1991). Childhood antecedents of conventional social accomplishment in midlife adults: A 36-year prospective study. *Journal of Personality and Social Psychology, 60,* 586–595.

Frederickson, N. (1986). Toward a broader conception of human intelligence. *American Psychologist, 41,* 445–452.

Frijda, N. H. (1988). The laws of emotion. *American Psychologist, 43,* 349–358.

Garner, D. M., & Garfinkel, P. E. (1979). The eating attitudes test: An index of the symptoms of anorexia nervosa. *Psychological Medicine, 9,* 273–279.

Gilovich, T., Vallone, R., & Tversky, A. (1985). The hot hand in basketball: On the misperception of random sequences. *Cognitive Psychology, 17,* 295–314.

Gladue, B. A., & Delaney, H. J. (1990). Gender differences in perception of attractiveness of men and women in bars. *Personality and Social Psychology Bulletin, 16,* 378–391.

Glass, D. C., & Singer, J. E. (1972). *Urban stress: Experiments on noise and social stressors.* New York: Academic Press.

Glick, P., Gottesman, D., & Jolton, J. (1989). The fault is not in the stars: Susceptibility of skeptics and believers in astrology to the Barnum effect. *Personality and Social Psychology Bulletin, 15,* 559–571.

Goldman, B. A., & Mitchell, D. F. (1990). *Directory of unpublished experimental mental measures* (Vol. 5). Dubuque, IA: Wm. C. Brown.

Gottman, J. M. (1993). *What predicts divorce? The relationship between marital processes and marital outcomes.* Hillsdale, NJ: Erlbaum.

Greenberger, E., & Steinberg, L. (1986). *When teenagers work: The psychological and social costs of adolescent employment.* New York: Basic Books.

Greenwald, A. G. (1975). Significance, nonsignificance, an interpretation of an ESP experiment. *Journal of Experimental Social Psychology, 11,* 180–191.

Greenwald, A. G. (1976). Within-subjects designs: To use or not to use? *Psychological Bulletin, 83,* 314–320.

Groves, R. M., & Kahn, R. L. (1979). *Surveys by telephone: A national comparison with personal interviews.* New York: Academic Press.

Hays, W. L. (1981). *Statistics* (3rd ed.). New York: Holt, Rinehart and Winston.

Hedges, L. (1987). How hard is hard science, how soft is soft science? *American Psychologist, 42,* 443–455.

High-handed professor's comments called hot error. (1985, August). *USA Today,* p. 2c.

Hill, C. A. (1991). Seeking emotional support: The influence of affiliative need and partner warmth. *Journal of Personality and Social Psychology, 60,* 112–121.

Hilton, J. L., & Fein, S. (1989). The role of typical diagnosticity on stereotype-based social judgments. *Journal of Personality and Social Psychology, 57,* 201–211.

Hilton, J. L., & von Hippel, W. (1990). The role of consistency in the judgment of stereotype-relevant behaviors. *Personality and Social Psychology Bulletin, 16,* 723–727.

Holmes, D. S., & Will, M. J. (1985). Expression of interpersonal aggression by angered and nonangered persons with Type A and Type B behavior patterns. *Journal of Personality and Social Psychology, 48,* 723–727.

Holmes, J. G., & Boon, S. D. (1990). Developments in the field of close relationships: Creating foundations for intervention strategies. *Personality and Social Psychology Bulletin, 16,* 23–41.

Honomichl, J. (1990, August 6). Answering machines threaten survey research. *Marketing News,* p. 11.

Ickes, W., & Barnes, R. D. (1978). Boys and girls together and alienated: On enacting stereotyped sex roles in mixed-sex dyads. *Journal of Personality and Social Psychology, 36,* 669–683.

Injury quiets rams. (1984, August 6). *USA Today,* p. 7c.

Jackson, J. M., & Williams, K. D. (1985). Social loafing on difficult tasks: Working collectively can improve performance. *Journal of Personality and Social Psychology, 49,* 937–942.

Janis, I. L., & Field, P. B. (1959). A behavioral assessment of persuasability: Consistency of individual differences. In C. I. Hovland & I. L. Janis (Eds.), *Personality and persuasability* (pp. 29–54). New Haven, CT: Yale University Press.

Jolley, J. M., Murray, J. D., & Keller, P. A. (1992). *How to write psychology papers: A student's survival guide for psychology and related fields.* Sarasota, FL.: Professional Resource Exchange.

Kenny, D. A., & Smith, E. R. (1980). A note on the analysis of designs in which subjects receive each stimulus only once. *Journal of Experimental Social Psychology, 16,* 497–507.

Kerlinger, F. N. (1986). *Foundations of behavioral research* (4th ed.). New York: Holt, Rinehart and Winston.

Keyser, D. J., & Sweetland, R. C. (Eds.) (1984). *Test critiques.* Kansas City, MO: Test Corporation of America.

Kiesler, C. A. (1982). Public and professional myths about mental hospitalization: An empirical reassessment of policy-related beliefs. *American Psychologist, 37,* 1323–1339.

Kiesler, C. A., & Sibulkin, A. E. (1987). *Mental hospitalization: Myths and facts about a national crisis.* Beverly Hills, CA: Sage.

Kimble, G. A. (1990). A search for principles in principles of psychology. *Psychological Science, 1,* 151–155.

Kincher, J. (1992). *The first honest book about lies.* Minneapolis, MN: Free Spirit Publishing.

Kohlberg, L. (1981). *The meaning and measurement of moral development.* Worcester, MA: Clark University Press.

Kohn, A. (1988). You know what they say: Are proverbs nuggets of truth or fool's gold? *Psychology Today, 22 (4),* 36–41.

Kramer, J. J., & Conoley, J. C. (Eds.). (1992). *The eleventh mental measurements yearbook.* Lincoln, NE: Buros Institute of Mental Measurements.

Krosnick, J. A., & Schuman, H. (1988). Attitude intensity, importance, and certainty and susceptibility to response effects. *Journal of Personality and Social Psychology, 54,* 940–952.

Kuehn, S. A. (1989). *Prospectus handbook for Comm 352.* Unpublished manuscript.

Langer, E. J., & Rodin, J. T. (1976). The effects of choice and enhanced personal responsibility for the aged: A field experiment in an institutional setting. *Journal of Personality and Social Psychology, 34,* 909–917.

Lardner, R. (1994, Feb. 21). Common nonsense: The age of reason (1974–1994). *The Nation, 258,* 232–234.

Latane, B., & Darley, J. M. (1968). Group inhibition of bystander intervention in emergencies. *Journal of Personality and Social Psychology, 10,* 215–221.

Latane, B., & Darley, J. M. (1970). *The unresponsive bystander: Why doesn't he help?* New York: Appleton-Century-Crofts.

Latane, B., Williams, K., & Harkins, S. (1979). Many hands make light the work: The causes and consequences of social loafing. *Journal of Personality and Social Psychology, 37,* 822–832.

Lehman, D. R., Lempert, R. O., & Nisbett, R. E. (1988). The effects of graduate training on reasoning: Formal discipline and thinking about everyday-life events. *American Psychologist, 43,* 431–442.

Levy-Leboyer, C. (1988). Success and failure in applying psychology. *American Psychologist, 43,* 779–785.

Lewis, D., & Greene, J. (1982). *Thinking better.* New York: Rawson, Wade.

Maslow, A. H. (1970). Cited in S. Cunningham, Humanist celebrate gains, goals. *APA Monitor, 16,* p. 16.

Milgram, S. (1974). *Obedience to authority: An experimental view.* New York: Harper and Row.

Miller, R. L., Wozniak, W. J., Rust, M. R., Miller, B. R., & Slezak, J. (1996). Counterattitudinal advocacy as a means of enhancing instructional effectiveness: How to teach students what they do not want to know. *Teaching of Psychology, 23,* 215–219.

Mitchell, J. V. (Ed.). (1983). *Tests in print III: An index to tests, test reviews, and the literature on specific tests.* Lincoln, NE: Buros Institute of Mental Measurements.

Morris, J. D. (1986). MTV in the classroom. *Chronicle of Higher Education, 32,* 25–26.

Myers, D. G. (1999). *Social psychology* (6th ed.). New York: McGraw-Hill.

Mynatt & Doherty (1999). *Understanding human behavior.* Needham Heights, MA: Allyn & Bacon.

Neisser, U. (1984). *Ecological movement in cognitive psychology.* Invited address at the 92nd Annual Convention of the American Psychological Association in Toronto, Canada.

Nisbett, R. E., & Ross, L. (1980). *Human inference: Strategies and shortcomings of social judgment.* Englewood Cliffs, NJ: Prentice-Hall.

Nisbett, R. E., & Wilson, T. D. (1977). Telling more than we can know: Verbal reports on mental processes. *Psychological Review, 84,* 231–259.

O'Keefe, M. K., Nesselhof-Kendall, S., & Baum, A. (1990). Behavior and prevention of AIDS: Bases of research and intervention. *Personality and Social Psychology Bulletin, 16,* 166–180.

Orne, M. (1962). On the social psychology of the psychological experiment: With particular reference to demand characteristics and their implications. *American Psychologist, 17,* 776–783.

Pennebaker, J. W., Dyer, M. A., Caulkins, R. S., Litowitz, D. L., Ackerman, P. L., Anderson, D. B., & McGraw, K. M. (1979). Don't the girls get prettier at closing time: A country and western application to psychology. *Personality and Social Psychology Bulletin, 5,* 122–125.

Pfungst, O. (1911). *Clever Hans.* New York: Henry Holt.

Pliner, P., Chaiken, S., & Flett, G. L. (1990). Gender differences in concern with body weight and physical appearance over the life span. *Personality and Social Psychology Bulletin, 16,* 263–273.

Plomin, R. (1993). Nature and nurture: Perspective and prospective. In R. Plomin, R. McClearn, & G. E. McClearn (Eds.), *Nature, Nurture, and Psychology.* Washington, DC: American Psychological Association.

Porter, T. M. (1997). *Trust in numbers: The pursuit of objectivity in science and public life.* Princeton, NJ: Princeton University Press.

Ralof, J. (September 19, 1998). The science of museums. *Science News,* 184–186.

Ranieri, D. J., & Zeiss, A. M. (1984). Induction of a depressed mood: A test of opponent-process theory. *Journal of Personality and Social Psychology, 47,* 1413–1422.

Reis, H. T., & Stiller, J. (1992). Publication trends in JPSP: A three-decade review. *Personality and Social Psychology Bulletin, 18,* 465–472.

Richter, M. L., & Seay, M. B. (1987). ANOVA designs with subjects and stimuli and random effects: Applications to prototype effects on recognition memory. *Journal of Personality and Social Psychology, 53,* 470–480.

Robins, C. J. (1988). Attributions and depression: Why is the literature so inconsistent? *Journal of Personality and Social Psychology, 54,* 880–889.

Roediger, H. L. (1980). The effectiveness of four mnemonics in ordering recall. *Journal of Experimental Psychology, 6,* 558–567.

Roethlisberger, F. J., & Dickson, W. J. (1939). *Management and the worker.* Cambridge, MA: Harvard University Press.

Rogers, C. R. (1985). Cited in S. Cunningham, Humanists celebrate gains, goals. *APA Monitor, 16,* p. 16.

Rosa, L. R., Rosa, E. R., Sarner, L. S., & Barrett, S. B. (1998). Close look at therapeutic touch. *Journal of the American Medical Association, 279,* 1005–1010.

Rosenthal, R. (1992, Fall). Computing contrasts: On sharpening psychological science. *Dialogue,* p. 3.

Rubin, Z. (1970). Measurement of romantic love. *Journal of Personality and Social Psychology, 16,* 265–273.

Ruchlis, H., & Oddo, S. (1990). *Clear thinking: A practical introduction.* Buffalo, NY: Prometheus.

Sagan, C. (1993). *Broca's brain.* New York: Ballantine.

Schachter, S. (1959). *The psychology of affiliation.* Stanford, CA: Stanford University Press.

Schultz, D., & Schultz, S. (1990). *Psychology and industry today: An introduction to industrial and organizational psychology* (5th ed.) New York: Macmillan.

Schwarz, N. (1999). Self-Reports: How the questions shape the answers. *American Psychologist, 54,* 93–105.

Seligman, M. E. P. (1990). *Learned optimism: How to change your mind and your life.* New York: Pocket.

Semon, T. (1990, April). Beware of bedazzling number mongers. *Marketing News, 13.*

Shedler, J., & Block, J. (1990). Adolescent drug use and psychological health: A longitudinal inquiry. *American Psychologist, 45,* 612–637.

Shefrin, H. M., & Statman, M. (1986). How not to make money in the stock market. *Psychology Today, 20,* 52–57.

Sherman, S. J. (1980). On the self-erasing nature of errors of prediction. *Journal of Personality and Social Psychology, 39,* 211–221.

Shorter, E. (1997). *A history of psychiatry.* New York: Wiley.

Shultz, K. S. (1994, July). *Type I error and multiple hypothesis tests of correlation coefficients.* Paper presented at the sixth annual American Psychological Society Convention, Washington, DC.

Shute, V. J. (1994, May/June). Learner's instruction: What's good for the goose may not be good for the gander. *Psychology Science Agenda,* pp. 8–9.

Sigall, H., & Mills, J. (1998). Measures of independent variables and mediators are useful in social psychology experiments: But are they necessary? *Personality and Social Psychology Review, 2,* 218–226.

Slovic, P. S., & Fischoff, B. (1977). On the psychology of experimental surprises. *Journal of Experimental Psychology: Human Perception and Performance, 3,* 455–471.

Snyder, M. (1984). When belief creates reality. In L. Berkowitz (Ed.), *Advances in experimental social psychology, Vol. 18.* New York: Academic Press.

Snyder, M., & Omoto, A. M. (1990). Basic research in action: Volunteerism and society's response to AIDS. *Personality and Social Psychology Bulletin, 16,* 133–151.

Stanovich, K. E. (1990). *How to think straight about psychology.* Glenview, IL: Scott, Foresman.

Steele, C. M., Southwick, L. L., & Critchlow, B. (1981). Dissonance and alcohol: Drinking your troubles away. *Journal of Personality and Social Psychology, 41,* 831–846.

Steinberg, L., & Dornbusch, S. M. (1991). Negative correlates of part-time employment during adolescence: Replication and elaboration. *Developmental Psychology, 27,* 304–313.

Stern, P. C. (1993). A second environmental science: Human-environmental interactions. *Science, 260,* 1997–1999.

Sternberg, R. J. (1986). *Intelligence applied: Understanding and increasing your intellectual skills.* New York: Harcourt Brace Jovanovich.

Sternberg, R. J. (1994, Spring). Love is a story. *The General Psychologist, 30,* 1–11.

Stone, J., Aronson, E., Crain, A. L., Winslow, M. P., & Fried, C. (1994). Introducing hypocrisy as a means of encouraging young adults to use condoms. *Personality and Social Psychology Bulletin, 20,* 116–128.

Stone, P. J., Dunphy, D. C., Smith, M. S., & Ogilvie, D. M. (1966). *The general inquirer: A computer approach to content analysis.* Cambridge, MA: M.I.T. Press.

Swets, J. A., & Bjork, R. A. (1990). Enhancing human performance: An evaluation of "new age" techniques considered by the U.S. Army. *Psychological Science, 1,* 85–96.

Tversky, A. (1985). Quoted by K. McKean, Decisions, decisions. *Discover,* pp. 22–31.

Tversky, B. (1973). Encoding processes in recognition and recall. *Cognitive Psychology, 5,* 275–287.

Ward, W. C., & Jenkins, H. M. (1965). The display of information and the judgment of contingency. *Canadian Journal of Psychology, 19,* 231–241.

Wedell, D. H., & Parducci, A. (1988). The category effect in social judgment: Experimental ratings of happiness. *Journal of Personality and Social Psychology, 55,* 341–356.

Weiten, W. (1992). *Psychology themes and variations.* Pacific Grove, CA: Brooks Cole.

Wickens, T. D., & Keppel, G. (1983). On the choice of design and of test statistic in the analysis of experiments with sampled materials. *Journal of Verbal Learning and Verbal Behavior, 22,* 296–309.

Wike, E. L., & Church, J. D. (1976). Comments on Clark's "The language-as-fixed-effect fallacy." *Journal of Verbal Learning and Verbal Behavior, 15,* 249–255.

Williams, R. L., & Long, J. D. (1983). *Toward a self-managed lifestyle* (3rd ed.). Boston: Houghton-Mifflin.

Wilson, T. D., & Schooler, J. W. (1991). Thinking too much: Introspection can reduce the quality of preferences and decisions. *Journal of Personality and Social Psychology, 60,* 181–192.

Winer, B. J. (1971). *Statistical principles in experimental design* (2nd ed.). New York: McGraw-Hill.

Wohlford, P. (1970). Initiation of cigarette smoking: Is it related to parental smoking behavior? *Journal of Consulting and Clinical Psychology, 34,* 148–151.

Woods, N. S., Eyler, F. D., Conlon, M., Behnke, M., & Wobie, K. (1998). Pygmalion in the cradle: Observer bias against cocaine-exposed infants. *Developmental and Behavioral Pediatrics, 19,* 283–285.

Zajonc, R. B. (1965). Social facilitation. *Science, 149,* 269–274.

Zajonc, R. B. (1968). The attitudinal effects of mere exposure. *Journal of Personality and Social Psychology, 9,* 1–27.

Zajonc, R. B., & Sales, S. M. (1966). Social facilitation of dominant and subordinate responses. *Journal of Experimental Social Psychology, 2,* 160–168.

Zebrowitz, L. A., Montepare, J. M., & Lee, H. K. (1993). They don't all look alike: Individual impressions of other racial groups. *Journal of Personality and Social Psychology, 65,* 85–101.

Zimbardo, P., Haney, C., Banks, W. C., & Jaffe, D. (1975). The psychology of imprisonment: Privation, power, and pathology. In D. Rosenhan & P. London (Eds.), *Theory and research in abnormal psychology* (pp. 272–287). New York: Holt, Rinehart and Winston.

Zuckerman, M. (1993). Out of sensory deprivation and into sensation seeking: A personal and scientific journey. In G. C. Brannigan & M. R. Merrens (Eds.), *The undaunted psychologist: Adventures in research.* New York: McGraw-Hill.

CREDITS

Figure 1-1
Garfield © 1999 Paws, Inc. Reprinted with permission of Universal Press Syndicate. All rights reserved.

Figure 1-3
Cathy © 1994 Cathy Guisewite. Reprinted with permission of Universal Press Syndicate. All rights reserved.

Table 1-3
Copyright © 1992 by the American Psychological Association. Reprinted with permission.

Table 1-5
Copyright © 1996 by the American Psychological Association. Reprinted with permission.

Figure 2-1
Dilbert reprinted by permission of United Feature Syndicate, Inc.

Table 13-1
VanAmburg Group, Inc.

Box A-3
Copyright © 1992 by the American Psychological Association. Reprinted with permission.

Box A-4
Copyright © 1996 by the American Psychological Association. Reprinted with permission.

Appendix D
Copyright © 1988 by the American Psychological Association. Adapted with permission. Adapted from Frank, M.G., A. & Gilovich, T. (1988). The dark side of self and social perception: Black uniforms and aggression in professional sports. *Journal of Personality and Social Psychology, 54,* 74-85. Used with the kind permission of Mark Frank and the American Psychological Association.

Table E-1
Condensed from Table 12 in Pearson, E. S. and Hartley, H. O. (Eds.). (1970). *Biometrika tables for statisticians.* (3rd ed., Vol. 1). New York: Cambridge University Press. Used with the kind permission of the Biometrika trustees.

Table E-2
Taken from Table 8 in Pearson, E. S. and Hartley, H. O. (Eds.). (1970). *Biometrika tables for statisticians.* (3rd ed., Vol. 1). New York: Cambridge University Press. Used with the kind permission of the Biometrika trustees.

Table E-3
Condensed from Table 18 in Pearson, E. S. and Hartley, H. O. (Eds.). (1970). *Biometrika tables for statisticians.* (3rd ed., Vol. 1). New York: Cambridge University Press. Used with the kind permission of the Biometrika trustees.

Table E-4
Reproduced from Table VII in Hays, W. L. (1981). *Statistics.* New York: Holt, Rinehart and Winston. Used with the kindly permission of W. L. Hays.

Table E-5
Abridged from Table 29 in Pearson, E. S. and Hartley, H. O. (Eds.). (1970). *Biometrika tables for statisticians.* (3rd ed., Vol. 1). New York: Cambridge University Press. Used with the kind permission of the Biometrika trustees.

Table E-6
Taken from the random numbers table of Appendix D in Kerlinger, F. N. (1973). *Foundations of behavioral research,* 2nd ed. New York: Holt, Rinehart and Winston. Used with the kindly permission of F. N. Kerlinger.

INDEX